S P I D E R -

DAILY  BUGLE

WRITERS:
Paul Grist, Bill Rosemann, Zeb Wells & Tom DeFalco with **Steven Grant**

PENCILERS:
Karl Kerschl, Guy Davis, Dean Haspiel &
Takeshi Miyazawa with **Walter McDaniel & co.**

INKERS:
Greg Adams, Guy Davis, Dean Haspiel & Takeshi Miyazawa with
Al Milgrom, Chris Ivy, Sam De La Rosa, Matt Banning & Vince Evans

COLORISTS:
Dave Stewart, Steve Buccellato &
Christina Strain with **Michael Higgins**

LETTERERS:
Jim Novak, John Costanza, Dave Sharpe,
Paul Tutrone & Clem Robins with
Sue Crespi, Michael Higgins & Joe Rosen

ASSISTANT EDITORS:
Glenn Greenberg, Marc Sumerak,
Jeff Youngquist, John Miesegaes &
Nick Lowe with **Mike Lackey**

EDITORS:
Tom Brevoort, Axel Alonso &
Ralph Macchio with **Mark Powers &**
Danny Fingeroth

FRONT COVER ARTISTS:
Mike Mayhew & Andy Troy

BACK COVER ARTIST:
Dean Haspiel

COLLECTION EDITOR:
Mark D. Beazley

ASSISTANT EDITOR:
Caitlin O'Connell

ASSOCIATE MANAGING EDITOR:
Kateri Woody

ASSOCIATE MANAGER, DIGITAL ASSETS:
Joe Hochstein

SENIOR EDITOR, SPECIAL PROJECTS:
Jennifer Grünwald

VP PRODUCTION & SPECIAL PROJECTS:
Jeff Youngquist

RESEARCH:
Daron Jensen

LAYOUT:
Jeph York

PRODUCTION:
ColorTek & Ryan Devall

BOOK DESIGNER:
Adam Del Re

SVP PRINT, SALES & MARKETING:
David Gabriel

EDITOR IN CHIEF:
Axel Alonso

CHIEF CREATIVE OFFICER:
Joe Quesada

PRESIDENT:
Dan Buckley

EXECUTIVE PRODUCER:
Alan Fine

SPECIAL THANKS TO
Mike Hansen

SPIDER-MAN: THE DAILY BUGLE. Contains material originally published in magazine form as DAILY BUGLE #1-3, DEADLINE #1-4, SPIDER-MAN'S TANGLED WEB #20, SPECTACULAR SPIDER-MAN #205-207 and MARVEL HOLIDAY SPECIAL 2004. First printing 2017. ISBN# 978-1-302-90793-8. Published by MARVEL WORLDWIDE, INC., a subsidiary of MARVEL ENTERTAINMENT, LLC. OFFICE OF PUBLICATION: 135 West 50th Street, New York, NY 10020. Copyright © 2017 MARVEL No similarity between any of the names, characters, persons, and/or institutions in this magazine with those of any living or dead person or institution is intended, and any such similarity which may exist is purely coincidental. **Printed in the U.S.A.** DAN BUCKLEY, President, Marvel Entertainment; JOE QUESADA, Chief Creative Officer; TOM BREVOORT, SVP of Publishing; DAVID BOGART, SVP of Business Affairs & Operations, Publishing & Partnership; C.B. CEBULSKI, VP of Brand Management & Development, Asia; DAVID GABRIEL, SVP of Sales & Marketing, Publishing; JEFF YOUNGQUIST, VP of Production & Special Projects; DAN CARR, Executive Director of Publishing Technology; ALEX MORALES, Director of Publishing Operations; SUSAN CRESPI, Production Manager; STAN LEE, Chairman Emeritus. For information regarding advertising in Marvel Comics or on Marvel.com, please contact Vit DeBellis, Integrated Sales Manager, at vdebellis@marvel.com. For Marvel subscription inquiries, please call 888-511-5480. **Manufactured between 8/4/2017 and 9/5/2017 by LSC COMMUNICATIONS INC., KENDALLVILLE, IN, USA.**

10 9 8 7 6 5 4 3 2 1

September 27, 2017 Vol. CMVMMCMXXXVIII

DAILY BUGLE

NEW YORK'S FINEST DAILY NEWSPAPER

INTRODUCTION

I'm so pleased Marvel is doing this fine collection of tales relating to the *Daily Bugle* newspaper and its incendiary publisher, J. Jonah Jameson. Spider-Man and his supporting cast of players are among the best in all of comicdom. The *Bugle* itself has been a staple in the series since the beginning, and it's time we devoted a trade paperback to some of the better stories spotlighting it.

Although he's basically an honorable journalist, Jameson has used his newspaper as a weapon aimed squarely at Your Friendly Neighborhood Spider-Man. And it's been quite an effective one in turning the public against the web-spinner. Frequently, its headlines would proclaim that Spider-Man was a threat or menace to the city; that he was actually in cahoots with the super villain he was purportedly battling. Jameson's editorials railed against this mysterious costumed figure who was terrorizing the populace. Jameson's paranoia knew no bounds. Looking back at the glory days of Stan Lee and Steve Ditko, you'd see how many of the real menaces our hero faced were actually bankrolled by the *Bugle*'s publisher. The great illusionist, Mysterio, went straight to the *Bugle* to issue a challenge to the web-slinger and expose him as a fraud. Jameson was only too happy to print the message. Jameson financed an actual robot that had his face imprinted on a front screen for the sole purpose of chasing down Spidey and humiliating him. And let's not forget Mac Gargan, who became the stronger-than-Spider-Man baddie called the Scorpion, whose mission was to take the web-spinner down big time. The *Bugle* supported him, too. And much as did Frankenstein's creation, Gargan wound up turning on his creator, who in a superb bit of irony, was saved by none other than the web-spinner himself.

It appears a pattern is developing here. J. Jonah Jameson is obviously obsessed with Spider-Man and will use any means available to discredit him or bring him down. Why? In all other aspects of the *Bugle*, Jameson is a practical, ethical publisher. He hired editor in chief Robbie Robertson, who upholds the highest standards. On many public issues, the *Bugle* has often taken courageous stands. Jameson, on occasion, has actually been an admirable, if not sympathetic figure. But on the subject of Spider-Man, he is blinded by hatred. There was a particularly revealing segment in a Lee/Ditko issue where Jameson had a private moment of revelation. He stood alone in his office and was, for once, brutally honest with himself. Apparently, in Jameson's mind, Spider-Man is everything he is not—brave, self-sacrificing, etc. Because Jameson feels he possesses none of those qualities and can never be the man the web-slinger is, all that's left is to tear him down—just because he's a better man than Jonah. That's not an incredibly complex motivation, but it served to make J.J.J. perhaps the most persistent foe in Spidey's young life. They have been at odds since the *Amazing Spider-Man* title first appeared and our nascent web-head saved the life of Jameson's astronaut son, John. Needless to say, our fearless publisher was not overflowing with gratitude.

Even though many of the stories I've referenced appeared in the 1960s, the issue of celebrity misrepresentation in the media, print or otherwise, remains highly relevant. Spider-Man is a victim of wildly unfair coverage by an obsessed publisher, yet there is very little he can do about it. No matter how heroic his actions, the *Bugle* will misconstrue them to negative ends. I don't know if Stan consciously intended it, but Jameson and the *Daily Bugle* are the inverse of the Distinguished Competition's Perry White and the *Daily Planet*. Whereas White and his newspaper lionize Superman, the reverse is the norm for Spider-Man. The Spidey/Jameson relationship is a distorted mirror image of the Superman/White dynamic. All this goes to the heart of the matter: The power of the media to make or break you, no matter who you are.

Now don't get the wrong idea, this collection isn't all about the buzzcutted blabbermouth publisher. The title of this tome is the *Daily Bugle* and several offerings more than do justice to the title. "Front Page" by Paul Grist and Karl Kerschl is a gritty, behind-the-scenes look at the inner workings our favorite major metropolitan newspaper. It's told in a film noir-ish fashion, with Kerschl's stark pencils the perfect complement to Grist's lean, hard storytelling. For me, a major selling point is that it's presented in black-and-white, which truly enhances its electrifying effect. Not only is it a cool crime drama, but it's also an on-point exploration of the clash between a grizzled veteran reporter and a young one just out to make his mark. It works beautifully on multiple levels and will hook you from page one.

Deadline is another tale centered on *Daily Bugle* doings. In this instance, we follow the adventures of young Katherine Farrell, an intrepid *Bugle* reporter hot on the trail of an elusive killer. My friend, former Marvel editor Bill Rosemann, writes it in first-person narration, and Guy Davis ably illustrates it. I recall how enthusiastic Bill was as he relayed elements of the story to me over lunch several years back. He knew just where he was going and I could only nod my approbation. In Bill's capable hands, Kat really comes alive as a fully fleshed-out protagonist. We come to care about her. Rosemann deftly works in a surprising supernatural angle that with a lesser writer could have backfired. Not here. I was especially happy to see one of Spider-Man's early foes play a strong part in the story—Phineas Mason, the Terrible Tinkerer. His role in the resolution is wholly unexpected and jaw-dropping. *Deadline* alone is worth the price of entry.

That excursion is followed by a Steven Grant story broken into three parts, in which J. Jonah Jameson suffers the ultimate insult: people not taking his beloved tabloid seriously. While writer Grant expertly weaves comedic elements into the tale, it's actually a fairly serious examination of a man who sees his life's work being ridiculed. Jameson stares into his own personal abyss, undergoes a dark night of the soul and reappears—well, I won't spoil it for you. It's quite startling, believe me.

Above, I mentioned Jameson's moment of truth, but our psychoanalysis of him goes much deeper in these stories. One of the terrific pieces reprinted herein actually has Jolly Jonah on the psychiatrist's couch. It's a wonderfully written tale by Zeb Wells with fine pencils by Dean Haspiel that delves into his relationship with his father and other adult figures, as well as classmates. It's a window into the inner workings of our cigar-chomping protagonist. And it's a glimpse into Jameson's early life that we rarely get, through a series of very powerful incidents. Jameson is his usual, irascible self, but gradually, against his own wishes, the truth emerges. Naturally, Jameson only agrees to the session under pain of financial penalty.

Tom DeFalco finishes the penetrating portrayal of the boisterous *Bugle* publisher in his fine fable, "Jonah's Holiday Carol." Tom is no stranger to Spidey's world, as he was editor of the Spider-Man titles for several memorable years. Also, Mr. D. had a distinguished run as an *Amazing Spider-Man* scripter. Here, in a highly effective pastiche of Dickens' "A Christmas Carol," we see the adult Jameson commenting on childhood incidents that helped shape him. You can't help but be moved by the poignancy of the events, as Jameson's initial blustering gives way to sober remembrance. What an illuminating path to a man's soul.

I love newspapers. I truly do. Despite the endless talk of news media bias and an effete Eastern Establishment, the truth is we need a vigilant Fourth Estate; some countervailing force is essential to keep politicians and other public officials at all levels aware that their misdeeds will see the light of day because some eagle-eyed investigative journalist will expose them. Yet, we also are aware of how the power of the press can be turned toward slanted coverage that can be exceedingly damaging to those involved. The entries in this unique collection probe many aspects of journalism in thoughtful, sophisticated style. You will discover lots of mind food here, folks.

So, as I take my leave, listen to the many sounds of the ever-active *Daily Bugle* newsroom, alive with men and women whose mission is to inform the public of current events. Catch the hum of the presses as they print the latest edition of New York's premiere tabloid. The ink is barely dry, but you grab a copy anyway, because you just can't wait to scan that cover story and be part of it all. Hey, save one for me.

Ralph Macchio

Enjoy,
Ralph Macchio

Ralph Macchio spent over 35 years at Marvel, starting as an assistant editor and later writing Avengers, Thor and many others. As editor, he oversaw books across the Marvel line, including shepherding the Ultimate line into existence, and editing all of Stephen King's Marvel adaptations.

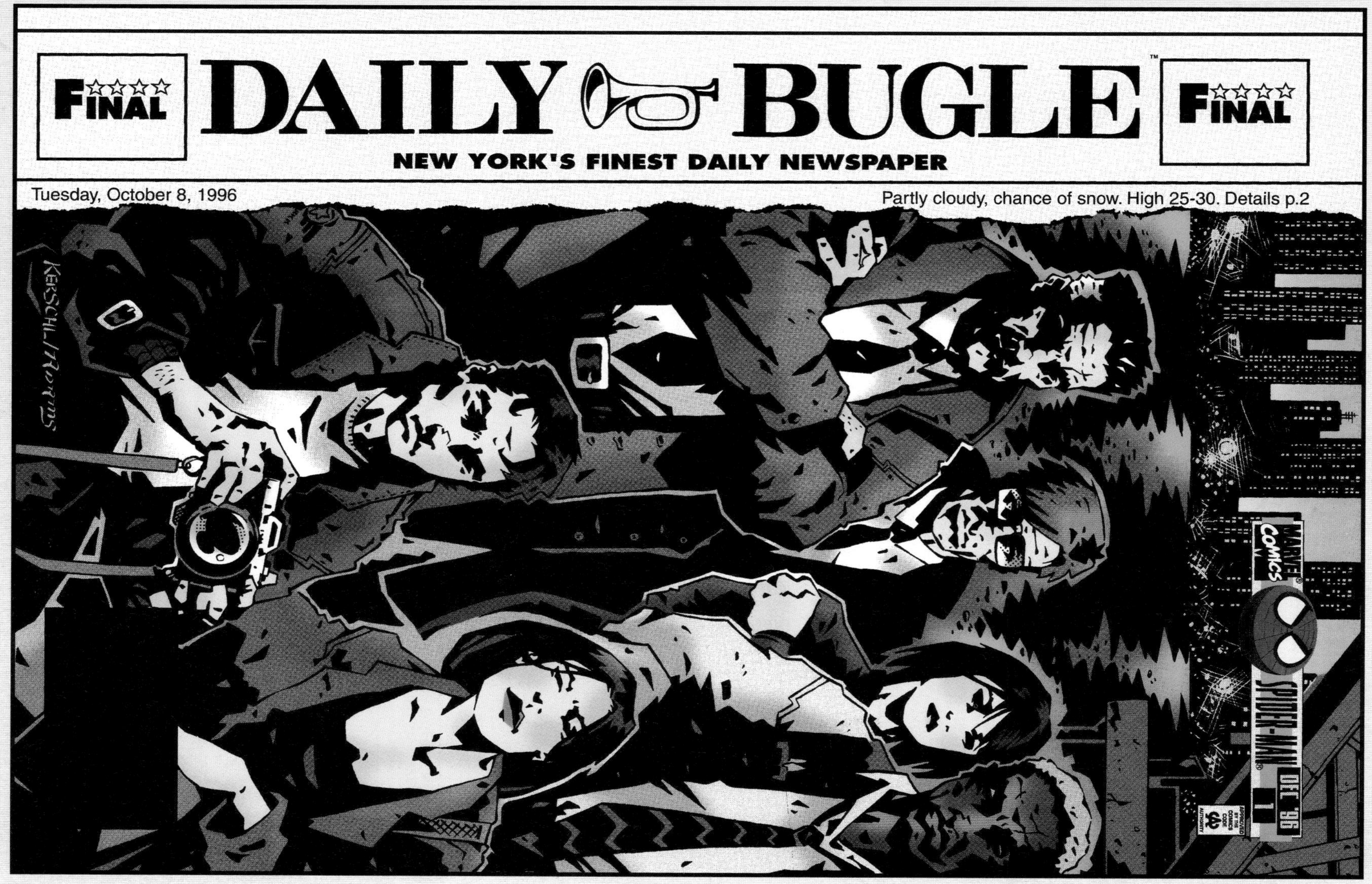
FINAL
DAILY BUGLE
FINAL
NEW YORK'S FINEST DAILY NEWSPAPER
Tuesday, October 8, 1996
Partly cloudy, chance of snow. High 25-30. Details p.2
MARVEL COMICS
SPIDER-MAN
DEC '96
1
APPROVED BY THE COMICS CODE AUTHORITY
KERSCHL/ADAMS

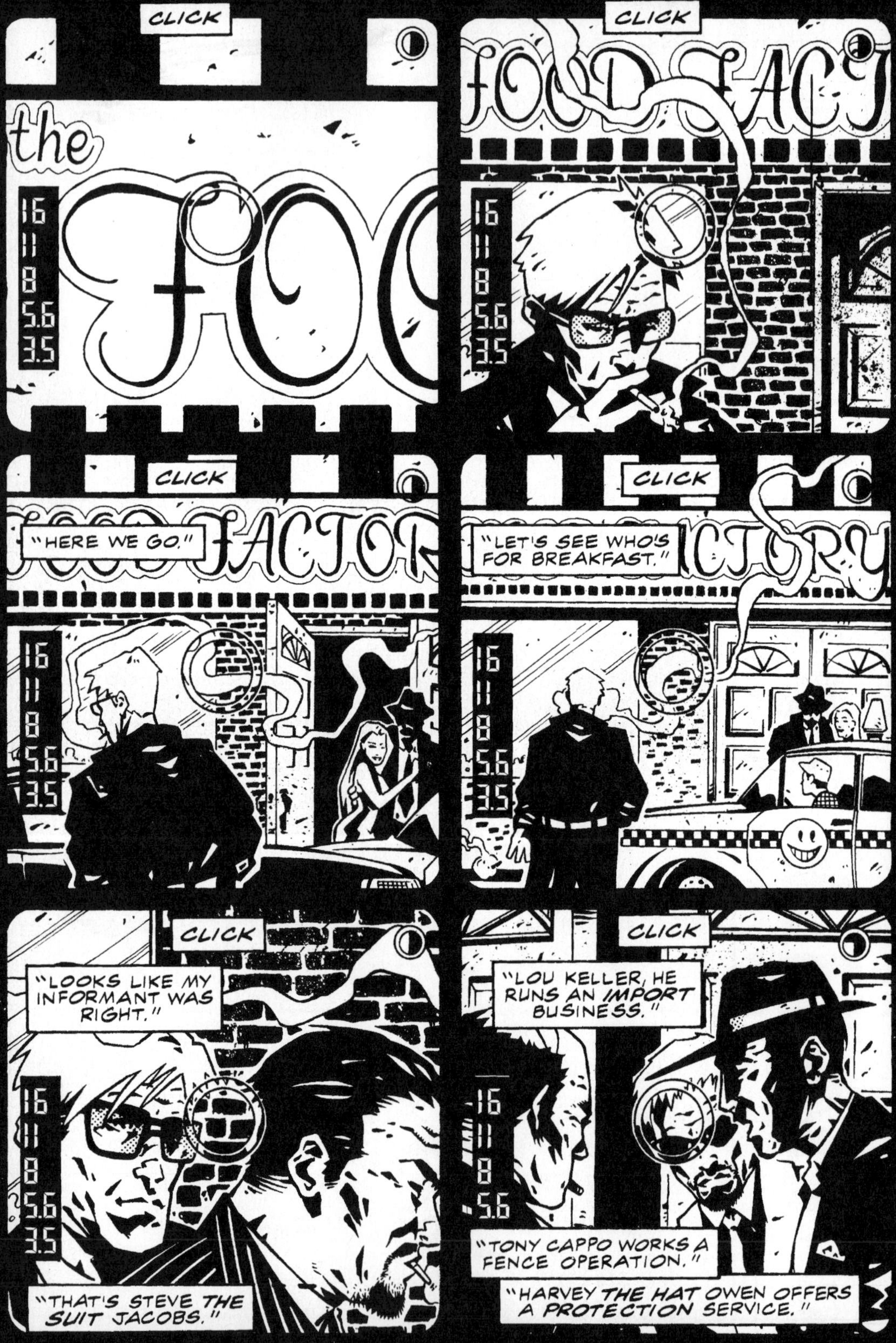
CLICK
the FOO
16
11
8
5.6
3.5
CLICK
FOOD FACT
16
11
8
5.6
3.5
CLICK
"HERE WE GO."
FOOD FACTOR
16
11
8
5.6
3.5
CLICK
"LET'S SEE WHO'S FOR BREAKFAST."
CTORY
16
11
8
5.6
3.5
CLICK
"LOOKS LIKE MY INFORMANT WAS RIGHT."
16
11
8
5.6
3.5
"THAT'S STEVE THE SUIT JACOBS."
CLICK
"LOU KELLER, HE RUNS AN IMPORT BUSINESS."
16
11
8
5.6
"TONY CAPPO WORKS A FENCE OPERATION."
"HARVEY THE HAT OWEN OFFERS A PROTECTION SERVICE."

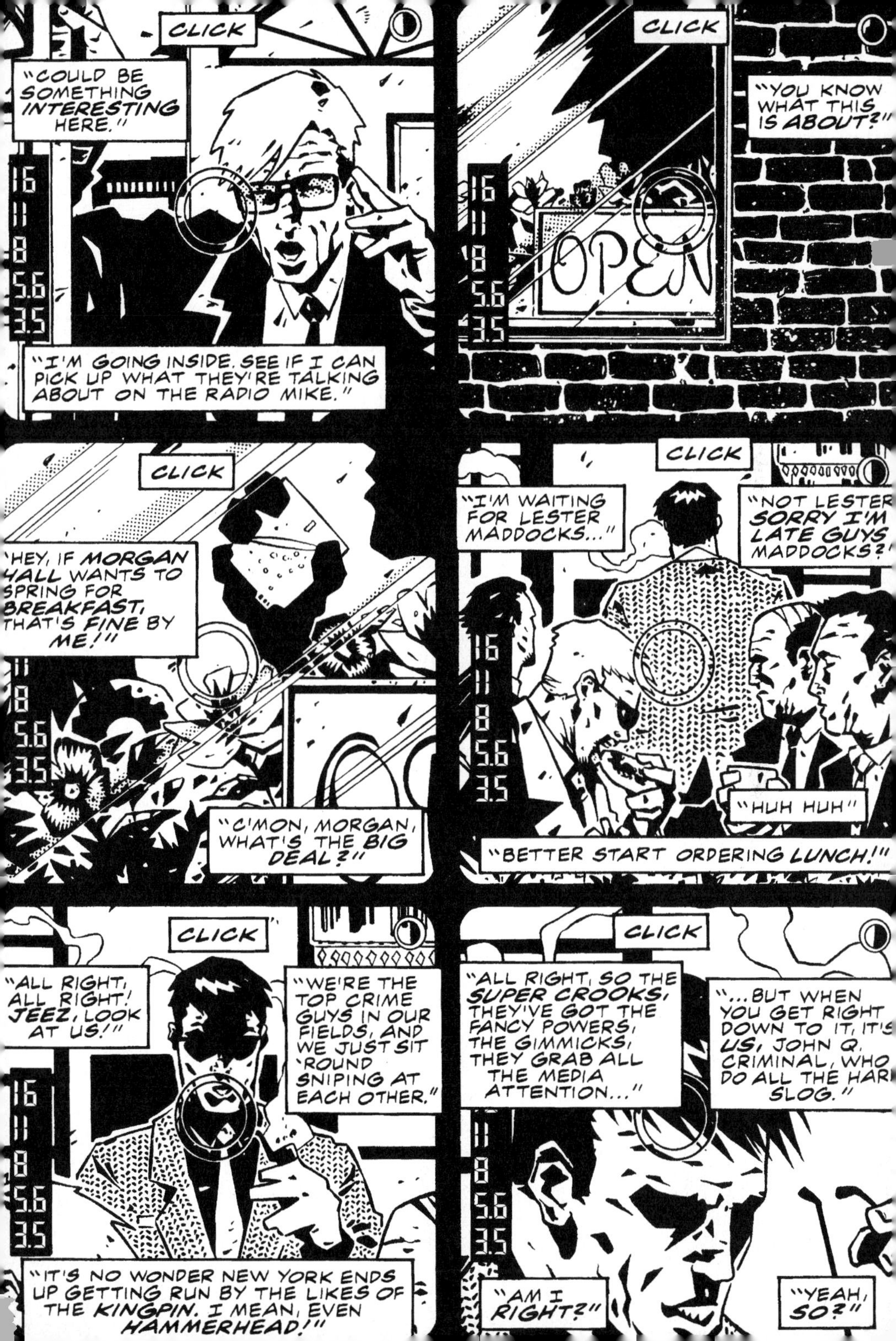
CLICK
"COULD BE SOMETHING INTERESTING HERE."
"I'M GOING INSIDE. SEE IF I CAN PICK UP WHAT THEY'RE TALKING ABOUT ON THE RADIO MIKE."
CLICK
"YOU KNOW WHAT THIS IS ABOUT?"
OPEN
CLICK
"HEY, IF MORGAN HALL WANTS TO SPRING FOR BREAKFAST, THAT'S FINE BY ME!"
"C'MON, MORGAN, WHAT'S THE BIG DEAL?"
CLICK
"I'M WAITING FOR LESTER MADDOCKS..."
"NOT LESTER SORRY I'M LATE GUYS MADDOCKS?"
"HUH HUH"
"BETTER START ORDERING LUNCH!"
CLICK
"ALL RIGHT, ALL RIGHT! JEEZ, LOOK AT US!"
"WE'RE THE TOP CRIME GUYS IN OUR FIELDS, AND WE JUST SIT 'ROUND SNIPING AT EACH OTHER."
"IT'S NO WONDER NEW YORK ENDS UP GETTING RUN BY THE LIKES OF THE KINGPIN. I MEAN, EVEN HAMMERHEAD!"
CLICK
"ALL RIGHT, SO THE SUPER CROOKS, THEY'VE GOT THE FANCY POWERS, THE GIMMICKS, THEY GRAB ALL THE MEDIA ATTENTION..."
"...BUT WHEN YOU GET RIGHT DOWN TO IT, IT'S US, JOHN Q. CRIMINAL, WHO DO ALL THE HAR SLOG."
"AM I RIGHT?"
"YEAH, SO?"

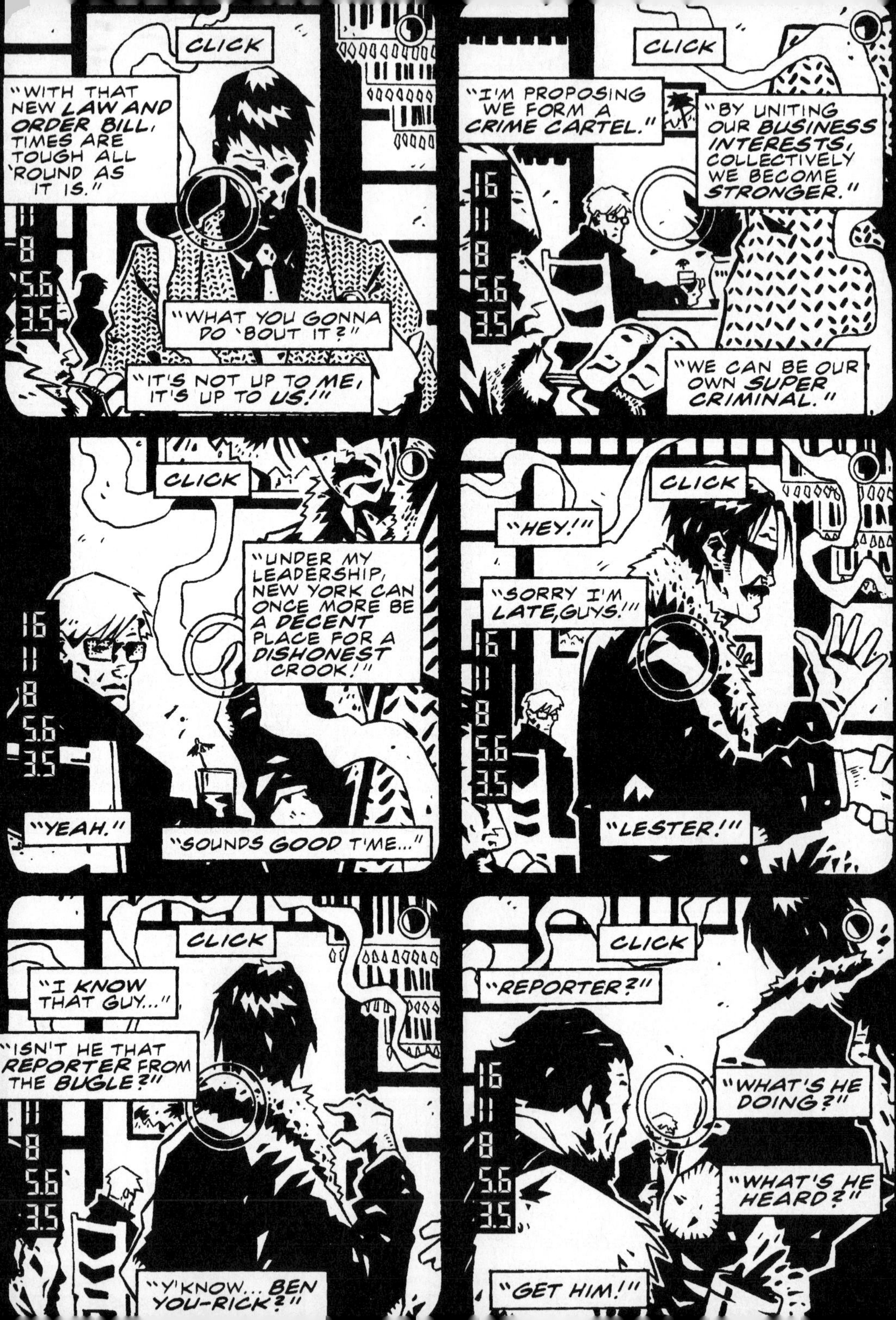
CLICK
"WITH THAT NEW LAW AND ORDER BILL, TIMES ARE TOUGH ALL 'ROUND AS IT IS."
"WHAT YOU GONNA DO 'BOUT IT?"
"IT'S NOT UP TO ME, IT'S UP TO US!"
CLICK
"I'M PROPOSING WE FORM A CRIME CARTEL."
"BY UNITING OUR BUSINESS INTERESTS, COLLECTIVELY WE BECOME STRONGER."
"WE CAN BE OUR OWN SUPER CRIMINAL."
CLICK
"UNDER MY LEADERSHIP, NEW YORK CAN ONCE MORE BE A DECENT PLACE FOR A DISHONEST CROOK!"
"YEAH."
"SOUNDS GOOD T'ME..."
CLICK
"HEY!"
"SORRY I'M LATE, GUYS!"
"LESTER!"
CLICK
"I KNOW THAT GUY..."
"ISN'T HE THAT REPORTER FROM THE BUGLE?"
"Y'KNOW... BEN YOU-RICK?"
CLICK
"REPORTER?"
"WHAT'S HE DOING?"
"WHAT'S HE HEARD?"
"GET HIM!"

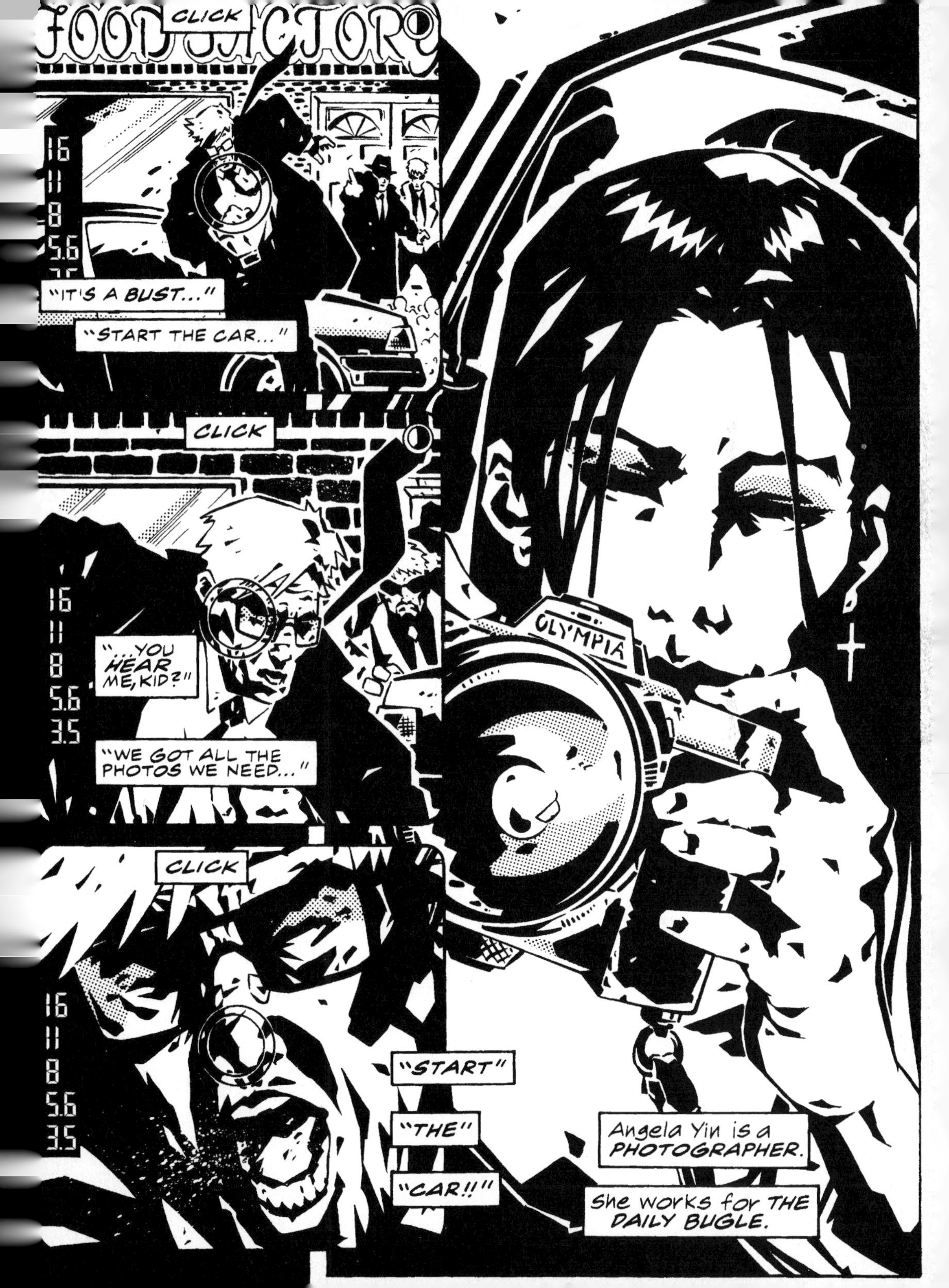

FOOD FACTORY
CLICK
16
11
8
5.6
"IT'S A BUST..."
"START THE CAR..."
CLICK
16
11
8
5.6
3.5
"...YOU HEAR ME, KID?"
"WE GOT ALL THE PHOTOS WE NEED..."
CLICK
16
11
8
5.6
3.5
"START"
"THE"
"CAR!!"
OLYMPIA
Angela Yin is a PHOTOGRAPHER.
She works for THE DAILY BUGLE.

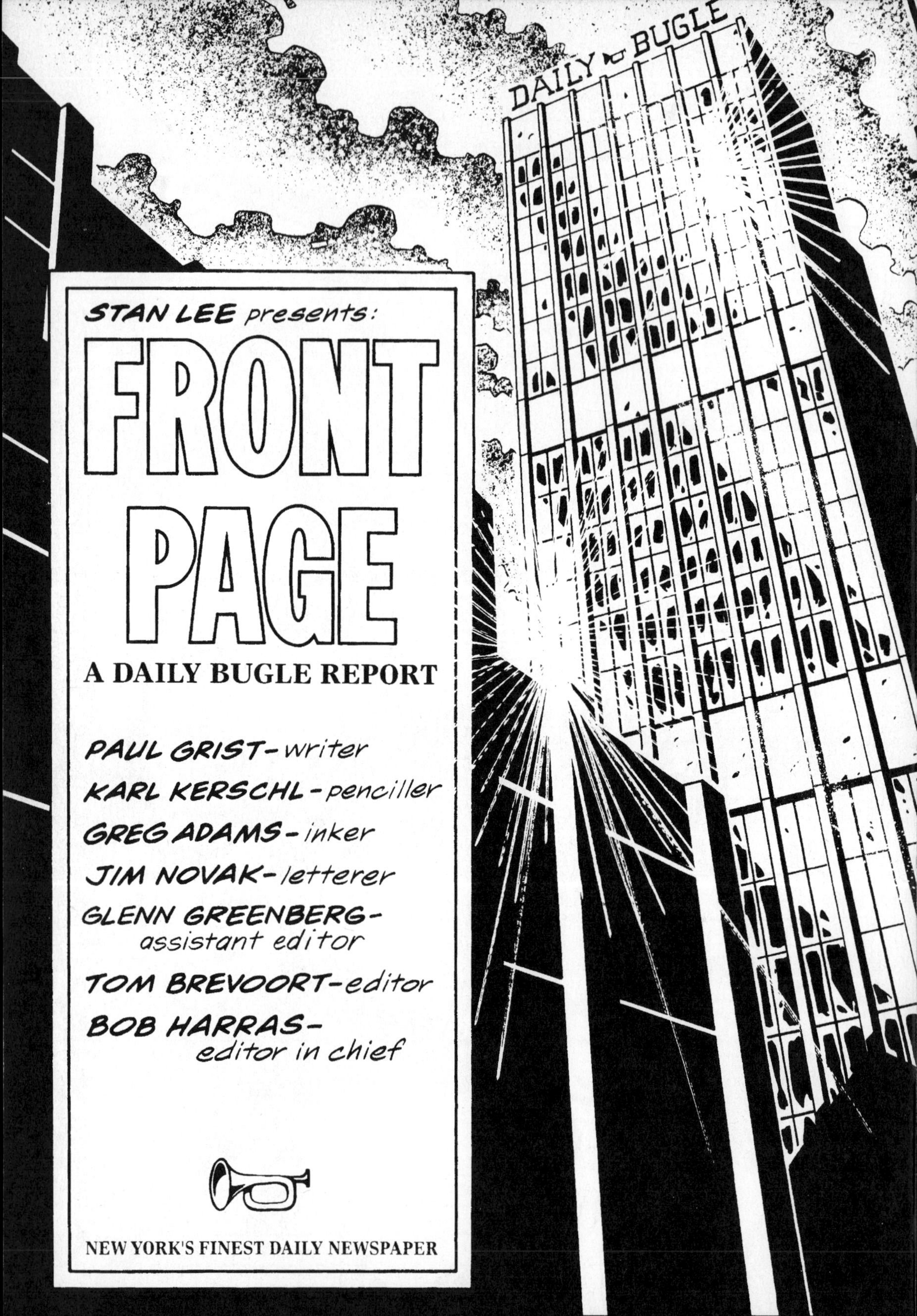
DAILY BUGLE
DAILY
STAN LEE presents:
FRONT PAGE
A DAILY BUGLE REPORT
PAUL GRIST - writer
KARL KERSCHL - penciller
GREG ADAMS - inker
JIM NOVAK - letterer
GLENN GREENBERG - assistant editor
TOM BREVOORT - editor
BOB HARRAS - editor in chief
NEW YORK'S FINEST DAILY NEWSPAPER

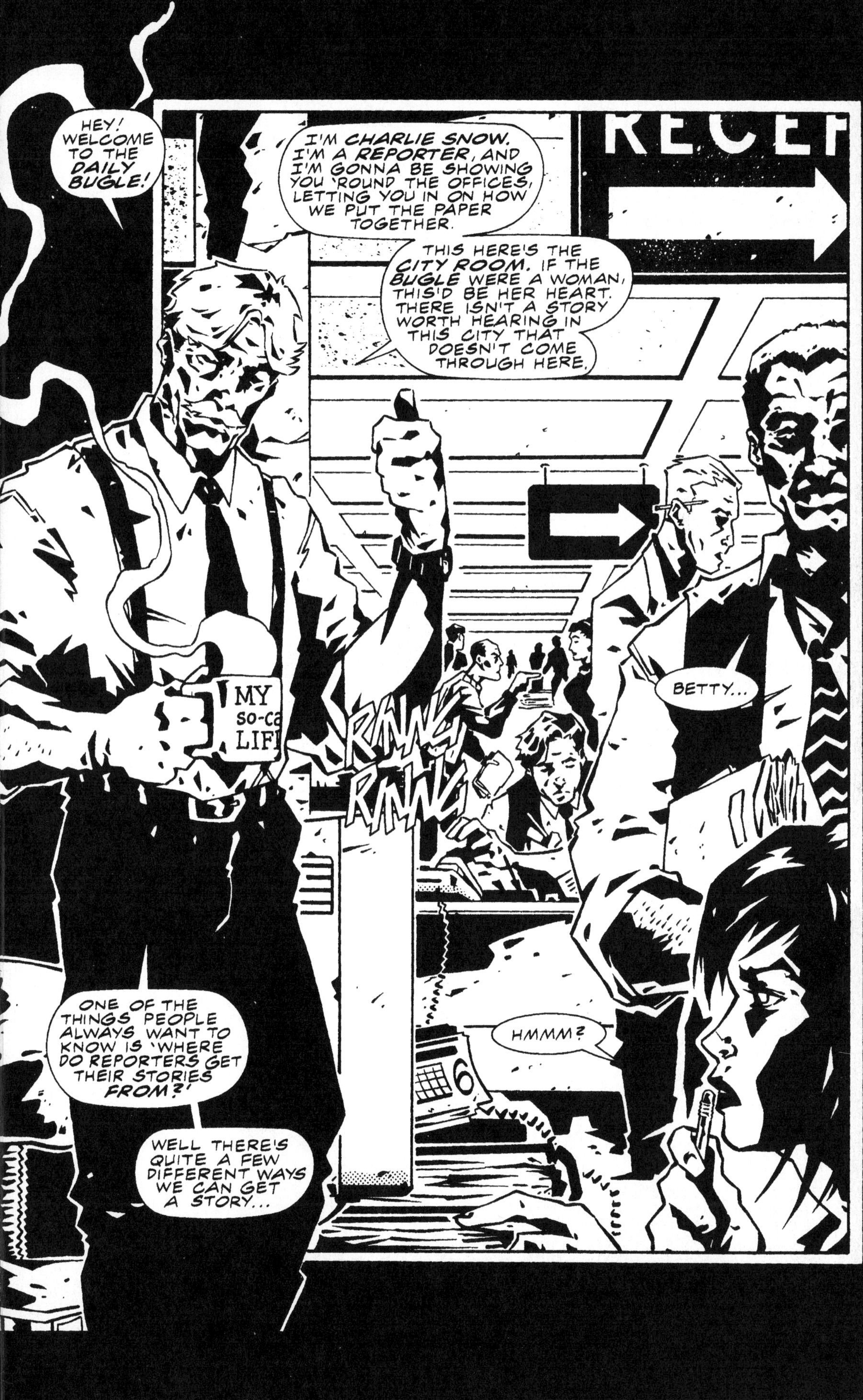

HEY! WELCOME TO THE DAILY BUGLE!
I'M CHARLIE SNOW. I'M A REPORTER, AND I'M GONNA BE SHOWING YOU 'ROUND THE OFFICES, LETTING YOU IN ON HOW WE PUT THE PAPER TOGETHER.
THIS HERE'S THE CITY ROOM. IF THE BUGLE WERE A WOMAN, THIS'D BE HER HEART. THERE ISN'T A STORY WORTH HEARING IN THIS CITY THAT DOESN'T COME THROUGH HERE.
RECEP
MY so-ca LIF
RING RING
BETTY...
HMMM?
ONE OF THE THINGS PEOPLE ALWAYS WANT TO KNOW IS 'WHERE DO REPORTERS GET THEIR STORIES FROM?'
WELL THERE'S QUITE A FEW DIFFERENT WAYS WE CAN GET A STORY...

I WANT AN INTERVIEW WITH *TOMMY FUDE,* THE OWNER OF THE *FOOD FACTORY* CHAIN, FOR THE THURSDAY FEATURE PAGE.

WHAT? I DON'T NEED *THIS,* ROBBIE...

FOR INSTANCE, YOU MIGHT GET ASSIGNED A PARTICULAR STORY TO COVER BY THE EDITOR.

YEAH? KEN ELLIS, DAILY BUGLE.

I'M SORRY, CHARLIE SNOW ISN'T AVAILABLE RIGHT NOW. HE'S DOING AN OFFICE TOUR...

OR MAYBE YOU GET A *TIP-OFF* FROM A MEMBER OF THE PUBLIC ABOUT SOMETHING UNUSUAL THAT'S HAPPENING.

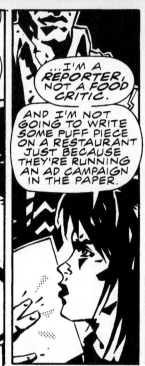

...I'M A *REPORTER,* NOT A FOOD CRITIC.

AND I'M NOT GOING TO WRITE SOME PUFF PIECE ON A RESTAURANT JUST BECAUSE THEY'RE RUNNING AN AD CAMPAIGN IN THE PAPER.

HOW'S THAT?

TRANSPORT AUTHORITIES FLOUTING GOVERNMENT REGULATIONS?

DO IT FOR THE *EXPERIENCE,* BETTY. DO IT TO SHOW YOUR VERSATILITY.

MOST OF ALL...

YEAH, YEAH. DON'T WORRY.

I'LL MAKE *SURE* HE GETS THAT...

BUT HOWEVER IT COMES, THE JOB OF THE REPORTER REMAINS THE SAME...

...DO IT BECAUSE *I'M* THE EDITOR.

RIGHT, CHIEF.

...TO TAKE THAT STORY, AND *RUN* WITH IT.

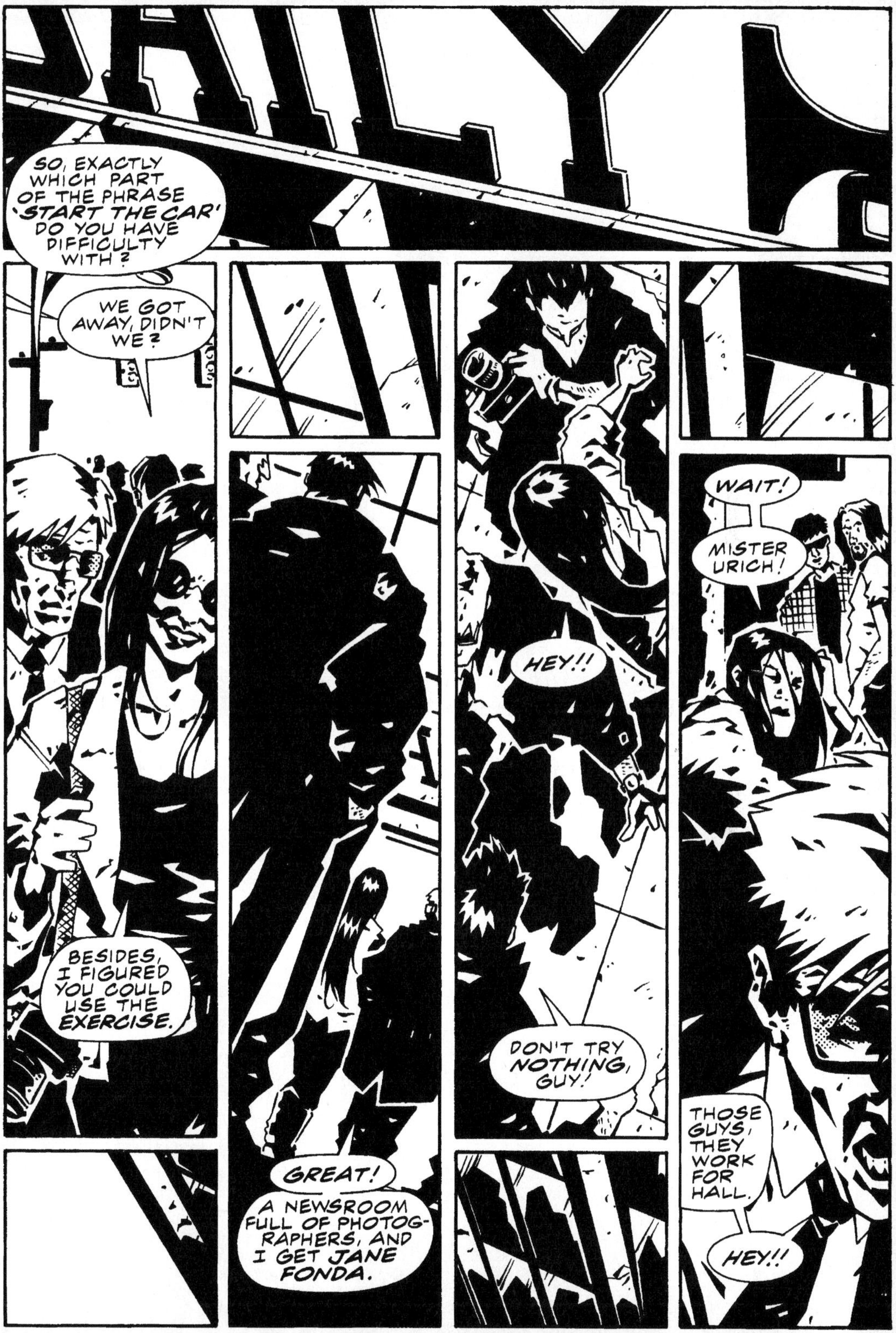
SO, EXACTLY WHICH PART OF THE PHRASE 'START THE CAR' DO YOU HAVE DIFFICULTY WITH?
WE GOT AWAY, DIDN'T WE?
BESIDES, I FIGURED YOU COULD USE THE EXERCISE.
HEY!!
DON'T TRY NOTHING, GUY!
WAIT!
MISTER URICH!
THOSE GUYS, THEY WORK FOR HALL.
GREAT!
A NEWSROOM FULL OF PHOTOGRAPHERS, AND I GET JANE FONDA.
HEY!!

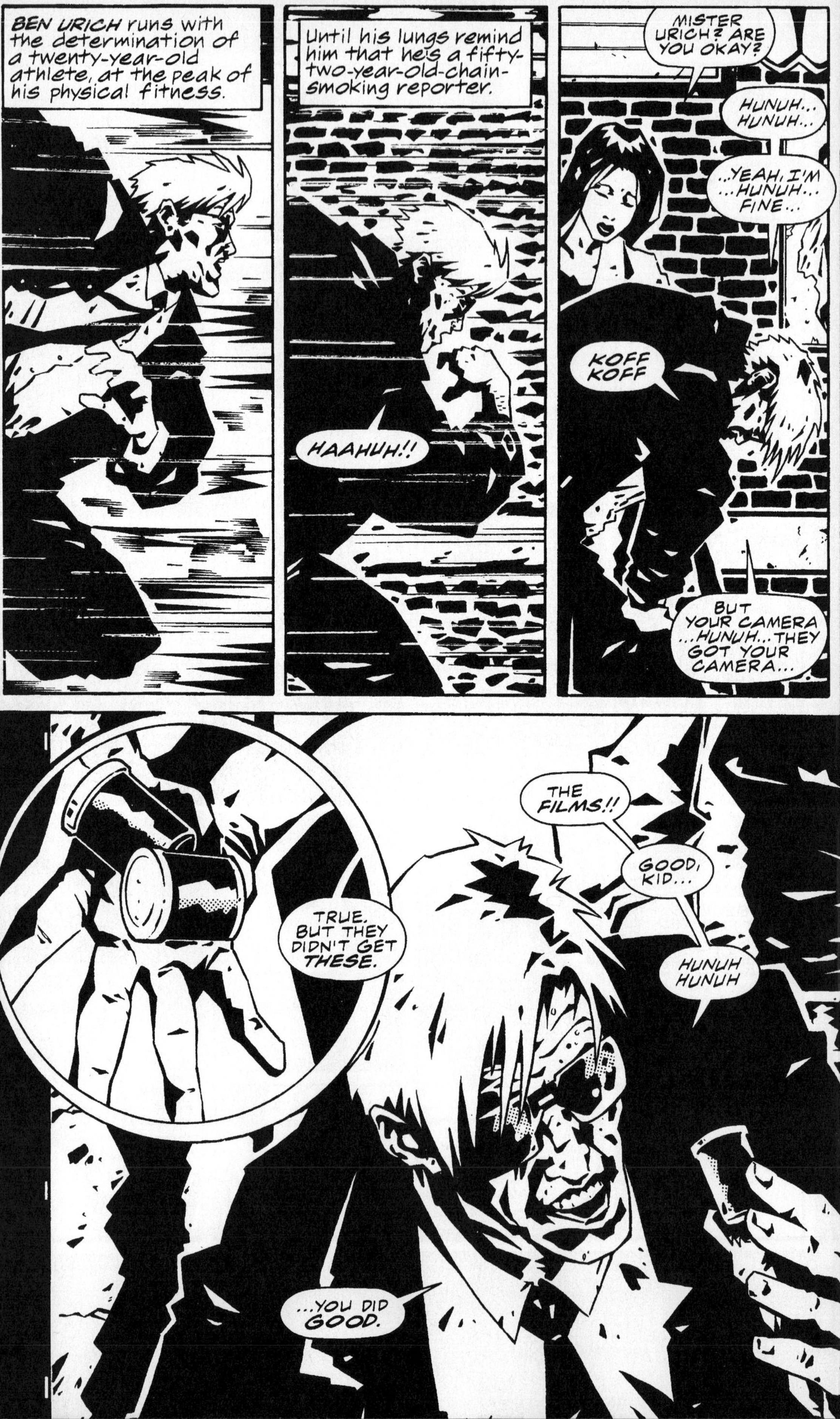
BEN URICH runs with the determination of a twenty-year-old athlete, at the peak of his physical fitness.
Until his lungs remind him that he's a fifty-two-year-old-chain-smoking reporter.
HAAHUH!!
MISTER URICH? ARE YOU OKAY?
HUNUH... HUNUH...
...YEAH, I'M ...HUNUH... FINE...
KOFF KOFF
BUT YOUR CAMERA ...HUNUH... THEY GOT YOUR CAMERA...
TRUE. BUT THEY DIDN'T GET THESE.
THE FILMS!!
GOOD, KID...
HUNUH HUNUH
...YOU DID GOOD.

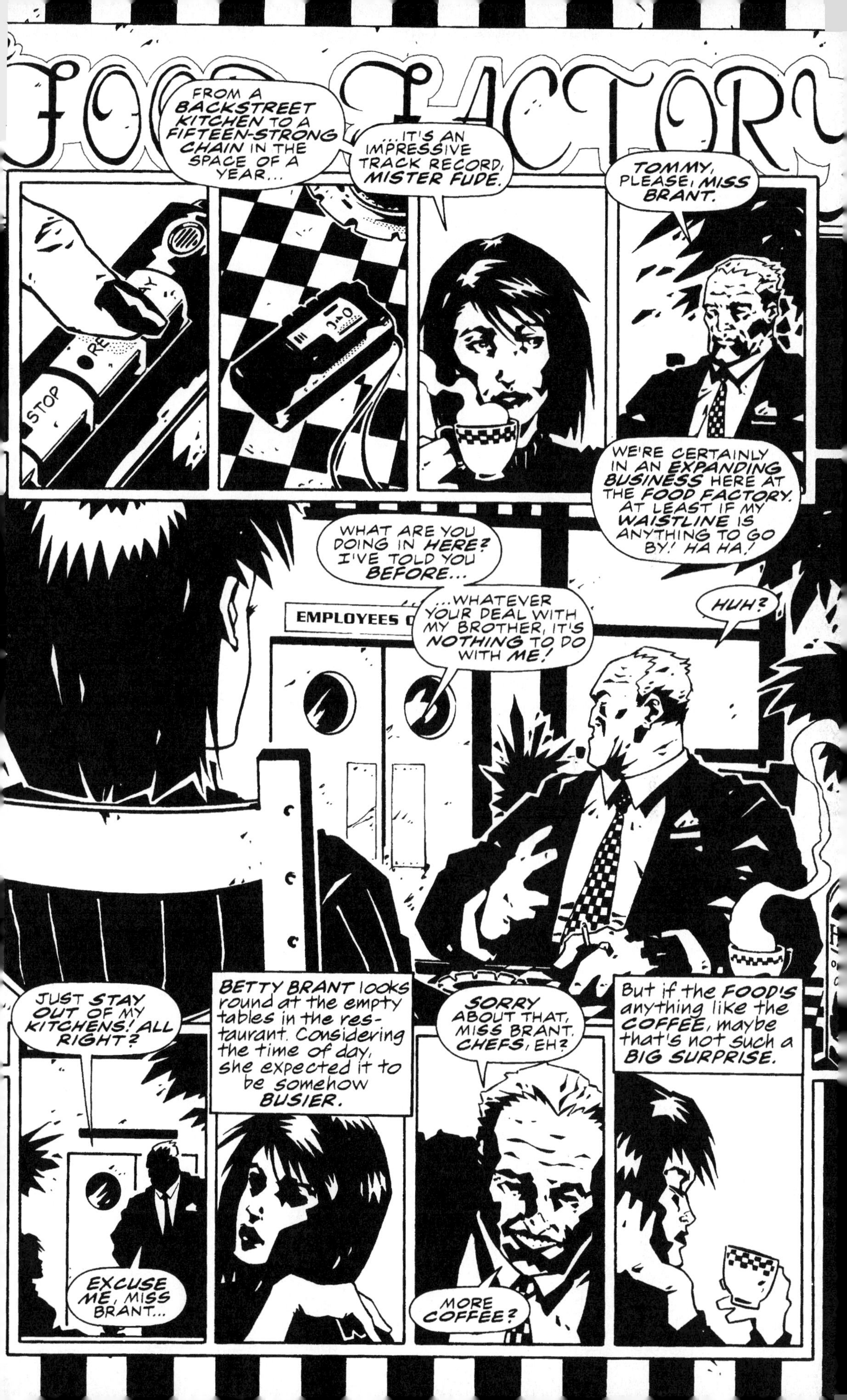
FOOD FACTORY
FROM A BACKSTREET KITCHEN TO A FIFTEEN-STRONG CHAIN IN THE SPACE OF A YEAR...
...IT'S AN IMPRESSIVE TRACK RECORD, MISTER FUDE.
TOMMY, PLEASE, MISS BRANT.
STOP
WE'RE CERTAINLY IN AN EXPANDING BUSINESS HERE AT THE FOOD FACTORY. AT LEAST IF MY WAISTLINE IS ANYTHING TO GO BY! HA HA!
WHAT ARE YOU DOING IN HERE? I'VE TOLD YOU BEFORE...
...WHATEVER YOUR DEAL WITH MY BROTHER, IT'S NOTHING TO DO WITH ME!
EMPLOYEES
HUH?
JUST STAY OUT OF MY KITCHENS! ALL RIGHT?
EXCUSE ME, MISS BRANT...
BETTY BRANT looks round at the empty tables in the restaurant. Considering the time of day, she expected it to be somehow BUSIER.
SORRY ABOUT THAT, MISS BRANT. CHEFS, EH?
MORE COFFEE?
But if the FOOD'S anything like the COFFEE, maybe that's not such a BIG SURPRISE.

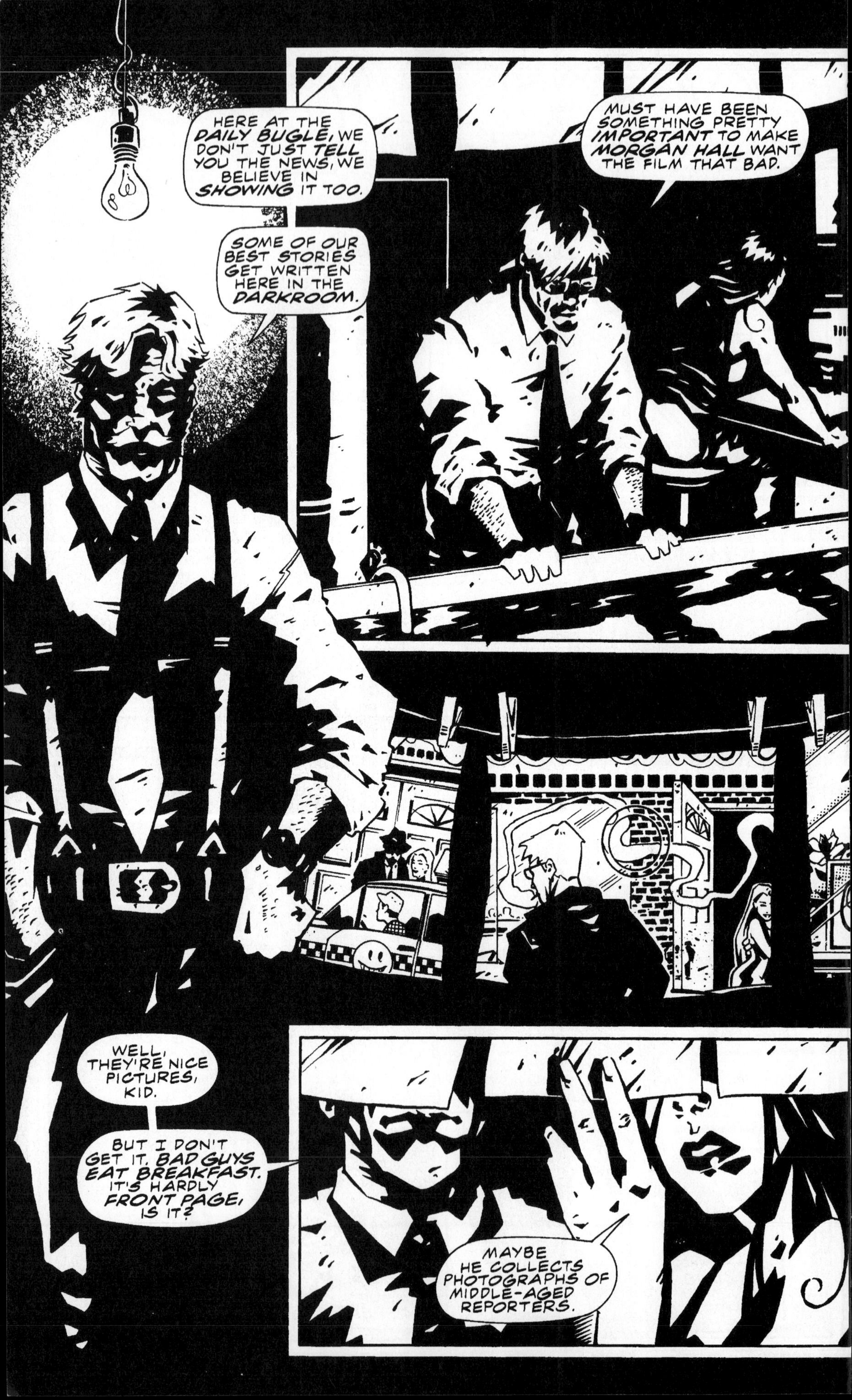
HERE AT THE DAILY BUGLE, WE DON'T JUST TELL YOU THE NEWS, WE BELIEVE IN SHOWING IT TOO.
SOME OF OUR BEST STORIES GET WRITTEN HERE IN THE DARKROOM.
MUST HAVE BEEN SOMETHING PRETTY IMPORTANT TO MAKE MORGAN HALL WANT THE FILM THAT BAD.
WELL, THEY'RE NICE PICTURES, KID.
BUT I DON'T GET IT. BAD GUYS EAT BREAKFAST. IT'S HARDLY FRONT PAGE, IS IT?
MAYBE HE COLLECTS PHOTOGRAPHS OF MIDDLE-AGED REPORTERS.

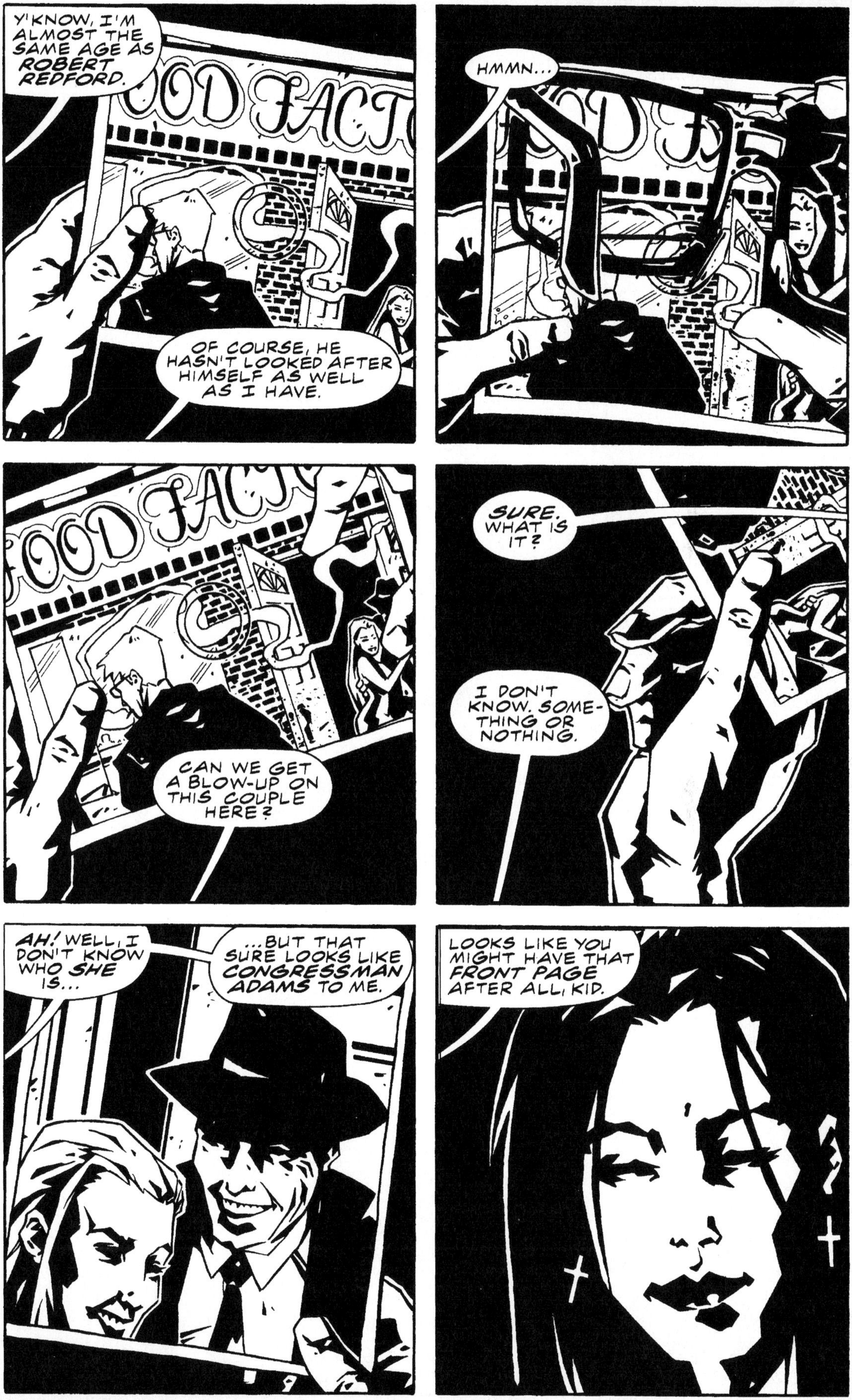
Y'KNOW, I'M ALMOST THE SAME AGE AS ROBERT REDFORD.
OF COURSE, HE HASN'T LOOKED AFTER HIMSELF AS WELL AS I HAVE.
HMMN...
CAN WE GET A BLOW-UP ON THIS COUPLE HERE?
SURE. WHAT IS IT?
I DON'T KNOW. SOME-THING OR NOTHING.
AH! WELL, I DON'T KNOW WHO SHE IS...
...BUT THAT SURE LOOKS LIKE CONGRESSMAN ADAMS TO ME.
LOOKS LIKE YOU MIGHT HAVE THAT FRONT PAGE AFTER ALL, KID.

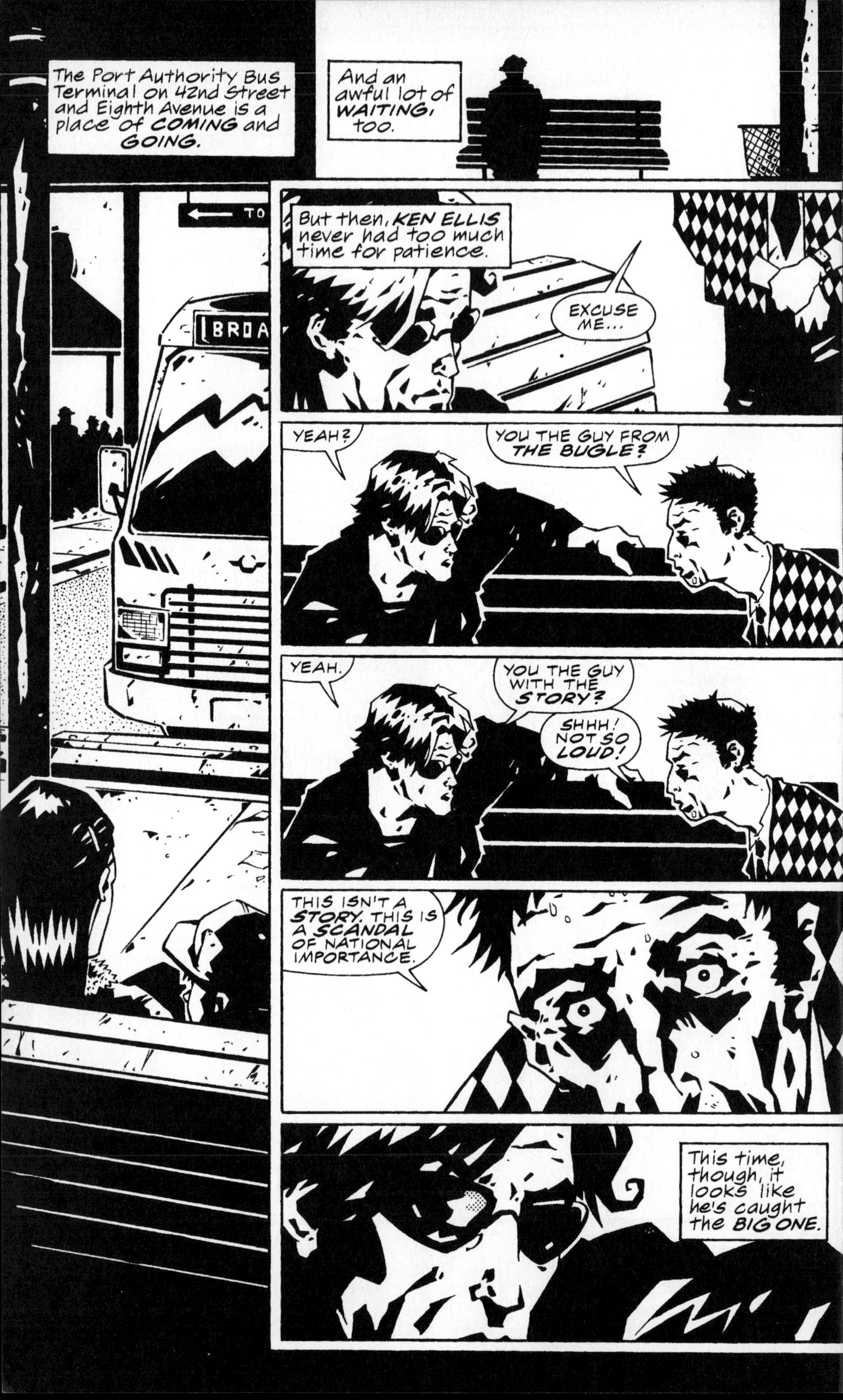
The Port Authority Bus Terminal on 42nd Street and Eighth Avenue is a place of COMING and GOING.
And an awful lot of WAITING, too.
TO
BROA
But then, KEN ELLIS never had too much time for patience.
EXCUSE ME...
YEAH?
YOU THE GUY FROM THE BUGLE?
YEAH.
YOU THE GUY WITH THE STORY?
SHHH! NOT SO LOUD!
THIS ISN'T A STORY. THIS IS A SCANDAL OF NATIONAL IMPORTANCE.
This time, though, it looks like he's caught the BIG ONE.

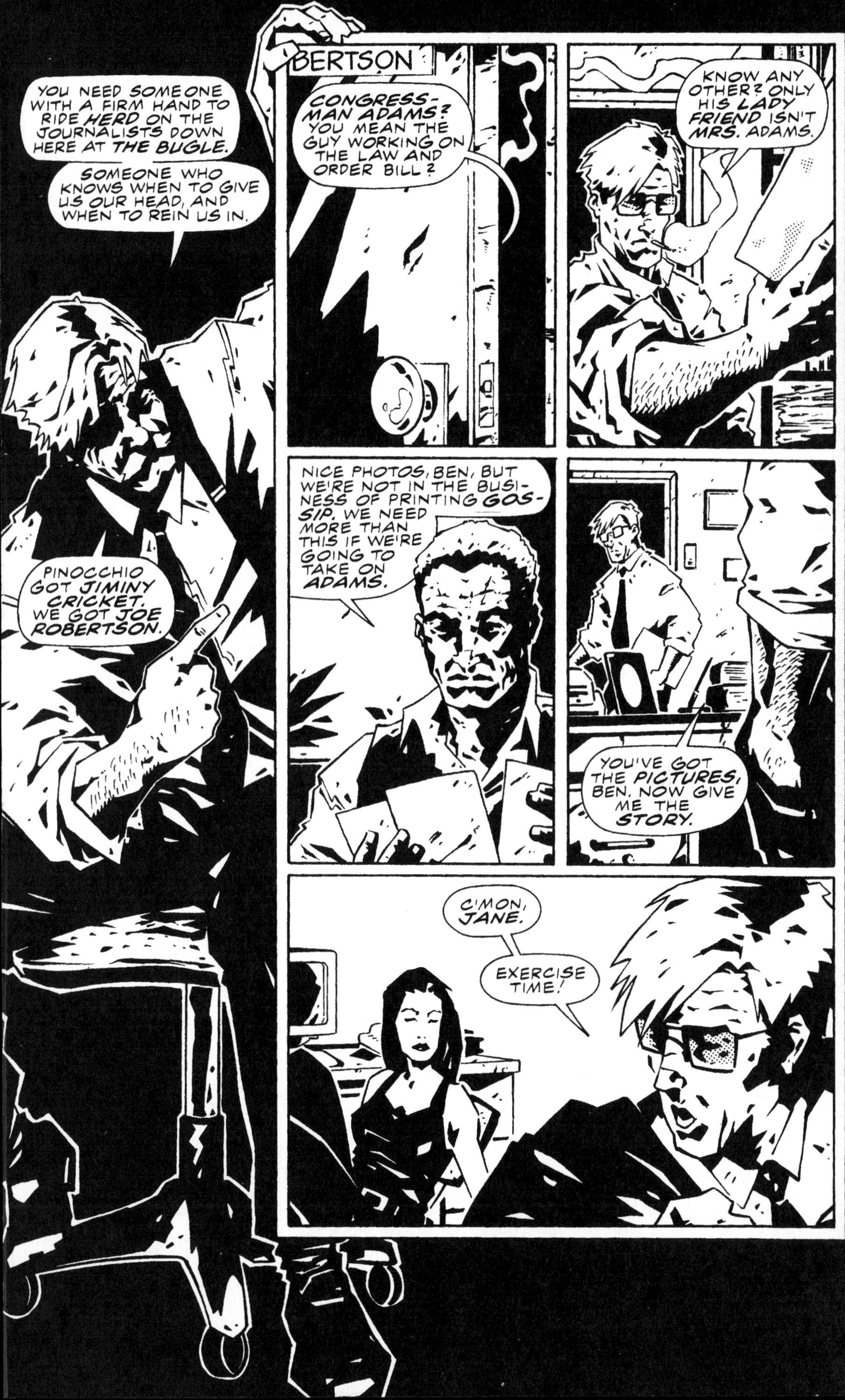
YOU NEED SOMEONE WITH A FIRM HAND TO RIDE HERD ON THE JOURNALISTS DOWN HERE AT THE BUGLE.
SOMEONE WHO KNOWS WHEN TO GIVE US OUR HEAD, AND WHEN TO REIN US IN.
PINOCCHIO GOT JIMINY CRICKET. WE GOT JOE ROBERTSON.
BERTSON
CONGRESS-MAN ADAMS? YOU MEAN THE GUY WORKING ON THE LAW AND ORDER BILL?
KNOW ANY OTHER? ONLY HIS LADY FRIEND ISN'T MRS. ADAMS.
NICE PHOTOS, BEN, BUT WE'RE NOT IN THE BUSI-NESS OF PRINTING GOS-SIP. WE NEED MORE THAN THIS IF WE'RE GOING TO TAKE ON ADAMS.
YOU'VE GOT THE PICTURES, BEN. NOW GIVE ME THE STORY.
C'MON, JANE.
EXERCISE TIME!

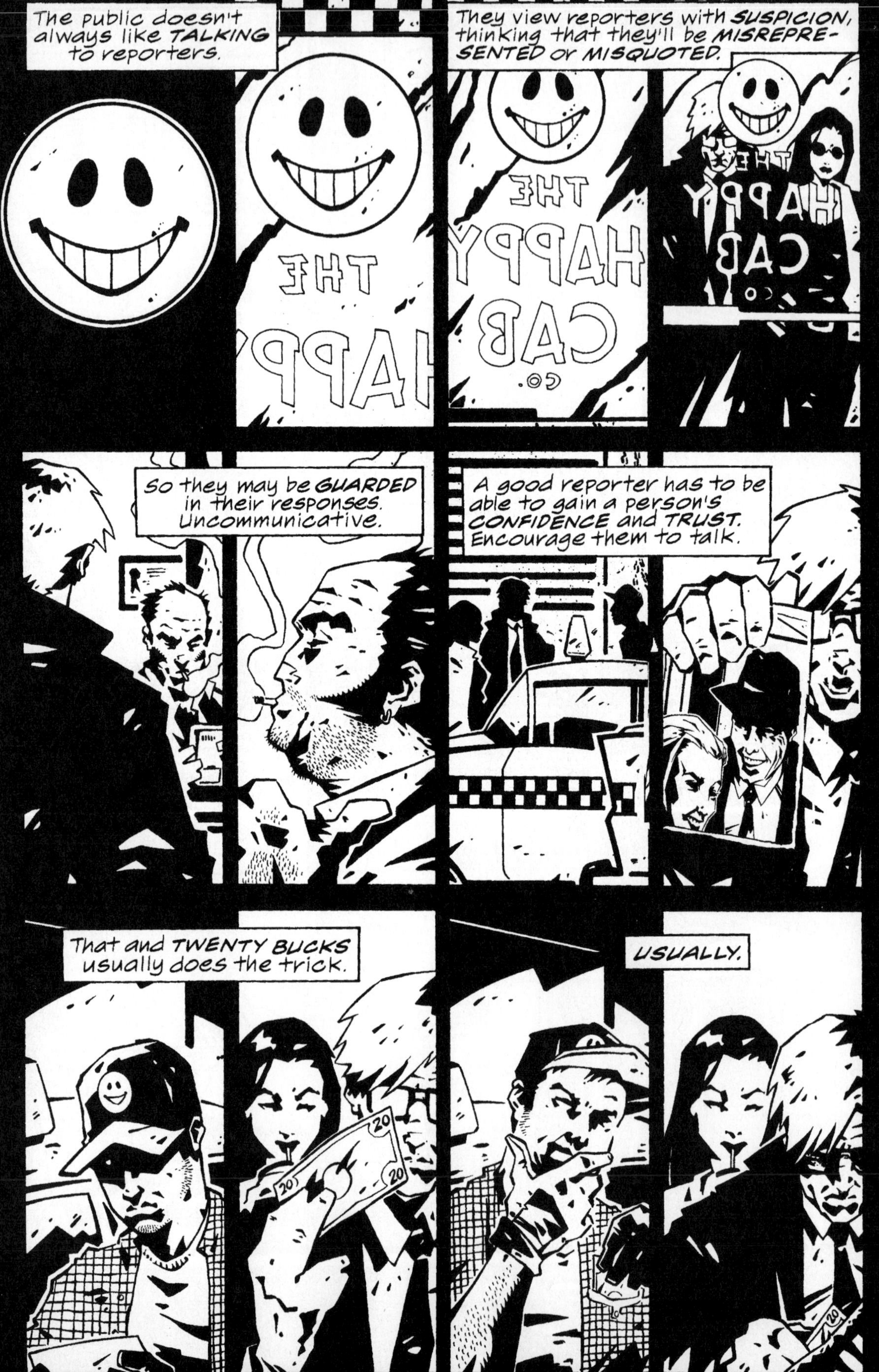

The public doesn't always like TALKING to reporters.
They view reporters with SUSPICION, thinking that they'll be MISREPRESENTED or MISQUOTED.
THE HAPPY CAB CO.
So they may be GUARDED in their responses. Uncommunicative.
A good reporter has to be able to gain a person's CONFIDENCE and TRUST. Encourage them to talk.
That and TWENTY BUCKS usually does the trick.
20
USUALLY.

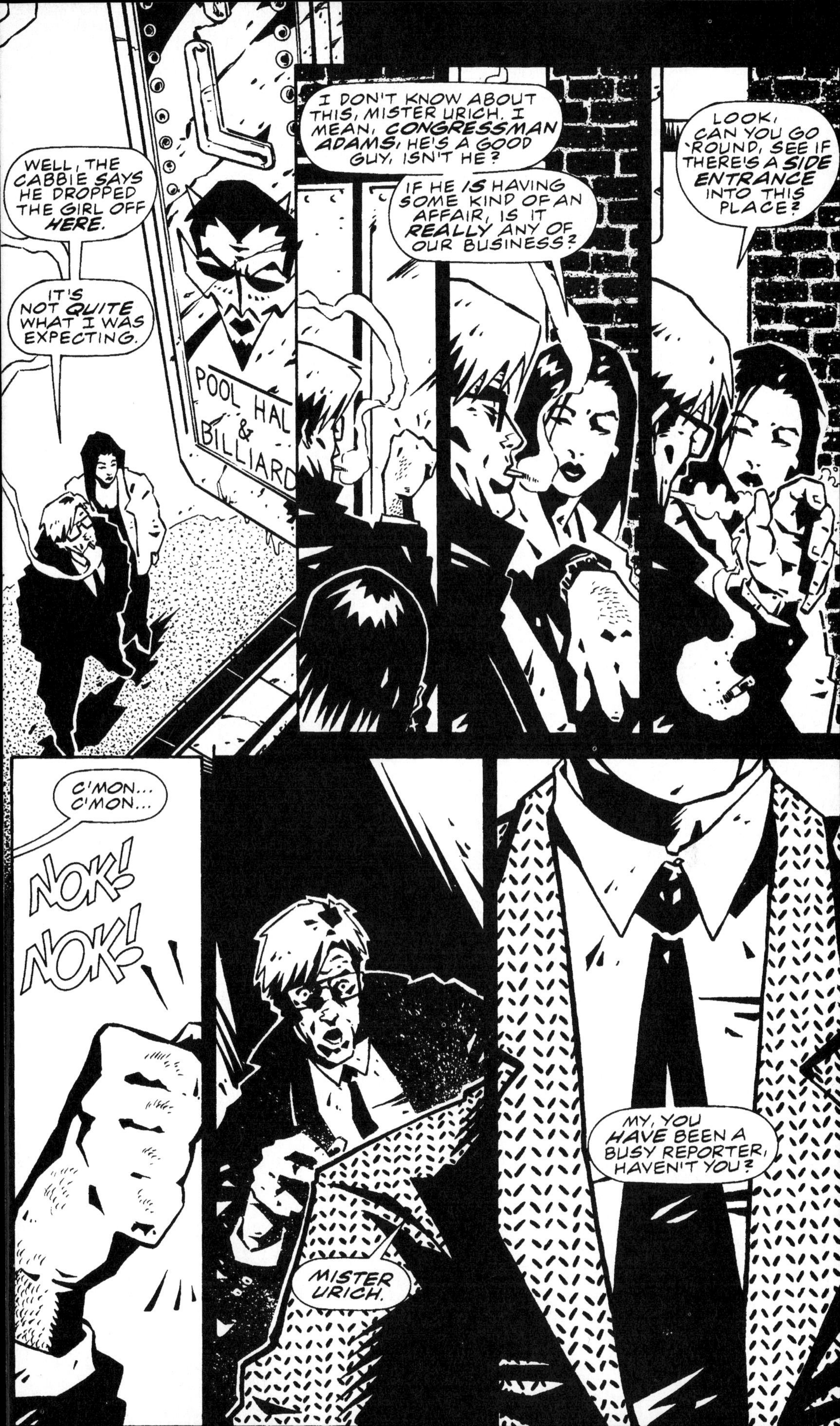
WELL, THE CABBIE SAYS HE DROPPED THE GIRL OFF HERE.
IT'S NOT QUITE WHAT I WAS EXPECTING.
POOL HAL & BILLIARD
I DON'T KNOW ABOUT THIS, MISTER URICH. I MEAN, CONGRESSMAN ADAMS, HE'S A GOOD GUY, ISN'T HE?
IF HE IS HAVING SOME KIND OF AN AFFAIR, IS IT REALLY ANY OF OUR BUSINESS?
LOOK, CAN YOU GO 'ROUND, SEE IF THERE'S A SIDE ENTRANCE INTO THIS PLACE?
C'MON... C'MON...
NOK! NOK!
MISTER URICH.
MY, YOU HAVE BEEN A BUSY REPORTER, HAVEN'T YOU?

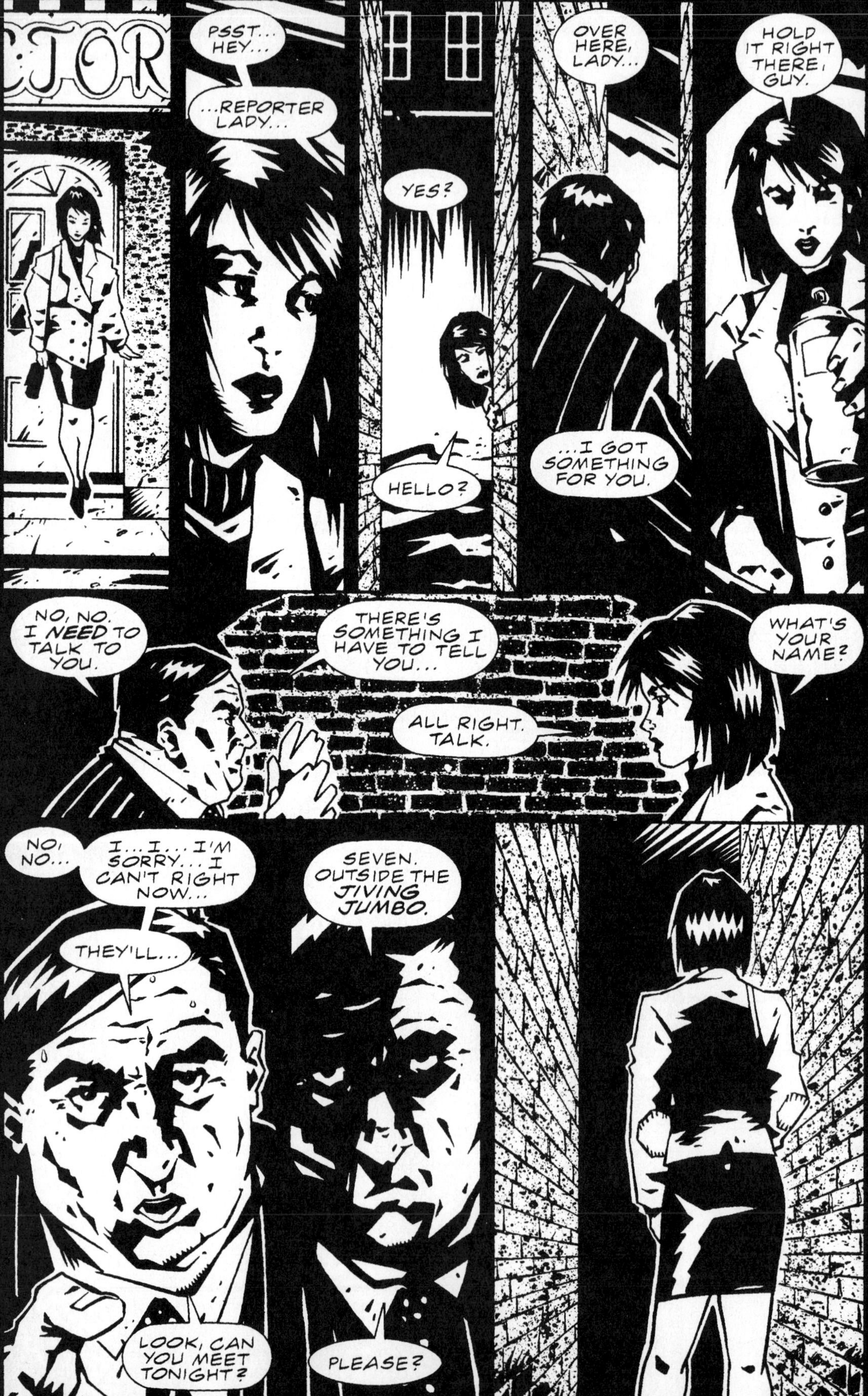

CTOR
PSST... HEY...
...REPORTER LADY...
YES?
HELLO?
OVER HERE, LADY...
...I GOT SOMETHING FOR YOU.
HOLD IT RIGHT THERE, GUY.
NO, NO. I NEED TO TALK TO YOU.
THERE'S SOMETHING I HAVE TO TELL YOU...
ALL RIGHT. TALK.
WHAT'S YOUR NAME?
NO, NO...
I... I... I'M SORRY... I CAN'T RIGHT NOW...
THEY'LL...
LOOK, CAN YOU MEET TONIGHT?
SEVEN. OUTSIDE THE JIVING JUMBO.
PLEASE?

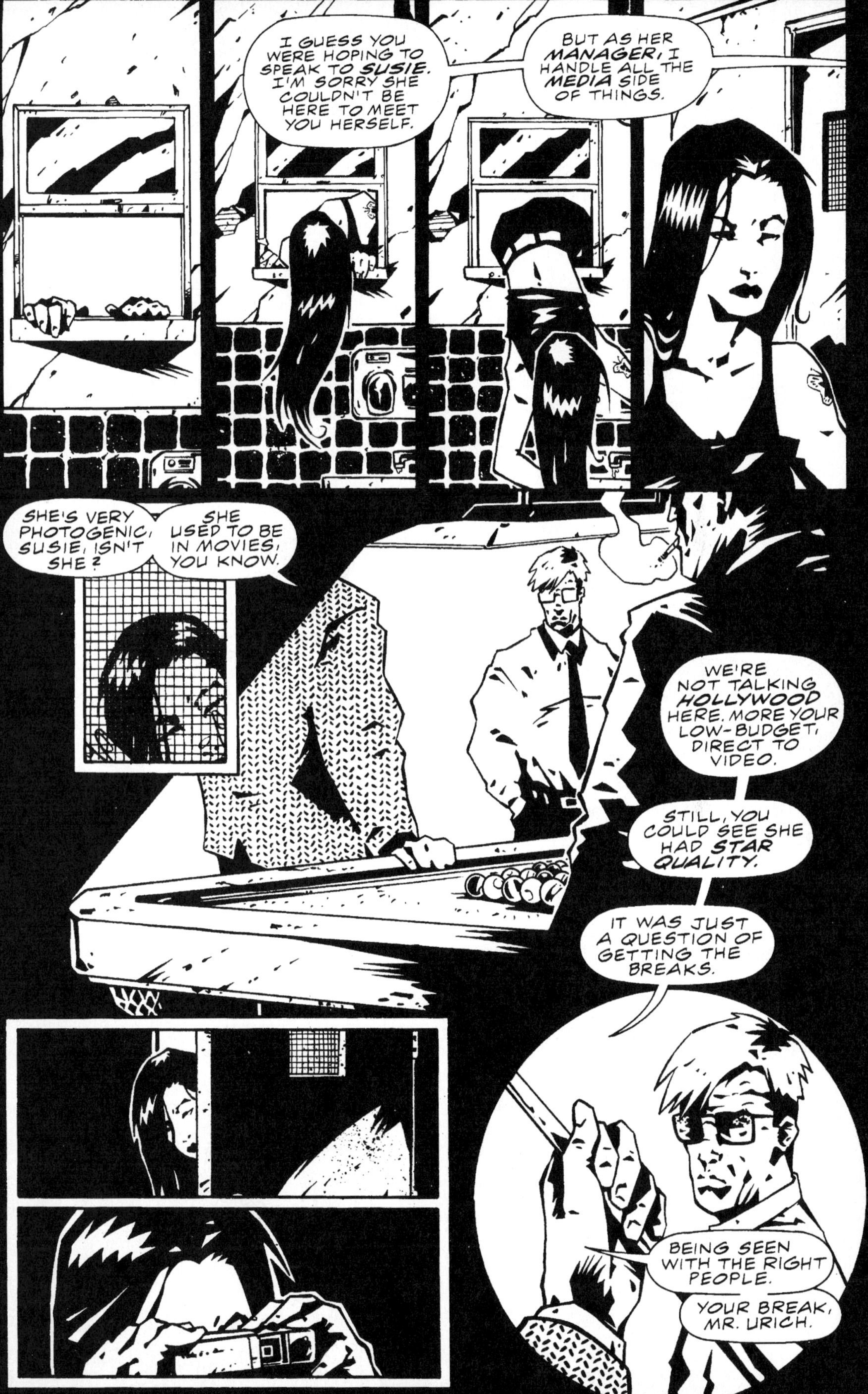
I GUESS YOU WERE HOPING TO SPEAK TO SUSIE. I'M SORRY SHE COULDN'T BE HERE TO MEET YOU HERSELF.
BUT AS HER MANAGER, I HANDLE ALL THE MEDIA SIDE OF THINGS.
SHE'S VERY PHOTOGENIC, SUSIE, ISN'T SHE?
SHE USED TO BE IN MOVIES, YOU KNOW.
WE'RE NOT TALKING HOLLYWOOD HERE. MORE YOUR LOW-BUDGET, DIRECT TO VIDEO.
STILL, YOU COULD SEE SHE HAD STAR QUALITY.
IT WAS JUST A QUESTION OF GETTING THE BREAKS.
BEING SEEN WITH THE RIGHT PEOPLE.
YOUR BREAK, MR. URICH.

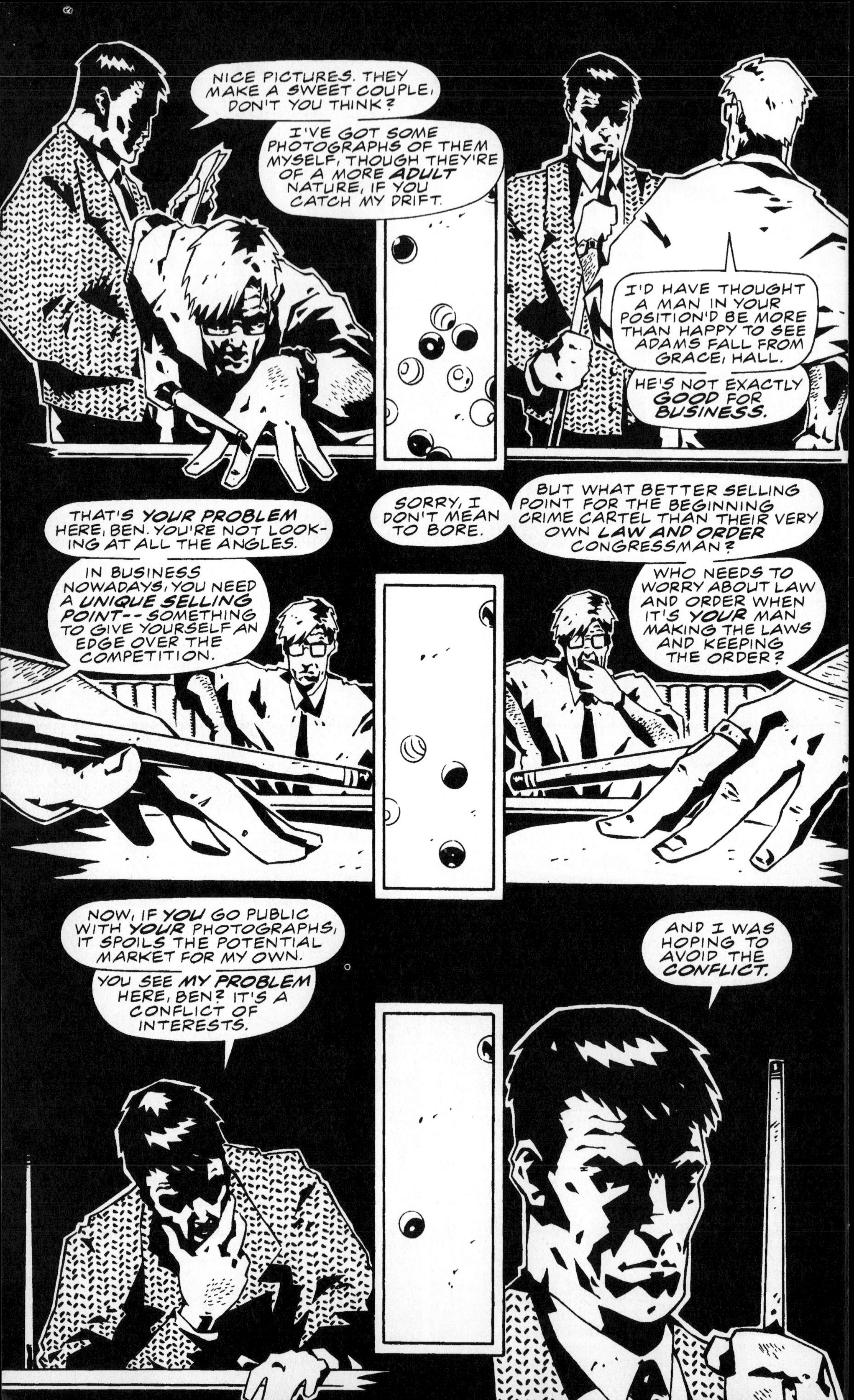

NICE PICTURES. THEY MAKE A SWEET COUPLE, DON'T YOU THINK?
I'VE GOT SOME PHOTOGRAPHS OF THEM MYSELF, THOUGH THEY'RE OF A MORE ADULT NATURE, IF YOU CATCH MY DRIFT.
I'D HAVE THOUGHT A MAN IN YOUR POSITION'D BE MORE THAN HAPPY TO SEE ADAMS FALL FROM GRACE, HALL.
HE'S NOT EXACTLY GOOD FOR BUSINESS.
THAT'S YOUR PROBLEM HERE, BEN. YOU'RE NOT LOOKING AT ALL THE ANGLES.
IN BUSINESS NOWADAYS, YOU NEED A UNIQUE SELLING POINT-- SOMETHING TO GIVE YOURSELF AN EDGE OVER THE COMPETITION.
SORRY, I DON'T MEAN TO BORE.
BUT WHAT BETTER SELLING POINT FOR THE BEGINNING CRIME CARTEL THAN THEIR VERY OWN LAW AND ORDER CONGRESSMAN?
WHO NEEDS TO WORRY ABOUT LAW AND ORDER WHEN IT'S YOUR MAN MAKING THE LAWS AND KEEPING THE ORDER?
NOW, IF YOU GO PUBLIC WITH YOUR PHOTOGRAPHS, IT SPOILS THE POTENTIAL MARKET FOR MY OWN.
YOU SEE MY PROBLEM HERE, BEN? IT'S A CONFLICT OF INTERESTS.
AND I WAS HOPING TO AVOID THE CONFLICT.

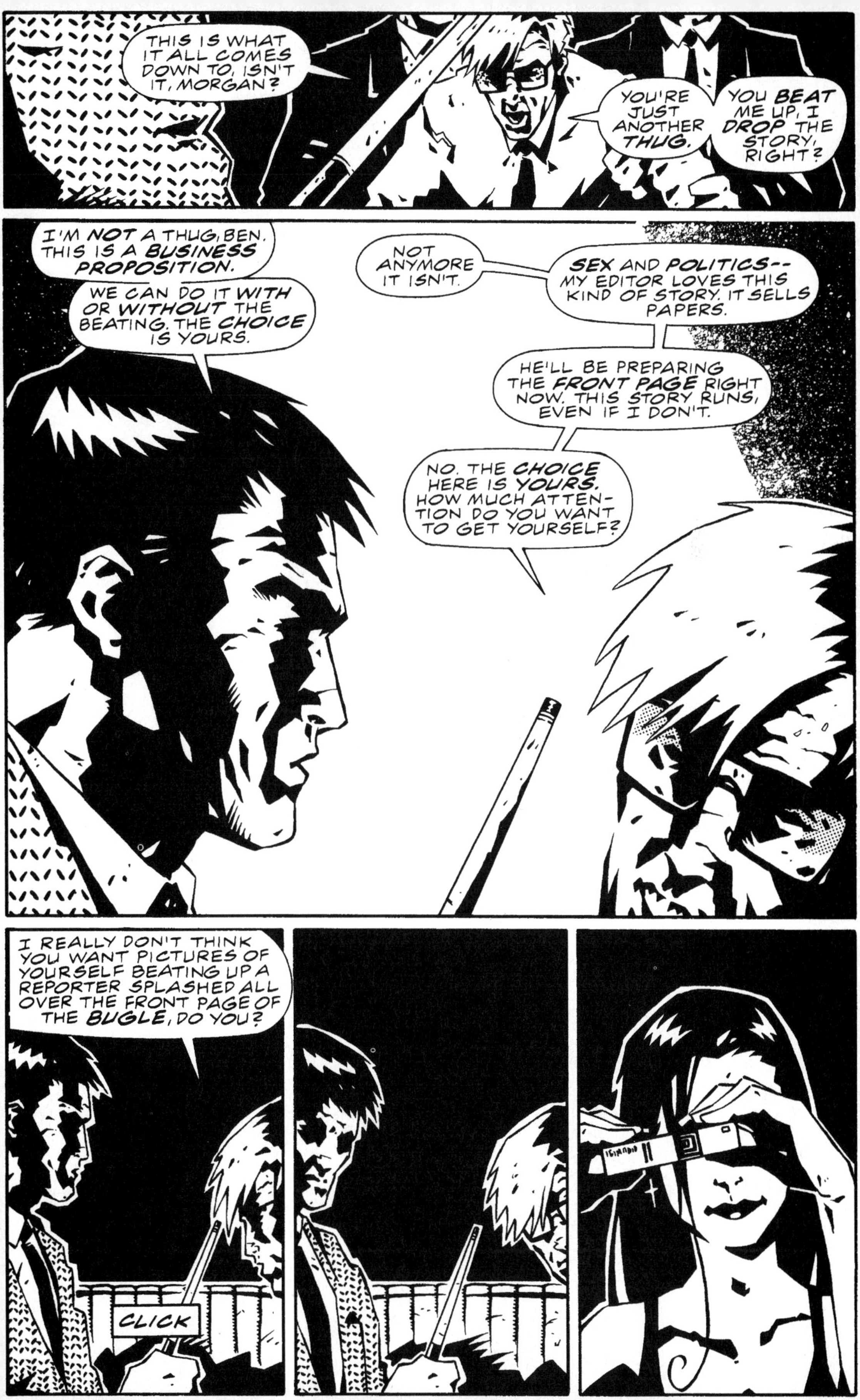

THIS IS WHAT IT ALL COMES DOWN TO, ISN'T IT, MORGAN?
YOU'RE JUST ANOTHER THUG.
YOU BEAT ME UP, I DROP THE STORY, RIGHT?
I'M NOT A THUG, BEN. THIS IS A BUSINESS PROPOSITION.
WE CAN DO IT WITH OR WITHOUT THE BEATING. THE CHOICE IS YOURS.
NOT ANYMORE IT ISN'T.
SEX AND POLITICS-- MY EDITOR LOVES THIS KIND OF STORY. IT SELLS PAPERS.
HE'LL BE PREPARING THE FRONT PAGE RIGHT NOW. THIS STORY RUNS, EVEN IF I DON'T.
NO. THE CHOICE HERE IS YOURS. HOW MUCH ATTEN- TION DO YOU WANT TO GET YOURSELF?
I REALLY DON'T THINK YOU WANT PICTURES OF YOURSELF BEATING UP A REPORTER SPLASHED ALL OVER THE FRONT PAGE OF THE BUGLE, DO YOU?
CLICK

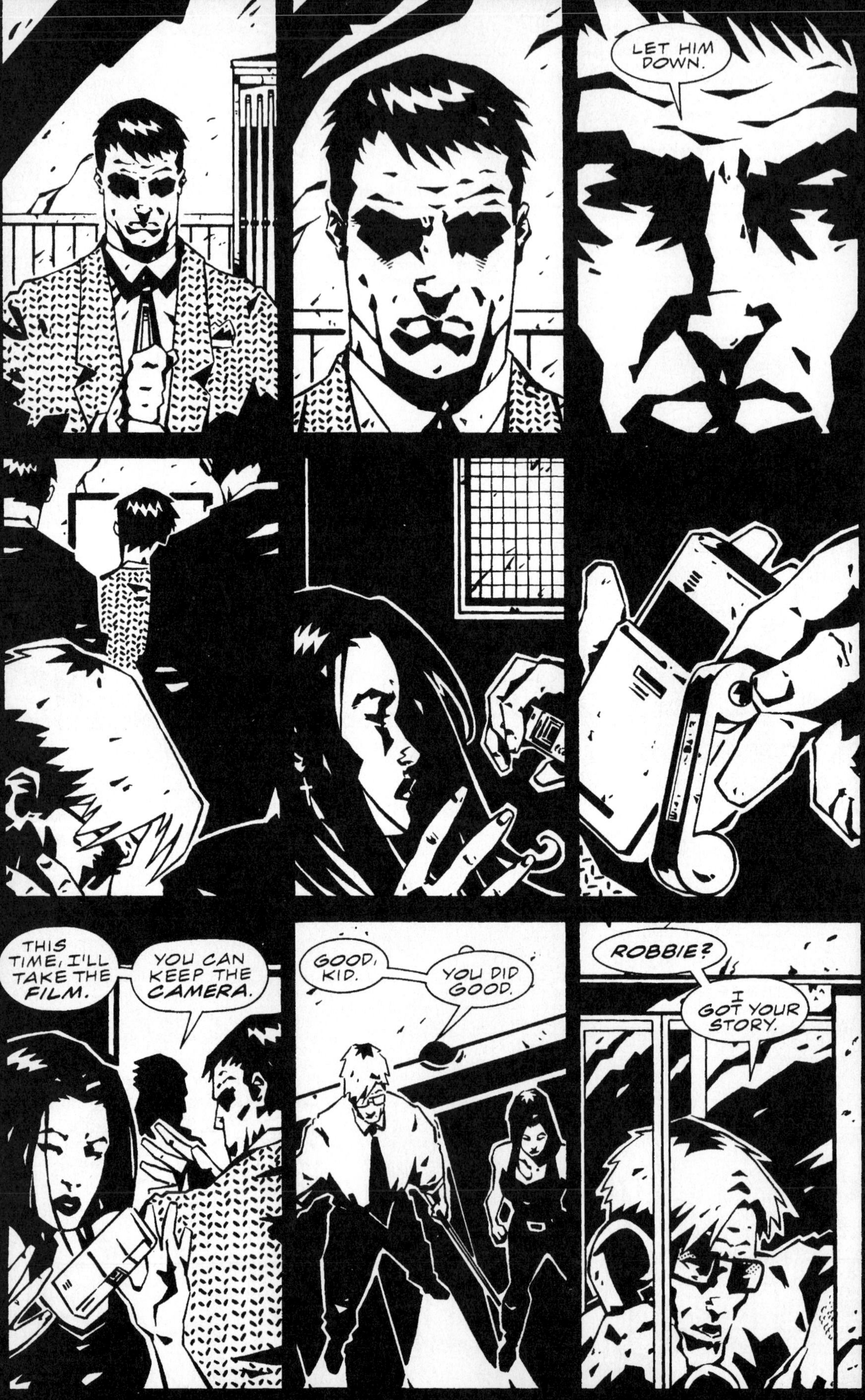
LET HIM DOWN.
THIS TIME, I'LL TAKE THE FILM.
YOU CAN KEEP THE CAMERA.
GOOD, KID.
YOU DID GOOD.
ROBBIE?
I GOT YOUR STORY.

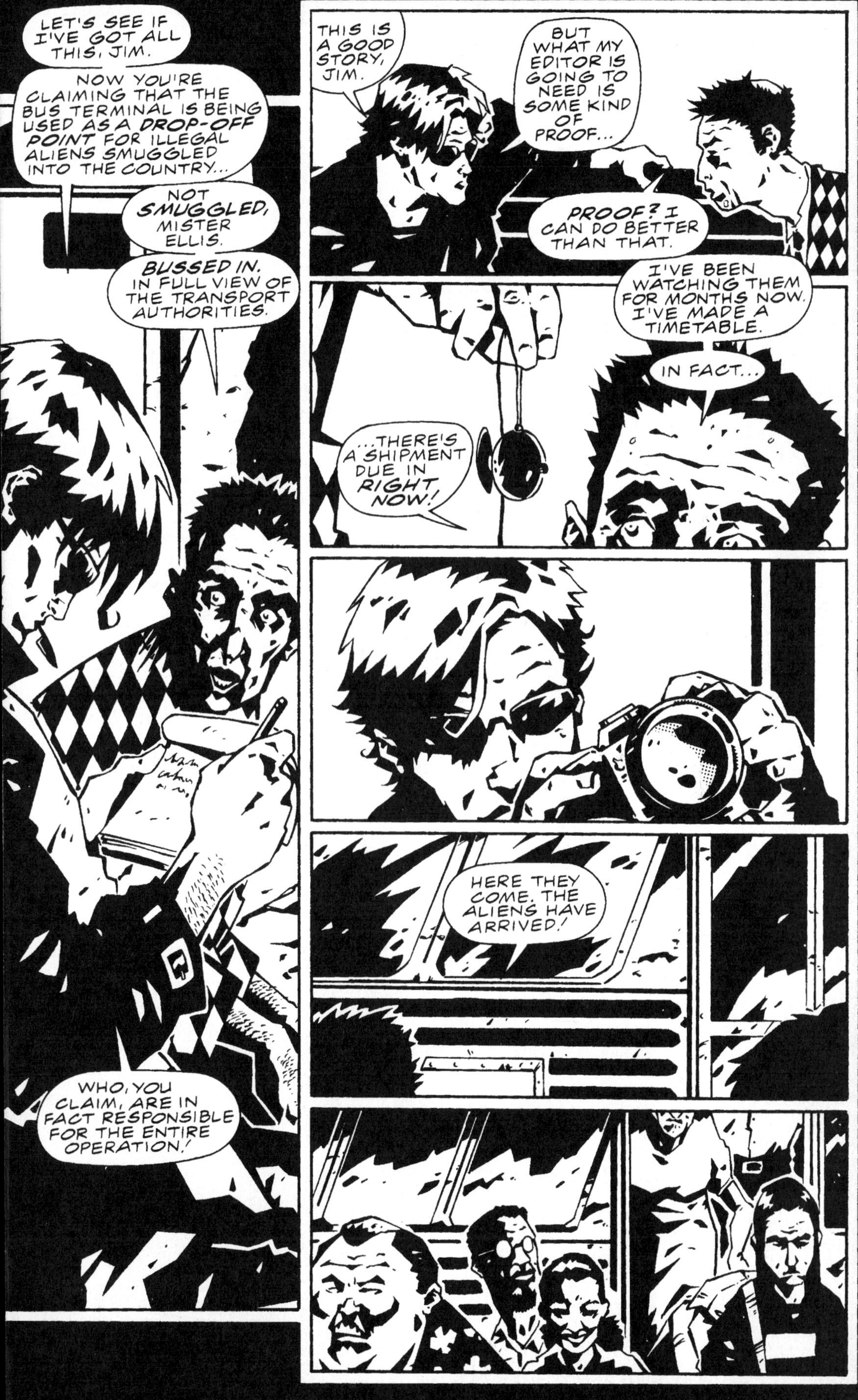
LET'S SEE IF I'VE GOT ALL THIS, JIM.
NOW YOU'RE CLAIMING THAT THE BUS TERMINAL IS BEING USED AS A DROP-OFF POINT FOR ILLEGAL ALIENS SMUGGLED INTO THE COUNTRY...
NOT SMUGGLED, MISTER ELLIS.
BUSSED IN. IN FULL VIEW OF THE TRANSPORT AUTHORITIES.
WHO, YOU CLAIM, ARE IN FACT RESPONSIBLE FOR THE ENTIRE OPERATION!
THIS IS A GOOD STORY, JIM.
BUT WHAT MY EDITOR IS GOING TO NEED IS SOME KIND OF PROOF...
PROOF? I CAN DO BETTER THAN THAT.
I'VE BEEN WATCHING THEM FOR MONTHS NOW. I'VE MADE A TIMETABLE.
IN FACT...
...THERE'S A SHIPMENT DUE IN RIGHT NOW!
HERE THEY COME. THE ALIENS HAVE ARRIVED!

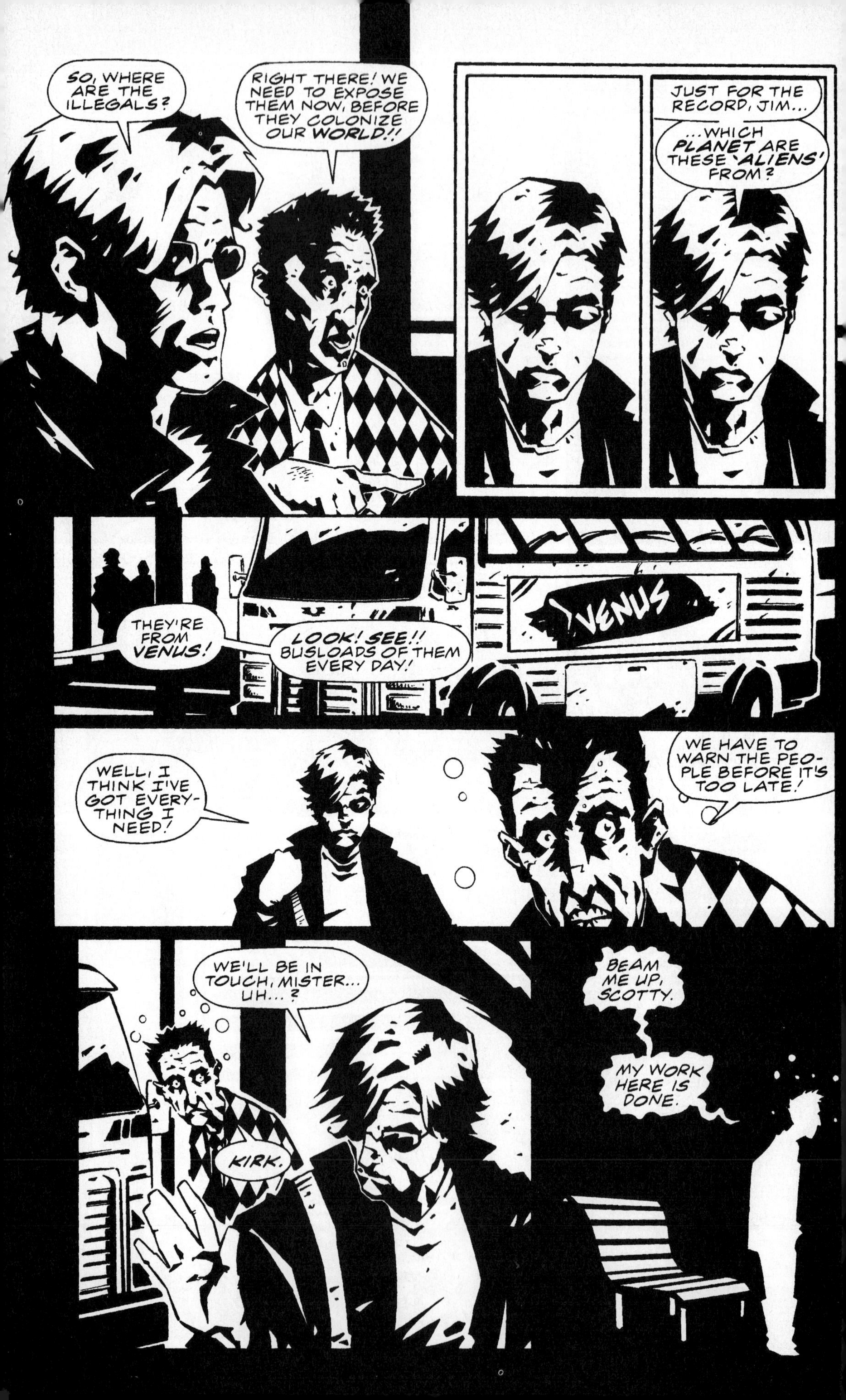
SO, WHERE ARE THE ILLEGALS?
RIGHT THERE! WE NEED TO EXPOSE THEM NOW, BEFORE THEY COLONIZE OUR WORLD!!
JUST FOR THE RECORD, JIM...
...WHICH PLANET ARE THESE 'ALIENS' FROM?
THEY'RE FROM VENUS!
LOOK! SEE!! BUSLOADS OF THEM EVERY DAY!
VENUS
WELL, I THINK I'VE GOT EVERYTHING I NEED!
WE HAVE TO WARN THE PEOPLE BEFORE IT'S TOO LATE!
WE'LL BE IN TOUCH, MISTER... UH...?
KIRK.
BEAM ME UP, SCOTTY.
MY WORK HERE IS DONE.

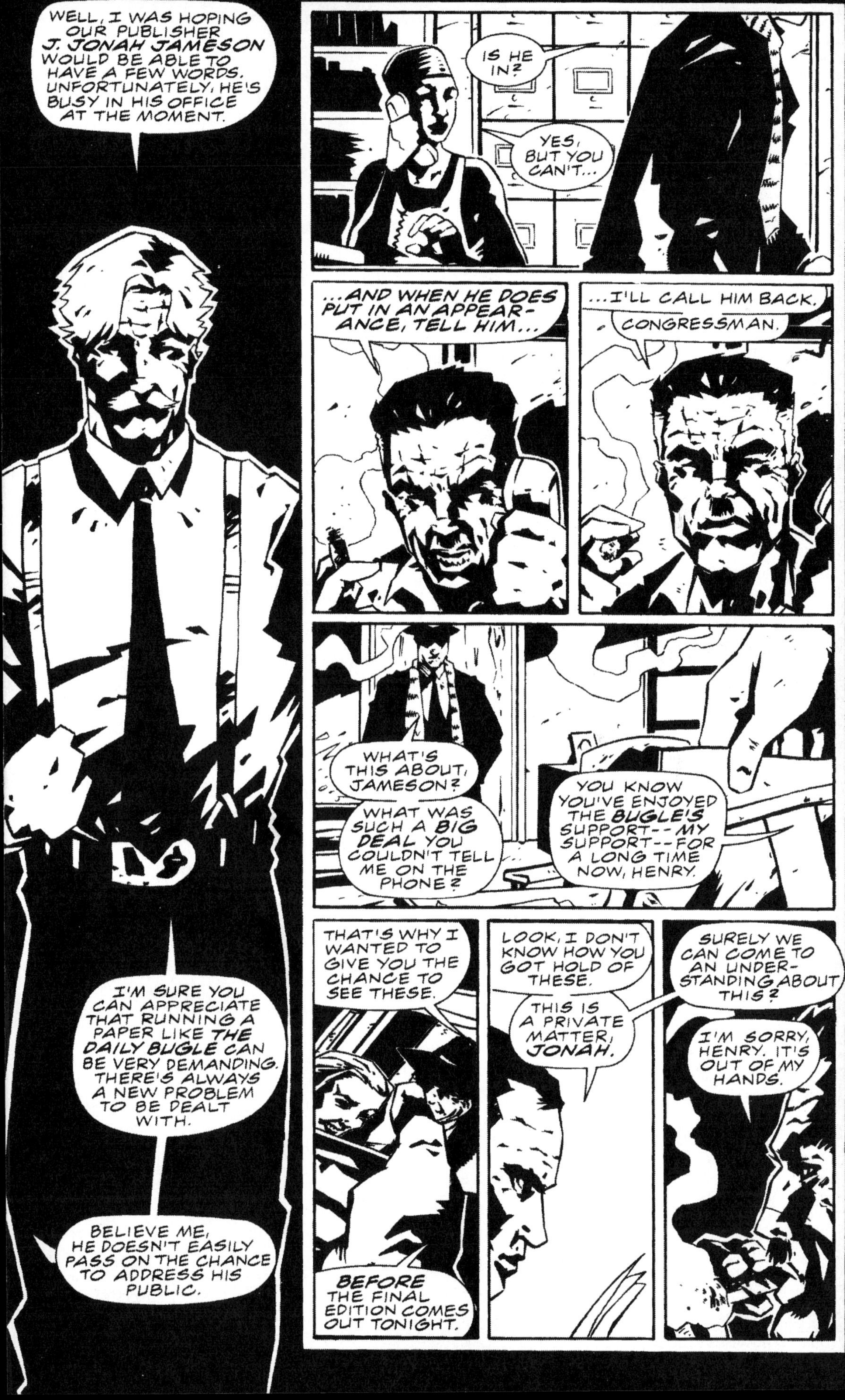
WELL, I WAS HOPING OUR PUBLISHER J. JONAH JAMESON WOULD BE ABLE TO HAVE A FEW WORDS. UNFORTUNATELY, HE'S BUSY IN HIS OFFICE AT THE MOMENT.
IS HE IN?
YES, BUT YOU CAN'T...
...AND WHEN HE DOES PUT IN AN APPEARANCE, TELL HIM...
...I'LL CALL HIM BACK.
CONGRESSMAN.
WHAT'S THIS ABOUT, JAMESON?
WHAT WAS SUCH A BIG DEAL YOU COULDN'T TELL ME ON THE PHONE?
YOU KNOW YOU'VE ENJOYED THE BUGLE'S SUPPORT-- MY SUPPORT-- FOR A LONG TIME NOW, HENRY.
THAT'S WHY I WANTED TO GIVE YOU THE CHANCE TO SEE THESE.
BEFORE THE FINAL EDITION COMES OUT TONIGHT.
LOOK, I DON'T KNOW HOW YOU GOT HOLD OF THESE.
THIS IS A PRIVATE MATTER, JONAH.
SURELY WE CAN COME TO AN UNDERSTANDING ABOUT THIS?
I'M SORRY, HENRY. IT'S OUT OF MY HANDS.
I'M SURE YOU CAN APPRECIATE THAT RUNNING A PAPER LIKE THE DAILY BUGLE CAN BE VERY DEMANDING. THERE'S ALWAYS A NEW PROBLEM TO BE DEALT WITH.
BELIEVE ME, HE DOESN'T EASILY PASS ON THE CHANCE TO ADDRESS HIS PUBLIC.

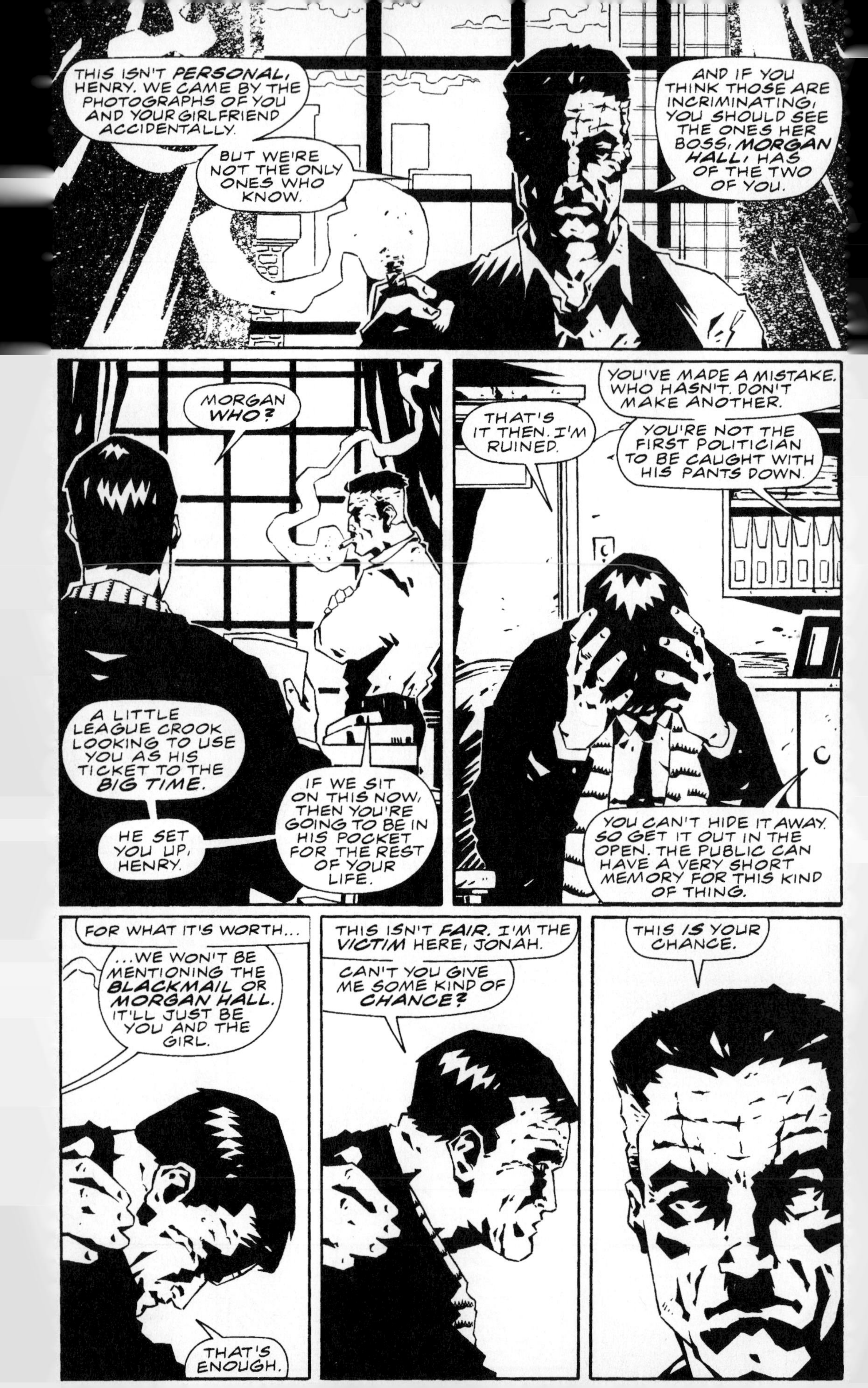
THIS ISN'T PERSONAL, HENRY. WE CAME BY THE PHOTOGRAPHS OF YOU AND YOUR GIRLFRIEND ACCIDENTALLY.
BUT WE'RE NOT THE ONLY ONES WHO KNOW.
AND IF YOU THINK THOSE ARE INCRIMINATING, YOU SHOULD SEE THE ONES HER BOSS, MORGAN HALL, HAS OF THE TWO OF YOU.
MORGAN WHO?
A LITTLE LEAGUE CROOK LOOKING TO USE YOU AS HIS TICKET TO THE BIG TIME.
HE SET YOU UP, HENRY.
IF WE SIT ON THIS NOW, THEN YOU'RE GOING TO BE IN HIS POCKET FOR THE REST OF YOUR LIFE.
THAT'S IT THEN. I'M RUINED.
YOU'VE MADE A MISTAKE. WHO HASN'T. DON'T MAKE ANOTHER.
YOU'RE NOT THE FIRST POLITICIAN TO BE CAUGHT WITH HIS PANTS DOWN.
YOU CAN'T HIDE IT AWAY. SO GET IT OUT IN THE OPEN. THE PUBLIC CAN HAVE A VERY SHORT MEMORY FOR THIS KIND OF THING.
FOR WHAT IT'S WORTH...
...WE WON'T BE MENTIONING THE BLACKMAIL OR MORGAN HALL. IT'LL JUST BE YOU AND THE GIRL.
THAT'S ENOUGH.
THIS ISN'T FAIR. I'M THE VICTIM HERE, JONAH.
CAN'T YOU GIVE ME SOME KIND OF CHANCE?
THIS IS YOUR CHANCE.

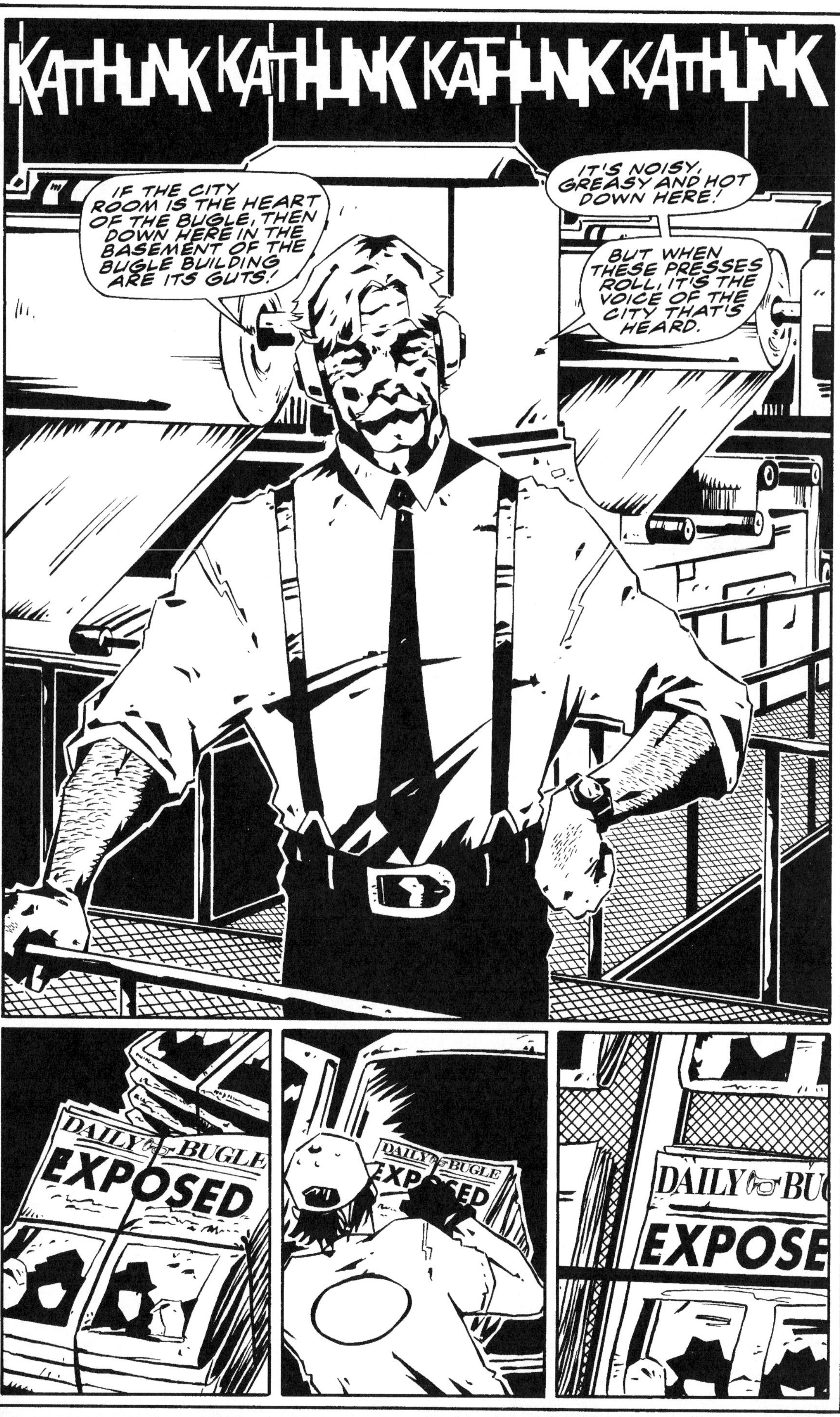
KATHUNK KATHUNK KATHUNK KATHUNK
IF THE CITY ROOM IS THE HEART OF THE BUGLE, THEN DOWN HERE IN THE BASEMENT OF THE BUGLE BUILDING ARE ITS GUTS!
IT'S NOISY, GREASY AND HOT DOWN HERE!
BUT WHEN THESE PRESSES ROLL, IT'S THE VOICE OF THE CITY THAT'S HEARD.
DAILY BUGLE
EXPOSED
DAILY BUGLE
EXPOSED
DAILY BU
EXPOSE

DAILY ☛ BUGLE ® 50¢

F★★★★INAL

NEW YORK'S FINEST DAILY NEWSPAPER

Tuesday, October 8, 1996 — Partly cloudy, chance of snow. High 25-30. Details p.2

EXPOSED

The Congressman and the Porn Star

Report by Ben Urich   Photographs by Angela Yin

Earlier today, The Dailly Bugle discovered evidence that Congressman Henry Adams has been conducting an affair with a former porn film star, Miss Susie Dawn.

Adams, 49, is the driving force behind a 'Law and Order' Bill currently going through Congress. This Bill is intends to give new powers to the police to kerb illegal activities such as pornography, and to keep people profiting from their involvement in these criminal acts.

In a statement to The Dailly Bugle, Congressman Adams said that he had only known Miss Dawn for a few weeks and was unaware of her background .

When asked to comment further , he said that his involvement with Miss Dawn was now over and he hoped for a reconciliation with his wife after a difficult time in his marriage caused by pressures of work.

Miss Dawn, 23, star of the film 'Naughty girls gone bad', was unavailable for comment.

DAILY ꮹ BU

THERE YOU GO, KID.

FRONT PAGE.

GOOD WORK.

DAILY BUGLE ROSED

SO WHAT DID WE DO HERE, MISTER URICH? THE *BAD GUYS* ARE STILL IN BUSINESS...

...AND WE'VE PROBABLY JUST GOT ONE OF THE FEW MEN WHO COULD HAVE MADE A *DIFFER- ENCE* THROWN OUT OF OFFICE.

AND THAT'S *GOOD* WORK?

SPOOKY

LOBSTER TALES

C.G.

GOOD NIGHT, ANGELA.

LOBSTER TALES

C.G.

DAILY EXPO

DAILY EXPOS

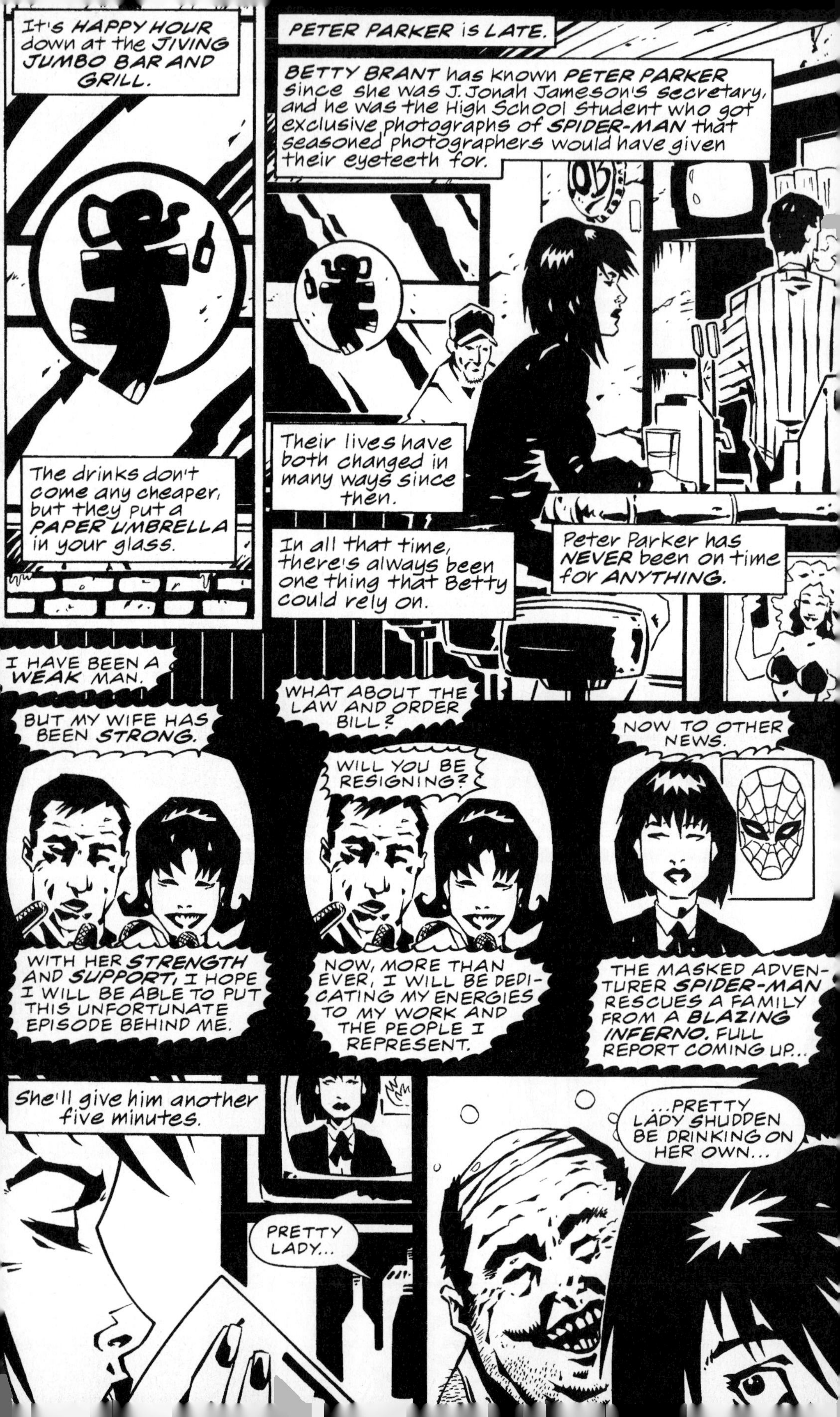

It's HAPPY HOUR down at the JIVING JUMBO BAR AND GRILL.
The drinks don't come any cheaper, but they put a PAPER UMBRELLA in your glass.
PETER PARKER is LATE.
BETTY BRANT has known PETER PARKER since she was J. Jonah Jameson's secretary, and he was the High School Student who got exclusive photographs of SPIDER-MAN that seasoned photographers would have given their eyeteeth for.
Their lives have both changed in many ways since then.
In all that time, there's always been one thing that Betty could rely on.
Peter Parker has NEVER been on time for ANYTHING.
I HAVE BEEN A WEAK MAN.
BUT MY WIFE HAS BEEN STRONG.
WITH HER STRENGTH AND SUPPORT, I HOPE I WILL BE ABLE TO PUT THIS UNFORTUNATE EPISODE BEHIND ME.
WHAT ABOUT THE LAW AND ORDER BILL?
WILL YOU BE RESIGNING?
NOW, MORE THAN EVER, I WILL BE DEDICATING MY ENERGIES TO MY WORK AND THE PEOPLE I REPRESENT.
NOW TO OTHER NEWS.
THE MASKED ADVENTURER SPIDER-MAN RESCUES A FAMILY FROM A BLAZING INFERNO. FULL REPORT COMING UP...
She'll give him another five minutes.
PRETTY LADY...
...PRETTY LADY SHUDDEN BE DRINKING ON HER OWN...

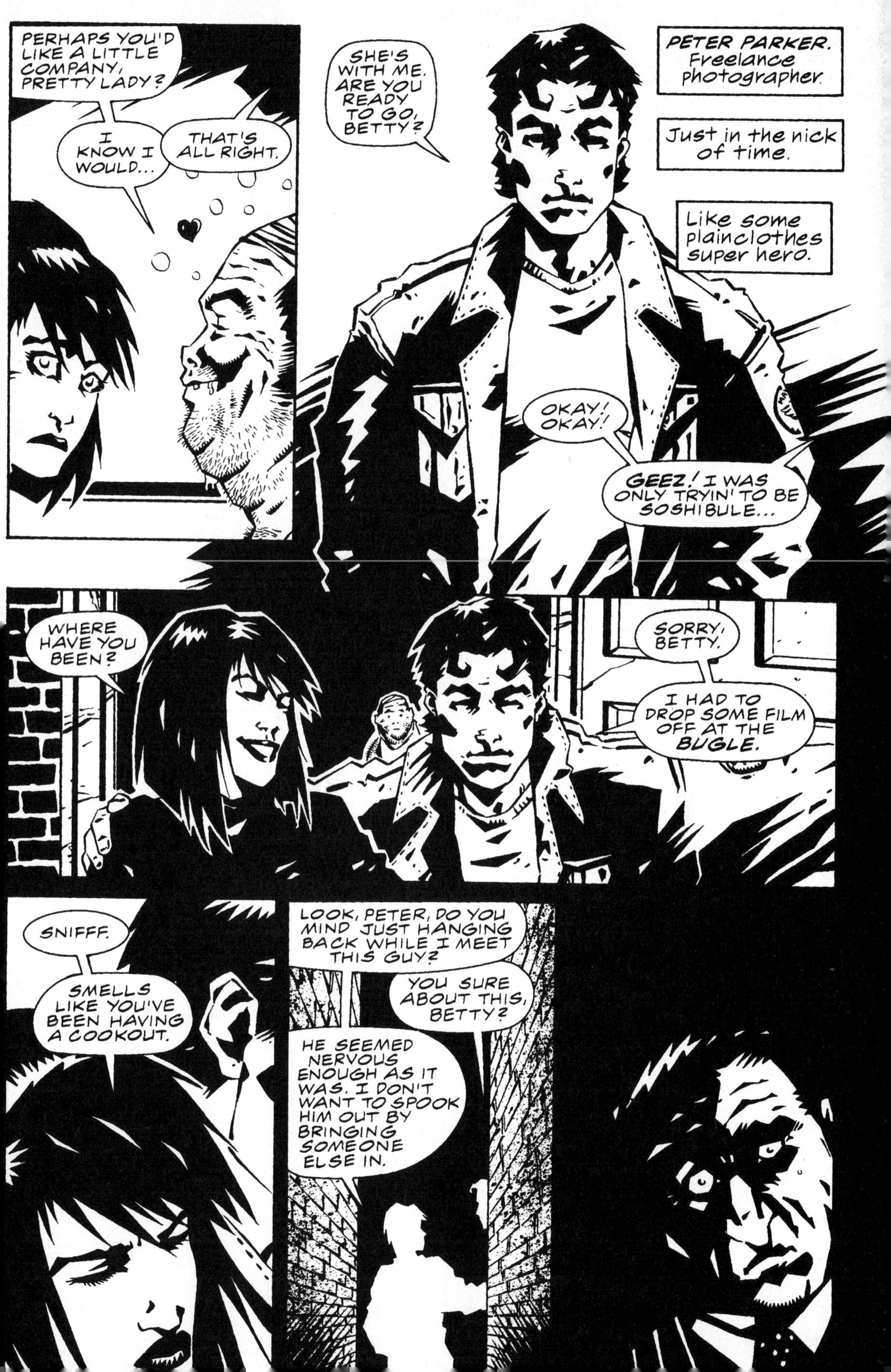

PERHAPS YOU'D LIKE A LITTLE COMPANY, PRETTY LADY?
I KNOW I WOULD...
THAT'S ALL RIGHT.
SHE'S WITH ME. ARE YOU READY TO GO, BETTY?
PETER PARKER. Freelance photographer.
Just in the nick of time.
Like some plainclothes super hero.
OKAY! OKAY!
GEEZ! I WAS ONLY TRYIN' TO BE SOSHIBULE...
WHERE HAVE YOU BEEN?
SORRY, BETTY.
I HAD TO DROP SOME FILM OFF AT THE BUGLE.
SNIFFF.
SMELLS LIKE YOU'VE BEEN HAVING A COOKOUT.
LOOK, PETER, DO YOU MIND JUST HANGING BACK WHILE I MEET THIS GUY?
YOU SURE ABOUT THIS, BETTY?
HE SEEMED NERVOUS ENOUGH AS IT WAS. I DON'T WANT TO SPOOK HIM OUT BY BRINGING SOMEONE ELSE IN.

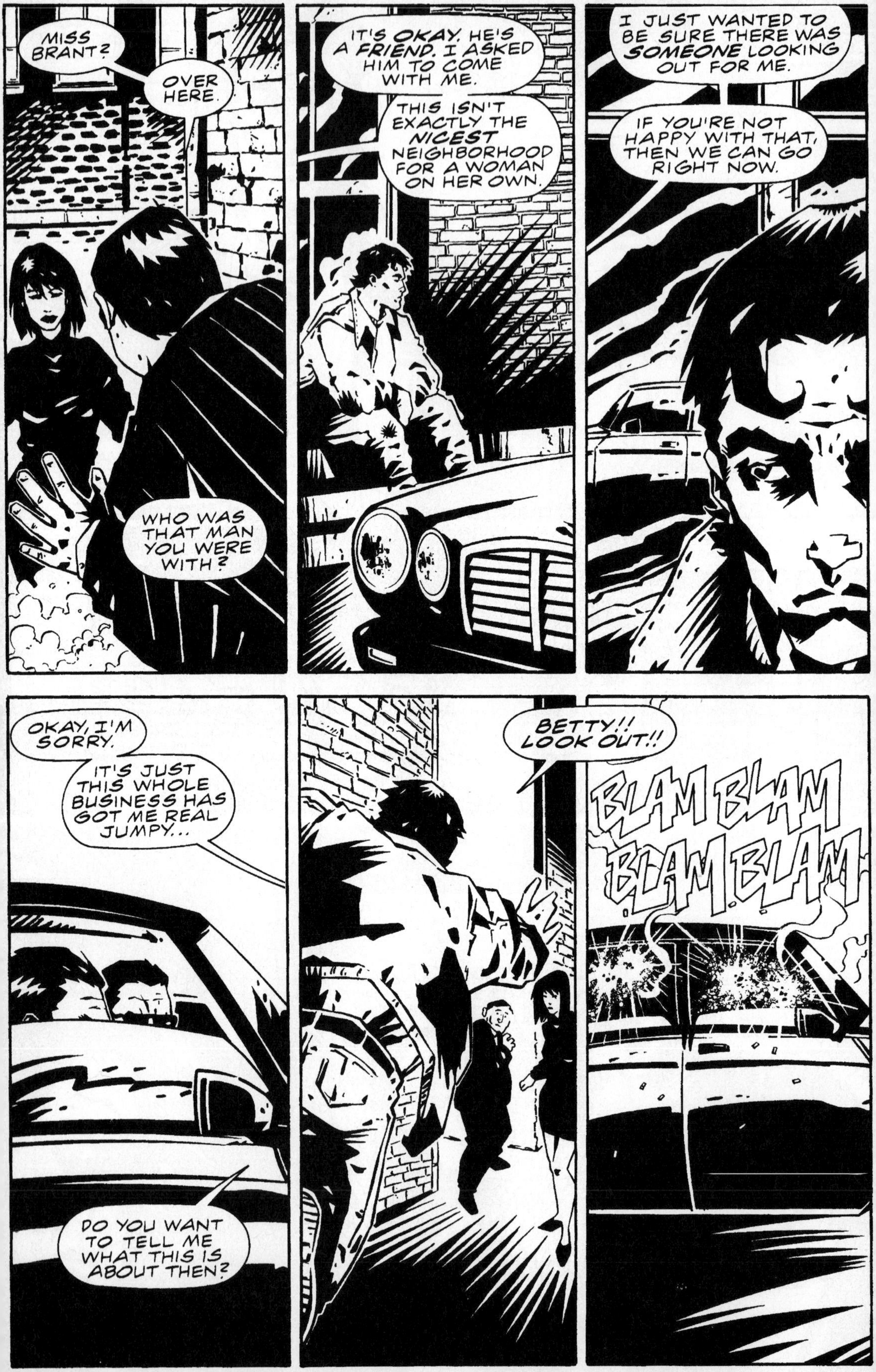
MISS BRANT?
OVER HERE.
WHO WAS THAT MAN YOU WERE WITH?
IT'S OKAY. HE'S A FRIEND. I ASKED HIM TO COME WITH ME.
THIS ISN'T EXACTLY THE NICEST NEIGHBORHOOD FOR A WOMAN ON HER OWN.
I JUST WANTED TO BE SURE THERE WAS SOMEONE LOOKING OUT FOR ME.
IF YOU'RE NOT HAPPY WITH THAT, THEN WE CAN GO RIGHT NOW.
OKAY, I'M SORRY.
IT'S JUST THIS WHOLE BUSINESS HAS GOT ME REAL JUMPY...
DO YOU WANT TO TELL ME WHAT THIS IS ABOUT THEN?
BETTY!! LOOK OUT!!
BLAM BLAM
BLAM BLAM

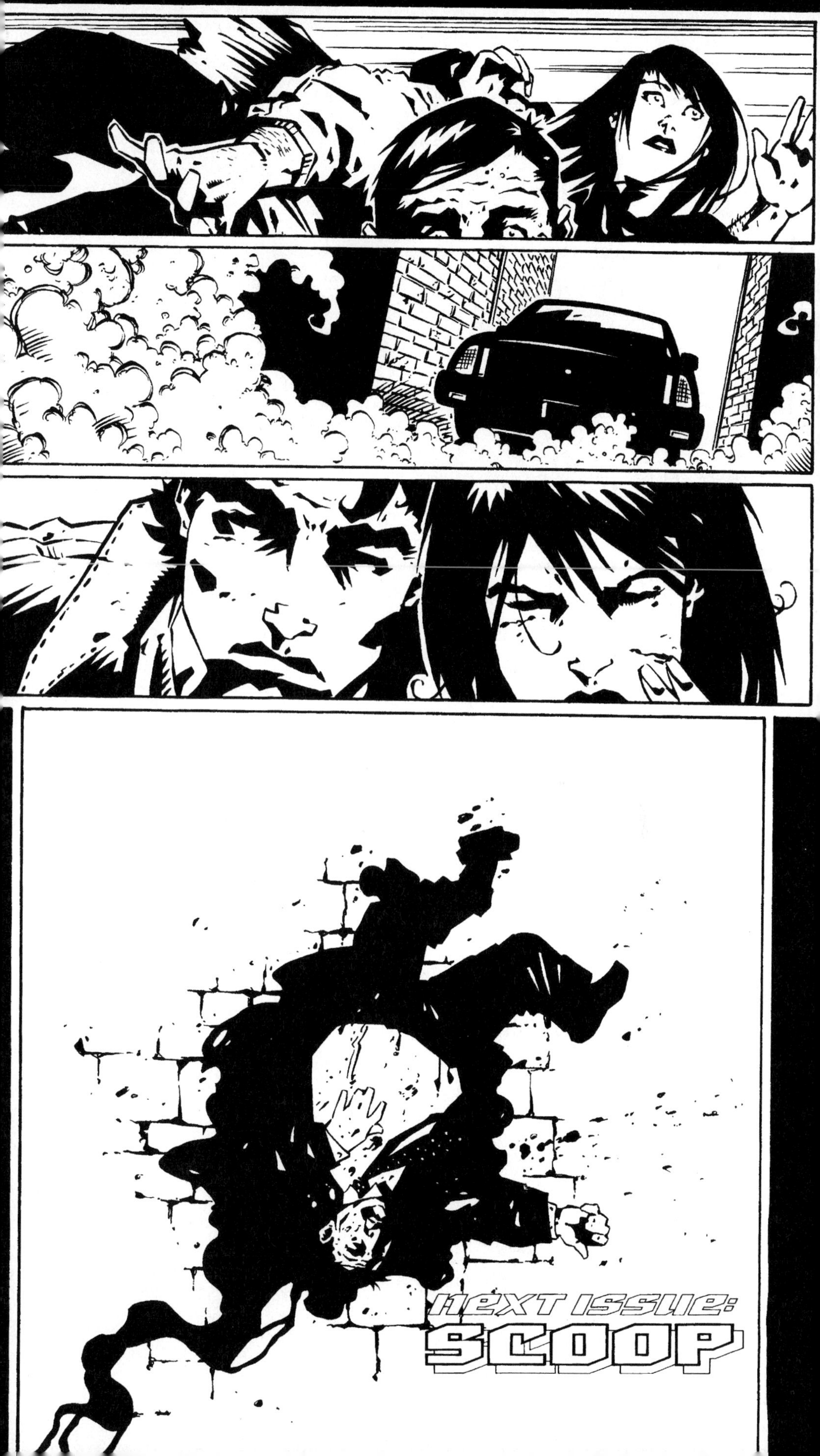
NEXT ISSUE:
SCOOP

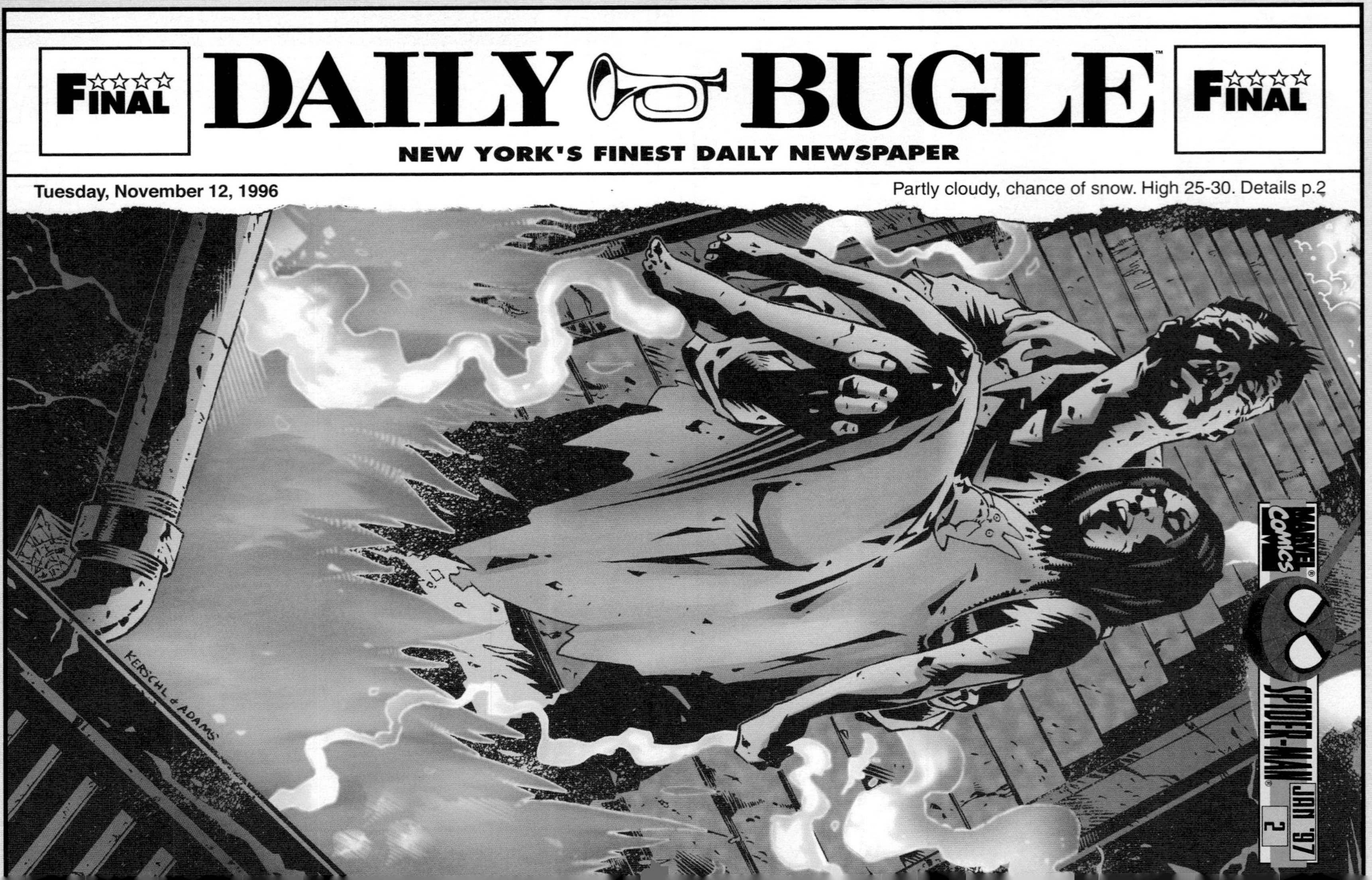
FINAL
DAILY BUGLE™
FINAL
NEW YORK'S FINEST DAILY NEWSPAPER
Tuesday, November 12, 1996
Partly cloudy, chance of snow. High 25-30. Details p.2
MARVEL® COMICS
SPIDER-MAN®
JAN '97
2
KERSCHL & ADAMS

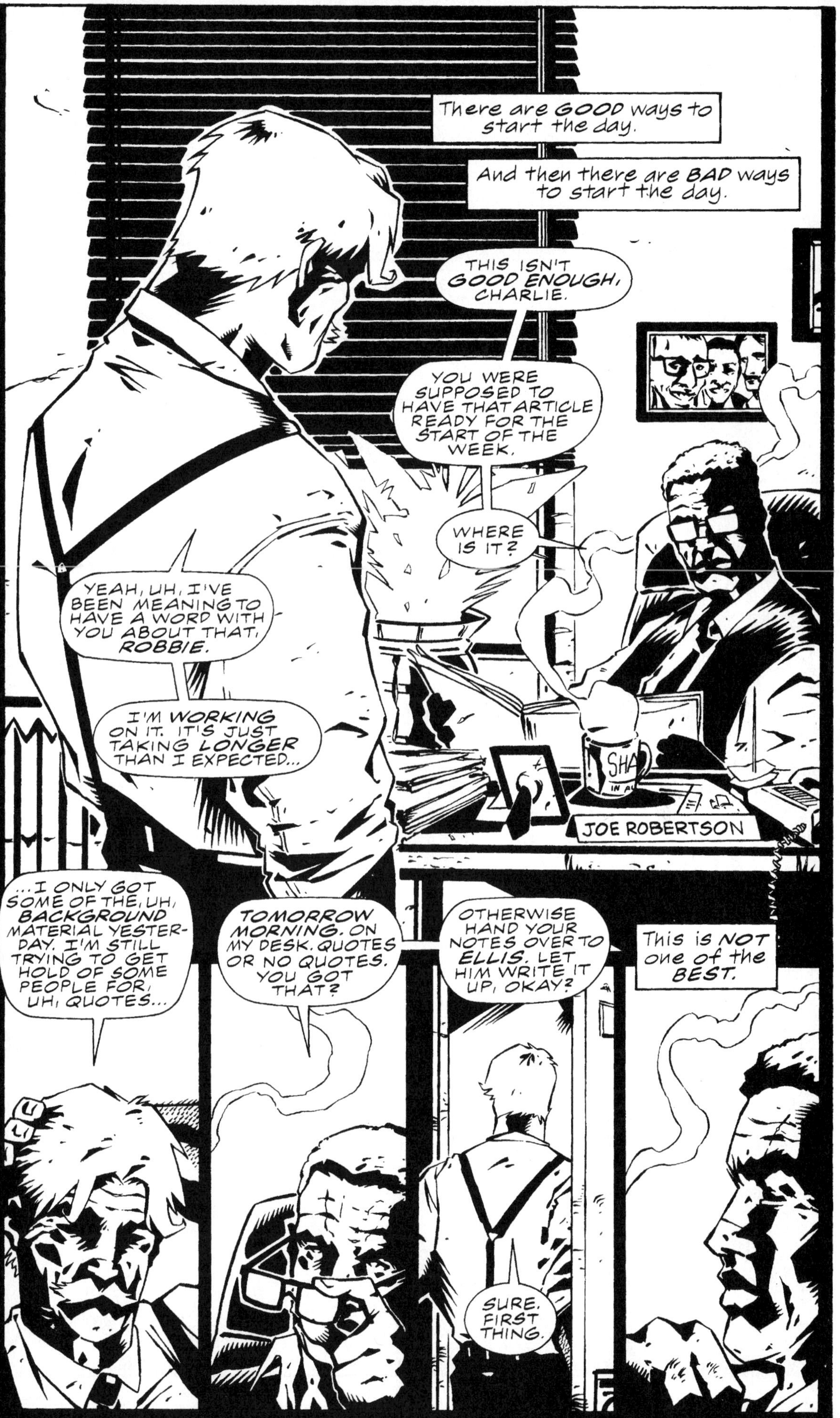
There are GOOD ways to start the day.
And then there are BAD ways to start the day.
THIS ISN'T GOOD ENOUGH, CHARLIE.
YOU WERE SUPPOSED TO HAVE THAT ARTICLE READY FOR THE START OF THE WEEK.
WHERE IS IT?
YEAH, UH, I'VE BEEN MEANING TO HAVE A WORD WITH YOU ABOUT THAT, ROBBIE.
I'M WORKING ON IT. IT'S JUST TAKING LONGER THAN I EXPECTED...
JOE ROBERTSON
...I ONLY GOT SOME OF THE, UH, BACKGROUND MATERIAL YESTER-DAY. I'M STILL TRYING TO GET HOLD OF SOME PEOPLE FOR, UH, QUOTES...
TOMORROW MORNING. ON MY DESK. QUOTES OR NO QUOTES. YOU GOT THAT?
OTHERWISE HAND YOUR NOTES OVER TO ELLIS. LET HIM WRITE IT UP, OKAY?
SURE. FIRST THING.
This is NOT one of the BEST.

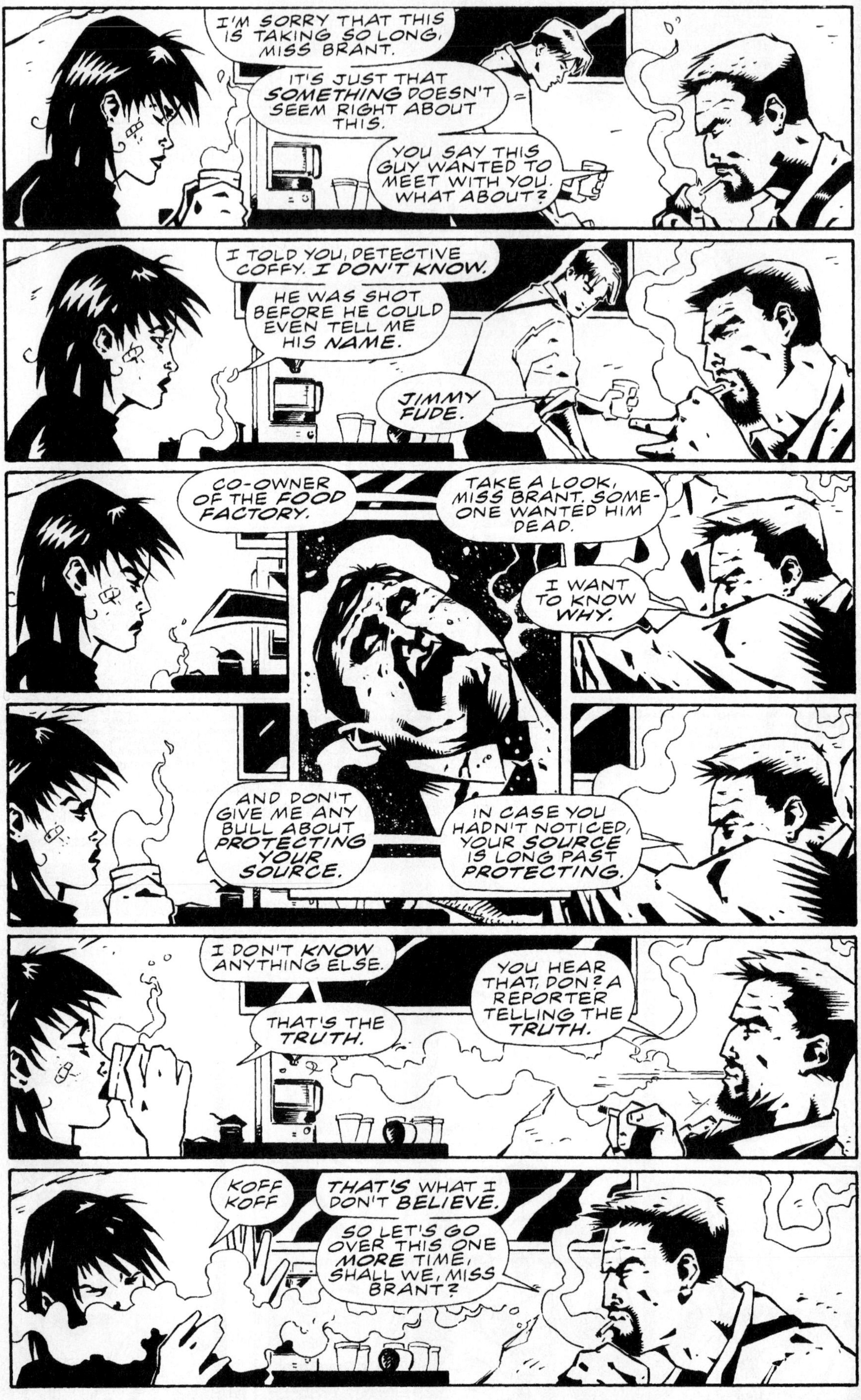
I'M SORRY THAT THIS IS TAKING SO LONG, MISS BRANT.
IT'S JUST THAT SOMETHING DOESN'T SEEM RIGHT ABOUT THIS.
YOU SAY THIS GUY WANTED TO MEET WITH YOU. WHAT ABOUT?
I TOLD YOU, DETECTIVE COFFY. I DON'T KNOW.
HE WAS SHOT BEFORE HE COULD EVEN TELL ME HIS NAME.
JIMMY FUDE.
CO-OWNER OF THE FOOD FACTORY.
TAKE A LOOK, MISS BRANT. SOME-ONE WANTED HIM DEAD.
I WANT TO KNOW WHY.
AND DON'T GIVE ME ANY BULL ABOUT PROTECTING YOUR SOURCE.
IN CASE YOU HADN'T NOTICED, YOUR SOURCE IS LONG PAST PROTECTING.
I DON'T KNOW ANYTHING ELSE.
THAT'S THE TRUTH.
YOU HEAR THAT, DON? A REPORTER TELLING THE TRUTH.
KOFF KOFF
THAT'S WHAT I DON'T BELIEVE.
SO LET'S GO OVER THIS ONE MORE TIME, SHALL WE, MISS BRANT?

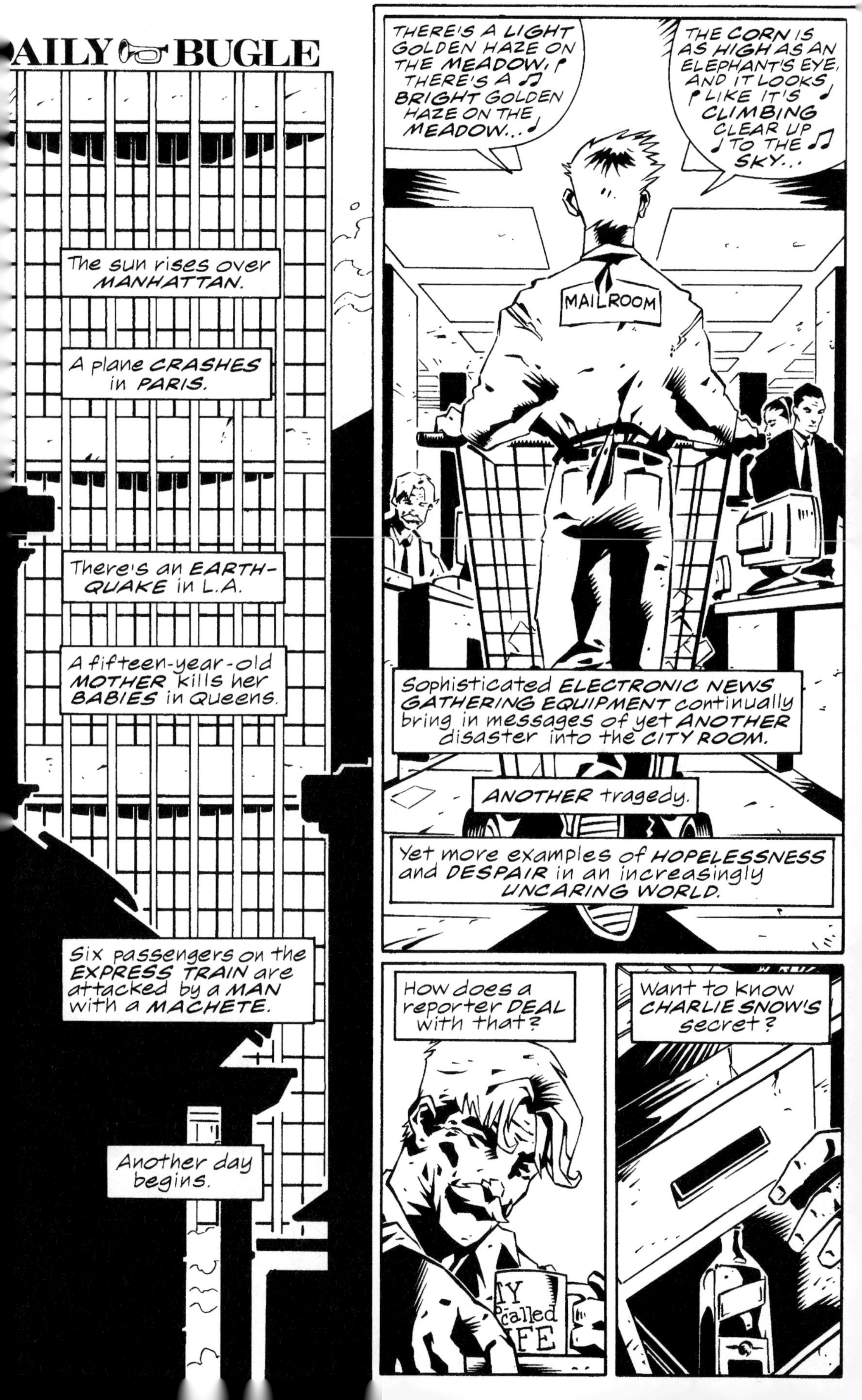
DAILY BUGLE
The sun rises over MANHATTAN.
A plane CRASHES in PARIS.
There's an EARTHQUAKE in L.A.
A fifteen-year-old MOTHER kills her BABIES in Queens.
Six passengers on the EXPRESS TRAIN are attacked by a MAN with a MACHETE.
Another day begins.
THERE'S A LIGHT GOLDEN HAZE ON THE MEADOW, THERE'S A BRIGHT GOLDEN HAZE ON THE MEADOW...
THE CORN IS AS HIGH AS AN ELEPHANT'S EYE, AND IT LOOKS LIKE IT'S CLIMBING CLEAR UP TO THE SKY...
MAILROOM
Sophisticated ELECTRONIC NEWS GATHERING EQUIPMENT continually bring in messages of yet ANOTHER disaster into the CITY ROOM.
ANOTHER tragedy.
Yet more examples of HOPELESSNESS and DESPAIR in an increasingly UNCARING WORLD.
How does a reporter DEAL with that?
Want to know CHARLIE SNOW'S secret?

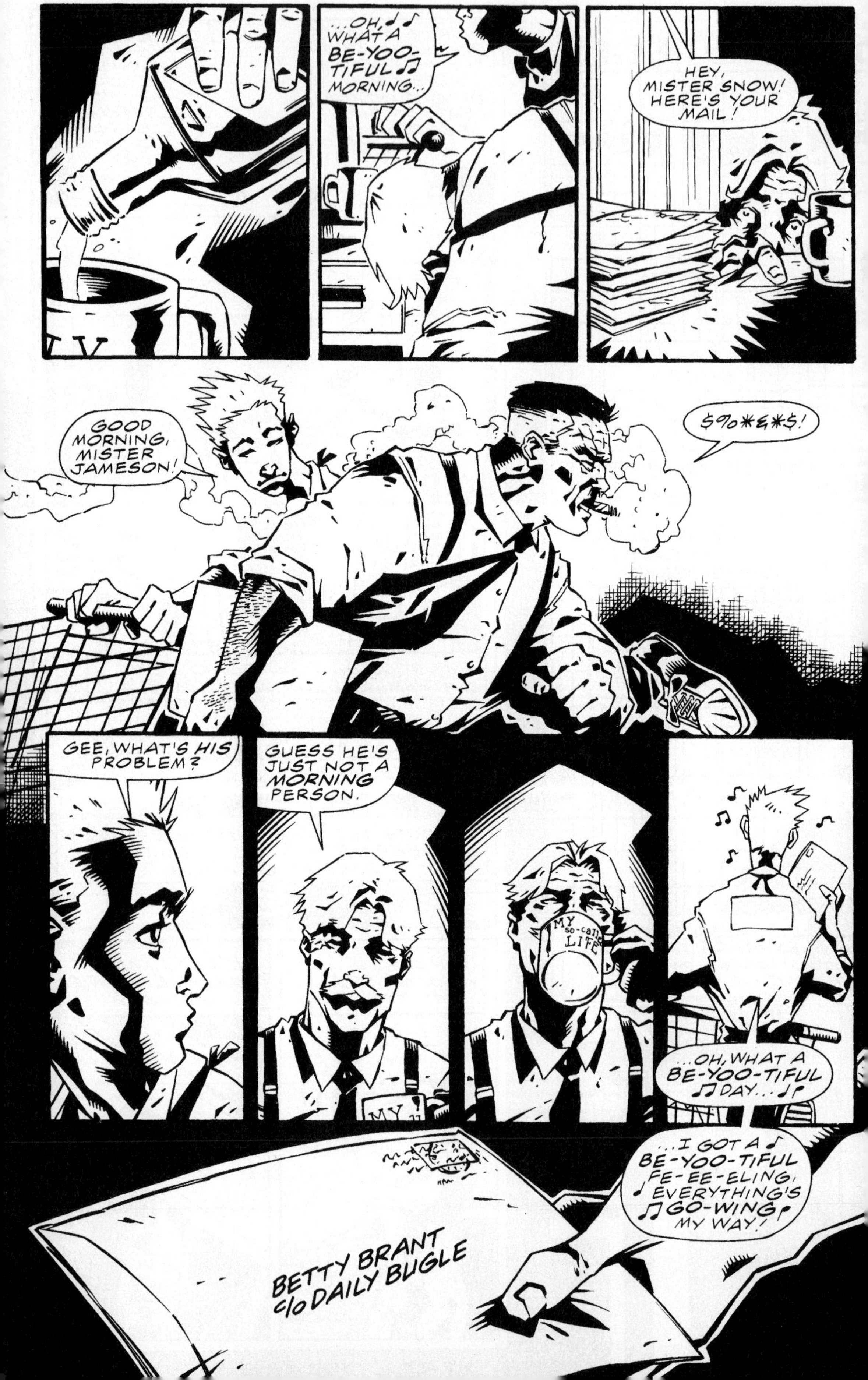
...OH, WHAT A BE-YOO-TIFUL MORNING...
HEY, MISTER SNOW! HERE'S YOUR MAIL!
GOOD MORNING, MISTER JAMESON!
$%*£*$!
GEE, WHAT'S HIS PROBLEM?
GUESS HE'S JUST NOT A MORNING PERSON.
MY so-called LIFE
...OH, WHAT A BE-YOO-TIFUL DAY...
...I GOT A BE-YOO-TIFUL FE-EE-ELING, EVERYTHING'S GO-WING MY WAY!
BETTY BRANT c/o DAILY BUGLE

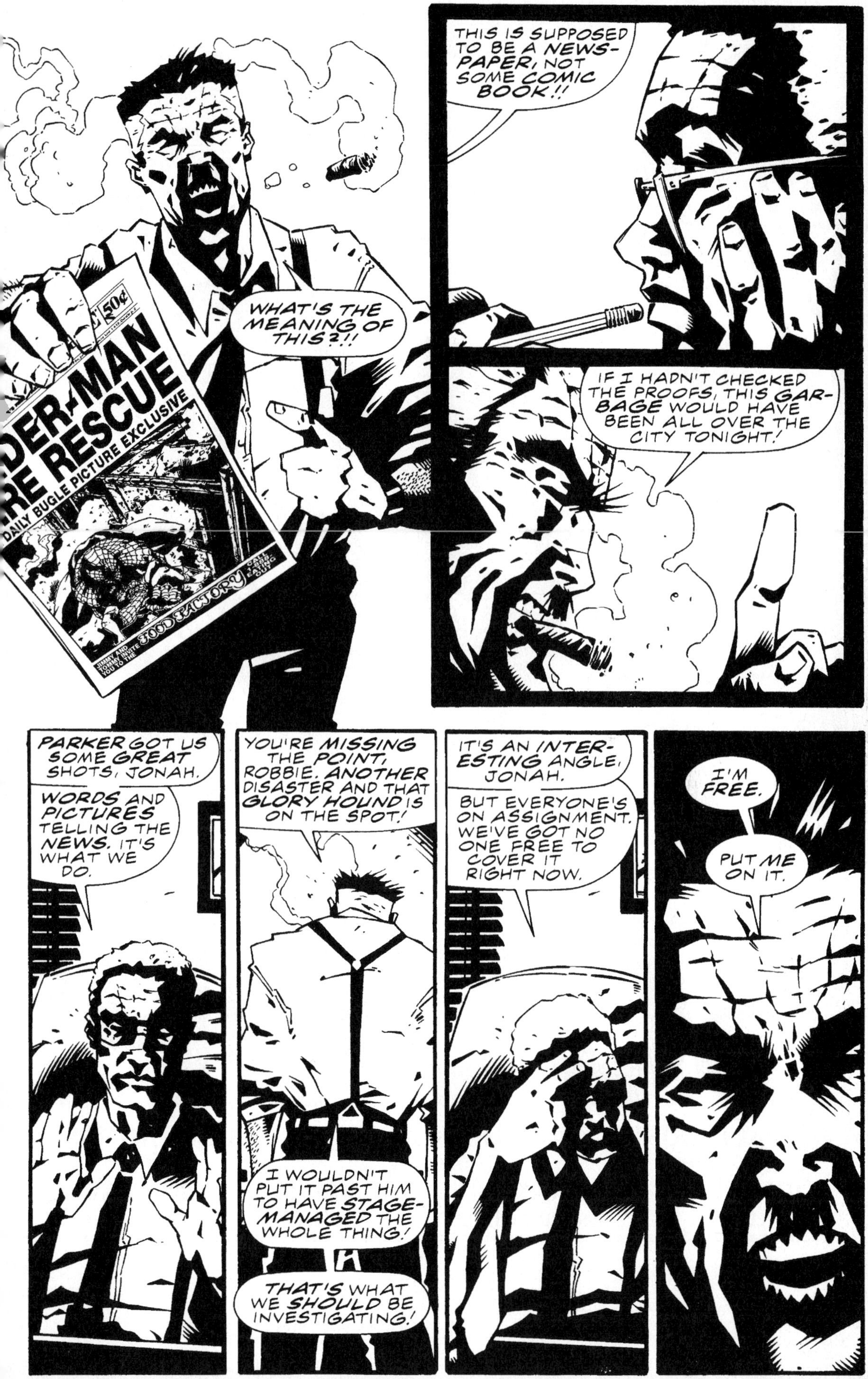
WHAT'S THE MEANING OF THIS?!!
DAILY BUGLE PICTURE EXCLUSIVE
50¢
DER-MAN
RE RESCUE
JIMMY AND TOMMY INVITE YOU TO THE FOOD FACTORY
THIS IS SUPPOSED TO BE A NEWS-PAPER, NOT SOME COMIC BOOK!!
IF I HADN'T CHECKED THE PROOFS, THIS GAR-BAGE WOULD HAVE BEEN ALL OVER THE CITY TONIGHT!
PARKER GOT US SOME GREAT SHOTS, JONAH.
WORDS AND PICTURES TELLING THE NEWS. IT'S WHAT WE DO.
YOU'RE MISSING THE POINT, ROBBIE. ANOTHER DISASTER AND THAT GLORY HOUND IS ON THE SPOT!
I WOULDN'T PUT IT PAST HIM TO HAVE STAGE-MANAGED THE WHOLE THING!
THAT'S WHAT WE SHOULD BE INVESTIGATING!
IT'S AN INTER-ESTING ANGLE, JONAH.
BUT EVERYONE'S ON ASSIGNMENT. WE'VE GOT NO ONE FREE TO COVER IT RIGHT NOW.
I'M FREE.
PUT ME ON IT.

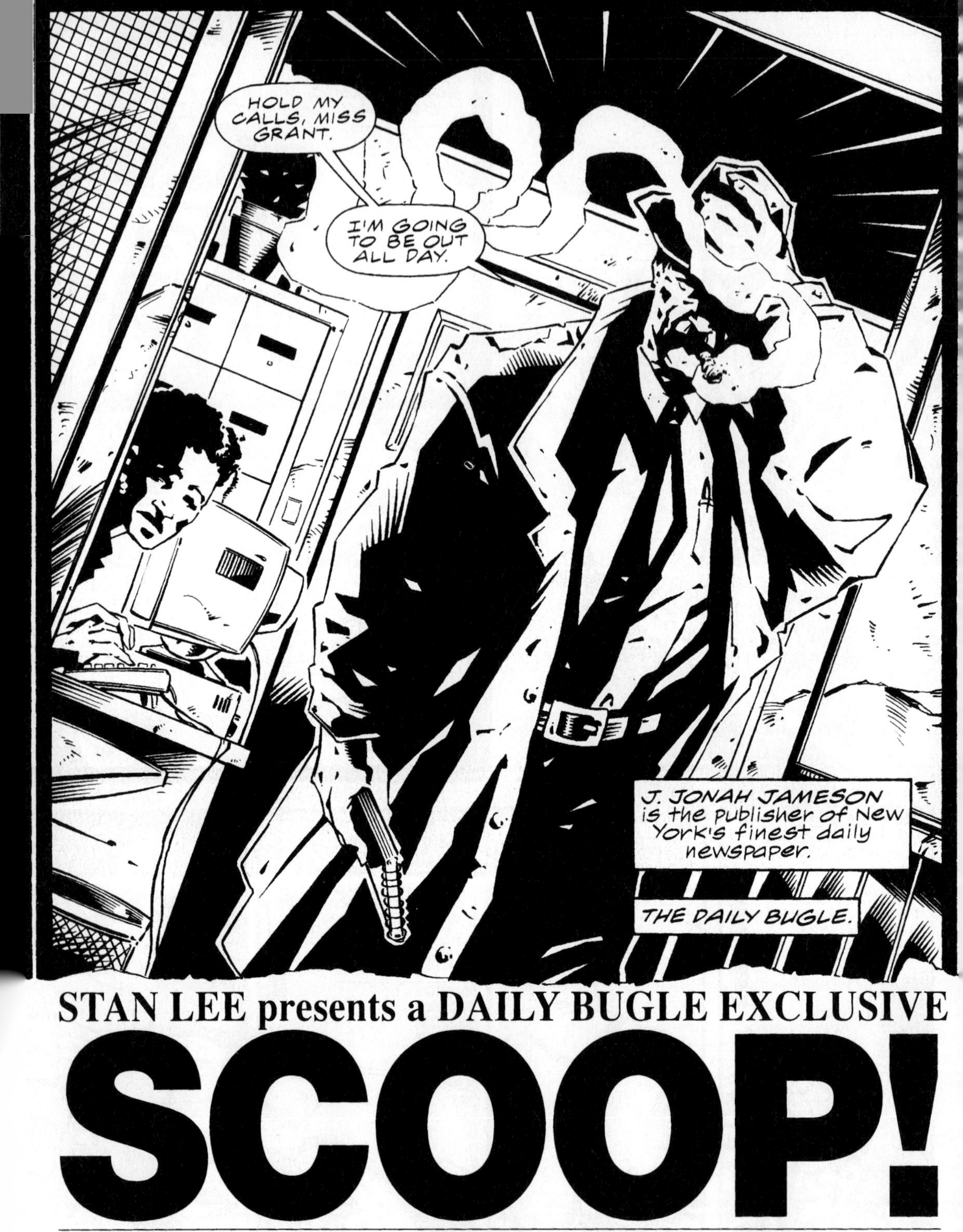
HOLD MY CALLS, MISS GRANT.
I'M GOING TO BE OUT ALL DAY.
J. JONAH JAMESON is the publisher of New York's finest daily newspaper.
THE DAILY BUGLE.

STAN LEE presents a DAILY BUGLE EXCLUSIVE

SCOOP!

PAUL GRIST writer	**KARL KERSCHL** penciler		**GREG ADAMS** inker
JIM NOVAK letters	**GLENN GREENBERG** assistant editor	**TOM BREVOORT** editor	**BOB HARRAS** editor in chief

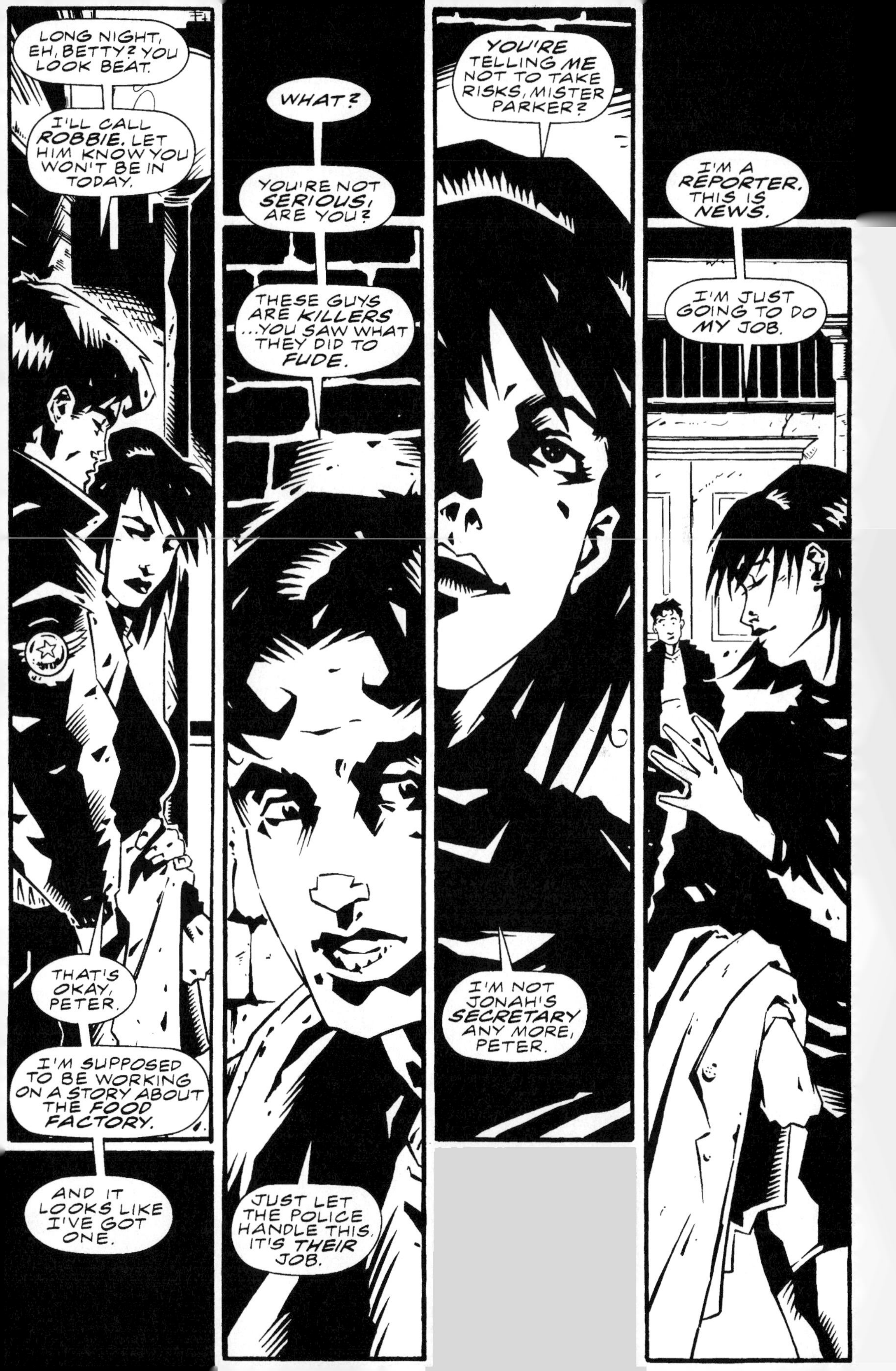
LONG NIGHT, EH, BETTY? YOU LOOK BEAT.
I'LL CALL ROBBIE. LET HIM KNOW YOU WON'T BE IN TODAY.
THAT'S OKAY, PETER.
I'M SUPPOSED TO BE WORKING ON A STORY ABOUT THE FOOD FACTORY.
AND IT LOOKS LIKE I'VE GOT ONE.
WHAT?
YOU'RE NOT SERIOUS, ARE YOU?
THESE GUYS ARE KILLERS ...YOU SAW WHAT THEY DID TO FUDE.
JUST LET THE POLICE HANDLE THIS. IT'S THEIR JOB.
YOU'RE TELLING ME NOT TO TAKE RISKS, MISTER PARKER?
I'M NOT JONAH'S SECRETARY ANY MORE, PETER.
I'M A REPORTER. THIS IS NEWS.
I'M JUST GOING TO DO MY JOB.

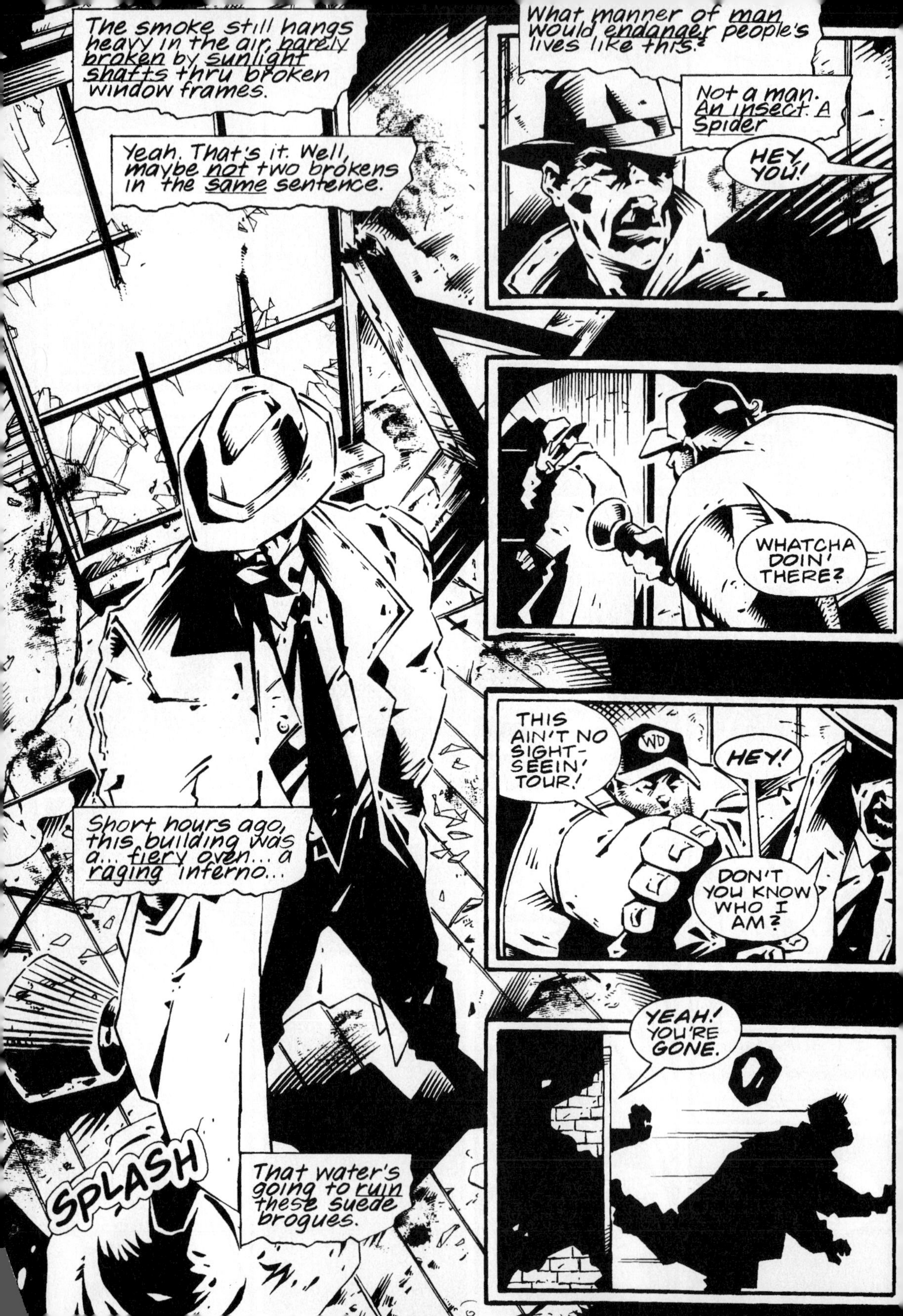
The smoke still hangs heavy in the air, barely broken by sunlight shafts thru broken window frames.
Yeah. That's it. Well, maybe not two brokens in the same sentence.
Short hours ago, this building was a... fiery oven... a raging inferno...
SPLASH
That water's going to ruin these suede brogues.
What manner of man would endanger people's lives like this?
Not a man. An insect. A Spider
HEY, YOU!
WHATCHA DOIN' THERE?
THIS AIN'T NO SIGHT-SEEIN' TOUR!
HEY!
DON'T YOU KNOW WHO I AM?
YEAH! YOU'RE GONE.

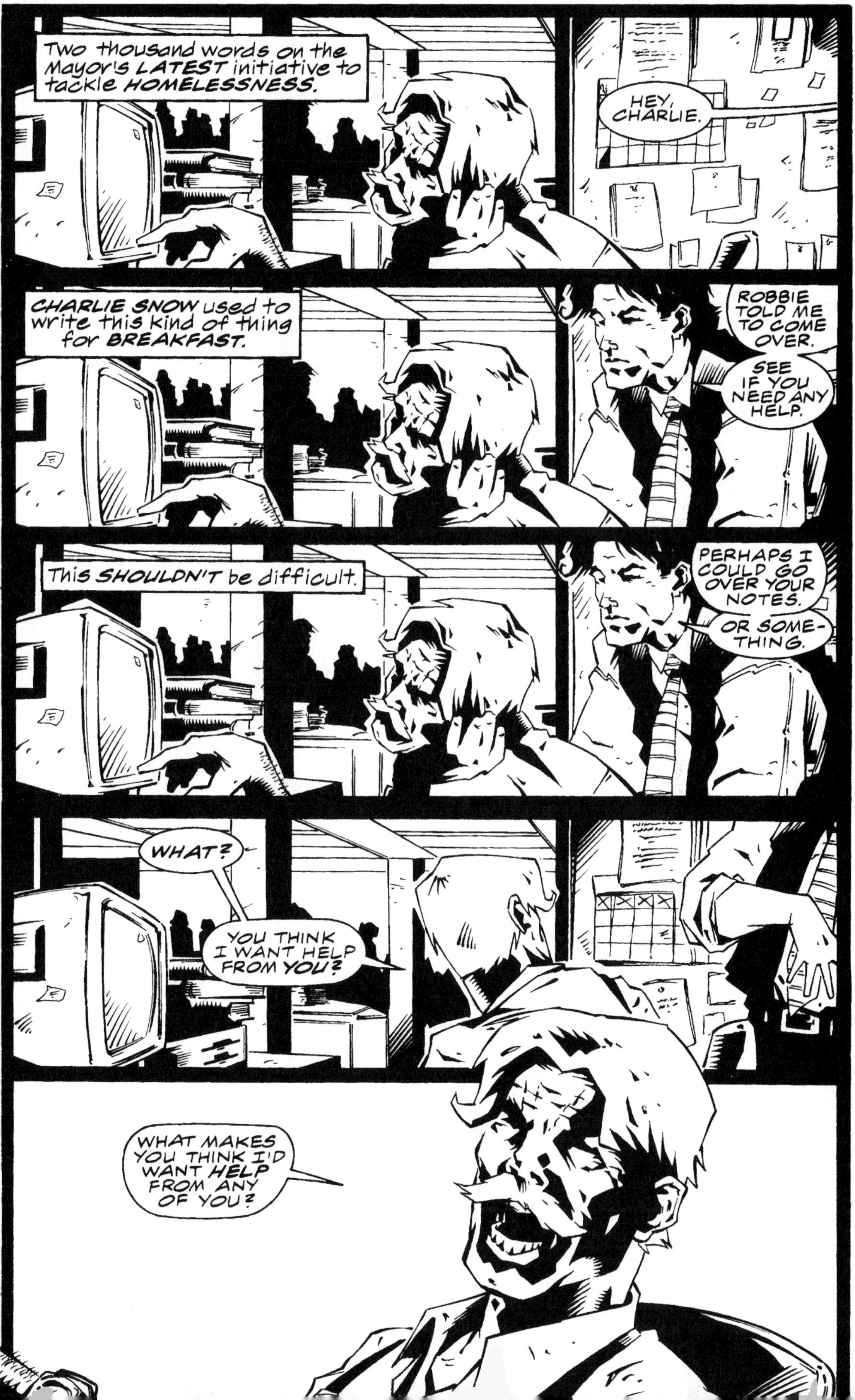

Two thousand words on the Mayor's LATEST initiative to tackle HOMELESSNESS.
HEY, CHARLIE.
CHARLIE SNOW used to write this kind of thing for BREAKFAST.
ROBBIE TOLD ME TO COME OVER.
SEE IF YOU NEED ANY HELP.
This SHOULDN'T be difficult.
PERHAPS I COULD GO OVER YOUR NOTES.
OR SOME-THING.
WHAT?
YOU THINK I WANT HELP FROM YOU?
WHAT MAKES YOU THINK I'D WANT HELP FROM ANY OF YOU?

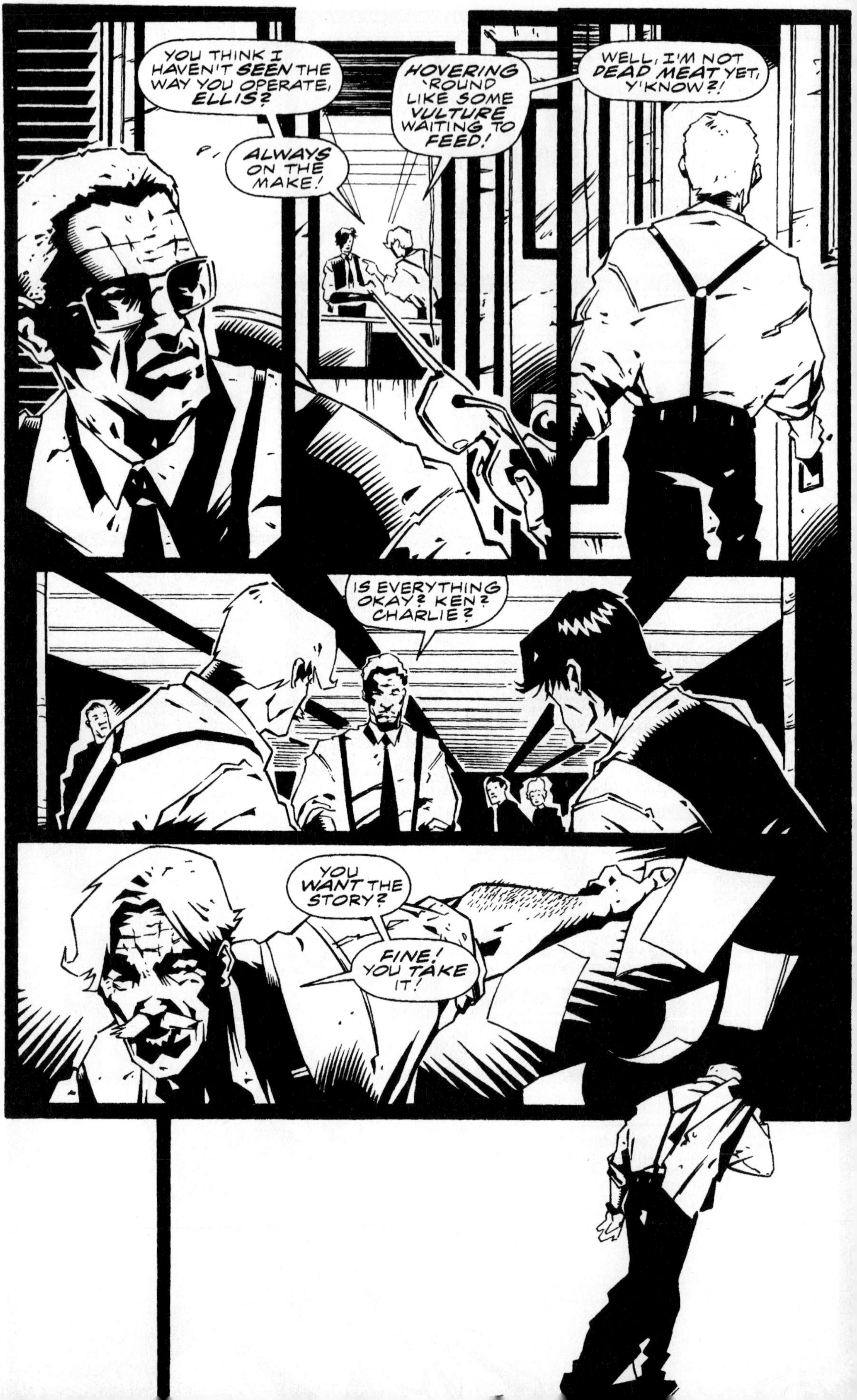
YOU THINK I HAVEN'T SEEN THE WAY YOU OPERATE, ELLIS?
ALWAYS ON THE MAKE!
HOVERING 'ROUND LIKE SOME VULTURE WAITING TO FEED!
WELL, I'M NOT DEAD MEAT YET, Y'KNOW?!
IS EVERYTHING OKAY? KEN? CHARLIE?
YOU WANT THE STORY?
FINE! YOU TAKE IT!

The Williams Development Office. Avenue of the Americas.

THIS WAY, MISTER JAMESON.

DON'T WORRY, THE ELEVATOR DOES TAKE PEOPLE BY *SURPRISE*. WE HAVE IT SOUNDPROOFED.

Twenty stories of mirrored glass and an elevator that has you at the *top* floor before you've *finished* admiring your reflection on the ground floor.

AIIEEK!

JONAH!

WELL, THIS IS A *PLEASANT* SURPRISE.

WE HAVEN'T SEEN MUCH OF YOU DOWN AT THE CLUB LATELY.

DRINK?

NO THANK YOU, NILES, THIS IS MORE OF A *BUSINESS* THAN A *SOCIAL* CALL.

I WAS JUST VISITING YOUR TENEMENT ON THE *LOWER EAST SIDE?* THE ONE THAT BURNED DOWN YESTERDAY.[2]

AND ONE OF YOUR SECURITY GUARDS HAD THE TEMERITY TO MANHANDLE ME OFF THE SITE.

THEY DID? WHAT CAN I SAY? I'M SORRY. YOU CAN BE SURE I'LL BE HAVING WORDS WITH THE MAN RESPONSIBLE.

MIND YOU, SECURITY IS HAVING TO BE ON THEIR TOES AT THE MOMENT. WE'VE HAD FOUR PROPERTIES BURN DOWN IN THE LAST SIX WEEKS.

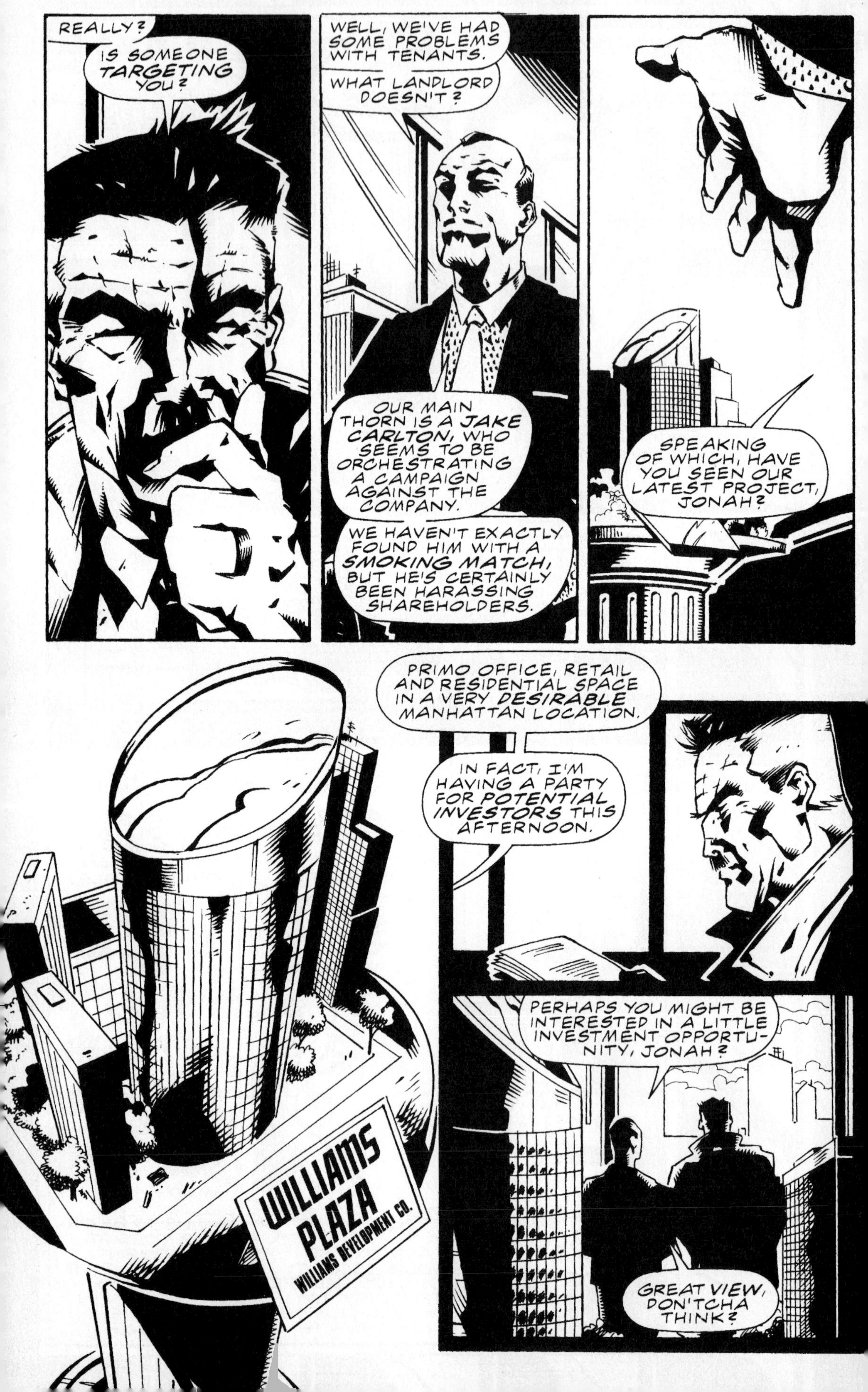
REALLY?
IS SOMEONE TARGETING YOU?
WELL, WE'VE HAD SOME PROBLEMS WITH TENANTS.
WHAT LANDLORD DOESN'T?
OUR MAIN THORN IS A JAKE CARLTON, WHO SEEMS TO BE ORCHESTRATING A CAMPAIGN AGAINST THE COMPANY.
WE HAVEN'T EXACTLY FOUND HIM WITH A SMOKING MATCH, BUT HE'S CERTAINLY BEEN HARASSING SHAREHOLDERS.
SPEAKING OF WHICH, HAVE YOU SEEN OUR LATEST PROJECT, JONAH?
WILLIAMS PLAZA
WILLIAMS DEVELOPMENT CO.
PRIMO OFFICE, RETAIL AND RESIDENTIAL SPACE IN A VERY DESIRABLE MANHATTAN LOCATION.
IN FACT, I'M HAVING A PARTY FOR POTENTIAL INVESTORS THIS AFTERNOON.
PERHAPS YOU MIGHT BE INTERESTED IN A LITTLE INVESTMENT OPPORTUNITY, JONAH?
GREAT VIEW, DON'TCHA THINK?

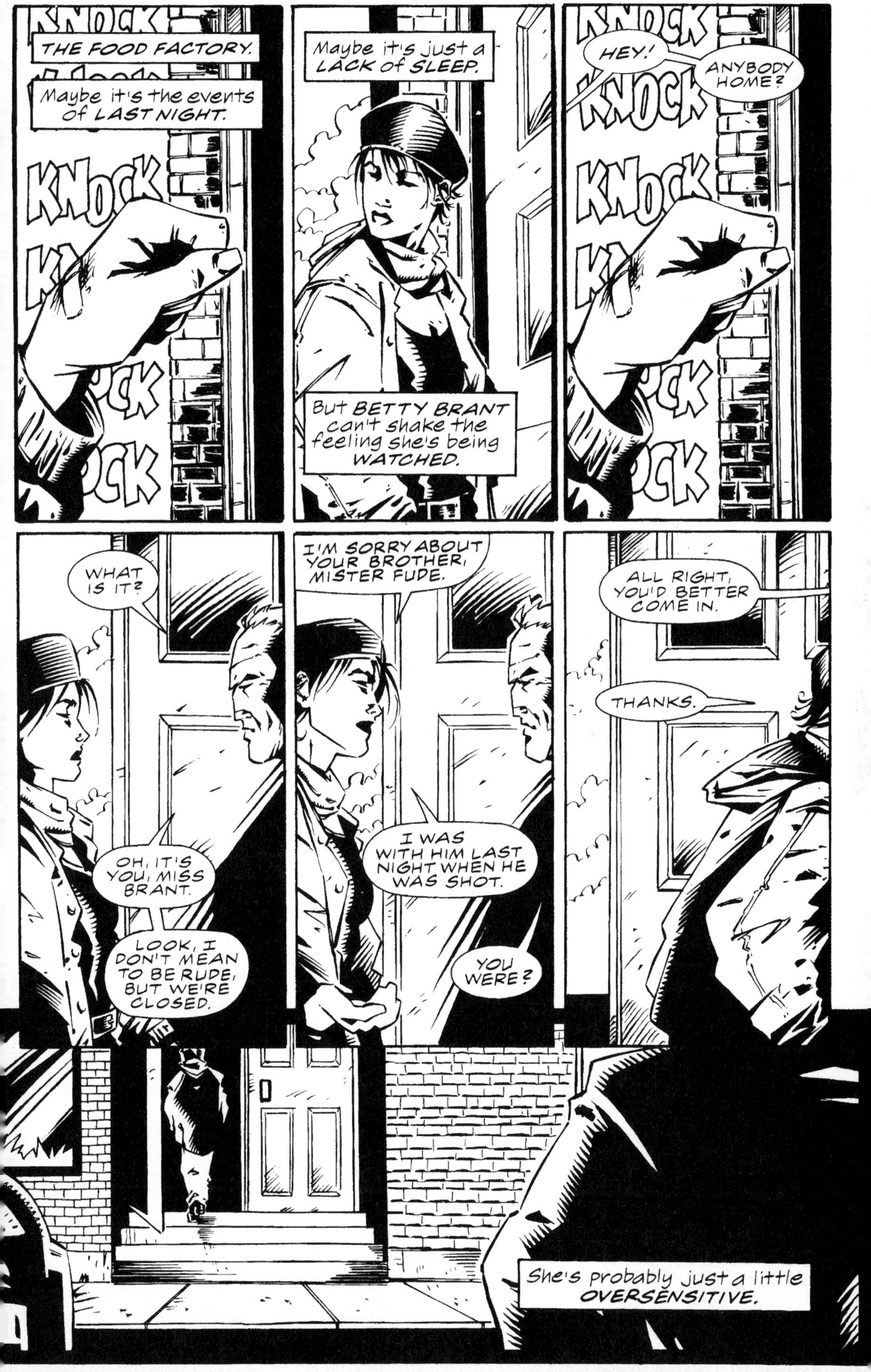
KNOCK
THE FOOD FACTORY.
Maybe it's the events of LAST NIGHT.
KNOCK
Maybe it's just a LACK of SLEEP.
But BETTY BRANT can't shake the feeling she's being WATCHED.
KNOCK
HEY!
ANYBODY HOME?
KNOCK
KNOCK
WHAT IS IT?
OH, IT'S YOU, MISS BRANT.
LOOK, I DON'T MEAN TO BE RUDE, BUT WE'RE CLOSED.
I'M SORRY ABOUT YOUR BROTHER, MISTER FUDE.
I WAS WITH HIM LAST NIGHT WHEN HE WAS SHOT.
YOU WERE?
ALL RIGHT, YOU'D BETTER COME IN.
THANKS.
She's probably just a little OVERSENSITIVE.

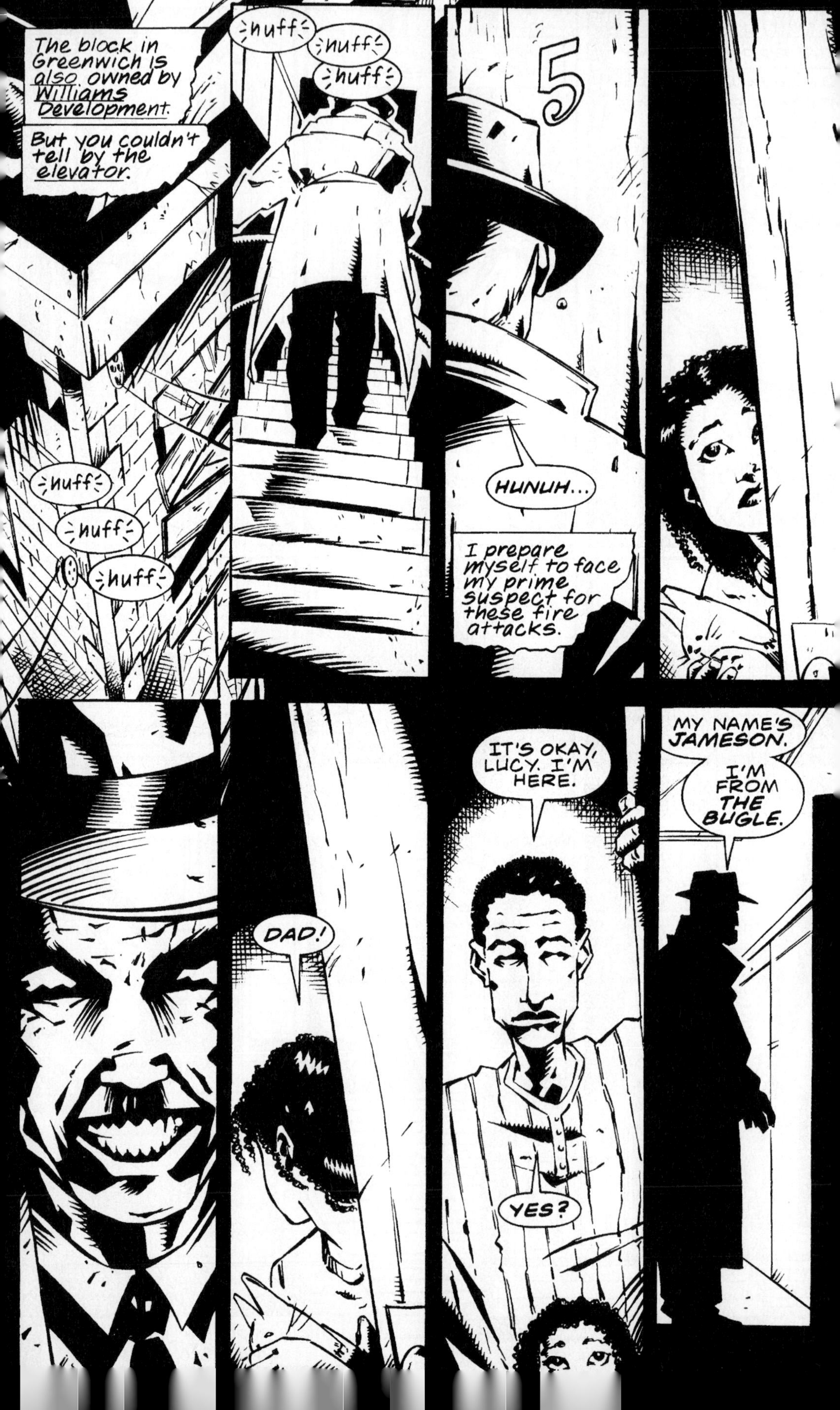

The block in Greenwich is also owned by Williams Development.
But you couldn't tell by the elevator.
huff
huff
huff
huff
huff
huff
5
HUNUH...
I prepare myself to face my prime suspect for these fire attacks.
DAD!
IT'S OKAY, LUCY. I'M HERE.
YES?
MY NAME'S JAMESON.
I'M FROM THE BUGLE.

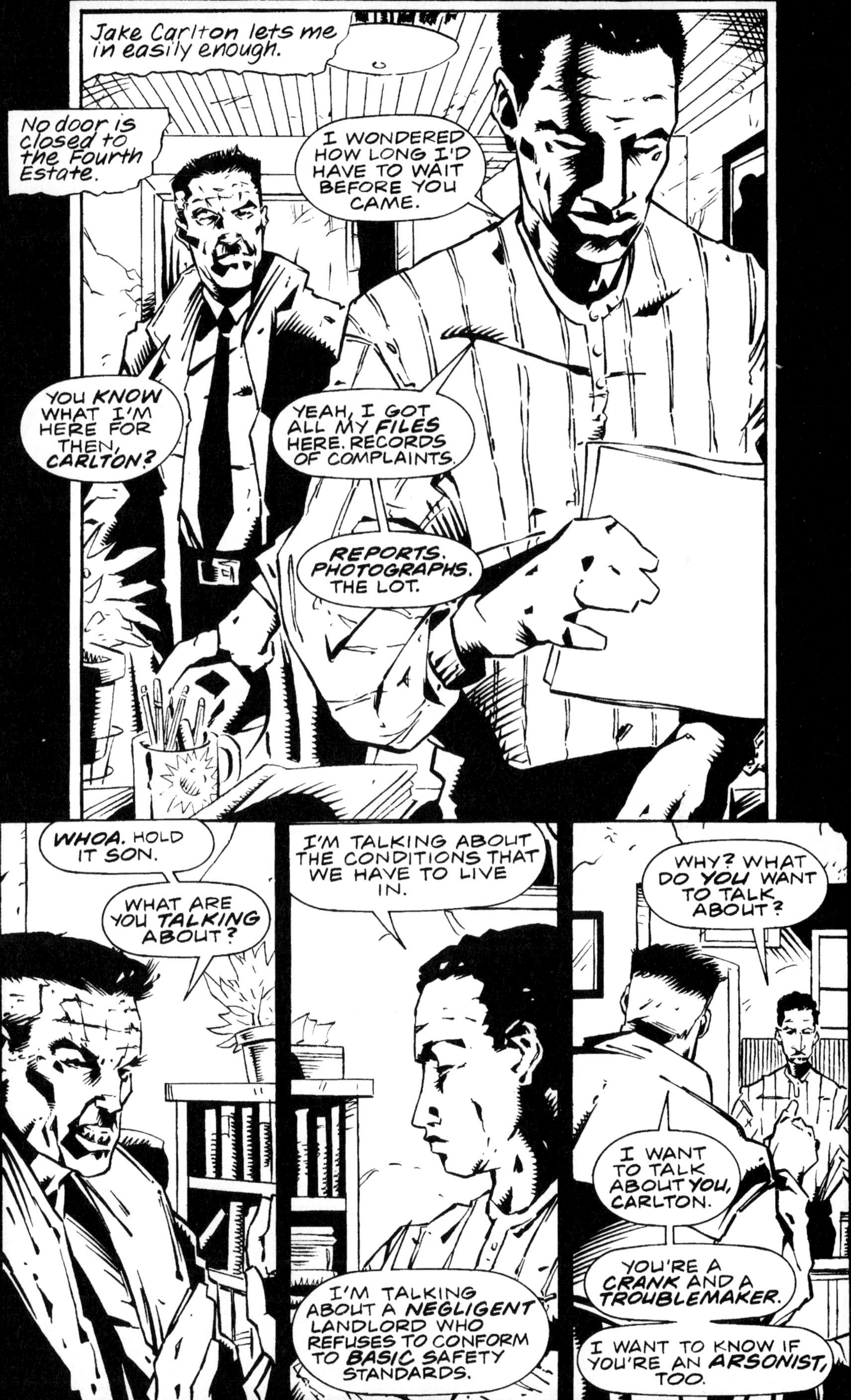
Jake Carlton lets me in easily enough.
No door is closed to the Fourth Estate.
I WONDERED HOW LONG I'D HAVE TO WAIT BEFORE YOU CAME.
YOU KNOW WHAT I'M HERE FOR THEN, CARLTON?
YEAH, I GOT ALL MY FILES HERE. RECORDS OF COMPLAINTS.
REPORTS. PHOTOGRAPHS. THE LOT.
WHOA. HOLD IT SON.
WHAT ARE YOU TALKING ABOUT?
I'M TALKING ABOUT THE CONDITIONS THAT WE HAVE TO LIVE IN.
I'M TALKING ABOUT A NEGLIGENT LANDLORD WHO REFUSES TO CONFORM TO BASIC SAFETY STANDARDS.
WHY? WHAT DO YOU WANT TO TALK ABOUT?
I WANT TO TALK ABOUT YOU, CARLTON.
YOU'RE A CRANK AND A TROUBLEMAKER.
I WANT TO KNOW IF YOU'RE AN ARSONIST, TOO.

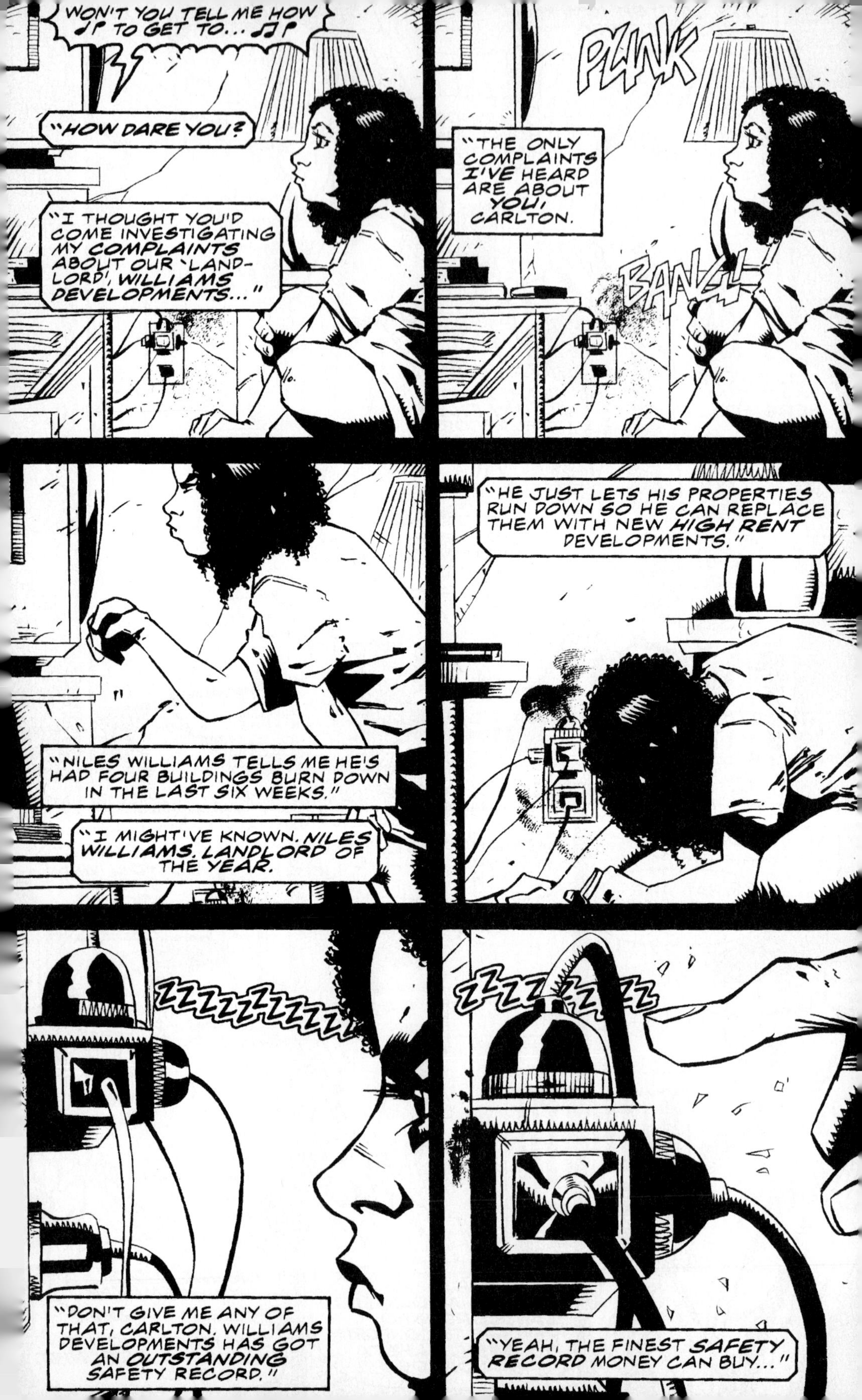
WON'T YOU TELL ME HOW ♪ TO GET TO... ♫
"HOW DARE YOU?
"I THOUGHT YOU'D COME INVESTIGATING MY COMPLAINTS ABOUT OUR 'LANDLORD', WILLIAMS DEVELOPMENTS..."
PLINK
"THE ONLY COMPLAINTS I'VE HEARD ARE ABOUT YOU, CARLTON.
BANG!
"NILES WILLIAMS TELLS ME HE'S HAD FOUR BUILDINGS BURN DOWN IN THE LAST SIX WEEKS."
"I MIGHT'VE KNOWN. NILES WILLIAMS. LANDLORD OF THE YEAR.
"HE JUST LETS HIS PROPERTIES RUN DOWN SO HE CAN REPLACE THEM WITH NEW HIGH RENT DEVELOPMENTS."
"DON'T GIVE ME ANY OF THAT, CARLTON. WILLIAMS DEVELOPMENTS HAS GOT AN OUTSTANDING SAFETY RECORD."
"YEAH, THE FINEST SAFETY RECORD MONEY CAN BUY..."

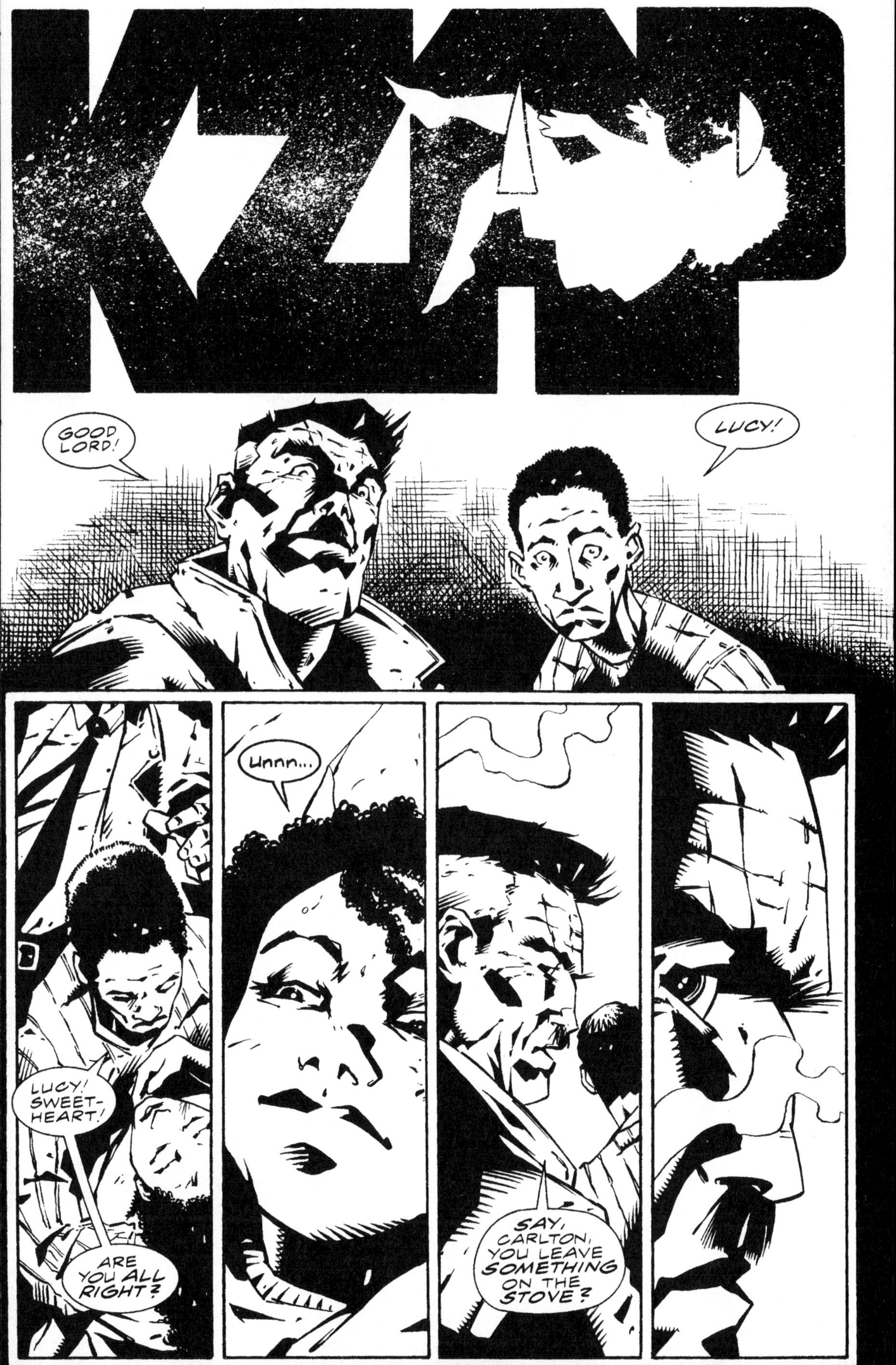
KZAP
GOOD LORD!
LUCY!
LUCY! SWEET-HEART!
ARE YOU ALL RIGHT?
Unnn...
SAY, CARLTON, YOU LEAVE SOMETHING ON THE STOVE?

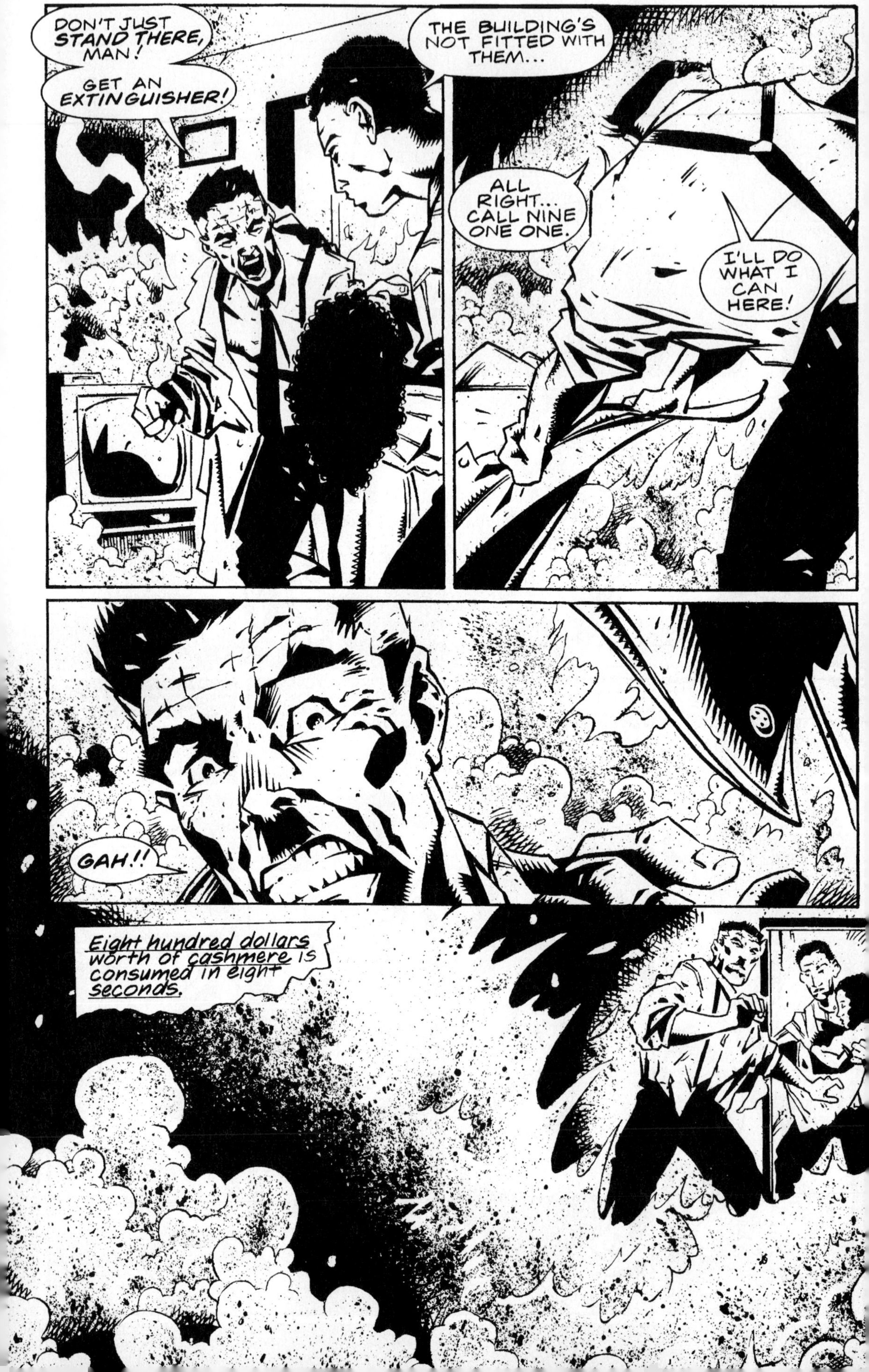
DON'T JUST STAND THERE, MAN!
GET AN EXTINGUISHER!
THE BUILDING'S NOT FITTED WITH THEM...
ALL RIGHT... CALL NINE ONE ONE.
I'LL DO WHAT I CAN HERE!
GAH!!
Eight hundred dollars worth of cashmere is consumed in eight seconds.

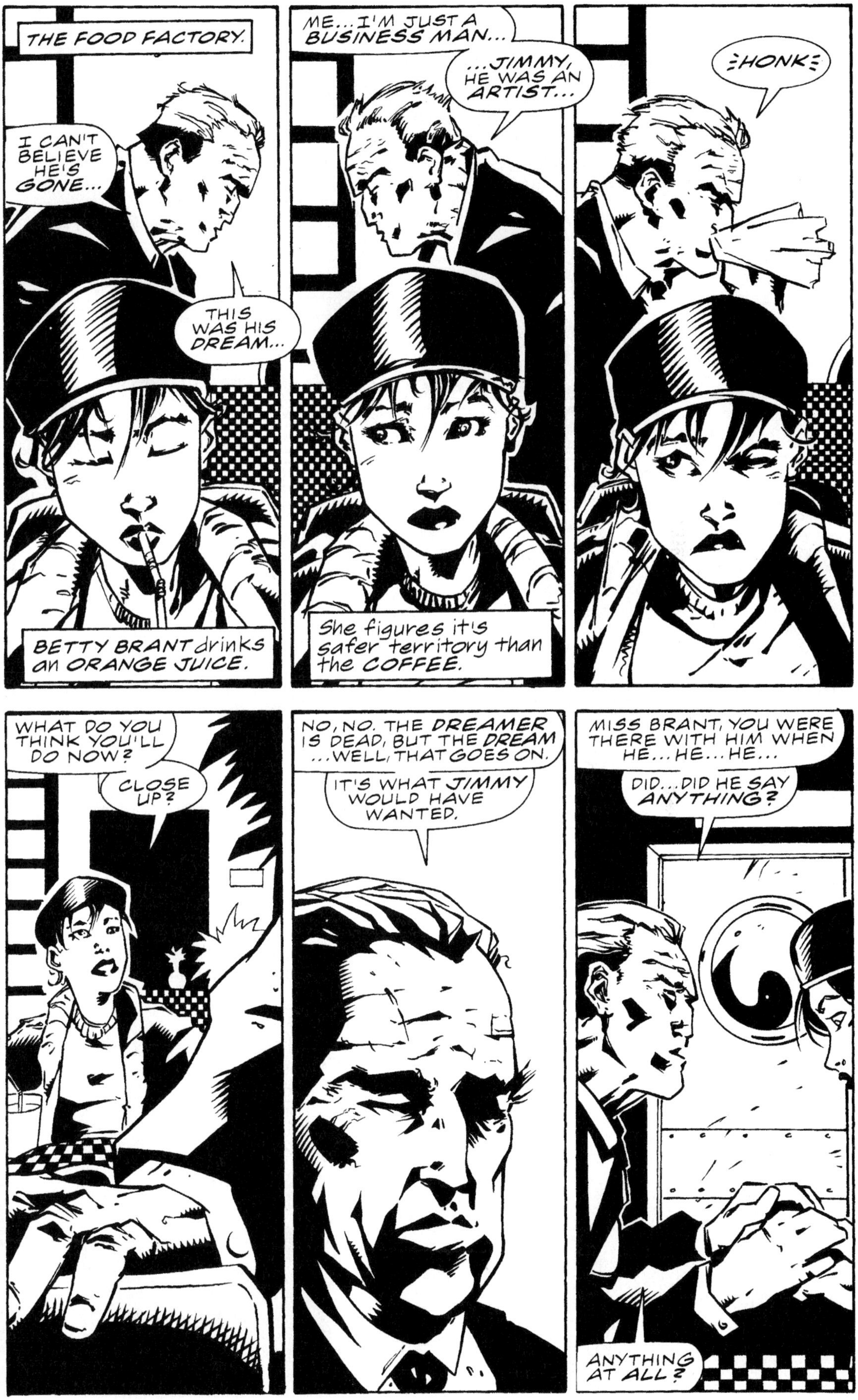
THE FOOD FACTORY.
I CAN'T BELIEVE HE'S GONE...
THIS WAS HIS DREAM...
BETTY BRANT drinks an ORANGE JUICE.
ME... I'M JUST A BUSINESS MAN...
...JIMMY, HE WAS AN ARTIST...
She figures it's safer territory than the COFFEE.
HONK
WHAT DO YOU THINK YOU'LL DO NOW?
CLOSE UP?
NO, NO. THE DREAMER IS DEAD, BUT THE DREAM ...WELL, THAT GOES ON.
IT'S WHAT JIMMY WOULD HAVE WANTED.
MISS BRANT, YOU WERE THERE WITH HIM WHEN HE... HE... HE...
DID... DID HE SAY ANYTHING?
ANYTHING AT ALL?

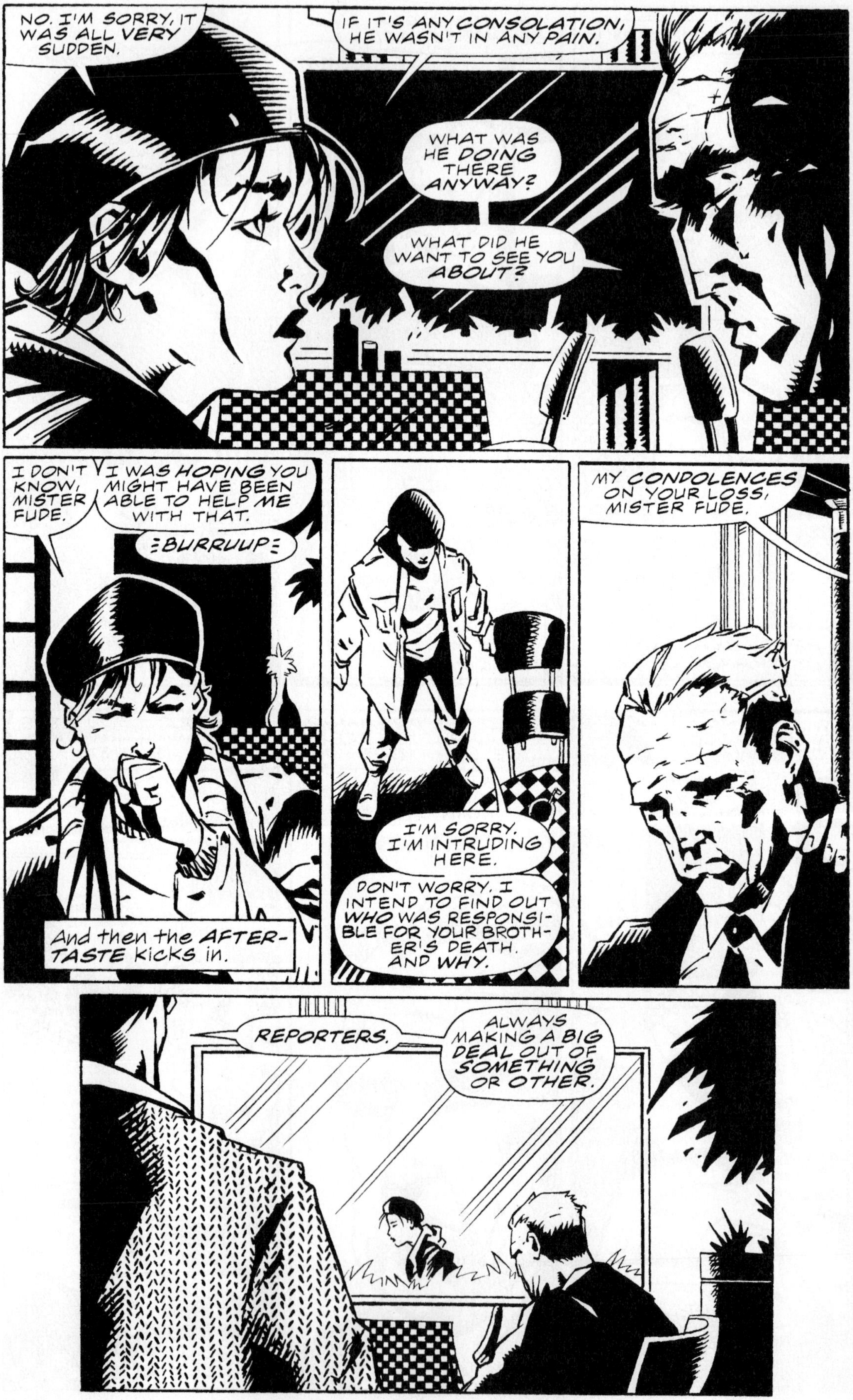
NO. I'M SORRY. IT WAS ALL VERY SUDDEN.
IF IT'S ANY CONSOLATION, HE WASN'T IN ANY PAIN.
WHAT WAS HE DOING THERE ANYWAY?
WHAT DID HE WANT TO SEE YOU ABOUT?
I DON'T KNOW, MISTER FUDE.
I WAS HOPING YOU MIGHT HAVE BEEN ABLE TO HELP ME WITH THAT.
BURRUUP
And then the AFTER-TASTE kicks in.
I'M SORRY. I'M INTRUDING HERE.
DON'T WORRY. I INTEND TO FIND OUT WHO WAS RESPONSI-BLE FOR YOUR BROTH-ER'S DEATH. AND WHY.
MY CONDOLENCES ON YOUR LOSS, MISTER FUDE.
REPORTERS.
ALWAYS MAKING A BIG DEAL OUT OF SOMETHING OR OTHER.

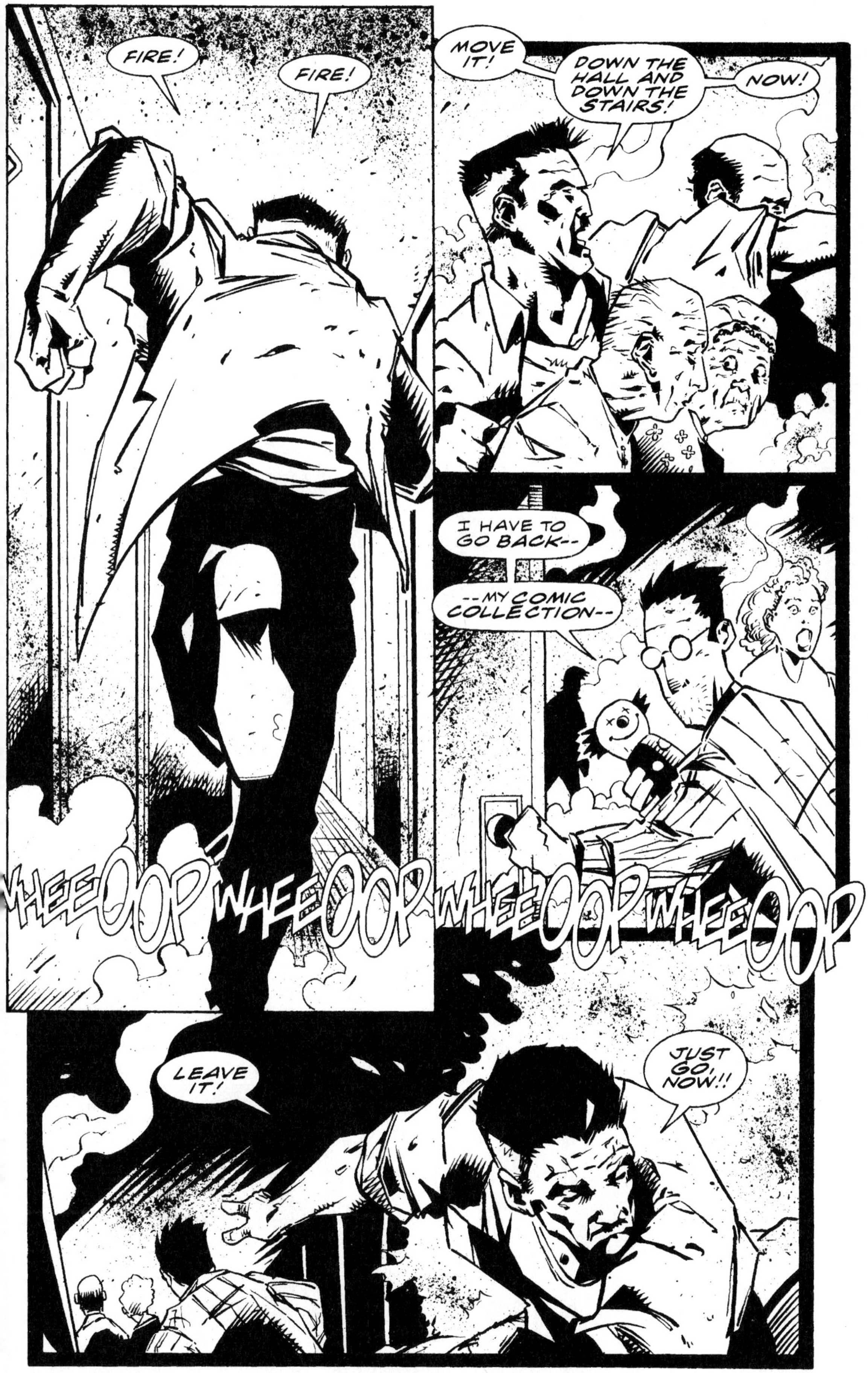
FIRE!
FIRE!
MOVE IT!
DOWN THE HALL AND DOWN THE STAIRS!
NOW!
I HAVE TO GO BACK--
--MY COMIC COLLECTION--
WHEEOOP WHEEOOP WHEEOOP WHEEOOP
LEAVE IT!
JUST GO, NOW!!

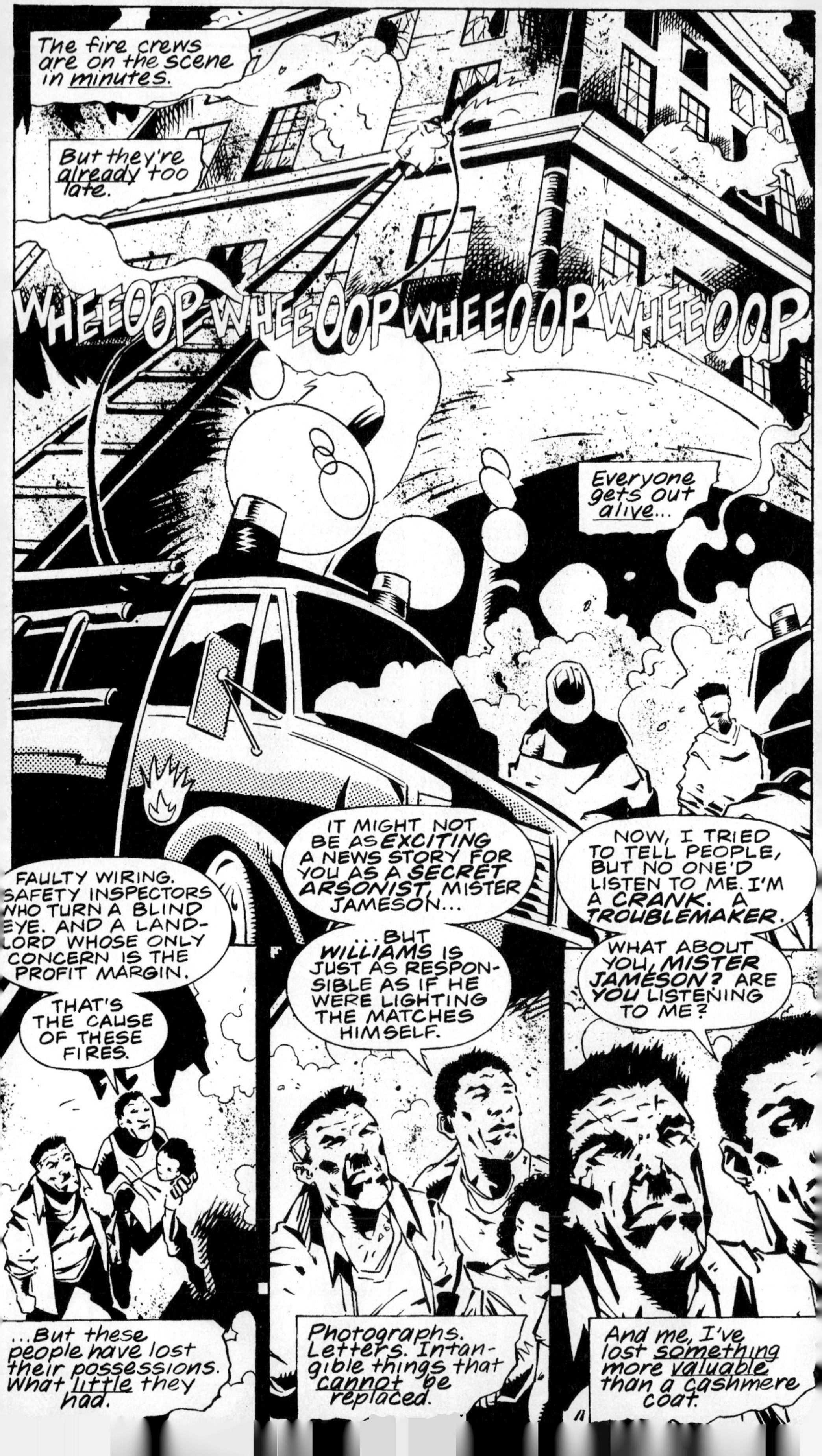
The fire crews are on the scene in minutes.
But they're already too late.
WHEEOOP WHEEOOP WHEEOOP WHEEOOP
Everyone gets out alive...
FAULTY WIRING. SAFETY INSPECTORS WHO TURN A BLIND EYE. AND A LANDLORD WHOSE ONLY CONCERN IS THE PROFIT MARGIN.
THAT'S THE CAUSE OF THESE FIRES.
...But these people have lost their possessions. What little they had.
IT MIGHT NOT BE AS EXCITING A NEWS STORY FOR YOU AS A SECRET ARSONIST, MISTER JAMESON...
...BUT WILLIAMS IS JUST AS RESPONSIBLE AS IF HE WERE LIGHTING THE MATCHES HIMSELF.
Photographs. Letters. Intangible things that cannot be replaced.
NOW, I TRIED TO TELL PEOPLE, BUT NO ONE'D LISTEN TO ME. I'M A CRANK. A TROUBLEMAKER.
WHAT ABOUT YOU, MISTER JAMESON? ARE YOU LISTENING TO ME?
And me, I've lost something more valuable than a cashmere coat.

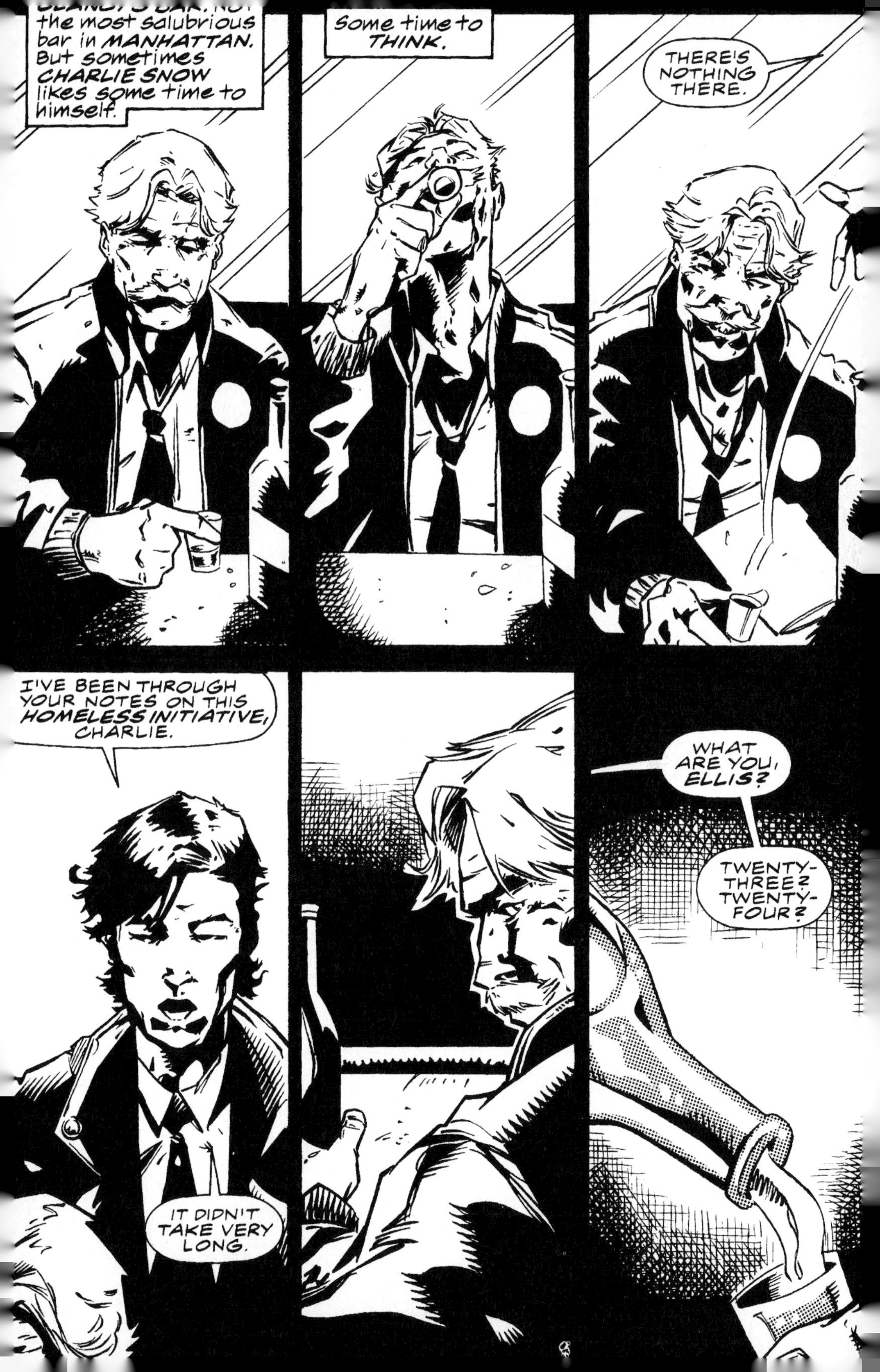

the most salubrious bar in MANHATTAN. But sometimes CHARLIE SNOW likes some time to himself.
Some time to THINK.
THERE'S NOTHING THERE.
I'VE BEEN THROUGH YOUR NOTES ON THIS HOMELESS INITIATIVE, CHARLIE.
IT DIDN'T TAKE VERY LONG.
WHAT ARE YOU, ELLIS?
TWENTY-THREE? TWENTY-FOUR?

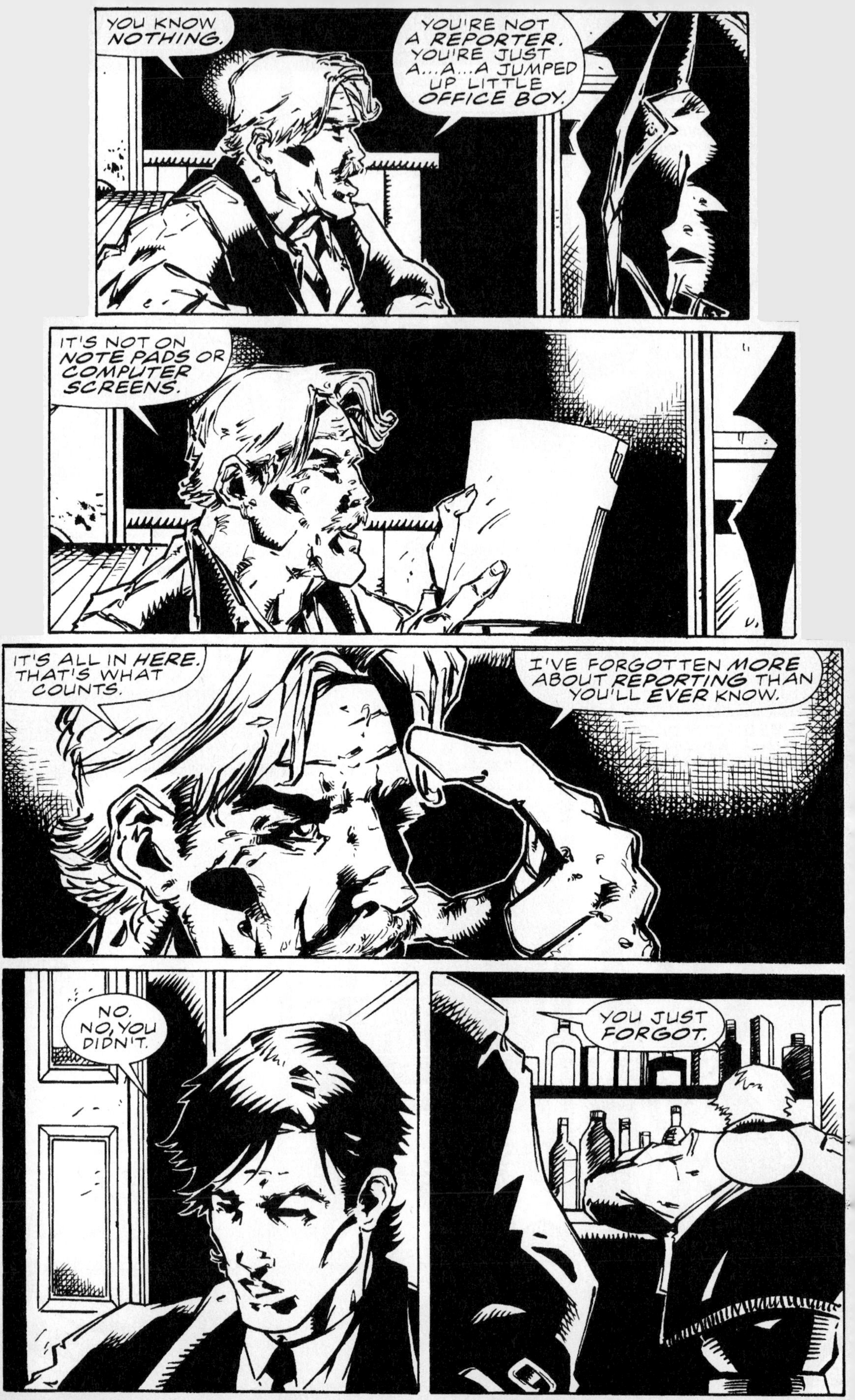
YOU KNOW NOTHING.
YOU'RE NOT A REPORTER. YOU'RE JUST A...A...A JUMPED UP LITTLE OFFICE BOY.
IT'S NOT ON NOTE PADS OR COMPUTER SCREENS.
IT'S ALL IN HERE. THAT'S WHAT COUNTS.
I'VE FORGOTTEN MORE ABOUT REPORTING THAN YOU'LL EVER KNOW.
NO. NO, YOU DIDN'T.
YOU JUST FORGOT.

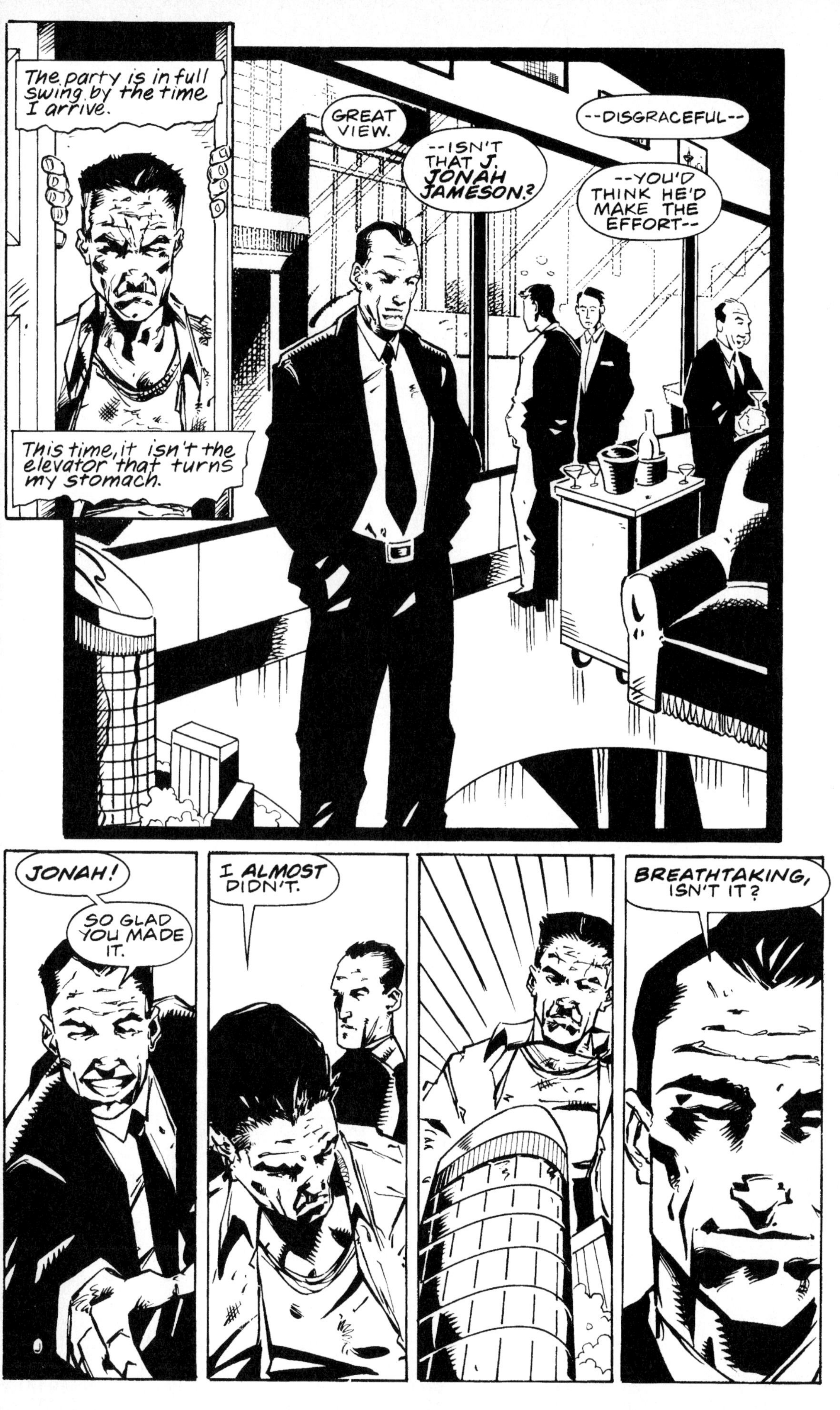
The party is in full swing by the time I arrive.
This time, it isn't the elevator that turns my stomach.
GREAT VIEW.
--ISN'T THAT J. JONAH JAMESON?
--DISGRACEFUL--
--YOU'D THINK HE'D MAKE THE EFFORT--
JONAH!
SO GLAD YOU MADE IT.
I ALMOST DIDN'T.
BREATHTAKING, ISN'T IT?

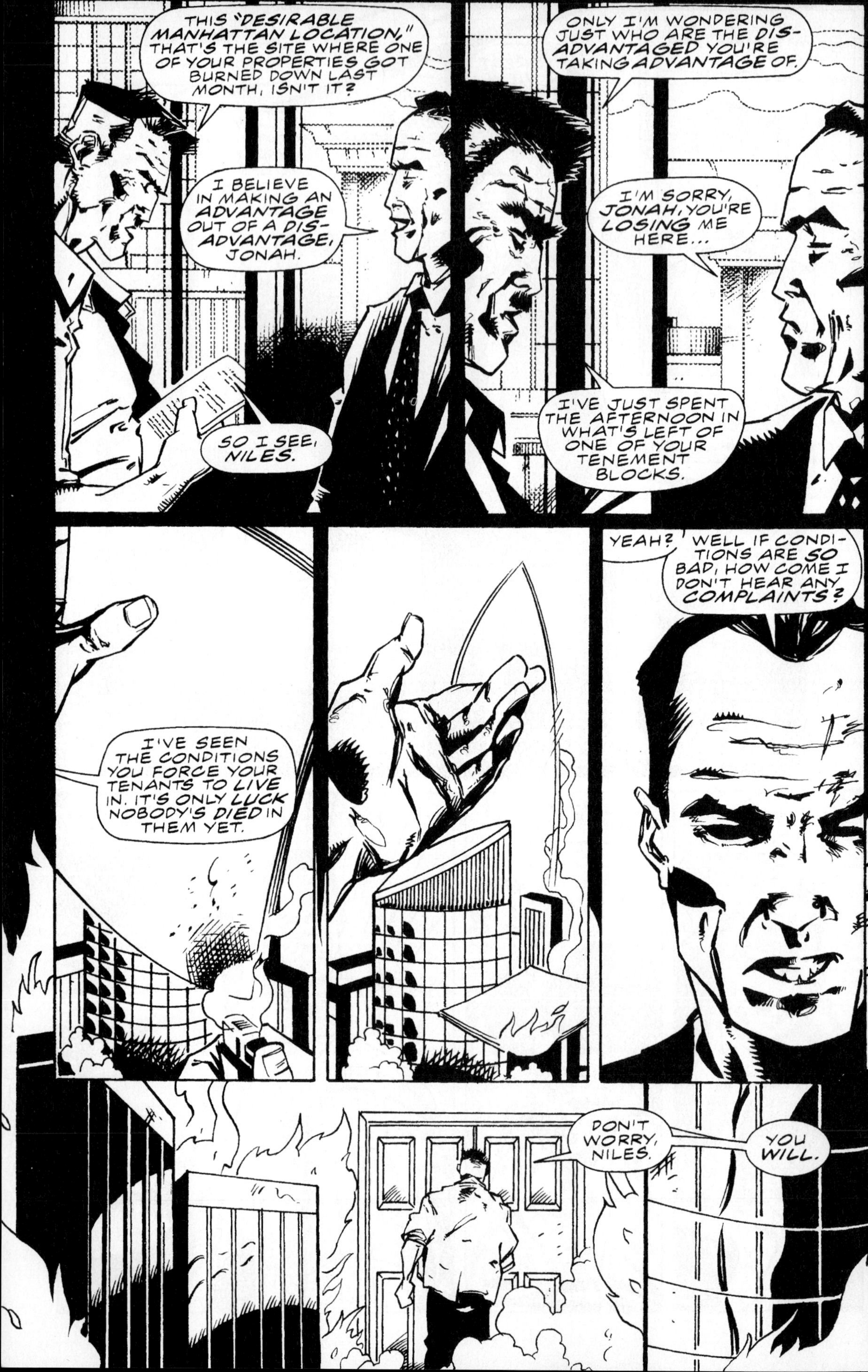
THIS "DESIRABLE MANHATTAN LOCATION," THAT'S THE SITE WHERE ONE OF YOUR PROPERTIES GOT BURNED DOWN LAST MONTH, ISN'T IT?
I BELIEVE IN MAKING AN ADVANTAGE OUT OF A DIS-ADVANTAGE, JONAH.
SO I SEE, NILES.
ONLY I'M WONDERING JUST WHO ARE THE DIS-ADVANTAGED YOU'RE TAKING ADVANTAGE OF.
I'M SORRY, JONAH, YOU'RE LOSING ME HERE...
I'VE JUST SPENT THE AFTERNOON IN WHAT'S LEFT OF ONE OF YOUR TENEMENT BLOCKS.
I'VE SEEN THE CONDITIONS YOU FORCE YOUR TENANTS TO LIVE IN. IT'S ONLY LUCK NOBODY'S DIED IN THEM YET.
YEAH?
WELL IF CONDITIONS ARE SO BAD, HOW COME I DON'T HEAR ANY COMPLAINTS?
DON'T WORRY, NILES.
YOU WILL.

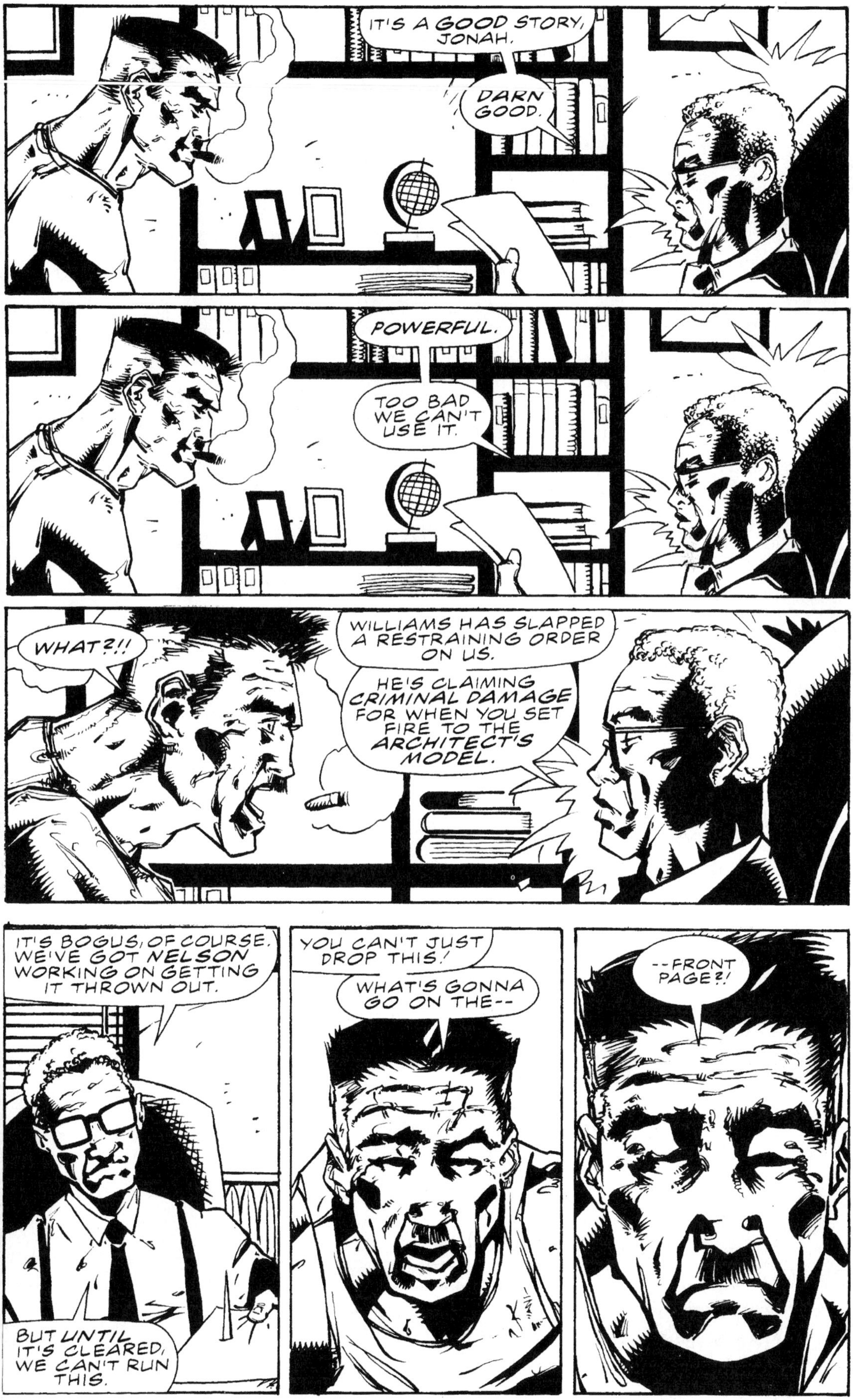
IT'S A GOOD STORY, JONAH.
DARN GOOD.
POWERFUL.
TOO BAD WE CAN'T USE IT.
WHAT?!!
WILLIAMS HAS SLAPPED A RESTRAINING ORDER ON US.
HE'S CLAIMING CRIMINAL DAMAGE FOR WHEN YOU SET FIRE TO THE ARCHITECT'S MODEL.
IT'S BOGUS, OF COURSE. WE'VE GOT NELSON WORKING ON GETTING IT THROWN OUT.
BUT UNTIL IT'S CLEARED, WE CAN'T RUN THIS.
YOU CAN'T JUST DROP THIS!
WHAT'S GONNA GO ON THE--
--FRONT PAGE?!

FINAL ☆☆☆☆

DAILY BUGLE®

NEW YORK'S FINEST DAILY NEWSPAPER

50¢

Wednesday, November 20th, 1996

Fine, possible showers. Low 14-19. Details p. 2

SPIDER-MAN FIRE RESCUE

A DAILY BUGLE PICTURE EXCLUSIVE

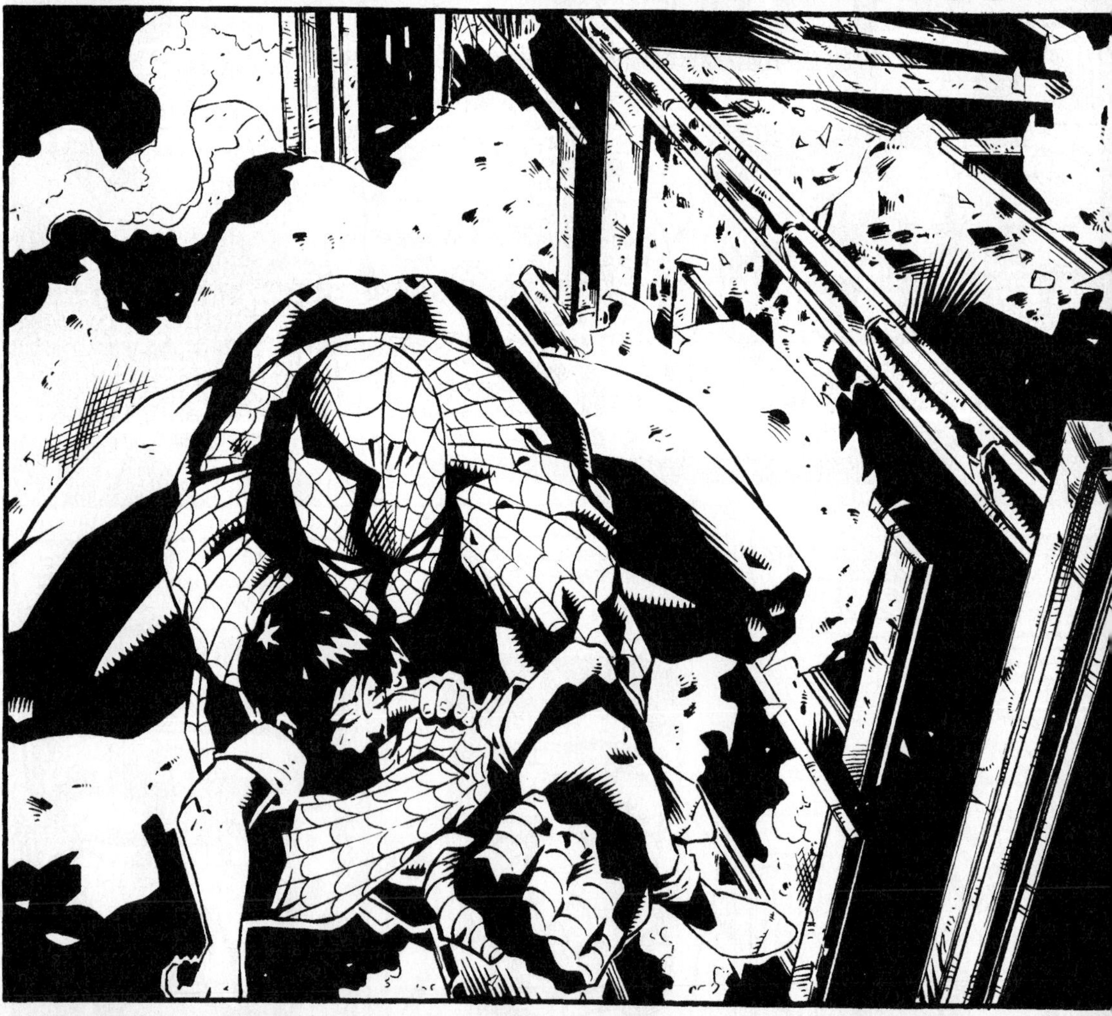

JIMMY AND TOMMY INVITE YOU TO THE FOOD FACTORY

CALL 1-888-EATING OUT

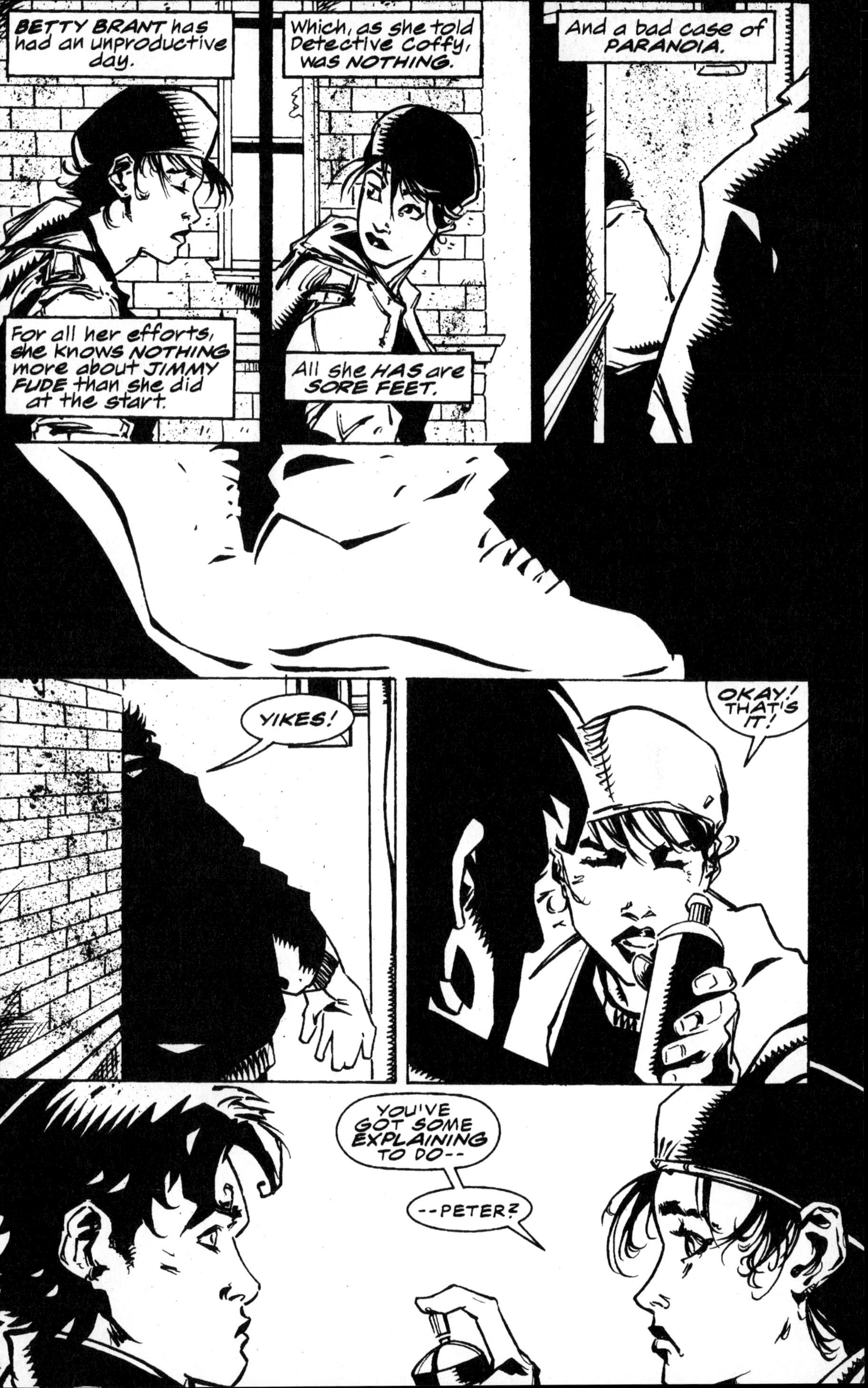
BETTY BRANT has had an unproductive day.
For all her efforts, she knows NOTHING more about JIMMY FUDE than she did at the start.
Which, as she told Detective Coffy, was NOTHING.
All she HAS are SORE FEET.
And a bad case of PARANOIA.
YIKES!
OKAY! THAT'S IT!
YOU'VE GOT SOME EXPLAINING TO DO--
--PETER?

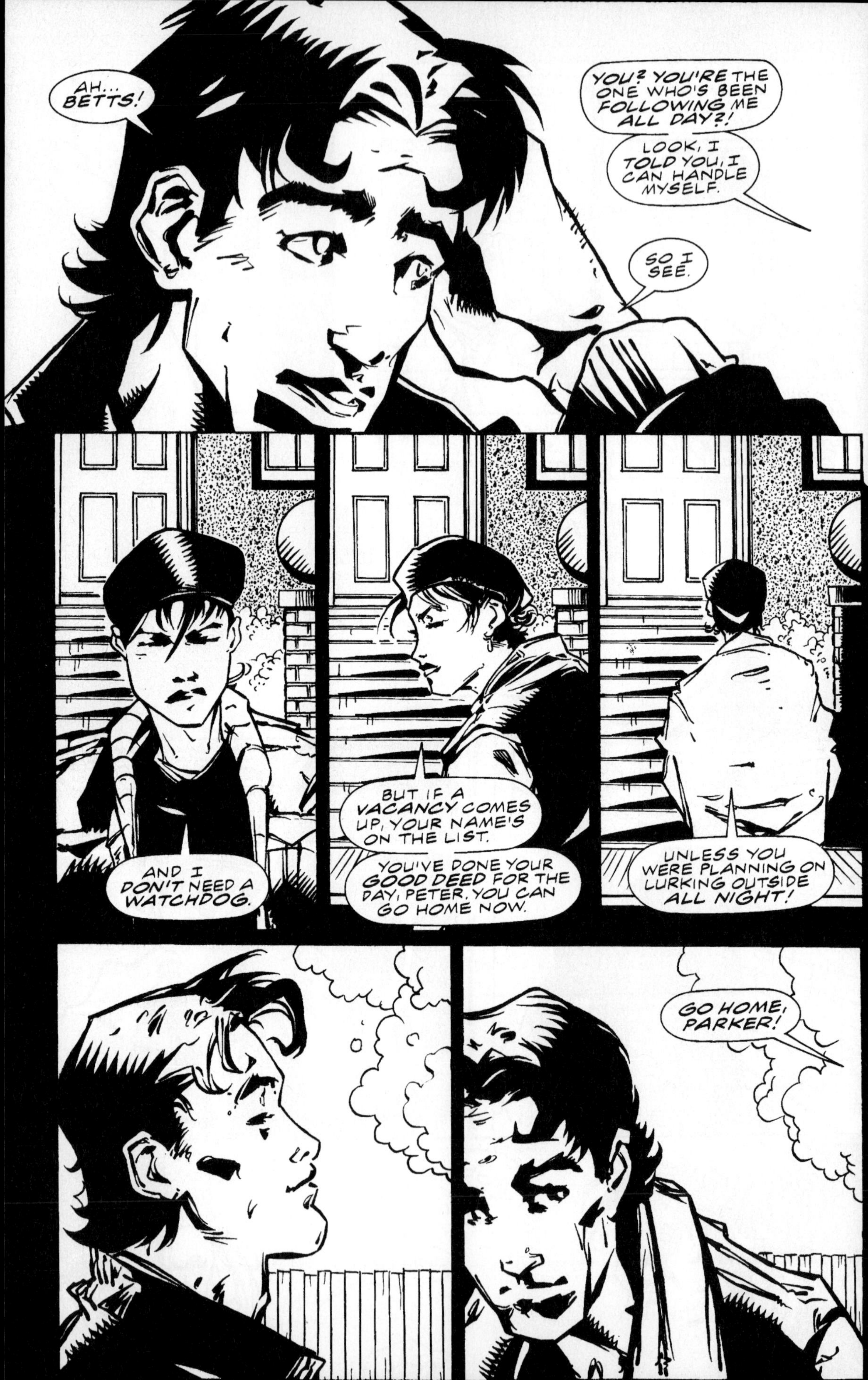
AH... BETTS!
YOU? YOU'RE THE ONE WHO'S BEEN FOLLOWING ME ALL DAY?!
LOOK, I TOLD YOU, I CAN HANDLE MYSELF.
SO I SEE.
AND I DON'T NEED A WATCHDOG.
BUT IF A VACANCY COMES UP, YOUR NAME'S ON THE LIST.
YOU'VE DONE YOUR GOOD DEED FOR THE DAY, PETER. YOU CAN GO HOME NOW.
UNLESS YOU WERE PLANNING ON LURKING OUTSIDE ALL NIGHT!
GO HOME, PARKER!

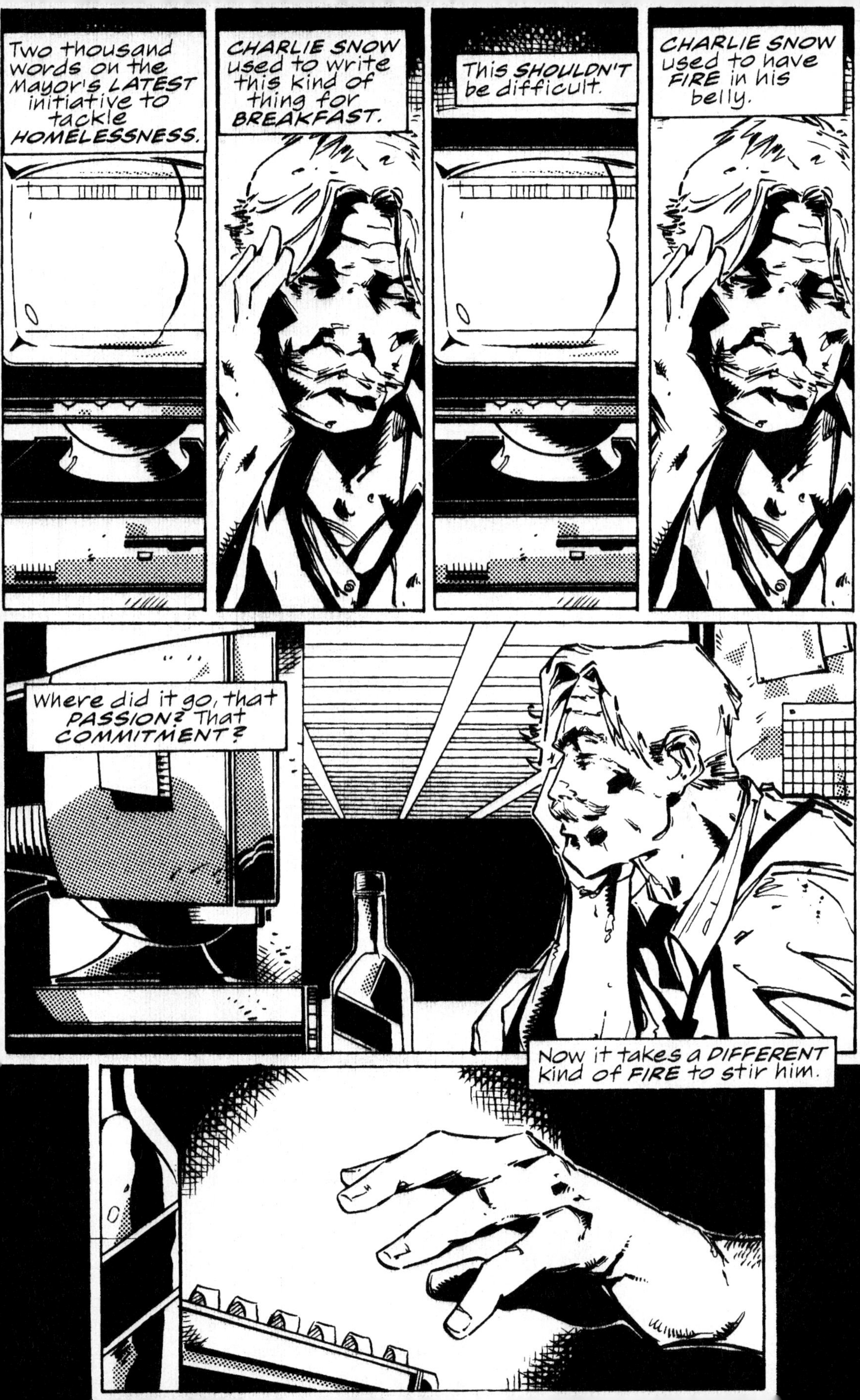
Two thousand words on the Mayor's LATEST initiative to tackle HOMELESSNESS.
CHARLIE SNOW used to write this kind of thing for BREAKFAST.
This SHOULDN'T be difficult.
CHARLIE SNOW used to have FIRE in his belly.
Where did it go, that PASSION? That COMMITMENT?
Now it takes a DIFFERENT kind of FIRE to stir him.

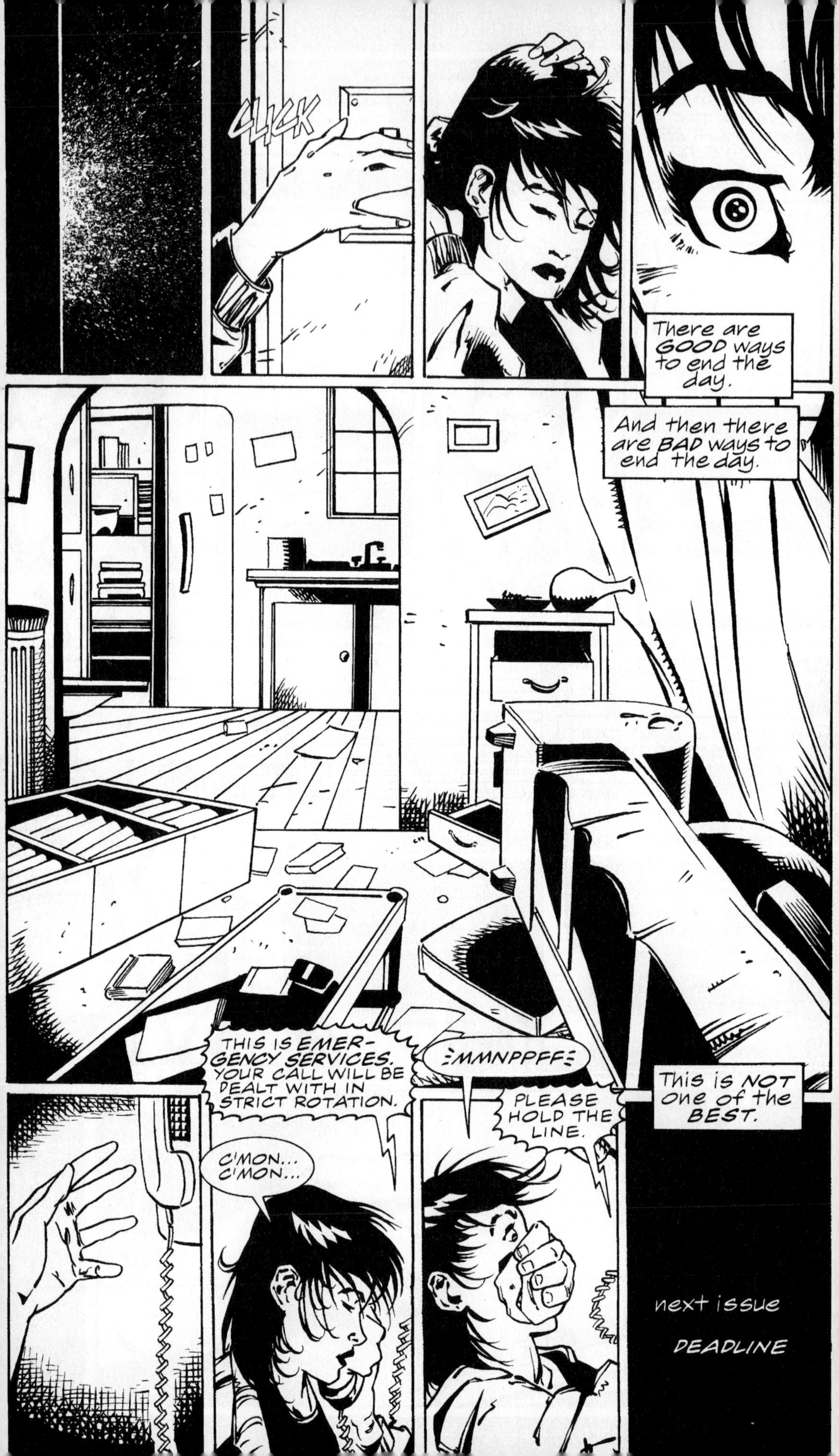
CLICK
There are GOOD ways to end the day.
And then there are BAD ways to end the day.
This is NOT one of the BEST.
THIS IS EMERGENCY SERVICES. YOUR CALL WILL BE DEALT WITH IN STRICT ROTATION.
MMNPPFF
PLEASE HOLD THE LINE.
C'MON... C'MON...
next issue
DEADLINE

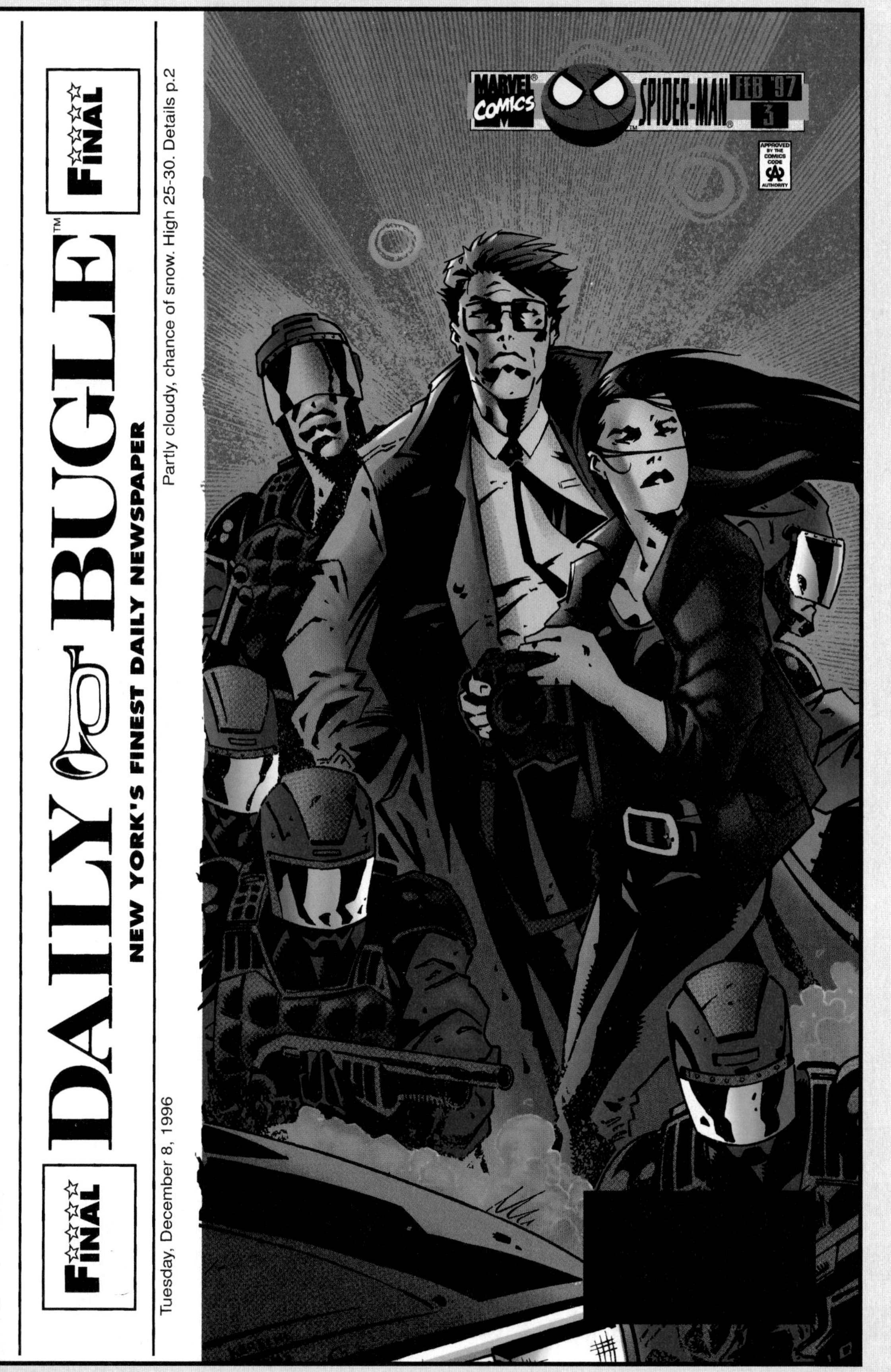
FINAL
DAILY BUGLE™
NEW YORK'S FINEST DAILY NEWSPAPER
Tuesday, December 8, 1996
Partly cloudy, chance of snow. High 25-30. Details p.2
FINAL
MARVEL COMICS
SPIDER-MAN
FEB '97
3
APPROVED BY THE COMICS CODE AUTHORITY

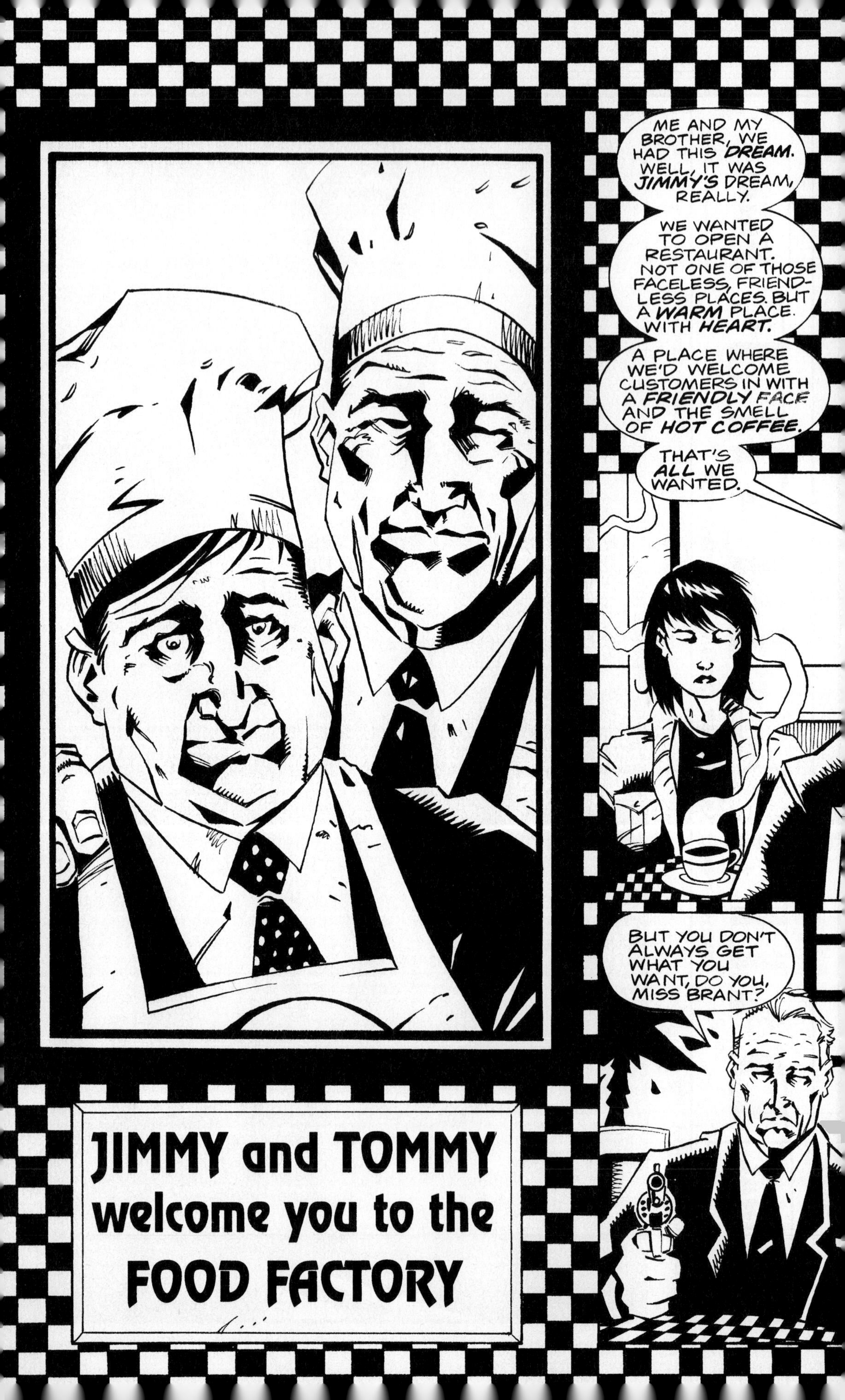

JIMMY and TOMMY
welcome you to the
FOOD FACTORY
ME AND MY BROTHER, WE HAD THIS DREAM. WELL, IT WAS JIMMY'S DREAM, REALLY.
WE WANTED TO OPEN A RESTAURANT. NOT ONE OF THOSE FACELESS, FRIEND-LESS PLACES. BUT A WARM PLACE. WITH HEART.
A PLACE WHERE WE'D WELCOME CUSTOMERS IN WITH A FRIENDLY FACE AND THE SMELL OF HOT COFFEE.
THAT'S ALL WE WANTED.
BUT YOU DON'T ALWAYS GET WHAT YOU WANT, DO YOU, MISS BRANT?

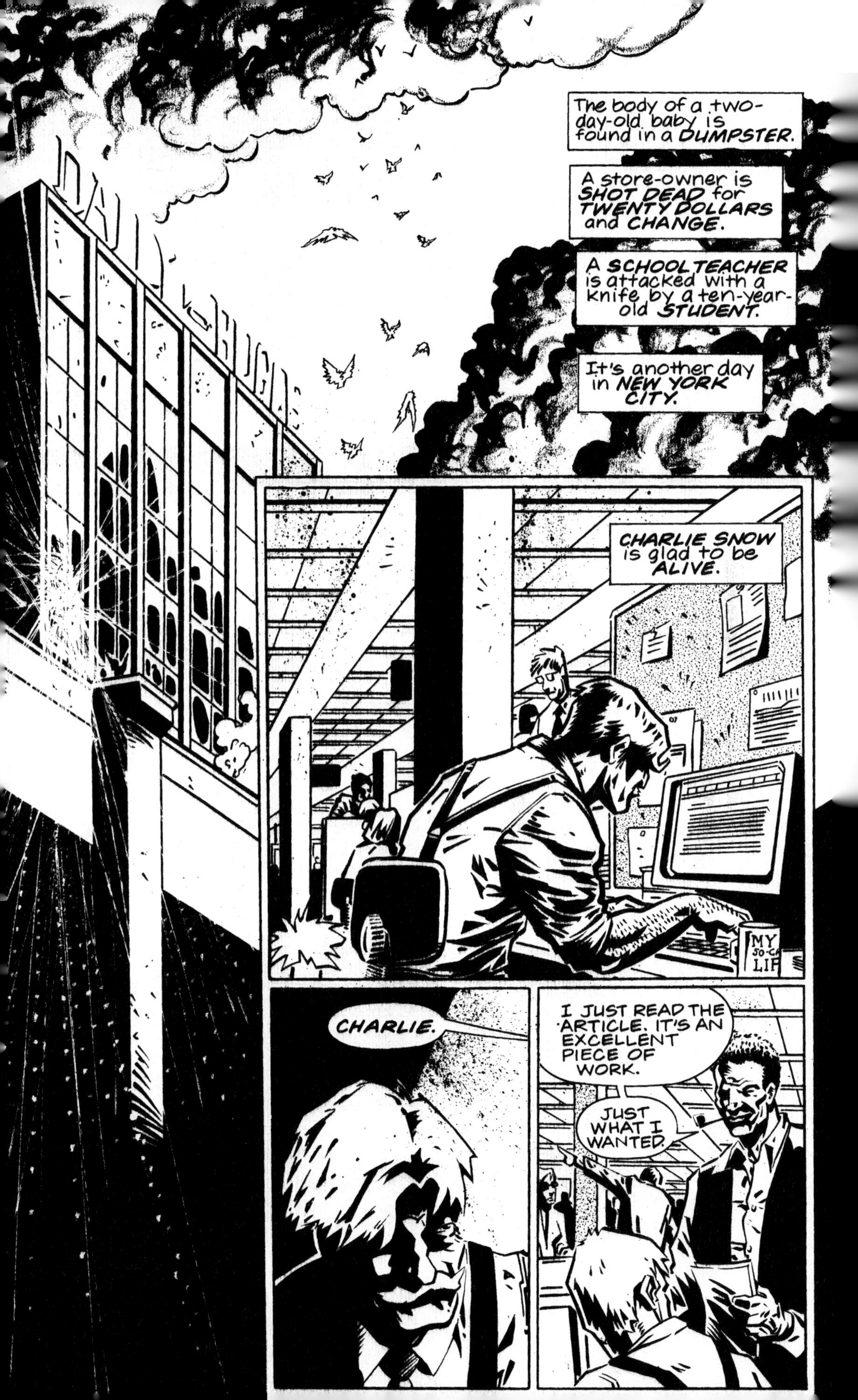
The body of a two-day-old baby is found in a DUMPSTER.
A store-owner is SHOT DEAD for TWENTY DOLLARS and CHANGE.
A SCHOOLTEACHER is attacked with a knife by a ten-year-old STUDENT.
It's another day in NEW YORK CITY.
CHARLIE SNOW is glad to be ALIVE.
CHARLIE.
I JUST READ THE ARTICLE. IT'S AN EXCELLENT PIECE OF WORK.
JUST WHAT I WANTED.

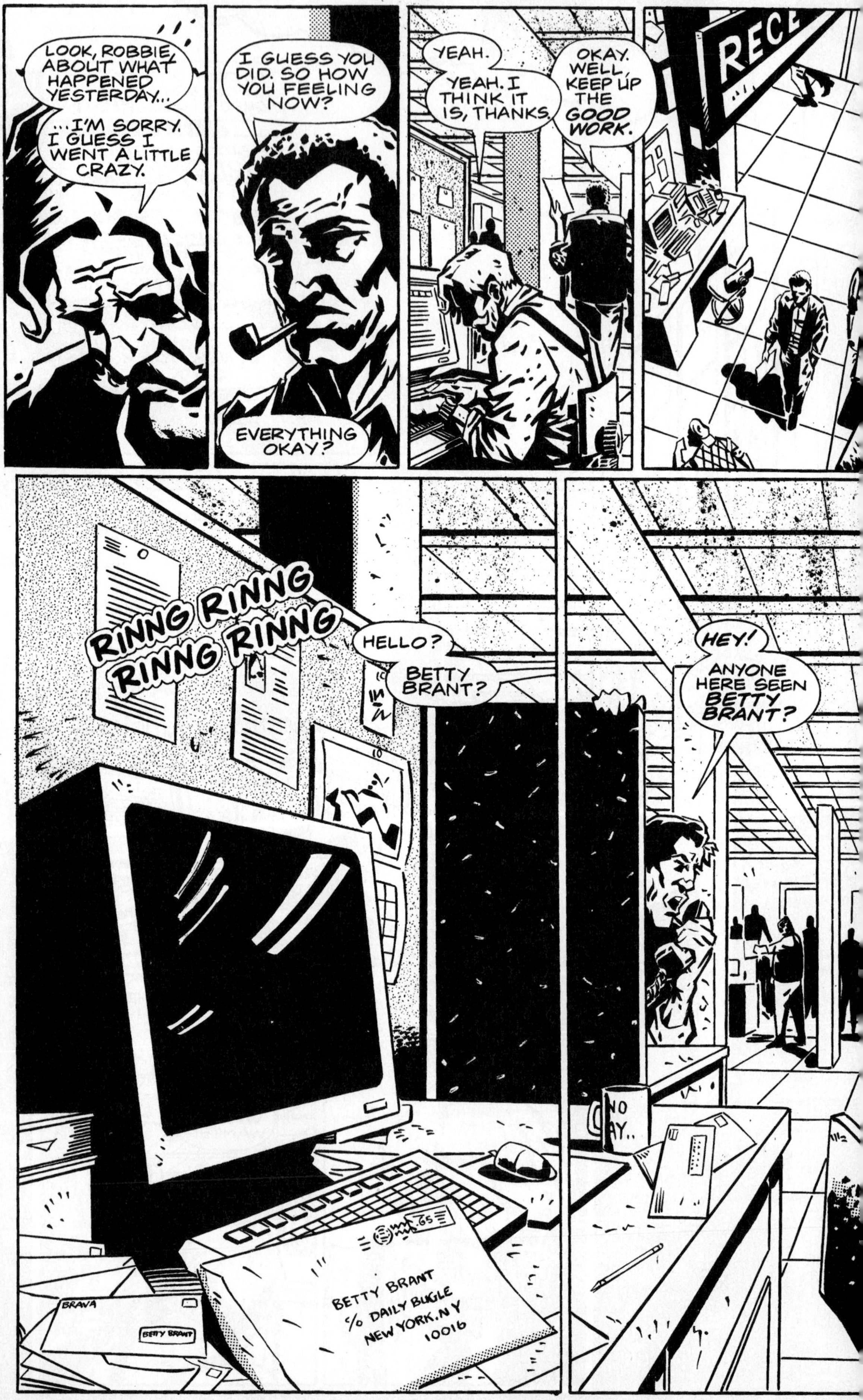

LOOK, ROBBIE, ABOUT WHAT HAPPENED YESTERDAY...
...I'M SORRY. I GUESS I WENT A LITTLE CRAZY.
I GUESS YOU DID. SO HOW YOU FEELING NOW?
EVERYTHING OKAY?
YEAH.
YEAH. I THINK IT IS, THANKS.
OKAY. WELL, KEEP UP THE GOOD WORK.
RECE
RINNG RINNG RINNG RINNG
HELLO?
BETTY BRANT?
HEY!
ANYONE HERE SEEN BETTY BRANT?
BETTY BRANT
% DAILY BUGLE
NEW YORK, N.Y
10016
BRAVA
BETTY BRANT

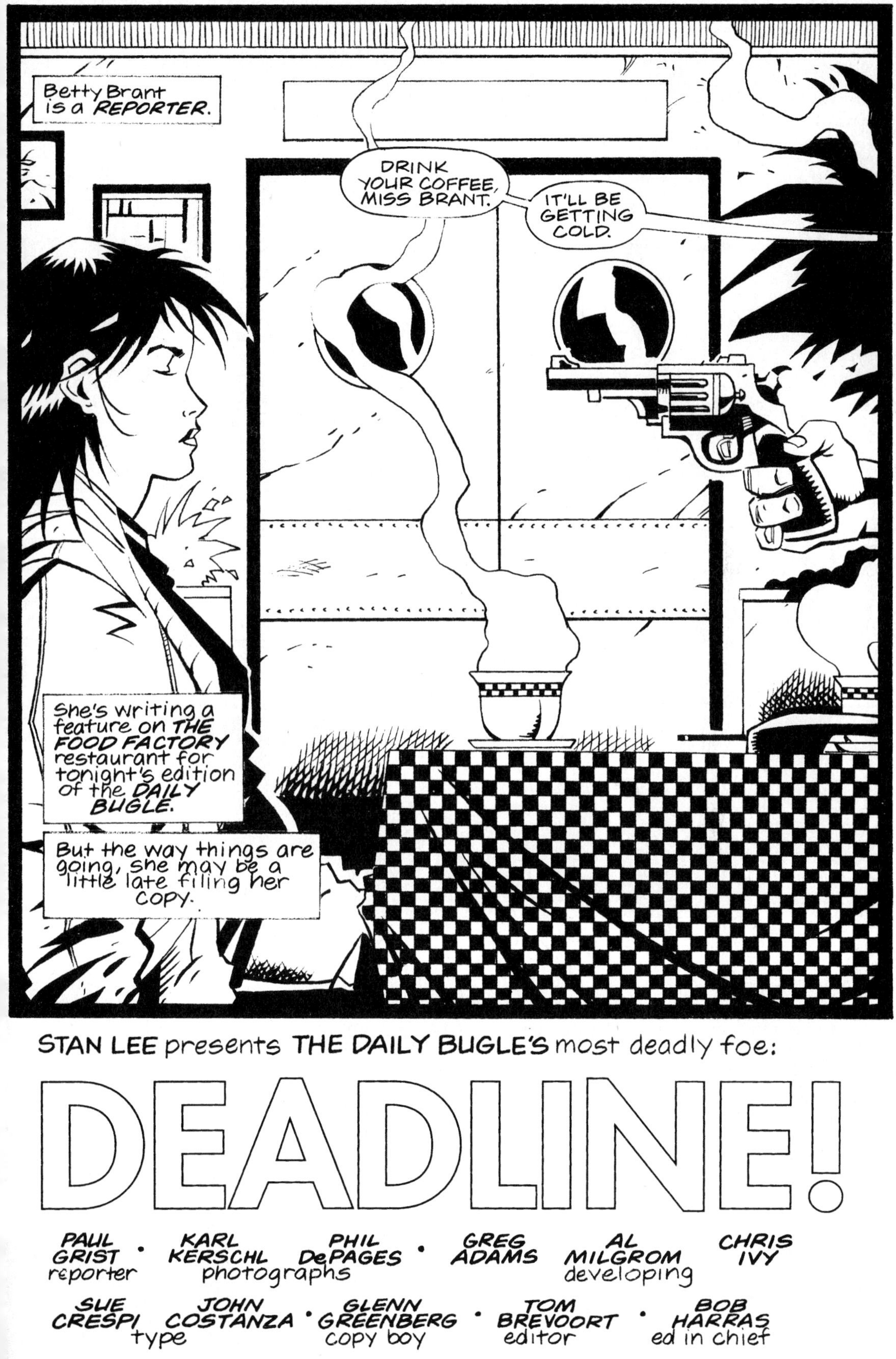
Betty Brant is a REPORTER.
DRINK YOUR COFFEE, MISS BRANT.
IT'LL BE GETTING COLD.
She's writing a feature on THE FOOD FACTORY restaurant for tonight's edition of the DAILY BUGLE.
But the way things are going, she may be a little late filing her copy.

STAN LEE presents THE DAILY BUGLE'S most deadly foe:

DEADLINE!

PAUL GRIST · reporter

KARL KERSCHL · PHIL DePAGES · photographs

GREG ADAMS · AL MILGROM · CHRIS IVY · developing

SUE CRESPI · JOHN COSTANZA · type

GLENN GREENBERG · copy boy

TOM BREVOORT · editor

BOB HARRAS · ed in chief

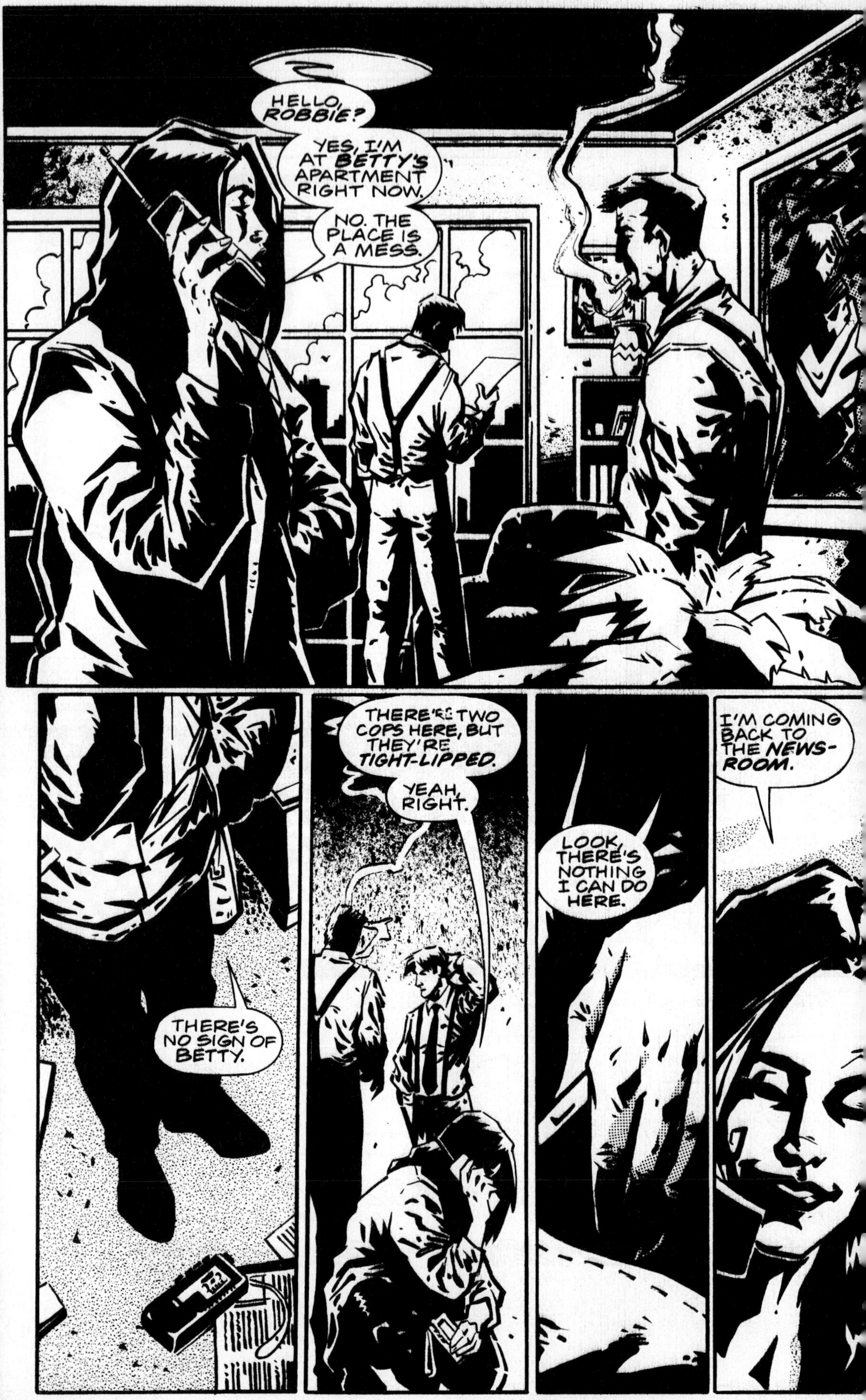
HELLO, ROBBIE?
YES, I'M AT BETTY'S APARTMENT RIGHT NOW.
NO. THE PLACE IS A MESS.
THERE'S NO SIGN OF BETTY.
THERE'RE TWO COPS HERE, BUT THEY'RE TIGHT-LIPPED.
YEAH, RIGHT.
LOOK, THERE'S NOTHING I CAN DO HERE.
I'M COMING BACK TO THE NEWS-ROOM.

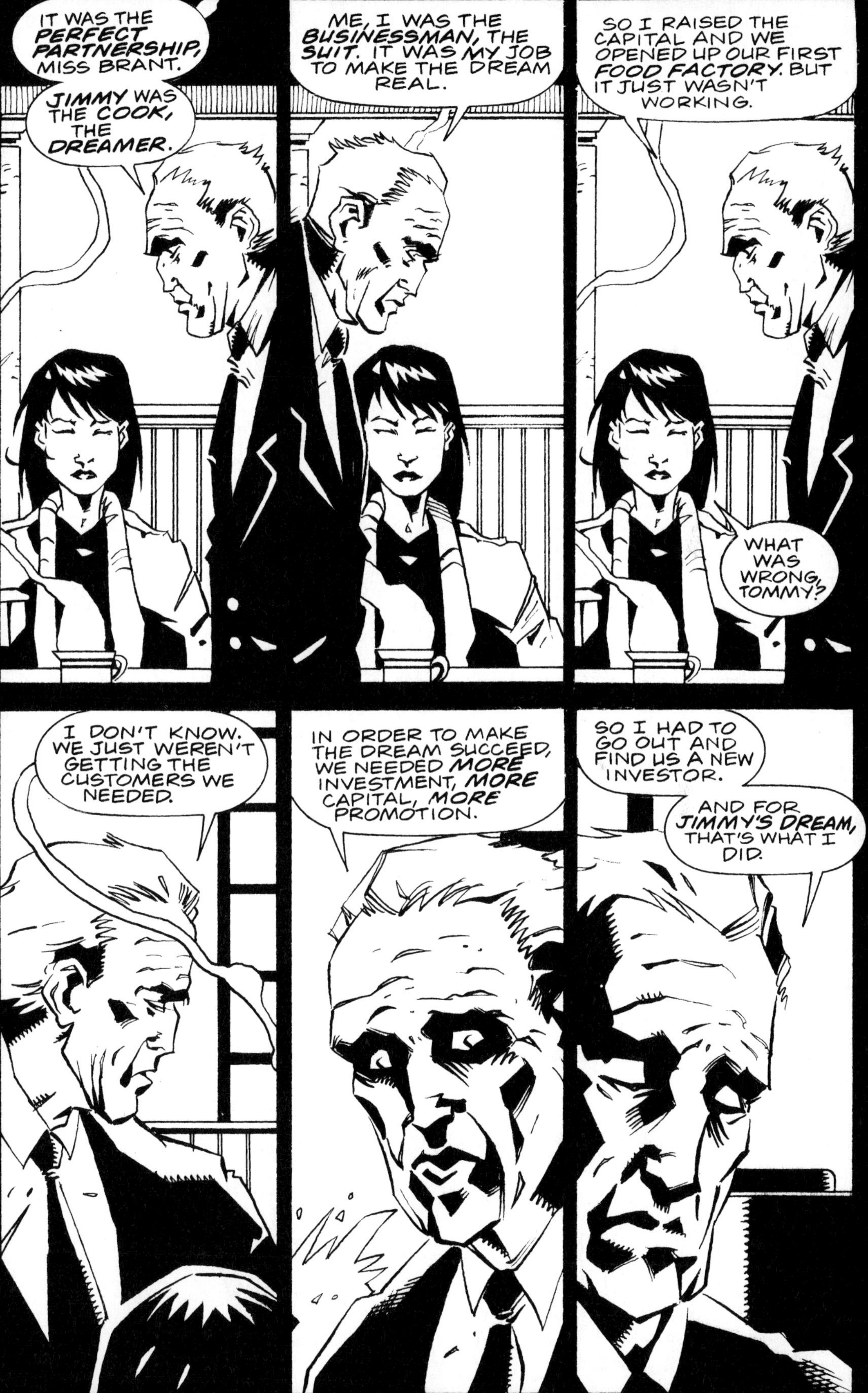
IT WAS THE PERFECT PARTNERSHIP, MISS BRANT.
JIMMY WAS THE COOK, THE DREAMER.
ME, I WAS THE BUSINESSMAN, THE SUIT. IT WAS MY JOB TO MAKE THE DREAM REAL.
SO I RAISED THE CAPITAL AND WE OPENED UP OUR FIRST FOOD FACTORY. BUT IT JUST WASN'T WORKING.
WHAT WAS WRONG, TOMMY?
I DON'T KNOW. WE JUST WEREN'T GETTING THE CUSTOMERS WE NEEDED.
IN ORDER TO MAKE THE DREAM SUCCEED, WE NEEDED MORE INVESTMENT, MORE CAPITAL, MORE PROMOTION.
SO I HAD TO GO OUT AND FIND US A NEW INVESTOR.
AND FOR JIMMY'S DREAM, THAT'S WHAT I DID.

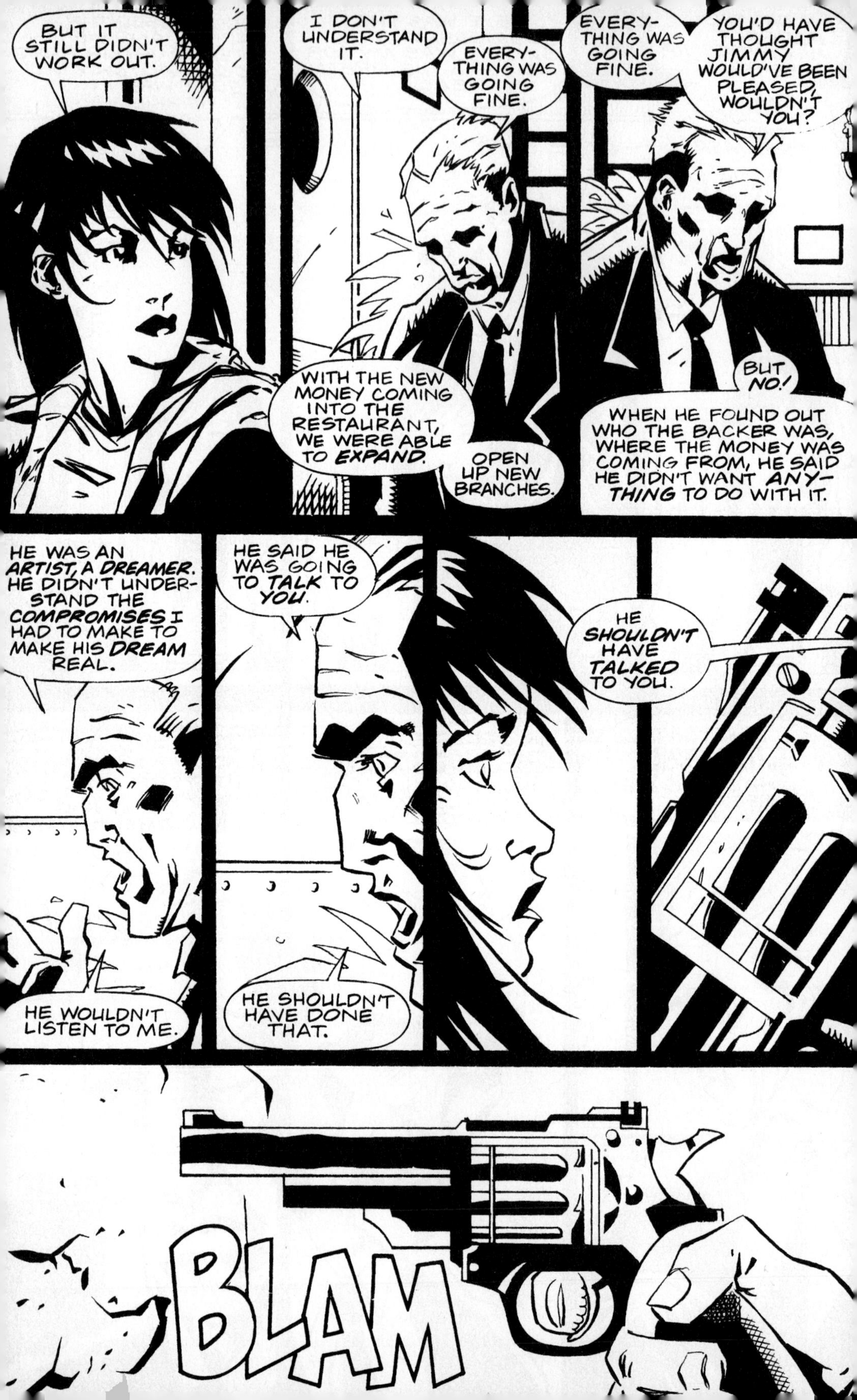

BUT IT STILL DIDN'T WORK OUT.
I DON'T UNDERSTAND IT.
EVERY-THING WAS GOING FINE.
WITH THE NEW MONEY COMING INTO THE RESTAURANT, WE WERE ABLE TO EXPAND.
OPEN UP NEW BRANCHES.
EVERY-THING WAS GOING FINE.
YOU'D HAVE THOUGHT JIMMY WOULD'VE BEEN PLEASED, WOULDN'T YOU?
BUT NO!
WHEN HE FOUND OUT WHO THE BACKER WAS, WHERE THE MONEY WAS COMING FROM, HE SAID HE DIDN'T WANT ANY-THING TO DO WITH IT.
HE WAS AN ARTIST, A DREAMER. HE DIDN'T UNDER-STAND THE COMPROMISES I HAD TO MAKE TO MAKE HIS DREAM REAL.
HE WOULDN'T LISTEN TO ME.
HE SAID HE WAS GOING TO TALK TO YOU.
HE SHOULDN'T HAVE DONE THAT.
HE SHOULDN'T HAVE TALKED TO YOU.
BLAM

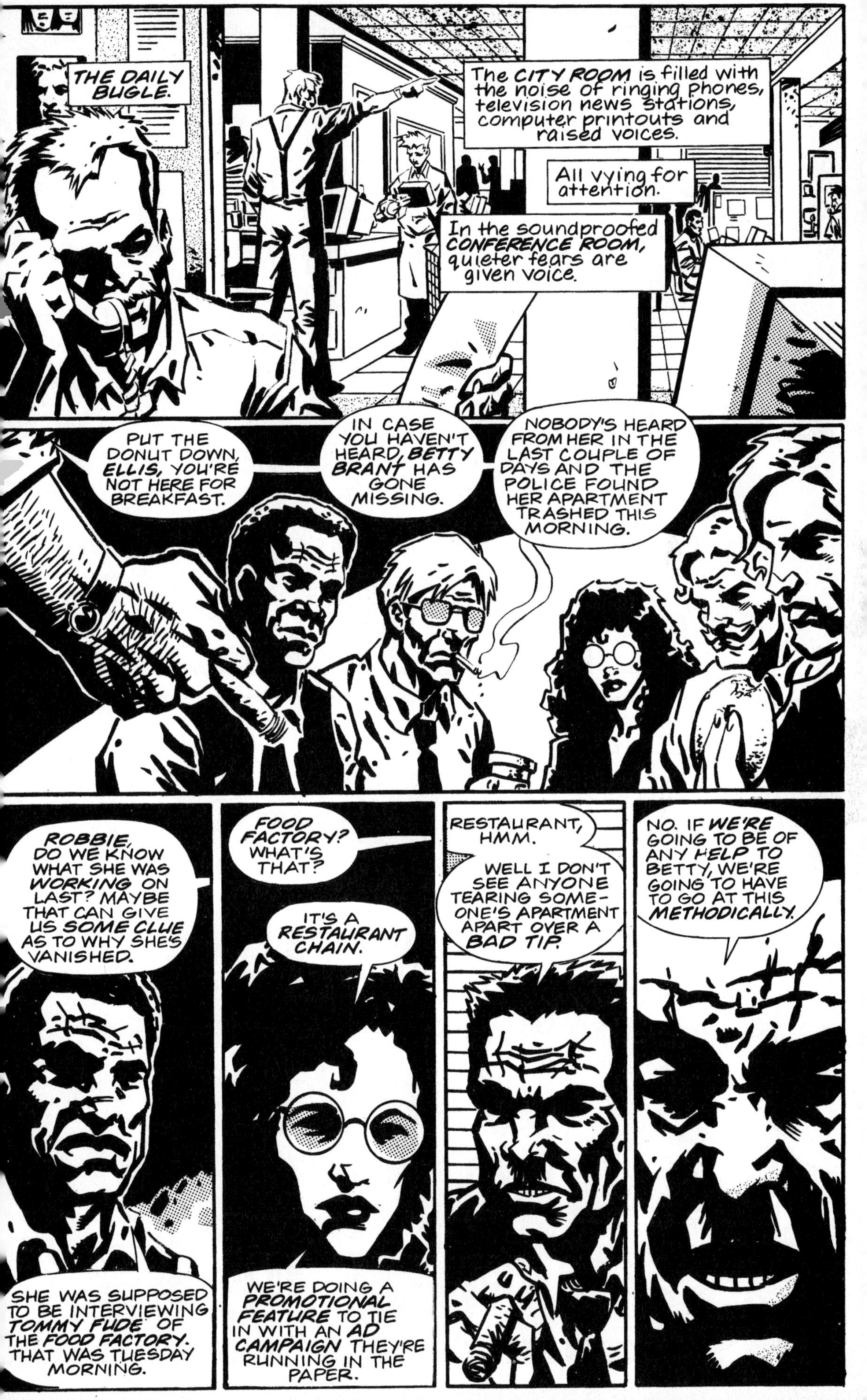
THE DAILY BUGLE.
The CITY ROOM is filled with the noise of ringing phones, television news stations, computer printouts and raised voices.
All vying for attention.
In the soundproofed CONFERENCE ROOM, quieter fears are given voice.
PUT THE DONUT DOWN, ELLIS, YOU'RE NOT HERE FOR BREAKFAST.
IN CASE YOU HAVEN'T HEARD, BETTY BRANT HAS GONE MISSING.
NOBODY'S HEARD FROM HER IN THE LAST COUPLE OF DAYS AND THE POLICE FOUND HER APARTMENT TRASHED THIS MORNING.
ROBBIE, DO WE KNOW WHAT SHE WAS WORKING ON LAST? MAYBE THAT CAN GIVE US SOME CLUE AS TO WHY SHE'S VANISHED.
SHE WAS SUPPOSED TO BE INTERVIEWING TOMMY FUDE OF THE FOOD FACTORY. THAT WAS TUESDAY MORNING.
FOOD FACTORY? WHAT'S THAT?
IT'S A RESTAURANT CHAIN.
WE'RE DOING A PROMOTIONAL FEATURE TO TIE IN WITH AN AD CAMPAIGN THEY'RE RUNNING IN THE PAPER.
RESTAURANT, HMM.
WELL I DON'T SEE ANYONE TEARING SOME-ONE'S APARTMENT APART OVER A BAD TIP.
NO. IF WE'RE GOING TO BE OF ANY HELP TO BETTY, WE'RE GOING TO HAVE TO GO AT THIS METHODICALLY.

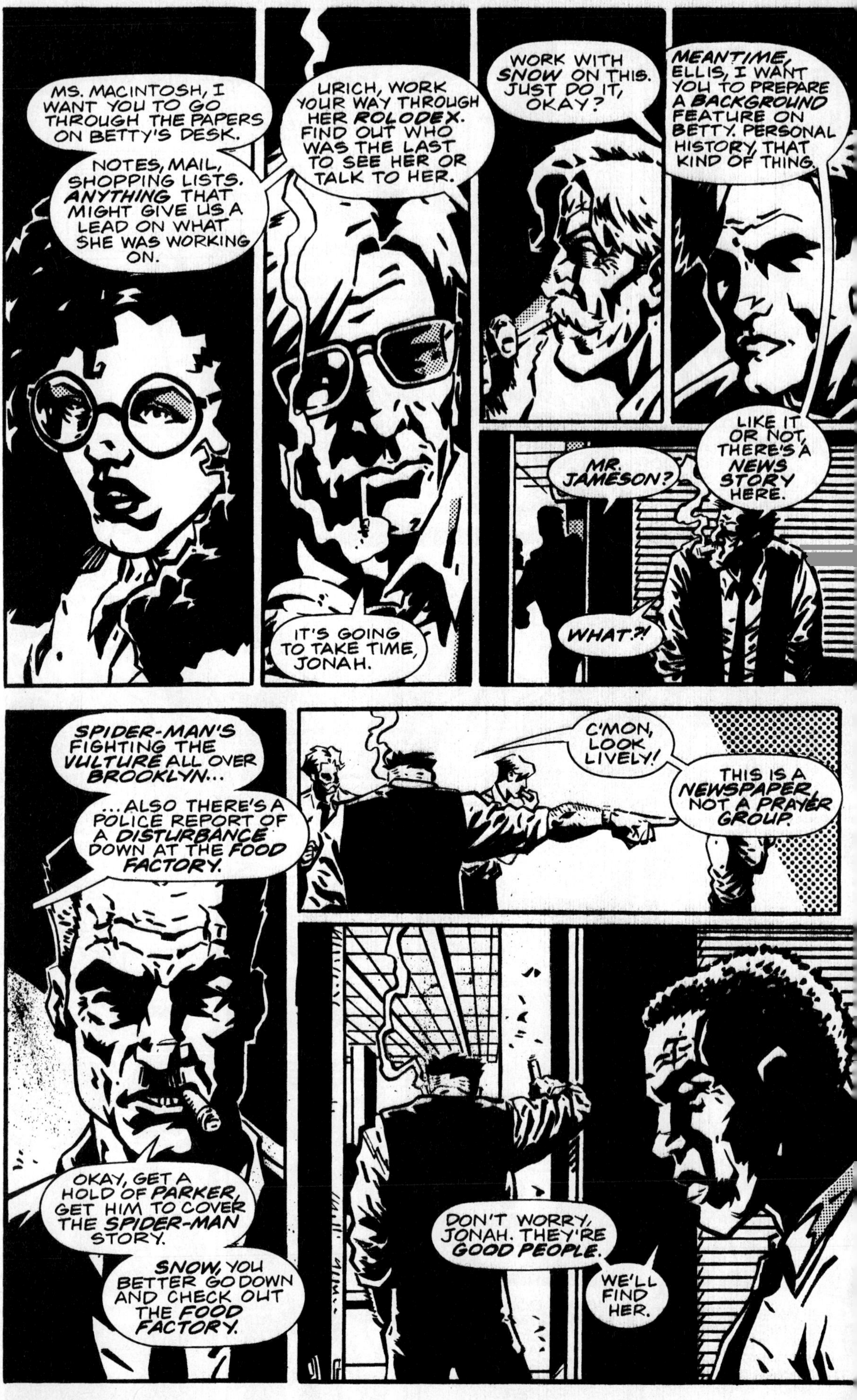

MS. MACINTOSH, I WANT YOU TO GO THROUGH THE PAPERS ON BETTY'S DESK.
NOTES, MAIL, SHOPPING LISTS. ANYTHING THAT MIGHT GIVE US A LEAD ON WHAT SHE WAS WORKING ON.
URICH, WORK YOUR WAY THROUGH HER ROLODEX. FIND OUT WHO WAS THE LAST TO SEE HER OR TALK TO HER.
IT'S GOING TO TAKE TIME, JONAH.
WORK WITH SNOW ON THIS. JUST DO IT, OKAY?
MEANTIME, ELLIS, I WANT YOU TO PREPARE A BACKGROUND FEATURE ON BETTY. PERSONAL HISTORY, THAT KIND OF THING.
MR. JAMESON?
WHAT?!
LIKE IT OR NOT, THERE'S A NEWS STORY HERE.
SPIDER-MAN'S FIGHTING THE VULTURE ALL OVER BROOKLYN...
...ALSO THERE'S A POLICE REPORT OF A DISTURBANCE DOWN AT THE FOOD FACTORY.
OKAY, GET A HOLD OF PARKER, GET HIM TO COVER THE SPIDER-MAN STORY.
SNOW, YOU BETTER GO DOWN AND CHECK OUT THE FOOD FACTORY.
C'MON, LOOK LIVELY!
THIS IS A NEWSPAPER, NOT A PRAYER GROUP.
DON'T WORRY, JONAH. THEY'RE GOOD PEOPLE.
WE'LL FIND HER.

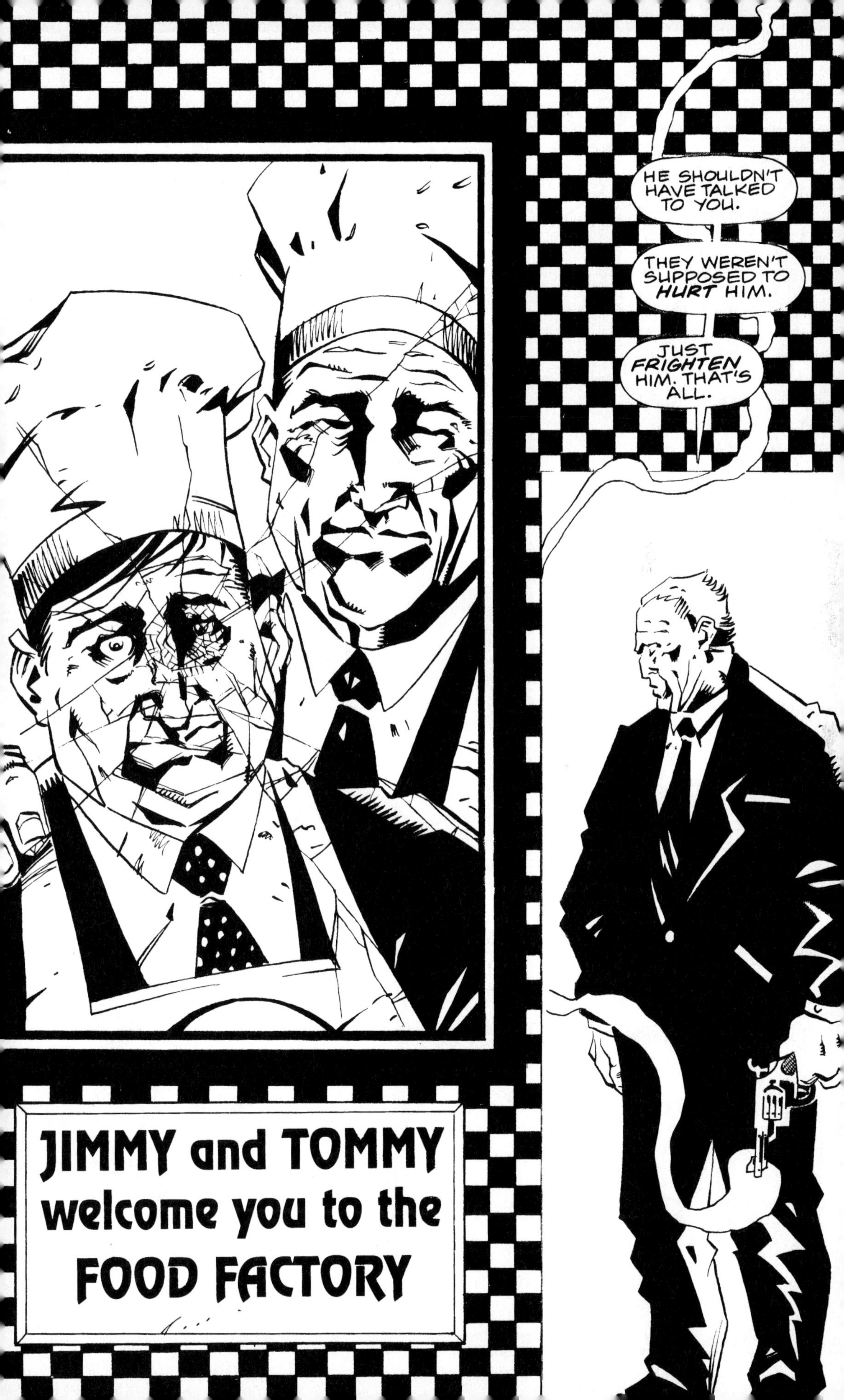

JIMMY and TOMMY welcome you to the FOOD FACTORY
HE SHOULDN'T HAVE TALKED TO YOU.
THEY WEREN'T SUPPOSED TO HURT HIM.
JUST FRIGHTEN HIM. THAT'S ALL.

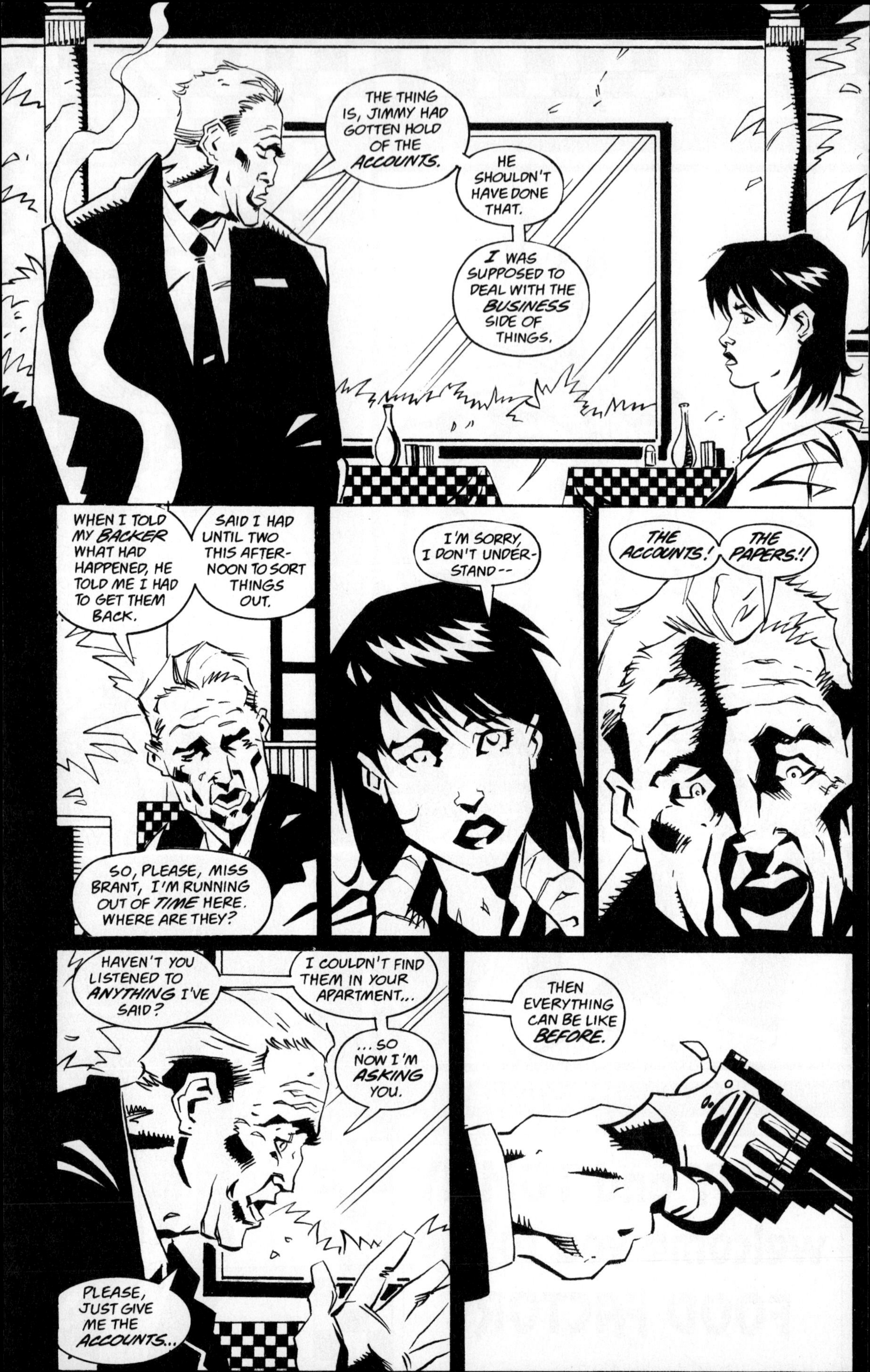
THE THING IS, JIMMY HAD GOTTEN HOLD OF THE ACCOUNTS.
HE SHOULDN'T HAVE DONE THAT.
I WAS SUPPOSED TO DEAL WITH THE BUSINESS SIDE OF THINGS.
WHEN I TOLD MY BACKER WHAT HAD HAPPENED, HE TOLD ME I HAD TO GET THEM BACK.
SAID I HAD UNTIL TWO THIS AFTER-NOON TO SORT THINGS OUT.
SO, PLEASE, MISS BRANT, I'M RUNNING OUT OF TIME HERE. WHERE ARE THEY?
I'M SORRY, I DON'T UNDER-STAND--
THE ACCOUNTS!
THE PAPERS!!
HAVEN'T YOU LISTENED TO ANYTHING I'VE SAID?
I COULDN'T FIND THEM IN YOUR APARTMENT...
...SO NOW I'M ASKING YOU.
PLEASE, JUST GIVE ME THE ACCOUNTS...
THEN EVERYTHING CAN BE LIKE BEFORE.

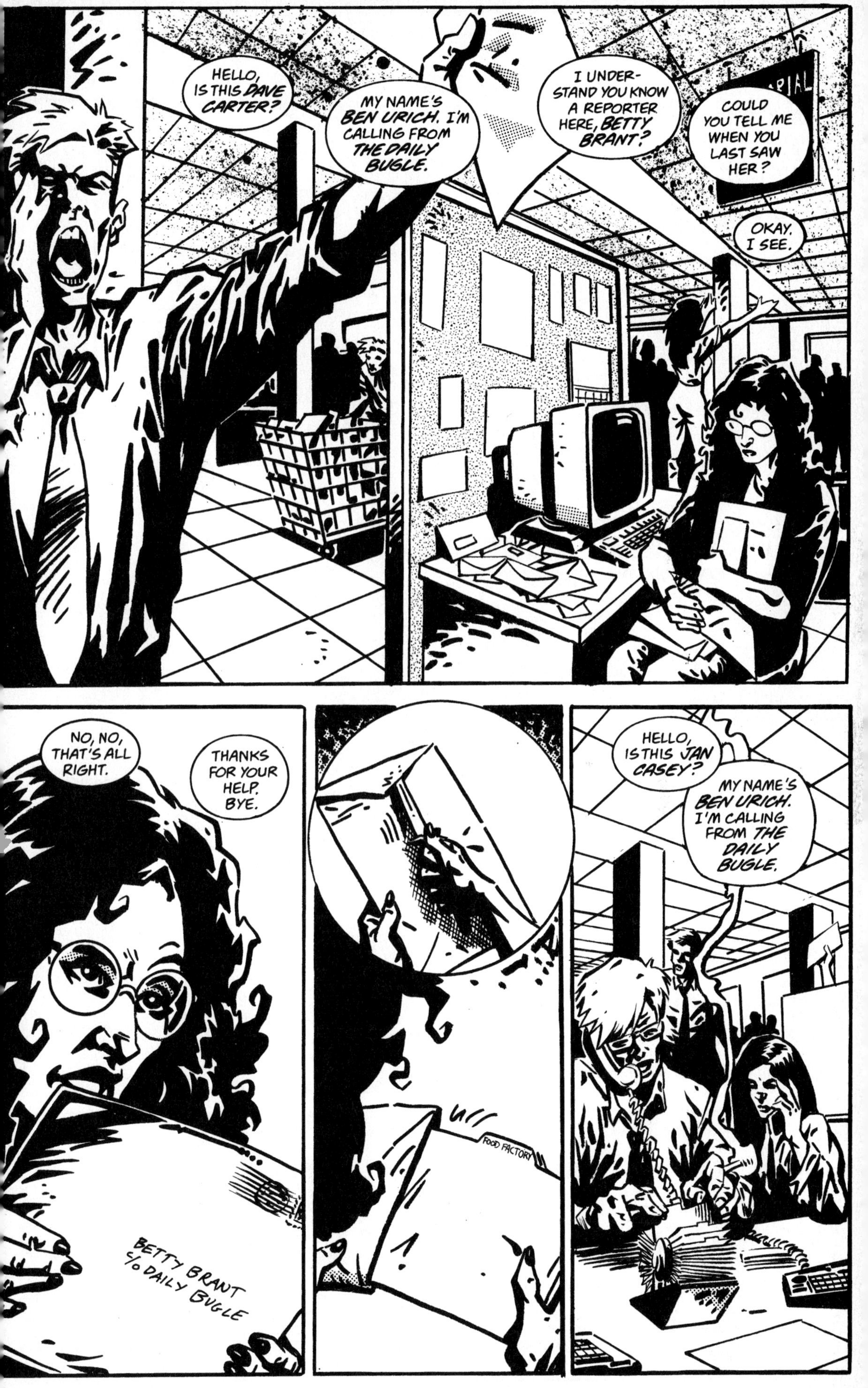
HELLO, IS THIS DAVE CARTER?
MY NAME'S BEN URICH. I'M CALLING FROM THE DAILY BUGLE.
I UNDER-STAND YOU KNOW A REPORTER HERE, BETTY BRANT?
COULD YOU TELL ME WHEN YOU LAST SAW HER?
OKAY. I SEE.
NO, NO, THAT'S ALL RIGHT.
THANKS FOR YOUR HELP. BYE.
BETTY BRANT c/o DAILY BUGLE
FOOD FACTORY
HELLO, IS THIS JAN CASEY?
MY NAME'S BEN URICH. I'M CALLING FROM THE DAILY BUGLE.

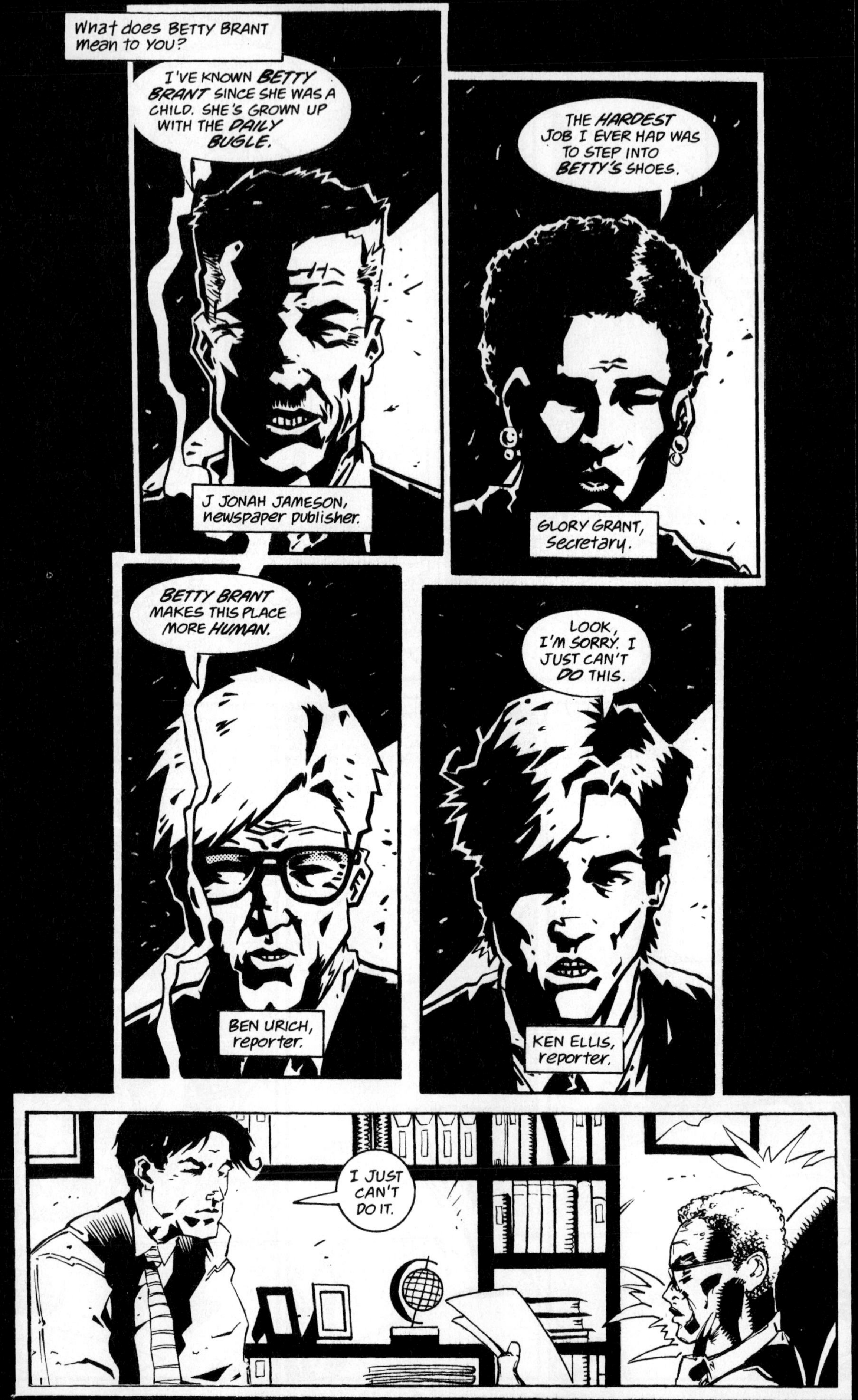
What does BETTY BRANT mean to you?
I'VE KNOWN BETTY BRANT SINCE SHE WAS A CHILD. SHE'S GROWN UP WITH THE DAILY BUGLE.
J JONAH JAMESON, newspaper publisher.
THE HARDEST JOB I EVER HAD WAS TO STEP INTO BETTY'S SHOES.
GLORY GRANT, Secretary.
BETTY BRANT MAKES THIS PLACE MORE HUMAN.
BEN URICH, reporter.
LOOK, I'M SORRY. I JUST CAN'T DO THIS.
KEN ELLIS, reporter.
I JUST CAN'T DO IT.

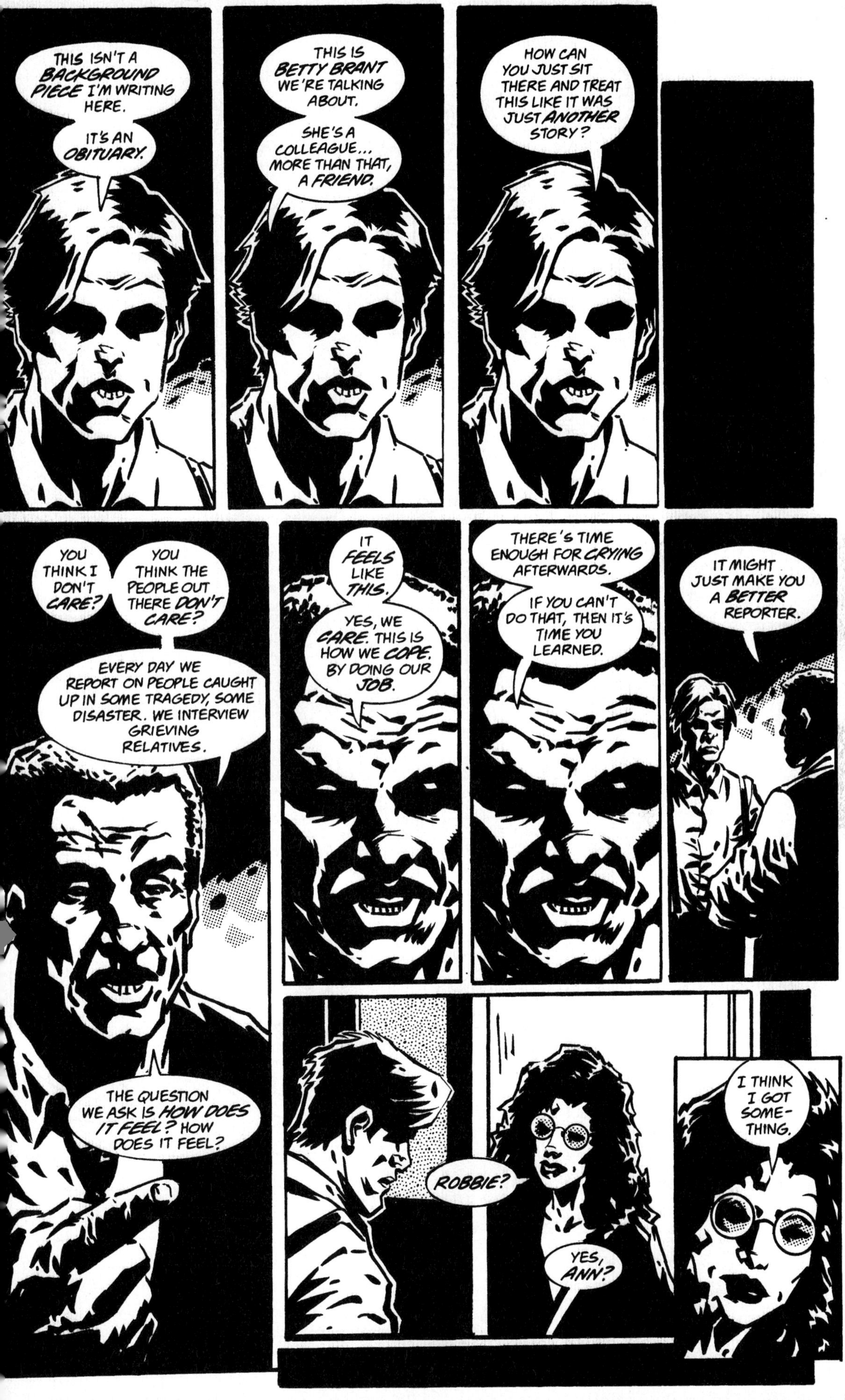

THIS ISN'T A BACKGROUND PIECE I'M WRITING HERE.
IT'S AN OBITUARY.
THIS IS BETTY BRANT WE'RE TALKING ABOUT.
SHE'S A COLLEAGUE... MORE THAN THAT, A FRIEND.
HOW CAN YOU JUST SIT THERE AND TREAT THIS LIKE IT WAS JUST ANOTHER STORY?
YOU THINK I DON'T CARE?
YOU THINK THE PEOPLE OUT THERE DON'T CARE?
EVERY DAY WE REPORT ON PEOPLE CAUGHT UP IN SOME TRAGEDY, SOME DISASTER. WE INTERVIEW GRIEVING RELATIVES.
THE QUESTION WE ASK IS HOW DOES IT FEEL? HOW DOES IT FEEL?
IT FEELS LIKE THIS.
YES, WE CARE. THIS IS HOW WE COPE. BY DOING OUR JOB.
THERE'S TIME ENOUGH FOR CRYING AFTERWARDS.
IF YOU CAN'T DO THAT, THEN IT'S TIME YOU LEARNED.
IT MIGHT JUST MAKE YOU A BETTER REPORTER.
ROBBIE?
YES, ANN?
I THINK I GOT SOME-THING.

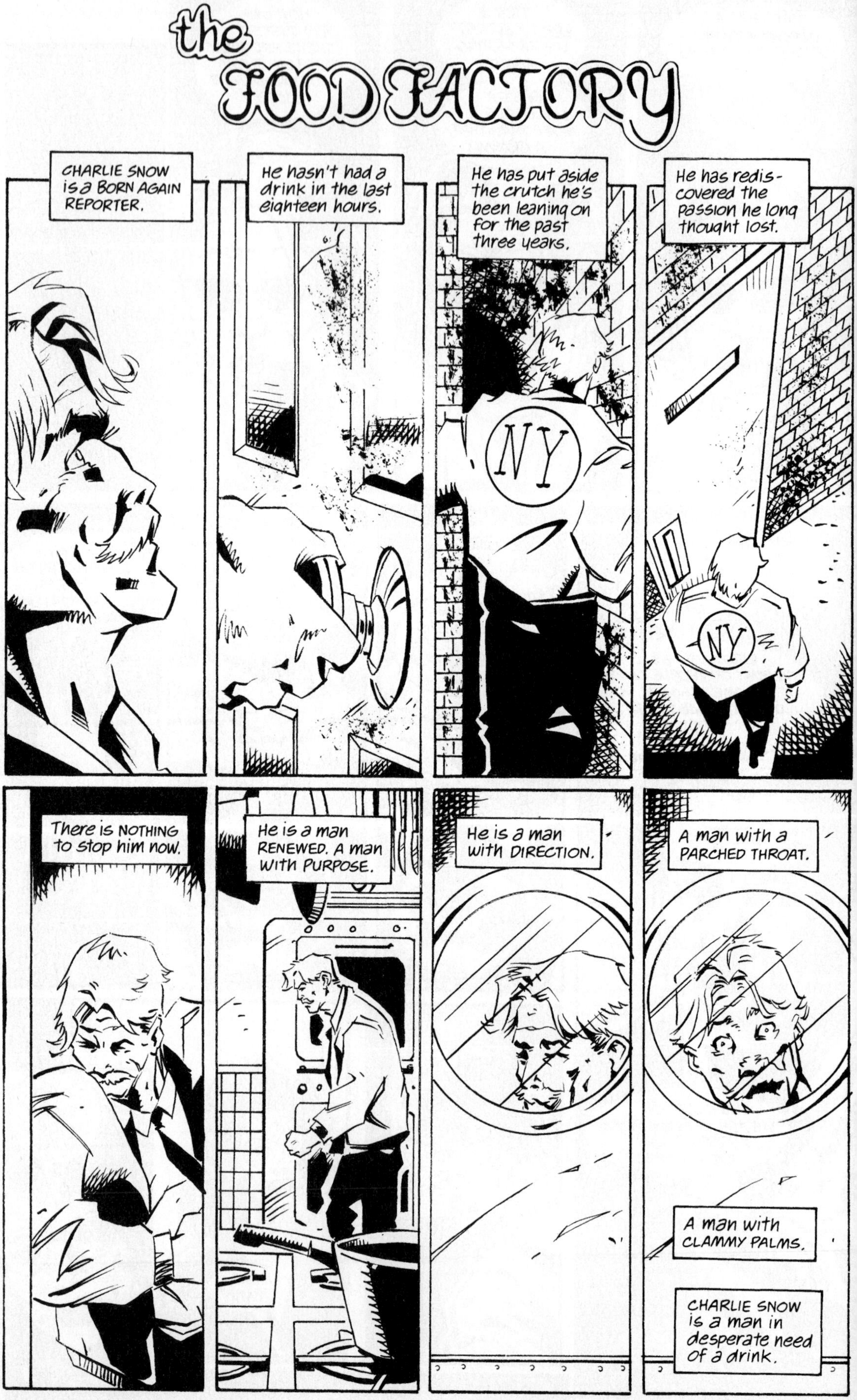
the FOOD FACTORY
CHARLIE SNOW is a BORN AGAIN REPORTER.
He hasn't had a drink in the last eighteen hours.
He has put aside the crutch he's been leaning on for the past three years.
He has rediscovered the passion he long thought lost.
NY
NY
There is NOTHING to stop him now.
He is a man RENEWED. A man with PURPOSE.
He is a man with DIRECTION.
A man with a PARCHED THROAT.
A man with CLAMMY PALMS.
CHARLIE SNOW is a man in desperate need of a drink.

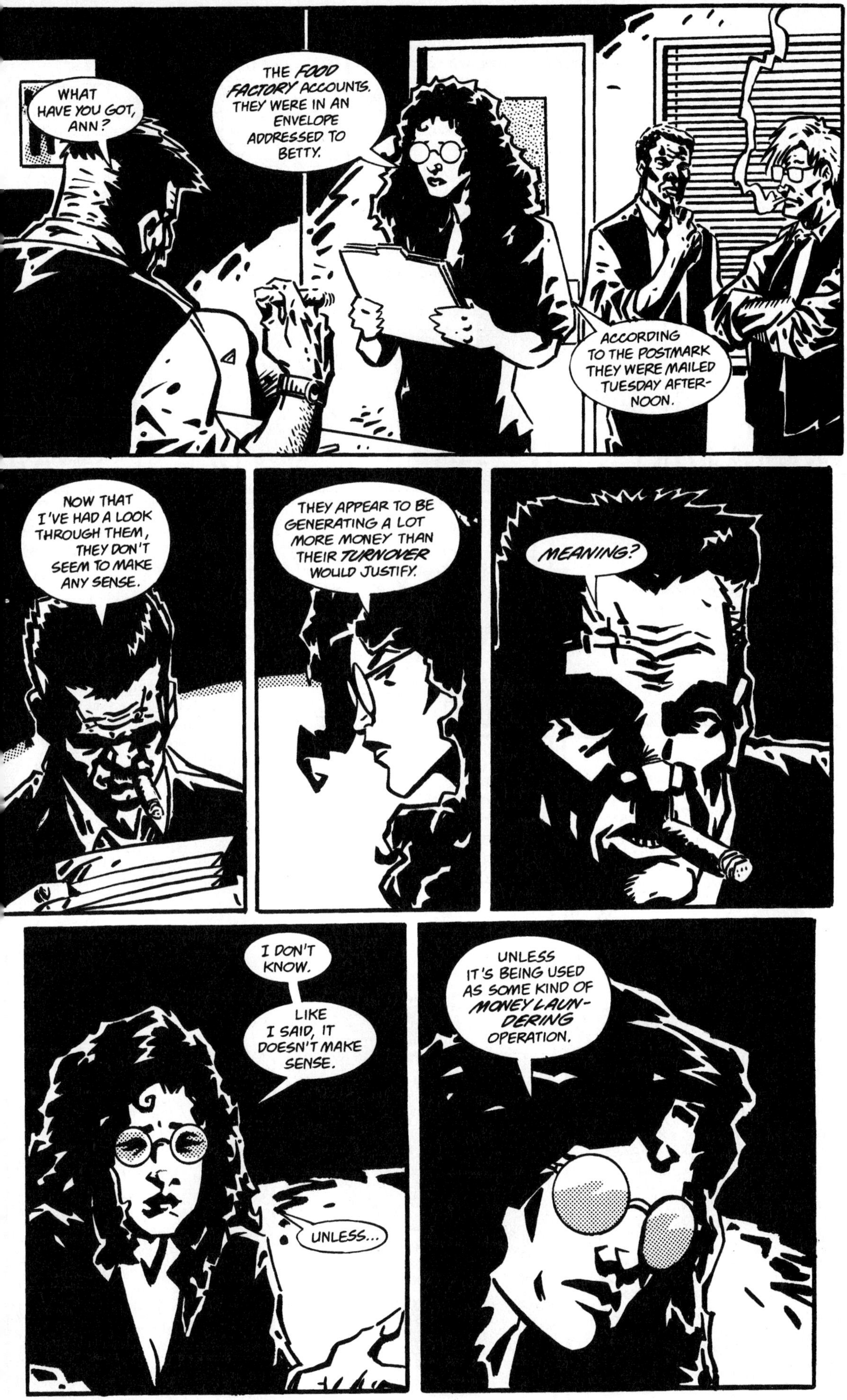
WHAT HAVE YOU GOT, ANN?
THE FOOD FACTORY ACCOUNTS. THEY WERE IN AN ENVELOPE ADDRESSED TO BETTY.
ACCORDING TO THE POSTMARK THEY WERE MAILED TUESDAY AFTER-NOON.
NOW THAT I'VE HAD A LOOK THROUGH THEM, THEY DON'T SEEM TO MAKE ANY SENSE.
THEY APPEAR TO BE GENERATING A LOT MORE MONEY THAN THEIR TURNOVER WOULD JUSTIFY.
MEANING?
I DON'T KNOW.
LIKE I SAID, IT DOESN'T MAKE SENSE.
UNLESS...
UNLESS IT'S BEING USED AS SOME KIND OF MONEY LAUN-DERING OPERATION.

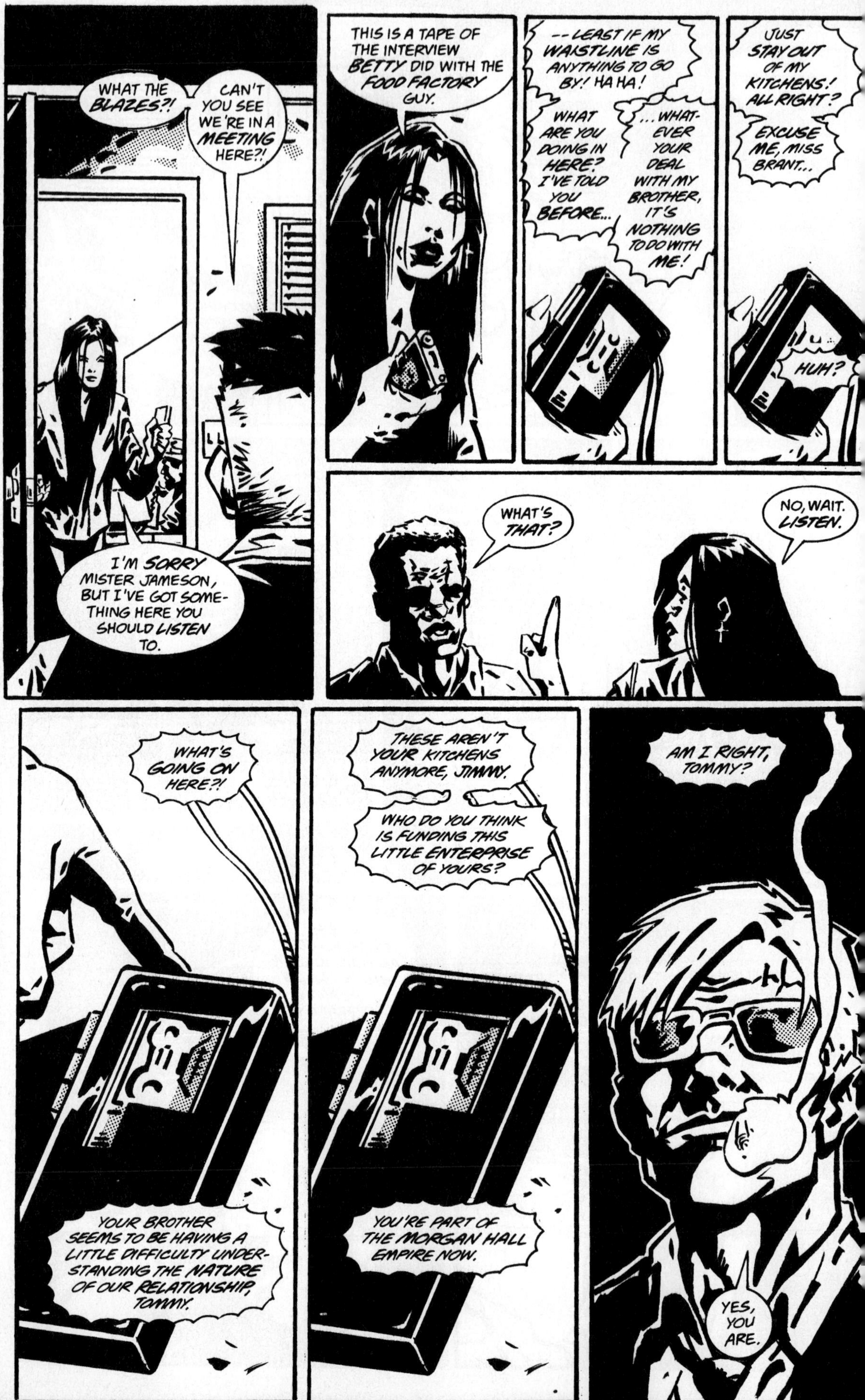
WHAT THE BLAZES?!
CAN'T YOU SEE WE'RE IN A MEETING HERE?!
I'M SORRY MISTER JAMESON, BUT I'VE GOT SOMETHING HERE YOU SHOULD LISTEN TO.
THIS IS A TAPE OF THE INTERVIEW BETTY DID WITH THE FOOD FACTORY GUY.
--LEAST IF MY WAISTLINE IS ANYTHING TO GO BY! HA HA!
WHAT ARE YOU DOING IN HERE? I'VE TOLD YOU BEFORE...
...WHATEVER YOUR DEAL WITH MY BROTHER, IT'S NOTHING TO DO WITH ME!
JUST STAY OUT OF MY KITCHENS! ALL RIGHT?
EXCUSE ME, MISS BRANT...
HUH?
WHAT'S THAT?
NO, WAIT. LISTEN.
WHAT'S GOING ON HERE?!
YOUR BROTHER SEEMS TO BE HAVING A LITTLE DIFFICULTY UNDERSTANDING THE NATURE OF OUR RELATIONSHIP, TOMMY.
THESE AREN'T YOUR KITCHENS ANYMORE, JIMMY.
WHO DO YOU THINK IS FUNDING THIS LITTLE ENTERPRISE OF YOURS?
YOU'RE PART OF THE MORGAN HALL EMPIRE NOW.
AM I RIGHT, TOMMY?
YES, YOU ARE.

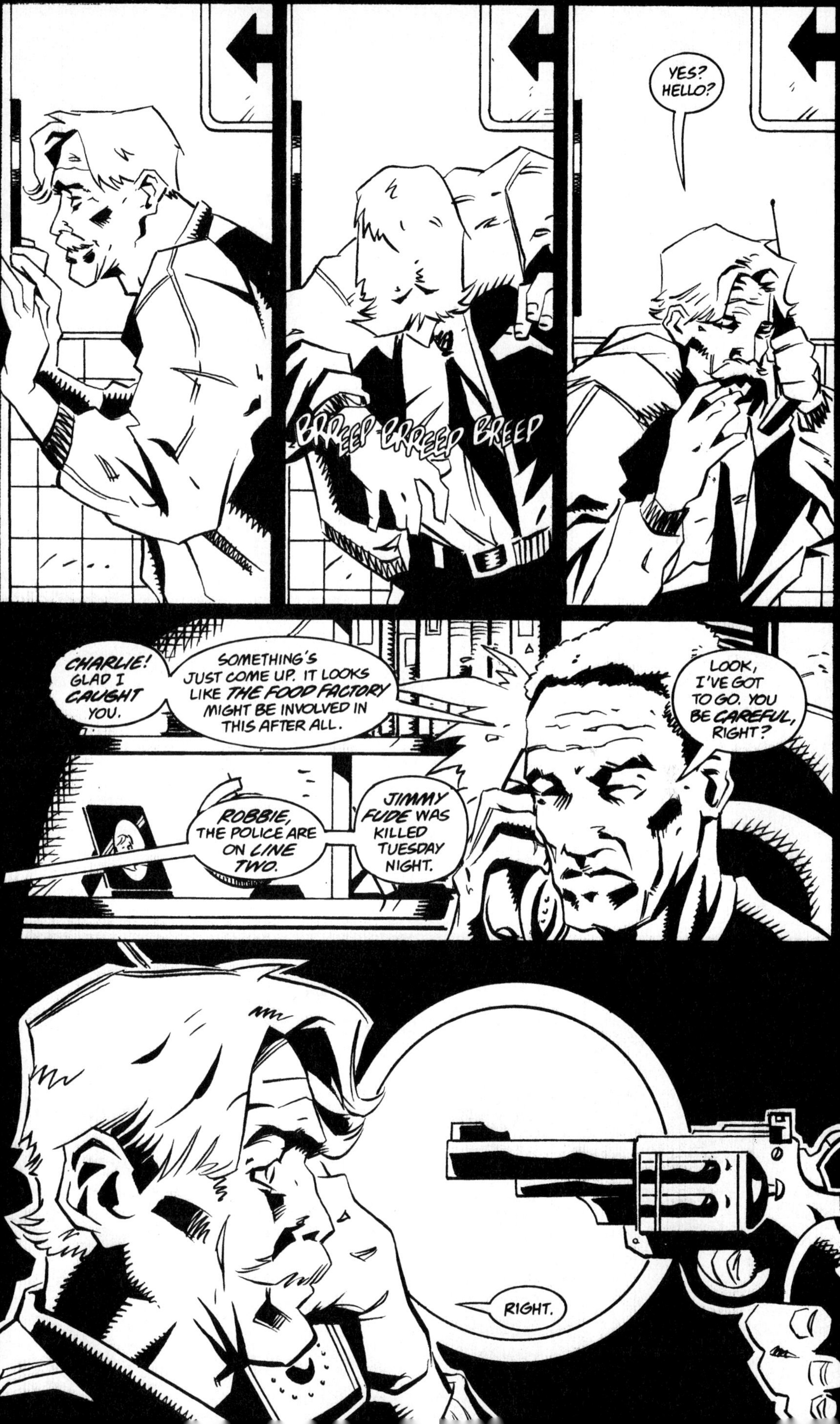

BRREEP BRREEP BREEP
YES? HELLO?
CHARLIE! GLAD I CAUGHT YOU.
SOMETHING'S JUST COME UP. IT LOOKS LIKE THE FOOD FACTORY MIGHT BE INVOLVED IN THIS AFTER ALL.
LOOK, I'VE GOT TO GO. YOU BE CAREFUL, RIGHT?
ROBBIE, THE POLICE ARE ON LINE TWO.
JIMMY FUDE WAS KILLED TUESDAY NIGHT.
RIGHT.

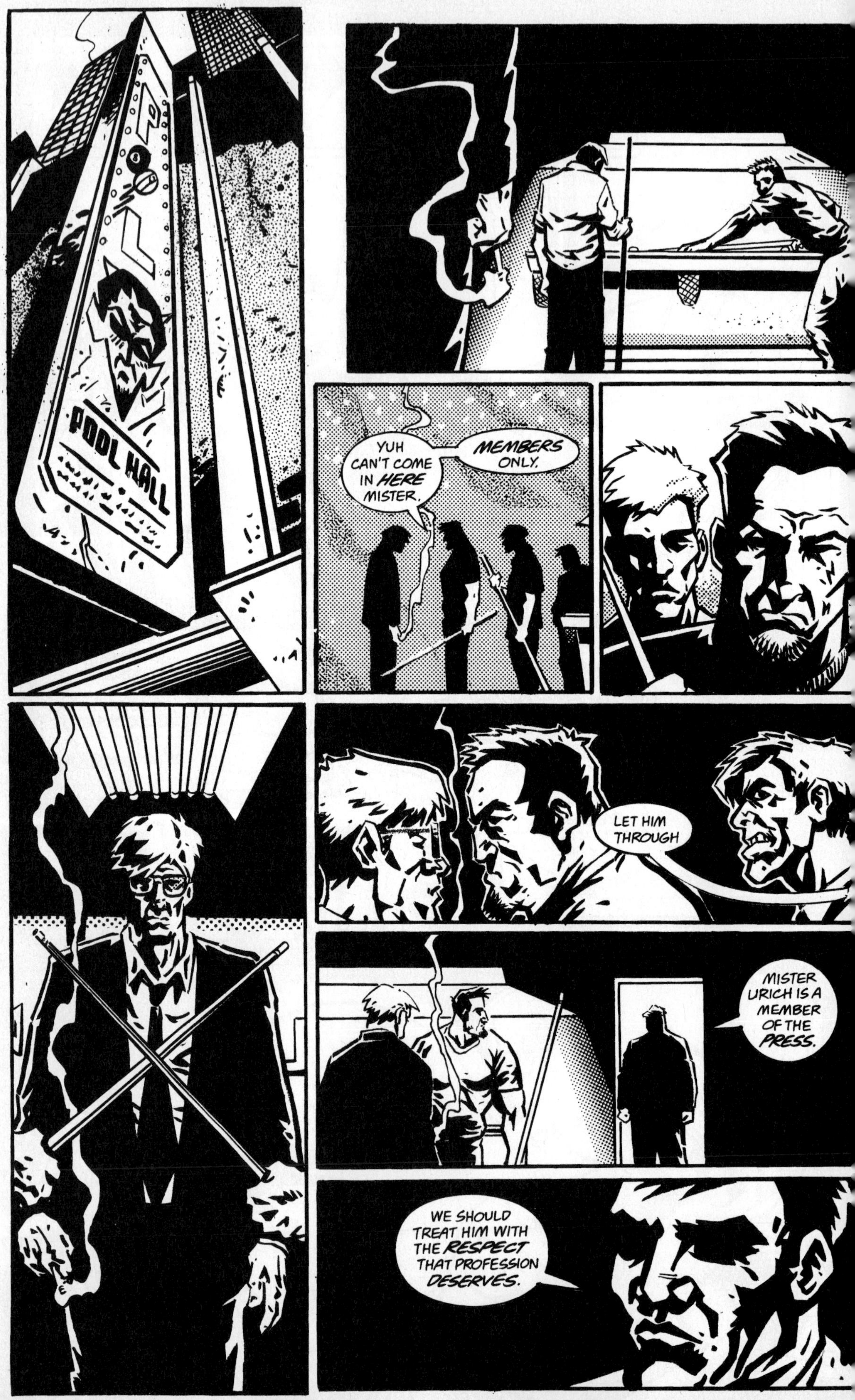
POOL HALL
YUH CAN'T COME IN *HERE* MISTER.
MEMBERS ONLY.
LET HIM THROUGH
MISTER URICH IS A MEMBER OF THE *PRESS*.
WE SHOULD TREAT HIM WITH THE *RESPECT* THAT PROFESSION *DESERVES*.

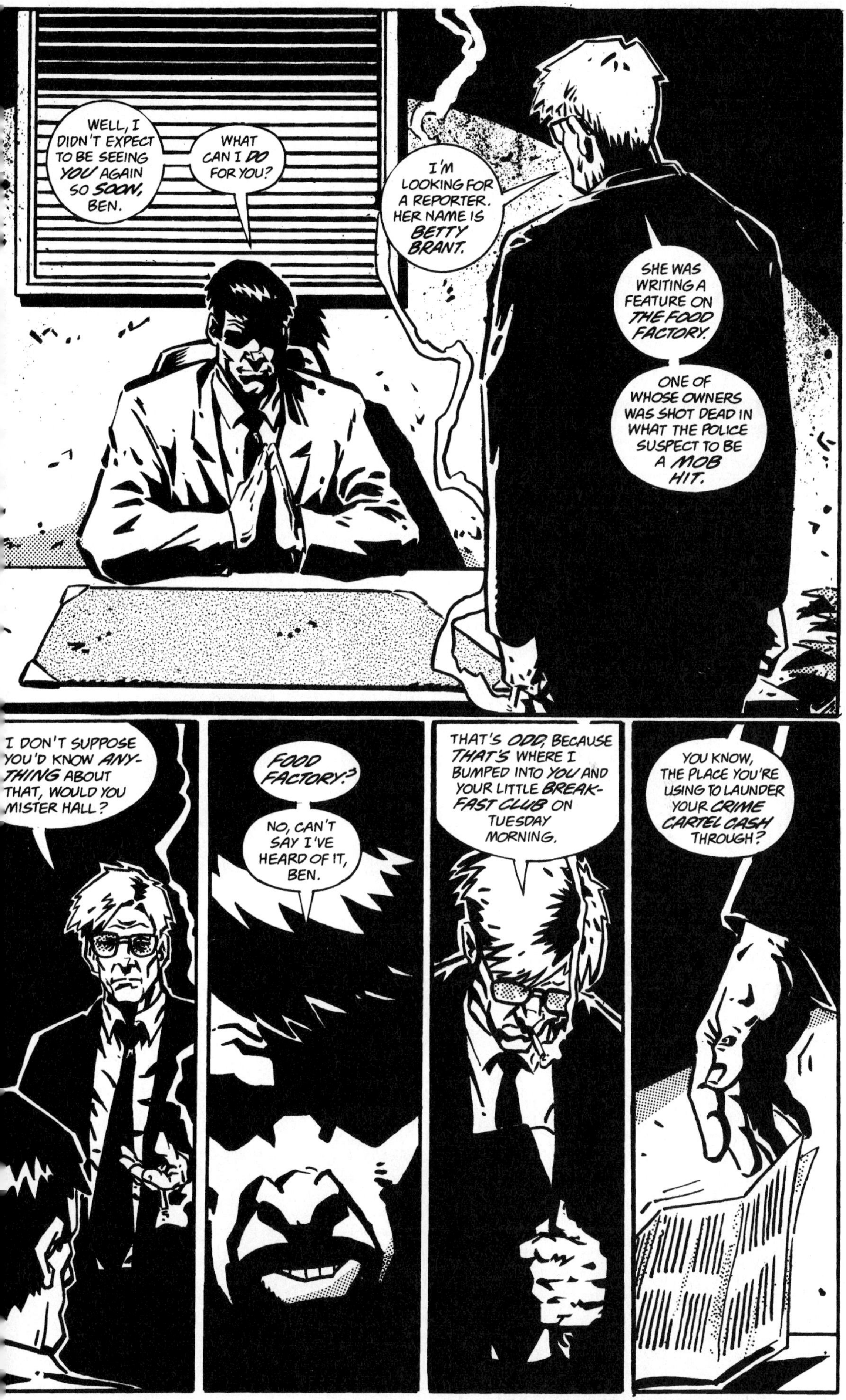
WELL, I DIDN'T EXPECT TO BE SEEING YOU AGAIN SO SOON, BEN.
WHAT CAN I DO FOR YOU?
I'M LOOKING FOR A REPORTER. HER NAME IS BETTY BRANT.
SHE WAS WRITING A FEATURE ON THE FOOD FACTORY.
ONE OF WHOSE OWNERS WAS SHOT DEAD IN WHAT THE POLICE SUSPECT TO BE A MOB HIT.
I DON'T SUPPOSE YOU'D KNOW ANYTHING ABOUT THAT, WOULD YOU MISTER HALL?
FOOD FACTORY?
NO, CAN'T SAY I'VE HEARD OF IT, BEN.
THAT'S ODD, BECAUSE THAT'S WHERE I BUMPED INTO YOU AND YOUR LITTLE BREAKFAST CLUB ON TUESDAY MORNING.
YOU KNOW, THE PLACE YOU'RE USING TO LAUNDER YOUR CRIME CARTEL CASH THROUGH?

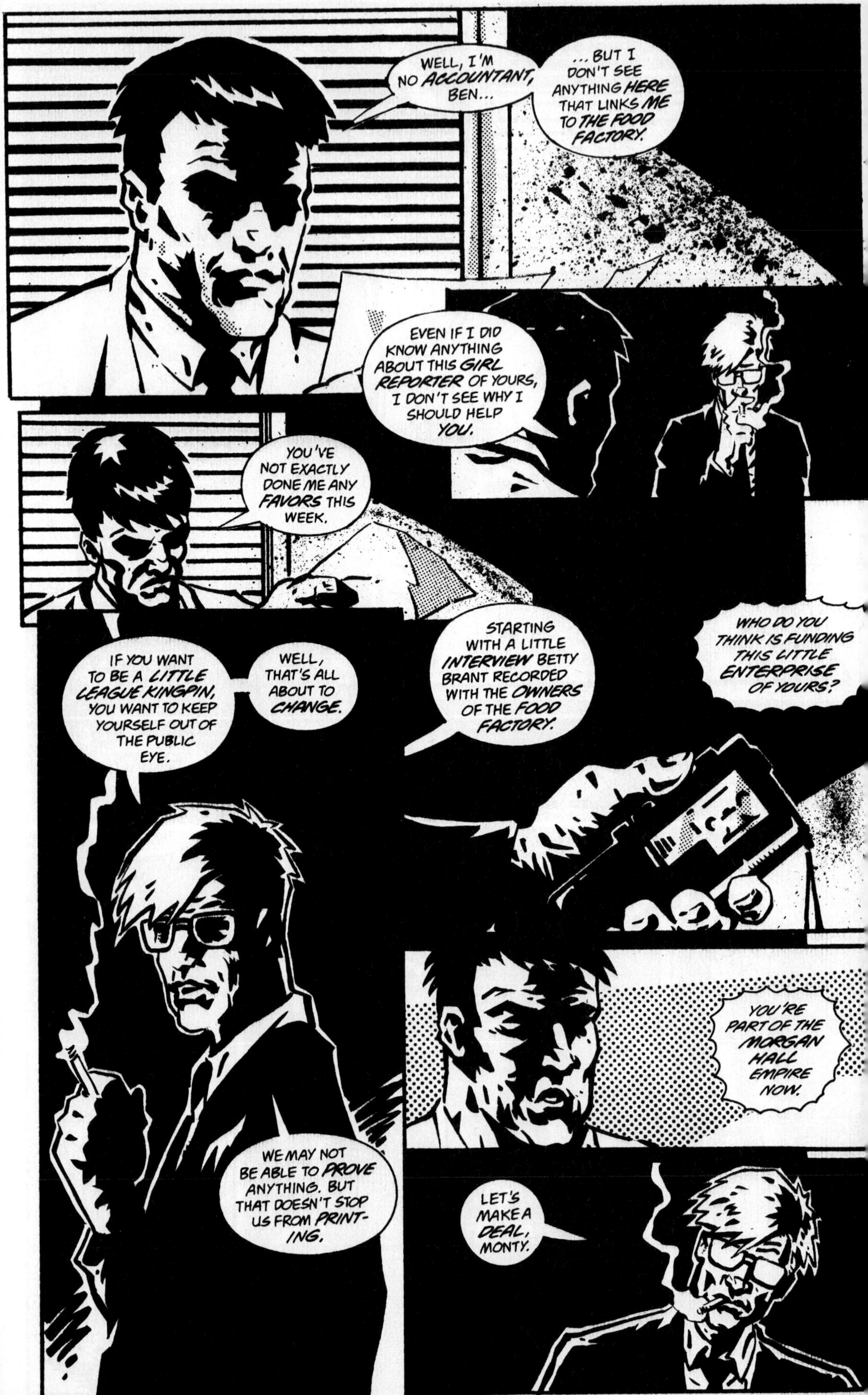
WELL, I'M NO ACCOUNTANT, BEN...
...BUT I DON'T SEE ANYTHING HERE THAT LINKS ME TO THE FOOD FACTORY.
EVEN IF I DID KNOW ANYTHING ABOUT THIS GIRL REPORTER OF YOURS, I DON'T SEE WHY I SHOULD HELP YOU.
YOU'VE NOT EXACTLY DONE ME ANY FAVORS THIS WEEK.
IF YOU WANT TO BE A LITTLE LEAGUE KINGPIN, YOU WANT TO KEEP YOURSELF OUT OF THE PUBLIC EYE.
WELL, THAT'S ALL ABOUT TO CHANGE.
WE MAY NOT BE ABLE TO PROVE ANYTHING. BUT THAT DOESN'T STOP US FROM PRINT-ING.
STARTING WITH A LITTLE INTERVIEW BETTY BRANT RECORDED WITH THE OWNERS OF THE FOOD FACTORY.
WHO DO YOU THINK IS FUNDING THIS LITTLE ENTERPRISE OF YOURS?
YOU'RE PART OF THE MORGAN HALL EMPIRE NOW.
LET'S MAKE A DEAL, MONTY.

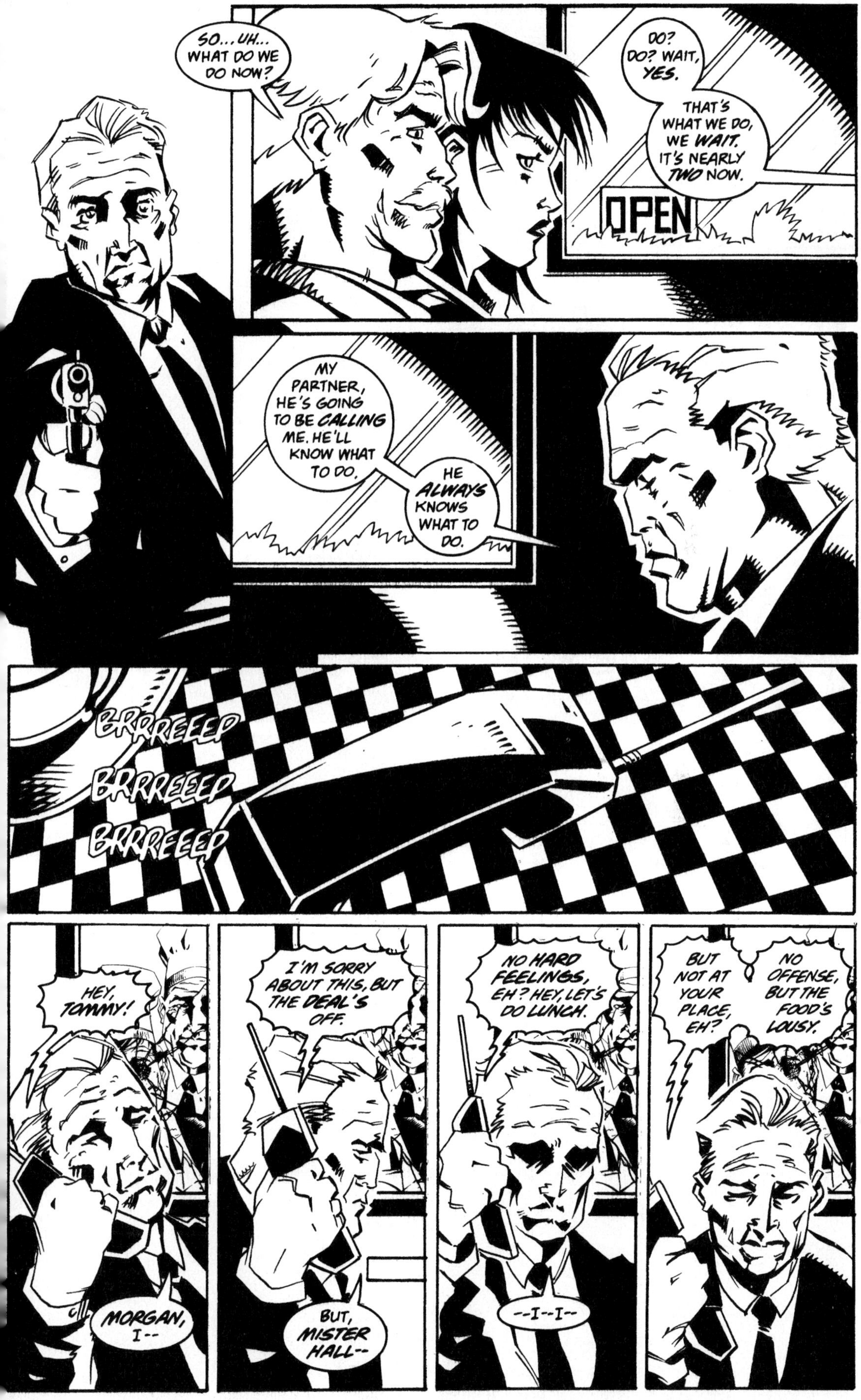

SO... UH... WHAT DO WE DO NOW?
DO? DO? WAIT, YES.
THAT'S WHAT WE DO, WE WAIT. IT'S NEARLY TWO NOW.
OPEN
MY PARTNER, HE'S GOING TO BE CALLING ME. HE'LL KNOW WHAT TO DO.
HE ALWAYS KNOWS WHAT TO DO.
BRRREEEP
BRRREEEP
BRRREEEP
HEY, TOMMY!
MORGAN, I--
I'M SORRY ABOUT THIS, BUT THE DEAL'S OFF.
BUT, MISTER HALL--
NO HARD FEELINGS, EH? HEY, LET'S DO LUNCH.
--I--I--
BUT NOT AT YOUR PLACE, EH?
NO OFFENSE, BUT THE FOOD'S LOUSY.

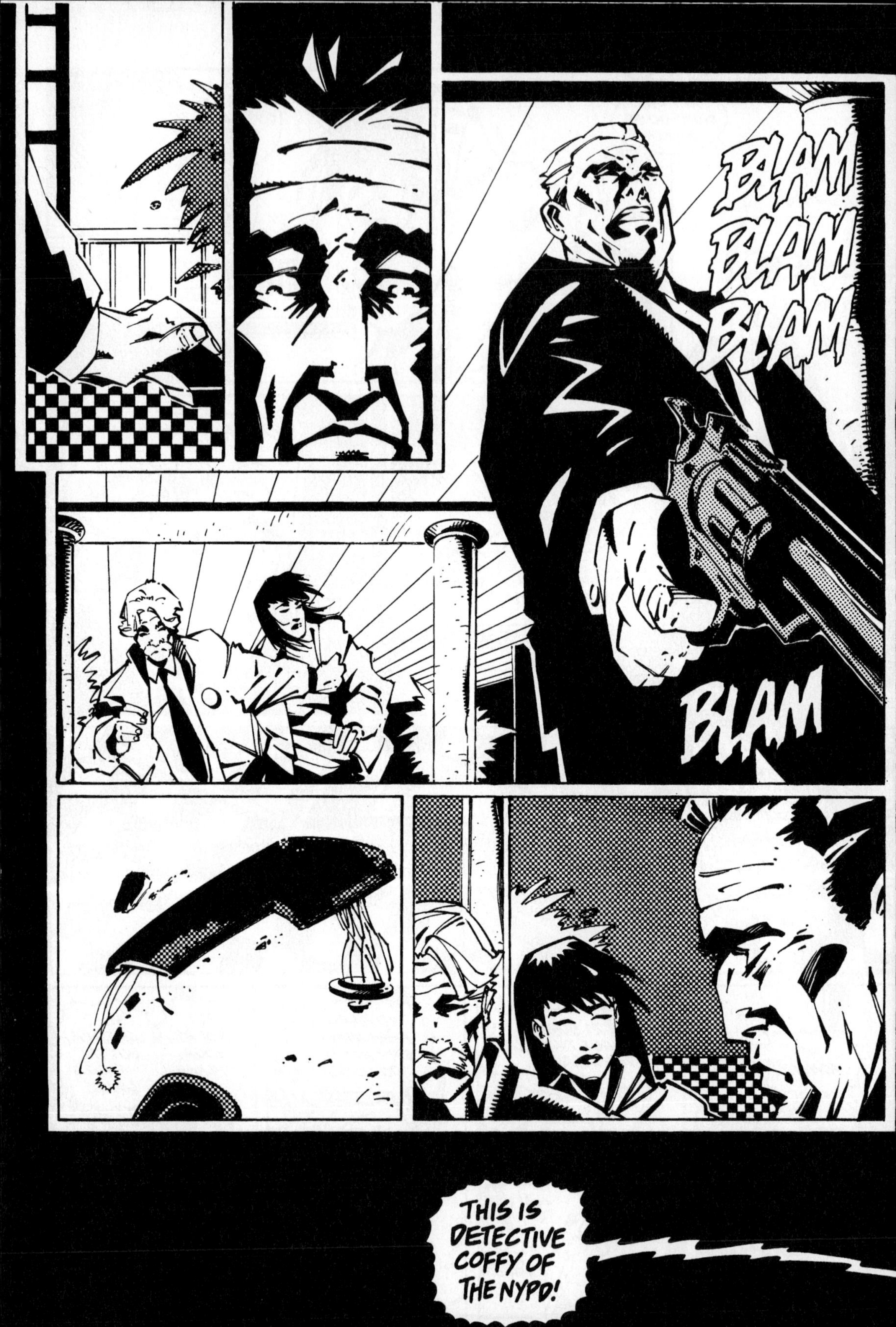
BLAM
BLAM
BLAM
BLAM
THIS IS DETECTIVE COFFY OF THE NYPD!

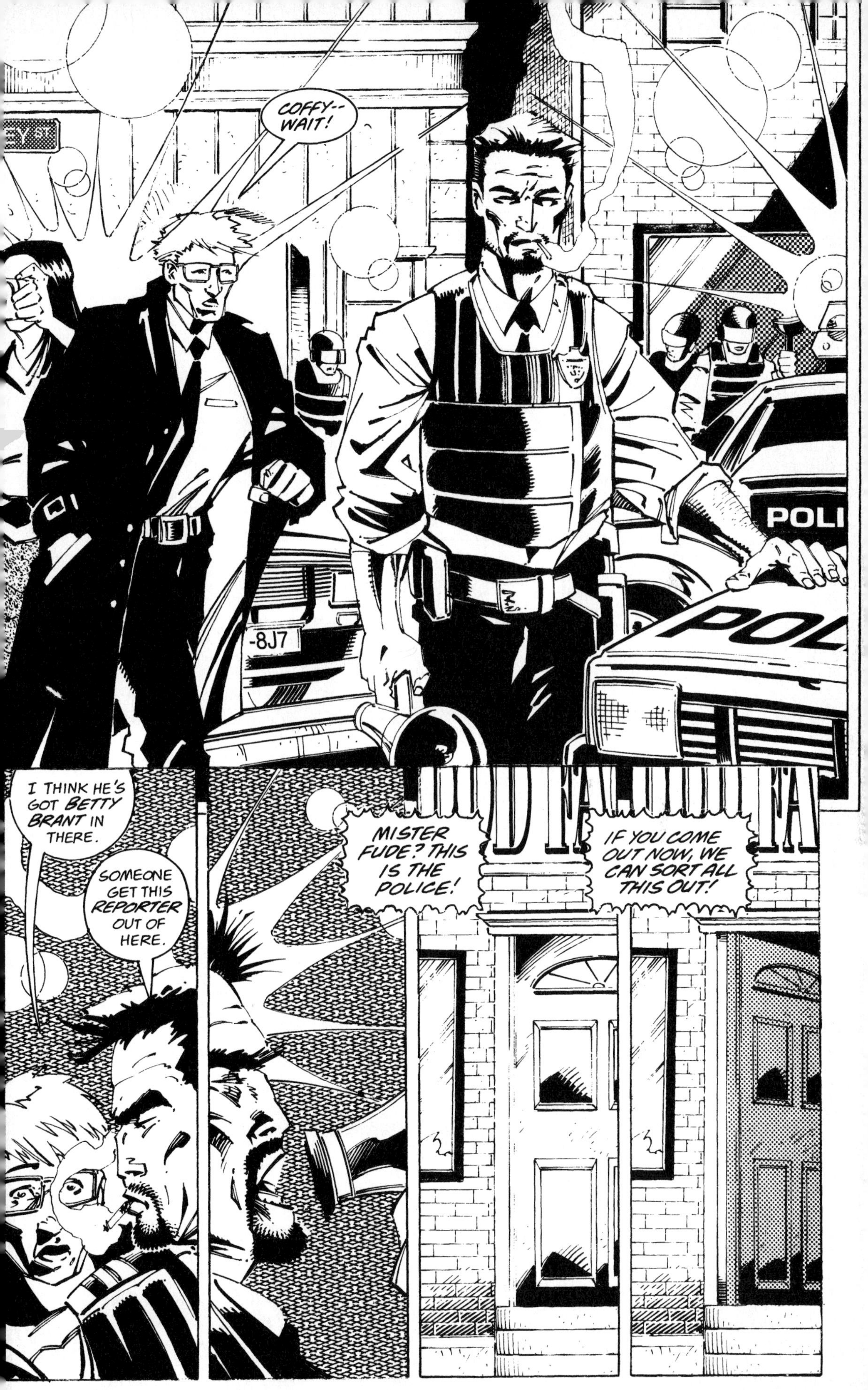
EY ST
COFFY--WAIT!
POLI
-8J7
POL
I THINK HE'S GOT BETTY BRANT IN THERE.
SOMEONE GET THIS REPORTER OUT OF HERE.
MISTER FUDE? THIS IS THE POLICE!
IF YOU COME OUT NOW, WE CAN SORT ALL THIS OUT!

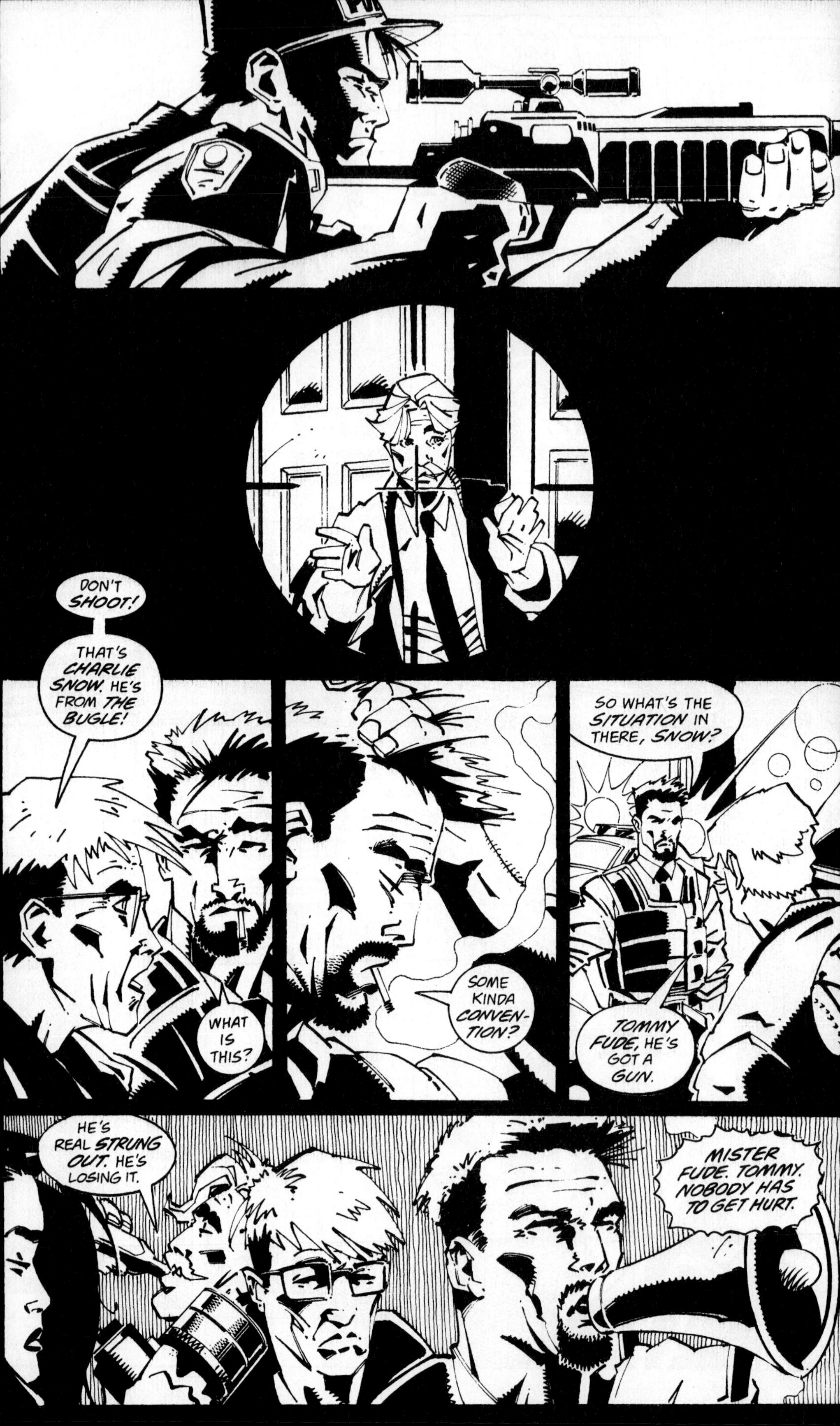
DON'T SHOOT!
THAT'S CHARLIE SNOW. HE'S FROM THE BUGLE!
WHAT IS THIS?
SOME KINDA CONVENTION?
SO WHAT'S THE SITUATION IN THERE, SNOW?
TOMMY FUDE, HE'S GOT A GUN.
HE'S REAL STRUNG OUT. HE'S LOSING IT.
MISTER FUDE. TOMMY. NOBODY HAS TO GET HURT.

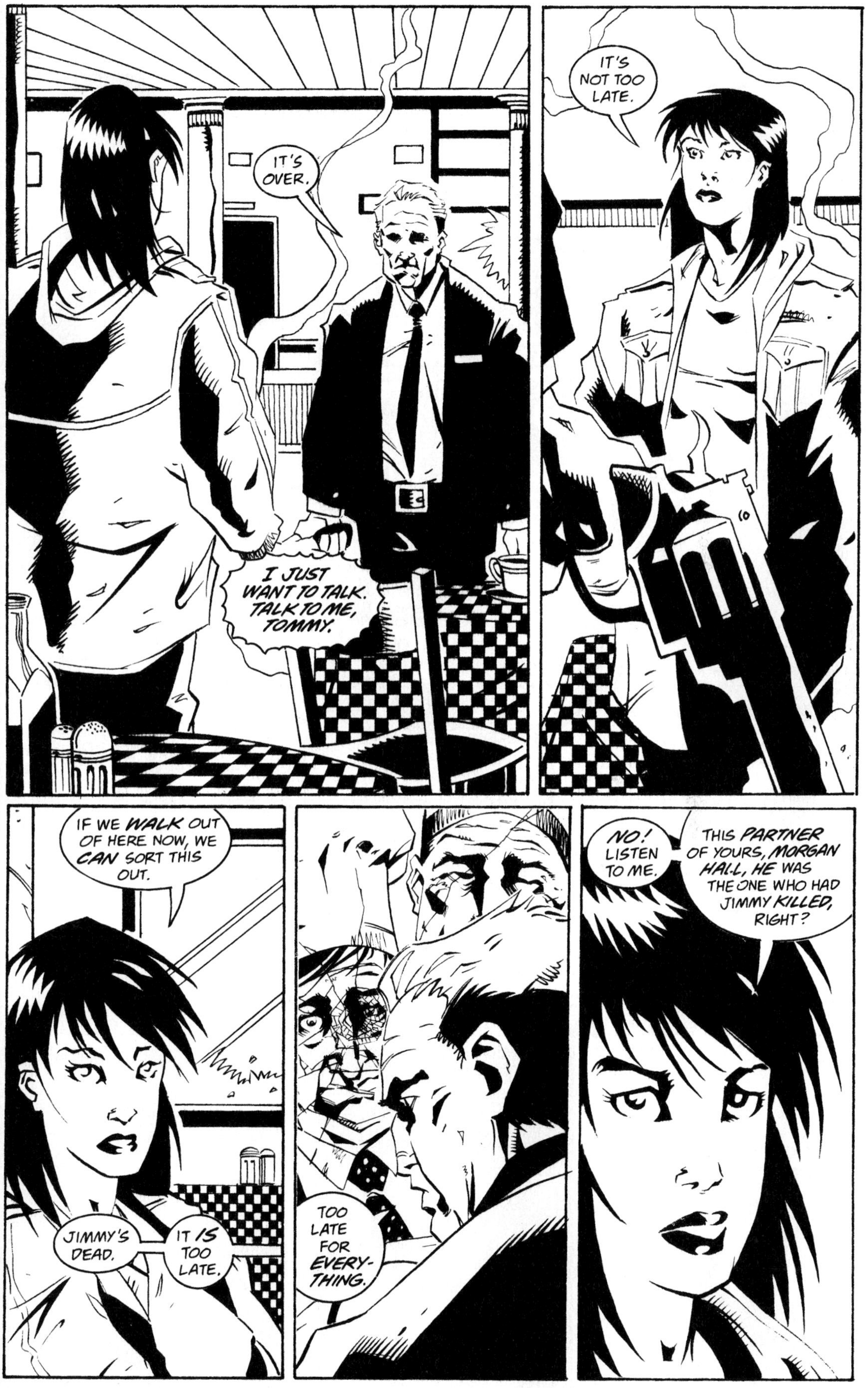

IT'S OVER.
I JUST WANT TO TALK. TALK TO ME, TOMMY.
IT'S NOT TOO LATE.
IF WE WALK OUT OF HERE NOW, WE CAN SORT THIS OUT.
JIMMY'S DEAD.
IT IS TOO LATE.
TOO LATE FOR EVERYTHING.
NO! LISTEN TO ME.
THIS PARTNER OF YOURS, MORGAN HALL, HE WAS THE ONE WHO HAD JIMMY KILLED, RIGHT?

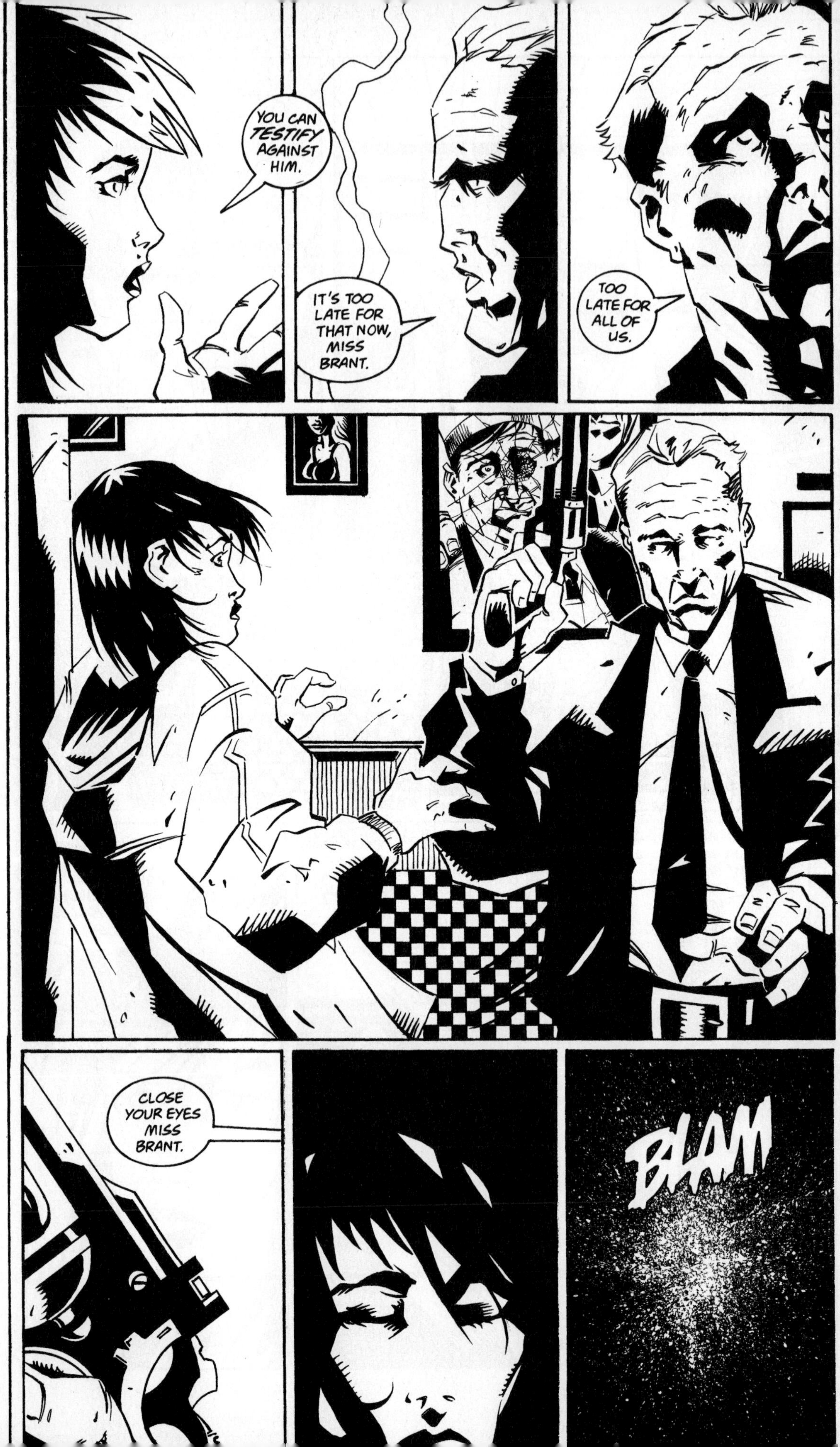
YOU CAN TESTIFY AGAINST HIM.
IT'S TOO LATE FOR THAT NOW, MISS BRANT.
TOO LATE FOR ALL OF US.
CLOSE YOUR EYES MISS BRANT.
BLAM

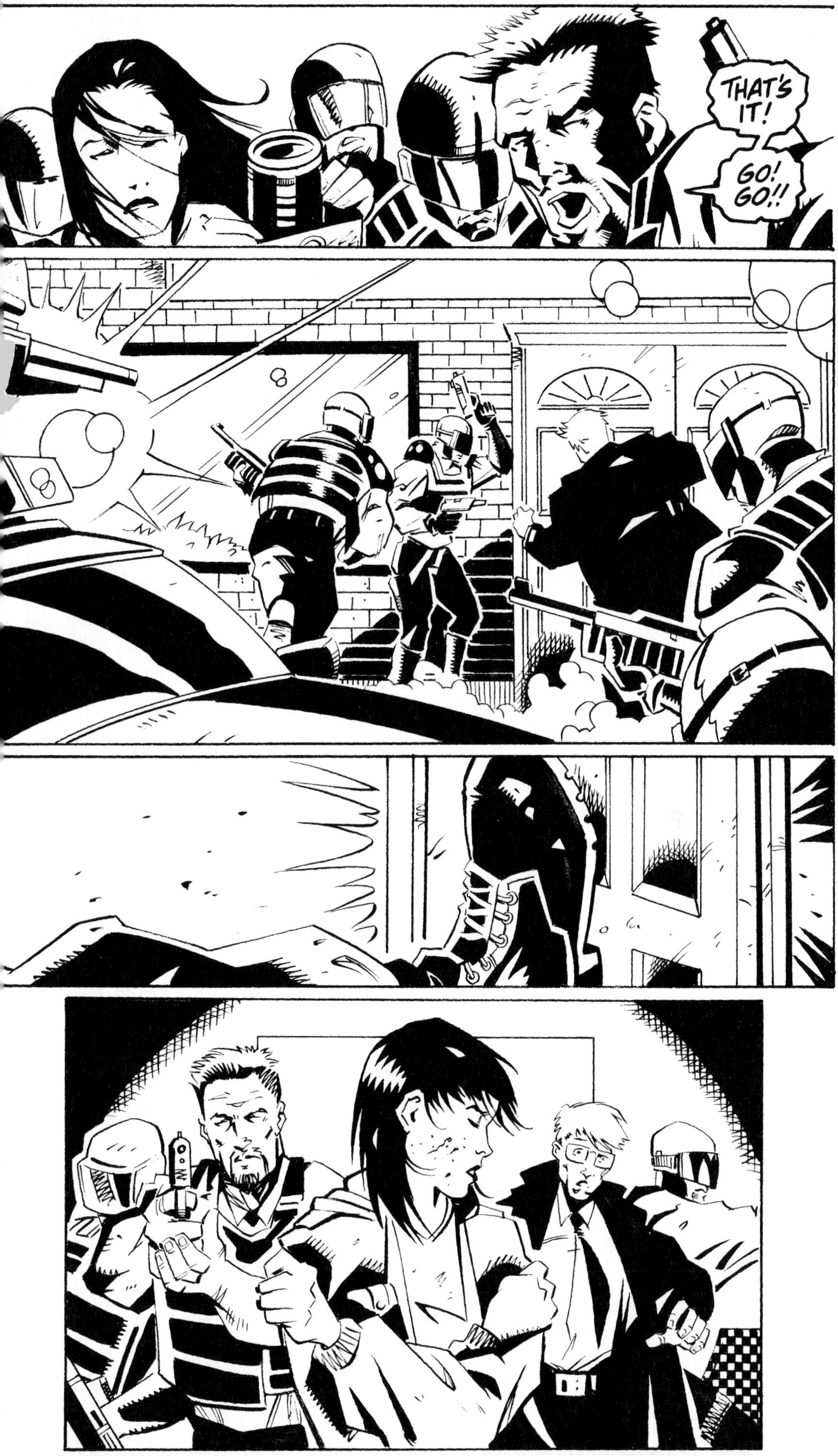
THAT'S IT!
GO! GO!!

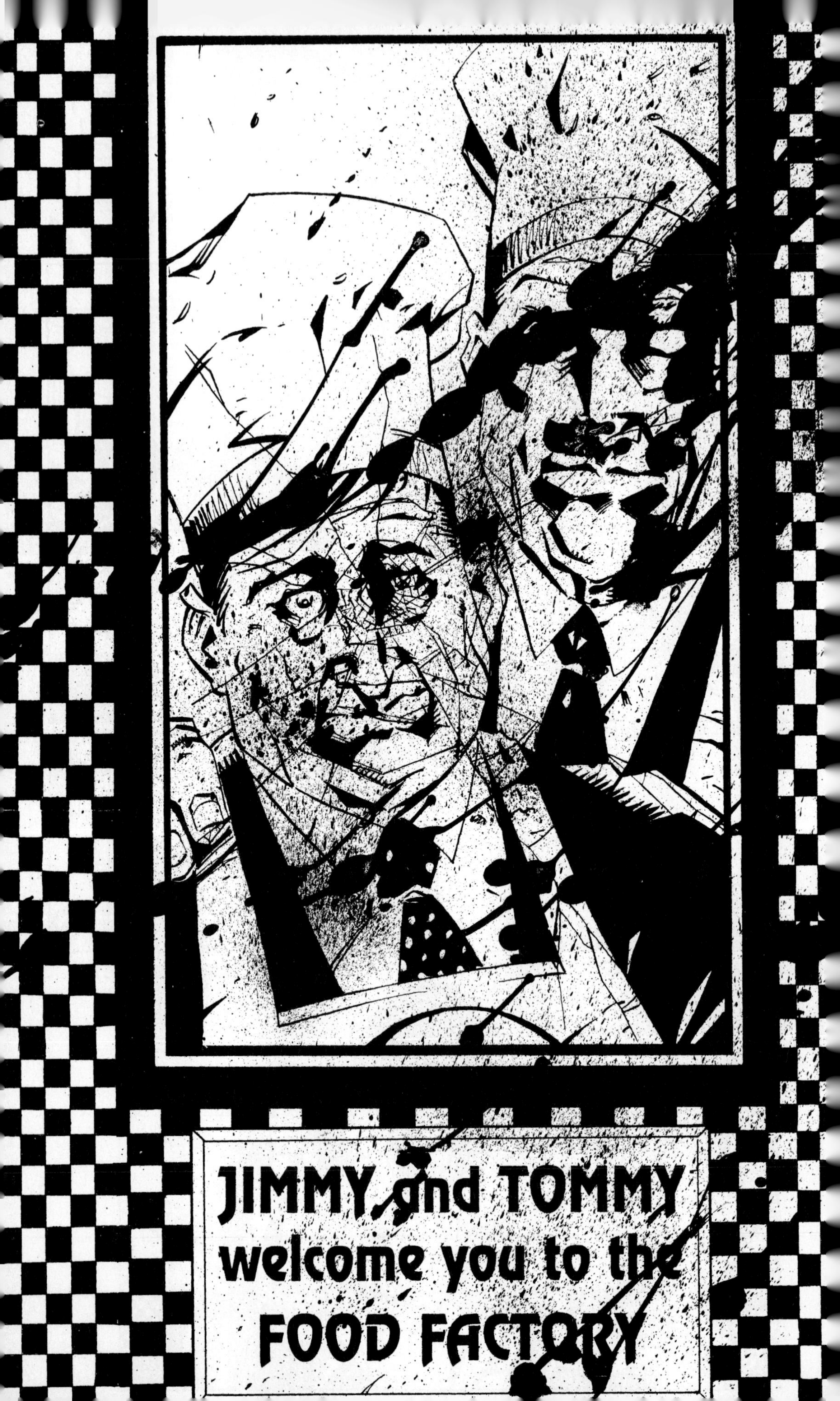
JIMMY and TOMMY
welcome you to the
FOOD FACTORY

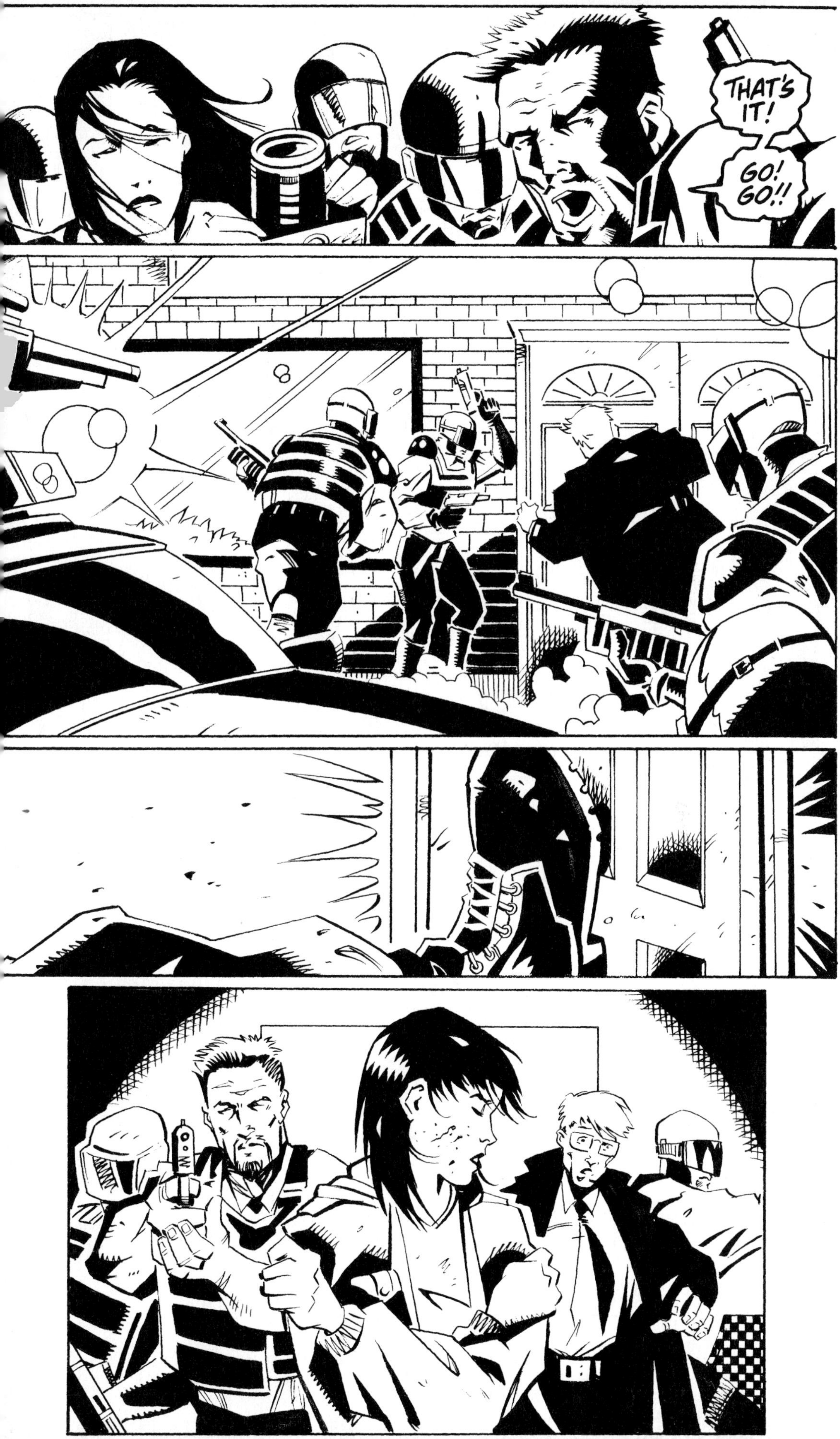
THAT'S IT!
GO! GO!!

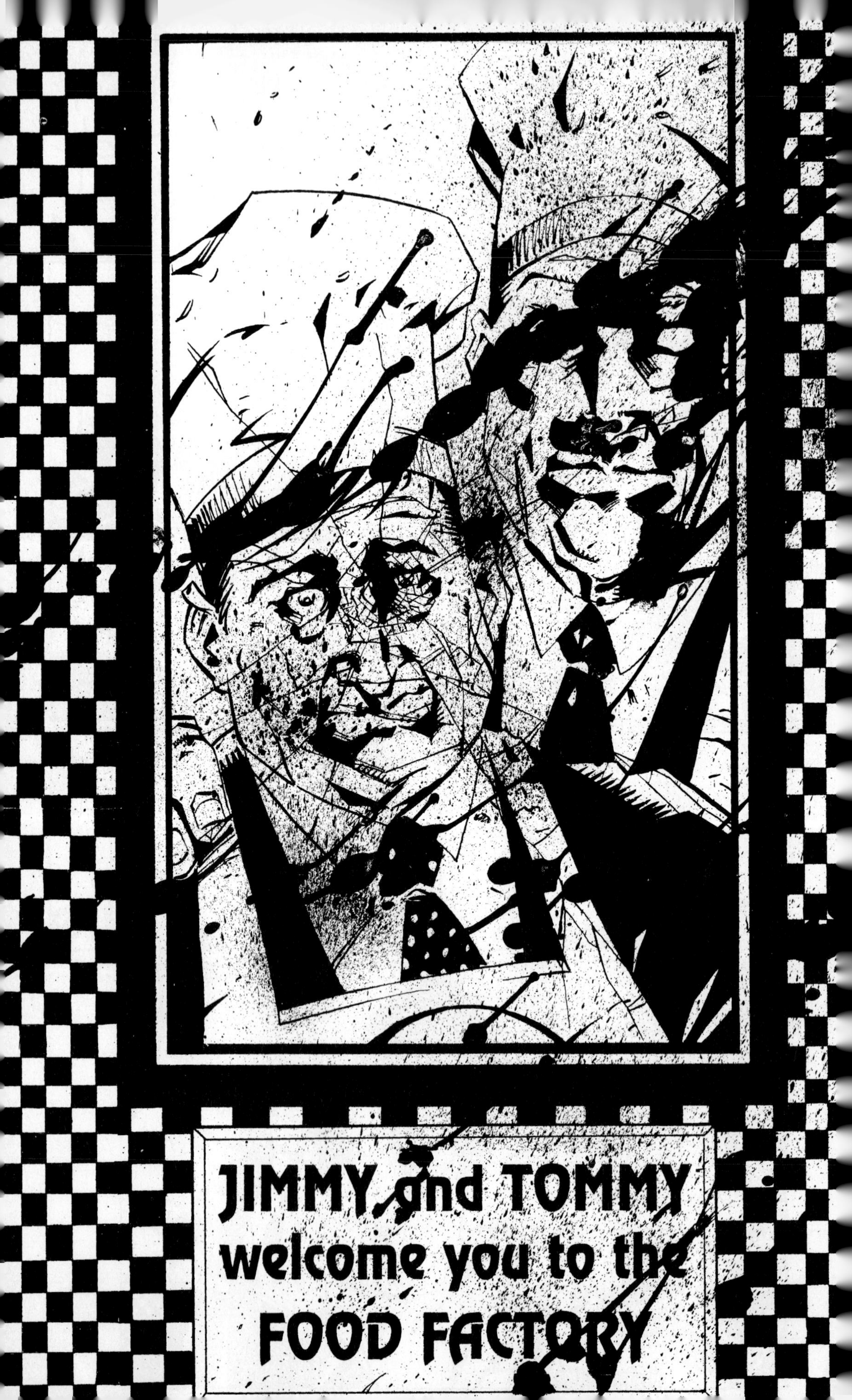
JIMMY and TOMMY
welcome you to the
FOOD FACTORY

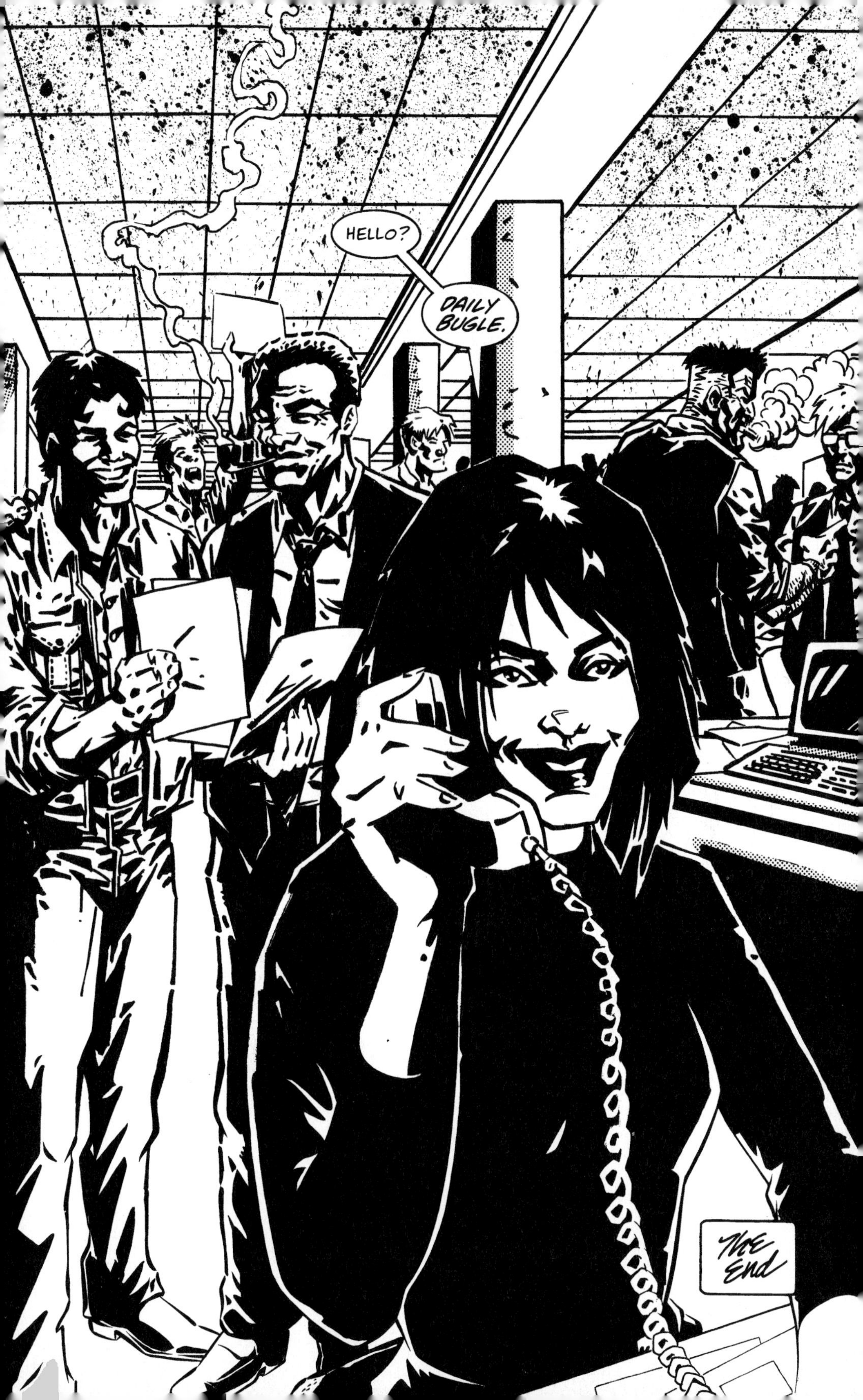
HELLO?
DAILY BUGLE.
THE END

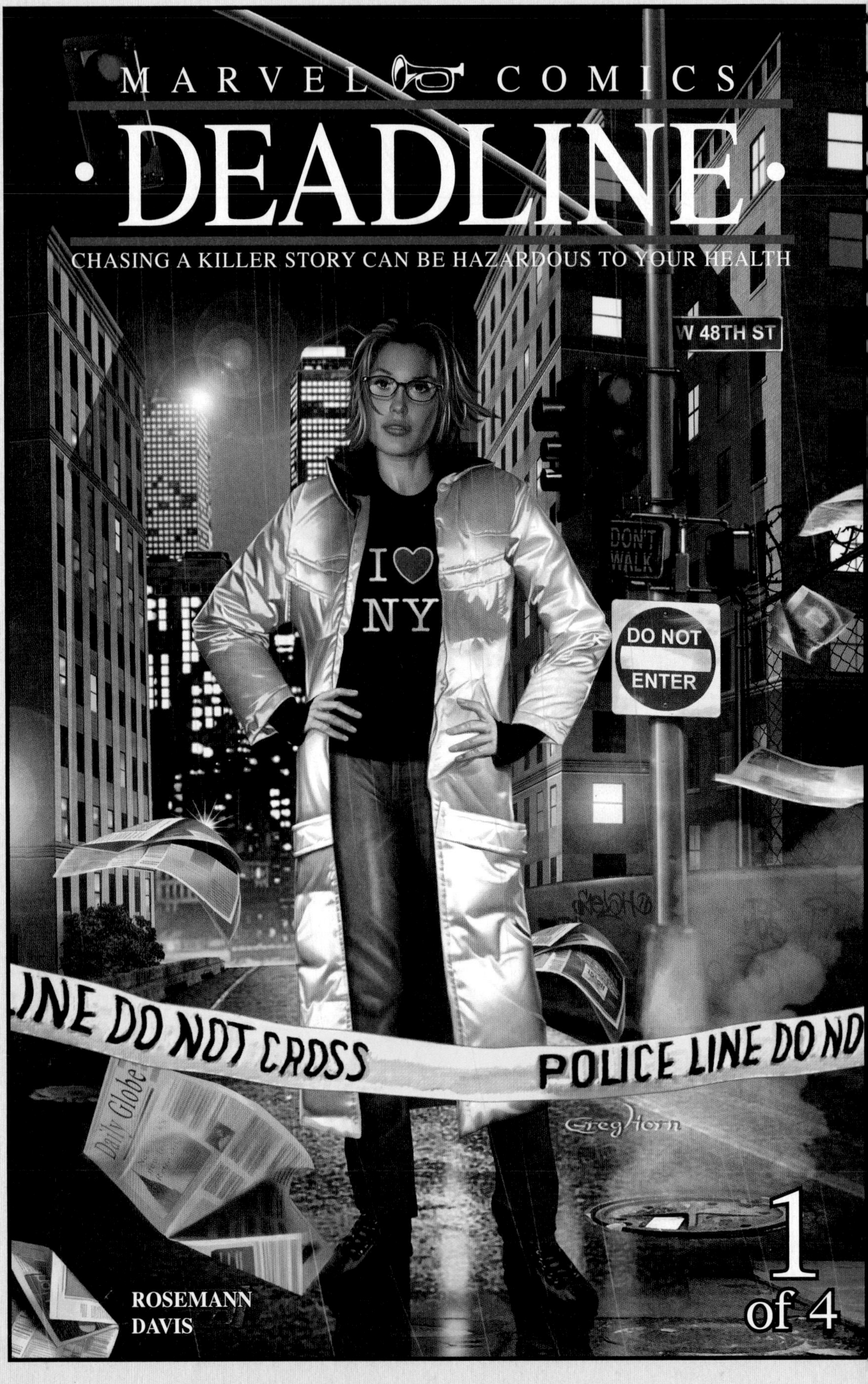
MARVEL COMICS
· DEADLINE ·
CHASING A KILLER STORY CAN BE HAZARDOUS TO YOUR HEALTH
W 48TH ST
DON'T WALK
I ♥ NY
DO NOT ENTER
LINE DO NOT CROSS
POLICE LINE DO NO
Daily Globe
Greg Horn
ROSEMANN
DAVIS
1 of 4

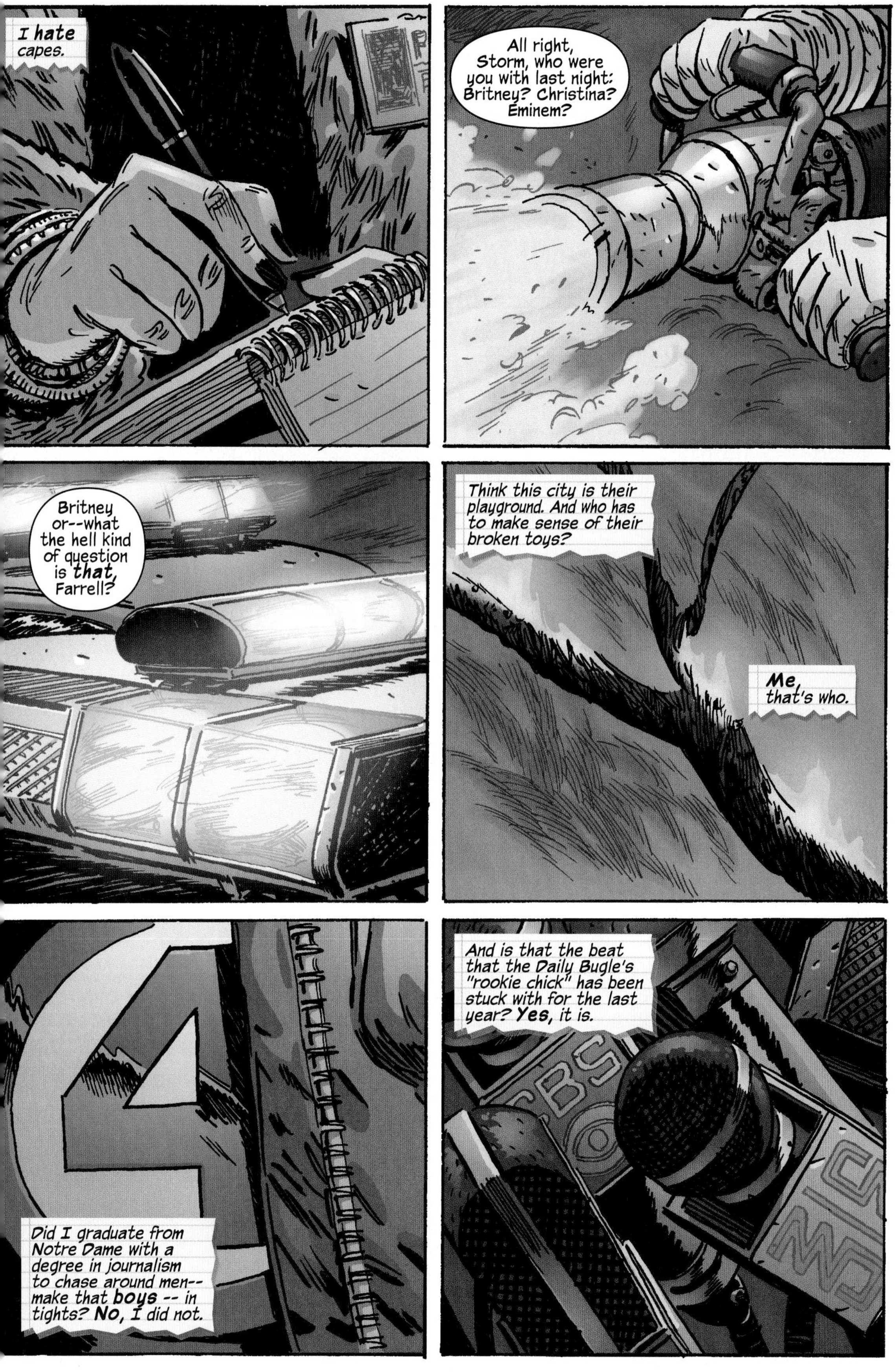
I hate capes.
All right, Storm, who were you with last night: Britney? Christina? Eminem?
Britney or--what the hell kind of question is that, Farrell?
Think this city is their playground. And who has to make sense of their broken toys?
Me, that's who.
Did I graduate from Notre Dame with a degree in journalism to chase around men--make that boys -- in tights? No, I did not.
And is that the beat that the Daily Bugle's "rookie chick" has been stuck with for the last year? Yes, it is.
CBS

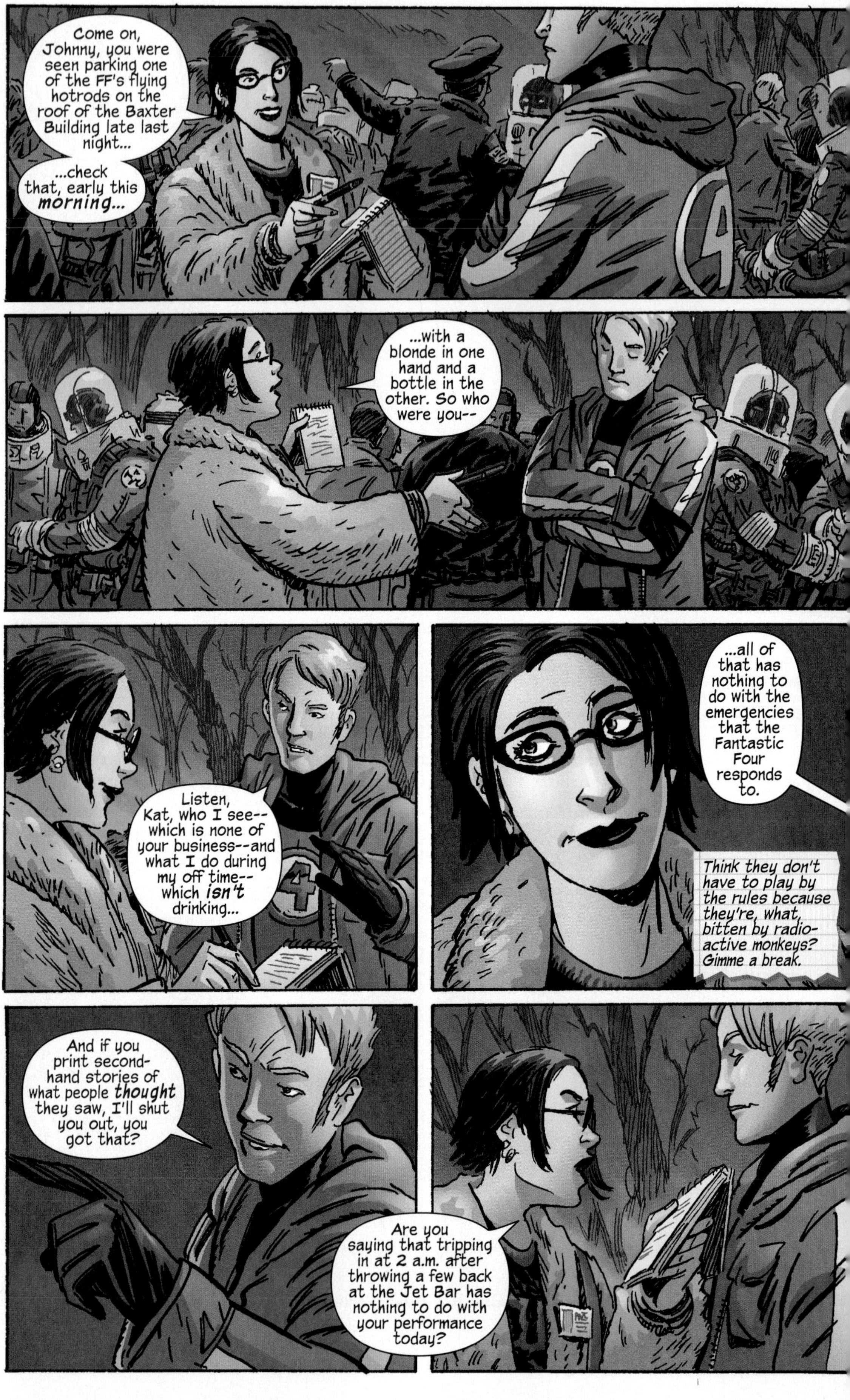
Come on, Johnny, you were seen parking one of the FF's flying hotrods on the roof of the Baxter Building late last night...
...check that, early this *morning*...
...with a blonde in one hand and a bottle in the other. So who were you--
Listen, Kat, who I see--which is none of your business--and what I do during my off time--which *isn't* drinking...
...all of that has nothing to do with the emergencies that the Fantastic Four responds to.
Think they don't have to play by the rules because they're, what, bitten by radio-active monkeys? Gimme a break.
And if you print second-hand stories of what people *thought* they saw, I'll shut you out, you got that?
Are you saying that tripping in at 2 a.m. after throwing a few back at the Jet Bar has nothing to do with your performance today?

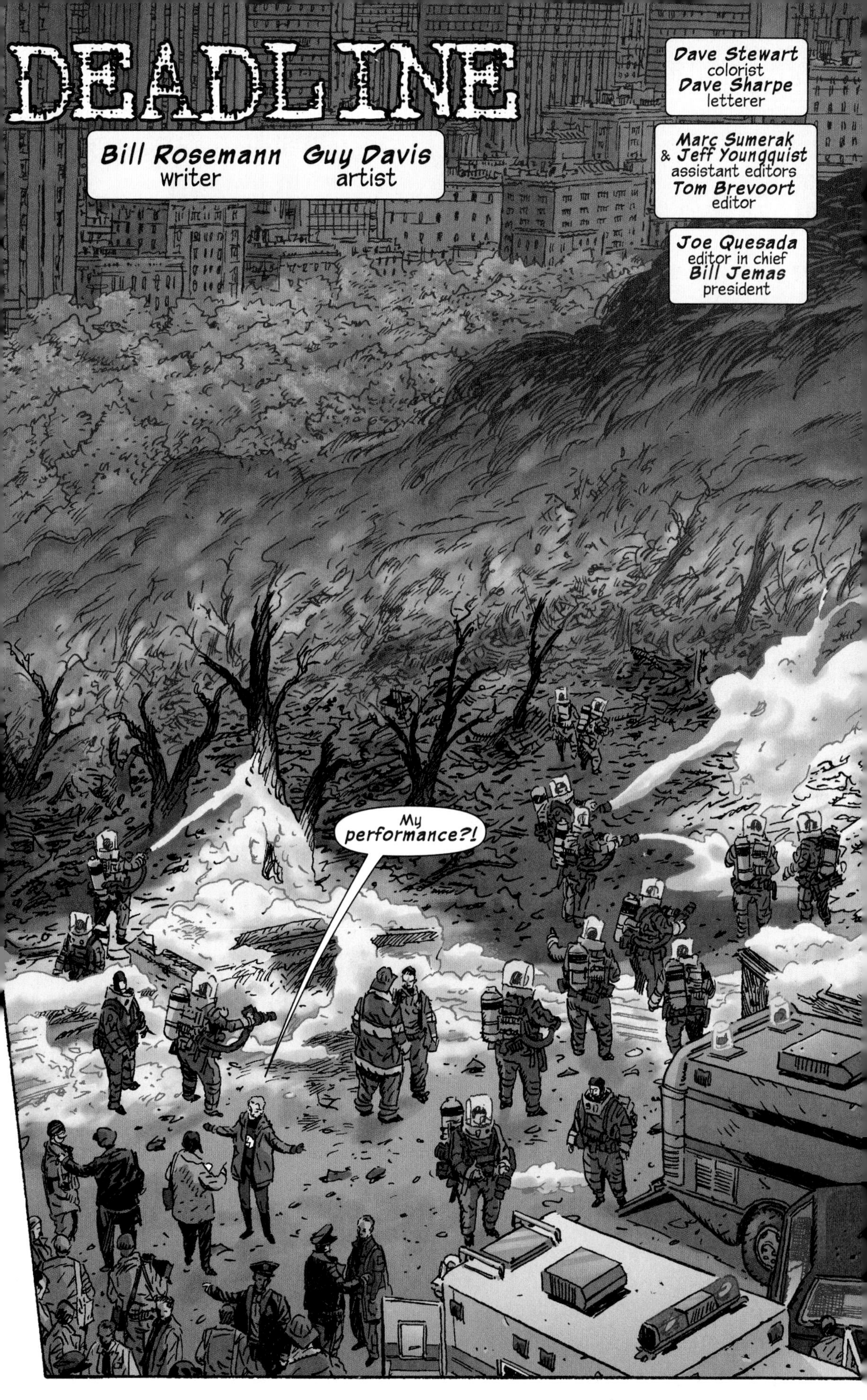
DEADLINE
Bill Rosemann writer Guy Davis artist
Dave Stewart colorist Dave Sharpe letterer
Marc Sumerak & Jeff Youngquist assistant editors Tom Brevoort editor
Joe Quesada editor in chief Bill Jemas president
My performance?!

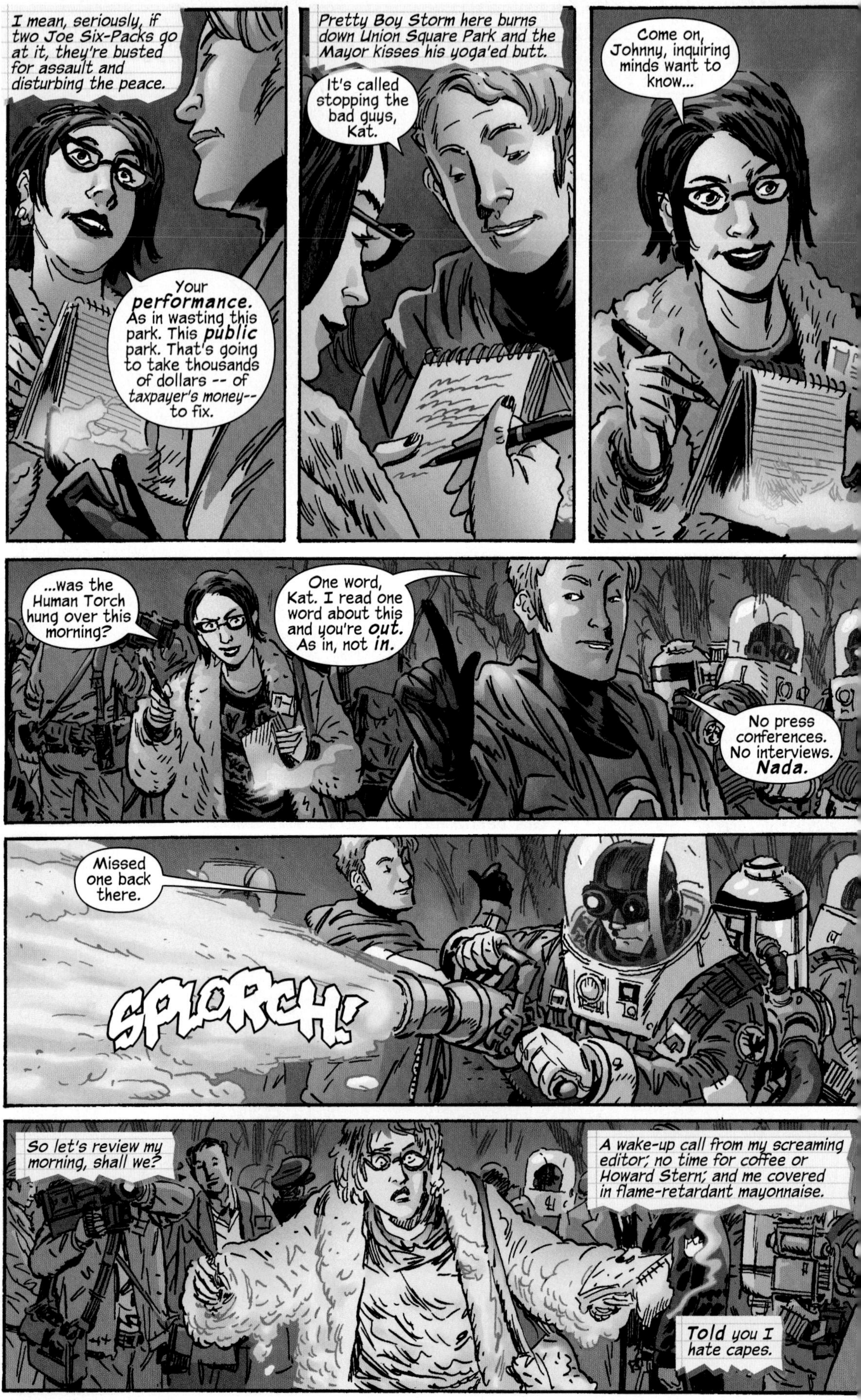

I mean, seriously, if two Joe Six-Packs go at it, they're busted for assault and disturbing the peace.
Your *performance.* As in wasting this park. This *public* park. That's going to take thousands of dollars -- of *taxpayer's money--* to fix.
Pretty Boy Storm here burns down Union Square Park and the Mayor kisses his yoga'ed butt.
It's called stopping the bad guys, Kat.
Come on, Johnny, inquiring minds want to know...
...was the Human Torch hung over this morning?
One word, Kat. I read one word about this and you're *out.* As in, not *in.*
No press conferences. No interviews. *Nada.*
Missed one back there.
SPLORCH!
So let's review my morning, shall we?
A wake-up call from my screaming editor; no time for coffee or Howard Stern; and me covered in flame-retardant mayonnaise.
Told you I hate capes.

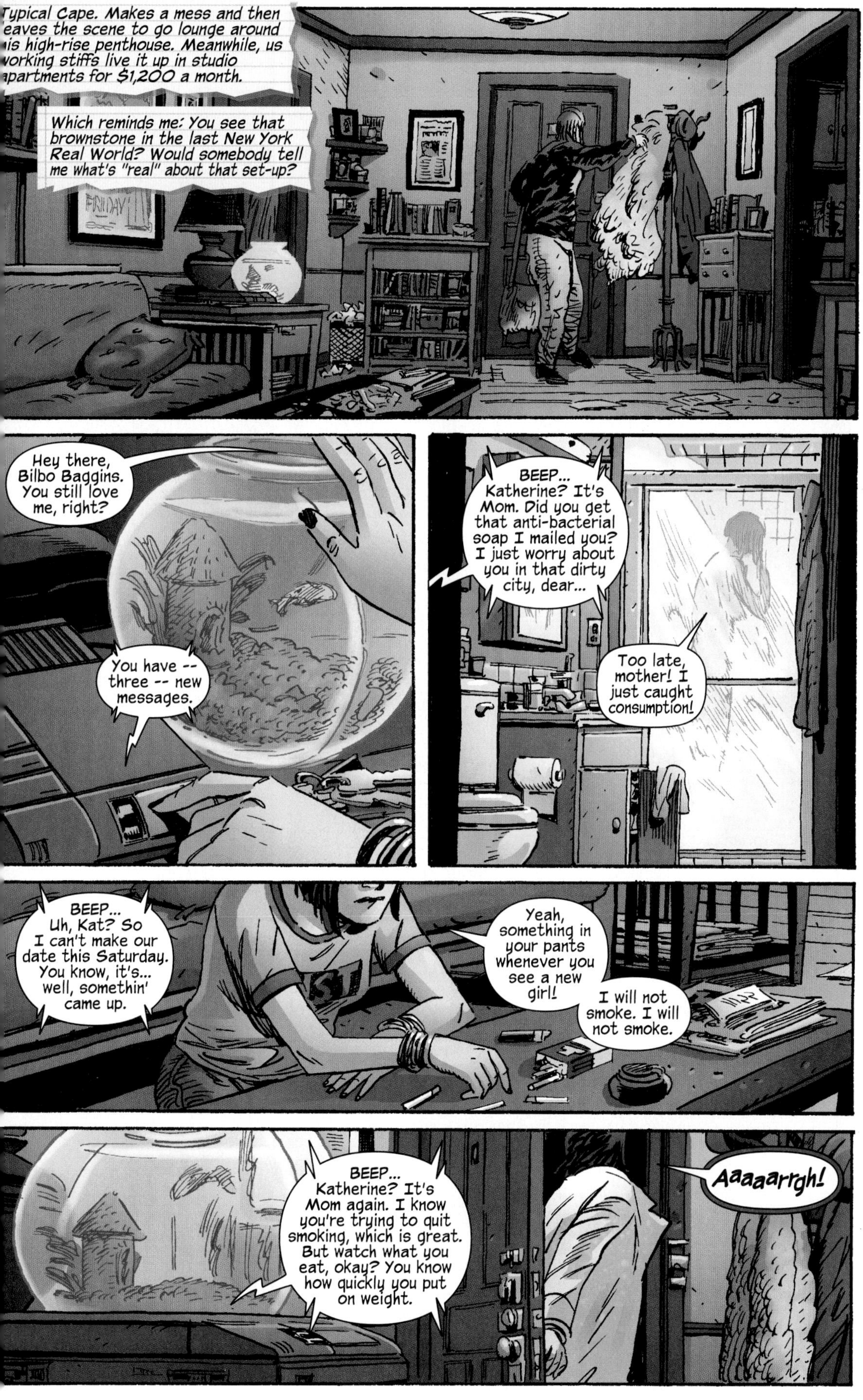
Typical Cape. Makes a mess and then leaves the scene to go lounge around his high-rise penthouse. Meanwhile, us working stiffs live it up in studio apartments for $1,200 a month.
Which reminds me: You see that brownstone in the last New York Real World? Would somebody tell me what's "real" about that set-up?
Hey there, Bilbo Baggins. You still love me, right?
You have -- three -- new messages.
BEEP... Katherine? It's Mom. Did you get that anti-bacterial soap I mailed you? I just worry about you in that dirty city, dear...
Too late, mother! I just caught consumption!
BEEP... Uh, Kat? So I can't make our date this Saturday. You know, it's... well, somethin' came up.
Yeah, something in your pants whenever you see a new girl!
I will not smoke. I will not smoke.
BEEP... Katherine? It's Mom again. I know you're trying to quit smoking, which is great. But watch what you eat, okay? You know how quickly you put on weight.
Aaaaarrgh!

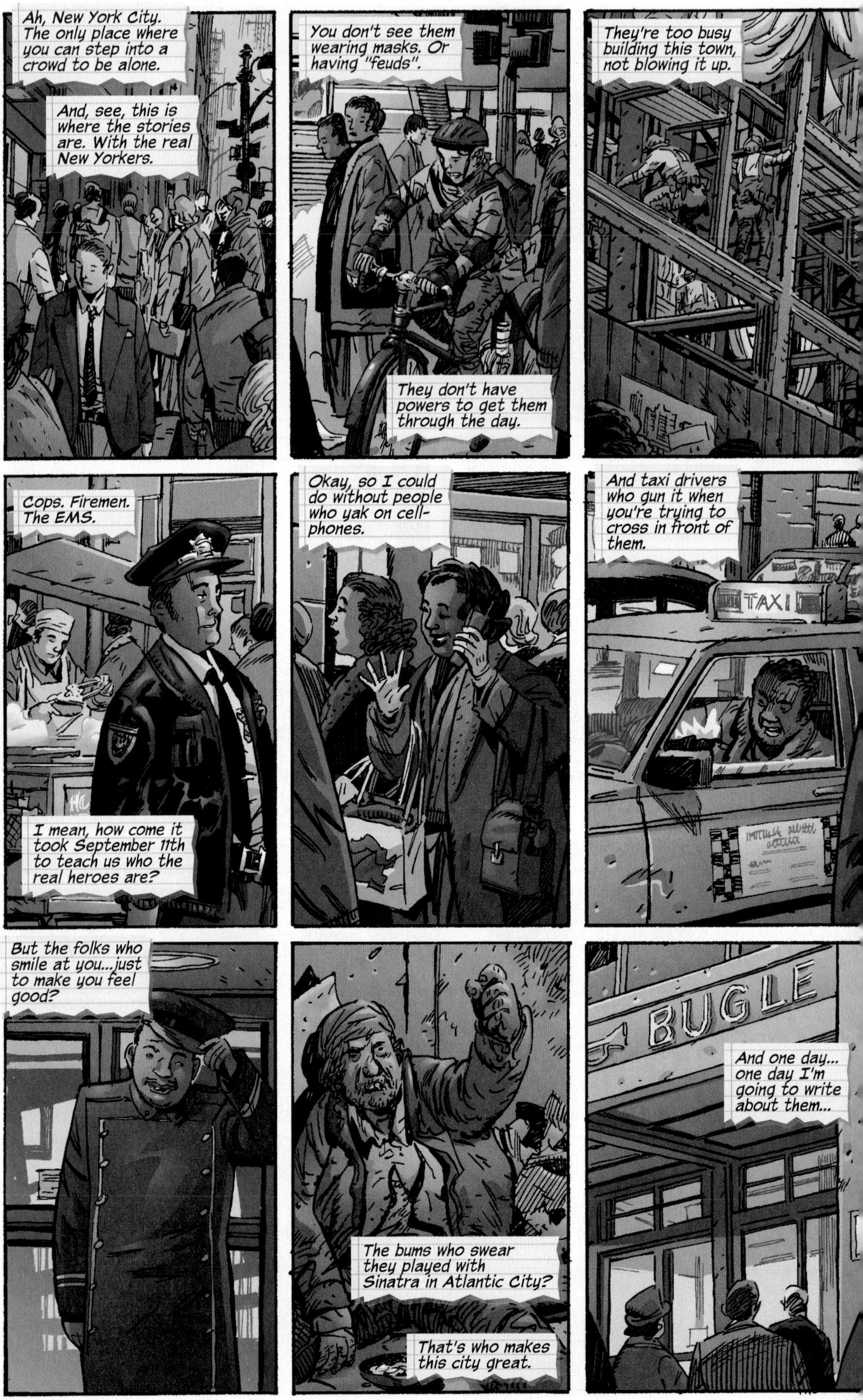
Ah, New York City. The only place where you can step into a crowd to be alone.
And, see, this is where the stories are. With the real New Yorkers.
You don't see them wearing masks. Or having "feuds".
They don't have powers to get them through the day.
They're too busy building this town, not blowing it up.
Cops. Firemen. The EMS.
I mean, how come it took September 11th to teach us who the real heroes are?
Okay, so I could do without people who yak on cell-phones.
And taxi drivers who gun it when you're trying to cross in front of them.
TAXI
But the folks who smile at you...just to make you feel good?
The bums who swear they played with Sinatra in Atlantic City?
That's who makes this city great.
BUGLE
And one day... one day I'm going to write about them...

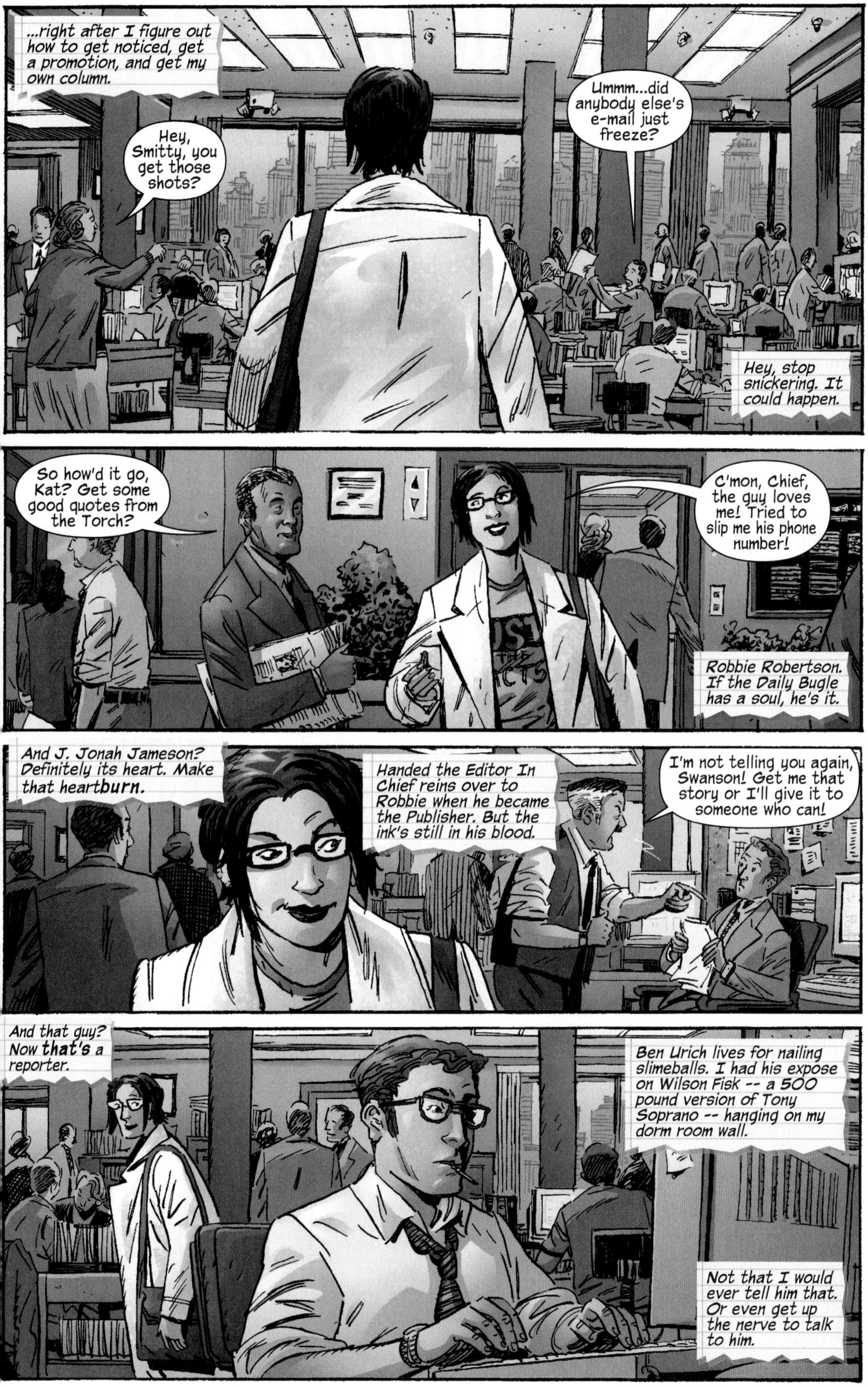
...right after I figure out how to get noticed, get a promotion, and get my own column.
Hey, Smitty, you get those shots?
Ummm...did anybody else's e-mail just freeze?
Hey, stop snickering. It could happen.
So how'd it go, Kat? Get some good quotes from the Torch?
C'mon, Chief, the guy loves me! Tried to slip me his phone number!
Robbie Robertson. If the Daily Bugle has a soul, he's it.
And J. Jonah Jameson? Definitely its heart. Make that heartburn.
Handed the Editor In Chief reins over to Robbie when he became the Publisher. But the ink's still in his blood.
I'm not telling you again, Swanson! Get me that story or I'll give it to someone who can!
And that guy? Now that's a reporter.
Ben Urich lives for nailing slimeballs. I had his expose on Wilson Fisk -- a 500 pound version of Tony Soprano -- hanging on my dorm room wall.
Not that I would ever tell him that. Or even get up the nerve to talk to him.

And this is my cubicle. Yeah, it's no corner office, but after a year of fetching coffee as an intern? It's heaven.

Hey, who left their subway map on my--

Holy tips, Batman.

CONNECT THE DOTS

Yo, Dickinson, you see who put this here?

Who put what now?

This map. On my desk.

Uh... the map fairy?

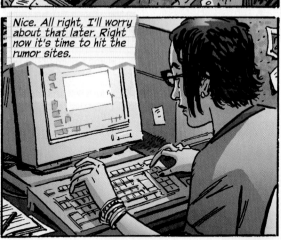

Nice. All right, I'll worry about that later. Right now it's time to hit the rumor sites.

Back   Forward   Reload
Location: www.superheronewsarama.home

SUPER HERO NEWSARAMA

CAPTAIN AMERICA: WHO'S UNDER THE MASK NOW?

WAITRESS: "I SLEPT WITH THOR!"

Yep, some people have no lives. Like me.

But if I can find another witness that saw the Torch last night--

Hell, if it's online it has to be true.

Hey, dig those bangs!

Thanks. Wanna get some caffeine?

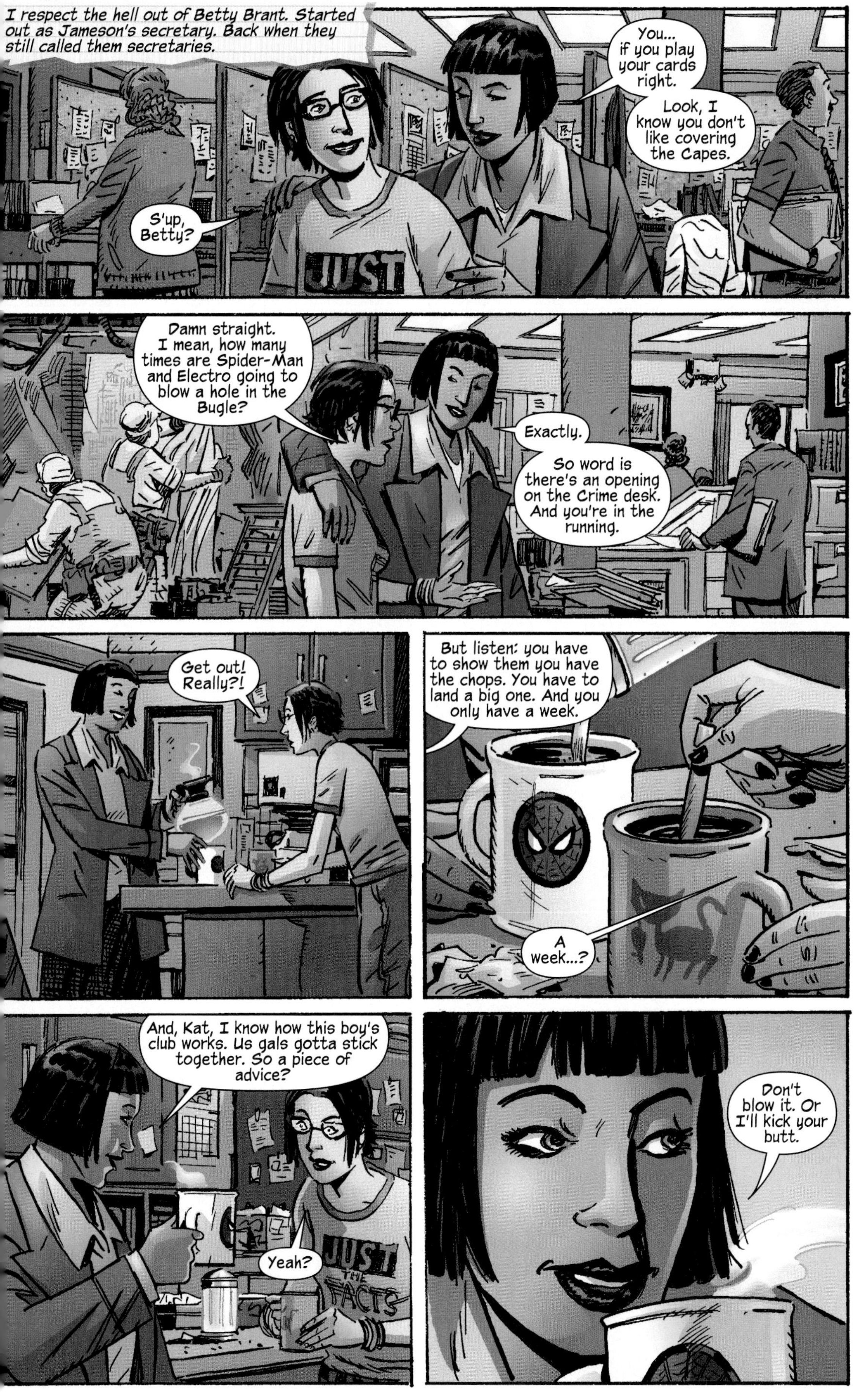
I respect the hell out of Betty Brant. Started out as Jameson's secretary. Back when they still called them secretaries.
S'up, Betty?
You... if you play your cards right.
Look, I know you don't like covering the Capes.
JUST
Damn straight. I mean, how many times are Spider-Man and Electro going to blow a hole in the Bugle?
Exactly.
So word is there's an opening on the Crime desk. And you're in the running.
Get out! Really?!
But listen: you have to show them you have the chops. You have to land a big one. And you only have a week.
A week...?
And, Kat, I know how this boy's club works. Us gals gotta stick together. So a piece of advice?
Yeah?
JUST THE FACTS
Don't blow it. Or I'll kick your butt.

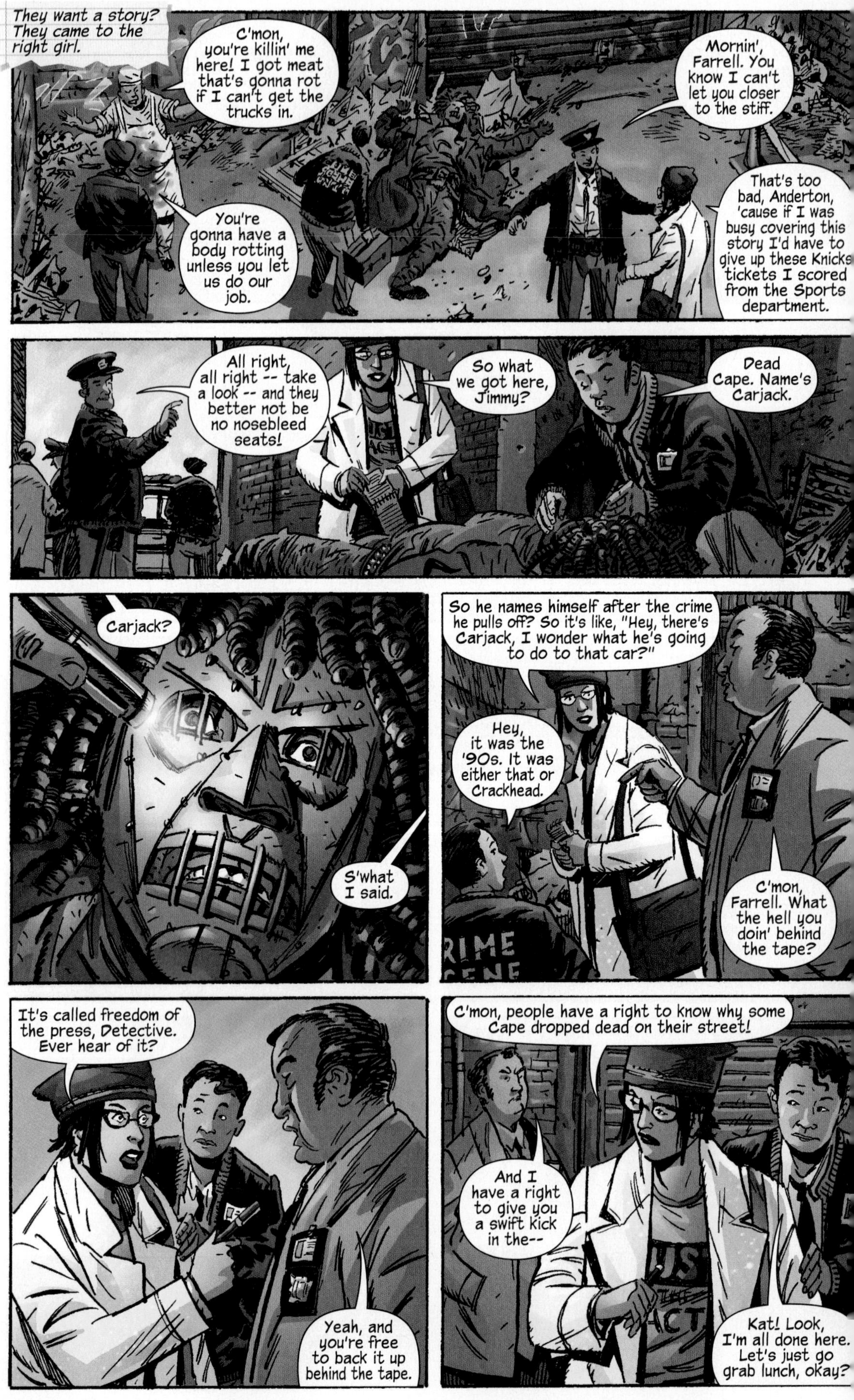
They want a story? They came to the right girl.
C'mon, you're killin' me here! I got meat that's gonna rot if I can't get the trucks in.
You're gonna have a body rotting unless you let us do our job.
Mornin', Farrell. You know I can't let you closer to the stiff.
That's too bad, Anderton, 'cause if I was busy covering this story I'd have to give up these Knicks tickets I scored from the Sports department.
All right, all right -- take a look -- and they better not be no nosebleed seats!
So what we got here, Jimmy?
Dead Cape. Name's Carjack.
Carjack?
S'what I said.
So he names himself after the crime he pulls off? So it's like, "Hey, there's Carjack, I wonder what he's going to do to that car?"
Hey, it was the '90s. It was either that or Crackhead.
C'mon, Farrell. What the hell you doin' behind the tape?
It's called freedom of the press, Detective. Ever hear of it?
Yeah, and you're free to back it up behind the tape.
C'mon, people have a right to know why some Cape dropped dead on their street!
And I have a right to give you a swift kick in the--
Kat! Look, I'm all done here. Let's just go grab lunch, okay?

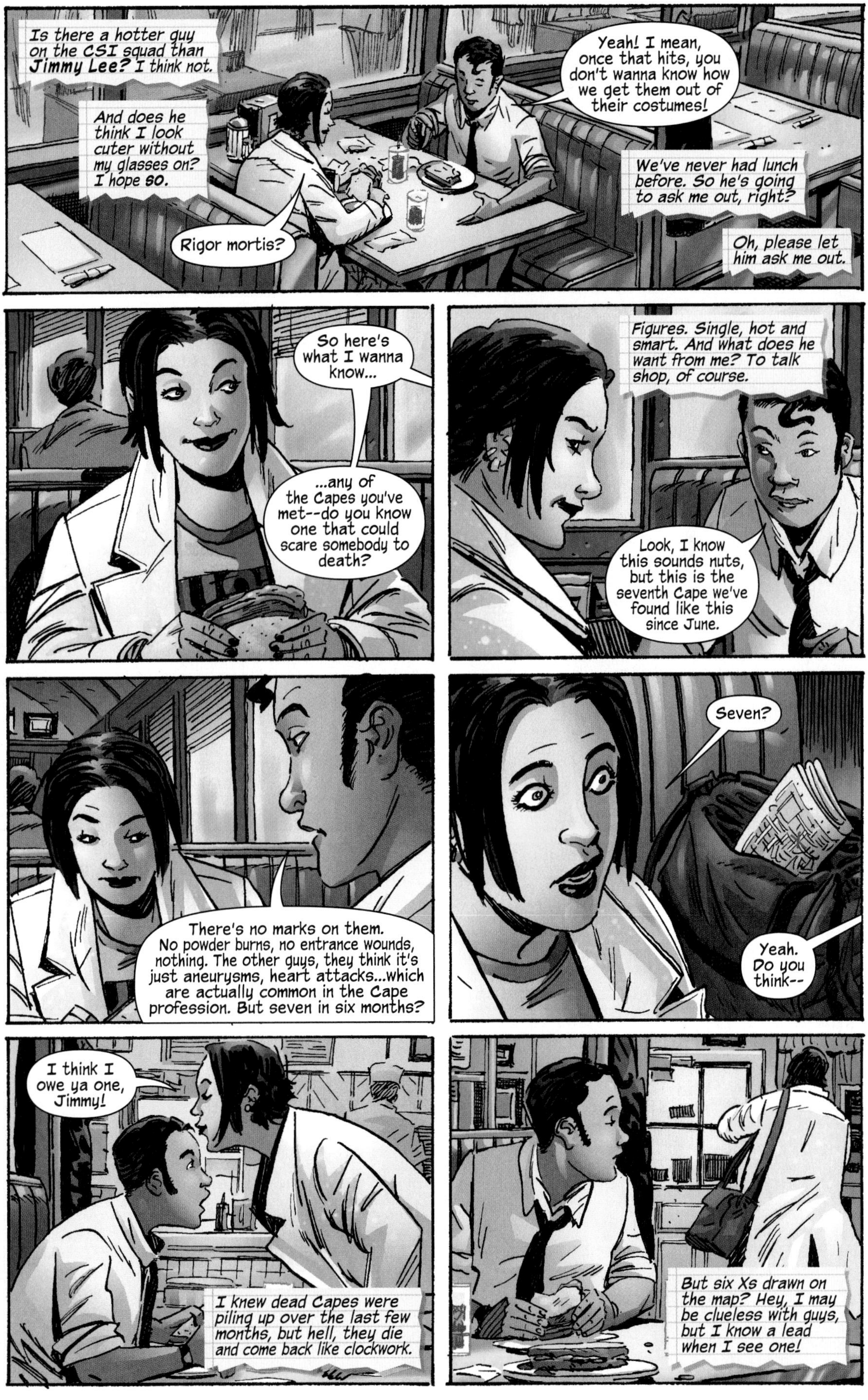
Is there a hotter guy on the CSI squad than Jimmy Lee? I think not.
And does he think I look cuter without my glasses on? I hope SO.
Rigor mortis?
Yeah! I mean, once that hits, you don't wanna know how we get them out of their costumes!
We've never had lunch before. So he's going to ask me out, right?
Oh, please let him ask me out.
So here's what I wanna know...
...any of the Capes you've met--do you know one that could scare somebody to death?
Figures. Single, hot and smart. And what does he want from me? To talk shop, of course.
Look, I know this sounds nuts, but this is the seventh Cape we've found like this since June.
There's no marks on them. No powder burns, no entrance wounds, nothing. The other guys, they think it's just aneurysms, heart attacks...which are actually common in the Cape profession. But seven in six months?
Seven?
Yeah. Do you think--
I think I owe ya one, Jimmy!
I knew dead Capes were piling up over the last few months, but hell, they die and come back like clockwork.
But six Xs drawn on the map? Hey, I may be clueless with guys, but I know a lead when I see one!

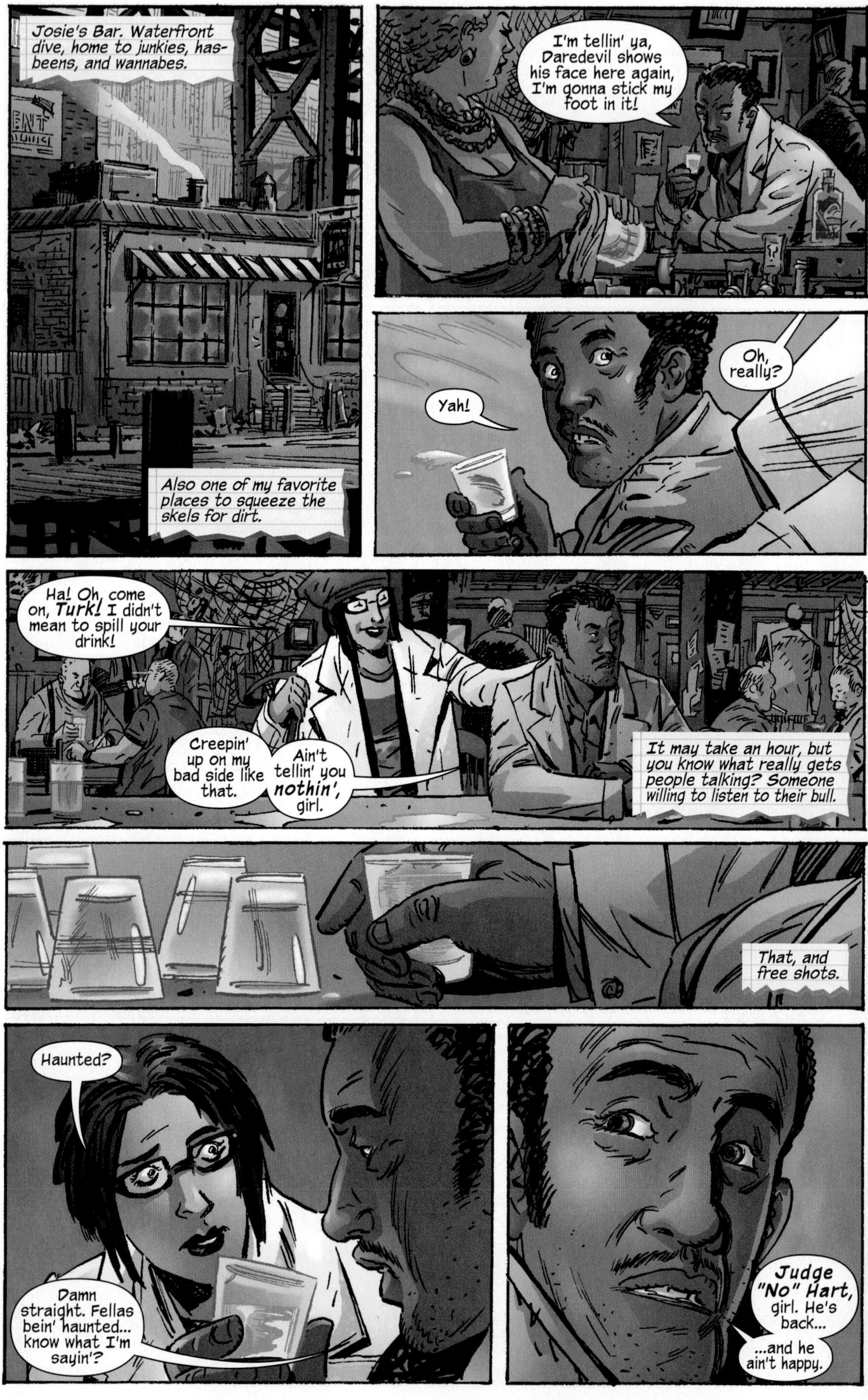
Josie's Bar. Waterfront dive, home to junkies, has-beens, and wannabes.
Also one of my favorite places to squeeze the skels for dirt.
I'm tellin' ya, Daredevil shows his face here again, I'm gonna stick my foot in it!
Yah!
Oh, really?
Ha! Oh, come on, Turk! I didn't mean to spill your drink!
Creepin' up on my bad side like that.
Ain't tellin' you nothin', girl.
It may take an hour, but you know what really gets people talking? Someone willing to listen to their bull.
That, and free shots.
Haunted?
Damn straight. Fellas bein' haunted... know what I'm sayin'?
Judge "No" Hart, girl. He's back...
...and he ain't happy.

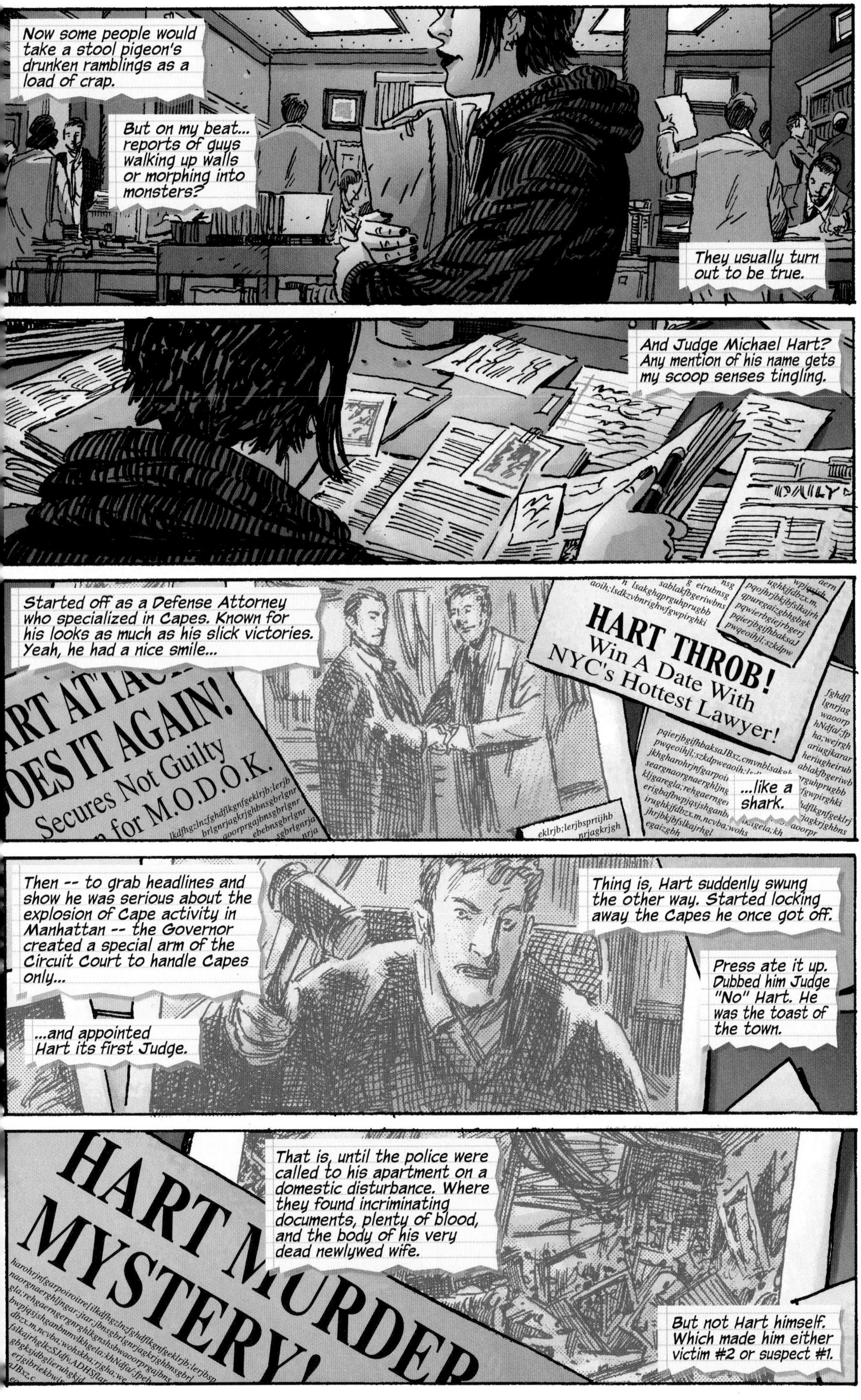
Now some people would take a stool pigeon's drunken ramblings as a load of crap.
But on my beat... reports of guys walking up walls or morphing into monsters?
They usually turn out to be true.
And Judge Michael Hart? Any mention of his name gets my scoop senses tingling.
DAILY
Started off as a Defense Attorney who specialized in Capes. Known for his looks as much as his slick victories. Yeah, he had a nice smile...
HART THROB! Win A Date With NYC's Hottest Lawyer!
ART ATTAC
OES IT AGAIN!
Secures Not Guilty
for M.O.D.O.K.
...like a shark.
Then -- to grab headlines and show he was serious about the explosion of Cape activity in Manhattan -- the Governor created a special arm of the Circuit Court to handle Capes only...
...and appointed Hart its first Judge.
Thing is, Hart suddenly swung the other way. Started locking away the Capes he once got off.
Press ate it up. Dubbed him Judge "No" Hart. He was the toast of the town.
HART MURDER MYSTERY!
That is, until the police were called to his apartment on a domestic disturbance. Where they found incriminating documents, plenty of blood, and the body of his very dead newlywed wife.
But not Hart himself. Which made him either victim #2 or suspect #1.

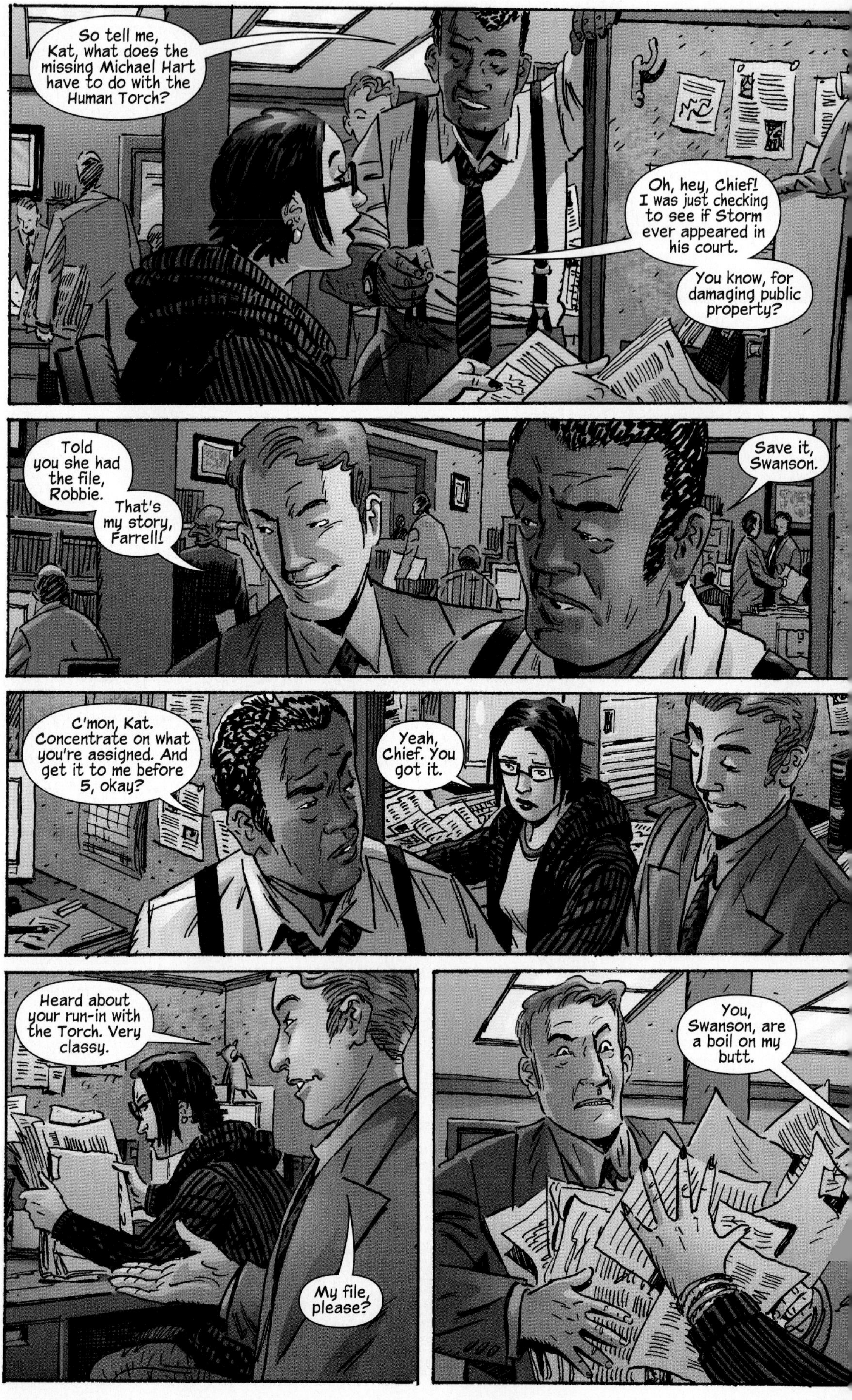
So tell me, Kat, what does the missing Michael Hart have to do with the Human Torch?
Oh, hey, Chief! I was just checking to see if Storm ever appeared in his court.
You know, for damaging public property?
Told you she had the file, Robbie.
That's my story, Farrell!
Save it, Swanson.
C'mon, Kat. Concentrate on what you're assigned. And get it to me before 5, okay?
Yeah, Chief. You got it.
Heard about your run-in with the Torch. Very classy.
My file, please?
You, Swanson, are a boil on my butt.

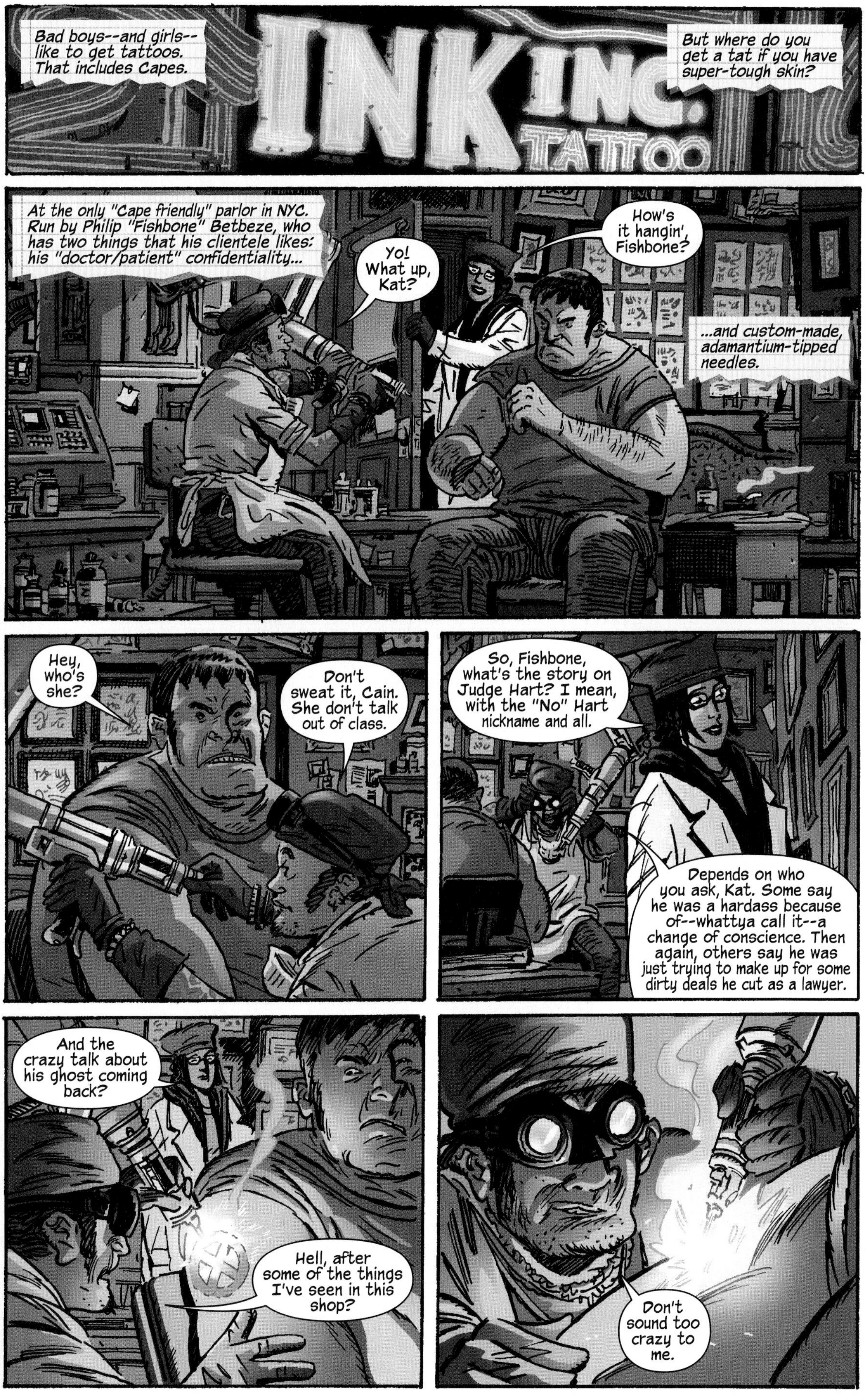

Bad boys--and girls--like to get tattoos. That includes Capes.
INK INC. TATTOO
But where do you get a tat if you have super-tough skin?
At the only "Cape friendly" parlor in NYC. Run by Philip "Fishbone" Betbeze, who has two things that his clientele likes: his "doctor/patient" confidentiality...
Yo! What up, Kat?
How's it hangin', Fishbone?
...and custom-made, adamantium-tipped needles.
Hey, who's she?
Don't sweat it, Cain. She don't talk out of class.
So, Fishbone, what's the story on Judge Hart? I mean, with the "No" Hart nickname and all.
Depends on who you ask, Kat. Some say he was a hardass because of--whattya call it--a change of conscience. Then again, others say he was just trying to make up for some dirty deals he cut as a lawyer.
And the crazy talk about his ghost coming back?
Hell, after some of the things I've seen in this shop?
Don't sound too crazy to me.

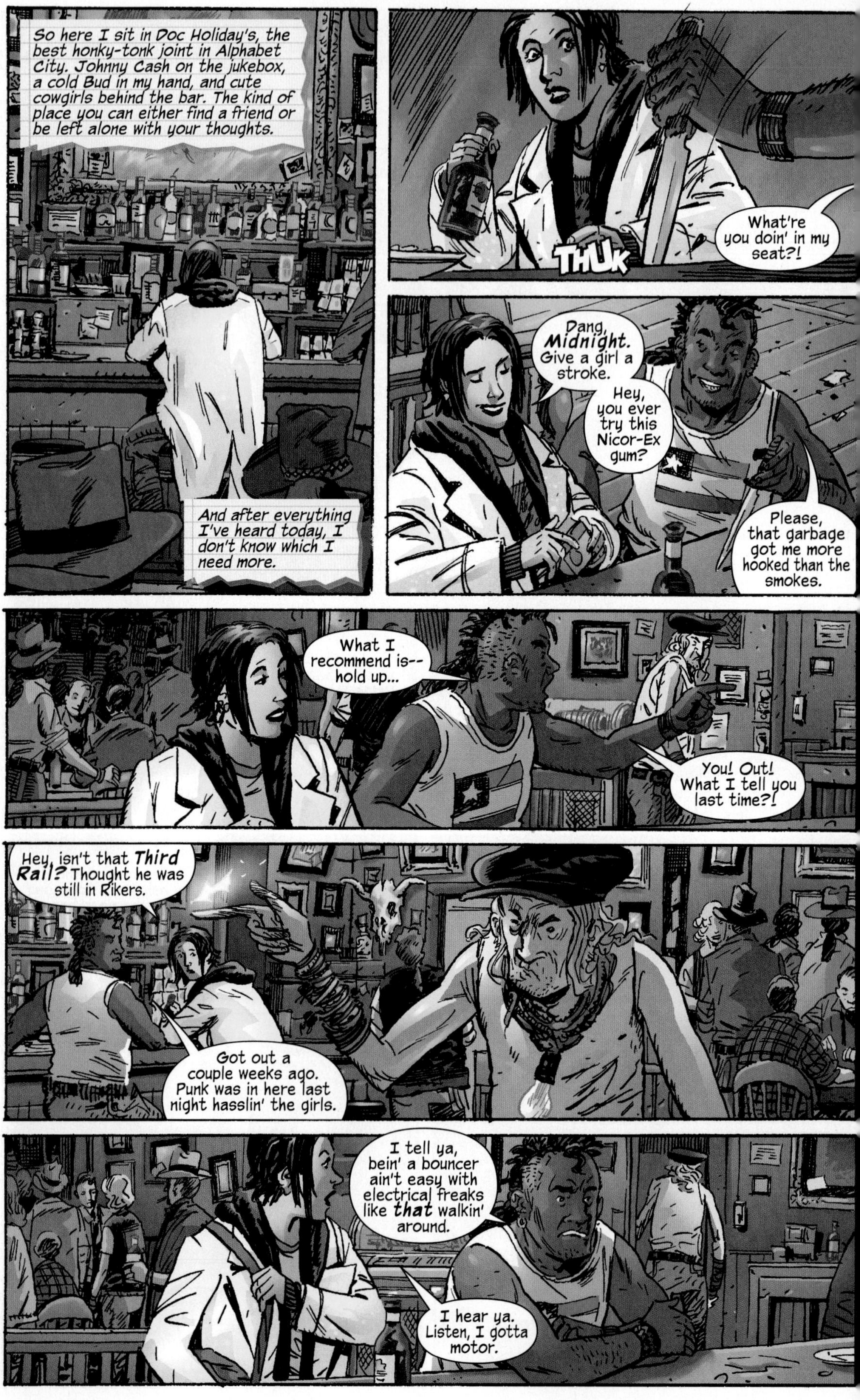
So here I sit in Doc Holiday's, the best honky-tonk joint in Alphabet City. Johnny Cash on the jukebox, a cold Bud in my hand, and cute cowgirls behind the bar. The kind of place you can either find a friend or be left alone with your thoughts.
And after everything I've heard today, I don't know which I need more.
THUK
What're you doin' in my seat?!
Dang, Midnight. Give a girl a stroke.
Hey, you ever try this Nicor-Ex gum?
Please, that garbage got me more hooked than the smokes.
What I recommend is-- hold up...
You! Out! What I tell you last time?!
Hey, isn't that Third Rail? Thought he was still in Rikers.
Got out a couple weeks ago. Punk was in here last night hasslin' the girls.
I tell ya, bein' a bouncer ain't easy with electrical freaks like that walkin' around.
I hear ya. Listen, I gotta motor.

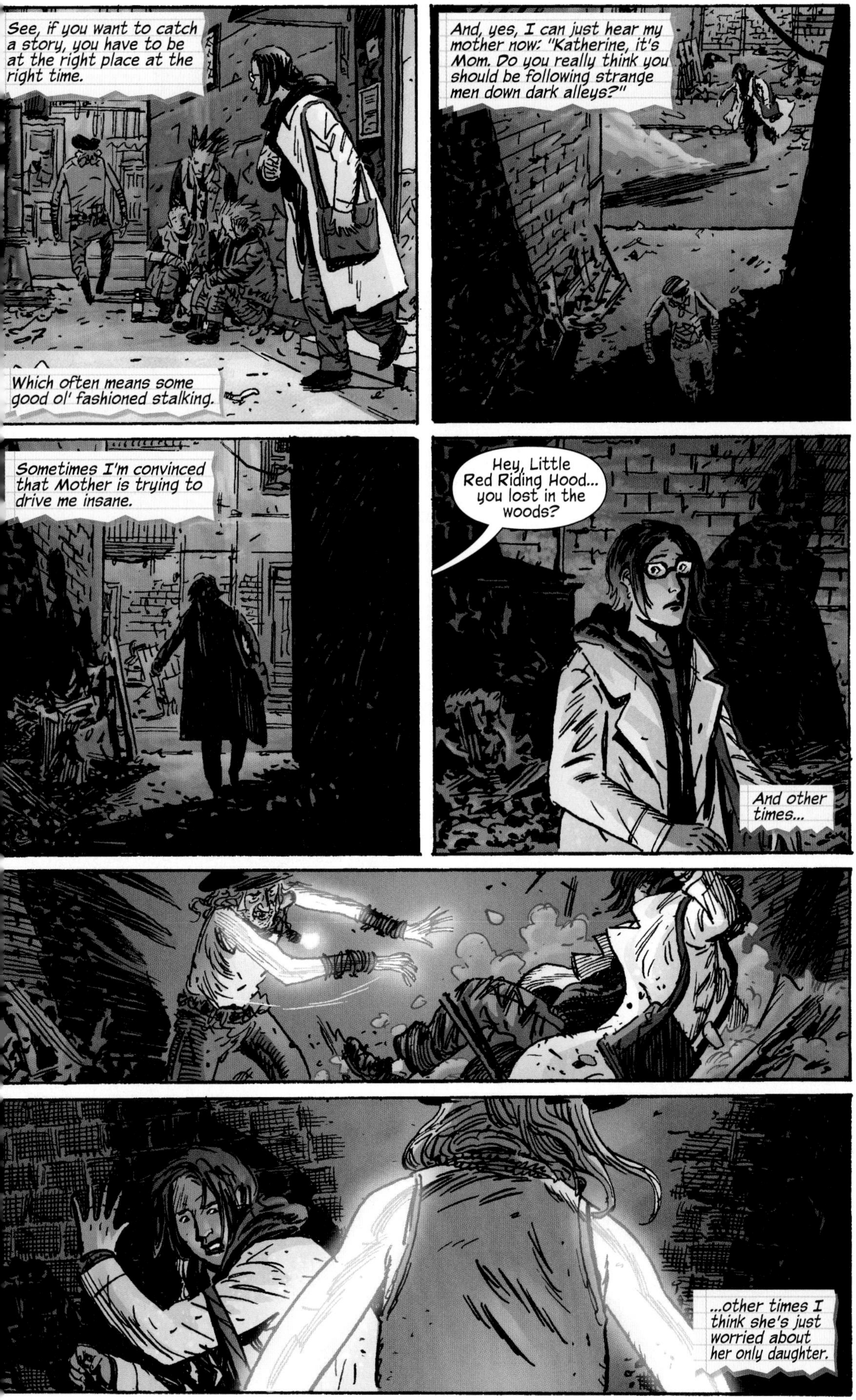
See, if you want to catch a story, you have to be at the right place at the right time.
Which often means some good ol' fashioned stalking.
And, yes, I can just hear my mother now: "Katherine, it's Mom. Do you really think you should be following strange men down dark alleys?"
Sometimes I'm convinced that Mother is trying to drive me insane.
Hey, Little Red Riding Hood... you lost in the woods?
And other times...
...other times I think she's just worried about her only daughter.

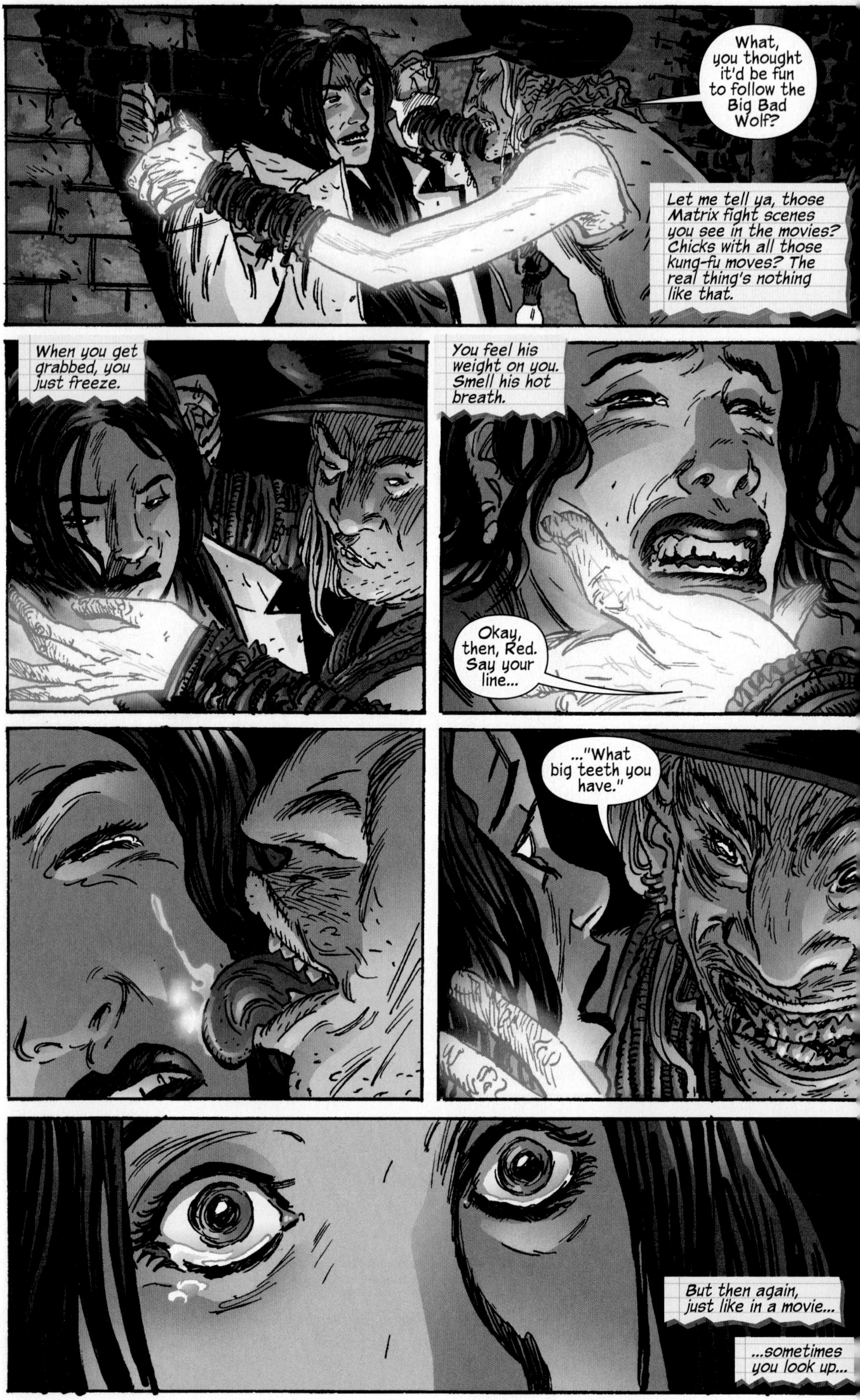
What, you thought it'd be fun to follow the Big Bad Wolf?
Let me tell ya, those Matrix fight scenes you see in the movies? Chicks with all those kung-fu moves? The real thing's nothing like that.
When you get grabbed, you just freeze.
You feel his weight on you. Smell his hot breath.
Okay, then, Red. Say your line...
..."What big teeth you have."
But then again, just like in a movie...
...sometimes you look up...

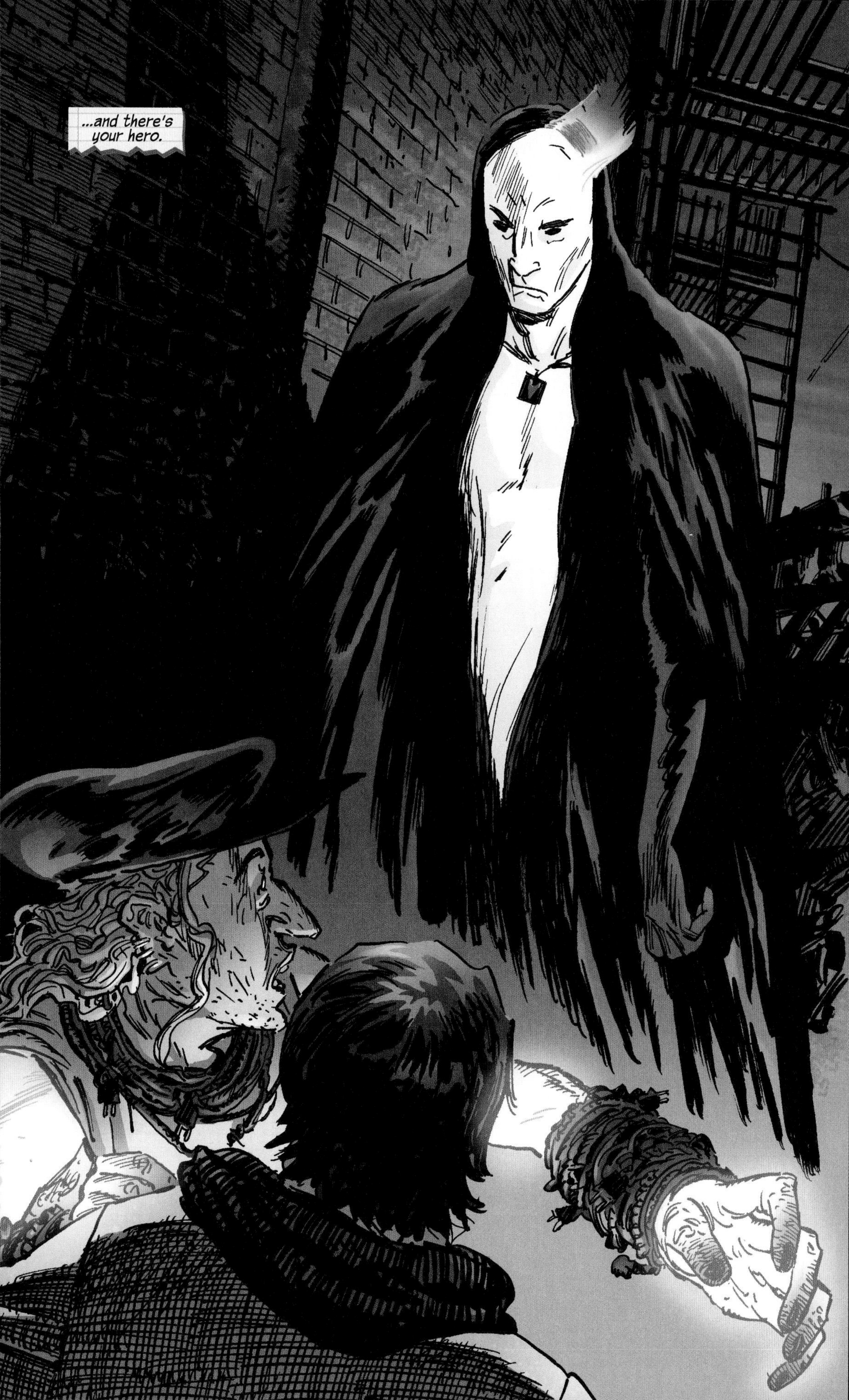
...and there's your hero.

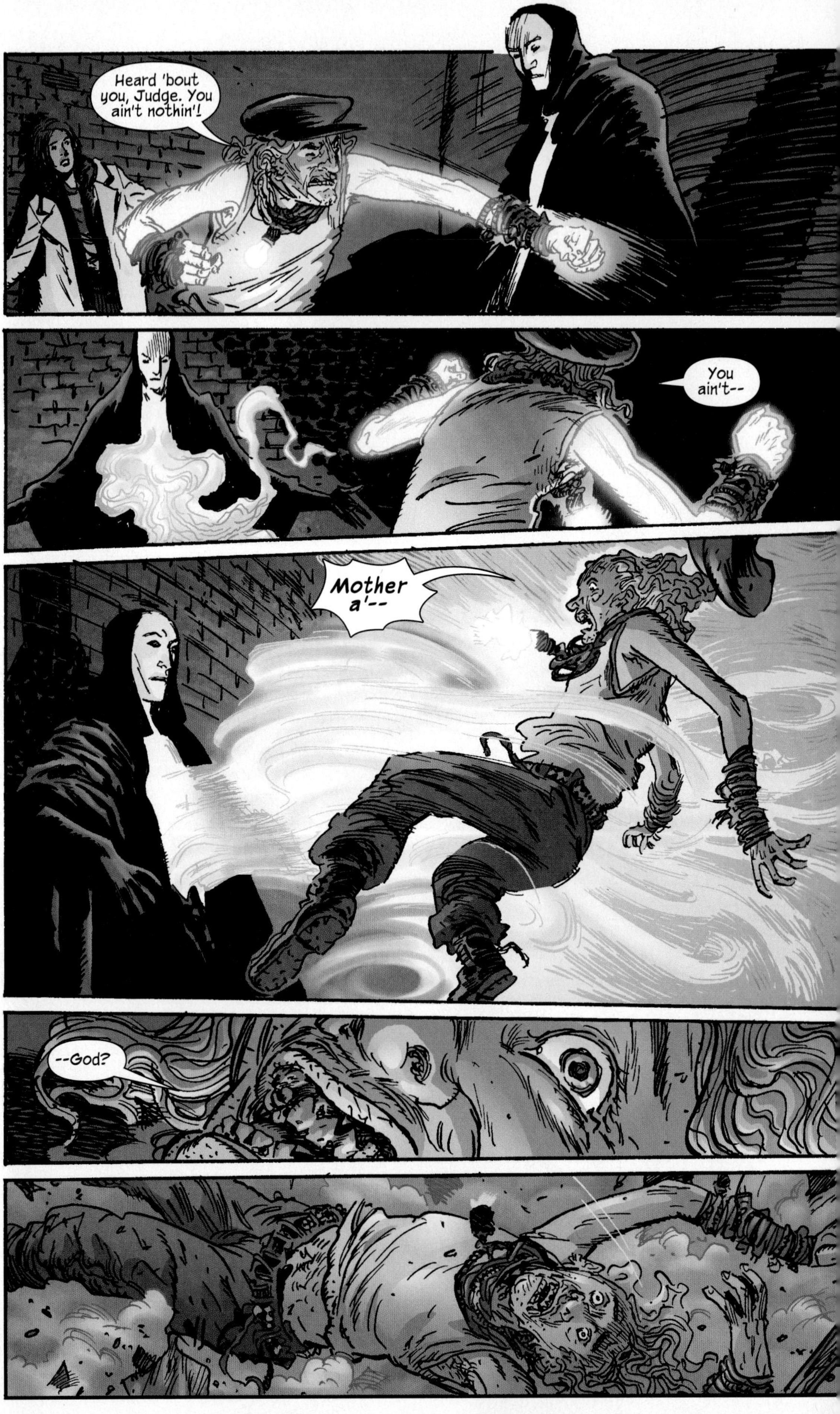
Heard 'bout you, Judge. You ain't nothin'!
You ain't--
Mother a'--
--God?

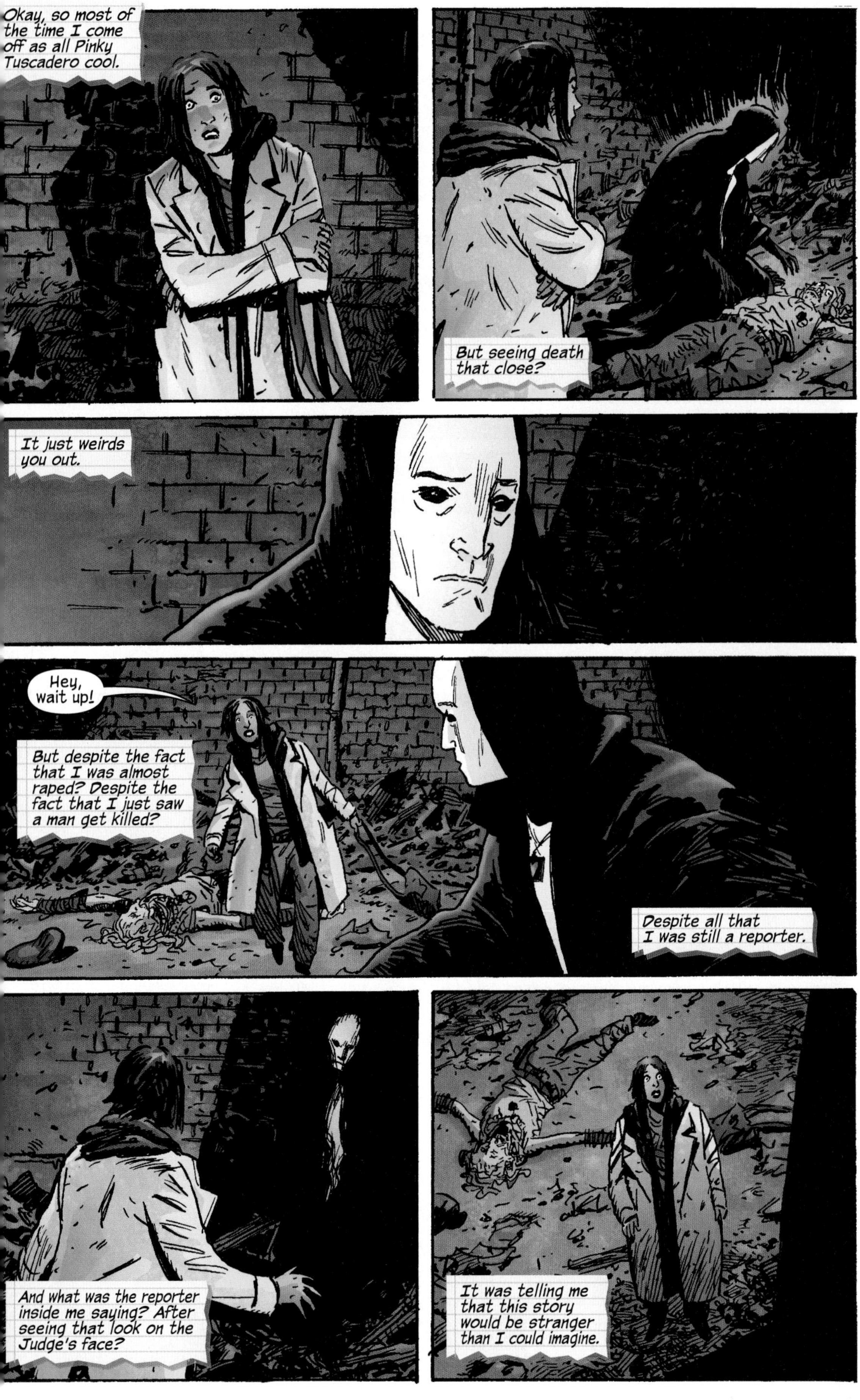
Okay, so most of the time I come off as all Pinky Tuscadero cool.
But seeing death that close?
It just weirds you out.
Hey, wait up!
But despite the fact that I was almost raped? Despite the fact that I just saw a man get killed?
Despite all that I was still a reporter.
And what was the reporter inside me saying? After seeing that look on the Judge's face?
It was telling me that this story would be stranger than I could imagine.

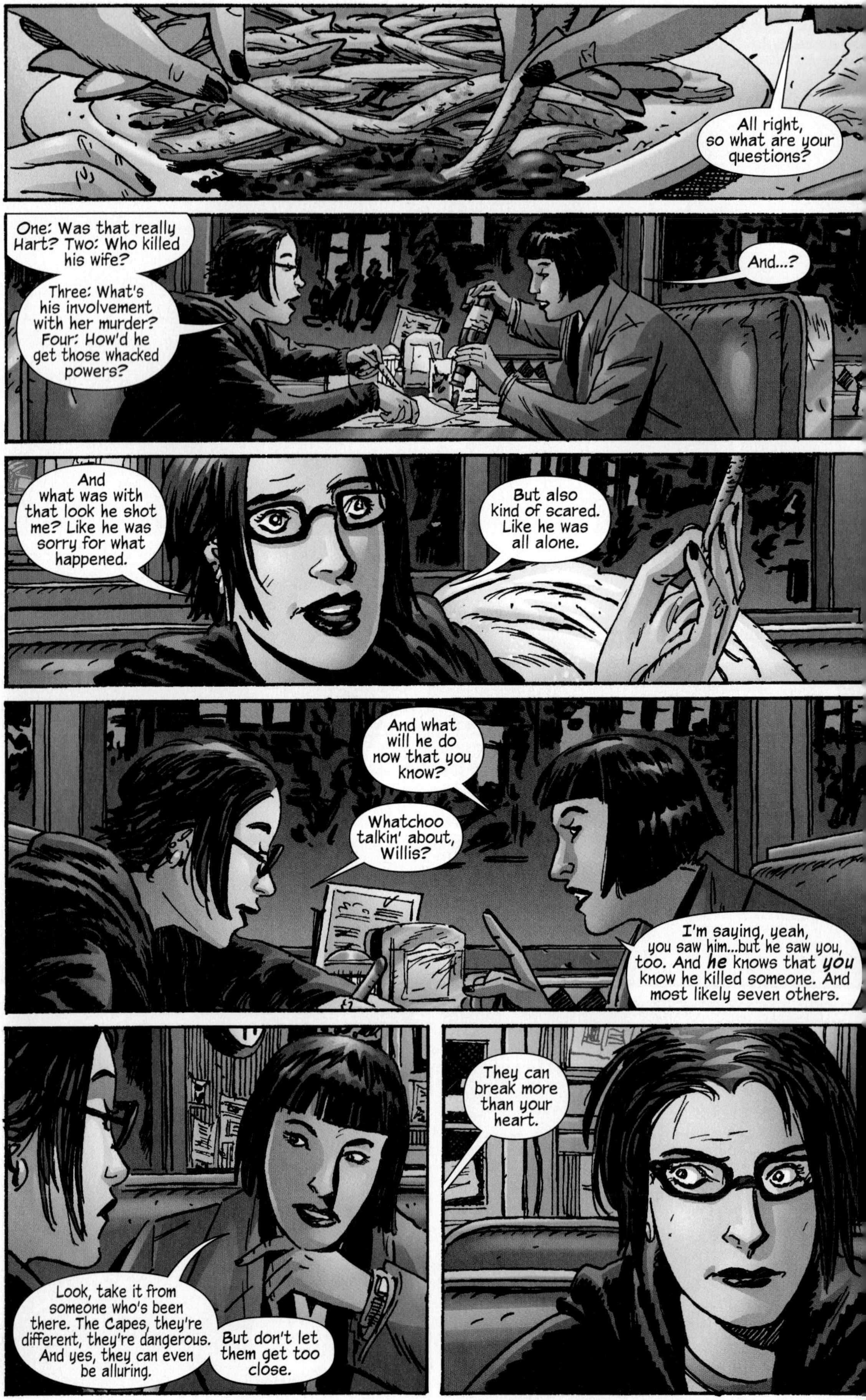
All right, so what are your questions?
One: Was that really Hart? Two: Who killed his wife?
Three: What's his involvement with her murder? Four: How'd he get those whacked powers?
And...?
And what was with that look he shot me? Like he was sorry for what happened.
But also kind of scared. Like he was all alone.
And what will he do now that you know?
Whatchoo talkin' about, Willis?
I'm saying, yeah, you saw him...but he saw you, too. And **he** knows that **you** know he killed someone. And most likely seven others.
Look, take it from someone who's been there. The Capes, they're different, they're dangerous. And yes, they can even be alluring.
But don't let them get too close.
They can break more than your heart.

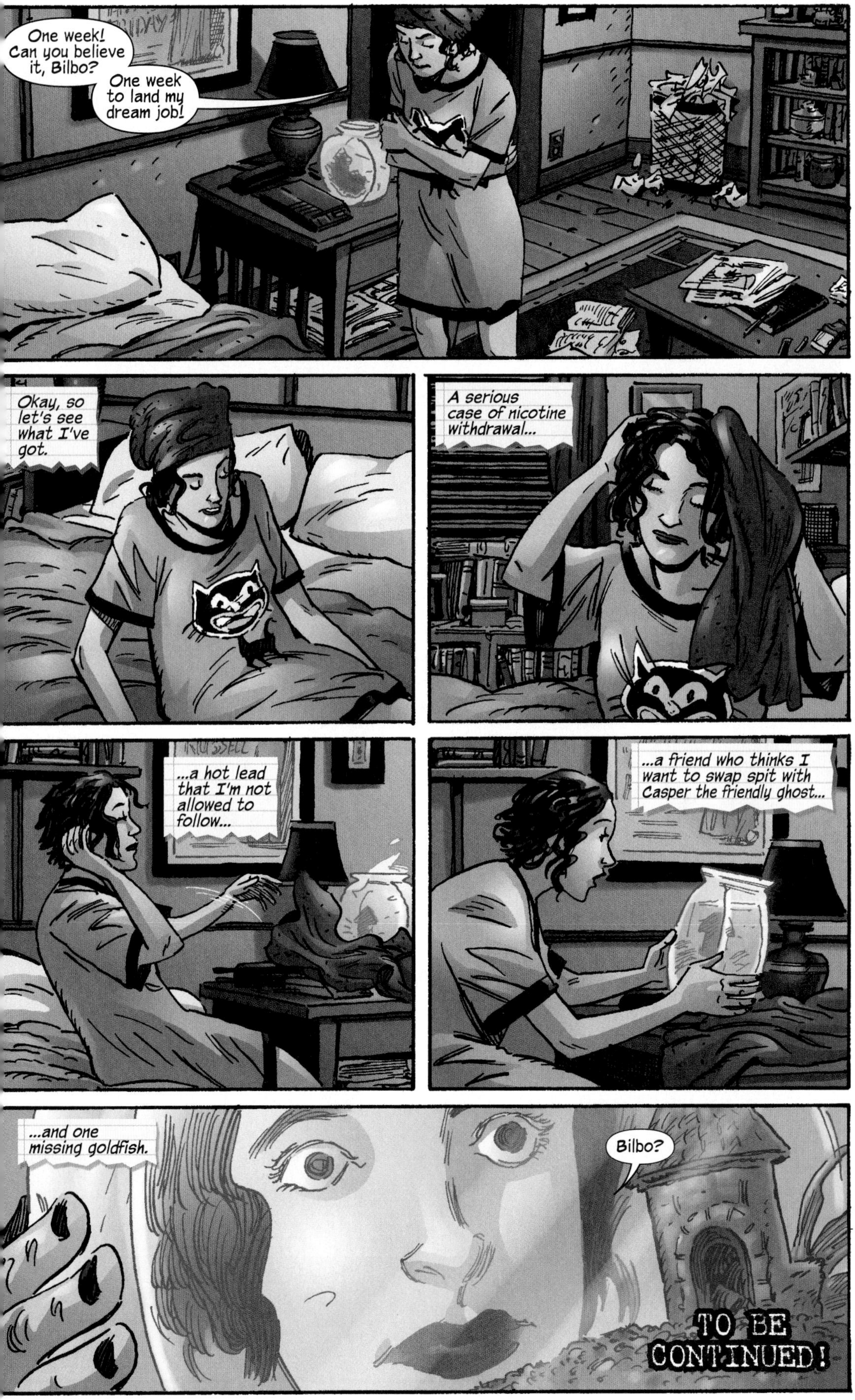
One week! Can you believe it, Bilbo?
One week to land my dream job!
Okay, so let's see what I've got.
A serious case of nicotine withdrawal...
...a hot lead that I'm not allowed to follow...
...a friend who thinks I want to swap spit with Casper the friendly ghost...
...and one missing goldfish.
Bilbo?
TO BE CONTINUED!

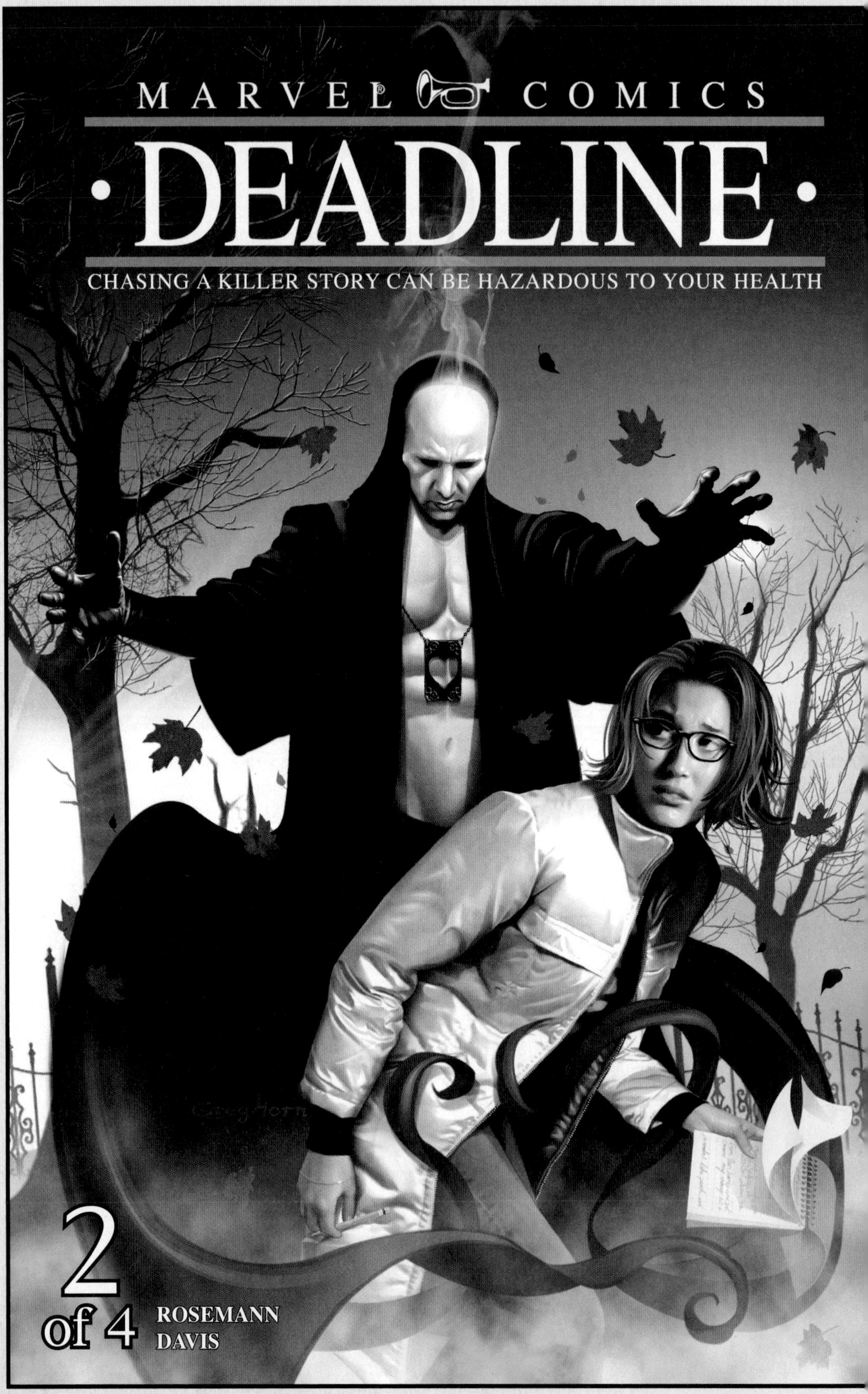
MARVEL COMICS
·DEADLINE·
CHASING A KILLER STORY CAN BE HAZARDOUS TO YOUR HEALTH
2 of 4
ROSEMANN
DAVIS

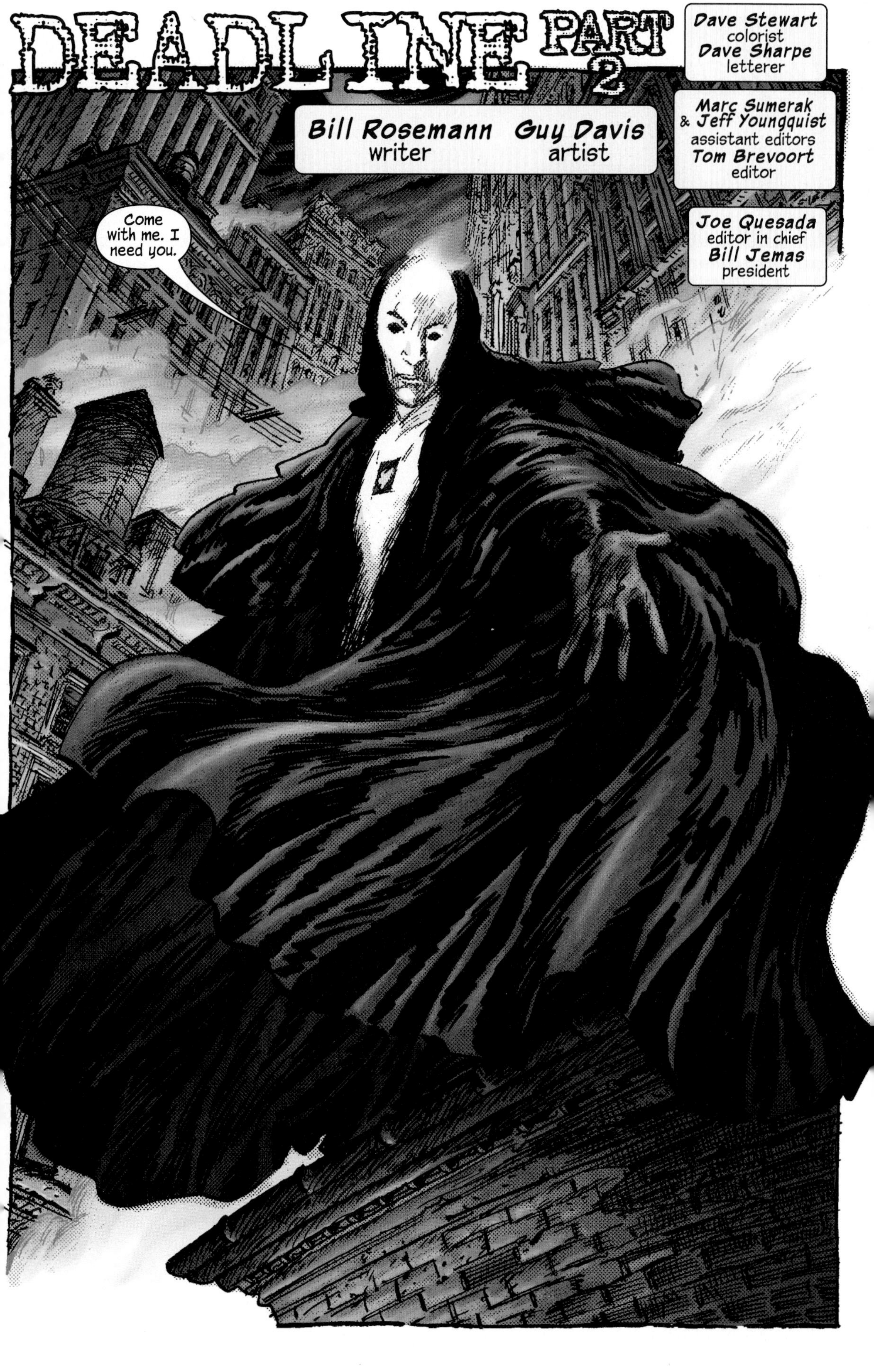
DEADLINE PART 2
Dave Stewart colorist
Dave Sharpe letterer
Bill Rosemann writer
Guy Davis artist
Marc Sumerak & Jeff Youngquist assistant editors
Tom Brevoort editor
Joe Quesada editor in chief
Bill Jemas president
Come with me. I need you.

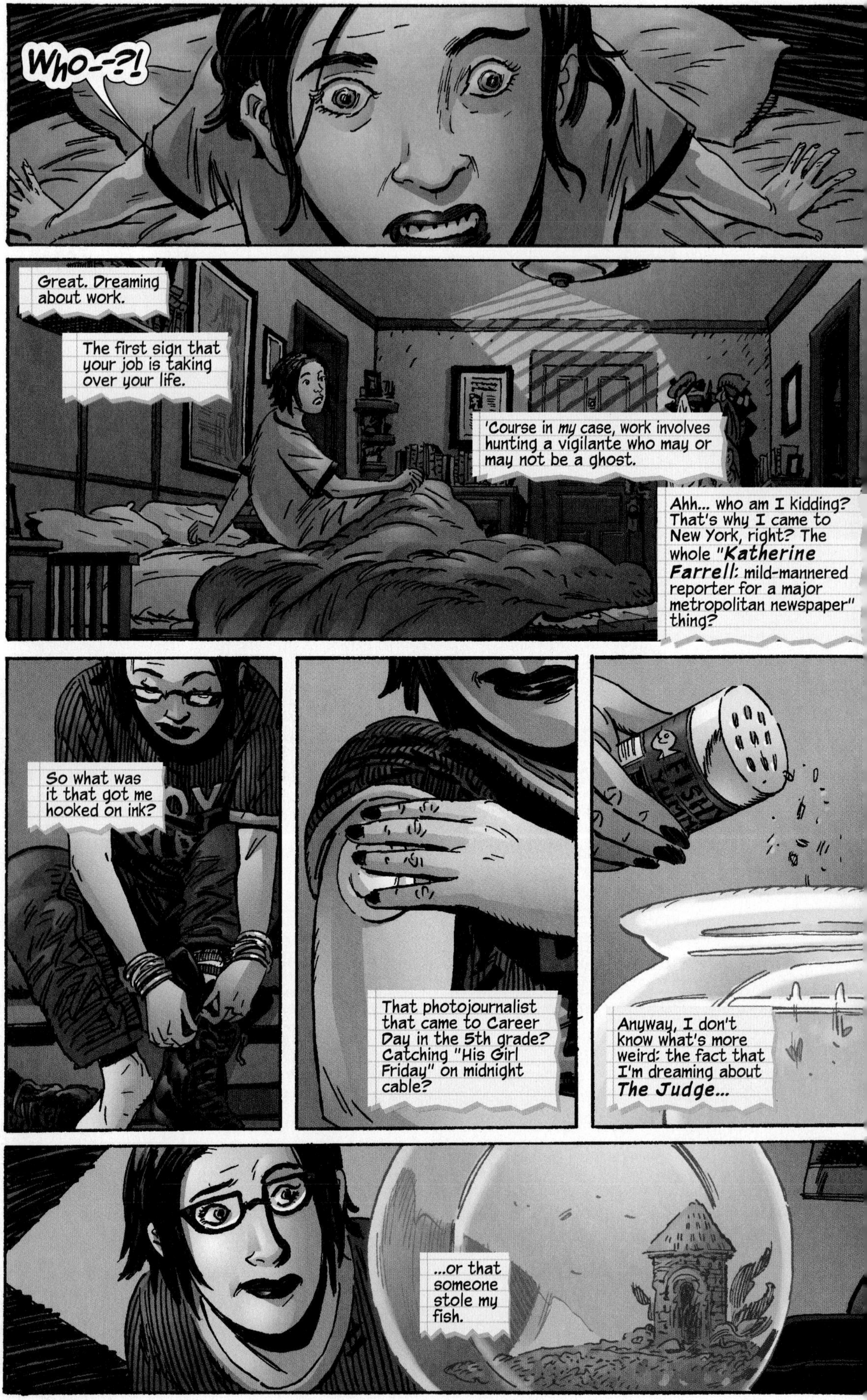
Who--?!
Great. Dreaming about work.
The first sign that your job is taking over your life.
'Course in my case, work involves hunting a vigilante who may or may not be a ghost.
Ahh... who am I kidding? That's why I came to New York, right? The whole "Katherine Farrell: mild-mannered reporter for a major metropolitan newspaper" thing?
So what was it that got me hooked on ink?
That photojournalist that came to Career Day in the 5th grade? Catching "His Girl Friday" on midnight cable?
FISH
Anyway, I don't know what's more weird: the fact that I'm dreaming about The Judge...
...or that someone stole my fish.

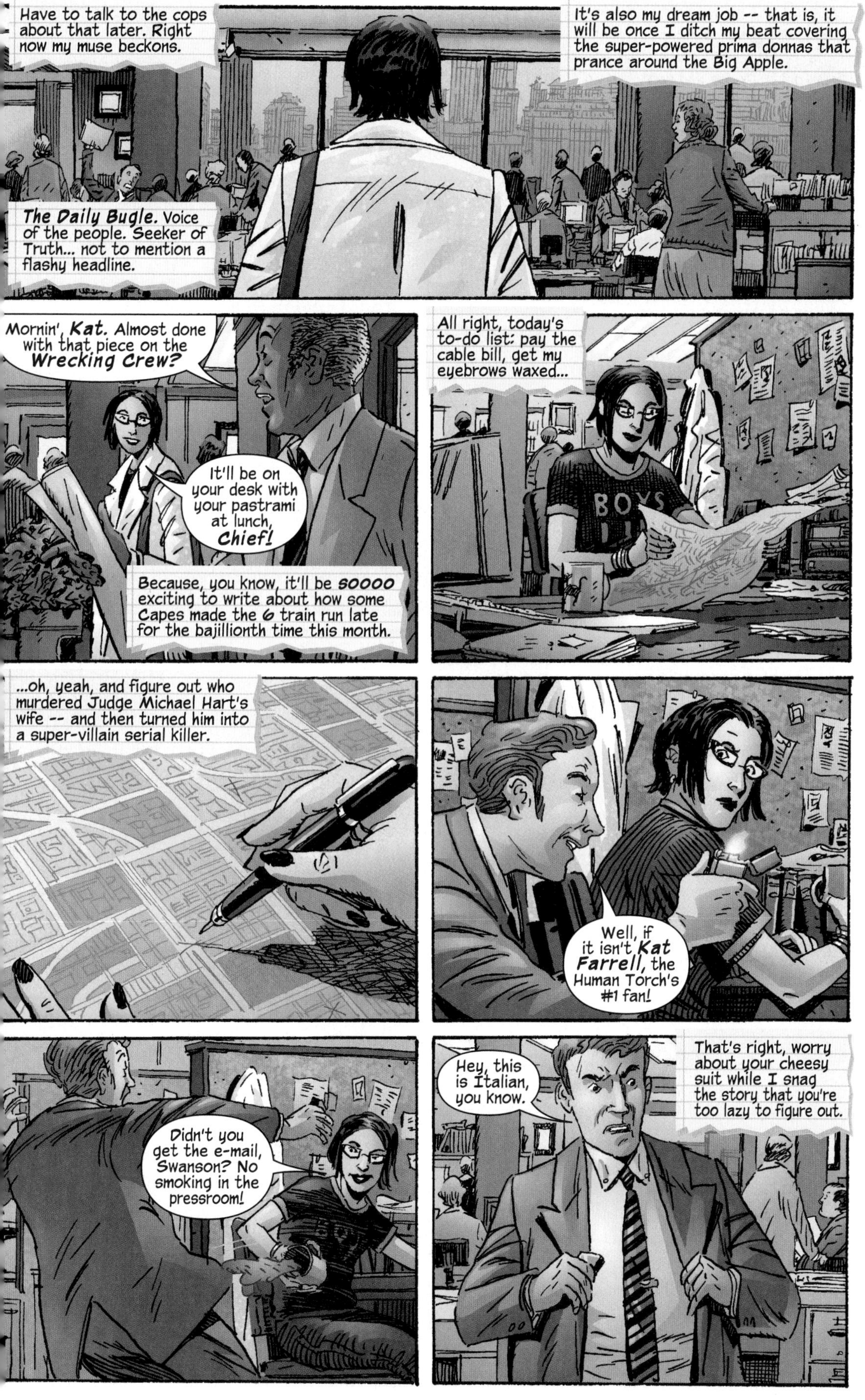

Have to talk to the cops about that later. Right now my muse beckons.
It's also my dream job -- that is, it will be once I ditch my beat covering the super-powered prima donnas that prance around the Big Apple.
The Daily Bugle. Voice of the people. Seeker of Truth... not to mention a flashy headline.
Mornin', Kat. Almost done with that piece on the Wrecking Crew?
It'll be on your desk with your pastrami at lunch, Chief!
Because, you know, it'll be SOOOO exciting to write about how some Capes made the 6 train run late for the bajillionth time this month.
All right, today's to-do list: pay the cable bill, get my eyebrows waxed...
BOYS
...oh, yeah, and figure out who murdered Judge Michael Hart's wife -- and then turned him into a super-villain serial killer.
Well, if it isn't Kat Farrell, the Human Torch's #1 fan!
Didn't you get the e-mail, Swanson? No smoking in the pressroom!
Hey, this is Italian, you know.
That's right, worry about your cheesy suit while I snag the story that you're too lazy to figure out.

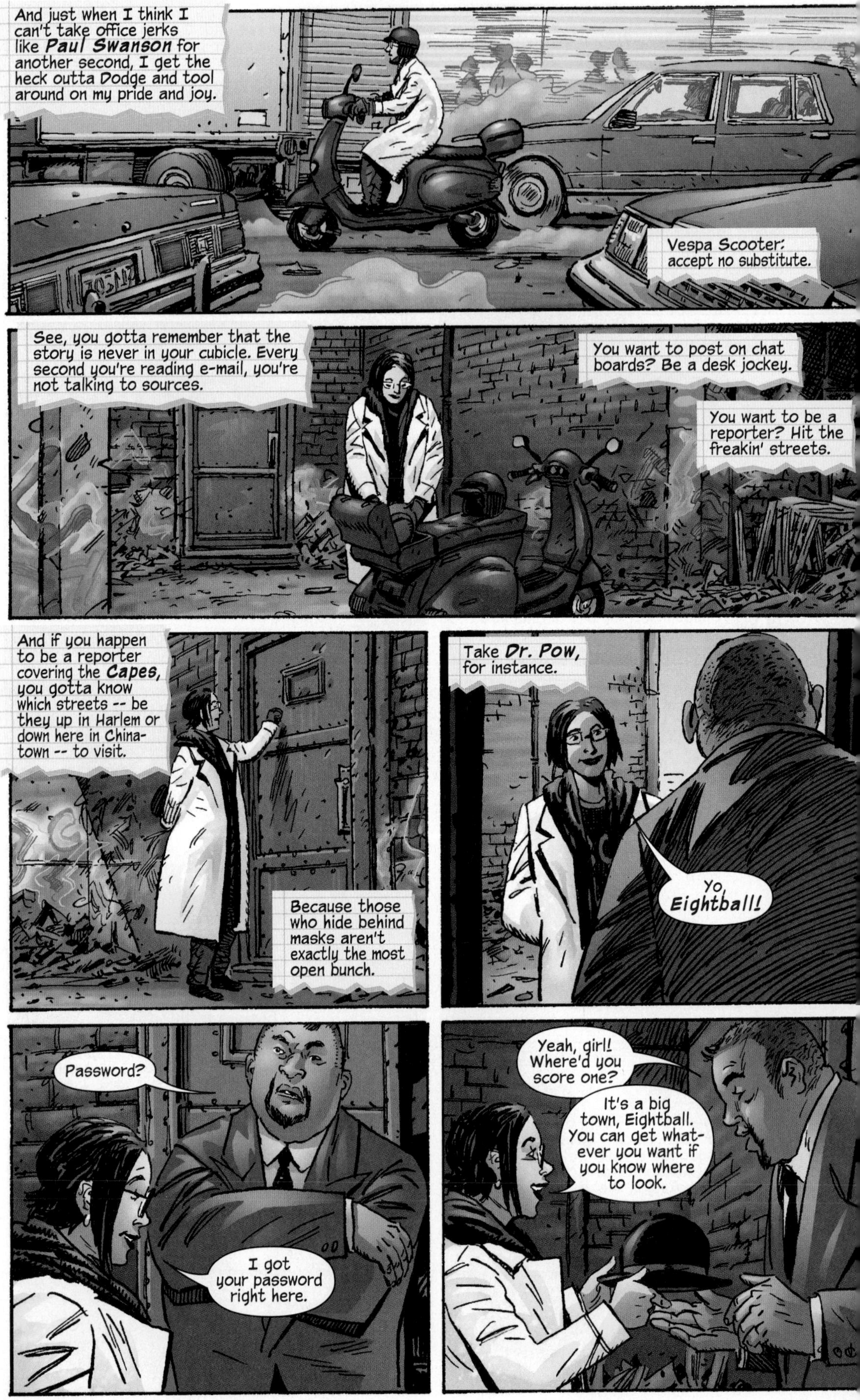
And just when I think I can't take office jerks like Paul Swanson for another second, I get the heck outta Dodge and tool around on my pride and joy.
Vespa Scooter: accept no substitute.
See, you gotta remember that the story is never in your cubicle. Every second you're reading e-mail, you're not talking to sources.
You want to post on chat boards? Be a desk jockey.
You want to be a reporter? Hit the freakin' streets.
And if you happen to be a reporter covering the Capes, you gotta know which streets -- be they up in Harlem or down here in China-town -- to visit.
Because those who hide behind masks aren't exactly the most open bunch.
Take Dr. Pow, for instance.
Yo, Eightball!
Password?
I got your password right here.
Yeah, girl! Where'd you score one?
It's a big town, Eightball. You can get what-ever you want if you know where to look.

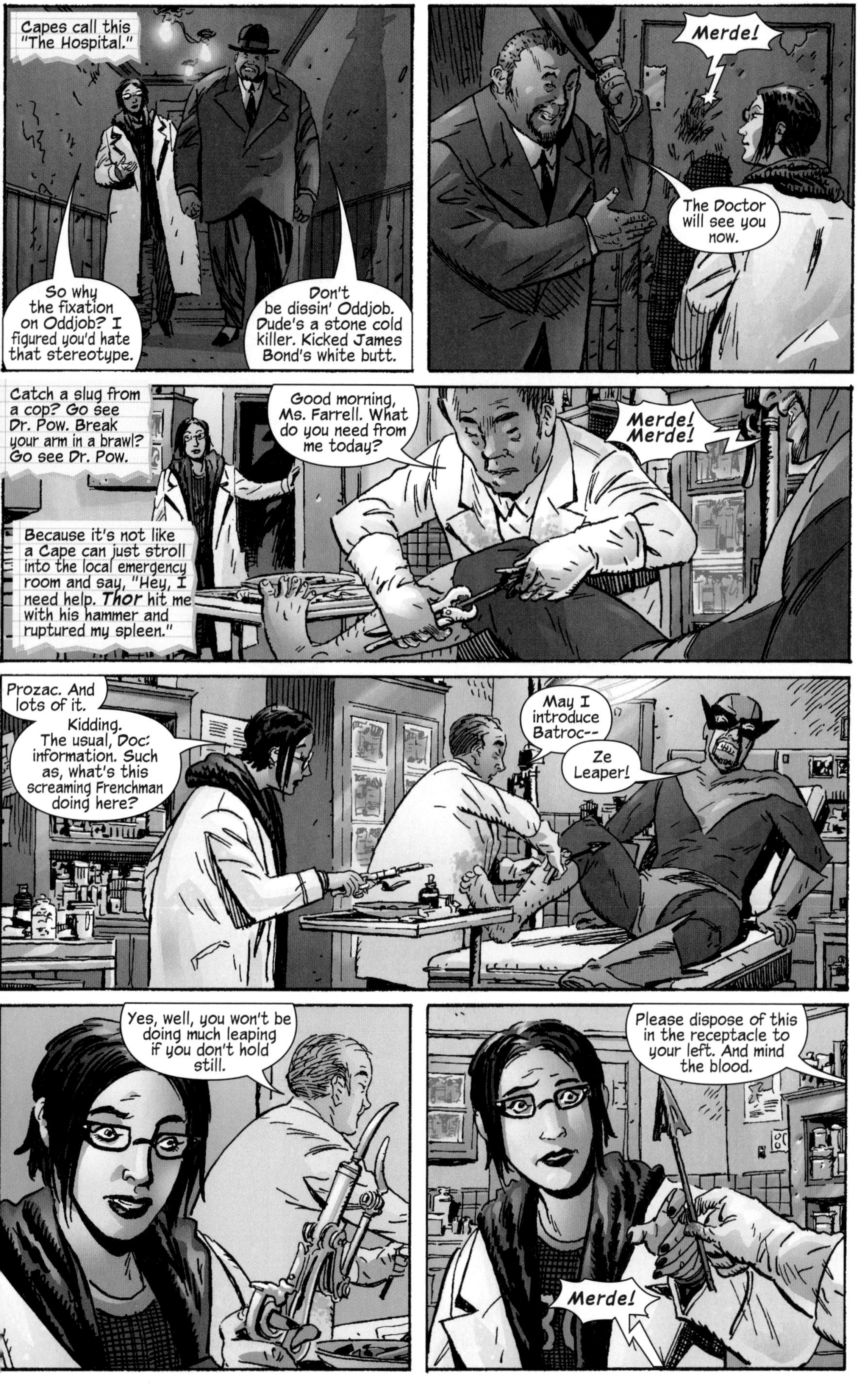
Capes call this "The Hospital."
So why the fixation on Oddjob? I figured you'd hate that stereotype.
Don't be dissin' Oddjob. Dude's a stone cold killer. Kicked James Bond's white butt.
Merde!
The Doctor will see you now.
Catch a slug from a cop? Go see Dr. Pow. Break your arm in a brawl? Go see Dr. Pow.
Because it's not like a Cape can just stroll into the local emergency room and say, "Hey, I need help. Thor hit me with his hammer and ruptured my spleen."
Good morning, Ms. Farrell. What do you need from me today?
Merde! Merde!
Prozac. And lots of it.
Kidding. The usual, Doc: information. Such as, what's this screaming Frenchman doing here?
May I introduce Batroc--
Ze Leaper!
Yes, well, you won't be doing much leaping if you don't hold still.
Please dispose of this in the receptacle to your left. And mind the blood.
Merde!

"Copyright and Trademark *Hawkeye* the Archer"?

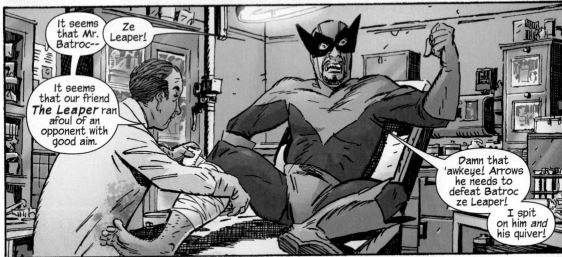

It seems that Mr. Batroc--

Ze Leaper!

It seems that our friend *The Leaper* ran afoul of an opponent with good aim.

Damn that 'awkeye! Arrows he needs to defeat Batroc ze Leaper! I spit on him *and* his quiver!

So listen, Doc, you know I respect the whole doctor/patient confidentiality thing and all, but... uh...

...you wouldn't happen to have patched up Judge Michael Hart a couple months ago?

No, but I heard that someone else helped him. A man who likes to tinker where he should not.

But now, storyteller, let me tell you a tale.

There once was a male and female fox that lived near a farm. And the farmer, he killed the lady fox.

And Mr. Fox?

He did not rest until he had killed every one of the farmer's chickens. Which he then laid on the farmer's doorstep.

An angry spirit is loose upon the city. Do not cross his path.

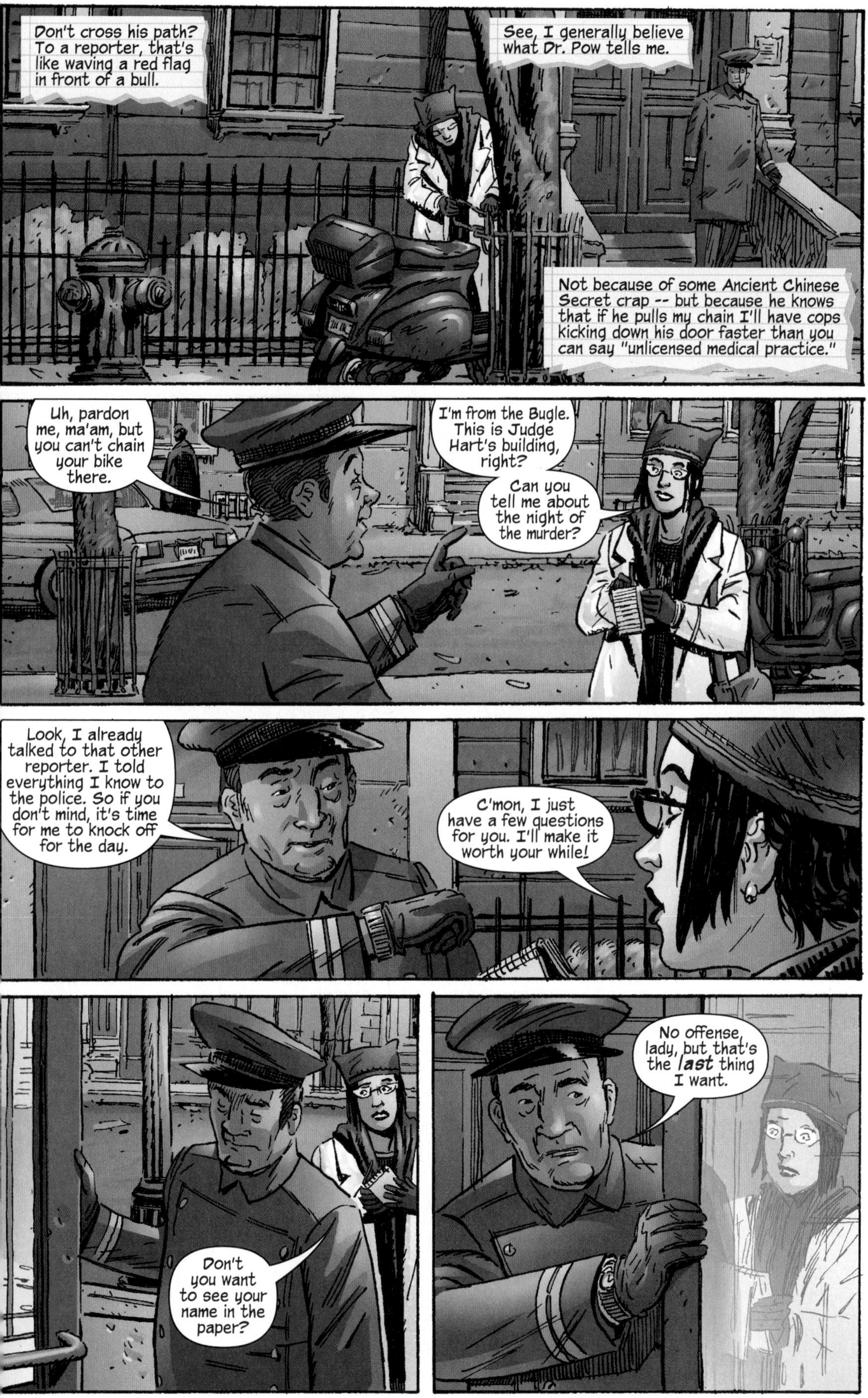

Don't cross his path? To a reporter, that's like waving a red flag in front of a bull.
See, I generally believe what Dr. Pow tells me.
Not because of some Ancient Chinese Secret crap -- but because he knows that if he pulls my chain I'll have cops kicking down his door faster than you can say "unlicensed medical practice."
Uh, pardon me, ma'am, but you can't chain your bike there.
I'm from the Bugle. This is Judge Hart's building, right?
Can you tell me about the night of the murder?
Look, I already talked to that other reporter. I told everything I know to the police. So if you don't mind, it's time for me to knock off for the day.
C'mon, I just have a few questions for you. I'll make it worth your while!
Don't you want to see your name in the paper?
No offense, lady, but that's the *last* thing I want.

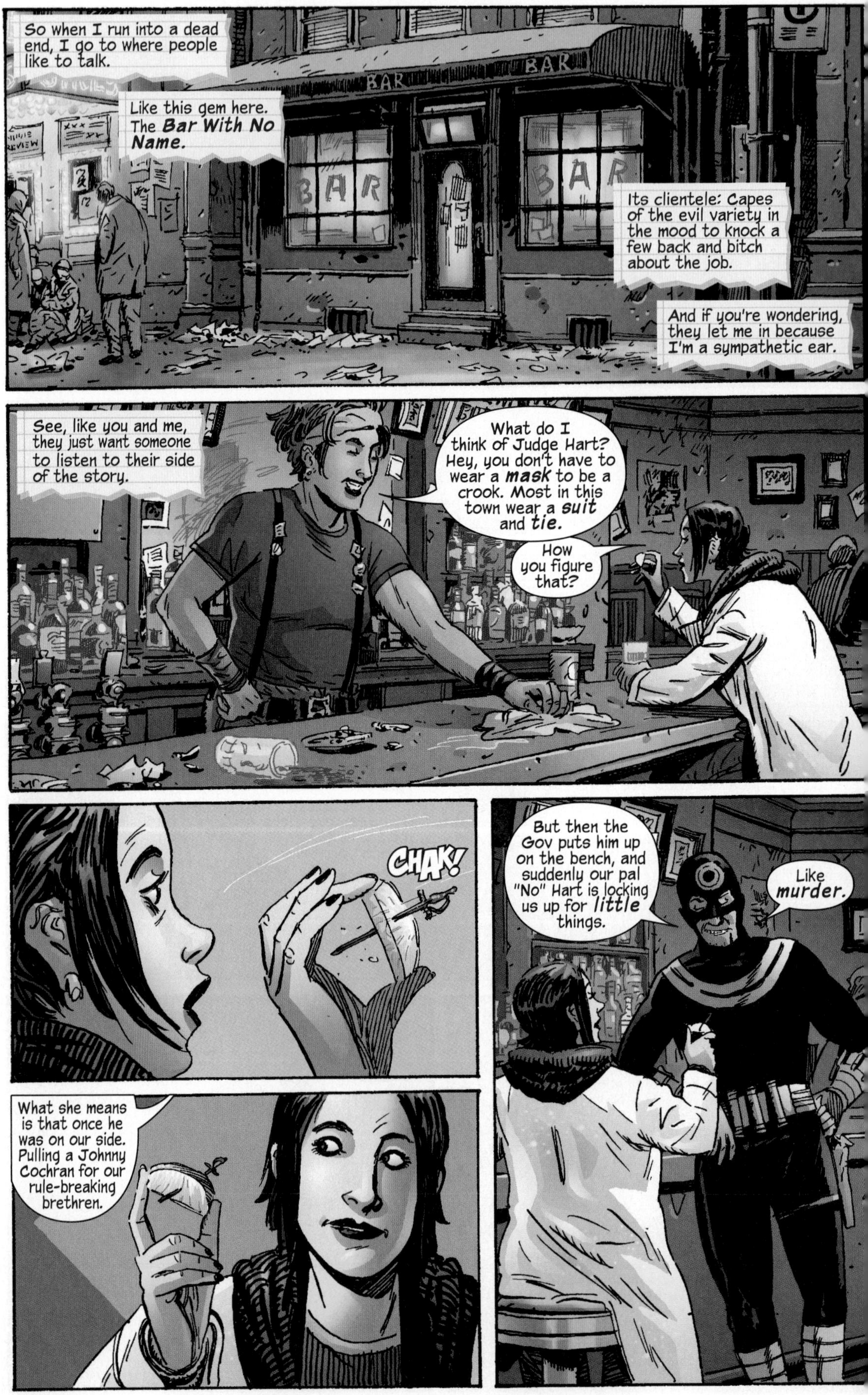
So when I run into a dead end, I go to where people like to talk.
Like this gem here. The Bar With No Name.
Its clientele: Capes of the evil variety in the mood to knock a few back and bitch about the job.
And if you're wondering, they let me in because I'm a sympathetic ear.
See, like you and me, they just want someone to listen to their side of the story.
What do I think of Judge Hart? Hey, you don't have to wear a mask to be a crook. Most in this town wear a suit and tie.
How you figure that?
CHAK!
But then the Gov puts him up on the bench, and suddenly our pal "No" Hart is locking us up for little things.
Like murder.
What she means is that once he was on our side. Pulling a Johnny Cochran for our rule-breaking brethren.

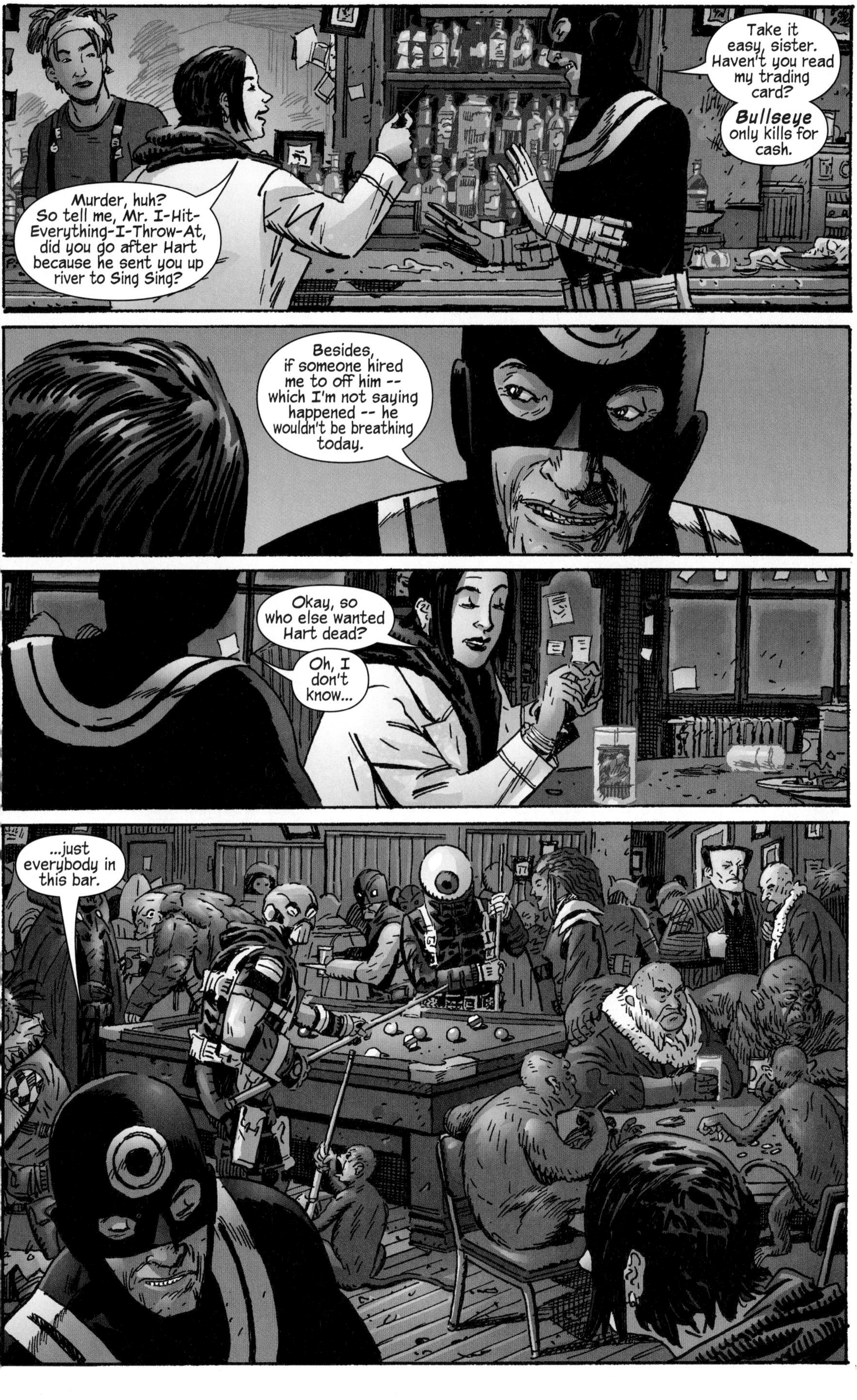
Take it easy, sister. Haven't you read my trading card?
Bullseye only kills for cash.
Murder, huh? So tell me, Mr. I-Hit-Everything-I-Throw-At, did you go after Hart because he sent you up river to Sing Sing?
Besides, if someone hired me to off him -- which I'm not saying happened -- he wouldn't be breathing today.
Okay, so who else wanted Hart dead?
Oh, I don't know...
...just everybody in this bar.

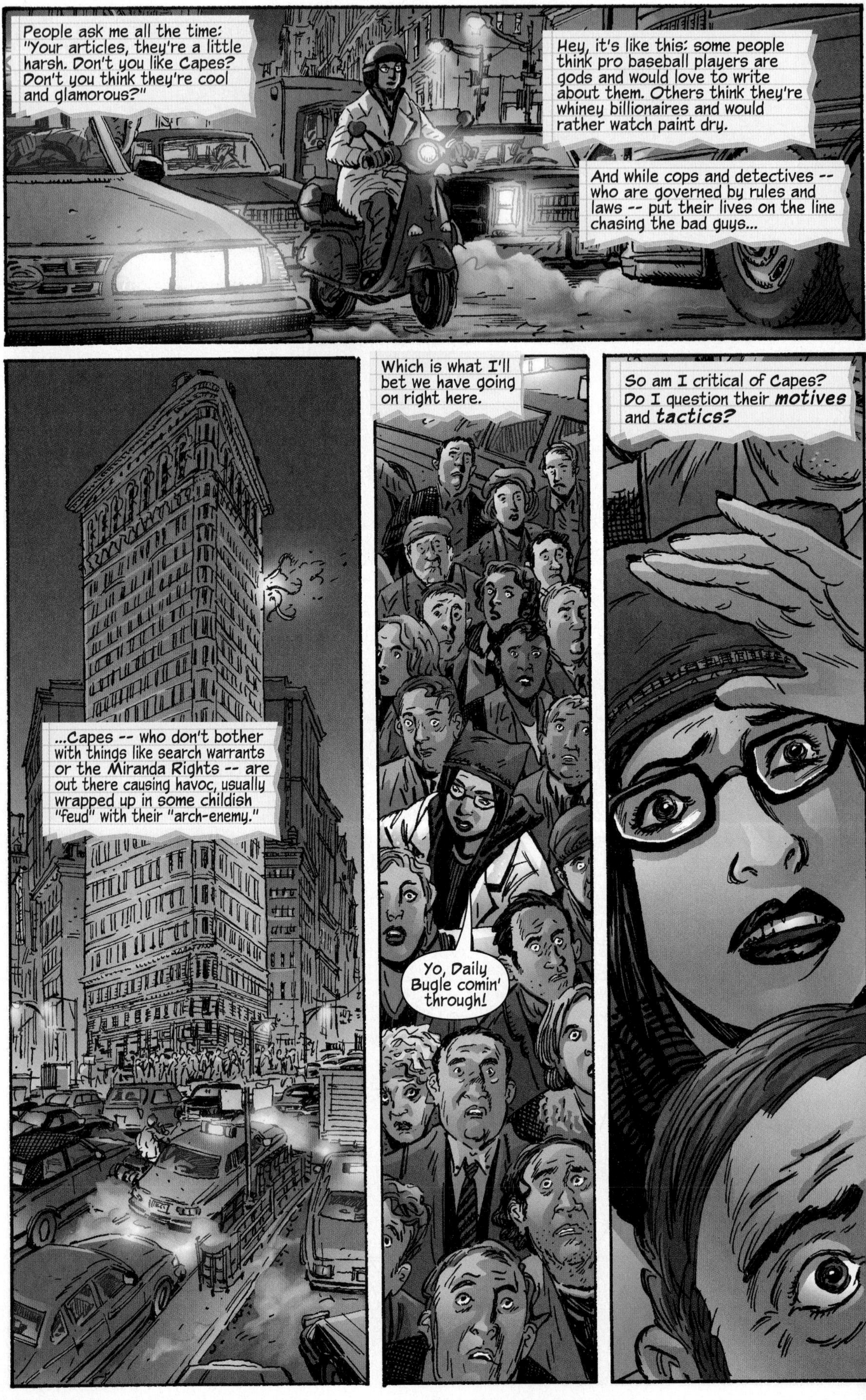
People ask me all the time: "Your articles, they're a little harsh. Don't you like Capes? Don't you think they're cool and glamorous?"
Hey, it's like this: some people think pro baseball players are gods and would love to write about them. Others think they're whiney billionaires and would rather watch paint dry.
And while cops and detectives -- who are governed by rules and laws -- put their lives on the line chasing the bad guys...
...Capes -- who don't bother with things like search warrants or the Miranda Rights -- are out there causing havoc, usually wrapped up in some childish "feud" with their "arch-enemy."
Which is what I'll bet we have going on right here.
Yo, Daily Bugle comin' through!
So am I critical of Capes? Do I question their *motives* and *tactics?*

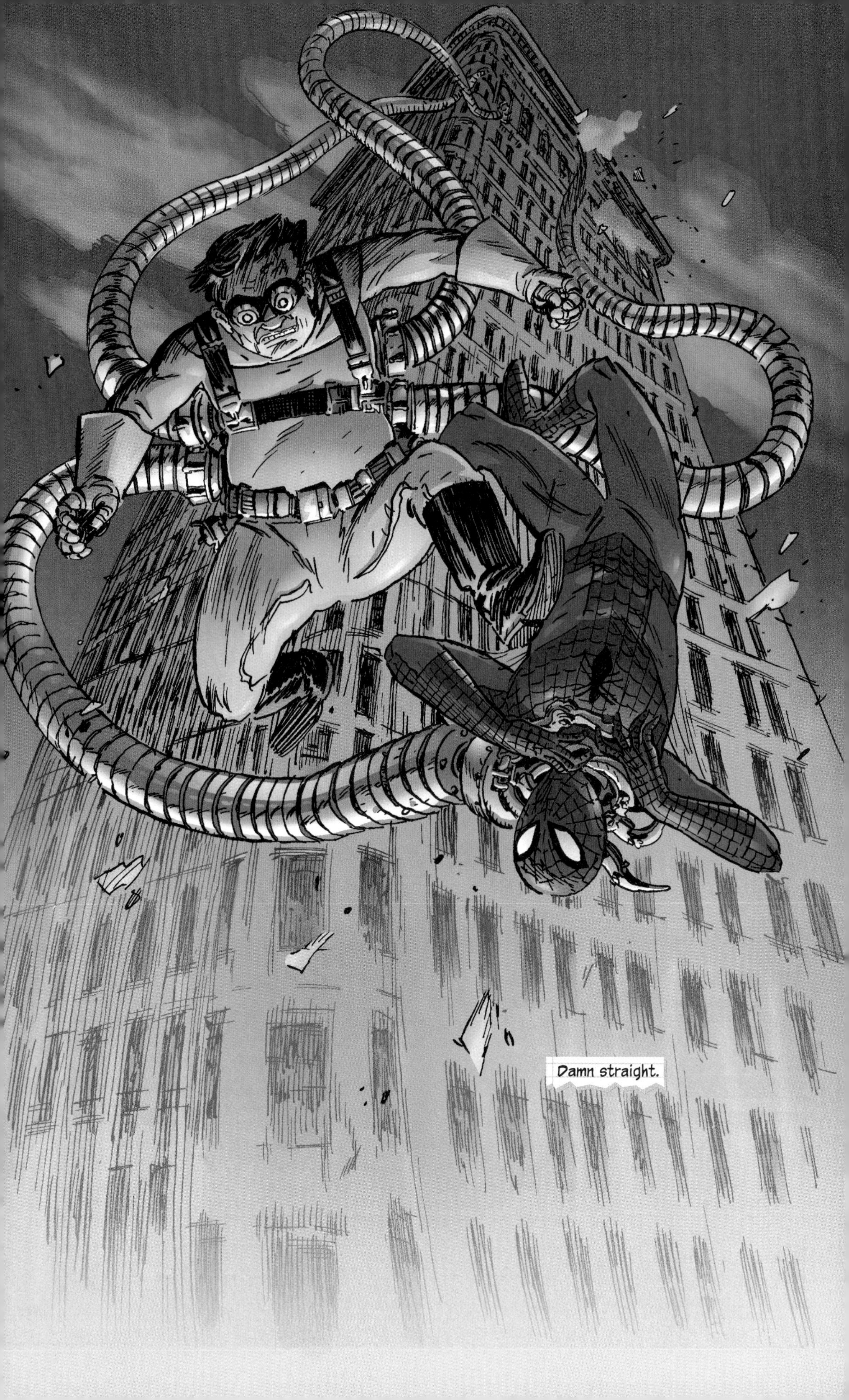
Damn straight.

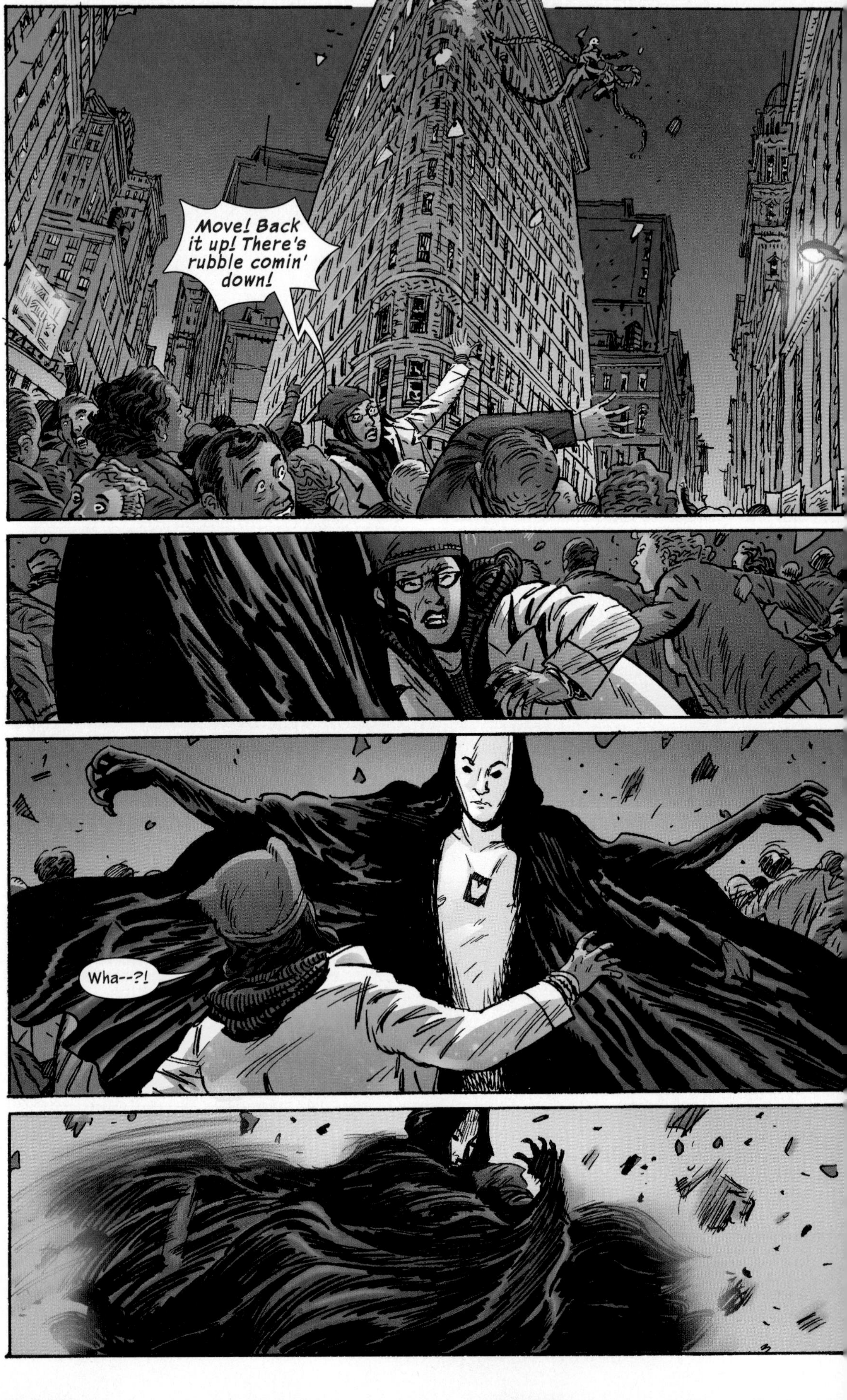
Move! Back it up! There's rubble comin' down!
Wha--?!

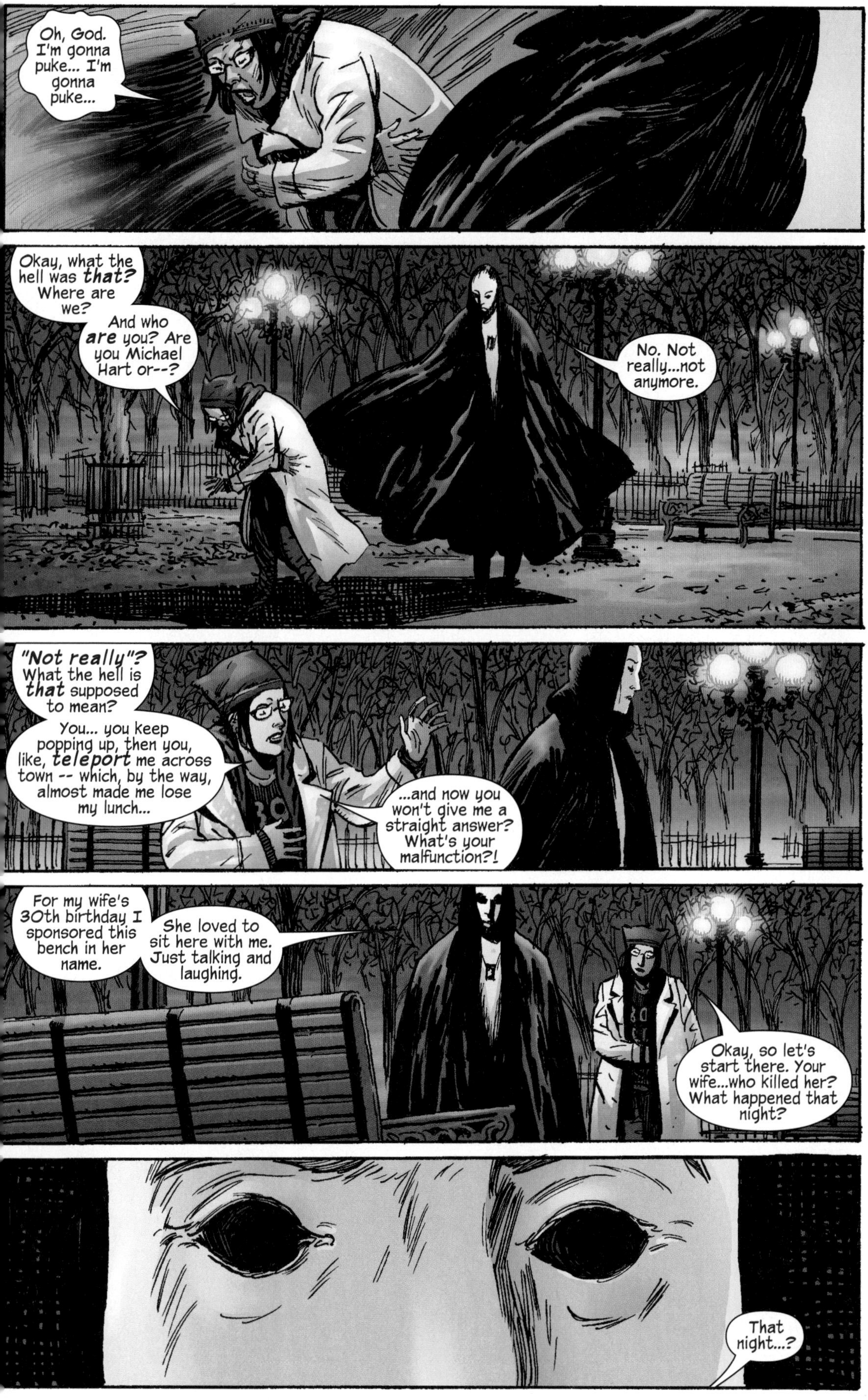
Oh, God. I'm gonna puke... I'm gonna puke...
Okay, what the hell was *that?* Where are we?
And who *are* you? Are you Michael Hart or--?
No. Not really...not anymore.
"Not really"? What the hell is *that* supposed to mean?
You... you keep popping up, then you, like, *teleport* me across town -- which, by the way, almost made me lose my lunch...
...and now you won't give me a straight answer? What's your malfunction?!
For my wife's 30th birthday I sponsored this bench in her name.
She loved to sit here with me. Just talking and laughing.
Okay, so let's start there. Your wife...who killed her? What happened that night?
That night...?

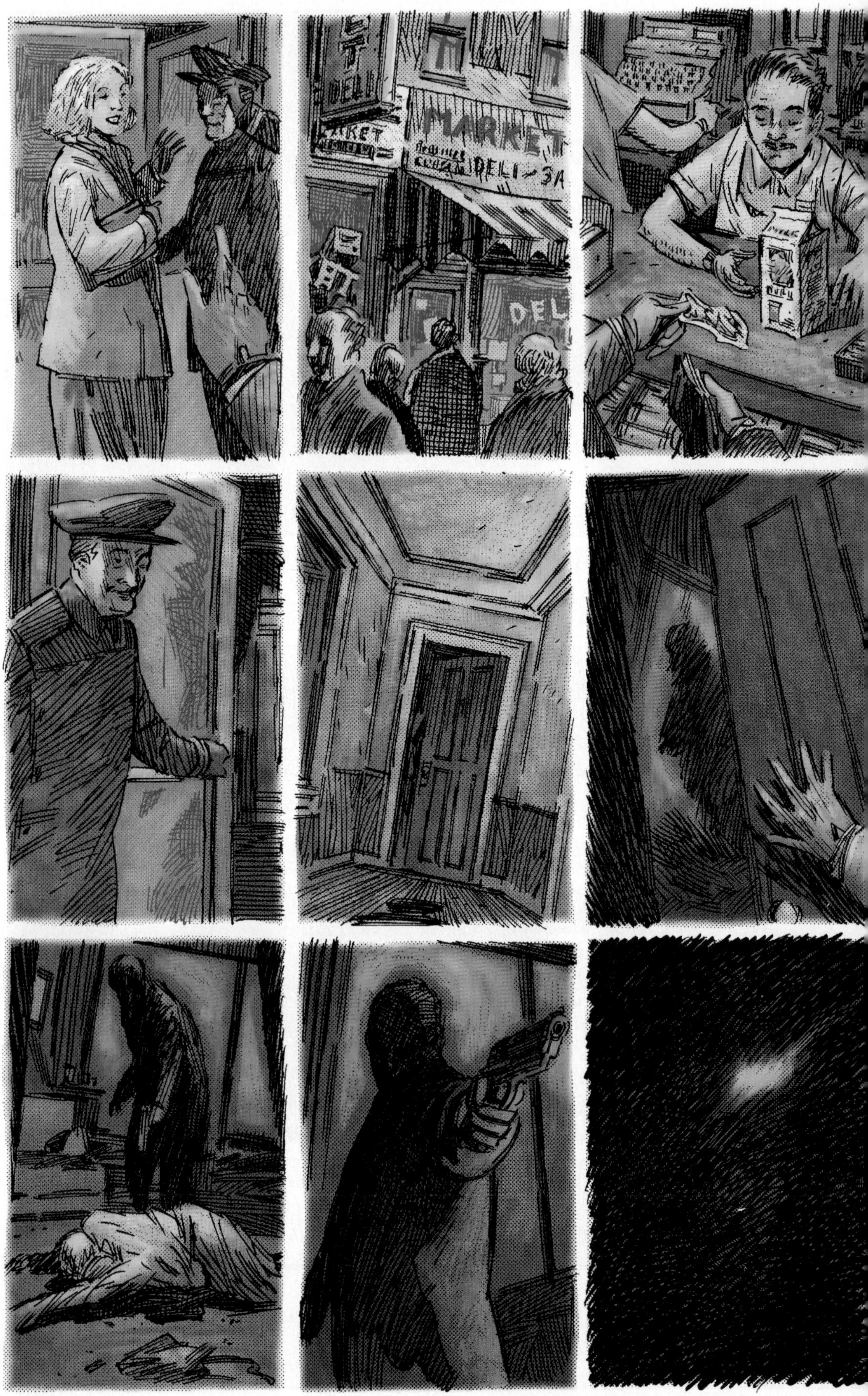
MARKET
DELI

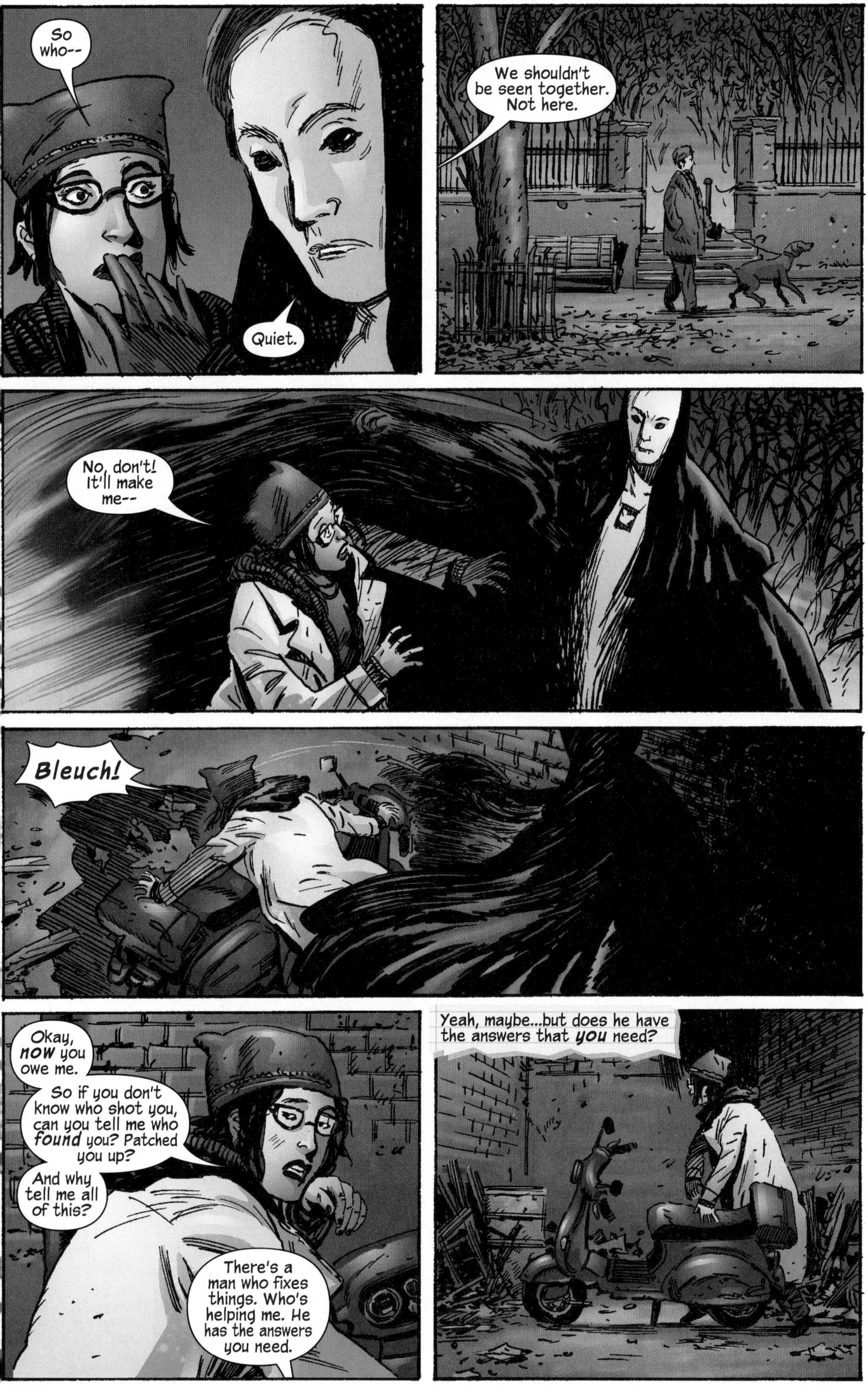
So who--
Quiet.
We shouldn't be seen together. Not here.
No, don't! It'll make me--
Bleuch!
Okay, NOW you owe me.
So if you don't know who shot you, can you tell me who found you? Patched you up?
And why tell me all of this?
There's a man who fixes things. Who's helping me. He has the answers you need.
Yeah, maybe...but does he have the answers that YOU need?

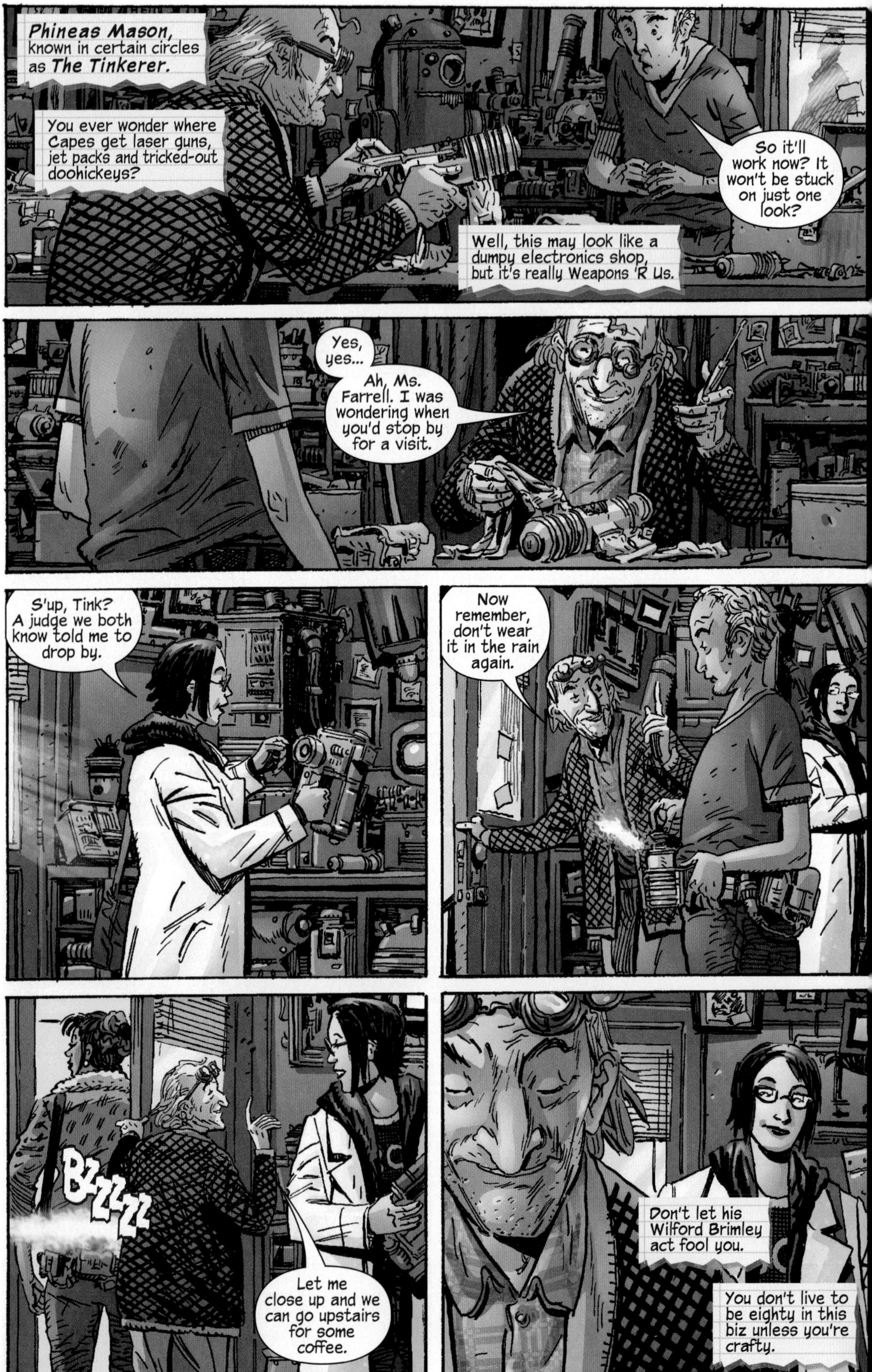
Phineas Mason, known in certain circles as The Tinkerer.
You ever wonder where Capes get laser guns, jet packs and tricked-out doohickeys?
Well, this may look like a dumpy electronics shop, but it's really Weapons 'R Us.
So it'll work now? It won't be stuck on just one look?
Yes, yes...
Ah, Ms. Farrell. I was wondering when you'd stop by for a visit.
S'up, Tink? A judge we both know told me to drop by.
Now remember, don't wear it in the rain again.
BZZZZZ
Let me close up and we can go upstairs for some coffee.
Don't let his Wilford Brimley act fool you.
You don't live to be eighty in this biz unless you're crafty.

Perhaps you'd like to see my greenhouse? I could get some pruning done as we talk.

Sounds like a plan.

TAPE SMACK-DOWN

EGGS
MILK
TOILET PAPER

FINAL
Tuesday, October 1
DAILY BUGLE
NEW YORK'S FINEST DAILY NEWSPAPER
Partly cloudy, chance of snow. High 25-3

"THE AGENT" FOUND DEAD

I imagine that many people you encounter lie or feign ignorance of their involvement with crimes.

But at my age I have neither the time nor the patience for games.

Uh-huh. So where'd you find Hart's body?

You're direct. How refreshing.

It was early, about three months ago. I was taking my morning walk down the West Side Promenade. That's when I get most of my good ideas.

And there -- washed up on the shore -- was a man.

I suppose my inquisitive nature got the best of me, because I turned him over and checked for a pulse. I found one, but just barely.

And you recognized him?

I'd have to be senile not to. After all, Hart had sentenced me once.

So then?

Then I put him in a taxi and brought him here.

Now why would you do that? Help a man who sent you to jail? And why not just take him to a hospital?

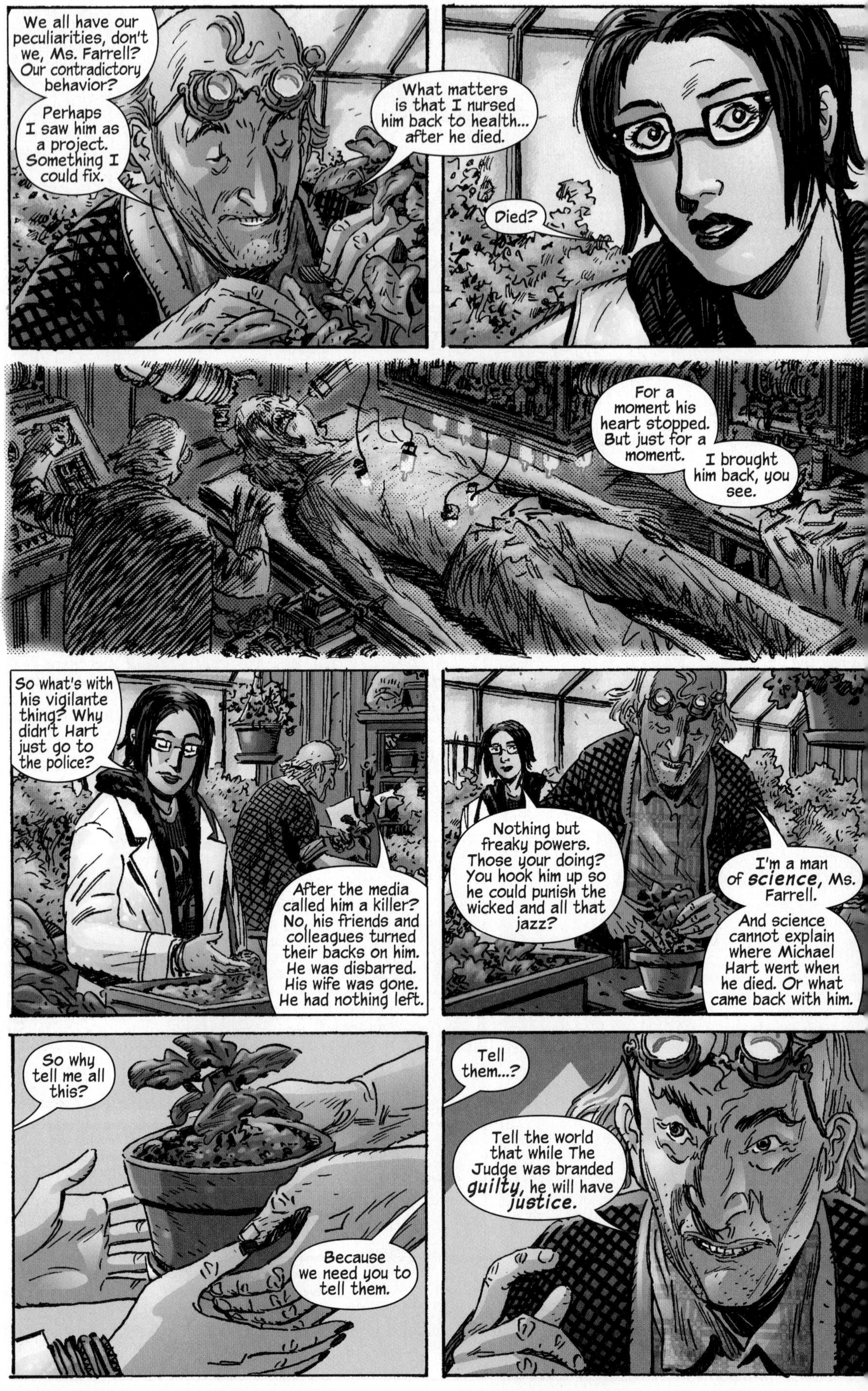
We all have our peculiarities, don't we, Ms. Farrell? Our contradictory behavior?
Perhaps I saw him as a project. Something I could fix.
What matters is that I nursed him back to health... after he died.
Died?
For a moment his heart stopped. But just for a moment.
I brought him back, you see.
So what's with his vigilante thing? Why didn't Hart just go to the police?
After the media called him a killer? No, his friends and colleagues turned their backs on him. He was disbarred. His wife was gone. He had nothing left.
Nothing but freaky powers. Those your doing? You hook him up so he could punish the wicked and all that jazz?
I'm a man of science, Ms. Farrell.
And science cannot explain where Michael Hart went when he died. Or what came back with him.
So why tell me all this?
Because we need you to tell them.
Tell them...?
Tell the world that while The Judge was branded guilty, he will have justice.

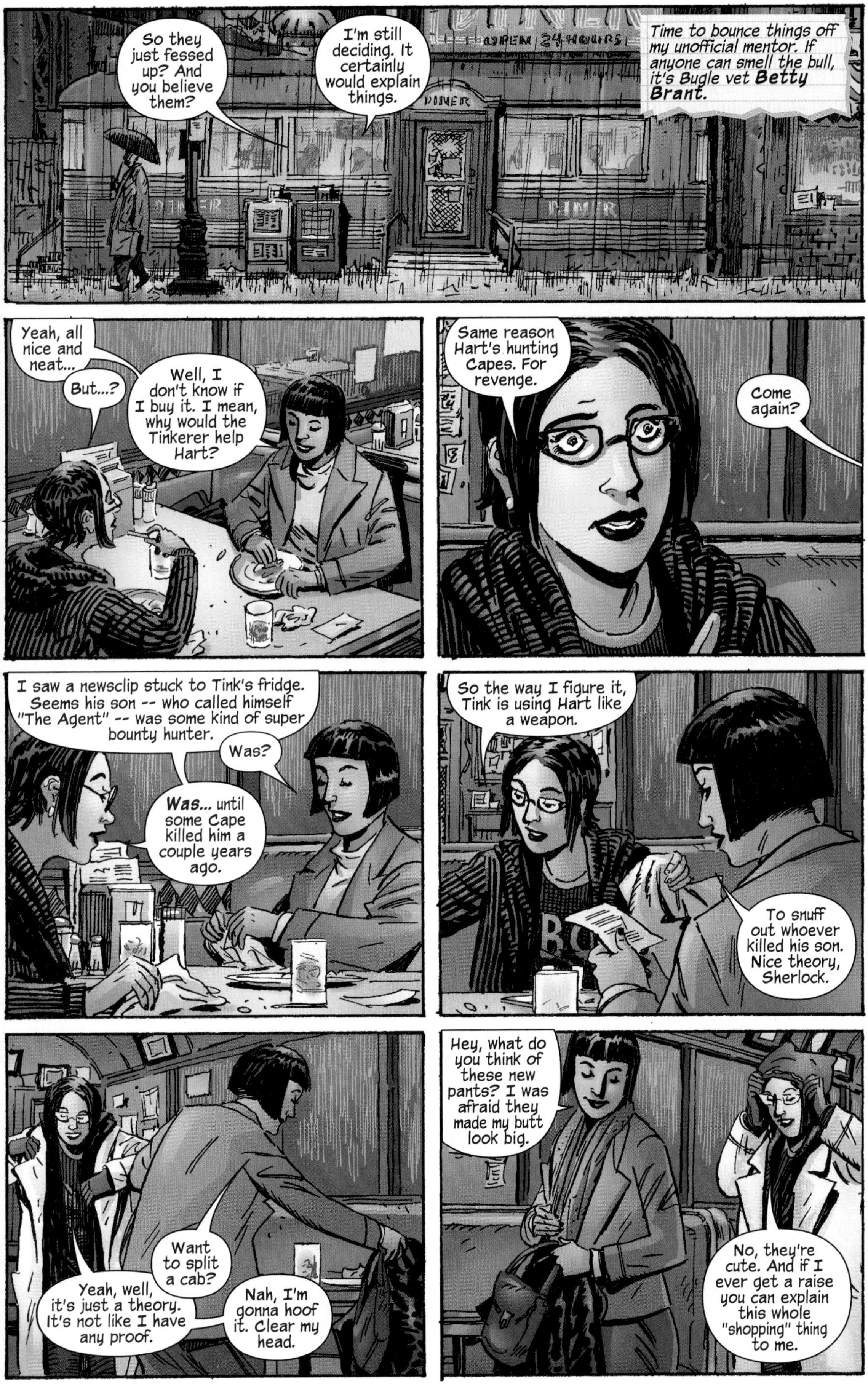
So they just fessed up? And you believe them?
I'm still deciding. It certainly would explain things.
OPEN 24 HOURS
DINER
Time to bounce things off my unofficial mentor. If anyone can smell the bull, it's Bugle vet Betty Brant.
Yeah, all nice and neat...
But...?
Well, I don't know if I buy it. I mean, why would the Tinkerer help Hart?
Same reason Hart's hunting Capes. For revenge.
Come again?
I saw a newsclip stuck to Tink's fridge. Seems his son -- who called himself "The Agent" -- was some kind of super bounty hunter.
Was?
Was... until some Cape killed him a couple years ago.
So the way I figure it, Tink is using Hart like a weapon.
To snuff out whoever killed his son. Nice theory, Sherlock.
Yeah, well, it's just a theory. It's not like I have any proof.
Want to split a cab?
Nah, I'm gonna hoof it. Clear my head.
Hey, what do you think of these new pants? I was afraid they made my butt look big.
No, they're cute. And if I ever get a raise you can explain this whole "shopping" thing to me.

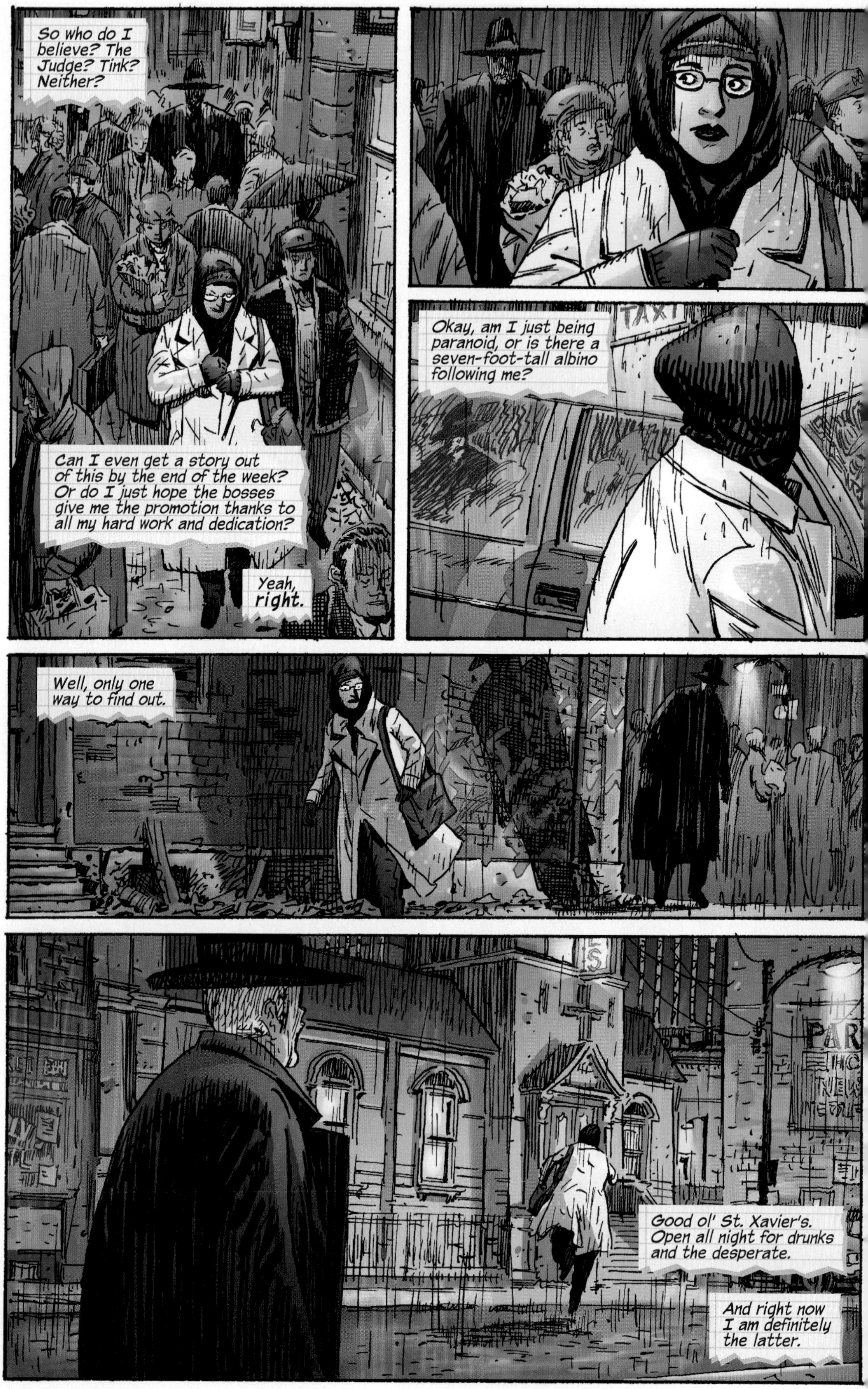
So who do I believe? The Judge? Tink? Neither?
Can I even get a story out of this by the end of the week? Or do I just hope the bosses give me the promotion thanks to all my hard work and dedication?
Yeah, right.
Okay, am I just being paranoid, or is there a seven-foot-tall albino following me?
TAXI
Well, only one way to find out.
Good ol' St. Xavier's. Open all night for drunks and the desperate.
And right now I am definitely the latter.

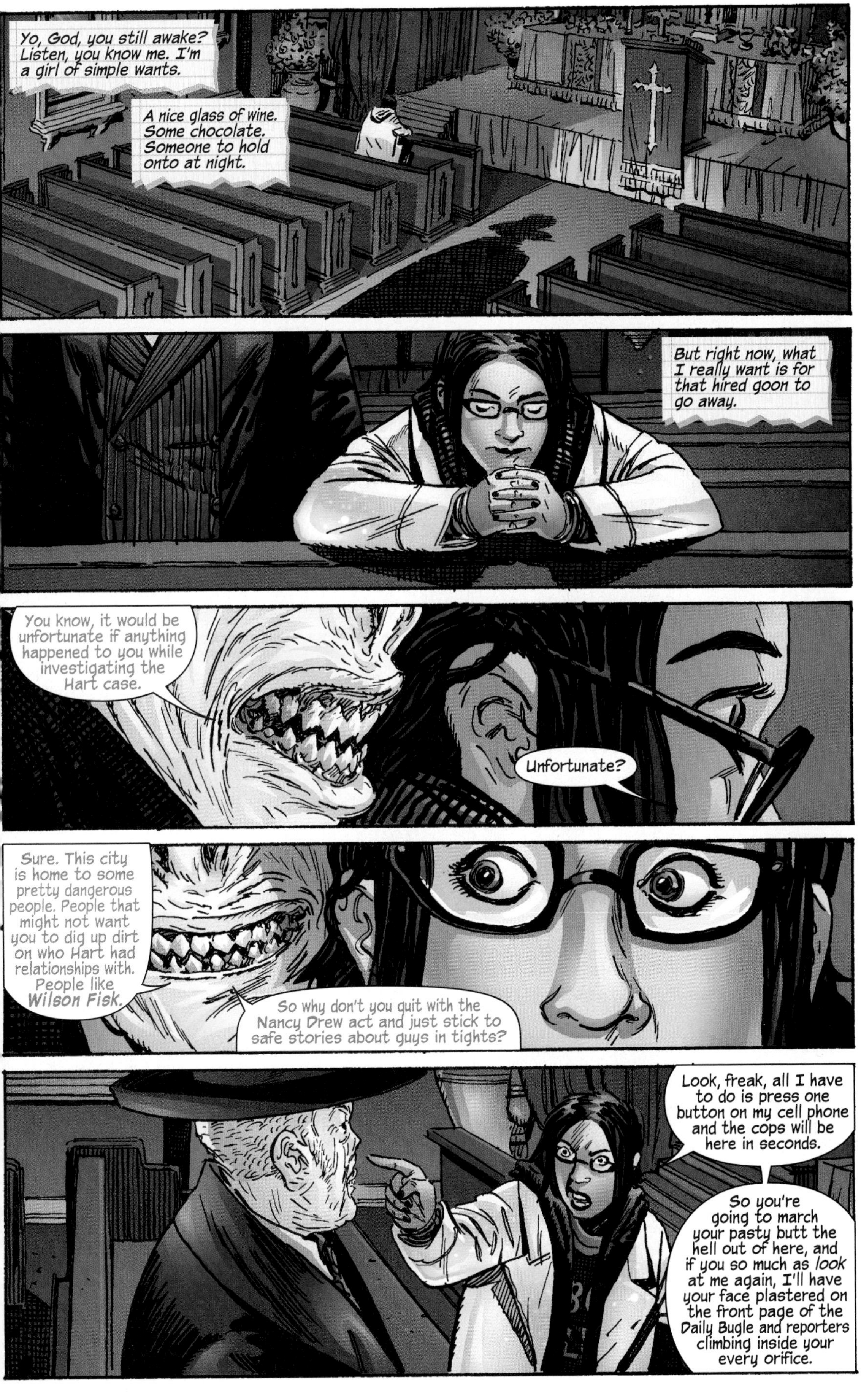
Yo, God, you still awake? Listen, you know me. I'm a girl of simple wants.
A nice glass of wine. Some chocolate. Someone to hold onto at night.
But right now, what I really want is for that hired goon to go away.
You know, it would be unfortunate if anything happened to you while investigating the Hart case.
Unfortunate?
Sure. This city is home to some pretty dangerous people. People that might not want you to dig up dirt on who Hart had relationships with. People like Wilson Fisk.
So why don't you quit with the Nancy Drew act and just stick to safe stories about guys in tights?
Look, freak, all I have to do is press one button on my cell phone and the cops will be here in seconds.
So you're going to march your pasty butt the hell out of here, and if you so much as look at me again, I'll have your face plastered on the front page of the Daily Bugle and reporters climbing inside your every orifice.

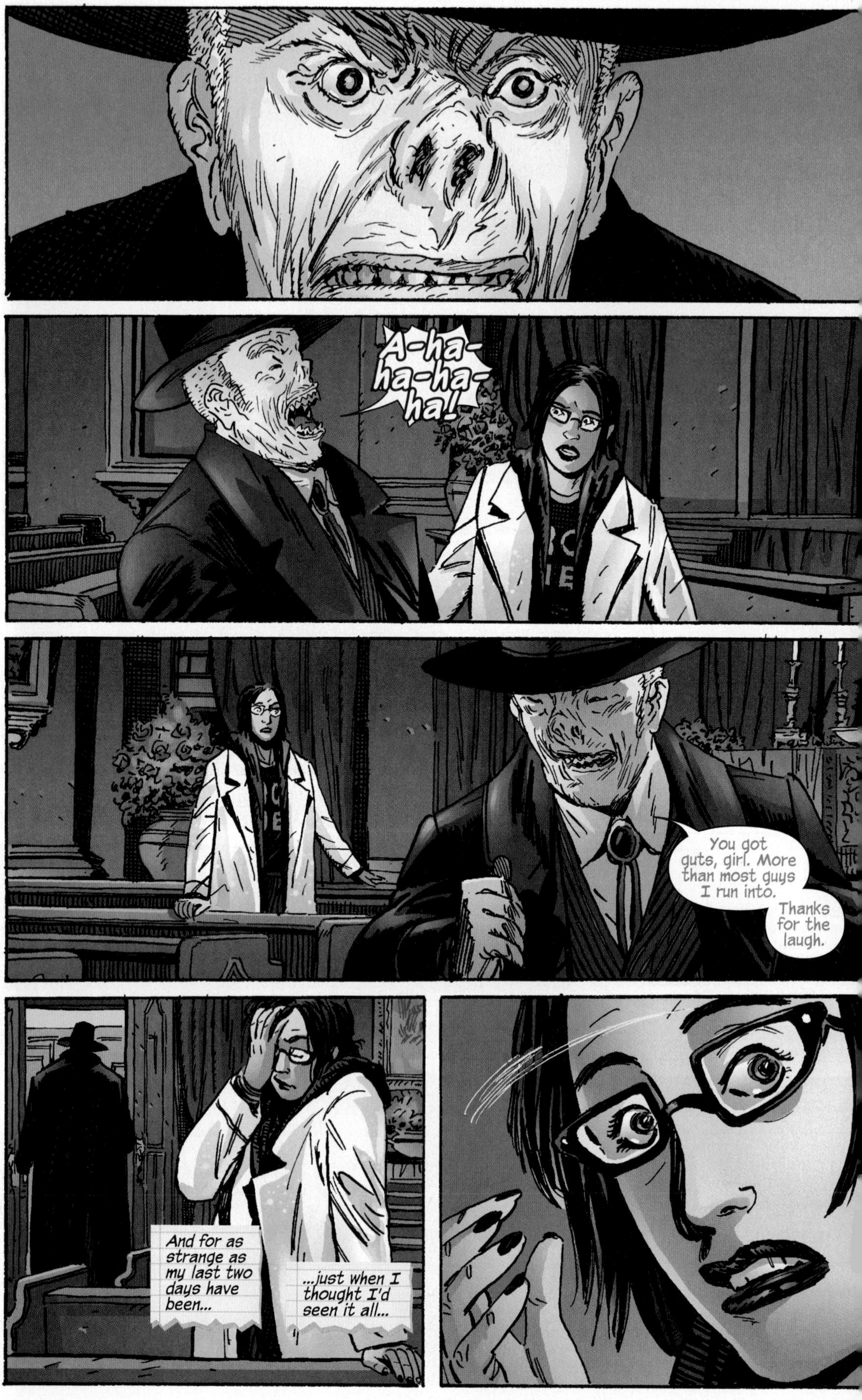
A-ha-ha-ha-ha-ha!
You got guts, girl. More than most guys I run into.
Thanks for the laugh.
And for as strange as my last two days have been...
...just when I thought I'd seen it all...

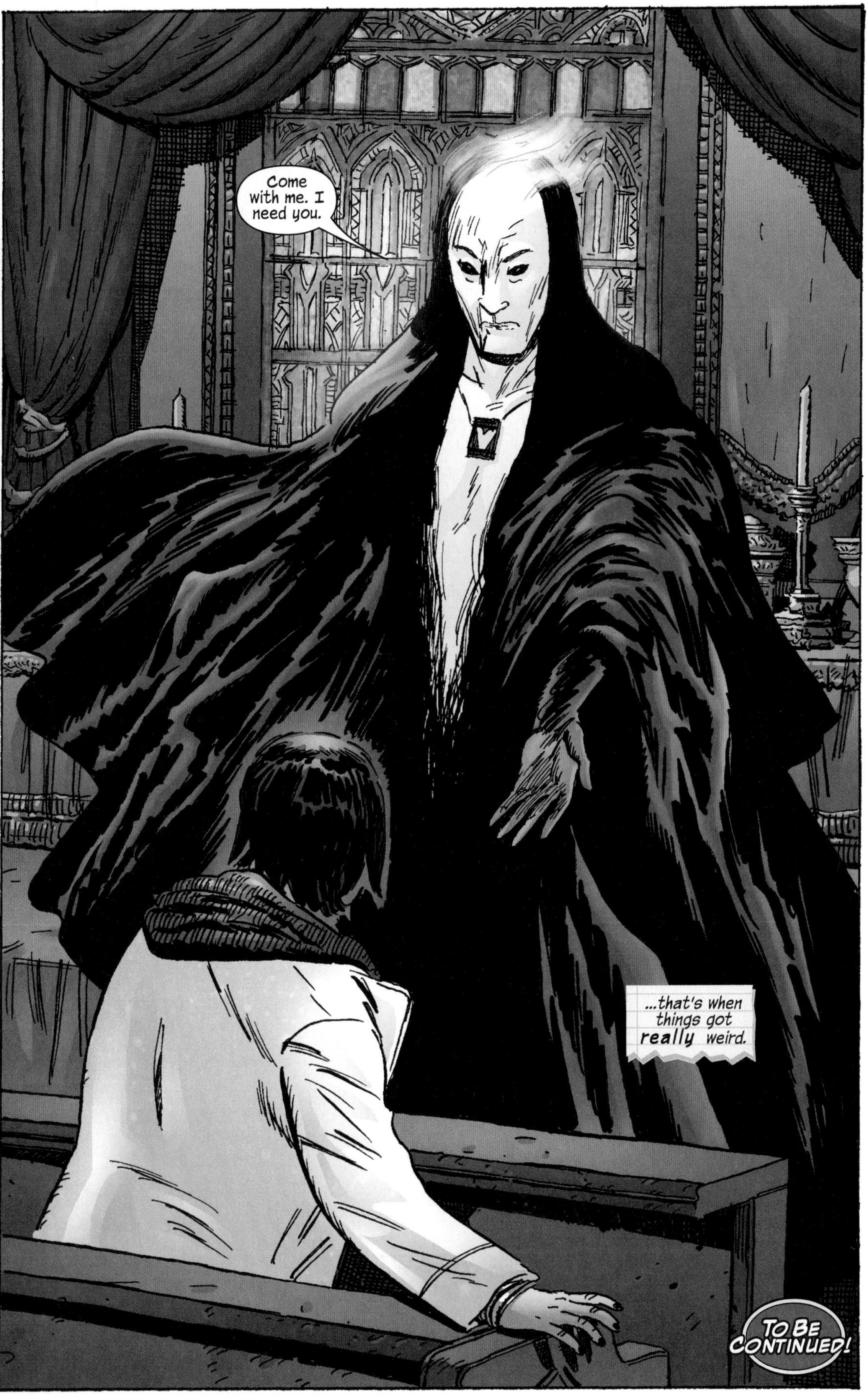
Come with me. I need you.
...that's when things got really weird.
TO BE CONTINUED!

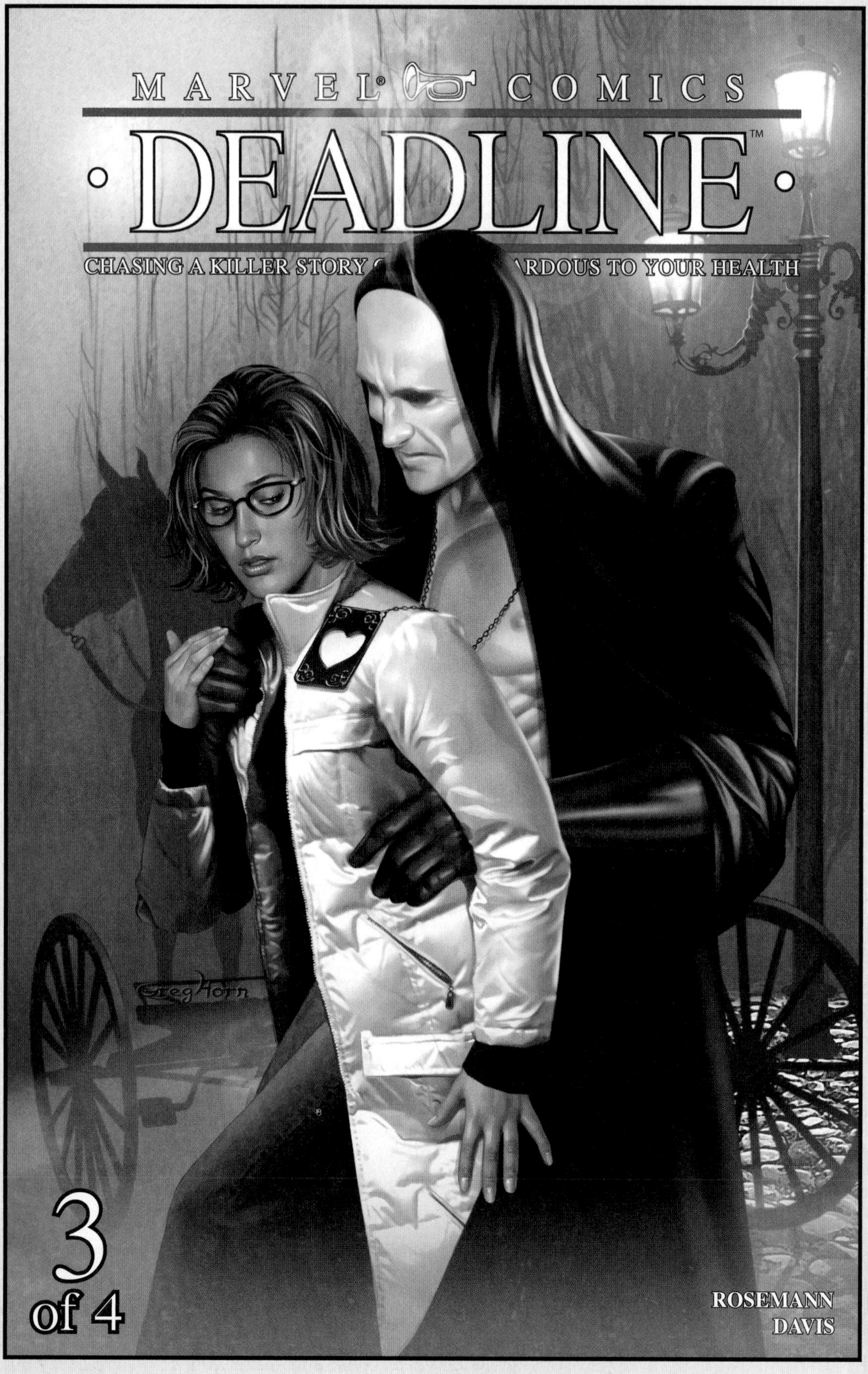
MARVEL COMICS
DEADLINE
CHASING A KILLER STORY
ARDOUS TO YOUR HEALTH
Greg Horn
3 of 4
ROSEMANN
DAVIS

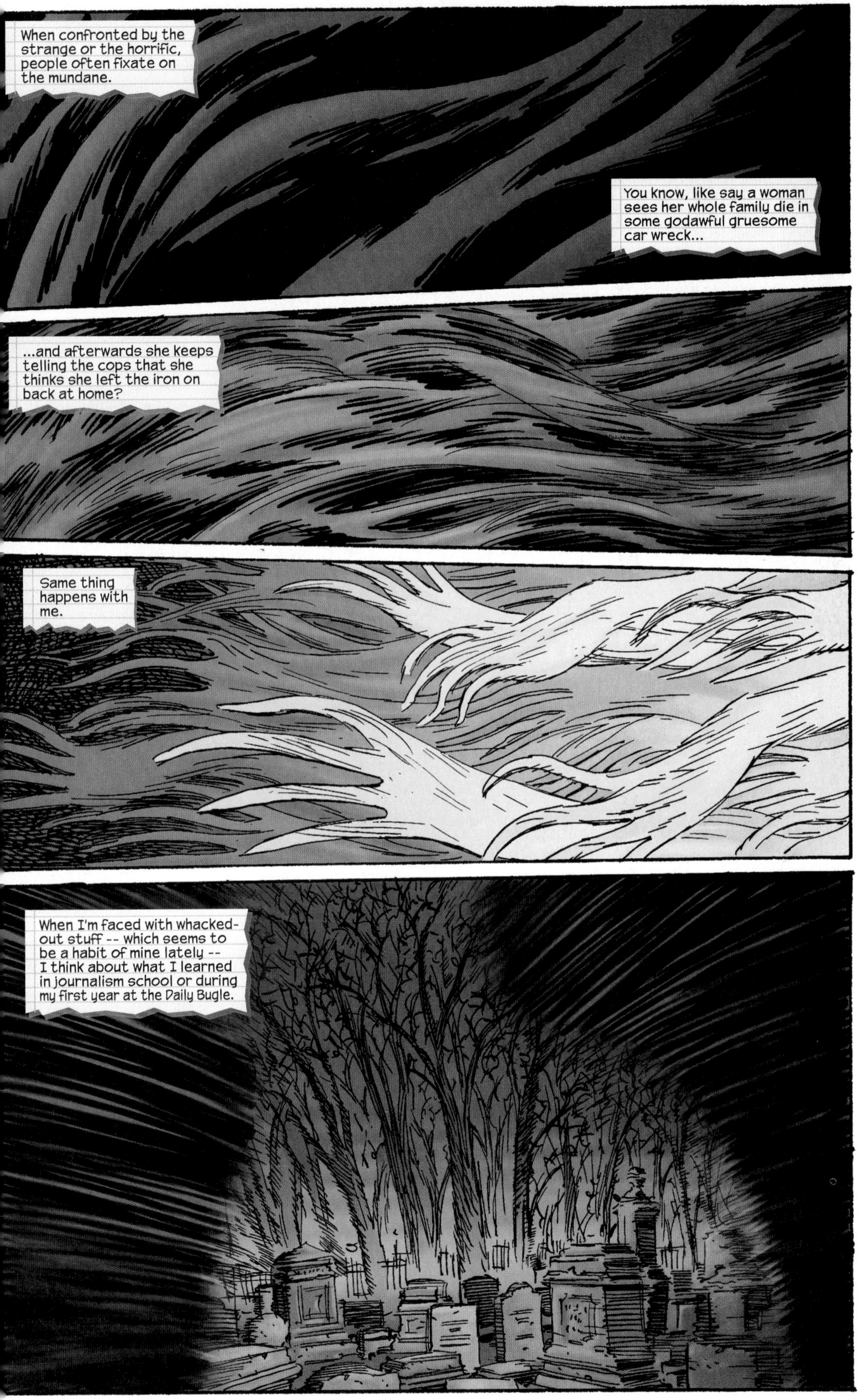
When confronted by the strange or the horrific, people often fixate on the mundane.
You know, like say a woman sees her whole family die in some godawful gruesome car wreck...
...and afterwards she keeps telling the cops that she thinks she left the iron on back at home?
Same thing happens with me.
When I'm faced with whacked-out stuff -- which seems to be a habit of mine lately -- I think about what I learned in journalism school or during my first year at the Daily Bugle.

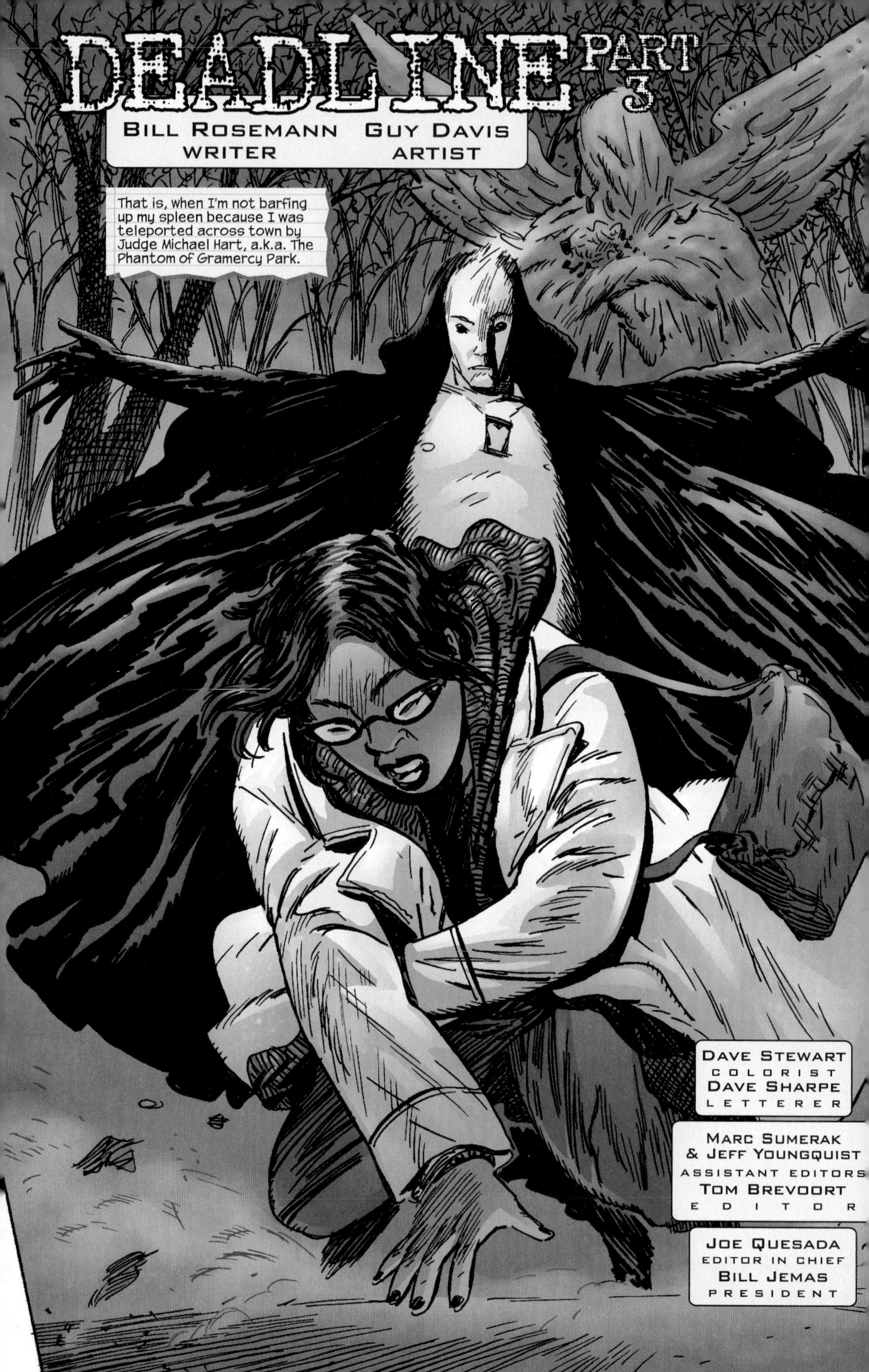
DEADLINE PART 3
BILL ROSEMANN WRITER
GUY DAVIS ARTIST
That is, when I'm not barfing up my spleen because I was teleported across town by Judge Michael Hart, a.k.a. The Phantom of Gramercy Park.
DAVE STEWART COLORIST
DAVE SHARPE LETTERER
MARC SUMERAK & JEFF YOUNGQUIST ASSISTANT EDITORS
TOM BREVOORT EDITOR
JOE QUESADA EDITOR IN CHIEF
BILL JEMAS PRESIDENT

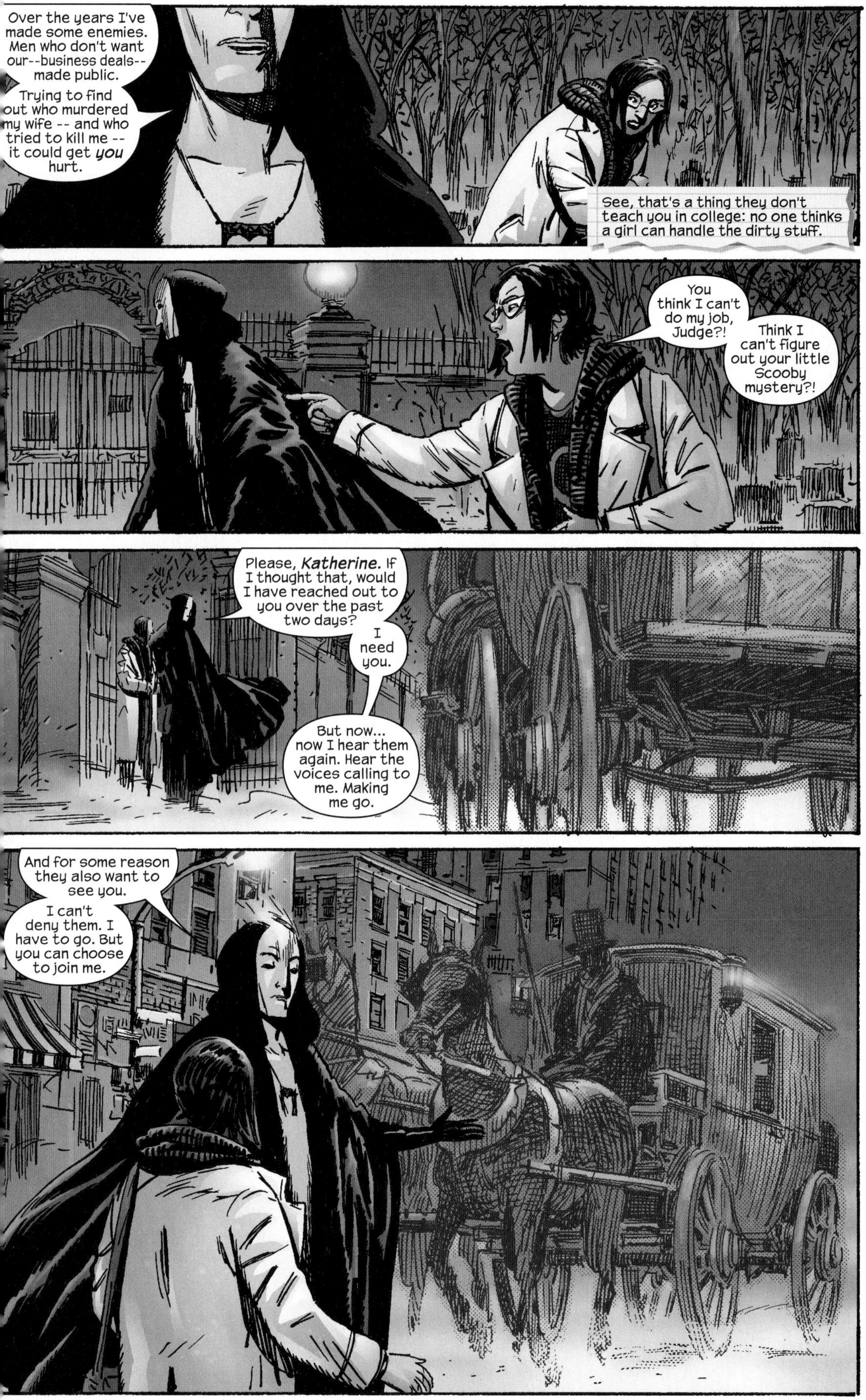
Over the years I've made some enemies. Men who don't want our--business deals--made public.
Trying to find out who murdered my wife -- and who tried to kill me -- it could get *you* hurt.
See, that's a thing they don't teach you in college: no one thinks a girl can handle the dirty stuff.
You think I can't do my job, Judge?!
Think I can't figure out your little Scooby mystery?!
Please, *Katherine.* If I thought that, would I have reached out to you over the past two days?
I need you.
But now... now I hear them again. Hear the voices calling to me. Making me go.
And for some reason they also want to see you.
I can't deny them. I have to go. But you can choose to join me.

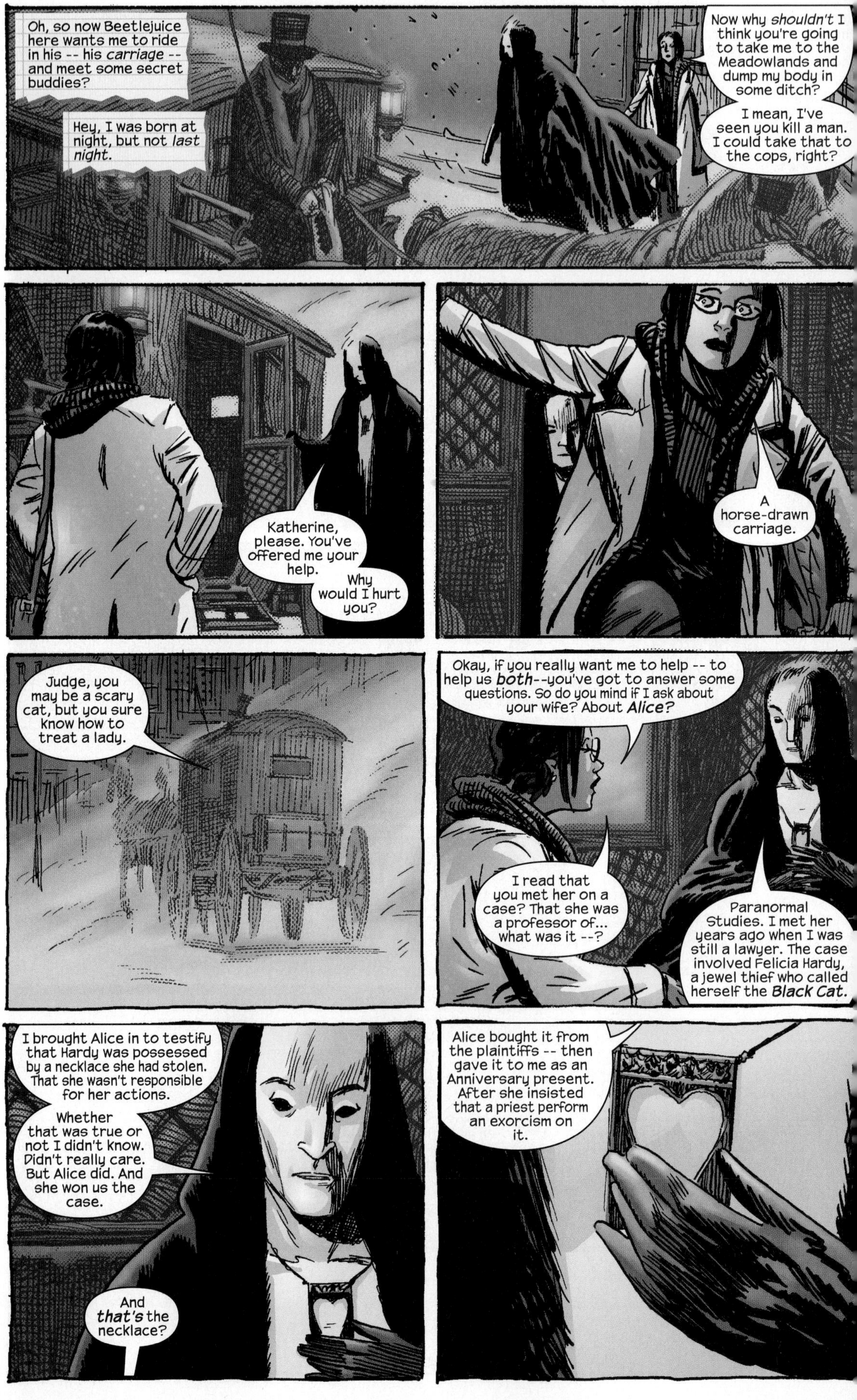

Oh, so now Beetlejuice here wants me to ride in his -- his *carriage* -- and meet some secret buddies?
Hey, I was born at night, but not *last night*.
Now why *shouldn't* I think you're going to take me to the Meadowlands and dump my body in some ditch?
I mean, I've seen you kill a man. I could take that to the cops, right?
Katherine, please. You've offered me your help.
Why would I hurt you?
A horse-drawn carriage.
Judge, you may be a scary cat, but you sure know how to treat a lady.
Okay, if you really want me to help -- to help us **both**--you've got to answer some questions. So do you mind if I ask about your wife? About ***Alice?***
I read that you met her on a case? That she was a professor of... what was it --?
Paranormal Studies. I met her years ago when I was still a lawyer. The case involved Felicia Hardy, a jewel thief who called herself the ***Black Cat.***
I brought Alice in to testify that Hardy was possessed by a necklace she had stolen. That she wasn't responsible for her actions.
Whether that was true or not I didn't know. Didn't really care. But Alice did. And she won us the case.
And ***that's*** the necklace?
Alice bought it from the plaintiffs -- then gave it to me as an Anniversary present. After she insisted that a priest perform an exorcism on it.

And -- no offense -- but how did you two fit together?

I mean, here you were this ambitious, slick lawyer and her the spiritual believer. Not exactly the perfect match.

Perfect? Wouldn't you describe saving a man's soul as perfect?

Saving him from his worst impulses? From himself?

But I couldn't save her.

Hey, you're trying now, right? Isn't that what this is all about? Getting her justice?

Okay, why am I crossing the line?

Am I just comforting him to keep him talking? Or do I really feel bad for him? Or something more?

Is that what you call this? Justice?

Don't you see the blood?

I see a man looking for answers.

And who's in serious need of help.

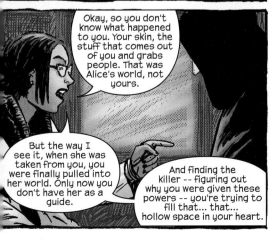

Okay, so you don't know what happened to you. Your skin, the stuff that comes out of you and grabs people. That was Alice's world, not yours.

But the way I see it, when she was taken from you, you were finally pulled into her world. Only now you don't have her as a guide.

And finding the killer -- figuring out why you were given these powers -- you're trying to fill that... that... hollow space in your heart.

You're very observant, Katherine. So keep watching.

All right, my whole little psychoanalysis there? That was just textbook profiling...

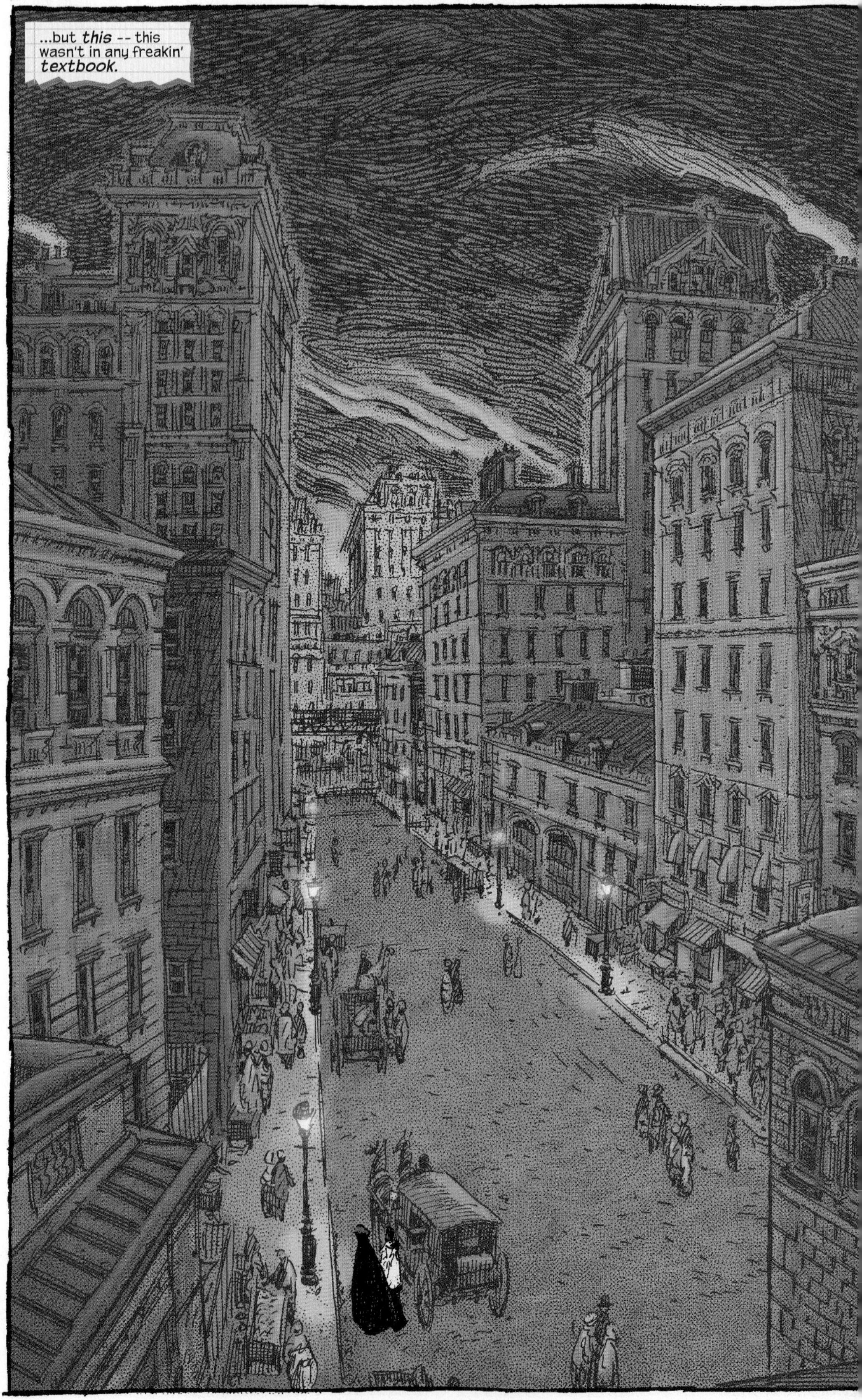
...but *this* -- this wasn't in any freakin' *textbook.*

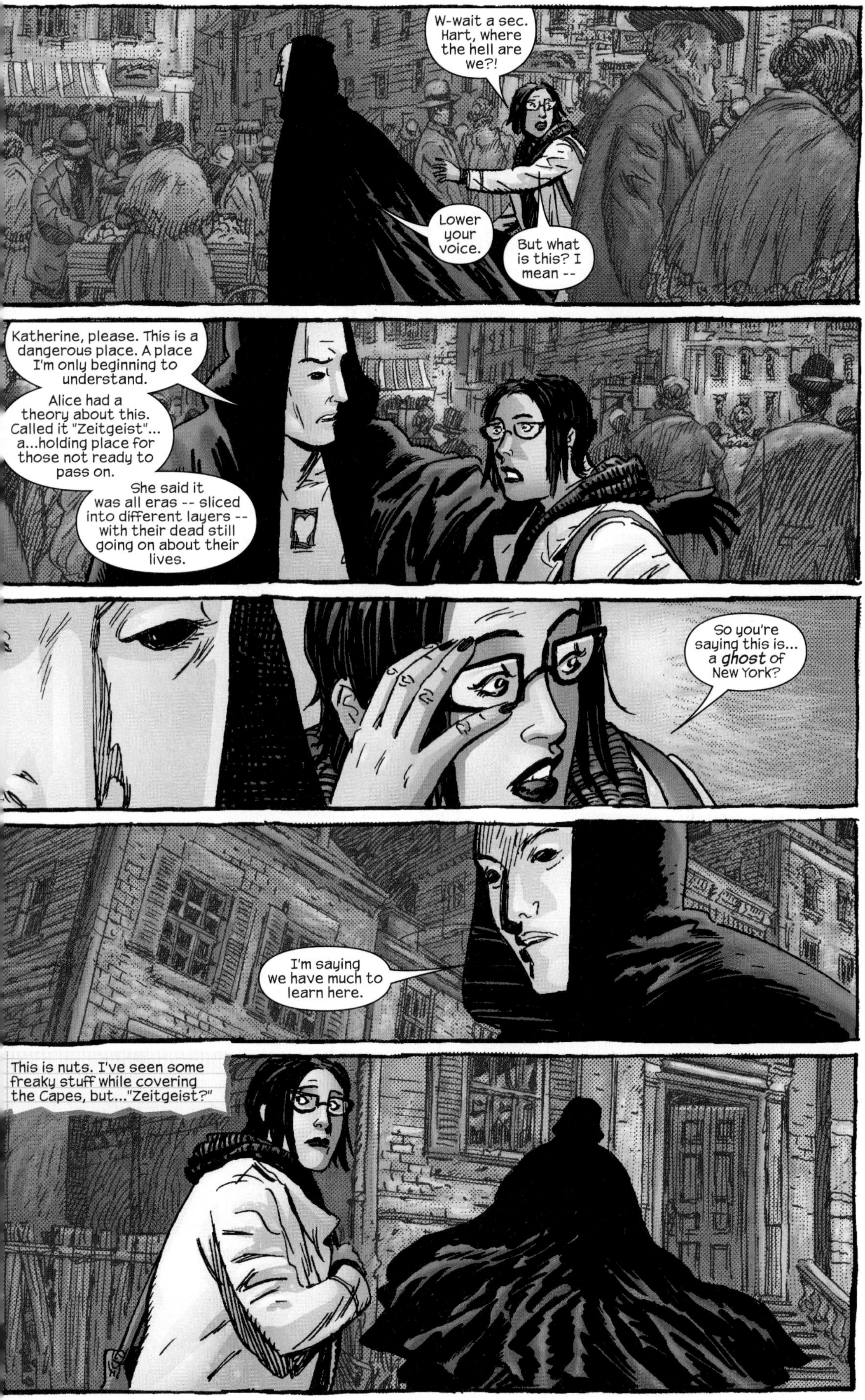
W-wait a sec. Hart, where the hell are we?!
Lower your voice.
But what is this? I mean --
Katherine, please. This is a dangerous place. A place I'm only beginning to understand.
Alice had a theory about this. Called it "Zeitgeist"... a...holding place for those not ready to pass on.
She said it was all eras -- sliced into different layers -- with their dead still going on about their lives.
So you're saying this is... a *ghost* of New York?
I'm saying we have much to learn here.
This is nuts. I've seen some freaky stuff while covering the Capes, but..."Zeitgeist?"

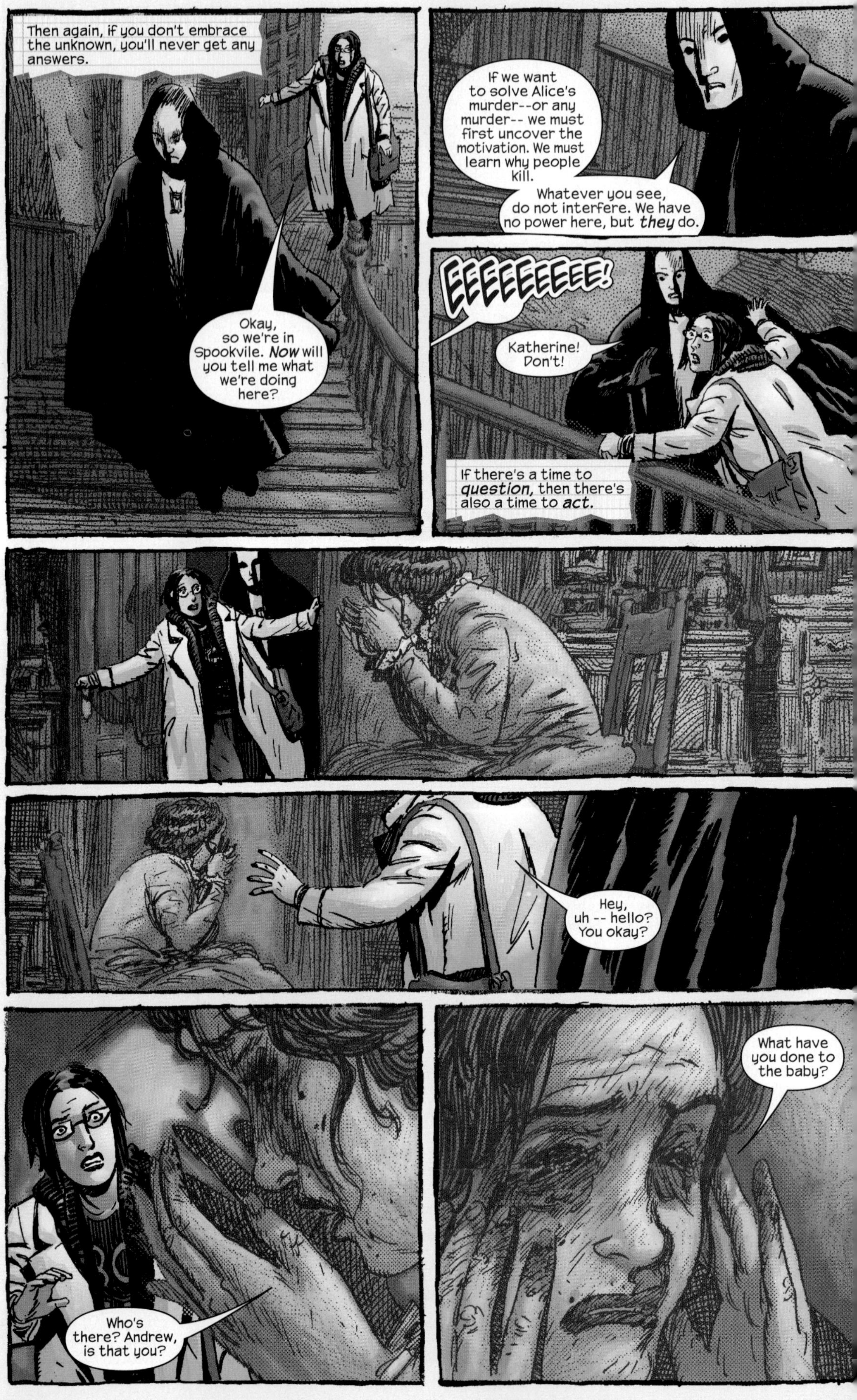
Then again, if you don't embrace the unknown, you'll never get any answers.
Okay, so we're in Spookvile. Now will you tell me what we're doing here?
If we want to solve Alice's murder--or any murder-- we must first uncover the motivation. We must learn why people kill.
Whatever you see, do not interfere. We have no power here, but they do.
EEEEEEEEE!
Katherine! Don't!
If there's a time to question, then there's also a time to act.
Hey, uh -- hello? You okay?
Who's there? Andrew, is that you?
What have you done to the baby?

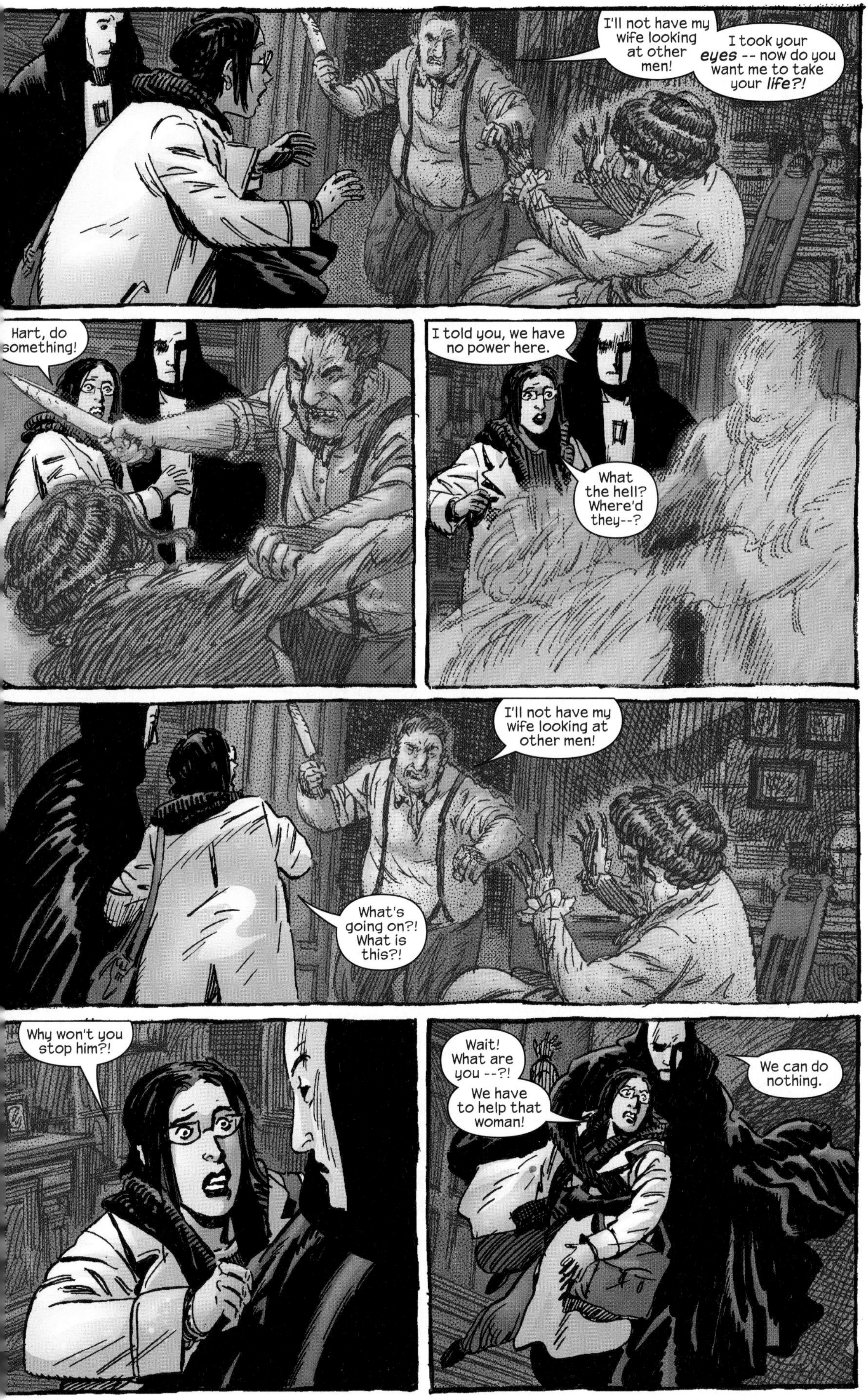
I'll not have my wife looking at other men!
I took your *eyes* -- now do you want me to take your *life?!*
Hart, do something!
I told you, we have no power here.
What the hell? Where'd they--?
I'll not have my wife looking at other men!
What's going on?! What is this?!
Why won't you stop him?!
Wait! What are you --?!
We can do nothing.
We have to help that woman!

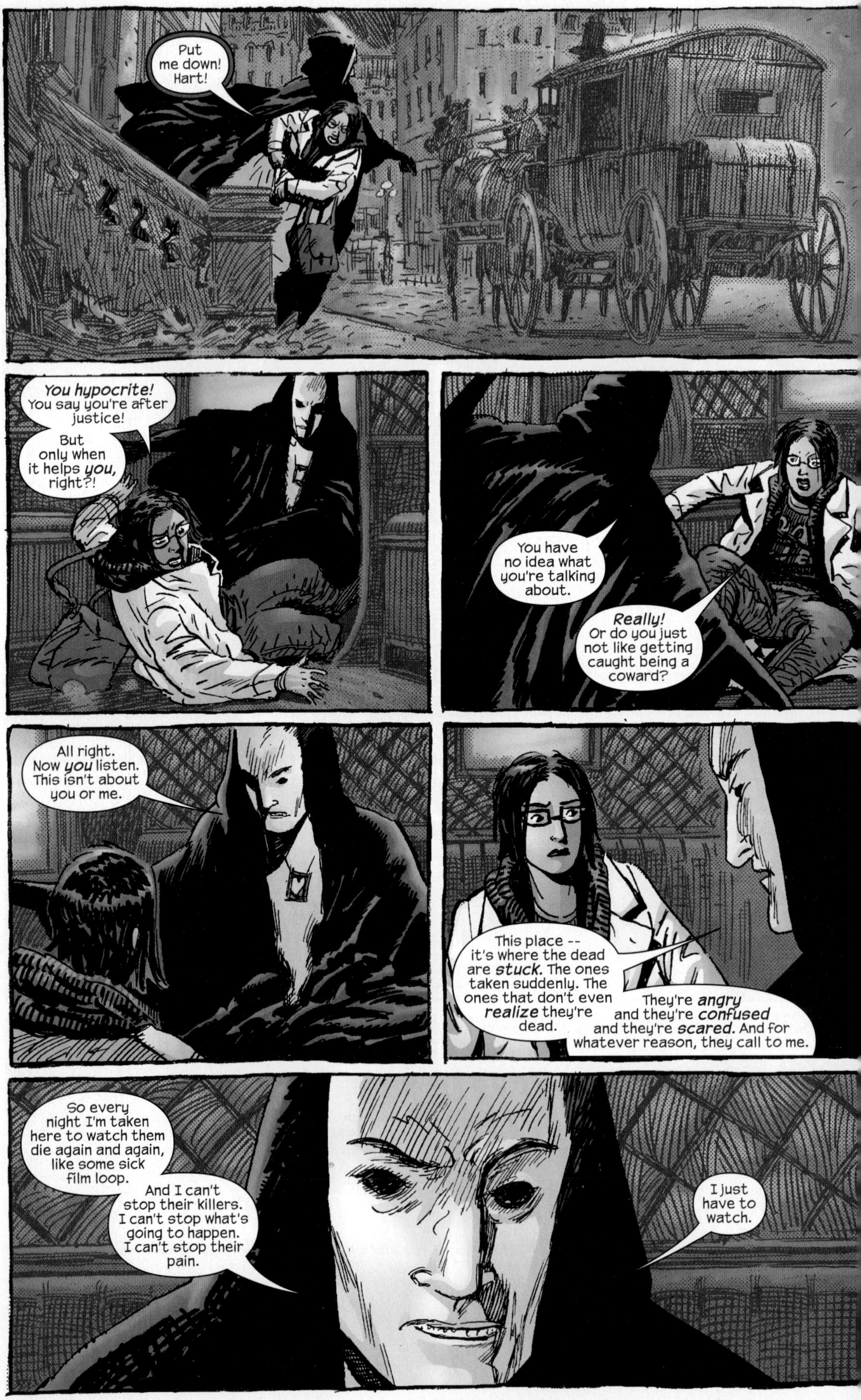
Put me down! Hart!
You hypocrite! You say you're after justice!
But only when it helps you, right?!
You have no idea what you're talking about.
Really! Or do you just not like getting caught being a coward?
All right. Now you listen. This isn't about you or me.
This place -- it's where the dead are stuck. The ones taken suddenly. The ones that don't even realize they're dead.
They're angry and they're confused and they're scared. And for whatever reason, they call to me.
So every night I'm taken here to watch them die again and again, like some sick film loop.
And I can't stop their killers. I can't stop what's going to happen. I can't stop their pain.
I just have to watch.

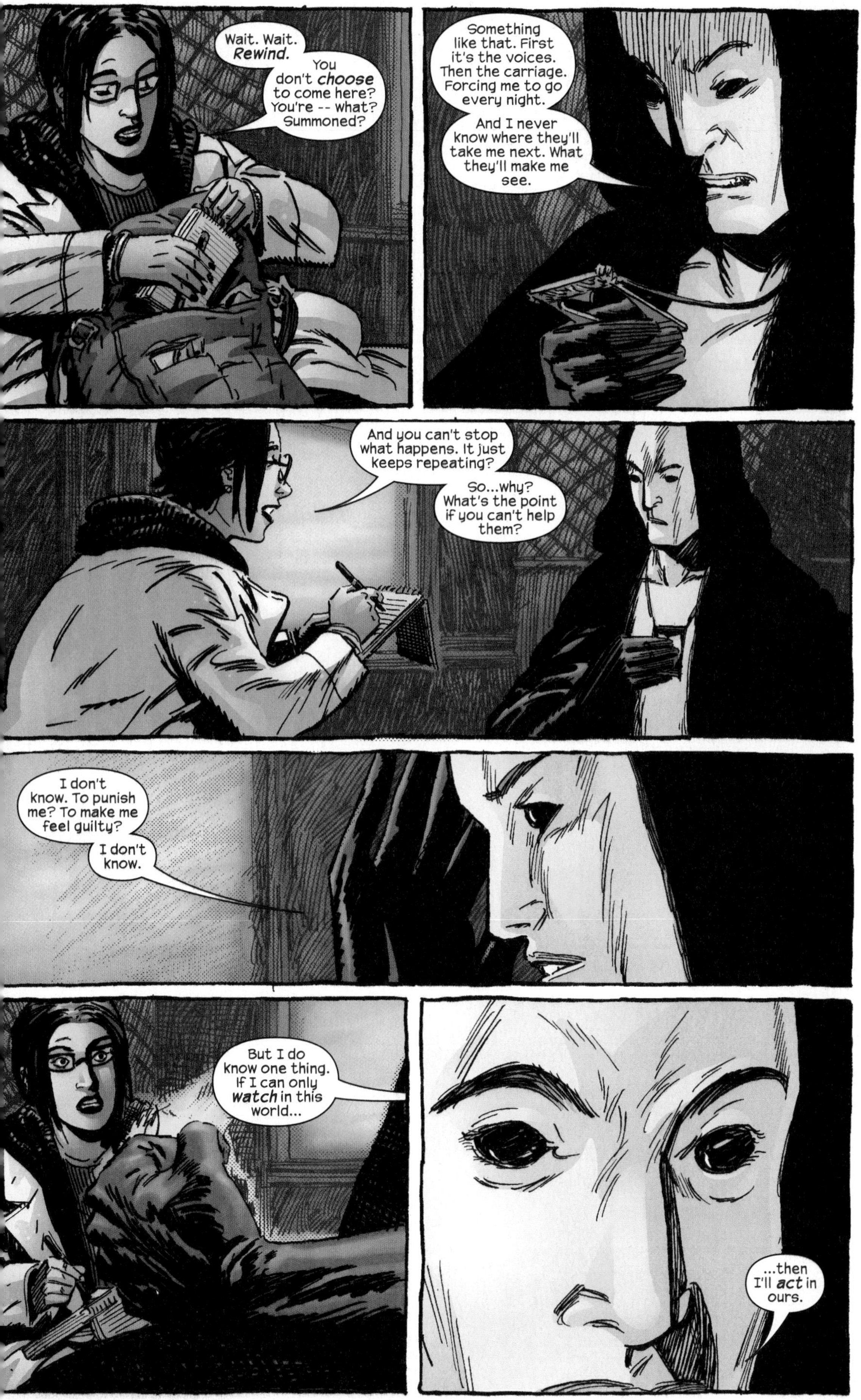

Wait. Wait. *Rewind.*
You don't *choose* to come here? You're -- what? Summoned?
Something like that. First it's the voices. Then the carriage. Forcing me to go every night.
And I never know where they'll take me next. What they'll make me see.
And you can't stop what happens. It just keeps repeating?
So...why? What's the point if you can't help them?
I don't know. To punish me? To make me feel guilty?
I don't know.
But I do know one thing. If I can only *watch* in this world...
...then I'll *act* in ours.

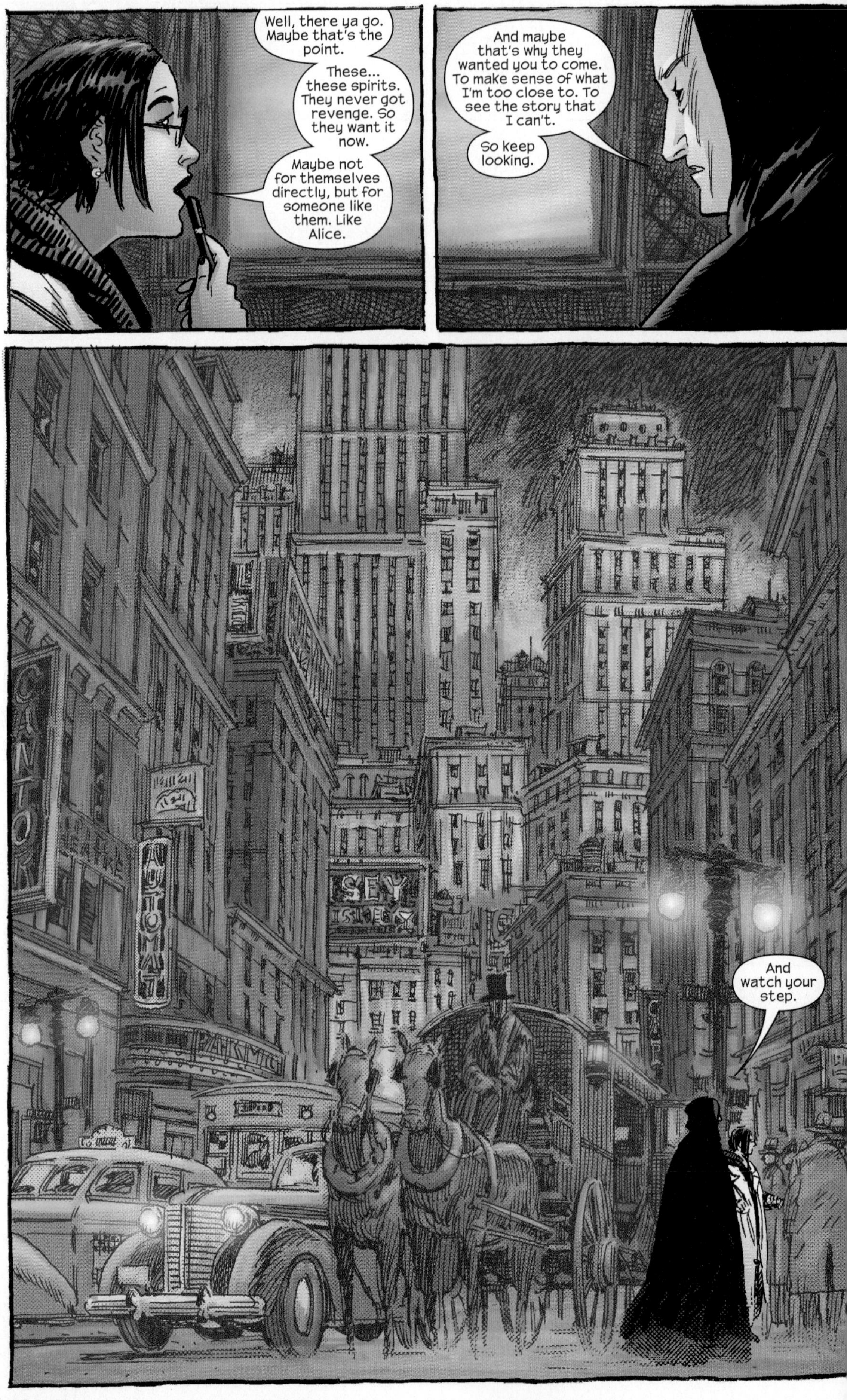
Well, there ya go. Maybe that's the point.
These... these spirits. They never got revenge. So they want it now.
Maybe not for themselves directly, but for someone like them. Like Alice.
And maybe that's why they wanted you to come. To make sense of what I'm too close to. To see the story that I can't.
So keep looking.
And watch your step.

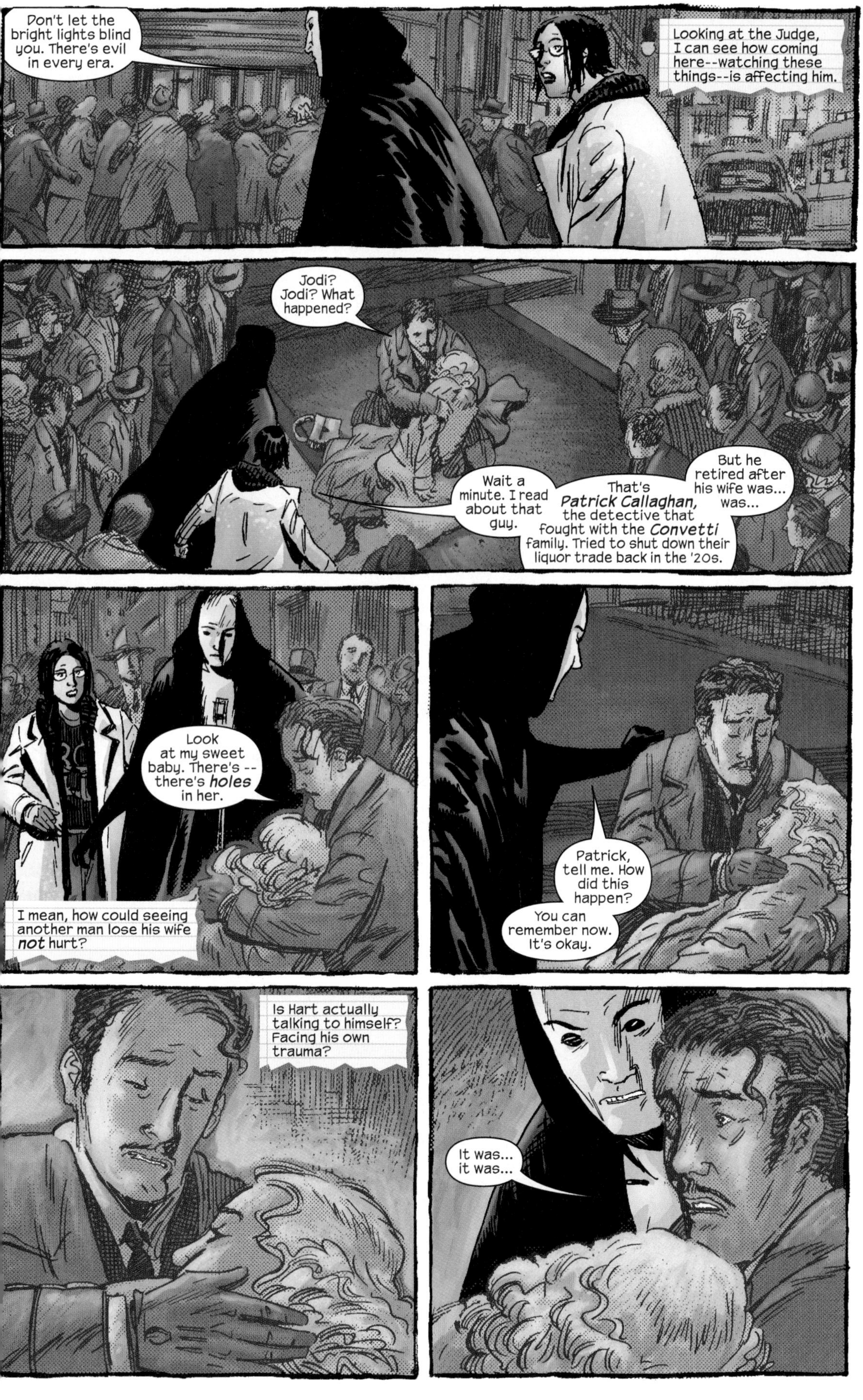
Don't let the bright lights blind you. There's evil in every era.
Looking at the Judge, I can see how coming here--watching these things--is affecting him.
Jodi? Jodi? What happened?
Wait a minute. I read about that guy.
That's *Patrick Callaghan,* the detective that fought with the *Convetti* family. Tried to shut down their liquor trade back in the '20s.
But he retired after his wife was... was...
Look at my sweet baby. There's -- there's *holes* in her.
I mean, how could seeing another man lose his wife ***not*** hurt?
Patrick, tell me. How did this happen?
You can remember now. It's okay.
Is Hart actually talking to himself? Facing his own trauma?
It was... it was...

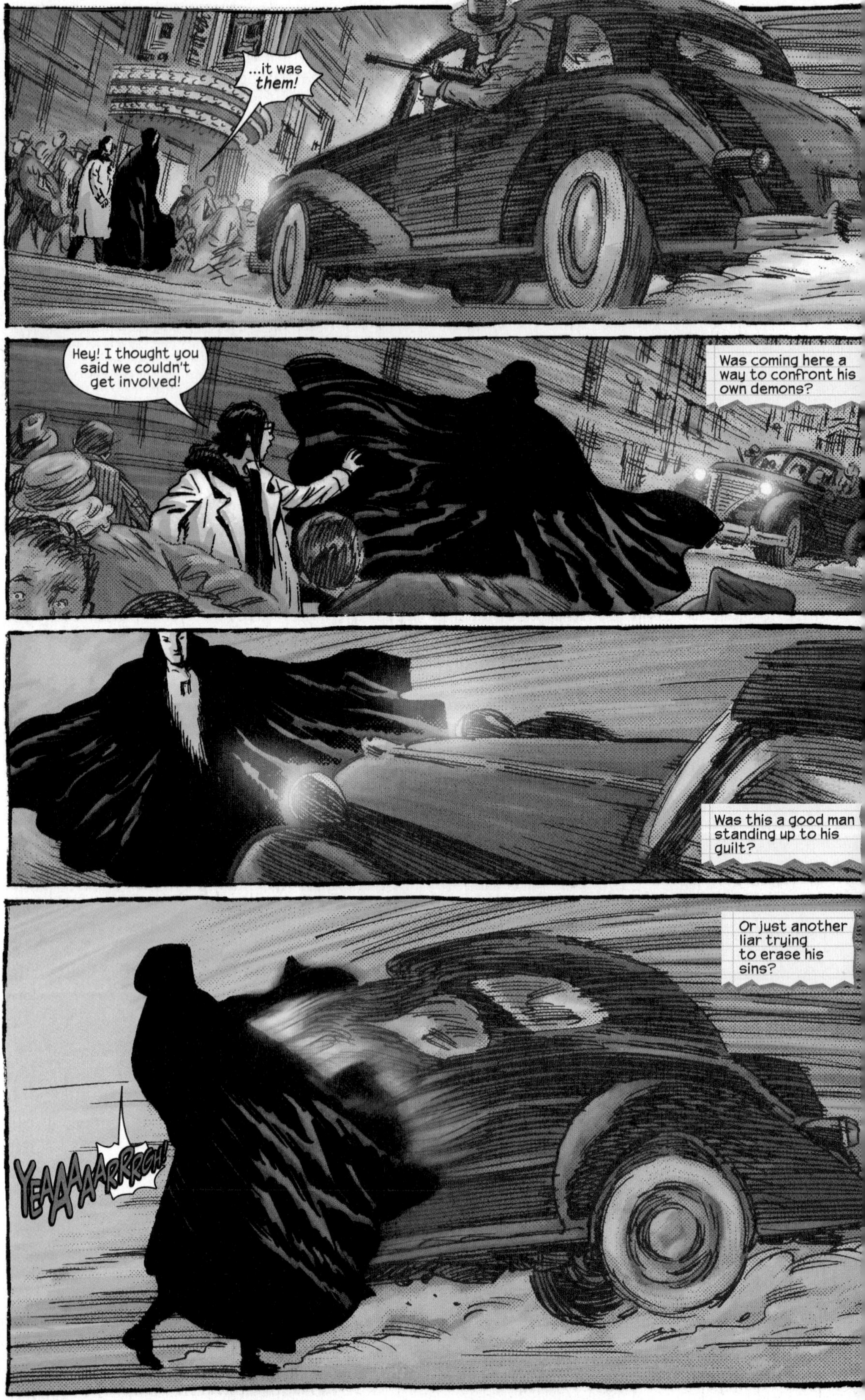

...it was them!
Hey! I thought you said we couldn't get involved!
Was coming here a way to confront his own demons?
Was this a good man standing up to his guilt?
Or just another liar trying to erase his sins?
YEAAAAARRRGH!

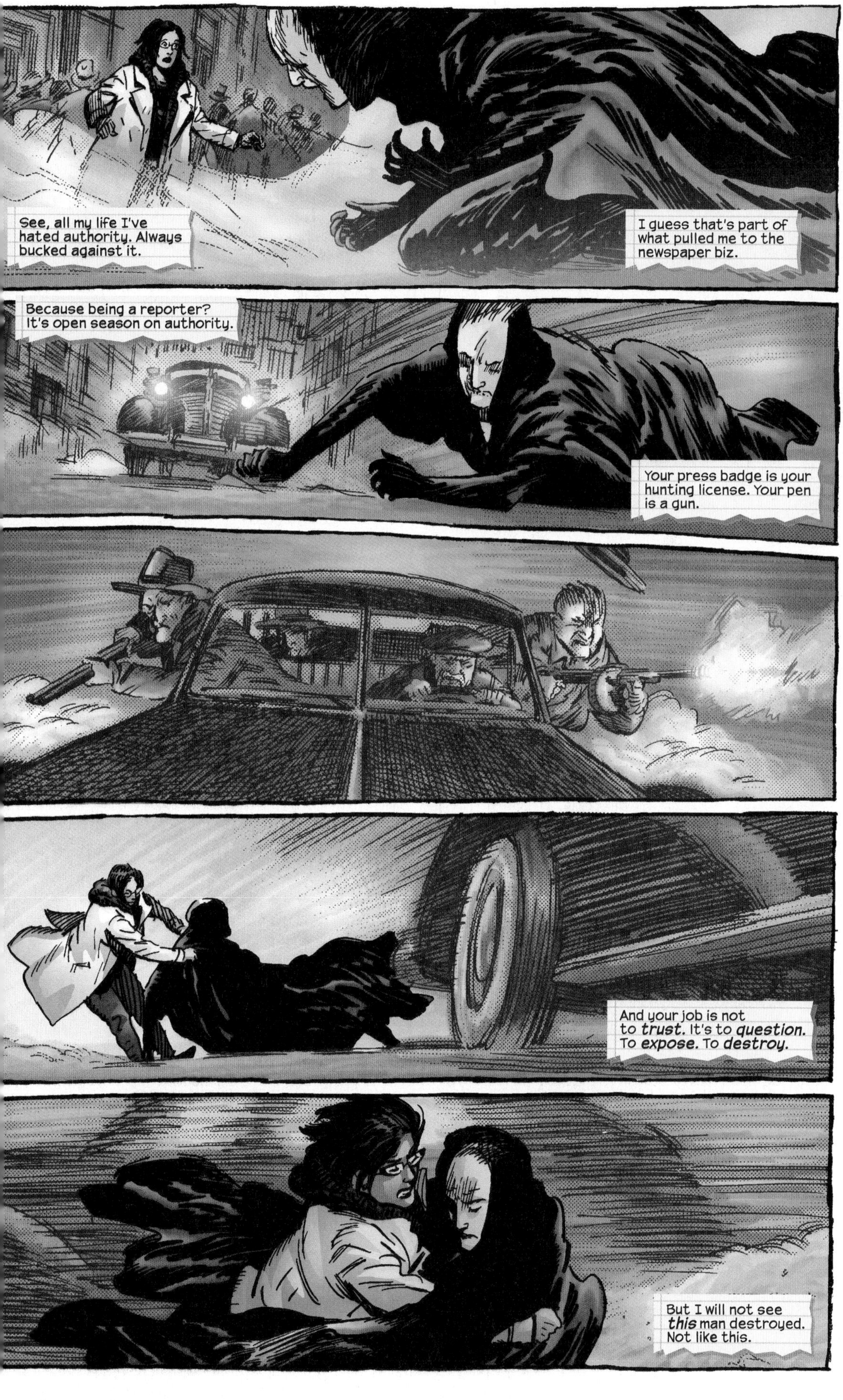

See, all my life I've hated authority. Always bucked against it.
I guess that's part of what pulled me to the newspaper biz.
Because being a reporter? It's open season on authority.
Your press badge is your hunting license. Your pen is a gun.
And your job is not to *trust*. It's to *question*. To *expose*. To *destroy*.
But I will not see *this* man destroyed. Not like this.

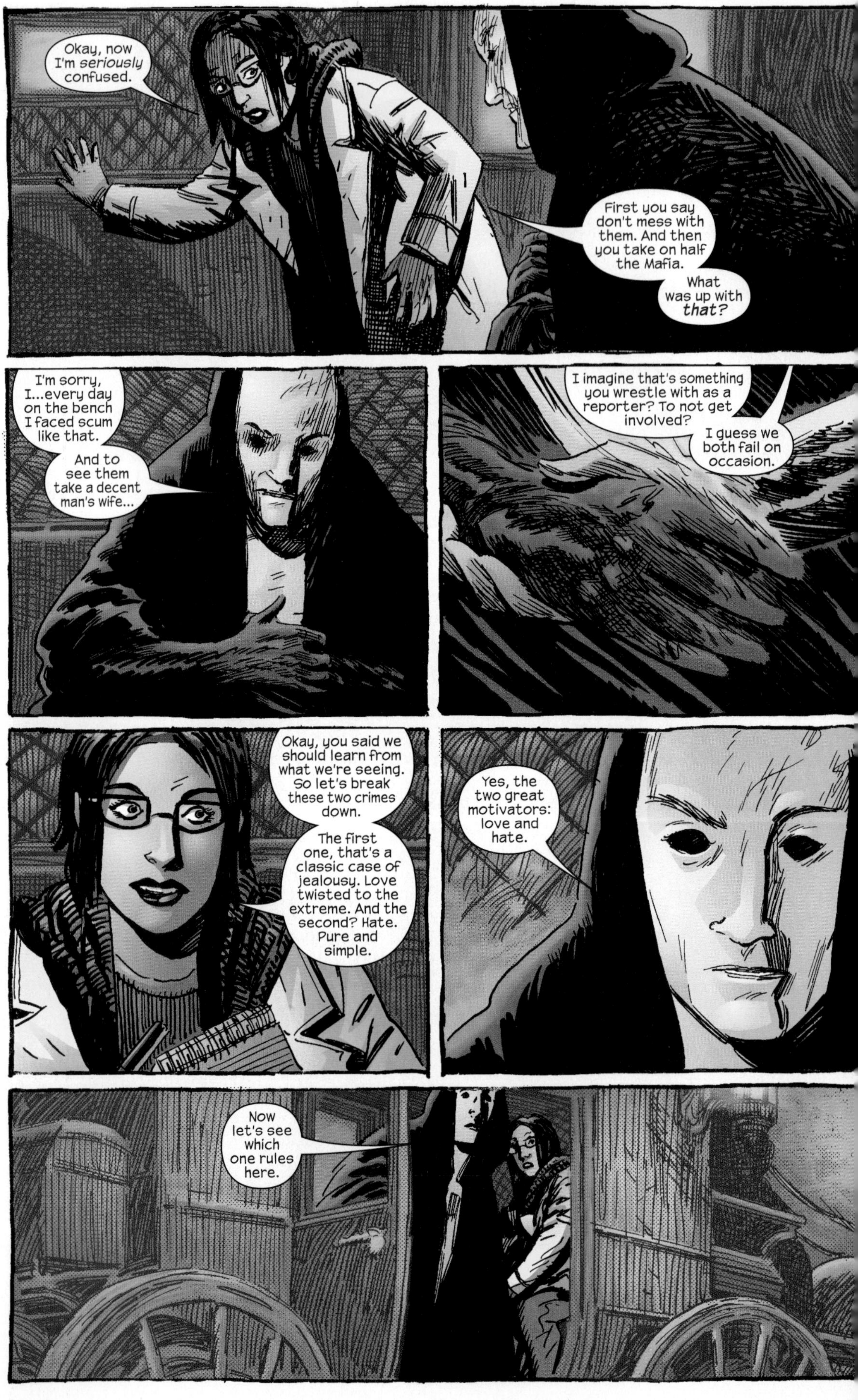
Okay, now I'm *seriously* confused.
First you say don't mess with them. And then you take on half the Mafia.
What was up with *that?*
I'm sorry, I...every day on the bench I faced scum like that.
And to see them take a decent man's wife...
I imagine that's something you wrestle with as a reporter? To not get involved?
I guess we both fail on occasion.
Okay, you said we should learn from what we're seeing. So let's break these two crimes down.
The first one, that's a classic case of jealousy. Love twisted to the extreme. And the second? Hate. Pure and simple.
Yes, the two great motivators: love and hate.
Now let's see which one rules here.

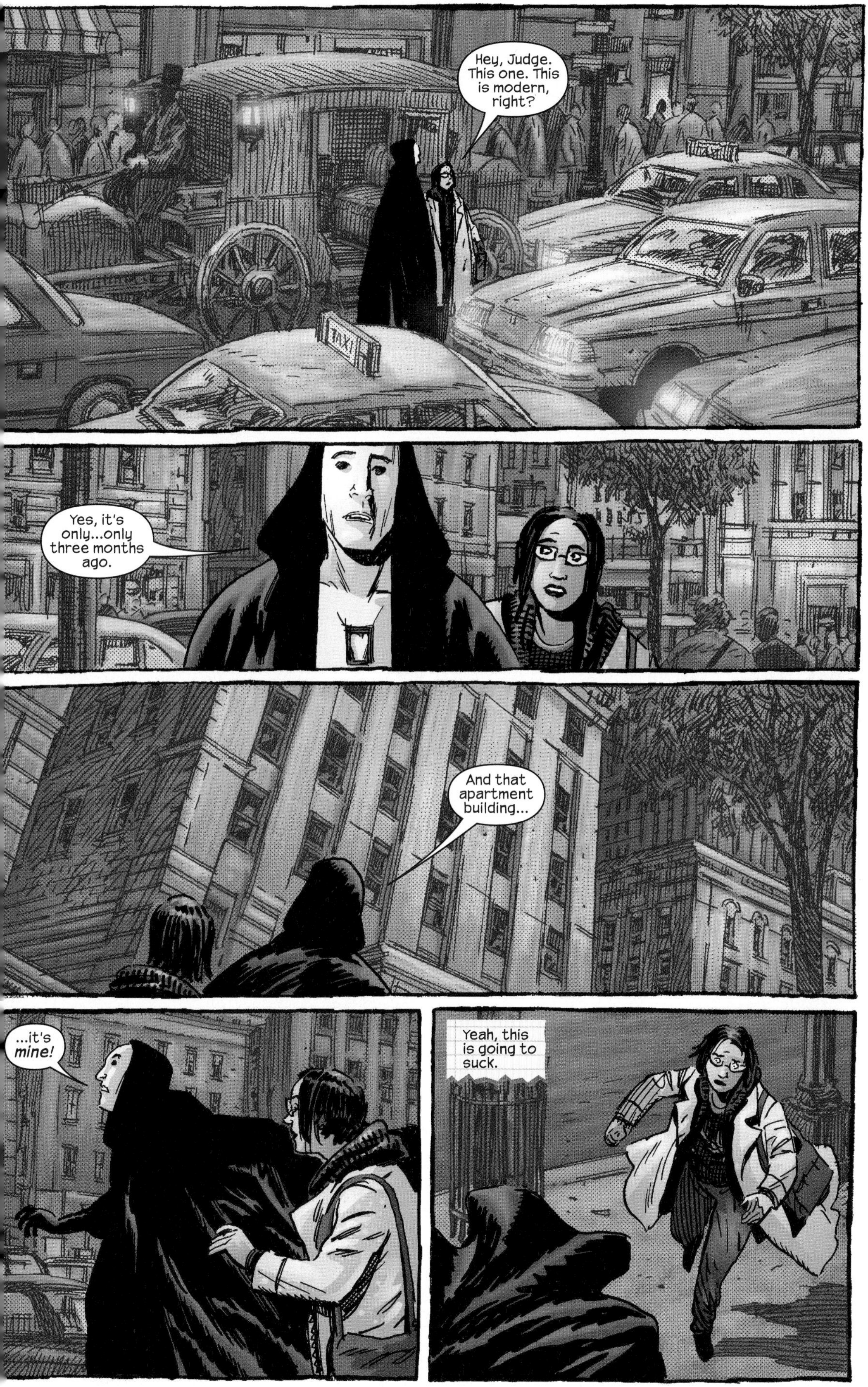
Hey, Judge. This one. This is modern, right?
Yes, it's only...only three months ago.
And that apartment building...
...it's *mine!*
Yeah, this is going to suck.

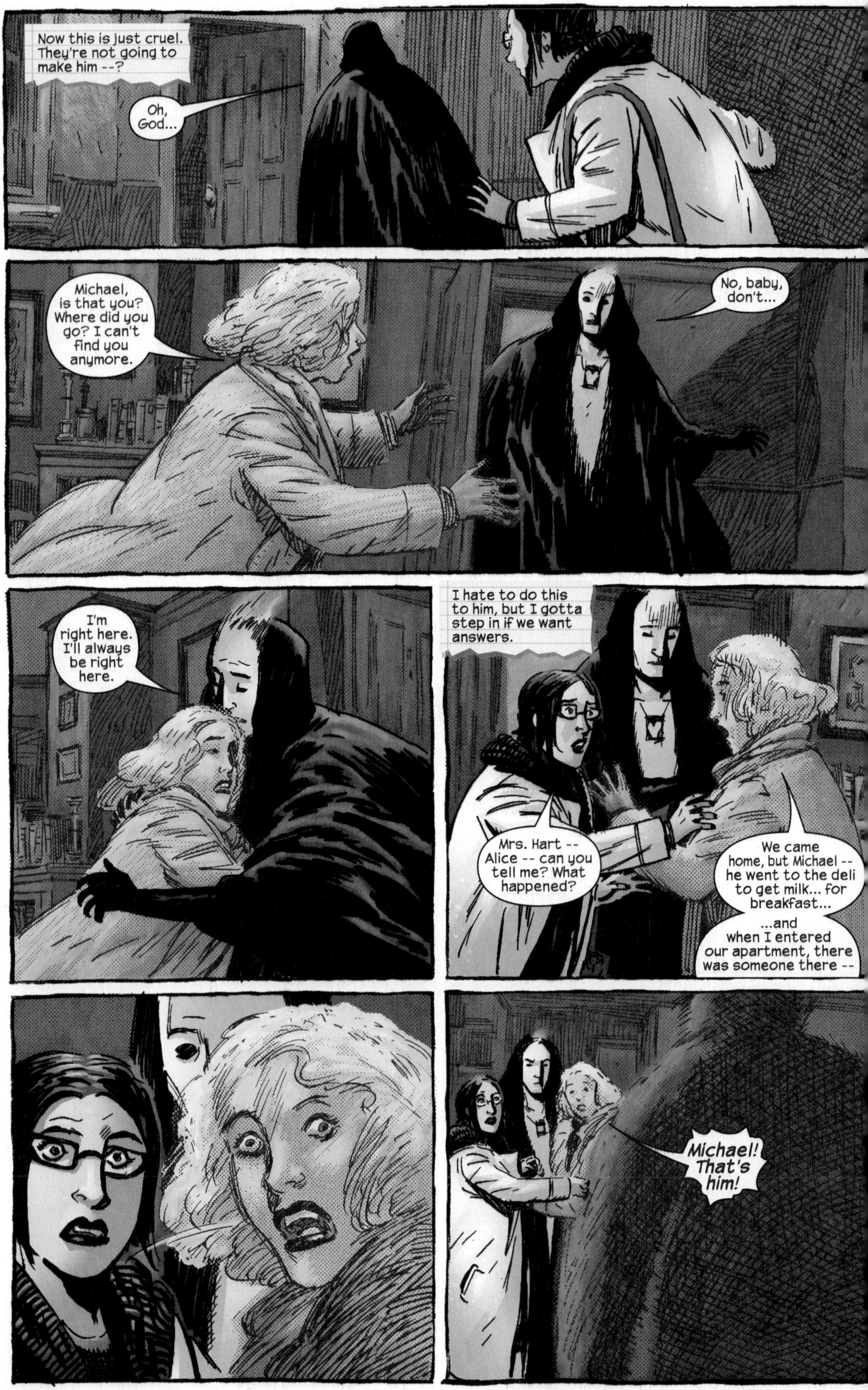
Now this is just cruel. They're not going to make him --?
Oh, God...
Michael, is that you? Where did you go? I can't find you anymore.
No, baby, don't...
I'm right here. I'll always be right here.
I hate to do this to him, but I gotta step in if we want answers.
Mrs. Hart -- Alice -- can you tell me? What happened?
We came home, but Michael -- he went to the deli to get milk... for breakfast...
...and when I entered our apartment, there was someone there --
Michael! That's him!

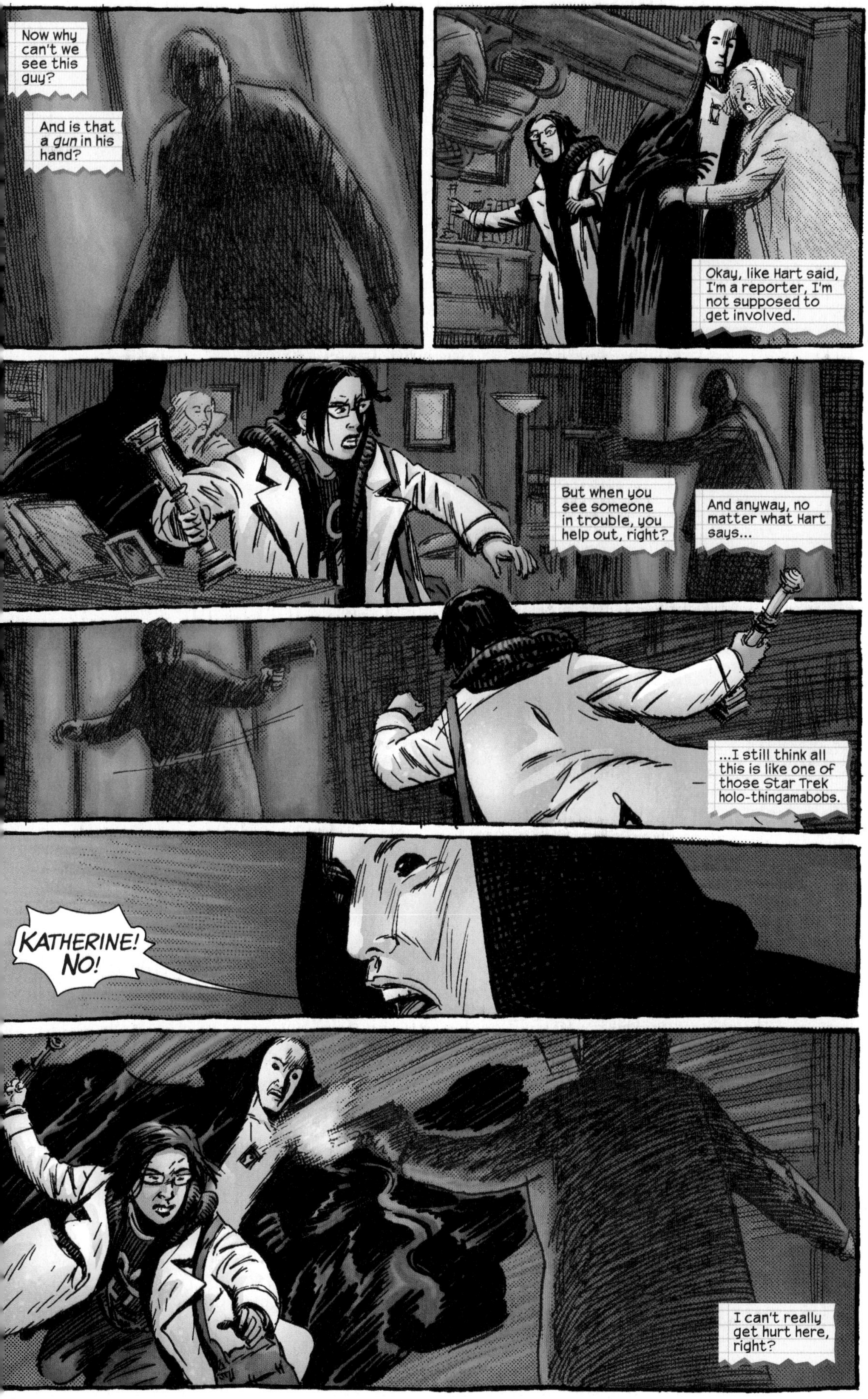
Now why can't we see this guy?
And is that a gun in his hand?
Okay, like Hart said, I'm a reporter, I'm not supposed to get involved.
But when you see someone in trouble, you help out, right?
And anyway, no matter what Hart says...
...I still think all this is like one of those Star Trek holo-thingamabobs.
KATHERINE! NO!
I can't really get hurt here, right?

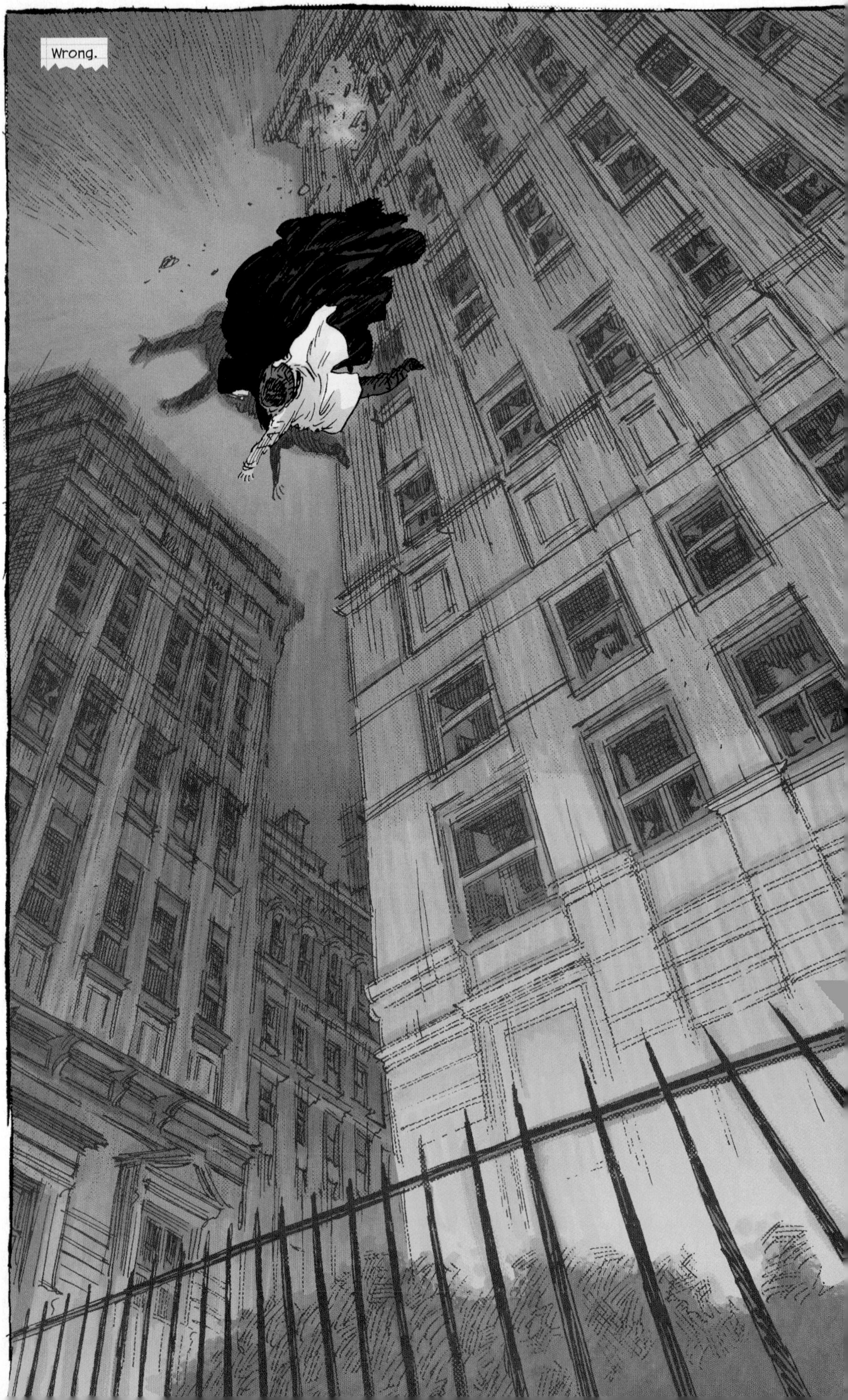
Wrong.

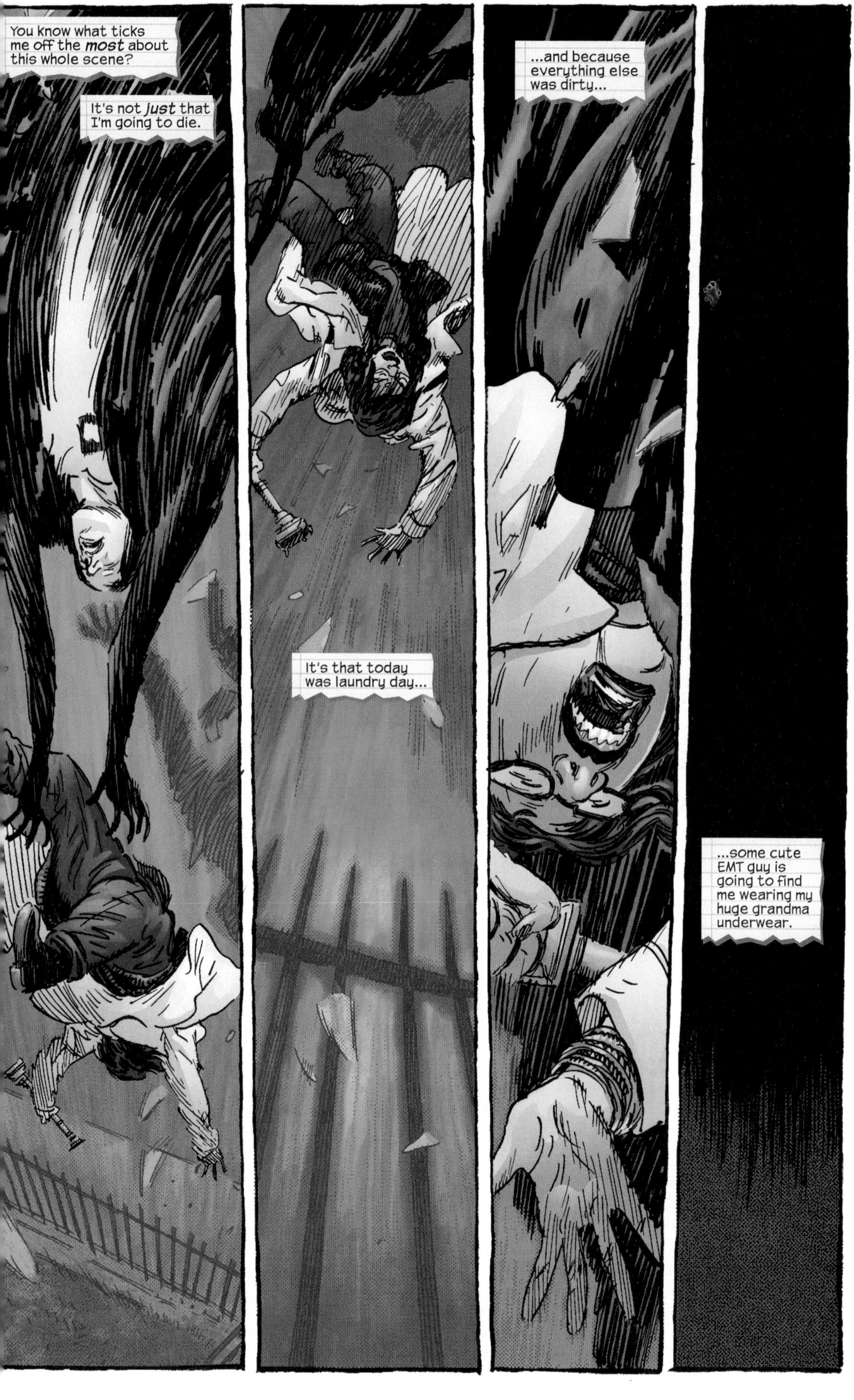
You know what ticks me off the *most* about this whole scene?
It's not *just* that I'm going to die.
It's that today was laundry day...
...and because everything else was dirty...
...some cute EMT guy is going to find me wearing my huge grandma underwear.

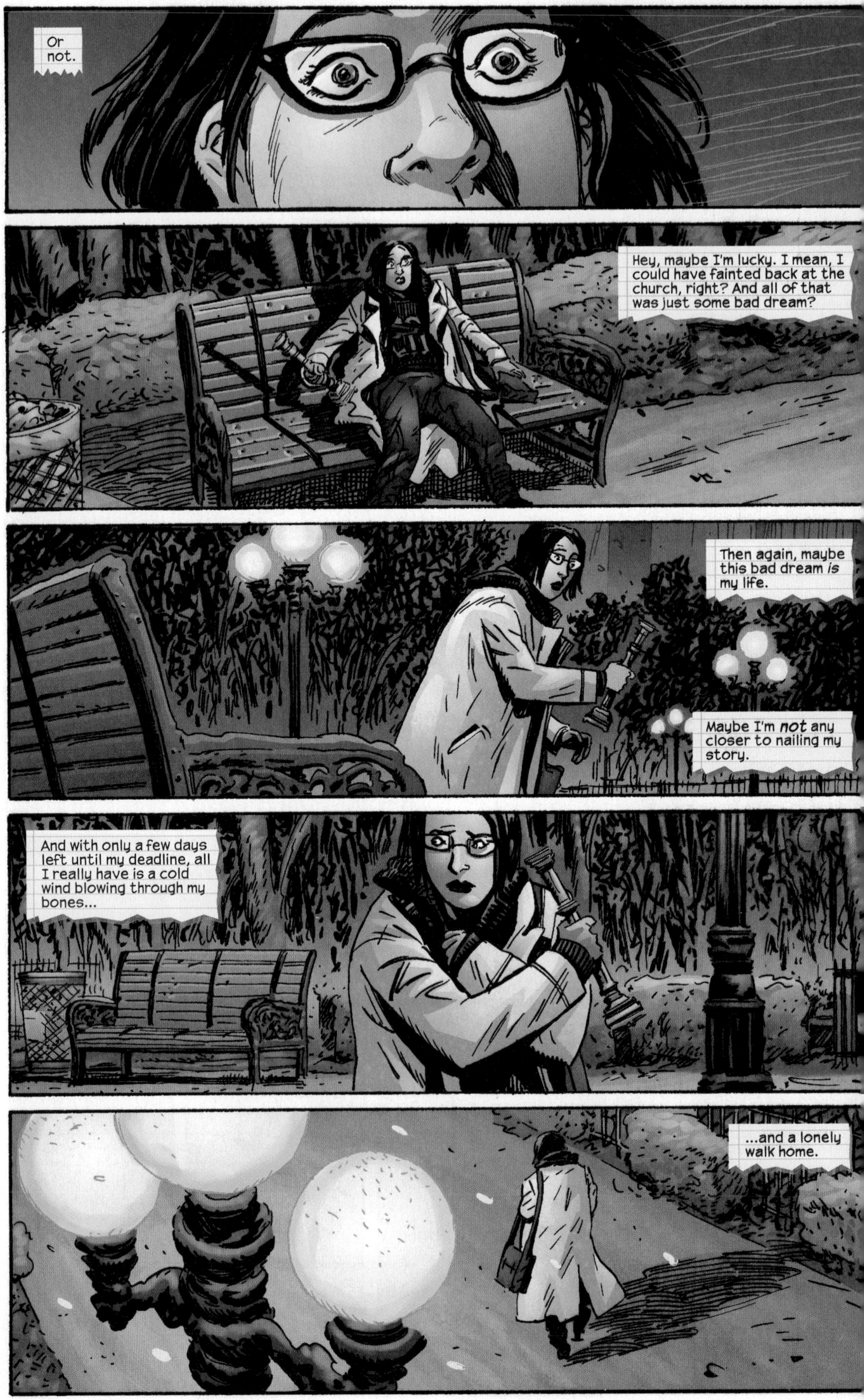

Or not.
Hey, maybe I'm lucky. I mean, I could have fainted back at the church, right? And all of that was just some bad dream?
Then again, maybe this bad dream *is* my life.
Maybe I'm ***not*** any closer to nailing my story.
And with only a few days left until my deadline, all I really have is a cold wind blowing through my bones...
...and a lonely walk home.

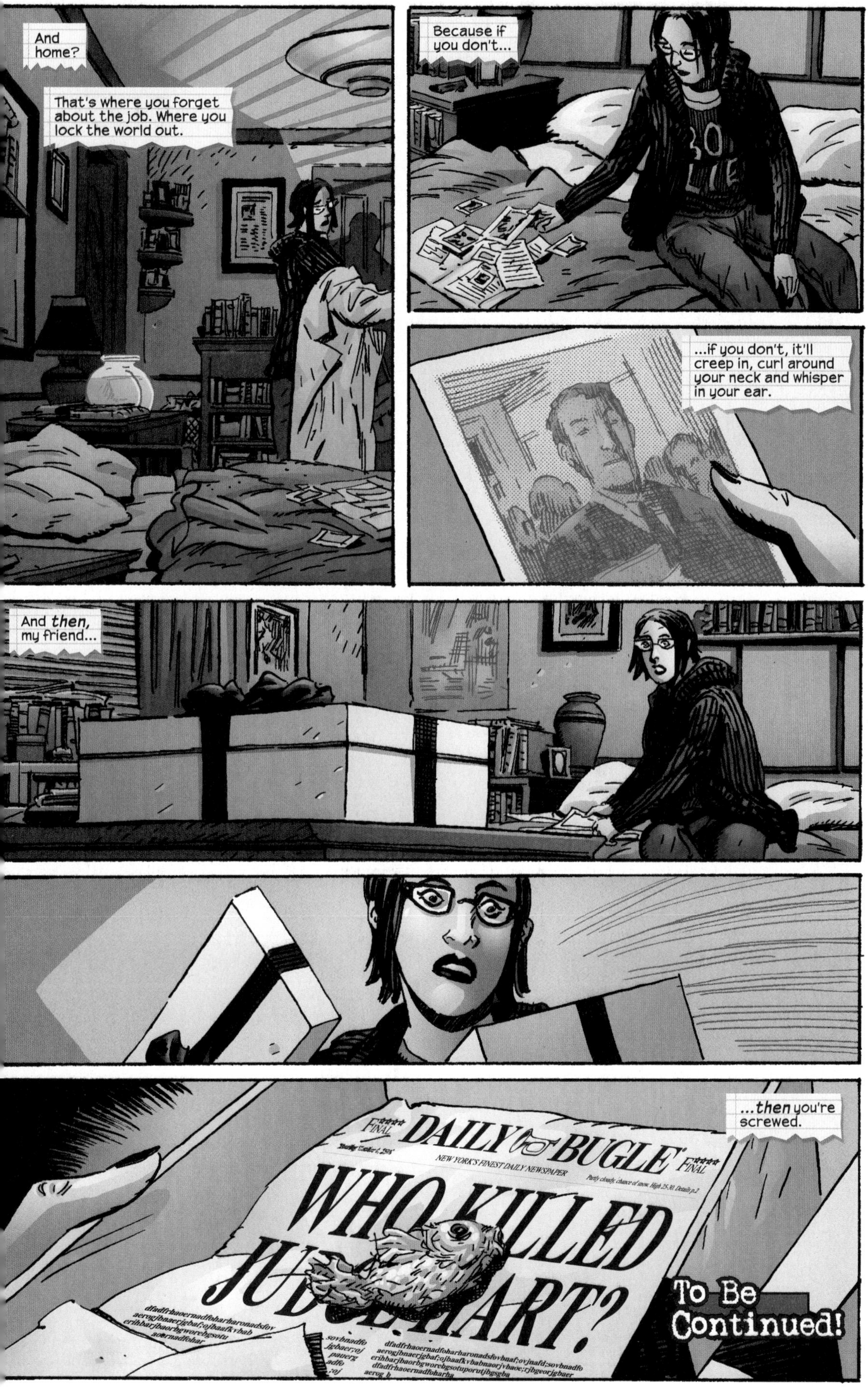

And home?
That's where you forget about the job. Where you lock the world out.
Because if you don't...
...if you don't, it'll creep in, curl around your neck and whisper in your ear.
And *then*, my friend...
...*then* you're screwed.
FINAL
DAILY BUGLE
NEW YORK'S FINEST DAILY NEWSPAPER
FINAL
Partly cloudy, chance of snow. High 25,30. Details p.2
WHO KILLED
To Be Continued!

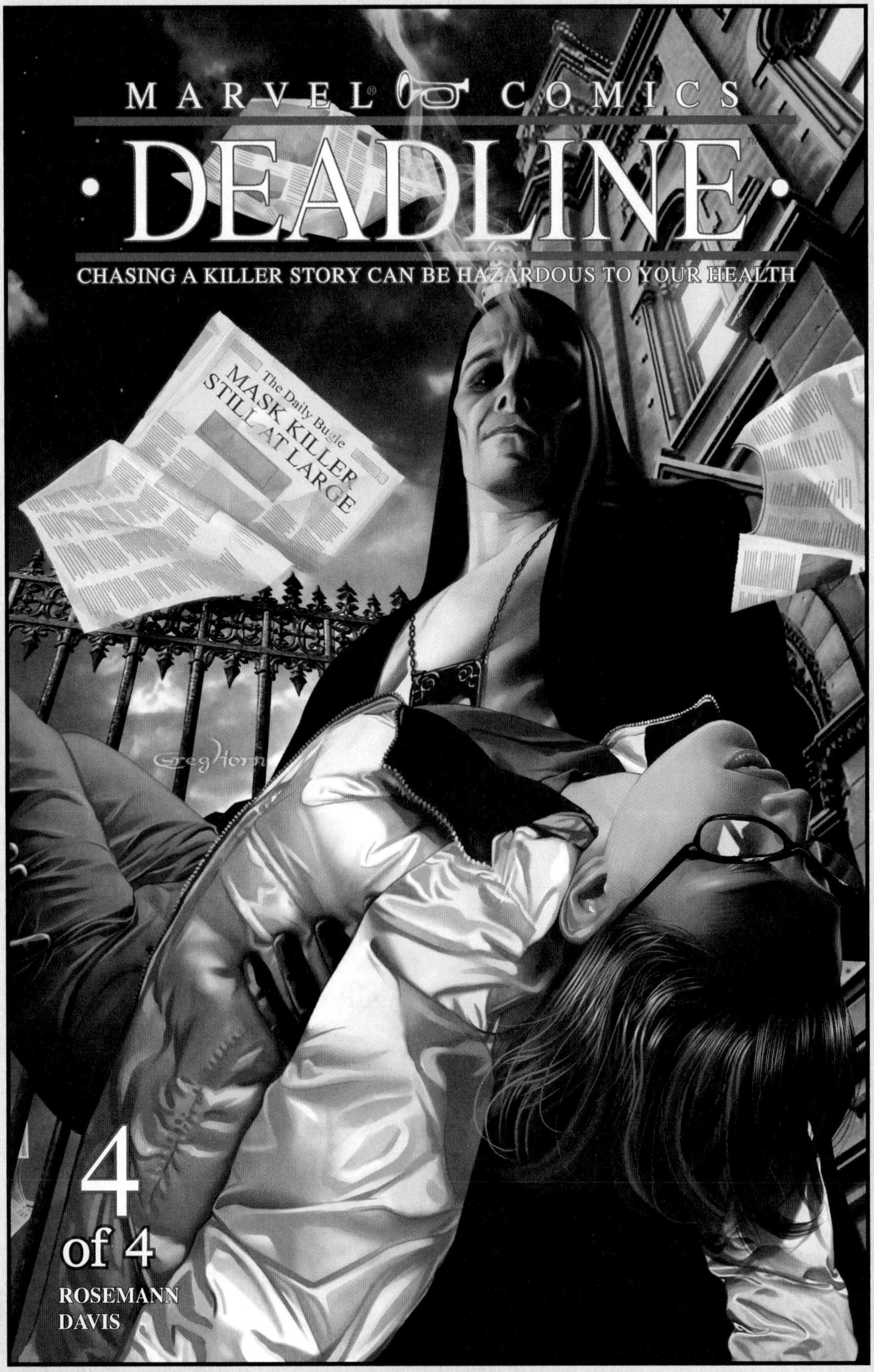

MARVEL® COMICS
DEADLINE™
CHASING A KILLER STORY CAN BE HAZARDOUS TO YOUR HEALTH
The Daily Bugle
MASK KILLER STILL AT LARGE
Greg Horn
4 of 4
ROSEMANN
DAVIS

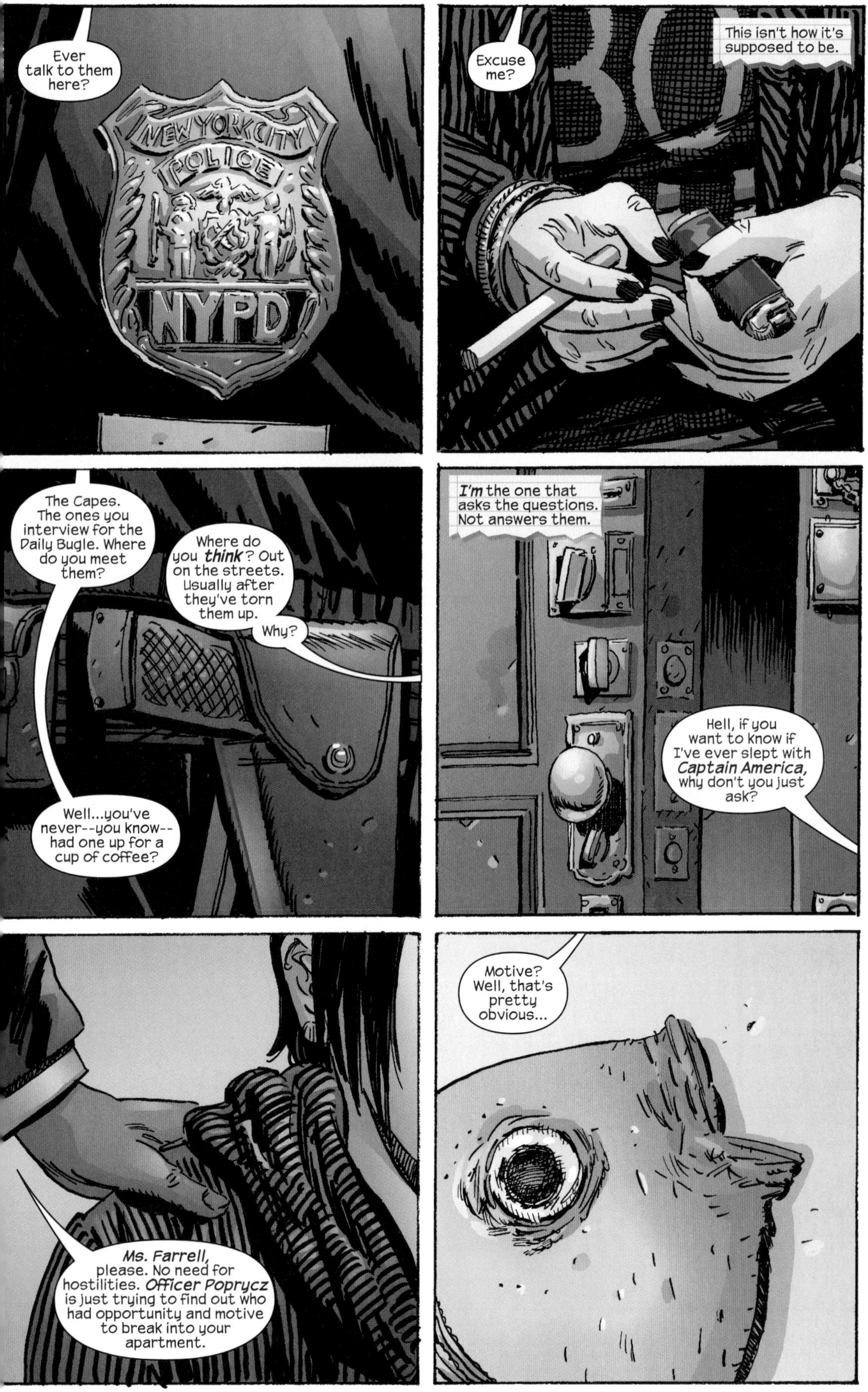
Ever talk to them here?
Excuse me?
This isn't how it's supposed to be.
The Capes. The ones you interview for the Daily Bugle. Where do you meet them?
Where do you *think*? Out on the streets. Usually after they've torn them up.
Why?
Well...you've never--you know--had one up for a cup of coffee?
I'm the one that asks the questions. Not answers them.
Hell, if you want to know if I've ever slept with *Captain America,* why don't you just ask?
Ms. Farrell, please. No need for hostilities. *Officer Poprycz* is just trying to find out who had opportunity and motive to break into your apartment.
Motive? Well, that's pretty obvious...

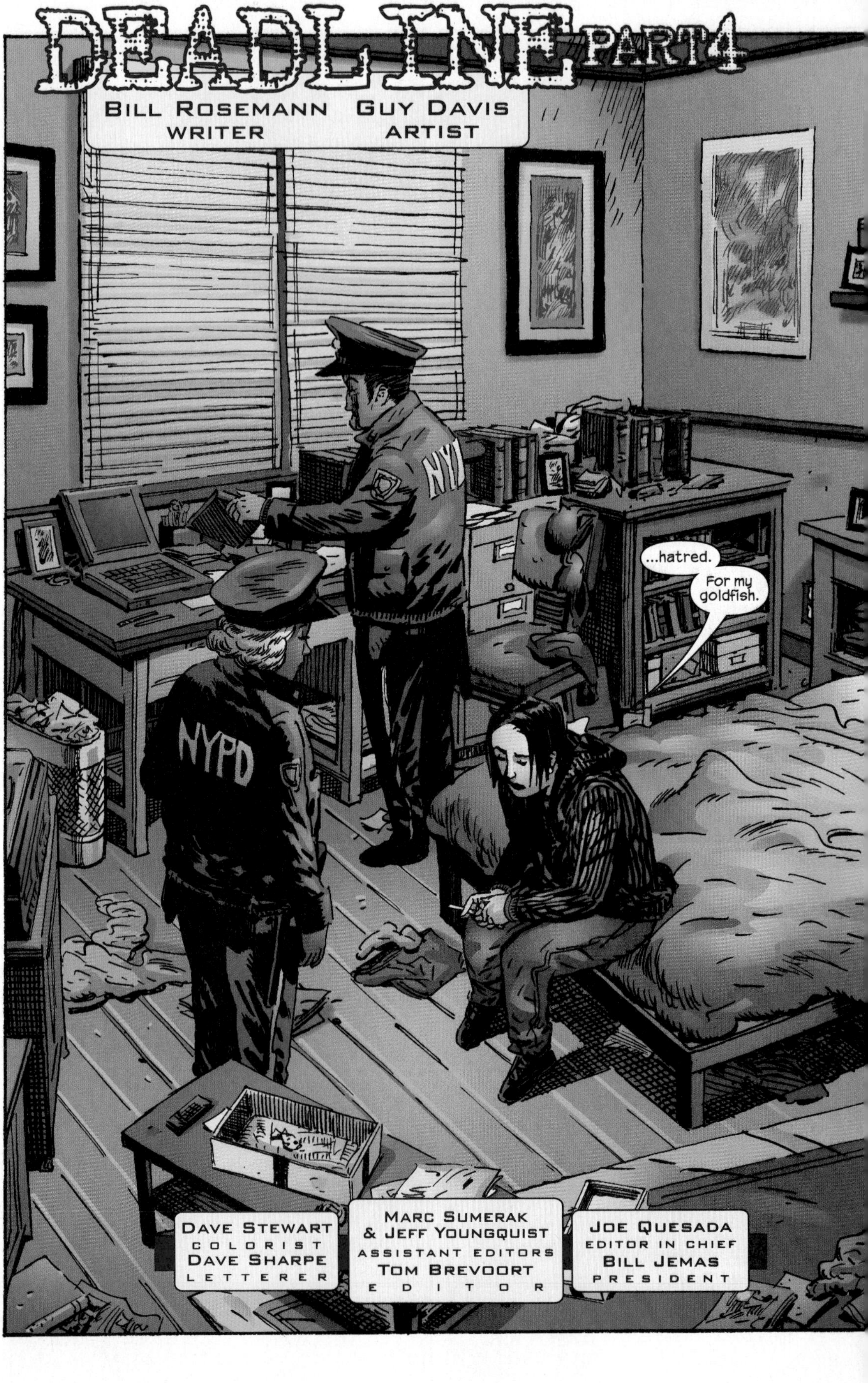
DEADLINE PART 4
BILL ROSEMANN WRITER
GUY DAVIS ARTIST
NYPD
NYPD
...hatred.
For my goldfish.
DAVE STEWART COLORIST
DAVE SHARPE LETTERER
MARC SUMERAK & JEFF YOUNGQUIST ASSISTANT EDITORS
TOM BREVOORT EDITOR
JOE QUESADA EDITOR IN CHIEF
BILL JEMAS PRESIDENT

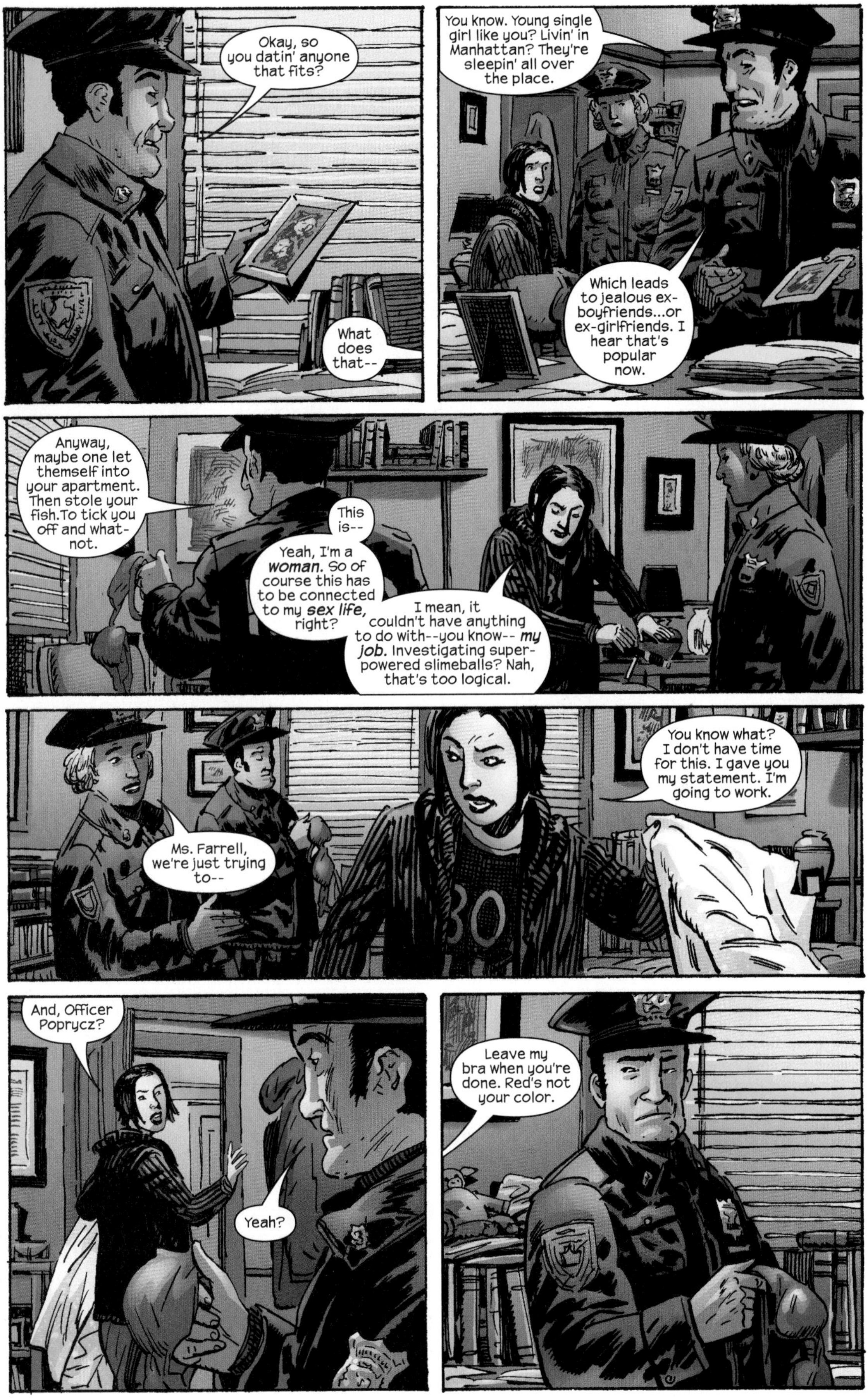
Okay, so you datin' anyone that fits?
What does that--
You know. Young single girl like you? Livin' in Manhattan? They're sleepin' all over the place.
Which leads to jealous ex-boyfriends...or ex-girlfriends. I hear that's popular now.
Anyway, maybe one let themself into your apartment. Then stole your fish. To tick you off and what-not.
This is--
Yeah, I'm a **woman.** So of course this has to be connected to my ***sex life,*** right?
I mean, it couldn't have anything to do with--you know-- ***my job.*** Investigating super-powered slimeballs? Nah, that's too logical.
Ms. Farrell, we're just trying to--
You know what? I don't have time for this. I gave you my statement. I'm going to work.
And, Officer Poprycz?
Yeah?
Leave my bra when you're done. Red's not your color.

Okay, I know they were just doing their jobs.

But the whole thing. Just the *idea* of being questioned. Snooping around my personal life.

Is that how I come off?

Did I make the *Human Torch* feel like *that* the other day?

C'mon, ya stupid lock...

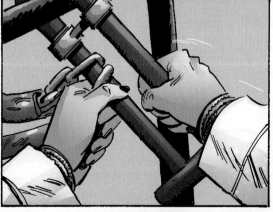

Damn it!

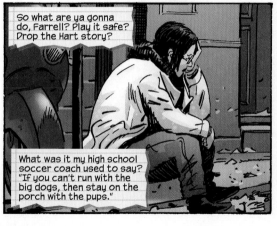

So what are ya gonna do, Farrell? Play it safe? Drop the Hart story?

What was it my high school soccer coach used to say? "If you can't run with the big dogs, then stay on the porch with the pups."

Yeah, well my momma didn't raise no pup.

All right then. Time to circle back to Hart's doorman, 'cause I'm betting he knows more about the murder of the Judge's wife than he's letting on.

And I've got a bluff that might get it out of him.

DAILY ◆ BUGLE FINAL
NEW YORK'S FINEST DAILY NEWSPAPER
Sunday, October 8, 2002
HELLFIRE CLUB SEX SCANDAL

You'd hate to have your name in the paper, huh? See yourself turned into water-cooler talk?

So I can understand why you didn't want to open up to me the other day.

But then again, I can also tell that you're a good guy. And that something's bothering you.

Botherin' me?

Yeah, like something you know? Something about the night Judge Hart went missing?

And if that was *me*-- and I knew what I saw could actually help someone? I'd want to tell somebody. Maybe anonymously.

Now what would I know about that night?

Well, I was thinking: Whoever hurt the Judge--how'd they get the body out of the apartment?

Hart's a good-sized guy, so you'd need help carrying him out, right? And maybe whoever *did* carry him out gave the person who helped him a present.

I mean, the guy who helped probably thought he was doing a good deed. So I could understand why he'd accept a little kickback.

Like maybe a shiny new Rolex watch?

Look, Miss, I got one year left to retirement. And if I get jammed up? Lose my pension?

The wife-- she's got a bad heart-- and I'm all she's got.

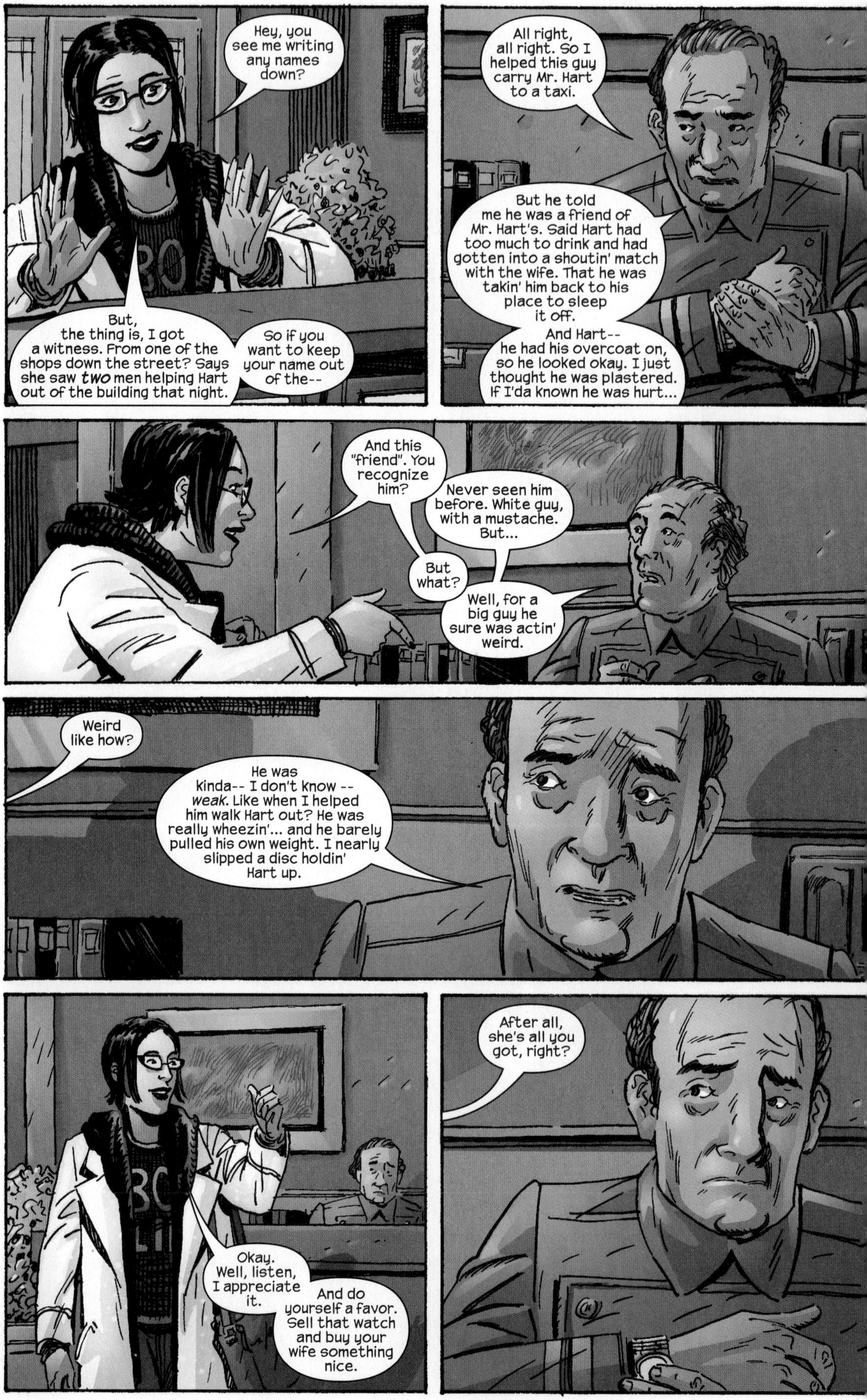
Hey, you see me writing any names down?
But, the thing is, I got a witness. From one of the shops down the street? Says she saw *two* men helping Hart out of the building that night.
So if you want to keep your name out of the--
All right, all right. So I helped this guy carry Mr. Hart to a taxi.
But he told me he was a friend of Mr. Hart's. Said Hart had too much to drink and had gotten into a shoutin' match with the wife. That he was takin' him back to his place to sleep it off.
And Hart-- he had his overcoat on, so he looked okay. I just thought he was plastered. If I'da known he was hurt...
And this "friend". You recognize him?
Never seen him before. White guy, with a mustache. But...
But what?
Well, for a big guy he sure was actin' weird.
Weird like how?
He was kinda-- I don't know -- *weak*. Like when I helped him walk Hart out? He was really wheezin'... and he barely pulled his own weight. I nearly slipped a disc holdin' Hart up.
Okay. Well, listen, I appreciate it.
And do yourself a favor. Sell that watch and buy your wife something nice.
After all, she's all you got, right?

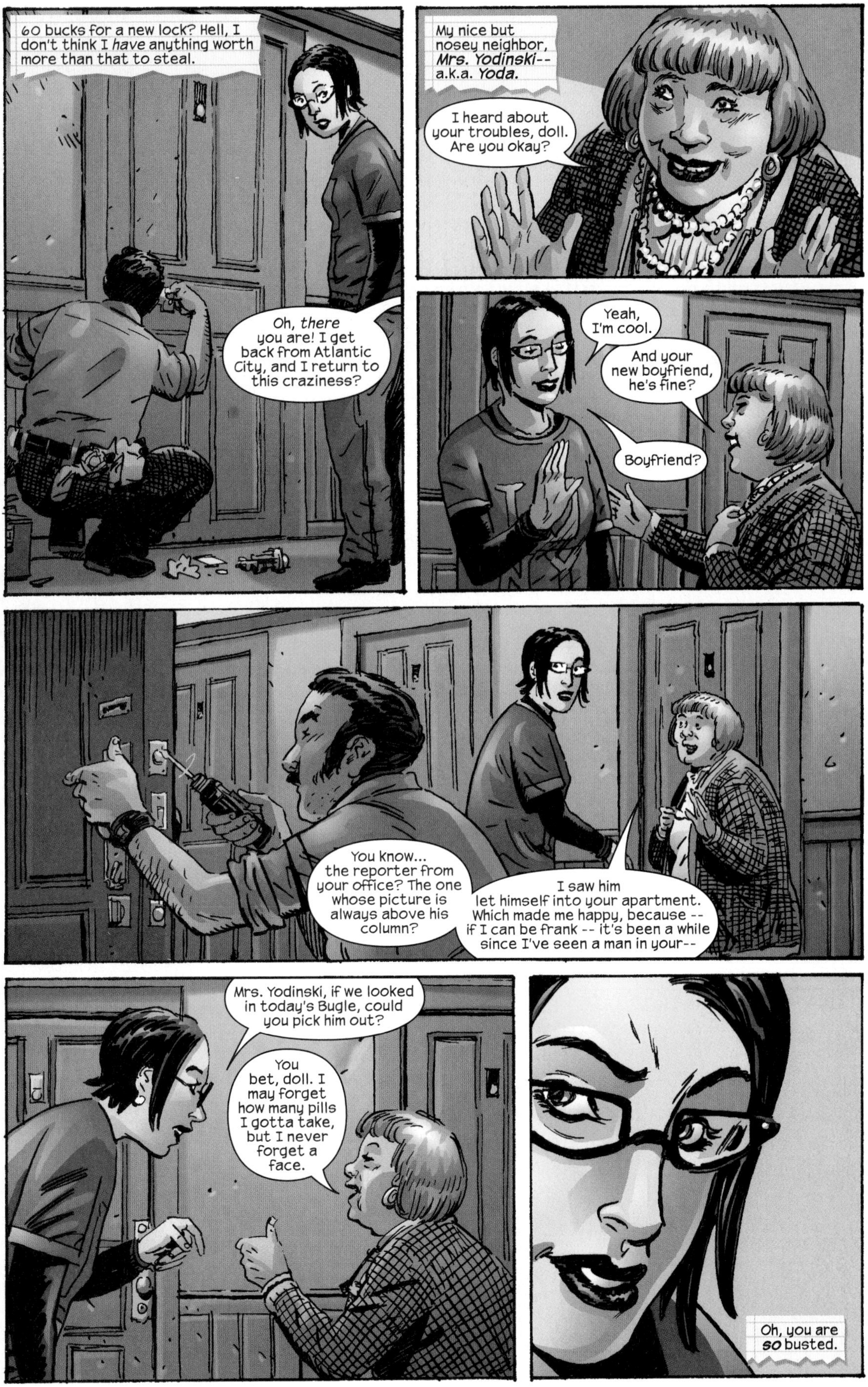
60 bucks for a new lock? Hell, I don't think I *have* anything worth more than that to steal.
Oh, *there* you are! I get back from Atlantic City, and I return to this craziness?
My nice but nosey neighbor, ***Mrs. Yodinski***-- a.k.a. ***Yoda.***
I heard about your troubles, doll. Are you okay?
Yeah, I'm cool.
And your new boyfriend, he's fine?
Boyfriend?
You know... the reporter from your office? The one whose picture is always above his column?
I saw him let himself into your apartment. Which made me happy, because -- if I can be frank -- it's been a while since I've seen a man in your--
Mrs. Yodinski, if we looked in today's Bugle, could you pick him out?
You bet, doll. I may forget how many pills I gotta take, but I never forget a face.
Oh, you are ***so*** busted.

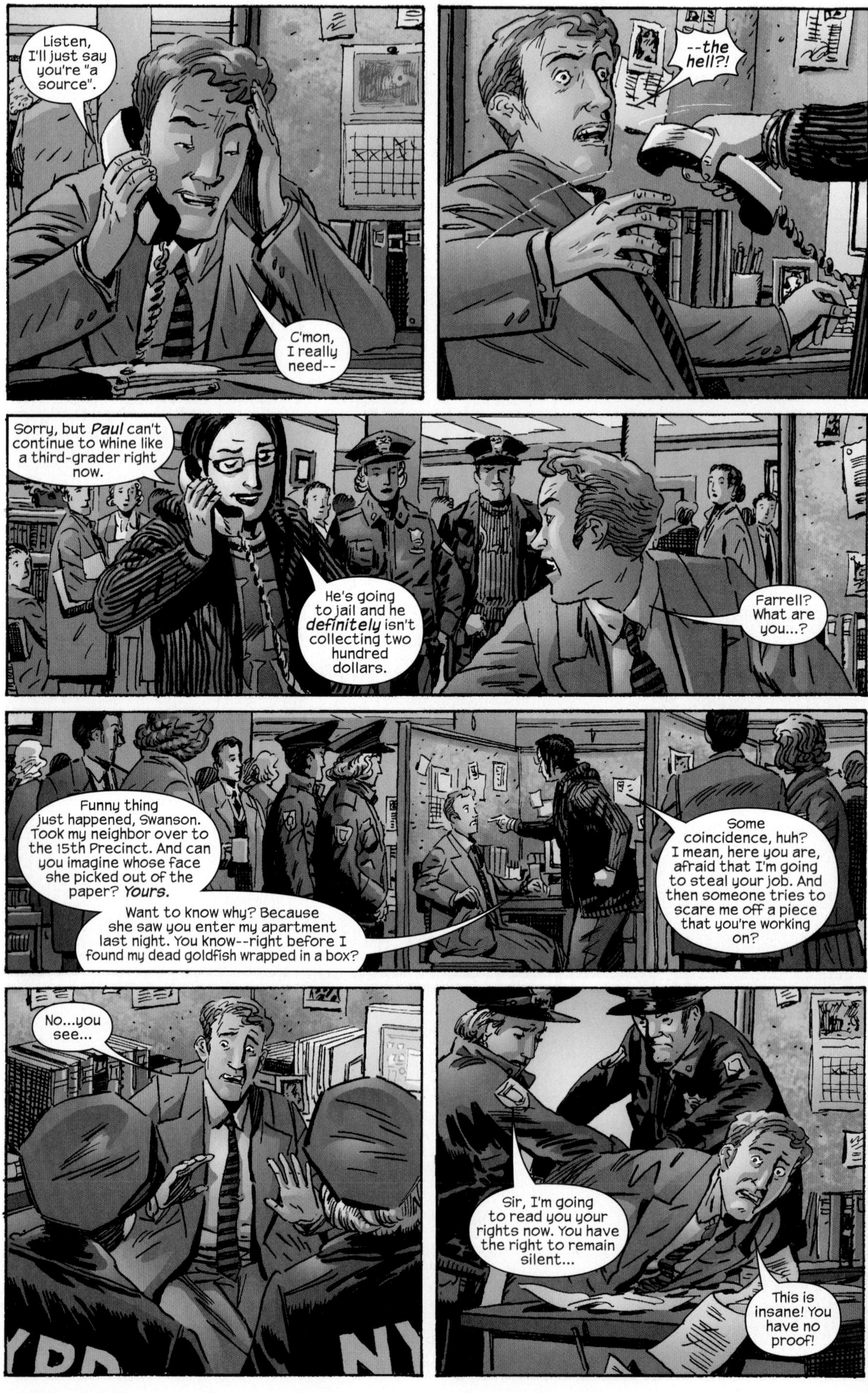
Listen, I'll just say you're "a source".
C'mon, I really need--
--the hell?!
Sorry, but *Paul* can't continue to whine like a third-grader right now.
He's going to jail and he *definitely* isn't collecting two hundred dollars.
Farrell? What are you...?
Funny thing just happened, Swanson. Took my neighbor over to the 15th Precinct. And can you imagine whose face she picked out of the paper? *Yours.*
Want to know why? Because she saw you enter my apartment last night. You know--right before I found my dead goldfish wrapped in a box?
Some coincidence, huh? I mean, here you are, afraid that I'm going to steal your job. And then someone tries to scare me off a piece that you're working on?
No...you see...
Sir, I'm going to read you your rights now. You have the right to remain silent...
This is insane! You have no proof!

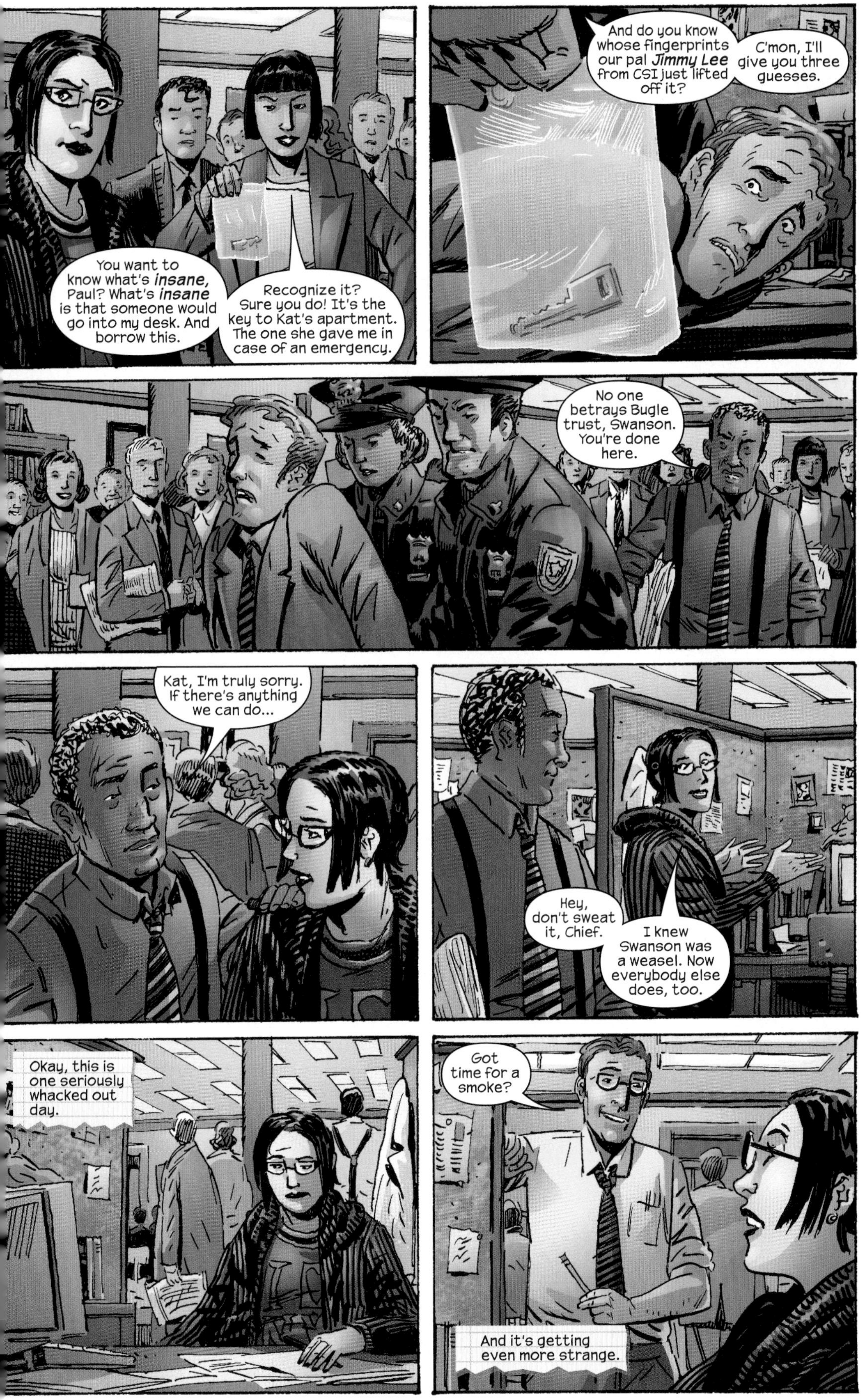
You want to know what's *insane,* Paul? What's *insane* is that someone would go into my desk. And borrow this.
Recognize it? Sure you do! It's the key to Kat's apartment. The one she gave me in case of an emergency.
And do you know whose fingerprints our pal *Jimmy Lee* from CSI just lifted off it?
C'mon, I'll give you three guesses.
No one betrays Bugle trust, Swanson. You're done here.
Kat, I'm truly sorry. If there's anything we can do...
Hey, don't sweat it, Chief.
I knew Swanson was a weasel. Now everybody else does, too.
Okay, this is one seriously whacked out day.
Got time for a smoke?
And it's getting even more strange.

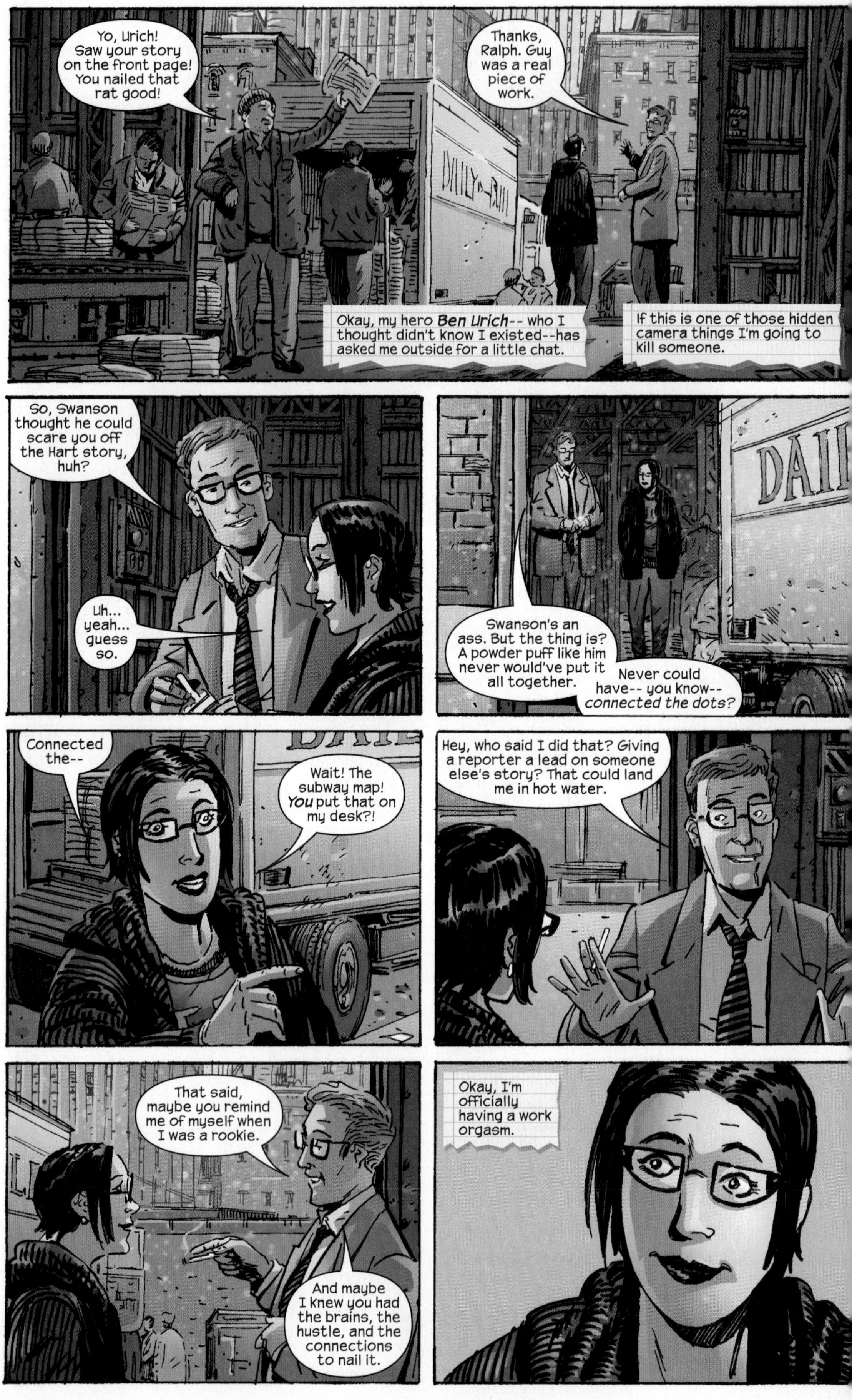

Yo, Urich! Saw your story on the front page! You nailed that rat good!
Thanks, Ralph. Guy was a real piece of work.
DAILY BUGLE
Okay, my hero *Ben Urich*-- who I thought didn't know I existed--has asked me outside for a little chat.
If this is one of those hidden camera things I'm going to kill someone.
So, Swanson thought he could scare you off the Hart story, huh?
Uh... yeah... guess so.
Swanson's an ass. But the thing is? A powder puff like him never would've put it all together.
Never could have-- you know-- *connected the dots?*
Connected the--
Wait! The subway map! *You* put that on my desk?!
Hey, who said I did that? Giving a reporter a lead on someone else's story? That could land me in hot water.
That said, maybe you remind me of myself when I was a rookie.
And maybe I knew you had the brains, the hustle, and the connections to nail it.
Okay, I'm officially having a work orgasm.

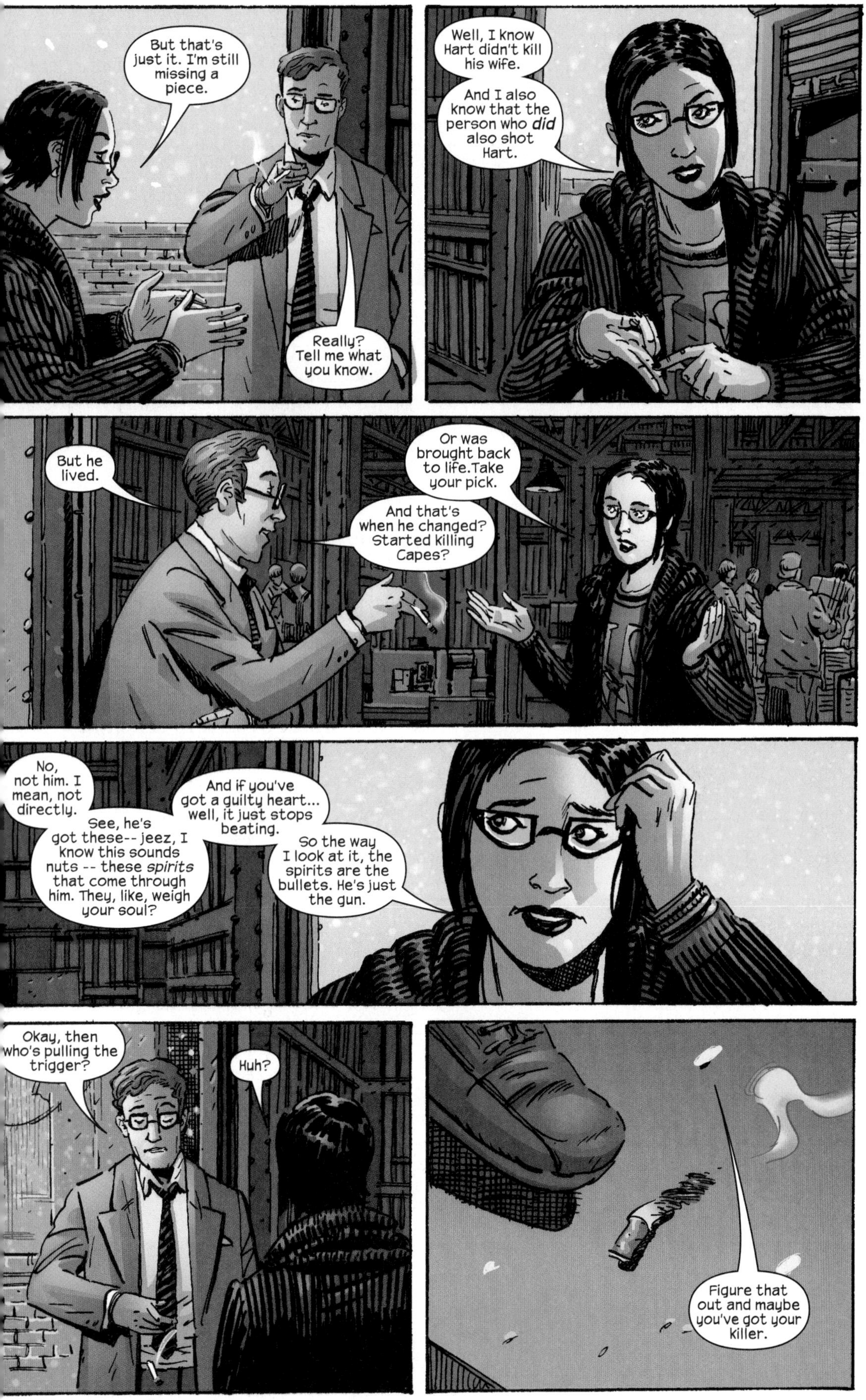
But that's just it. I'm still missing a piece.
Really? Tell me what you know.
Well, I know Hart didn't kill his wife.
And I also know that the person who *did* also shot Hart.
But he lived.
Or was brought back to life.Take your pick.
And that's when he changed? Started killing Capes?
No, not him. I mean, not directly.
See, he's got these-- jeez, I know this sounds nuts -- these *spirits* that come through him. They, like, weigh your soul?
And if you've got a guilty heart... well, it just stops beating.
So the way I look at it, the spirits are the bullets. He's just the gun.
Okay, then who's pulling the trigger?
Huh?
Figure that out and maybe you've got your killer.

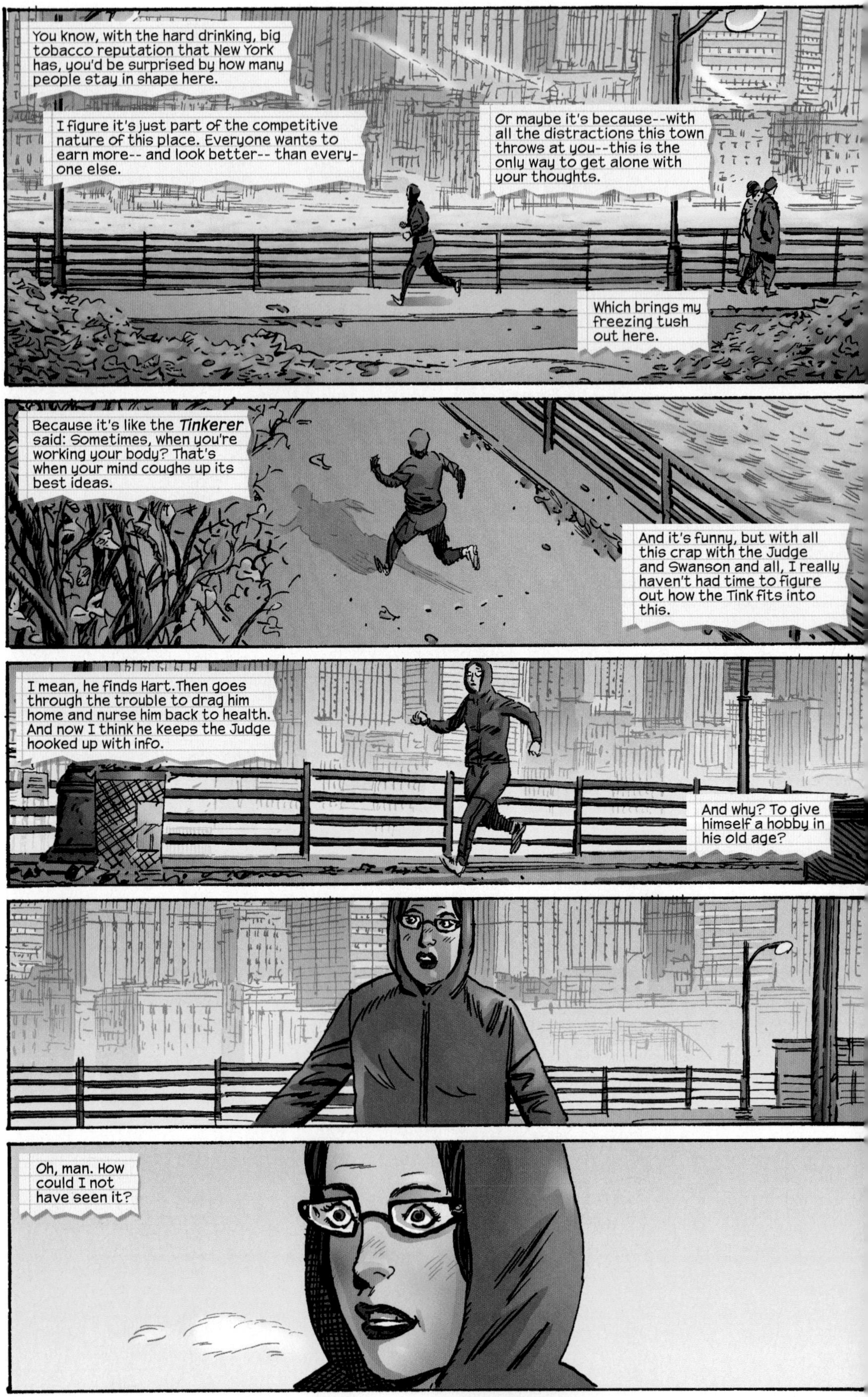
You know, with the hard drinking, big tobacco reputation that New York has, you'd be surprised by how many people stay in shape here.
I figure it's just part of the competitive nature of this place. Everyone wants to earn more-- and look better-- than every-one else.
Or maybe it's because--with all the distractions this town throws at you--this is the only way to get alone with your thoughts.
Which brings my freezing tush out here.
Because it's like the *Tinkerer* said: Sometimes, when you're working your body? That's when your mind coughs up its best ideas.
And it's funny, but with all this crap with the Judge and Swanson and all, I really haven't had time to figure out how the Tink fits into this.
I mean, he finds Hart. Then goes through the trouble to drag him home and nurse him back to health. And now I think he keeps the Judge hooked up with info.
And why? To give himself a hobby in his old age?
Oh, man. How could I not have seen it?

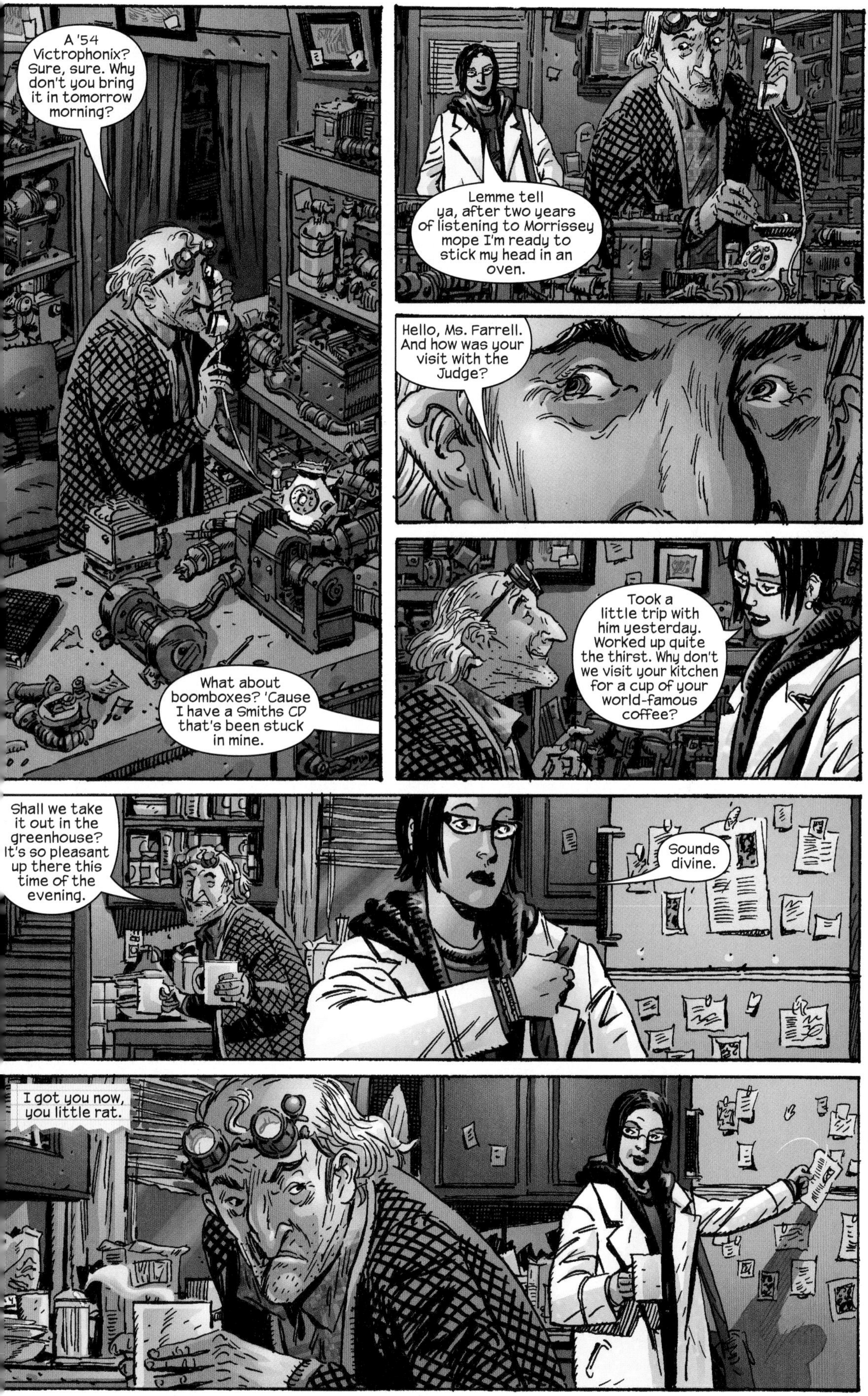
A '54 Victrophonix? Sure, sure. Why don't you bring it in tomorrow morning?
What about boomboxes? 'Cause I have a Smiths CD that's been stuck in mine.
Lemme tell ya, after two years of listening to Morrissey mope I'm ready to stick my head in an oven.
Hello, Ms. Farrell. And how was your visit with the Judge?
Took a little trip with him yesterday. Worked up quite the thirst. Why don't we visit your kitchen for a cup of your world-famous coffee?
Shall we take it out in the greenhouse? It's so pleasant up there this time of the evening.
Sounds divine.
I got you now, you little rat.

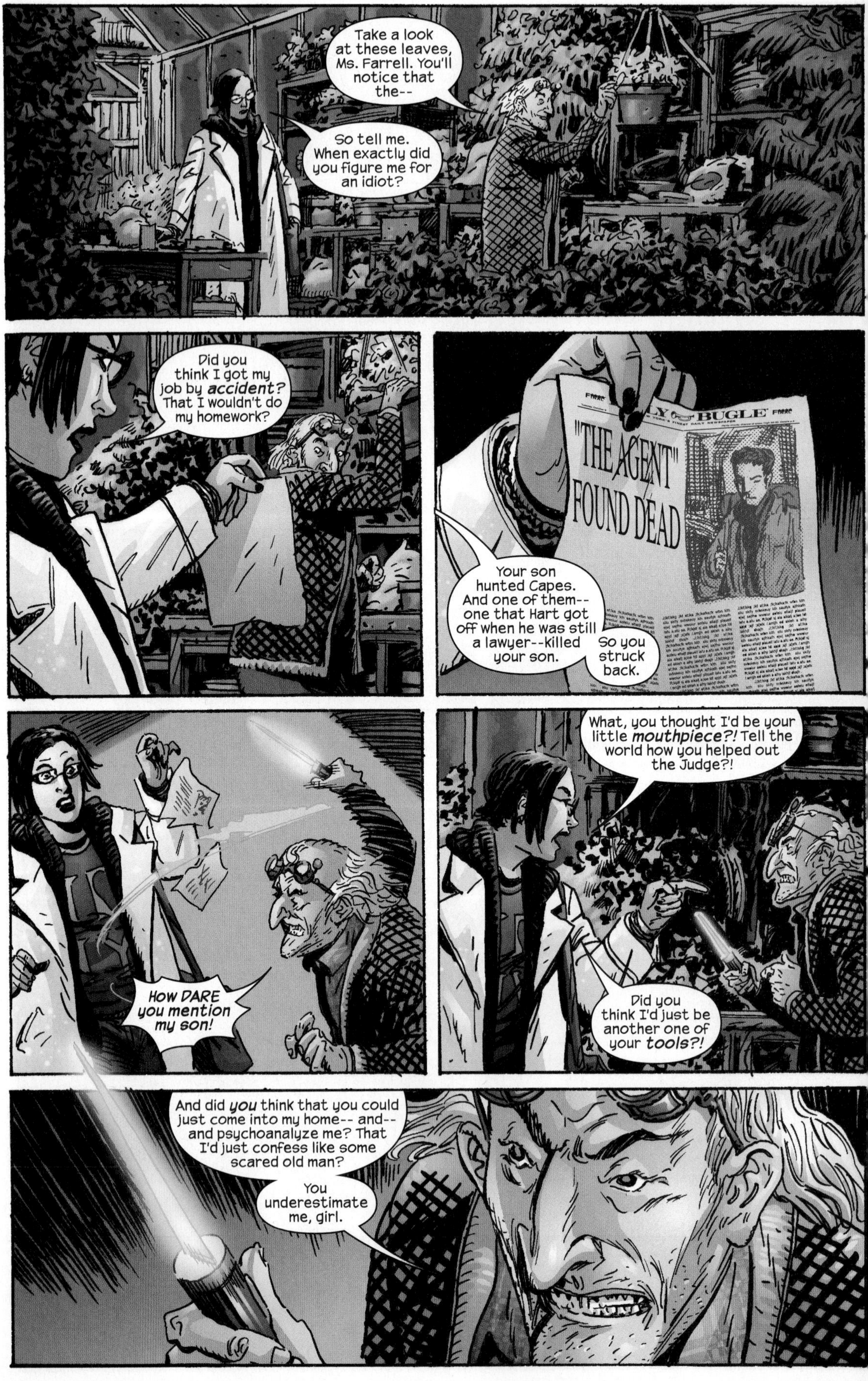
Take a look at these leaves, Ms. Farrell. You'll notice that the--
So tell me. When exactly did you figure me for an idiot?
Did you think I got my job by *accident?* That I wouldn't do my homework?
BUGLE
"THE AGENT" FOUND DEAD
Your son hunted Capes. And one of them-- one that Hart got off when he was still a lawyer--killed your son.
So you struck back.
HOW DARE you mention my son!
What, you thought I'd be your little *mouthpiece?!* Tell the world how you helped out the Judge?!
Did you think I'd just be another one of your *tools?!*
And did *you* think that you could just come into my home-- and-- and psychoanalyze me? That I'd just confess like some scared old man?
You underestimate me, girl.

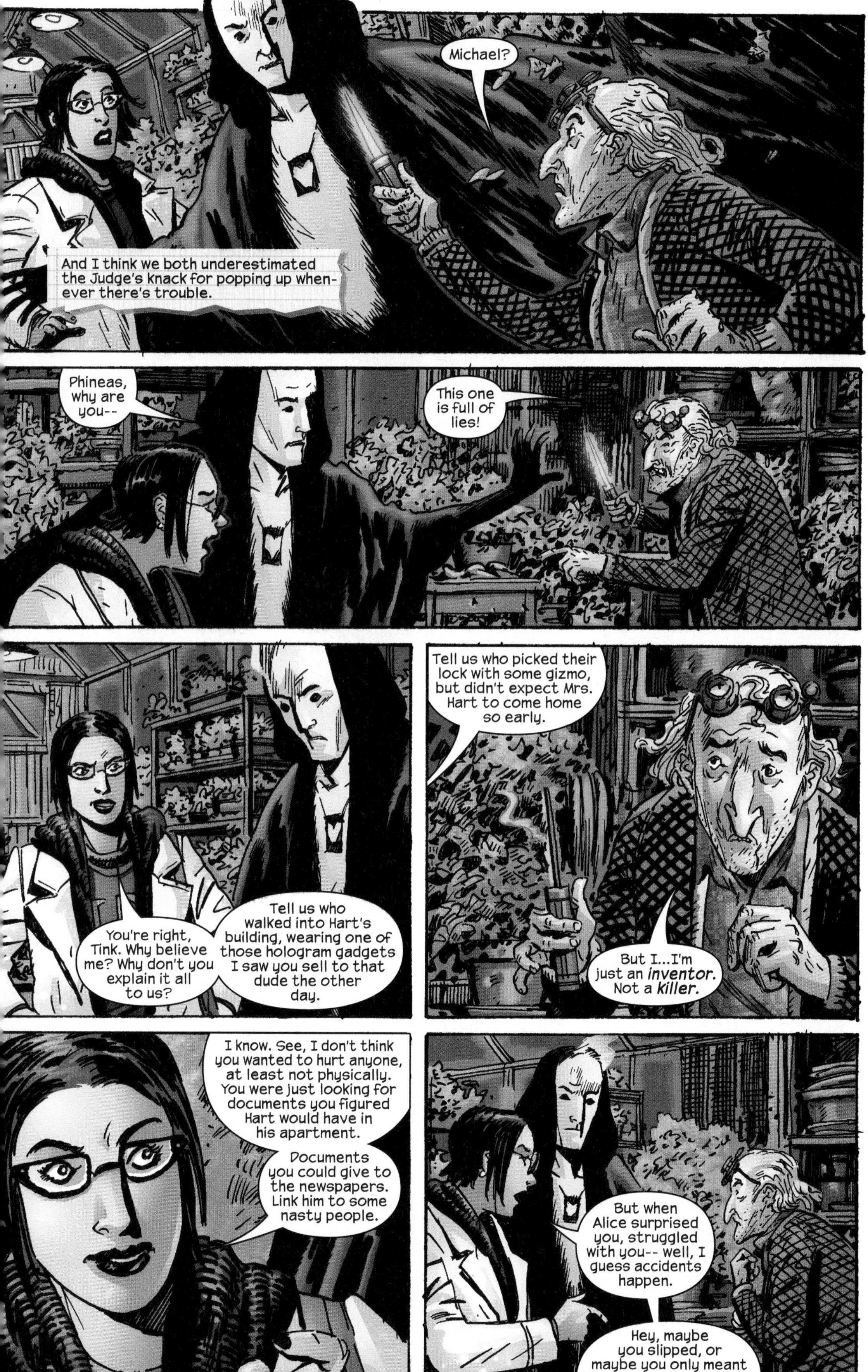
Michael?
And I think we both underestimated the Judge's knack for popping up whenever there's trouble.
Phineas, why are you--
This one is full of lies!
Tell us who picked their lock with some gizmo, but didn't expect Mrs. Hart to come home so early.
You're right, Tink. Why believe me? Why don't you explain it all to us?
Tell us who walked into Hart's building, wearing one of those hologram gadgets I saw you sell to that dude the other day.
But I...I'm just an *inventor*. Not a *killer*.
I know. See, I don't think you wanted to hurt anyone, at least not physically. You were just looking for documents you figured Hart would have in his apartment.
Documents you could give to the newspapers. Link him to some nasty people.
But when Alice surprised you, struggled with you-- well, I guess accidents happen.
Hey, maybe you slipped, or maybe you only meant to graze her. Whatever happened, she was dead.

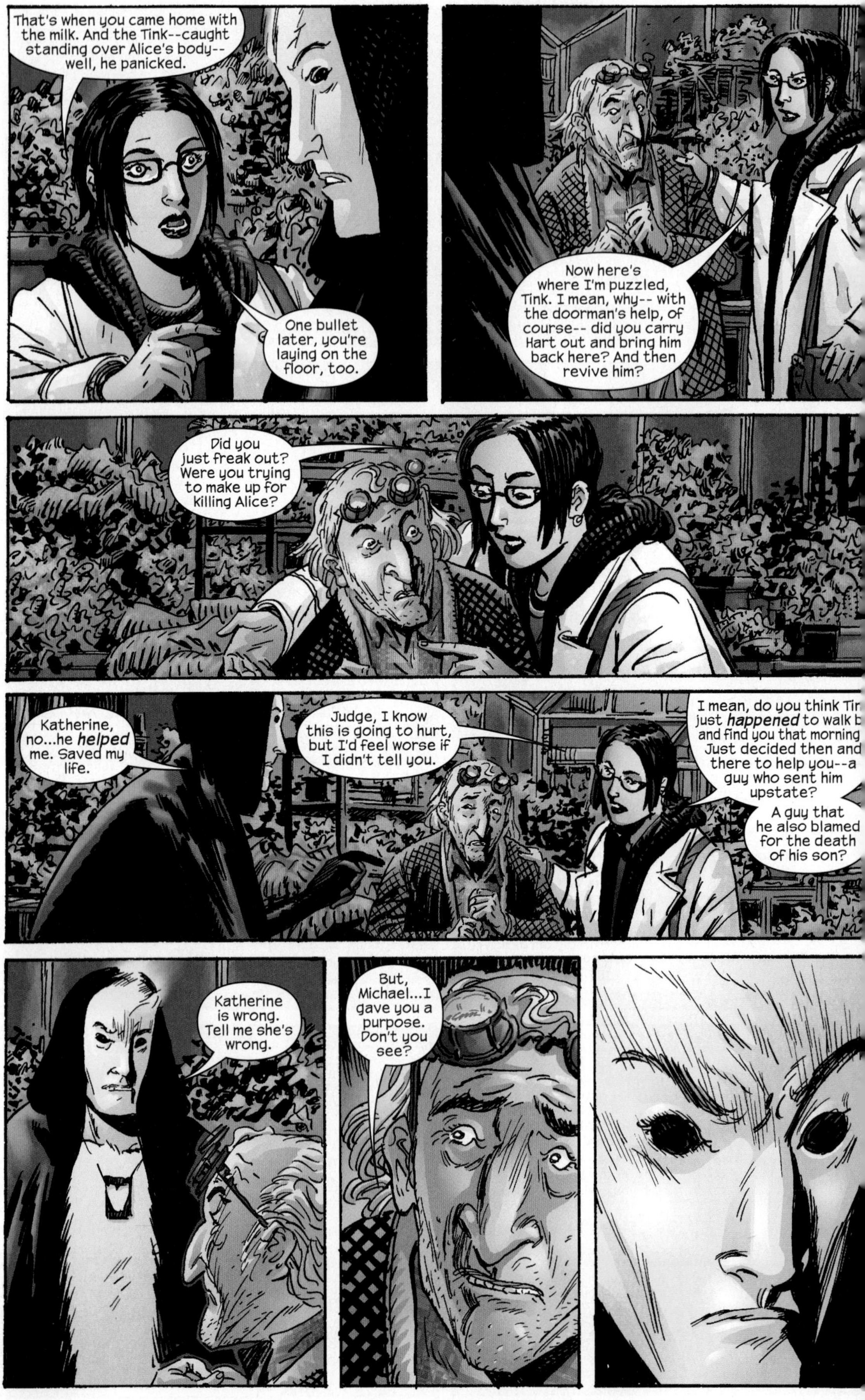
That's when you came home with the milk. And the Tink--caught standing over Alice's body-- well, he panicked.
One bullet later, you're laying on the floor, too.
Now here's where I'm puzzled, Tink. I mean, why-- with the doorman's help, of course-- did you carry Hart out and bring him back here? And then revive him?
Did you just freak out? Were you trying to make up for killing Alice?
Katherine, no...he *helped* me. Saved my life.
Judge, I know this is going to hurt, but I'd feel worse if I didn't tell you.
I mean, do you think Tin just *happened* to walk b and find you that morning Just decided then and there to help you--a guy who sent him upstate?
A guy that he also blamed for the death of his son?
Katherine is wrong. Tell me she's wrong.
But, Michael...I gave you a purpose. Don't you see?

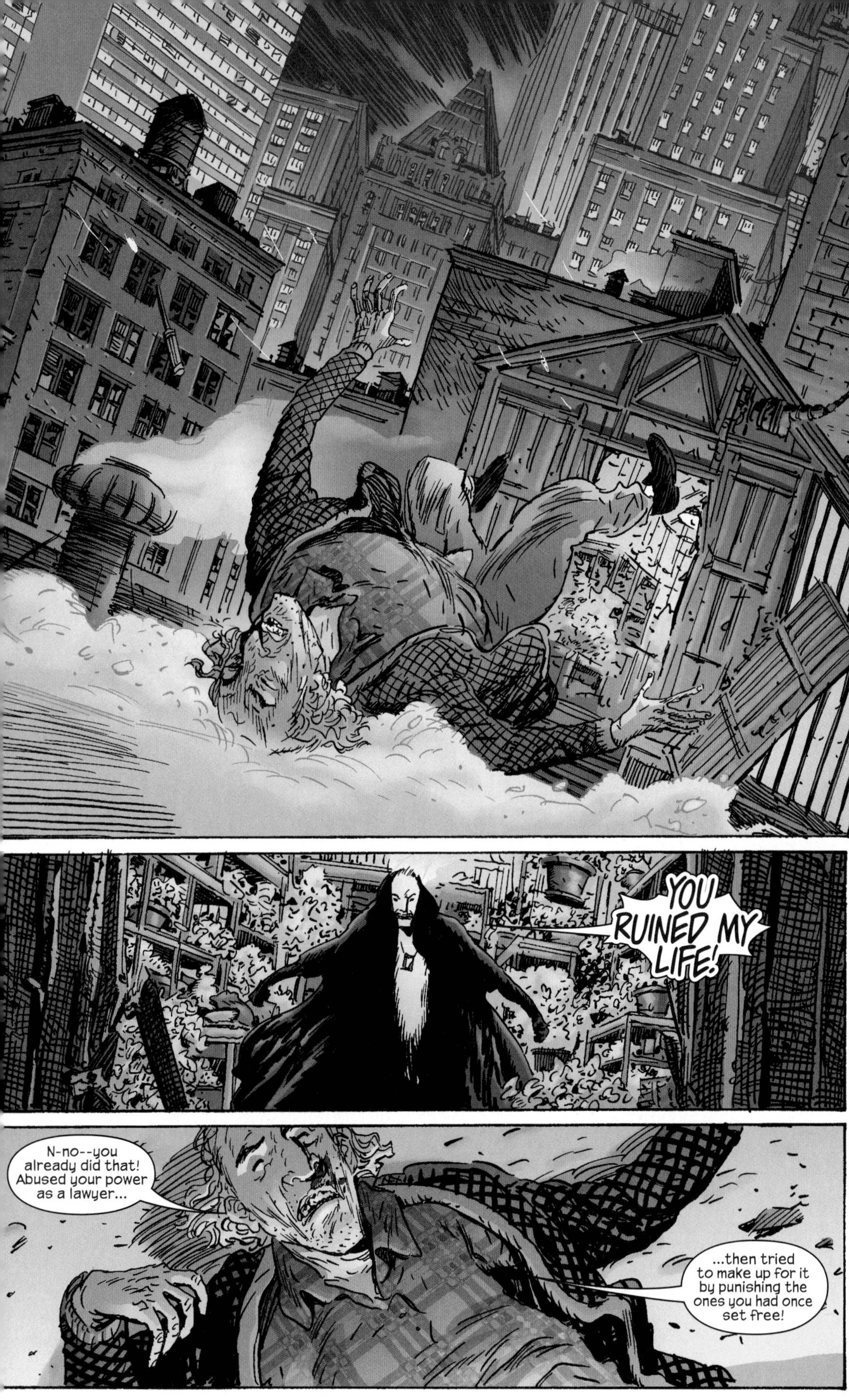
YOU RUINED MY LIFE!
N-no--you already did that! Abused your power as a lawyer...
...then tried to make up for it by punishing the ones you had once set free!

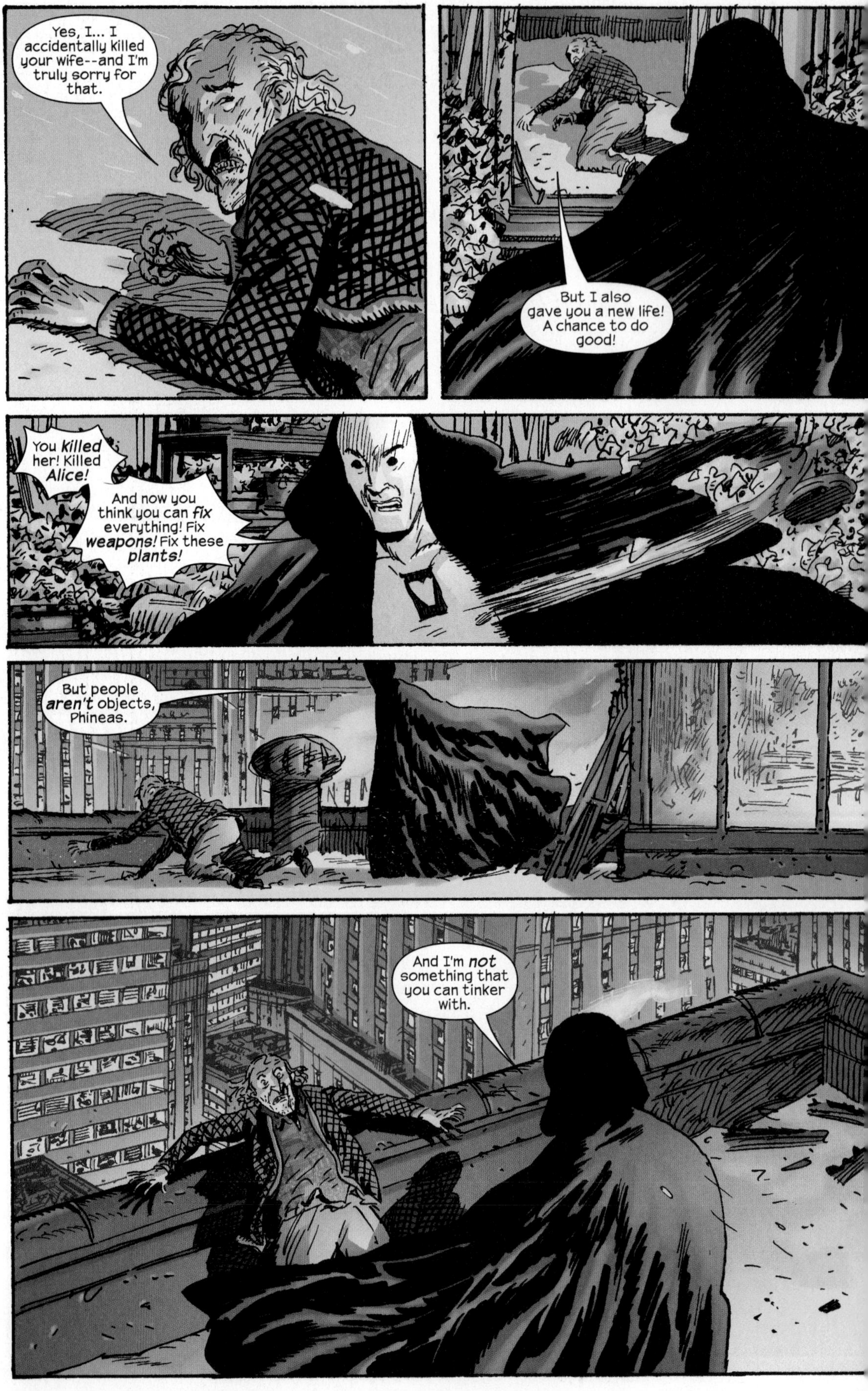
Yes, I... I accidentally killed your wife--and I'm truly sorry for that.
But I also gave you a new life! A chance to do good!
You *killed* her! Killed *Alice!*
And now you think you can *fix* everything! Fix *weapons!* Fix these *plants!*
But people *aren't* objects, Phineas.
And I'm *not* something that you can tinker with.

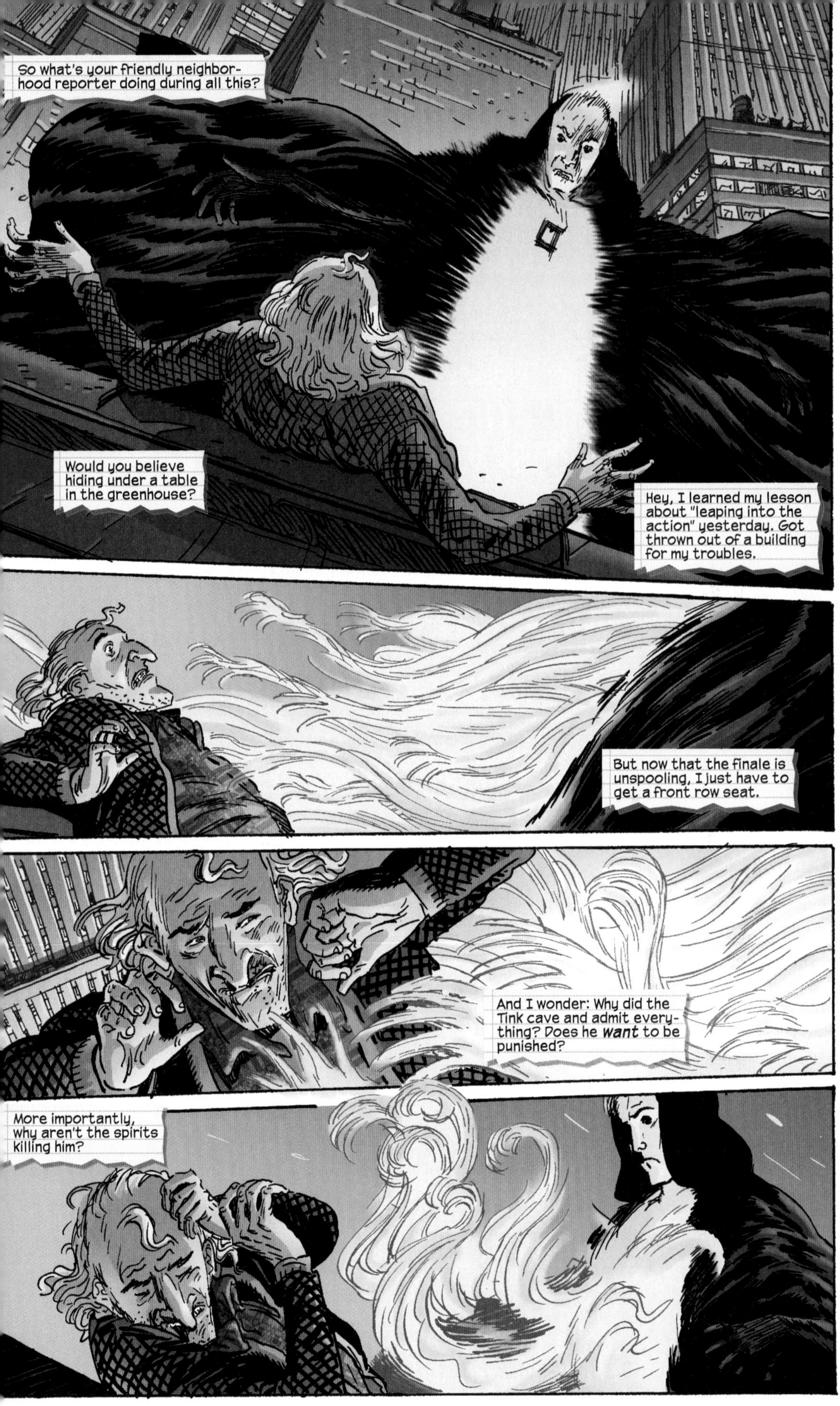
So what's your friendly neighbor-hood reporter doing during all this?
Would you believe hiding under a table in the greenhouse?
Hey, I learned my lesson about "leaping into the action" yesterday. Got thrown out of a building for my troubles.
But now that the finale is unspooling, I just have to get a front row seat.
And I wonder: Why did the Tink cave and admit every-thing? Does he *want* to be punished?
More importantly, why aren't the spirits killing him?

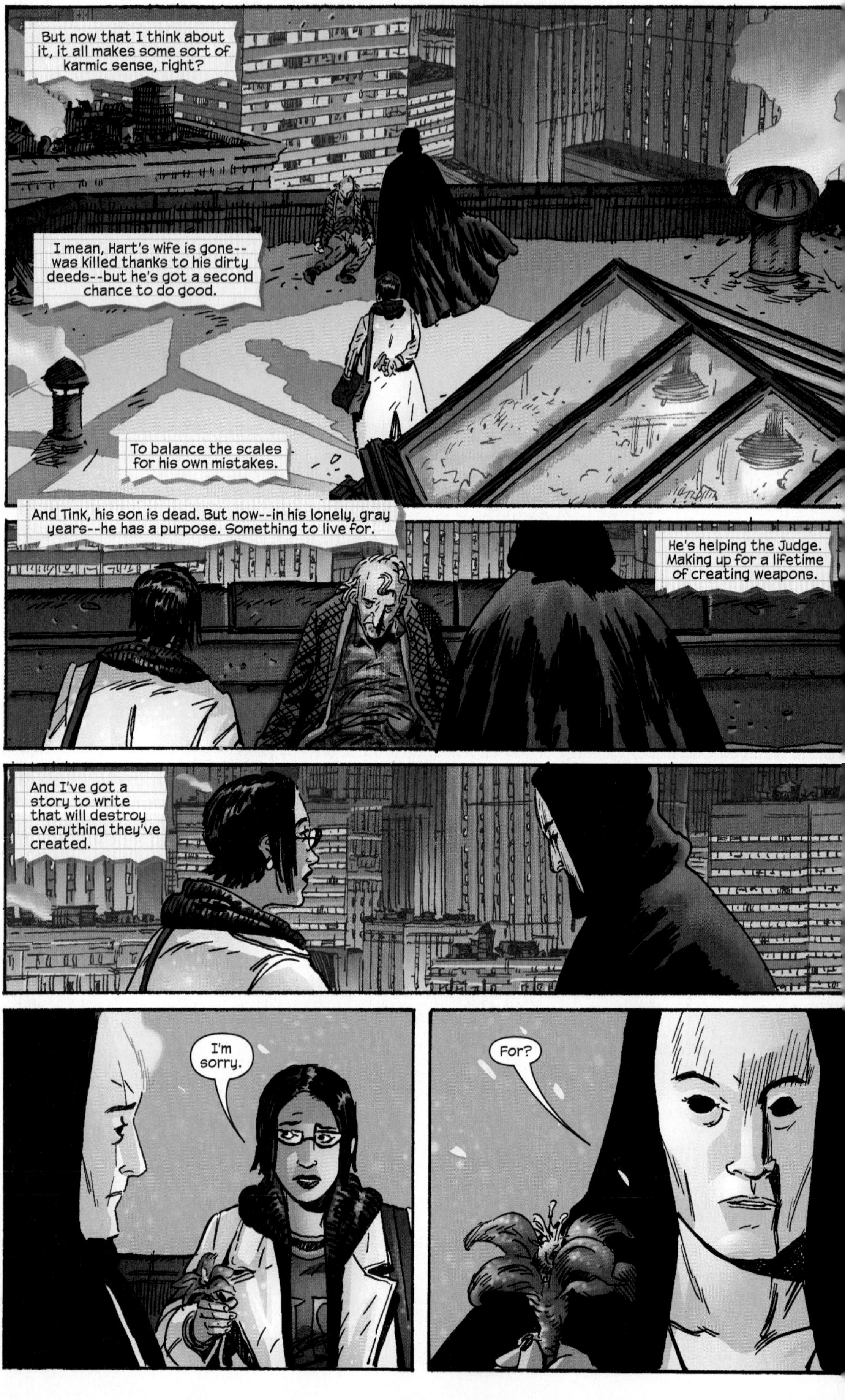

But now that I think about it, it all makes some sort of karmic sense, right?
I mean, Hart's wife is gone--was killed thanks to his dirty deeds--but he's got a second chance to do good.
To balance the scales for his own mistakes.
And Tink, his son is dead. But now--in his lonely, gray years--he has a purpose. Something to live for.
He's helping the Judge. Making up for a lifetime of creating weapons.
And I've got a story to write that will destroy everything they've created.
I'm sorry.
For?

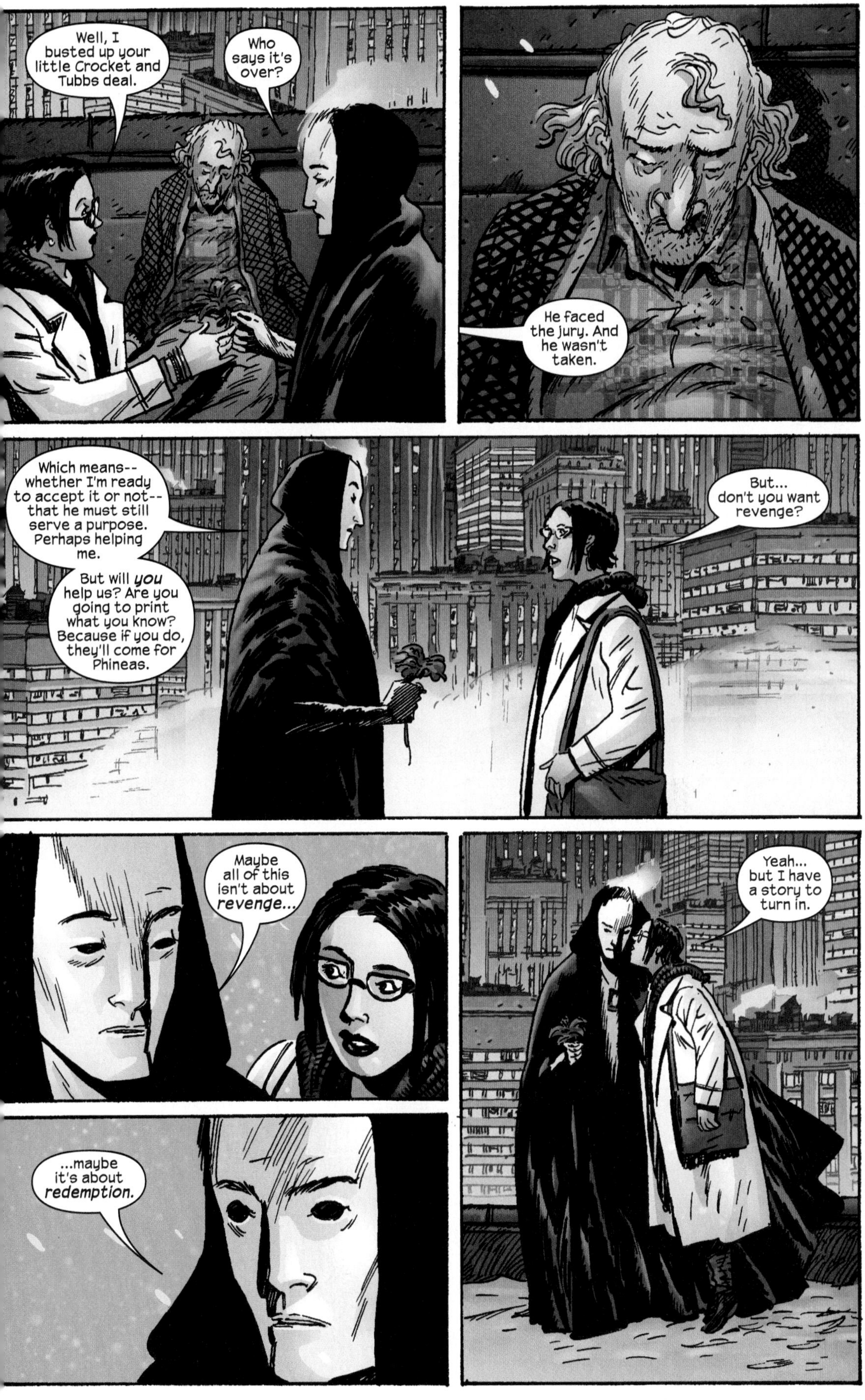
Well, I busted up your little Crocket and Tubbs deal.
Who says it's over?
He faced the jury. And he wasn't taken.
Which means--whether I'm ready to accept it or not--that he must still serve a purpose. Perhaps helping me.
But will *you* help us? Are you going to print what you know? Because if you do, they'll come for Phineas.
But... don't you want revenge?
Maybe all of this isn't about *revenge...*
...maybe it's about *redemption.*
Yeah... but I have a story to turn in.

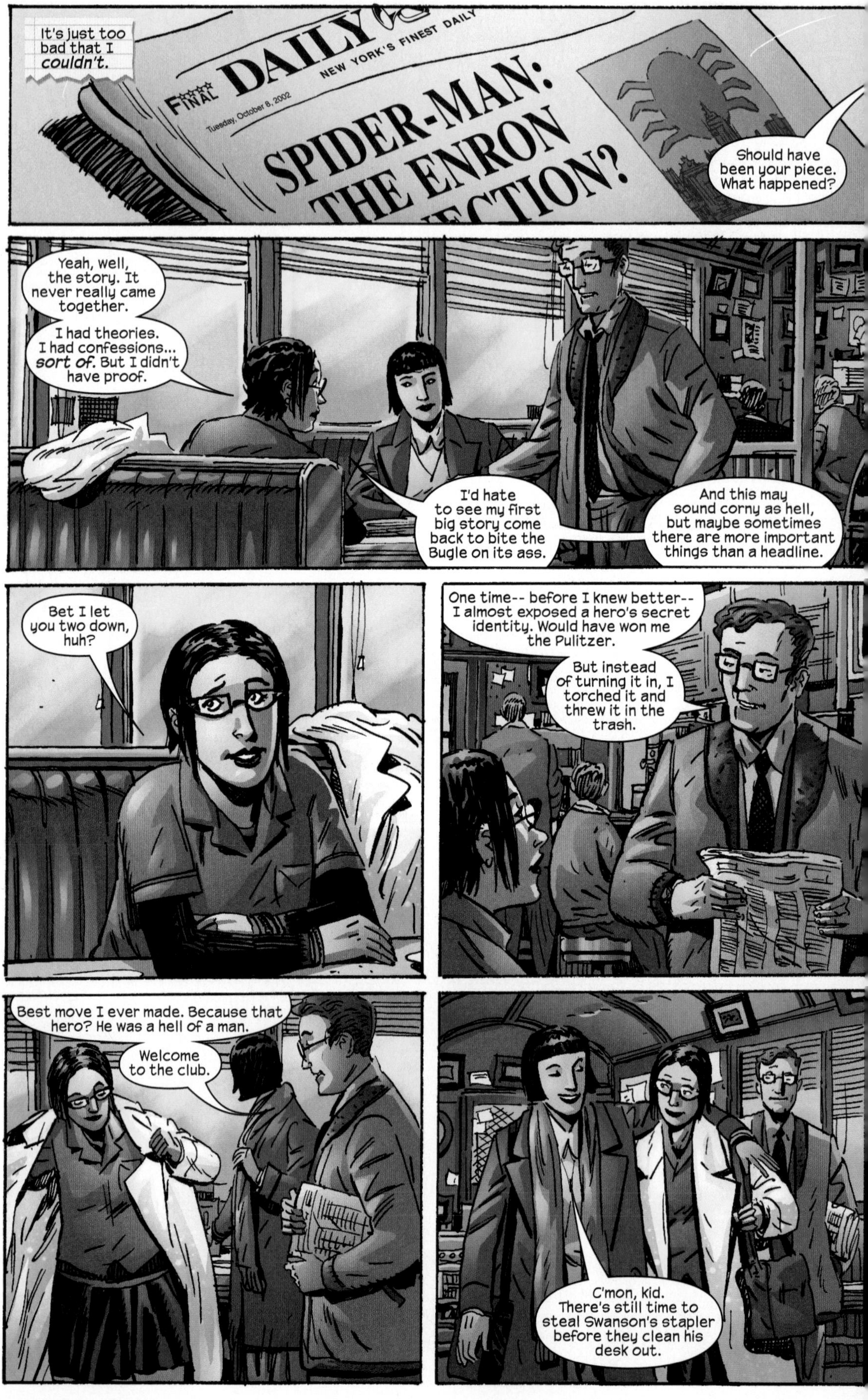
It's just too bad that I couldn't.
DAILY
NEW YORK'S FINEST DAILY
FINAL
Tuesday, October 8, 2002
SPIDER-MAN: THE ENRON
Should have been your piece. What happened?
Yeah, well, the story. It never really came together.
I had theories. I had confessions... sort of. But I didn't have proof.
I'd hate to see my first big story come back to bite the Bugle on its ass.
And this may sound corny as hell, but maybe sometimes there are more important things than a headline.
Bet I let you two down, huh?
One time-- before I knew better-- I almost exposed a hero's secret identity. Would have won me the Pulitzer.
But instead of turning it in, I torched it and threw it in the trash.
Best move I ever made. Because that hero? He was a hell of a man.
Welcome to the club.
C'mon, kid. There's still time to steal Swanson's stapler before they clean his desk out.

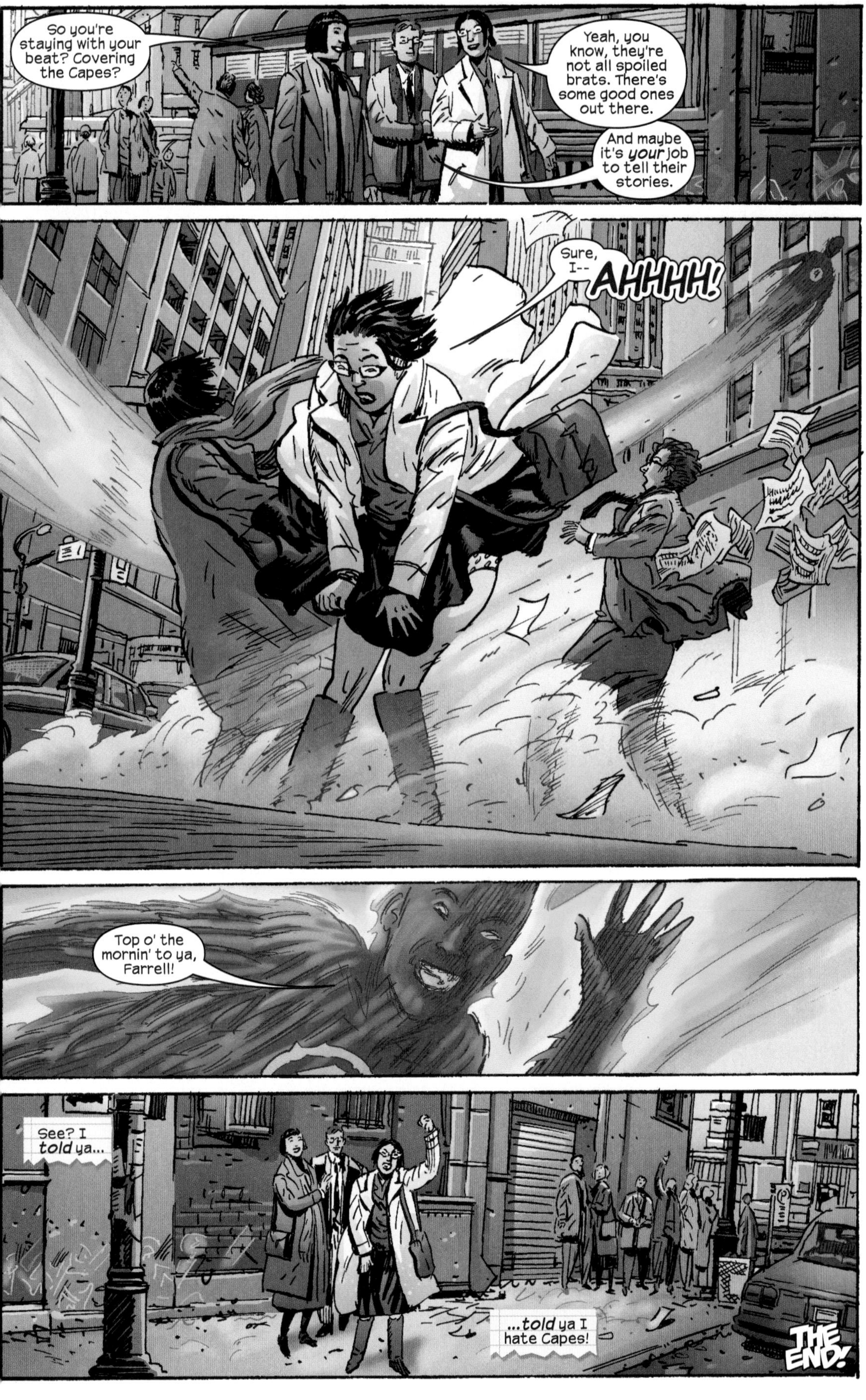
So you're staying with your beat? Covering the Capes?
Yeah, you know, they're not all spoiled brats. There's some good ones out there.
And maybe it's *your* job to tell their stories.
Sure, I--
AHHHH!
Top o' the mornin' to ya, Farrell!
See? I *told* ya...
...*told* ya I hate Capes!
THE END!

The following three-part *Daily Bugle* story was originally published as a backup feature in *Spectacular Spider-Man #205-207*.

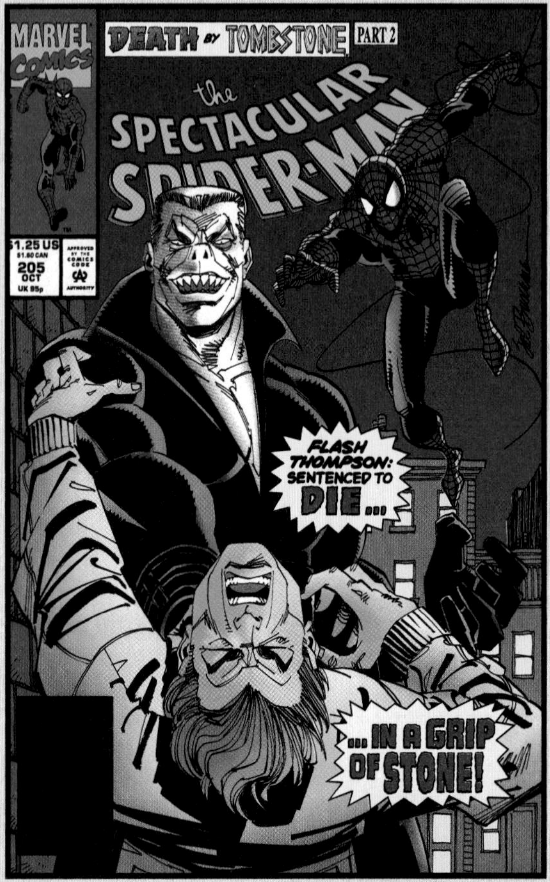
MARVEL COMICS
DEATH BY TOMBSTONE PART 2
the SPECTACULAR SPIDER-MAN
$1.25 US
205
OCT
UK 85p
FLASH THOMPSON: SENTENCED TO DIE...
...IN A GRIP OF STONE!

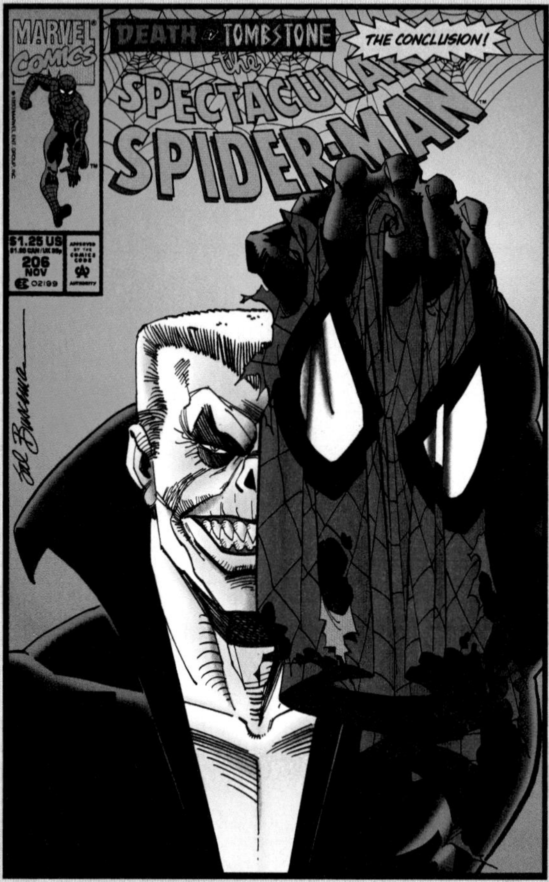
MARVEL COMICS
DEATH BY TOMBSTONE
THE CONCLUSION!
the SPECTACULAR SPIDER-MAN
$1.25 US
206
NOV

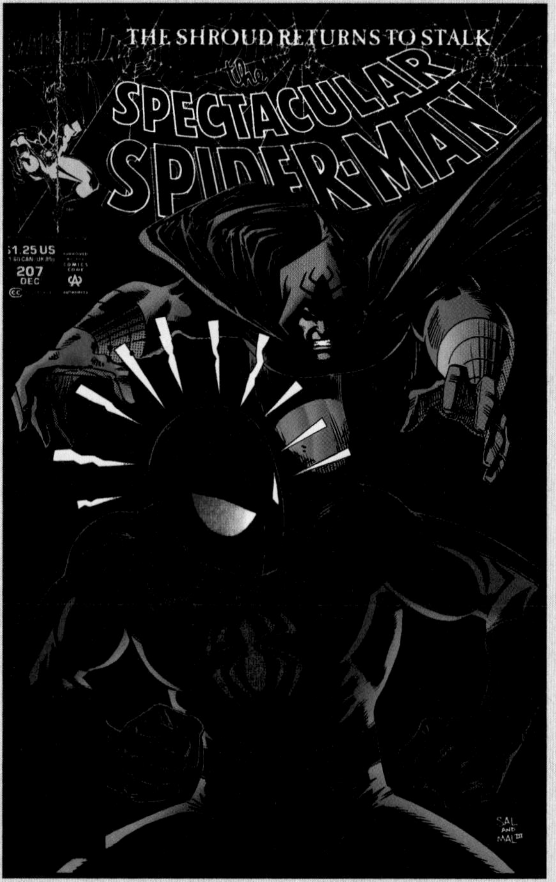
THE SHROUD RETURNS TO STALK
the SPECTACULAR SPIDER-MAN
$1.25 US
207
DEC
SAL AND MAL

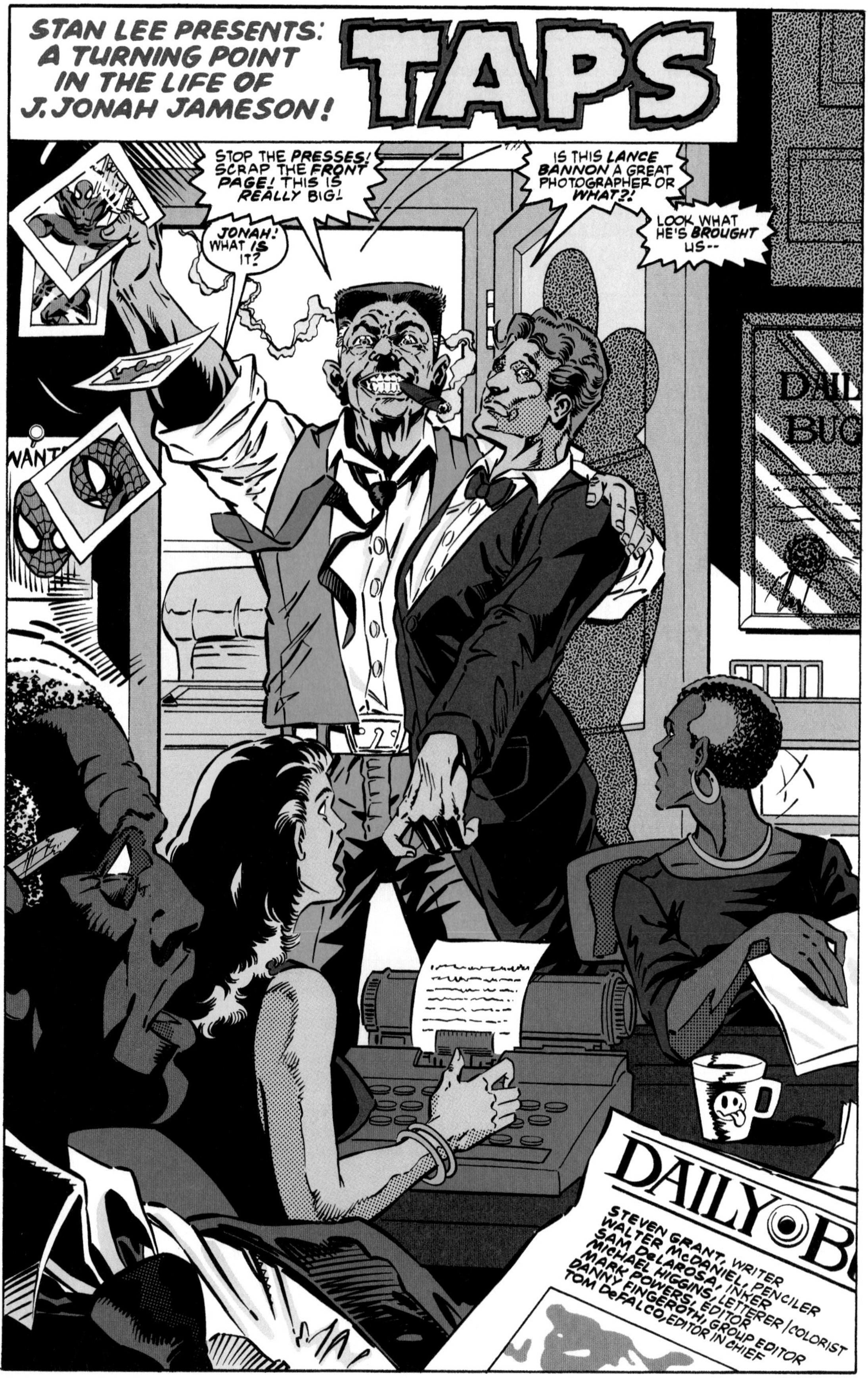
STAN LEE PRESENTS: A TURNING POINT IN THE LIFE OF J. JONAH JAMESON!
TAPS
STOP THE PRESSES! SCRAP THE FRONT PAGE! THIS IS REALLY BIG!
JONAH! WHAT IS IT?
IS THIS LANCE BANNON A GREAT PHOTOGRAPHER OR WHAT?!
LOOK WHAT HE'S BROUGHT US--
DAILY BUGLE
DAILY
STEVEN GRANT, WRITER
WALTER McDANIEL, PENCILER
SAM DeLAROSA, INKER
MICHAEL HIGGINS, LETTERER/COLORIST
MARK POWERS, EDITOR
DANNY FINGEROTH, GROUP EDITOR
TOM DeFALCO, EDITOR IN CHIEF

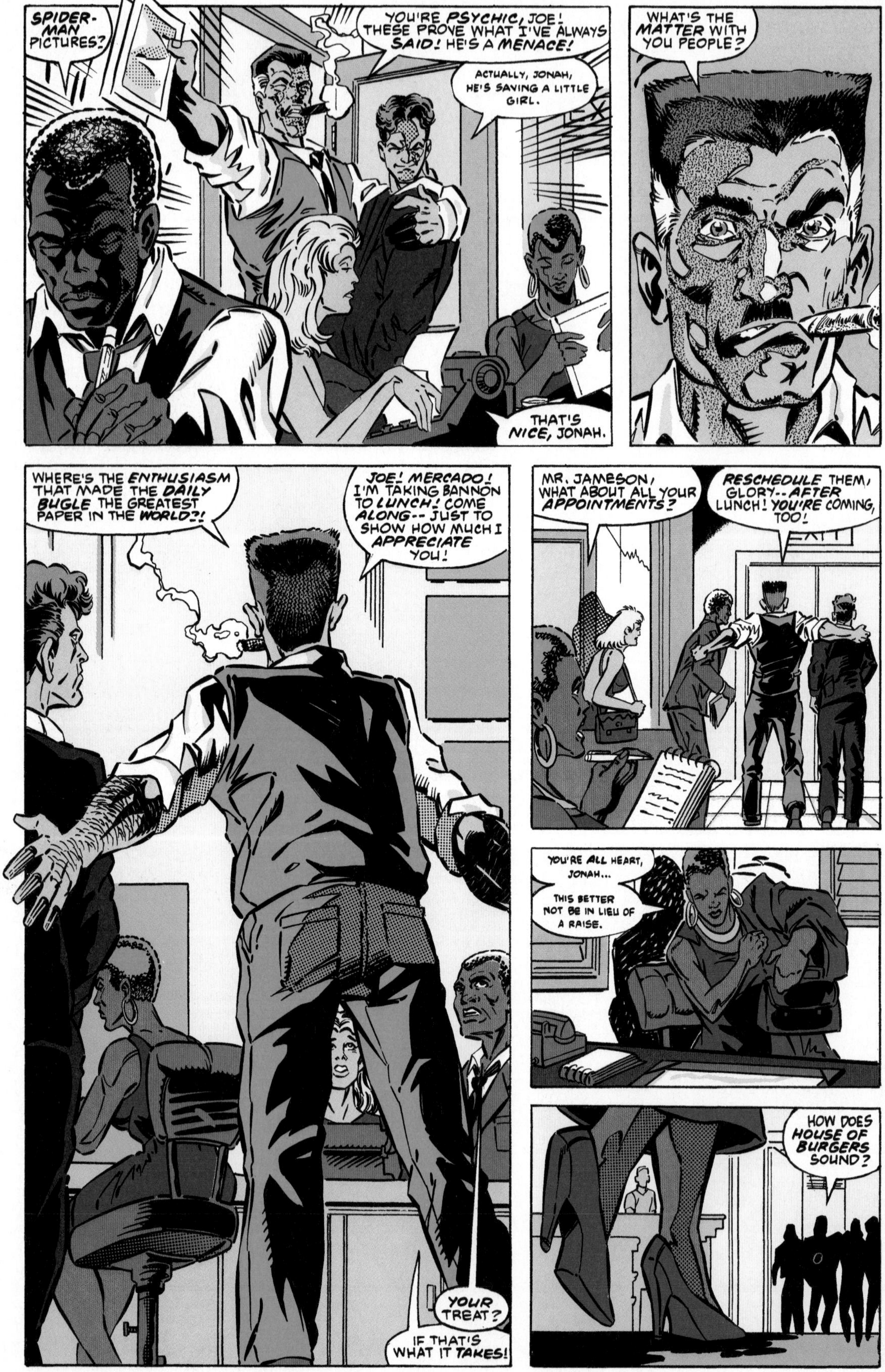
SPIDER-MAN PICTURES?
YOU'RE PSYCHIC, JOE! THESE PROVE WHAT I'VE ALWAYS SAID! HE'S A MENACE!
ACTUALLY, JONAH, HE'S SAVING A LITTLE GIRL.
THAT'S NICE, JONAH.
WHAT'S THE MATTER WITH YOU PEOPLE?
WHERE'S THE ENTHUSIASM THAT MADE THE DAILY BUGLE THE GREATEST PAPER IN THE WORLD?!
JOE! MERCADO! I'M TAKING BANNON TO LUNCH! COME ALONG-- JUST TO SHOW HOW MUCH I APPRECIATE YOU!
YOUR TREAT?
IF THAT'S WHAT IT TAKES!
MR. JAMESON, WHAT ABOUT ALL YOUR APPOINTMENTS?
RESCHEDULE THEM, GLORY-- AFTER LUNCH! YOU'RE COMING, TOO!
YOU'RE ALL HEART, JONAH...
THIS BETTER NOT BE IN LIEU OF A RAISE.
HOW DOES HOUSE OF BURGERS SOUND?

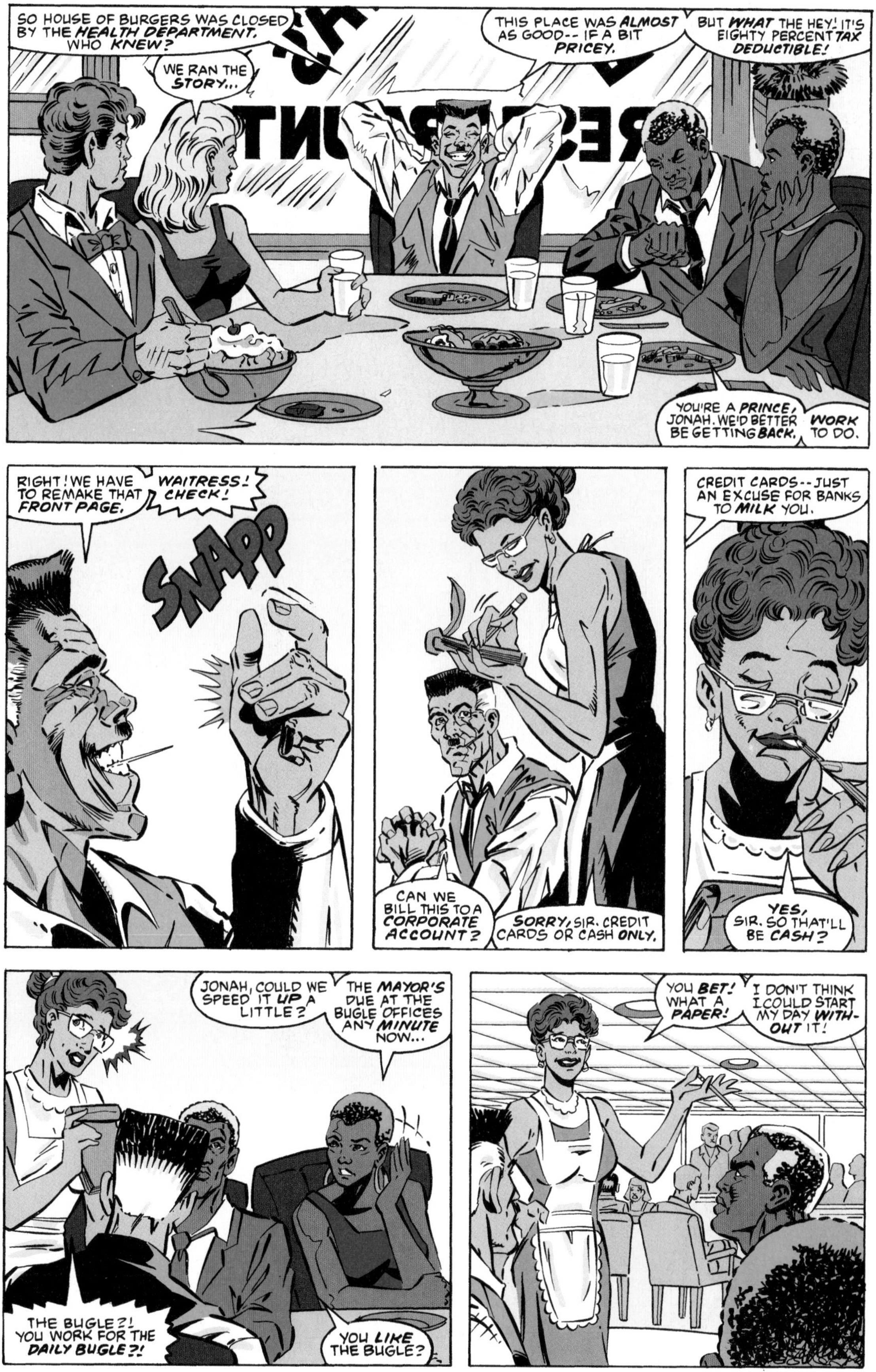
SO HOUSE OF BURGERS WAS CLOSED BY THE HEALTH DEPARTMENT. WHO KNEW?
WE RAN THE STORY...
THIS PLACE WAS ALMOST AS GOOD-- IF A BIT PRICEY.
BUT WHAT THE HEY! IT'S EIGHTY PERCENT TAX DEDUCTIBLE!
YOU'RE A PRINCE, JONAH. WE'D BETTER BE GETTING BACK.
WORK TO DO.
RIGHT! WE HAVE TO REMAKE THAT FRONT PAGE.
WAITRESS! CHECK!
SNAPP
CAN WE BILL THIS TO A CORPORATE ACCOUNT?
SORRY, SIR. CREDIT CARDS OR CASH ONLY.
CREDIT CARDS--JUST AN EXCUSE FOR BANKS TO MILK YOU.
YES, SIR. SO THAT'LL BE CASH?
JONAH, COULD WE SPEED IT UP A LITTLE?
THE MAYOR'S DUE AT THE BUGLE OFFICES ANY MINUTE NOW...
THE BUGLE?! YOU WORK FOR THE DAILY BUGLE?!
YOU LIKE THE BUGLE?
YOU BET! WHAT A PAPER!
I DON'T THINK I COULD START MY DAY WITHOUT IT!

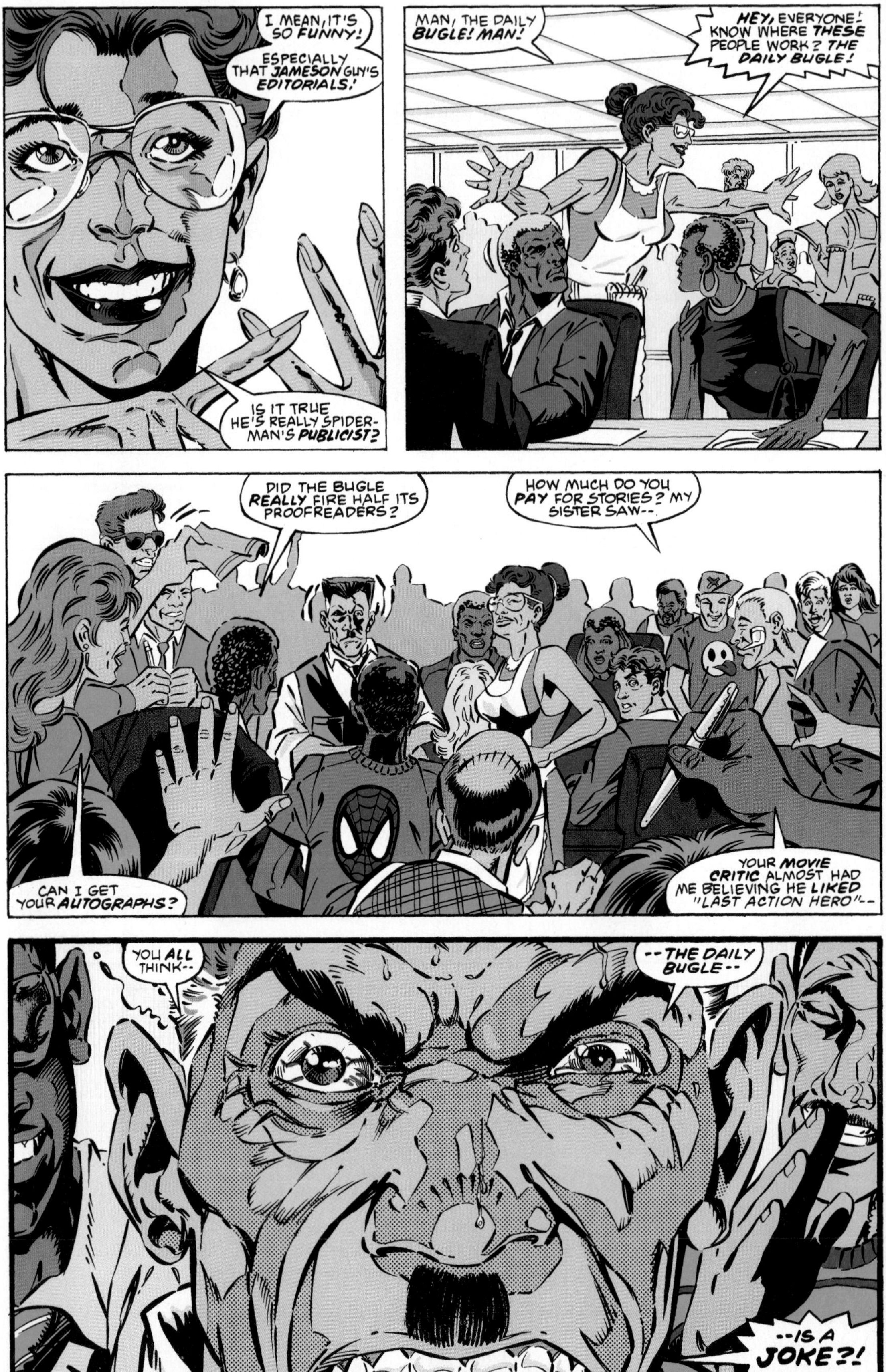
I MEAN, IT'S SO FUNNY!
ESPECIALLY THAT JAMESON GUY'S EDITORIALS!
IS IT TRUE HE'S REALLY SPIDER-MAN'S PUBLICIST?
MAN, THE DAILY BUGLE! MAN!
HEY, EVERYONE! KNOW WHERE THESE PEOPLE WORK? THE DAILY BUGLE!
DID THE BUGLE REALLY FIRE HALF ITS PROOFREADERS?
HOW MUCH DO YOU PAY FOR STORIES? MY SISTER SAW--
CAN I GET YOUR AUTOGRAPHS?
YOUR MOVIE CRITIC ALMOST HAD ME BELIEVING HE LIKED "LAST ACTION HERO"--
YOU ALL THINK--
--THE DAILY BUGLE--
--IS A JOKE?!

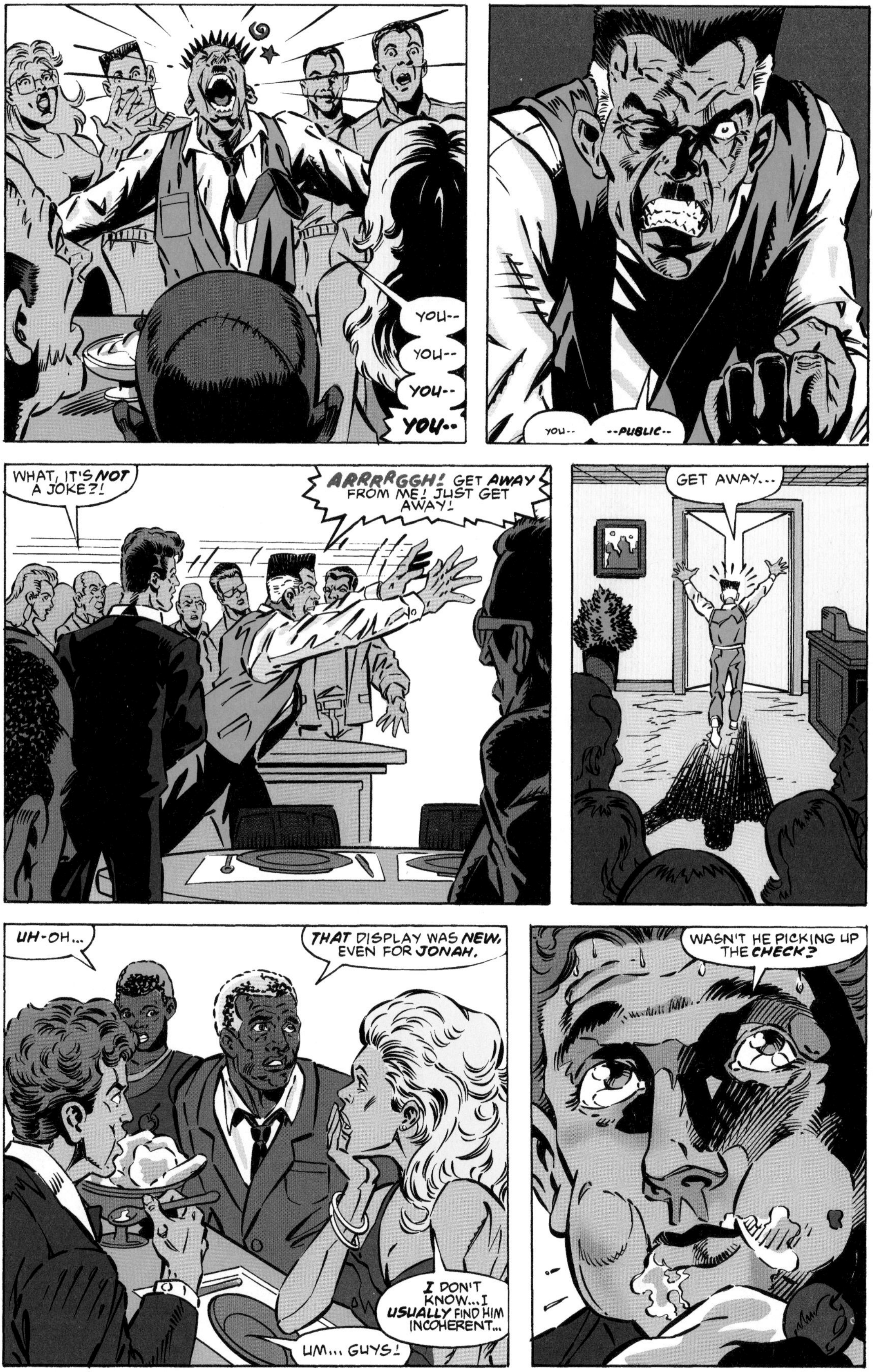
YOU--
YOU--
YOU--
YOU--
YOU--
--PUBLIC--
WHAT, IT'S NOT A JOKE?!
ARRRRGGH! GET AWAY FROM ME! JUST GET AWAY!
GET AWAY...
UH-OH...
THAT DISPLAY WAS NEW, EVEN FOR JONAH.
I DON'T KNOW...I USUALLY FIND HIM INCOHERENT...
UM... GUYS!
WASN'T HE PICKING UP THE CHECK?

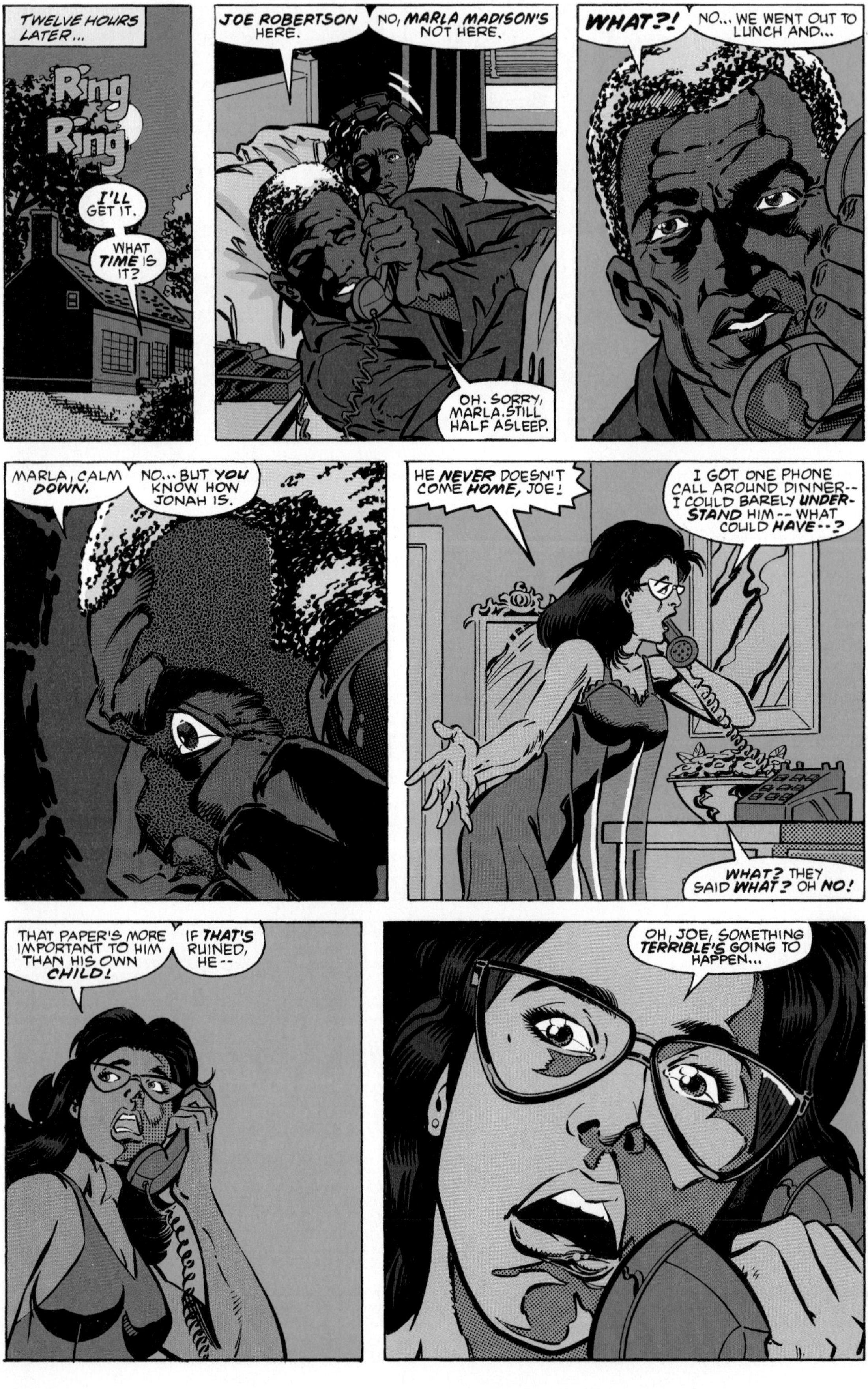

TWELVE HOURS LATER...
Ring Ring
I'LL GET IT.
WHAT TIME IS IT?
JOE ROBERTSON HERE.
NO, MARLA MADISON'S NOT HERE.
OH. SORRY, MARLA. STILL HALF ASLEEP.
WHAT?!
NO... WE WENT OUT TO LUNCH AND...
MARLA, CALM DOWN.
NO... BUT YOU KNOW HOW JONAH IS.
HE NEVER DOESN'T COME HOME, JOE!
I GOT ONE PHONE CALL AROUND DINNER-- I COULD BARELY UNDERSTAND HIM -- WHAT COULD HAVE--?
WHAT? THEY SAID WHAT? OH NO!
THAT PAPER'S MORE IMPORTANT TO HIM THAN HIS OWN CHILD!
IF THAT'S RUINED, HE--
OH, JOE, SOMETHING TERRIBLE'S GOING TO HAPPEN...

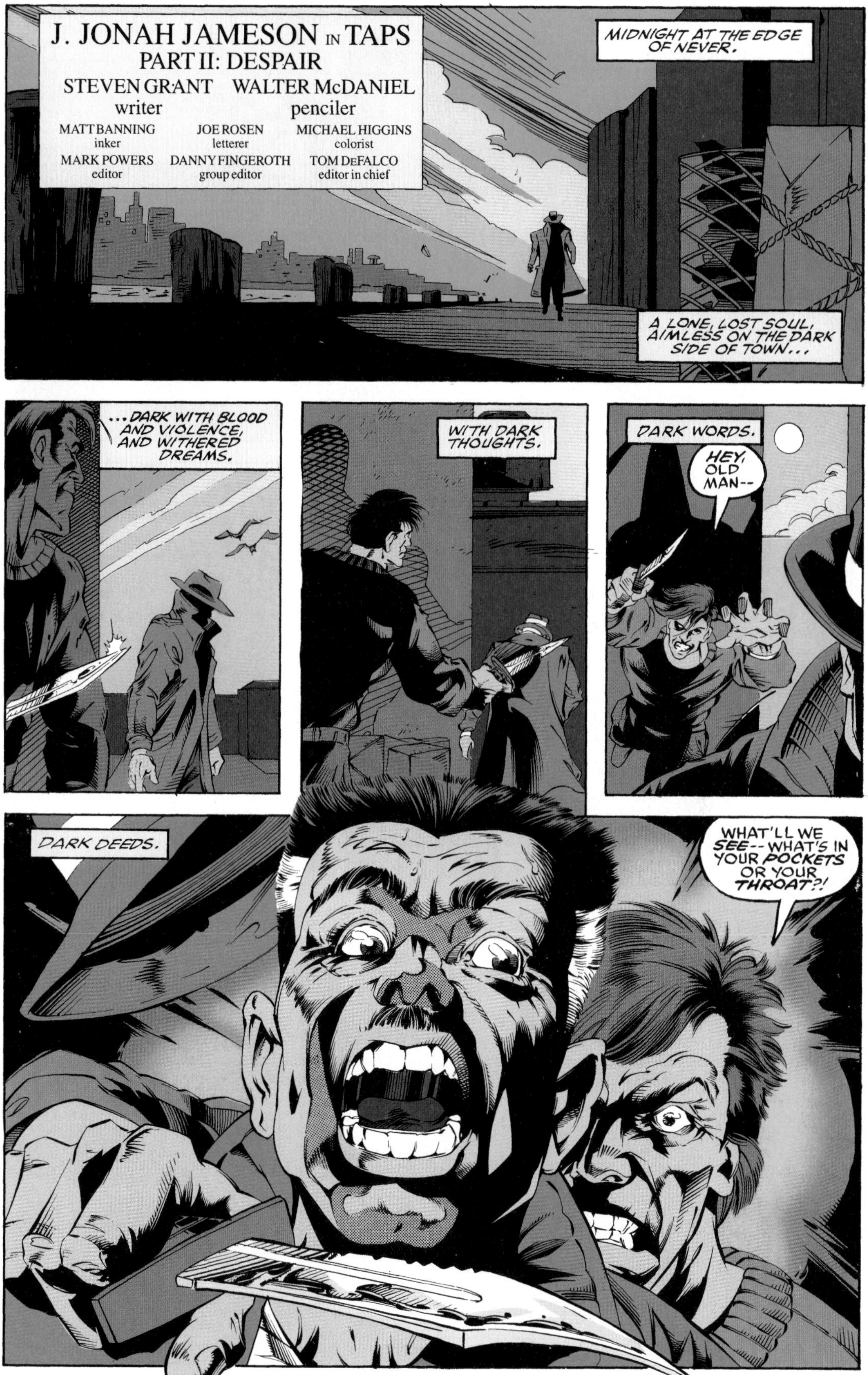

J. JONAH JAMESON IN TAPS
PART II: DESPAIR
STEVEN GRANT writer WALTER McDANIEL penciler
MATT BANNING inker JOE ROSEN letterer MICHAEL HIGGINS colorist
MARK POWERS editor DANNY FINGEROTH group editor TOM DeFALCO editor in chief
MIDNIGHT AT THE EDGE OF NEVER.
A LONE, LOST SOUL, AIMLESS ON THE DARK SIDE OF TOWN...
...DARK WITH BLOOD AND VIOLENCE, AND WITHERED DREAMS.
WITH DARK THOUGHTS.
DARK WORDS.
HEY, OLD MAN--
DARK DEEDS.
WHAT'LL WE SEE-- WHAT'S IN YOUR POCKETS OR YOUR THROAT?!

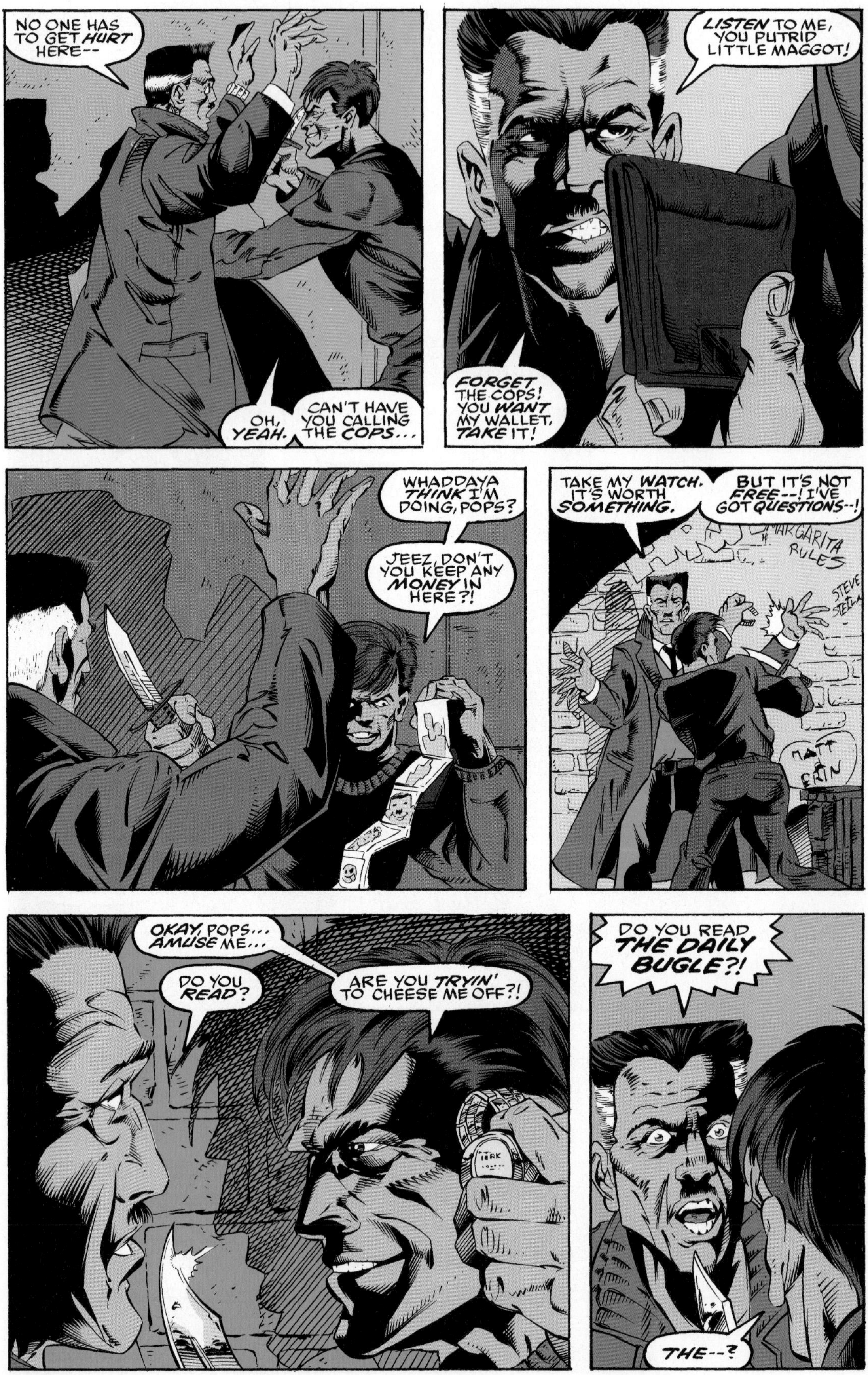

NO ONE HAS TO GET HURT HERE--
OH, YEAH.
CAN'T HAVE YOU CALLING THE COPS...
LISTEN TO ME, YOU PUTRID LITTLE MAGGOT!
FORGET THE COPS! YOU WANT MY WALLET, TAKE IT!
WHADDAYA THINK I'M DOING, POPS?
JEEZ, DON'T YOU KEEP ANY MONEY IN HERE?!
TAKE MY WATCH. IT'S WORTH SOMETHING.
BUT IT'S NOT FREE--! I'VE GOT QUESTIONS--!
MARGARITA RULES
STEVE
MATT ERIN
OKAY, POPS... AMUSE ME...
DO YOU READ?
ARE YOU TRYIN' TO CHEESE ME OFF?!
DO YOU READ THE DAILY BUGLE?!
THE--?

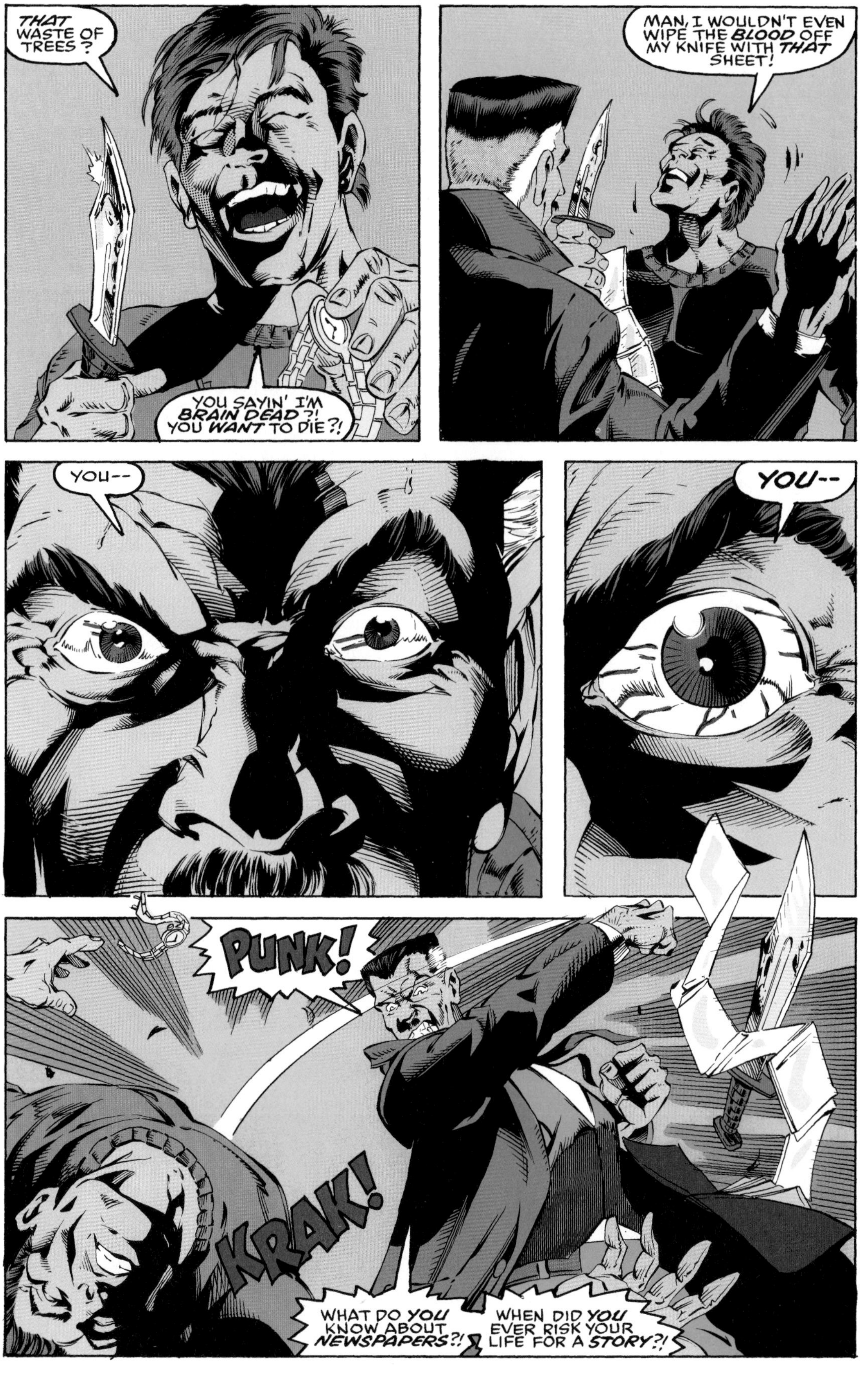
THAT WASTE OF TREES?
YOU SAYIN' I'M BRAIN DEAD?! YOU WANT TO DIE?!
MAN, I WOULDN'T EVEN WIPE THE BLOOD OFF MY KNIFE WITH THAT SHEET!
YOU--
YOU--
PUNK!
KRAK!
WHAT DO YOU KNOW ABOUT NEWSPAPERS?!
WHEN DID YOU EVER RISK YOUR LIFE FOR A STORY?!

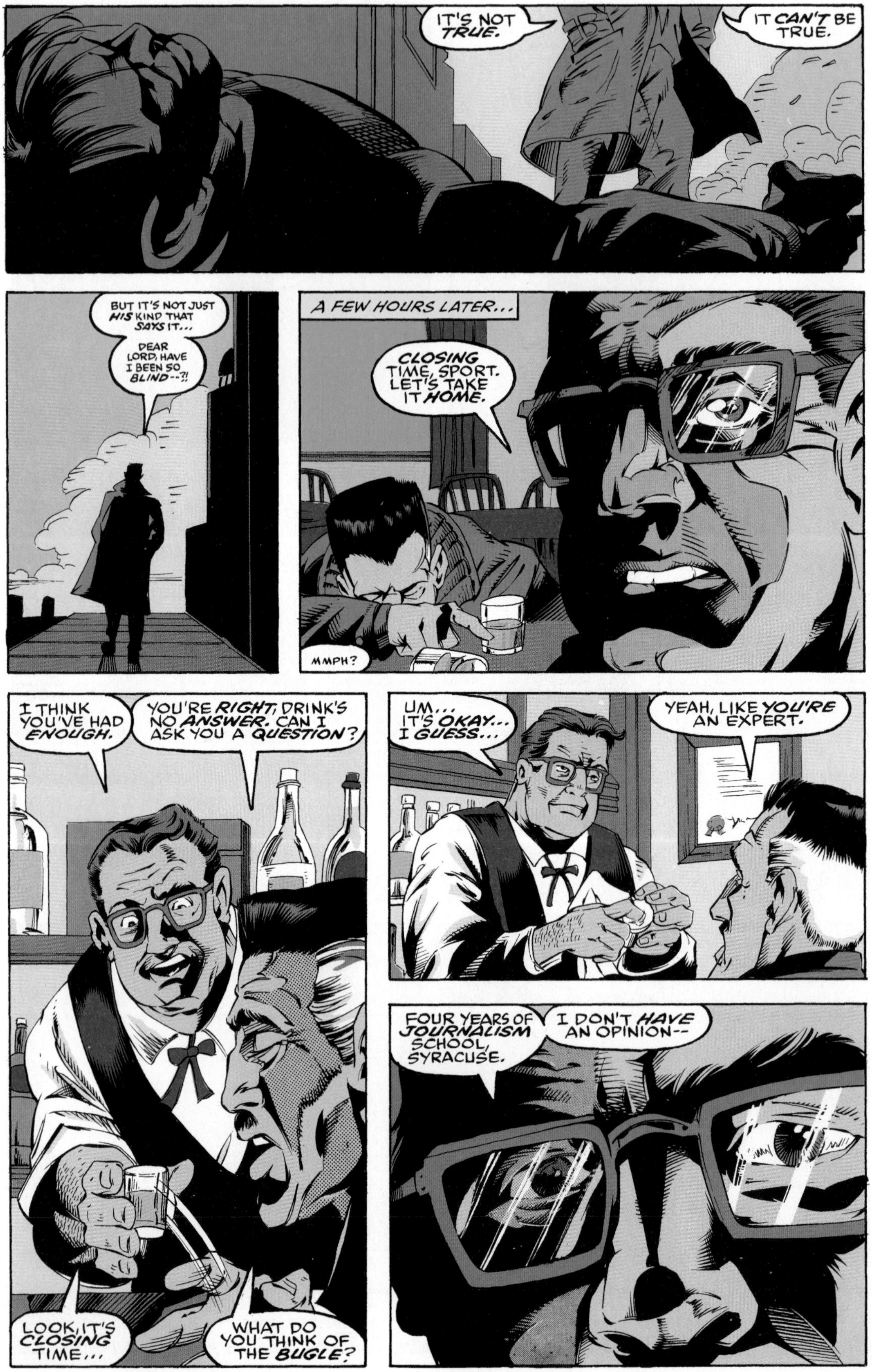
IT'S NOT TRUE.
IT CAN'T BE TRUE.
BUT IT'S NOT JUST HIS KIND THAT SAYS IT...
DEAR LORD, HAVE I BEEN SO BLIND--?!
A FEW HOURS LATER...
CLOSING TIME, SPORT. LET'S TAKE IT HOME.
MMPH?
I THINK YOU'VE HAD ENOUGH.
YOU'RE RIGHT; DRINK'S NO ANSWER. CAN I ASK YOU A QUESTION?
LOOK, IT'S CLOSING TIME...
WHAT DO YOU THINK OF THE BUGLE?
UM... IT'S OKAY... I GUESS...
YEAH, LIKE YOU'RE AN EXPERT.
FOUR YEARS OF JOURNALISM SCHOOL, SYRACUSE.
I DON'T HAVE AN OPINION--

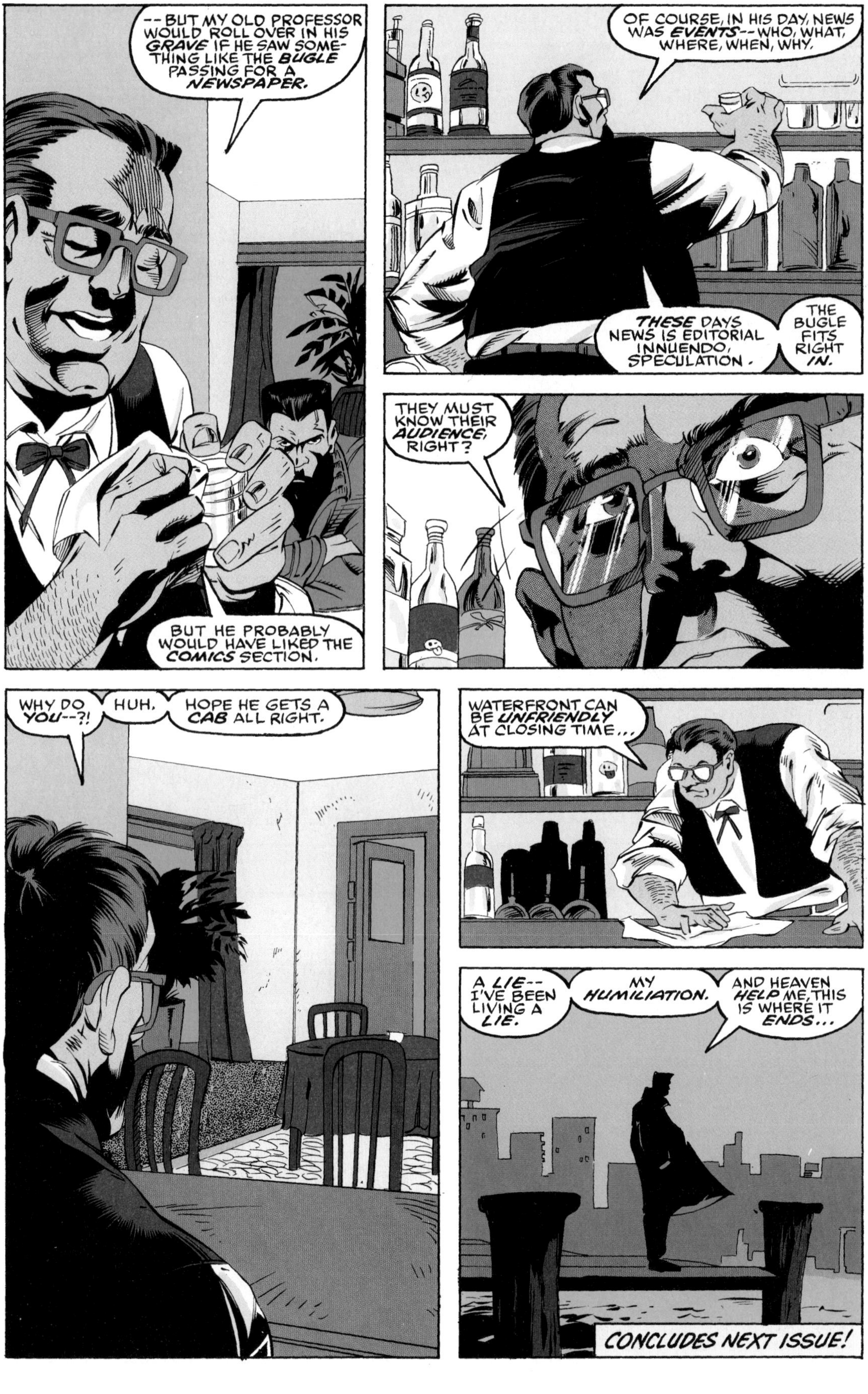

--BUT MY OLD PROFESSOR WOULD ROLL OVER IN HIS GRAVE IF HE SAW SOMETHING LIKE THE BUGLE PASSING FOR A NEWSPAPER.
BUT HE PROBABLY WOULD HAVE LIKED THE COMICS SECTION.
OF COURSE, IN HIS DAY, NEWS WAS EVENTS--WHO, WHAT, WHERE, WHEN, WHY.
THESE DAYS NEWS IS EDITORIAL INNUENDO, SPECULATION.
THE BUGLE FITS RIGHT IN.
THEY MUST KNOW THEIR AUDIENCE, RIGHT?
WHY DO YOU--?!
HUH.
HOPE HE GETS A CAB ALL RIGHT.
WATERFRONT CAN BE UNFRIENDLY AT CLOSING TIME...
A LIE--I'VE BEEN LIVING A LIE.
MY HUMILIATION.
AND HEAVEN HELP ME, THIS IS WHERE IT ENDS...
CONCLUDES NEXT ISSUE!

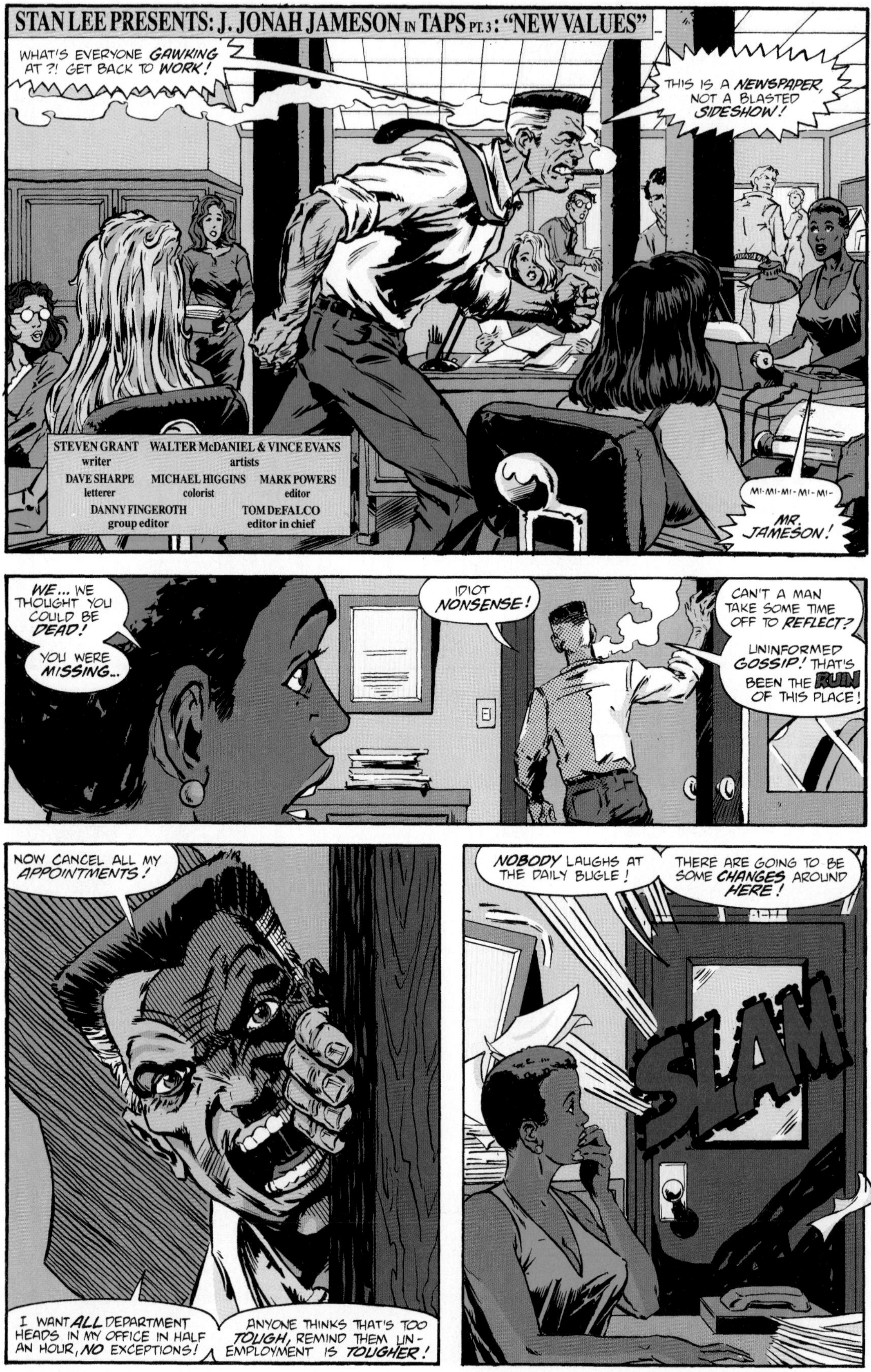
STAN LEE PRESENTS: J. JONAH JAMESON IN TAPS PT. 3: "NEW VALUES"
WHAT'S EVERYONE GAWKING AT ?! GET BACK TO WORK!
THIS IS A NEWSPAPER, NOT A BLASTED SIDESHOW!
STEVEN GRANT writer
WALTER McDANIEL & VINCE EVANS artists
DAVE SHARPE letterer
MICHAEL HIGGINS colorist
MARK POWERS editor
DANNY FINGEROTH group editor
TOM DeFALCO editor in chief
MI-MI-MI-MI-MI-
MR. JAMESON!
WE... WE THOUGHT YOU COULD BE DEAD!
YOU WERE MISSING...
IDIOT NONSENSE!
CAN'T A MAN TAKE SOME TIME OFF TO REFLECT?
UNINFORMED GOSSIP! THAT'S BEEN THE RUIN OF THIS PLACE!
NOW CANCEL ALL MY APPOINTMENTS!
I WANT ALL DEPARTMENT HEADS IN MY OFFICE IN HALF AN HOUR, NO EXCEPTIONS!
ANYONE THINKS THAT'S TOO TOUGH, REMIND THEM UN-EMPLOYMENT IS TOUGHER!
NOBODY LAUGHS AT THE DAILY BUGLE!
THERE ARE GOING TO BE SOME CHANGES AROUND HERE!
SLAM

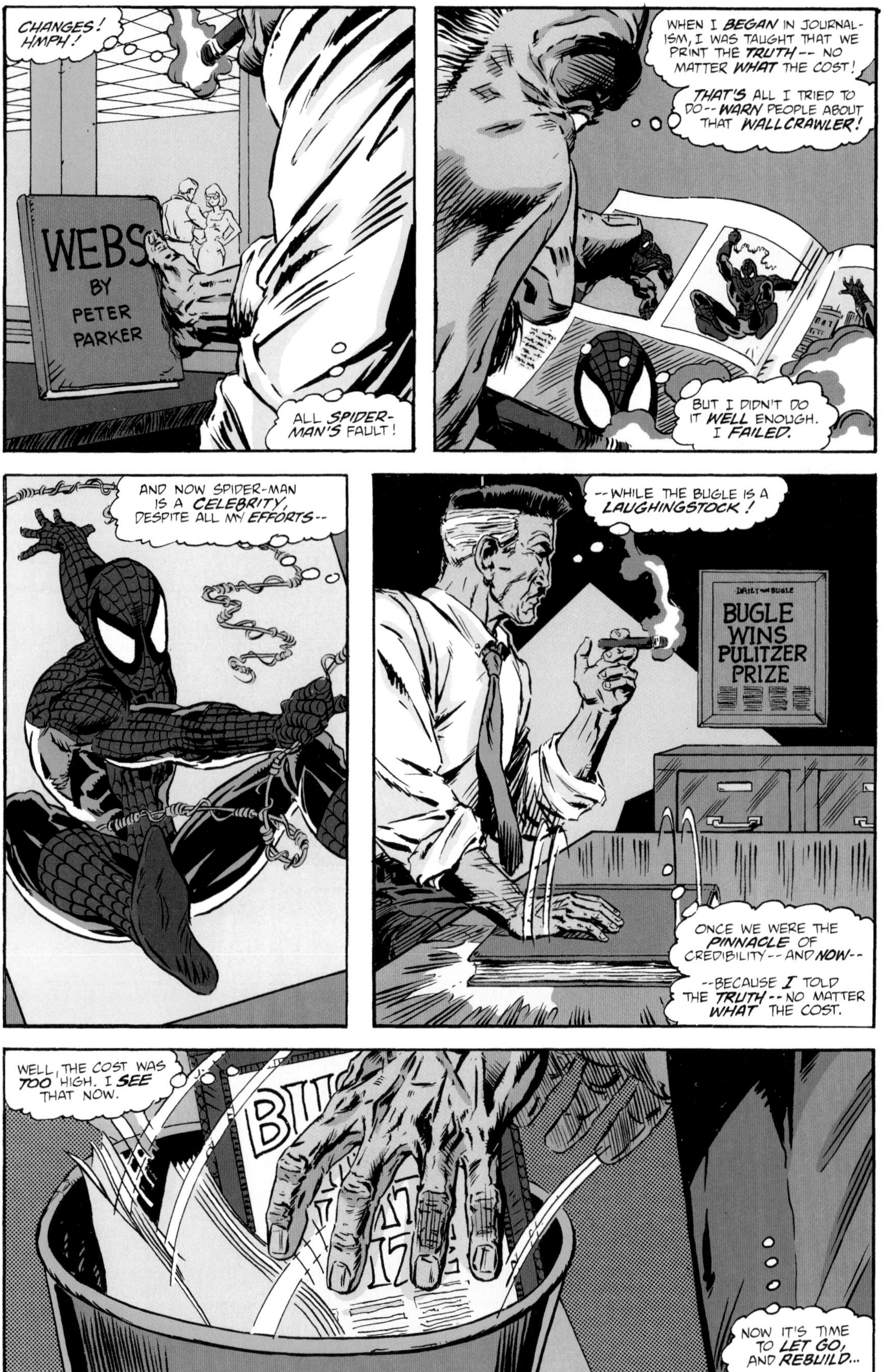
CHANGES! HMPH!
WEBS BY PETER PARKER
ALL SPIDER-MAN'S FAULT!
WHEN I BEGAN IN JOURNALISM, I WAS TAUGHT THAT WE PRINT THE TRUTH -- NO MATTER WHAT THE COST!
THAT'S ALL I TRIED TO DO -- WARN PEOPLE ABOUT THAT WALLCRAWLER!
BUT I DIDN'T DO IT WELL ENOUGH. I FAILED.
AND NOW SPIDER-MAN IS A CELEBRITY, DESPITE ALL MY EFFORTS--
--WHILE THE BUGLE IS A LAUGHINGSTOCK!
DAILY BUGLE
BUGLE WINS PULITZER PRIZE
ONCE WE WERE THE PINNACLE OF CREDIBILITY -- AND NOW--
--BECAUSE I TOLD THE TRUTH -- NO MATTER WHAT THE COST.
WELL, THE COST WAS TOO HIGH. I SEE THAT NOW.
NOW IT'S TIME TO LET GO, AND REBUILD...

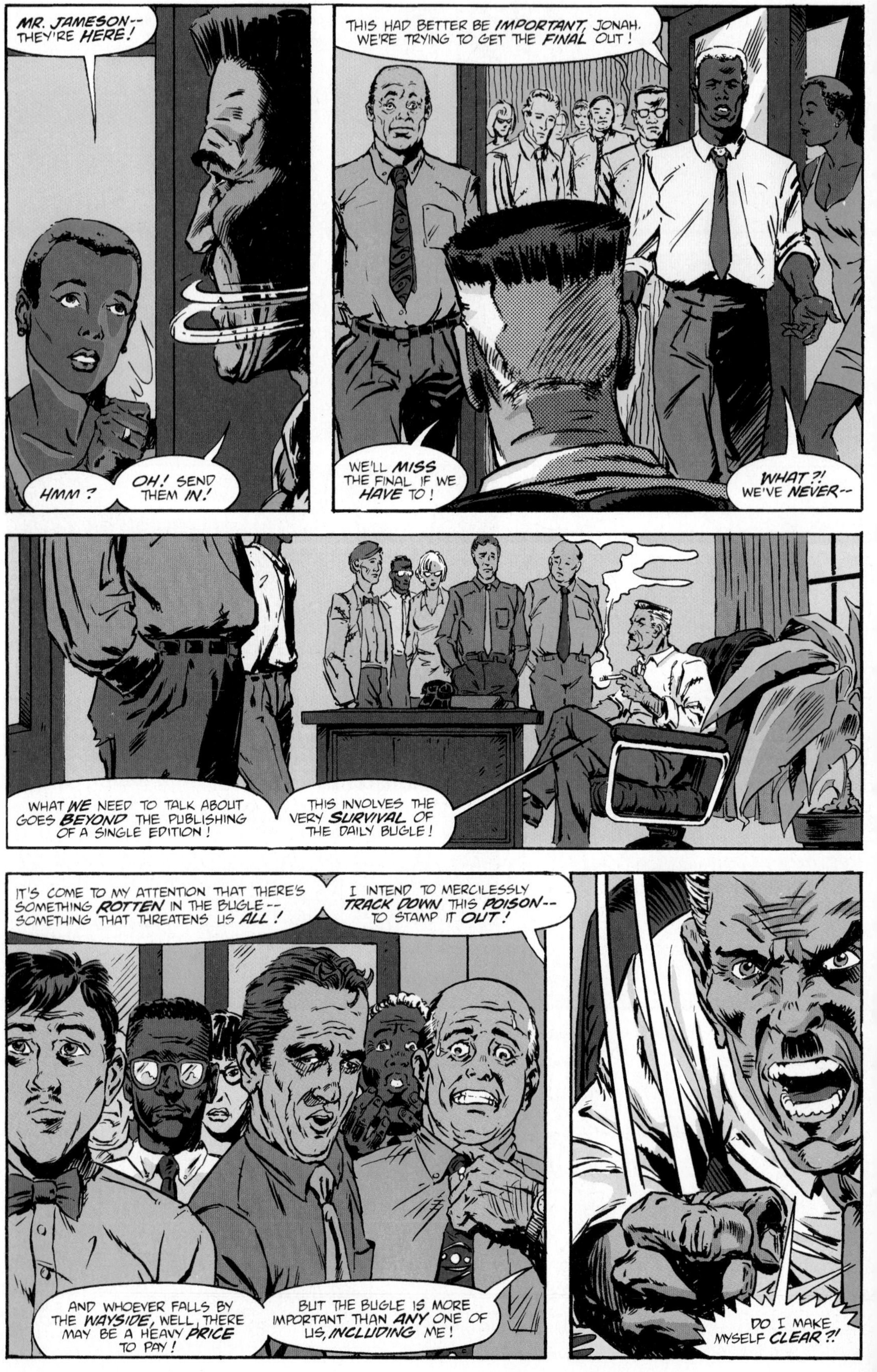
MR. JAMESON-- THEY'RE HERE!
HMM?
OH! SEND THEM IN!
THIS HAD BETTER BE IMPORTANT, JONAH. WE'RE TRYING TO GET THE FINAL OUT!
WE'LL MISS THE FINAL IF WE HAVE TO!
WHAT?! WE'VE NEVER--
WHAT WE NEED TO TALK ABOUT GOES BEYOND THE PUBLISHING OF A SINGLE EDITION!
THIS INVOLVES THE VERY SURVIVAL OF THE DAILY BUGLE!
IT'S COME TO MY ATTENTION THAT THERE'S SOMETHING ROTTEN IN THE BUGLE-- SOMETHING THAT THREATENS US ALL!
I INTEND TO MERCILESSLY TRACK DOWN THIS POISON-- TO STAMP IT OUT!
AND WHOEVER FALLS BY THE WAYSIDE, WELL, THERE MAY BE A HEAVY PRICE TO PAY!
BUT THE BUGLE IS MORE IMPORTANT THAN ANY ONE OF US, INCLUDING ME!
DO I MAKE MYSELF CLEAR?!

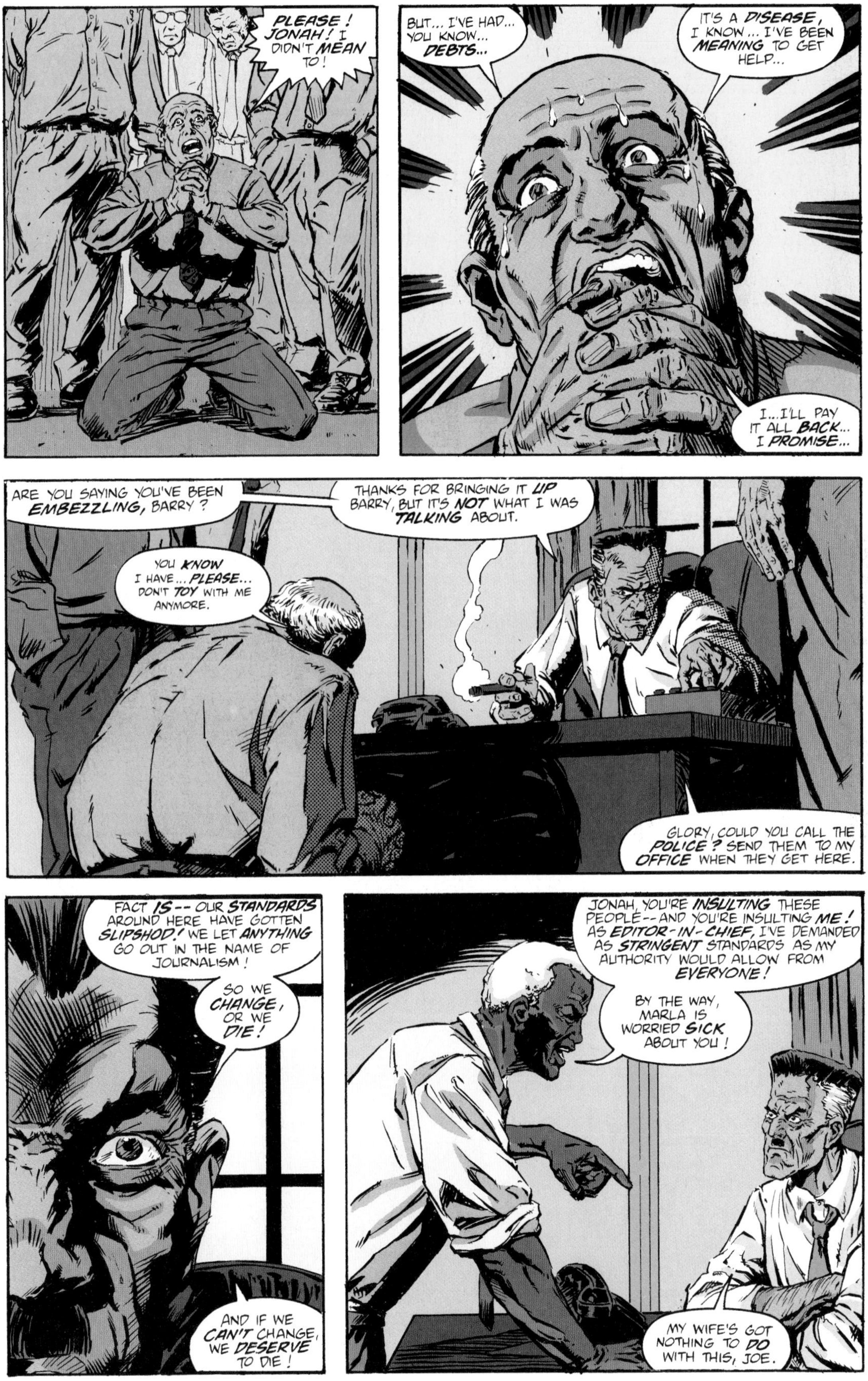
PLEASE! JONAH! I DIDN'T MEAN TO!
BUT... I'VE HAD... YOU KNOW... DEBTS...
IT'S A DISEASE, I KNOW... I'VE BEEN MEANING TO GET HELP...
I...I'LL PAY IT ALL BACK... I PROMISE...
ARE YOU SAYING YOU'VE BEEN EMBEZZLING, BARRY?
THANKS FOR BRINGING IT UP BARRY, BUT IT'S NOT WHAT I WAS TALKING ABOUT.
YOU KNOW I HAVE... PLEASE... DON'T TOY WITH ME ANYMORE.
GLORY, COULD YOU CALL THE POLICE? SEND THEM TO MY OFFICE WHEN THEY GET HERE.
FACT IS -- OUR STANDARDS AROUND HERE HAVE GOTTEN SLIPSHOD! WE LET ANYTHING GO OUT IN THE NAME OF JOURNALISM!
SO WE CHANGE, OR WE DIE!
AND IF WE CAN'T CHANGE, WE DESERVE TO DIE!
JONAH, YOU'RE INSULTING THESE PEOPLE -- AND YOU'RE INSULTING ME! AS EDITOR-IN-CHIEF, I'VE DEMANDED AS STRINGENT STANDARDS AS MY AUTHORITY WOULD ALLOW FROM EVERYONE!
BY THE WAY, MARLA IS WORRIED SICK ABOUT YOU!
MY WIFE'S GOT NOTHING TO DO WITH THIS, JOE.

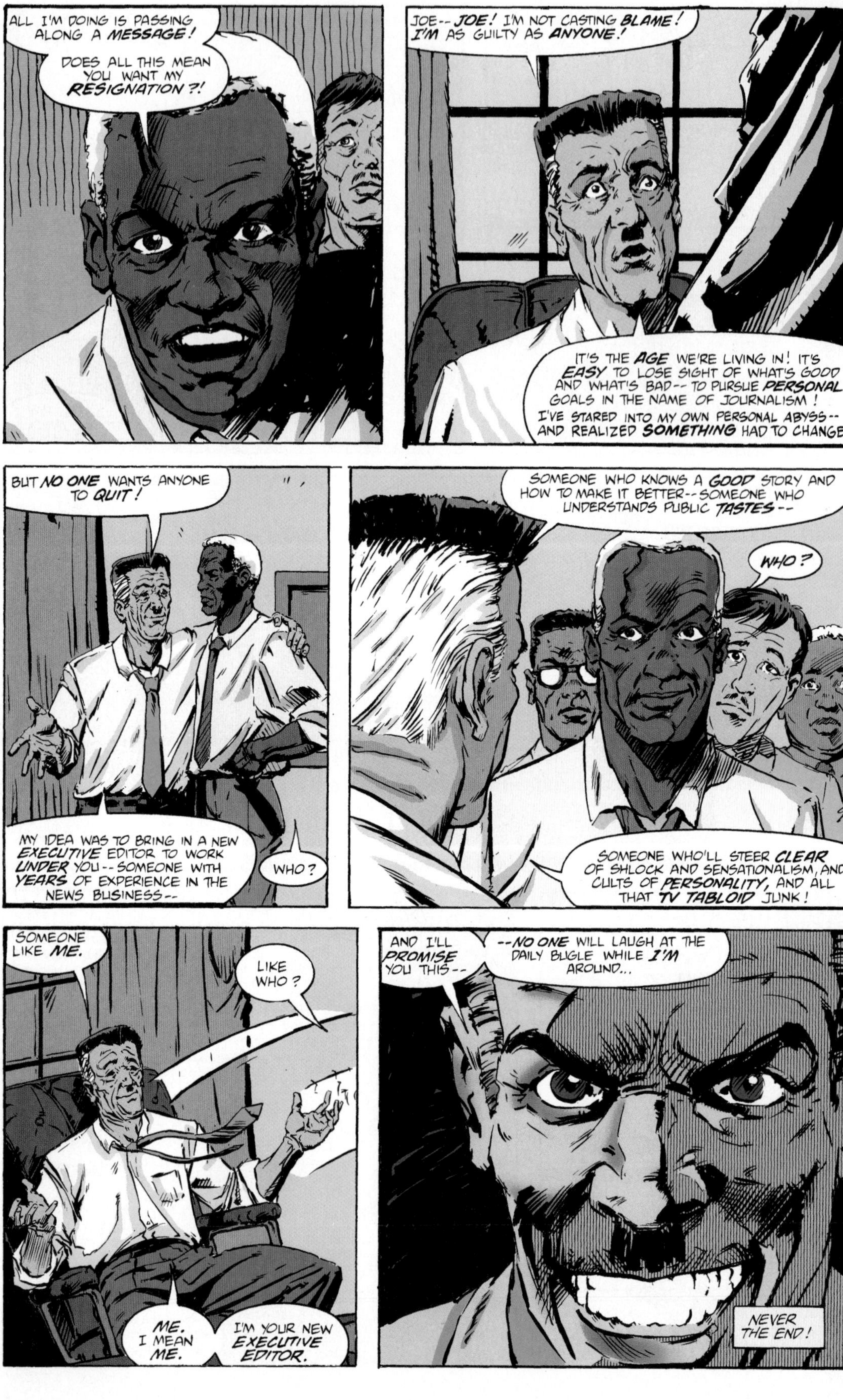
ALL I'M DOING IS PASSING ALONG A MESSAGE!
DOES ALL THIS MEAN YOU WANT MY RESIGNATION?!
JOE-- JOE! I'M NOT CASTING BLAME! I'M AS GUILTY AS ANYONE!
IT'S THE AGE WE'RE LIVING IN! IT'S EASY TO LOSE SIGHT OF WHAT'S GOOD AND WHAT'S BAD-- TO PURSUE PERSONAL GOALS IN THE NAME OF JOURNALISM!
I'VE STARED INTO MY OWN PERSONAL ABYSS-- AND REALIZED SOMETHING HAD TO CHANGE.
BUT NO ONE WANTS ANYONE TO QUIT!
MY IDEA WAS TO BRING IN A NEW EXECUTIVE EDITOR TO WORK UNDER YOU-- SOMEONE WITH YEARS OF EXPERIENCE IN THE NEWS BUSINESS--
WHO?
SOMEONE WHO KNOWS A GOOD STORY AND HOW TO MAKE IT BETTER-- SOMEONE WHO UNDERSTANDS PUBLIC TASTES--
WHO?
SOMEONE WHO'LL STEER CLEAR OF SHLOCK AND SENSATIONALISM, AND CULTS OF PERSONALITY, AND ALL THAT TV TABLOID JUNK!
SOMEONE LIKE ME.
LIKE WHO?
ME. I MEAN ME.
I'M YOUR NEW EXECUTIVE EDITOR.
AND I'LL PROMISE YOU THIS--
--NO ONE WILL LAUGH AT THE DAILY BUGLE WHILE I'M AROUND...
NEVER THE END!

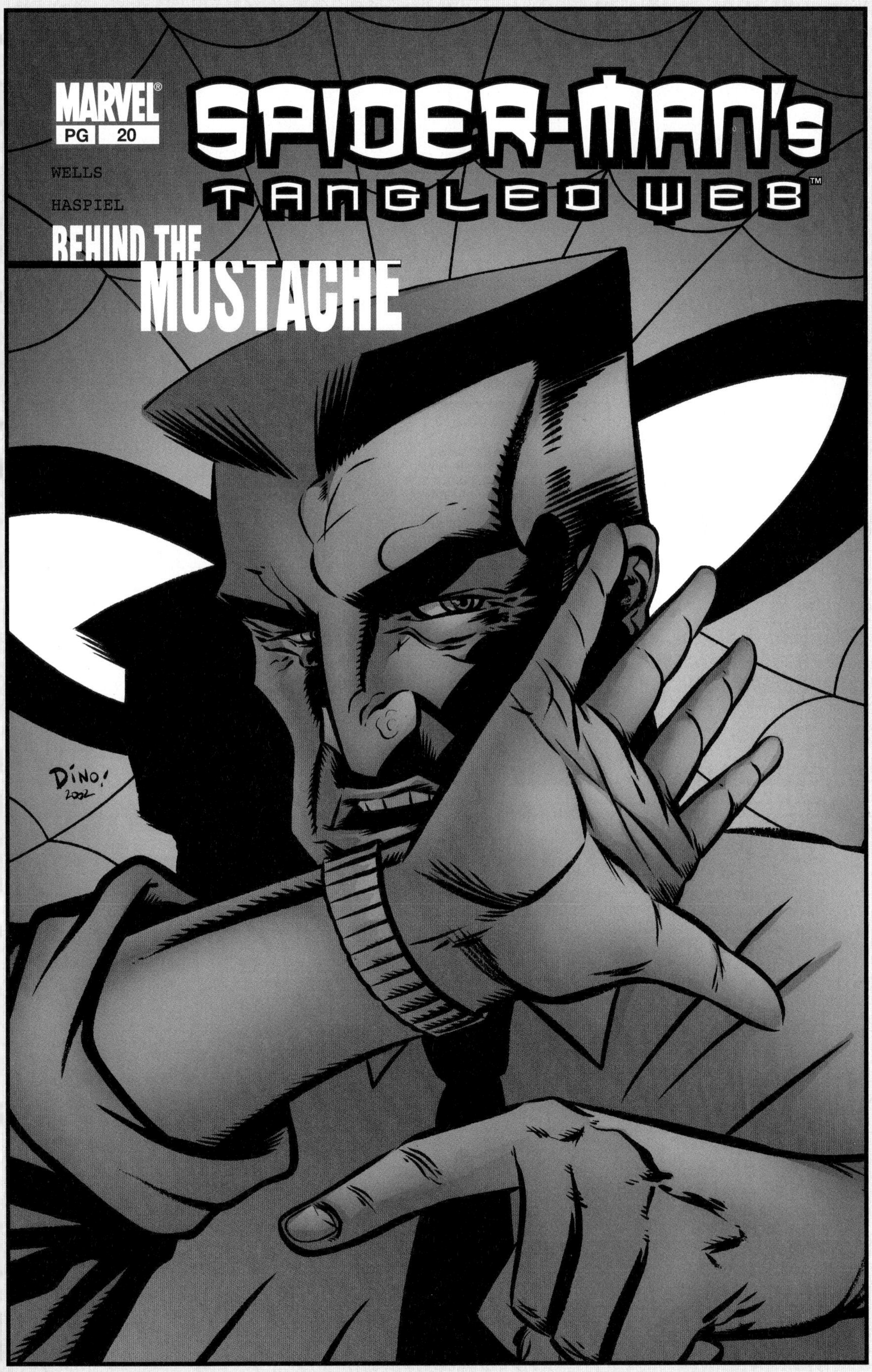

MARVEL®
PG 20
SPIDER-MAN'S
TANGLED WEB™
WELLS
HASPIEL
BEHIND THE
MUSTACHE
DINO! 2002

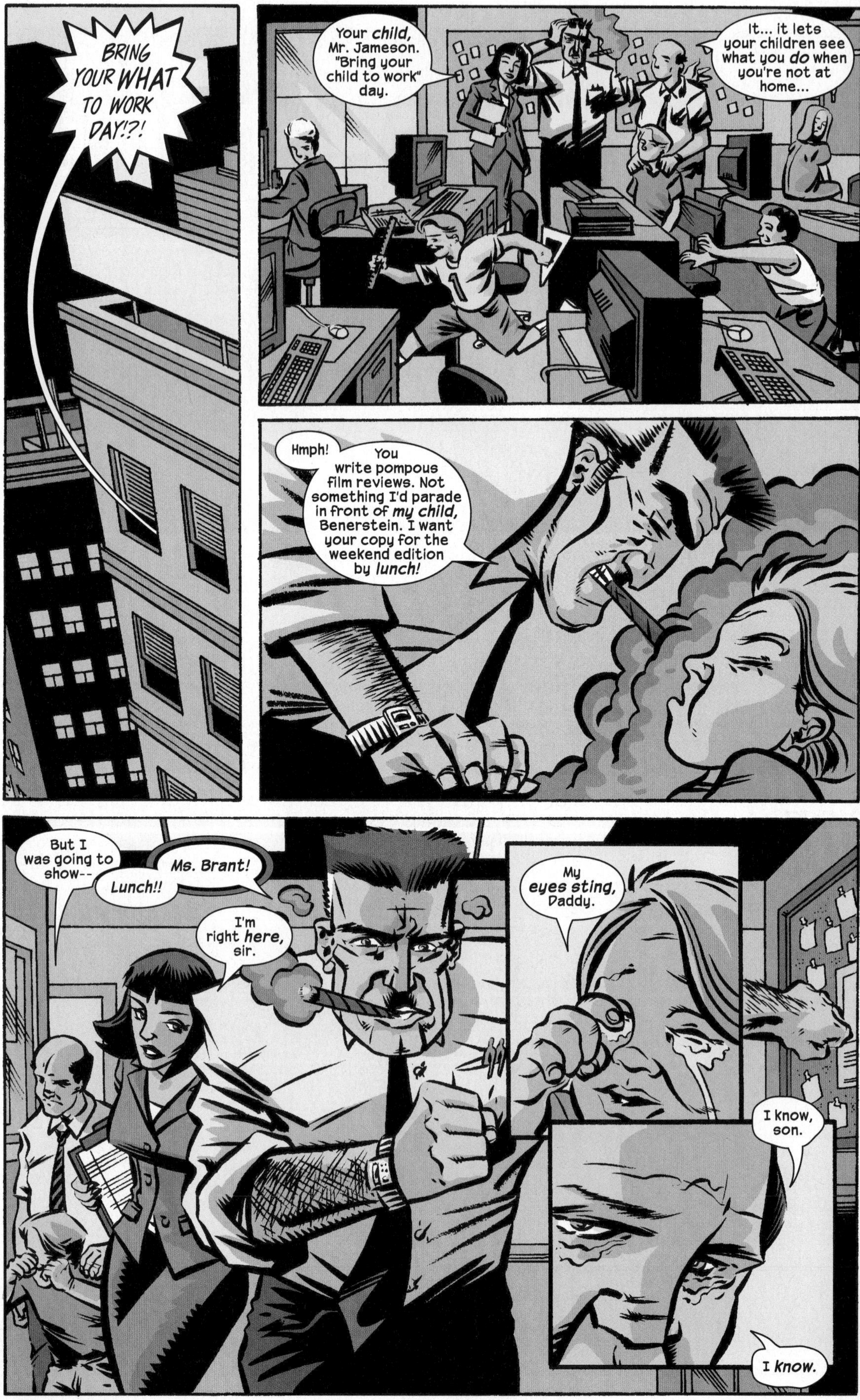

BRING YOUR WHAT TO WORK DAY!?!
Your child, Mr. Jameson. "Bring your child to work" day.
It... it lets your children see what you do when you're not at home...
Hmph!
You write pompous film reviews. Not something I'd parade in front of my child, Benerstein. I want your copy for the weekend edition by lunch!
But I was going to show--
Lunch!!
Ms. Brant!
I'm right here, sir.
My eyes sting, Daddy.
I know, son.
I know.

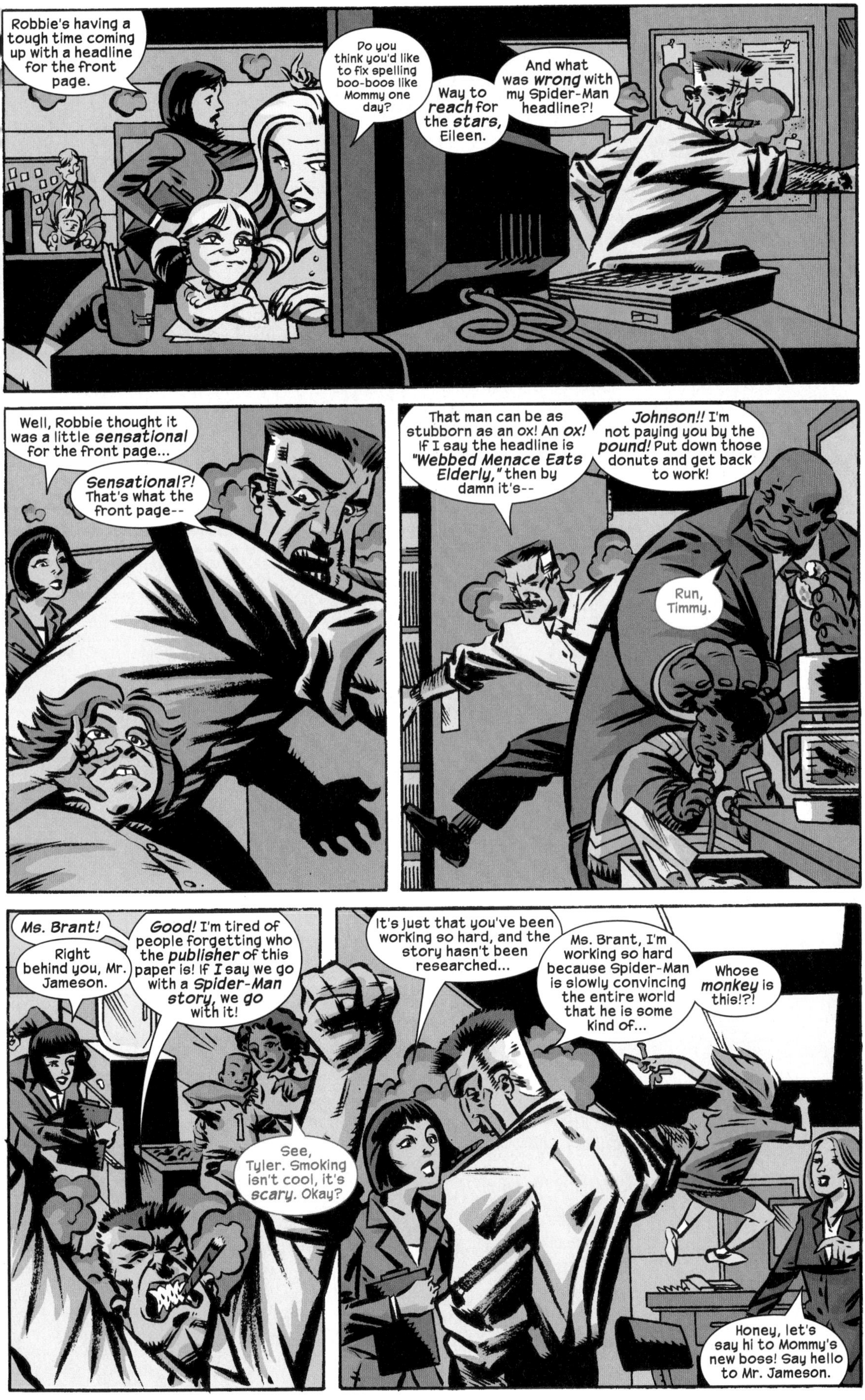
Robbie's having a tough time coming up with a headline for the front page.
Do you think you'd like to fix spelling boo-boos like Mommy one day?
Way to *reach* for the *stars,* Eileen.
And what was *wrong* with my Spider-Man headline?!
Well, Robbie thought it was a little *sensational* for the front page...
Sensational?! That's what the front page--
That man can be as stubborn as an ox! An *ox!* If I say the headline is *"Webbed Menace Eats Elderly,"* then by damn it's--
Johnson!! I'm not paying you by the *pound!* Put down those donuts and get back to work!
Run, Timmy.
Ms. Brant!
Right behind you, Mr. Jameson.
Good! I'm tired of people forgetting who the *publisher* of this paper is! If *I* say we go with a *Spider-Man story,* we *go* with it!
See, Tyler. Smoking isn't cool, it's *scary.* Okay?
It's just that you've been working so hard, and the story hasn't been researched...
Ms. Brant, I'm working so hard because Spider-Man is slowly convincing the entire world that he is some kind of...
Whose *monkey* is this!?!
Honey, let's say hi to Mommy's new boss! Say hello to Mr. Jameson.

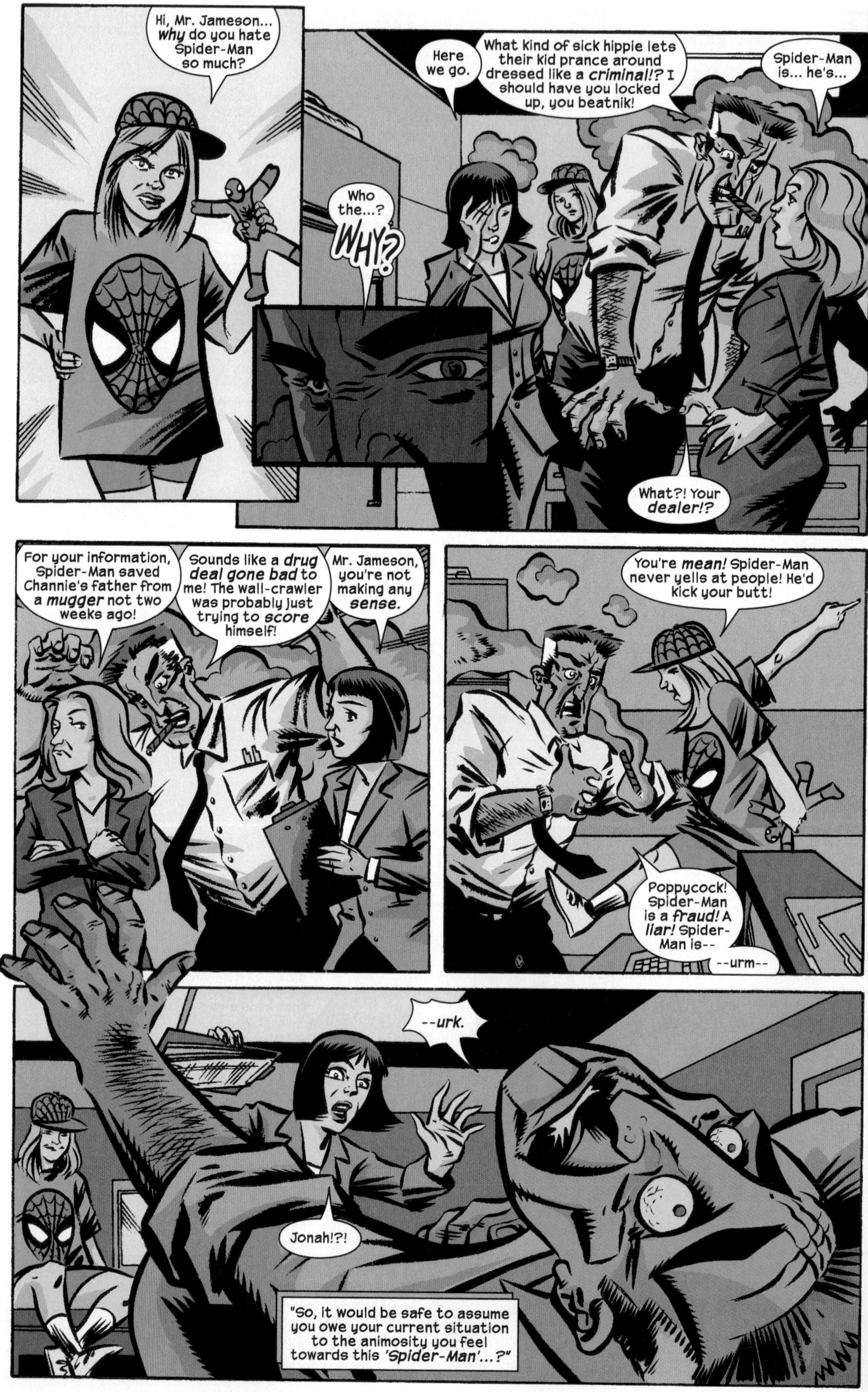

Hi, Mr. Jameson... why do you hate Spider-Man so much?
Who the...?
WHY?
Here we go.
What kind of sick hippie lets their kid prance around dressed like a criminal!? I should have you locked up, you beatnik!
Spider-Man is... he's...
What?! Your dealer!?
For your information, Spider-Man saved Channie's father from a mugger not two weeks ago!
Sounds like a drug deal gone bad to me! The wall-crawler was probably just trying to score himself!
Mr. Jameson, you're not making any sense.
You're mean! Spider-Man never yells at people! He'd kick your butt!
Poppycock! Spider-Man is a fraud! A liar! Spider-Man is--
--urm--
--urk.
Jonah!?!
"So, it would be safe to assume you owe your current situation to the animosity you feel towards this 'Spider-Man'...?"

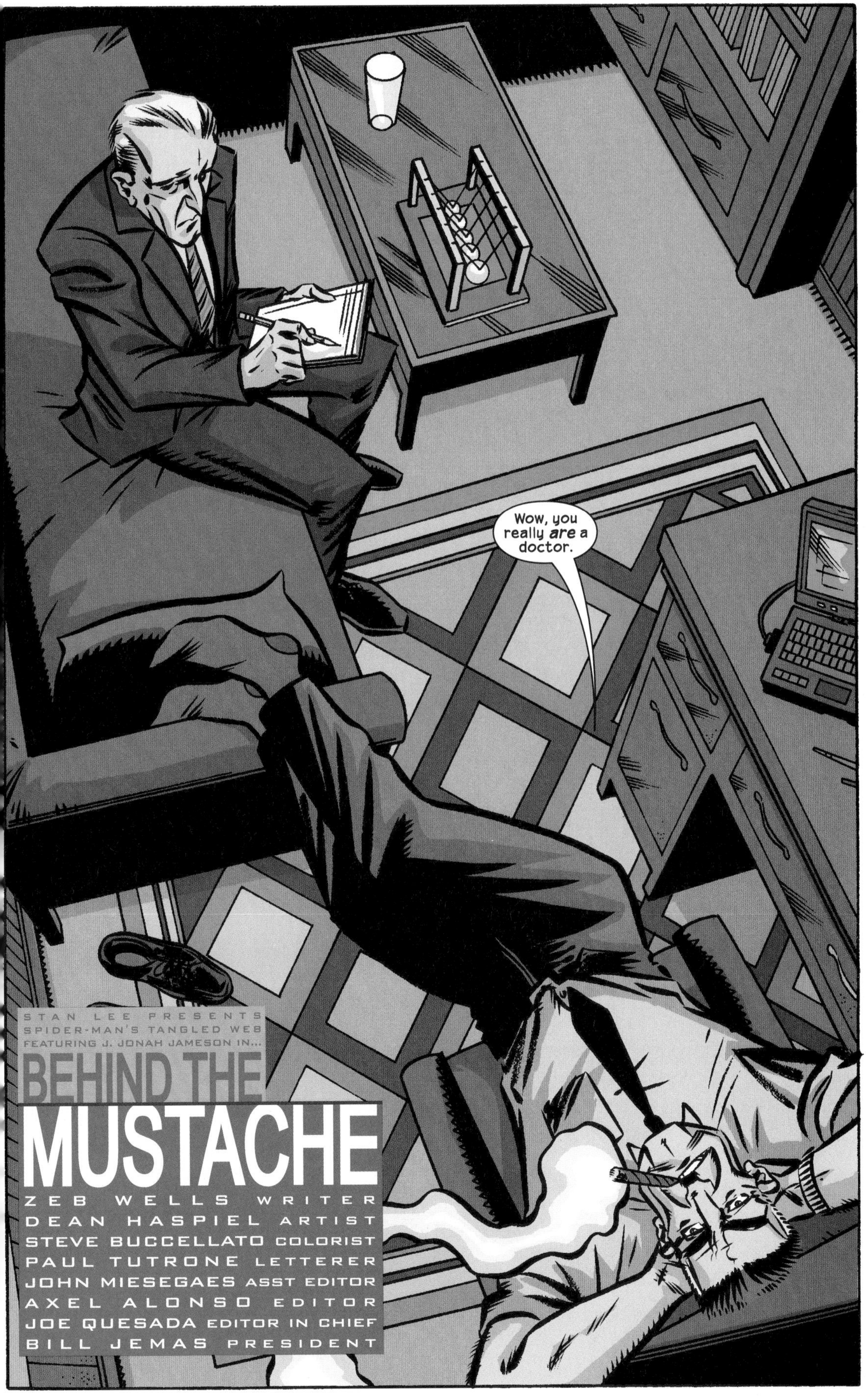

Wow, you really *are* a doctor.
STAN LEE PRESENTS
SPIDER-MAN'S TANGLED WEB
FEATURING J. JONAH JAMESON IN...
BEHIND THE
MUSTACHE
ZEB WELLS WRITER
DEAN HASPIEL ARTIST
STEVE BUCCELLATO COLORIST
PAUL TUTRONE LETTERER
JOHN MIESEGAES ASST EDITOR
AXEL ALONSO EDITOR
JOE QUESADA EDITOR IN CHIEF
BILL JEMAS PRESIDENT

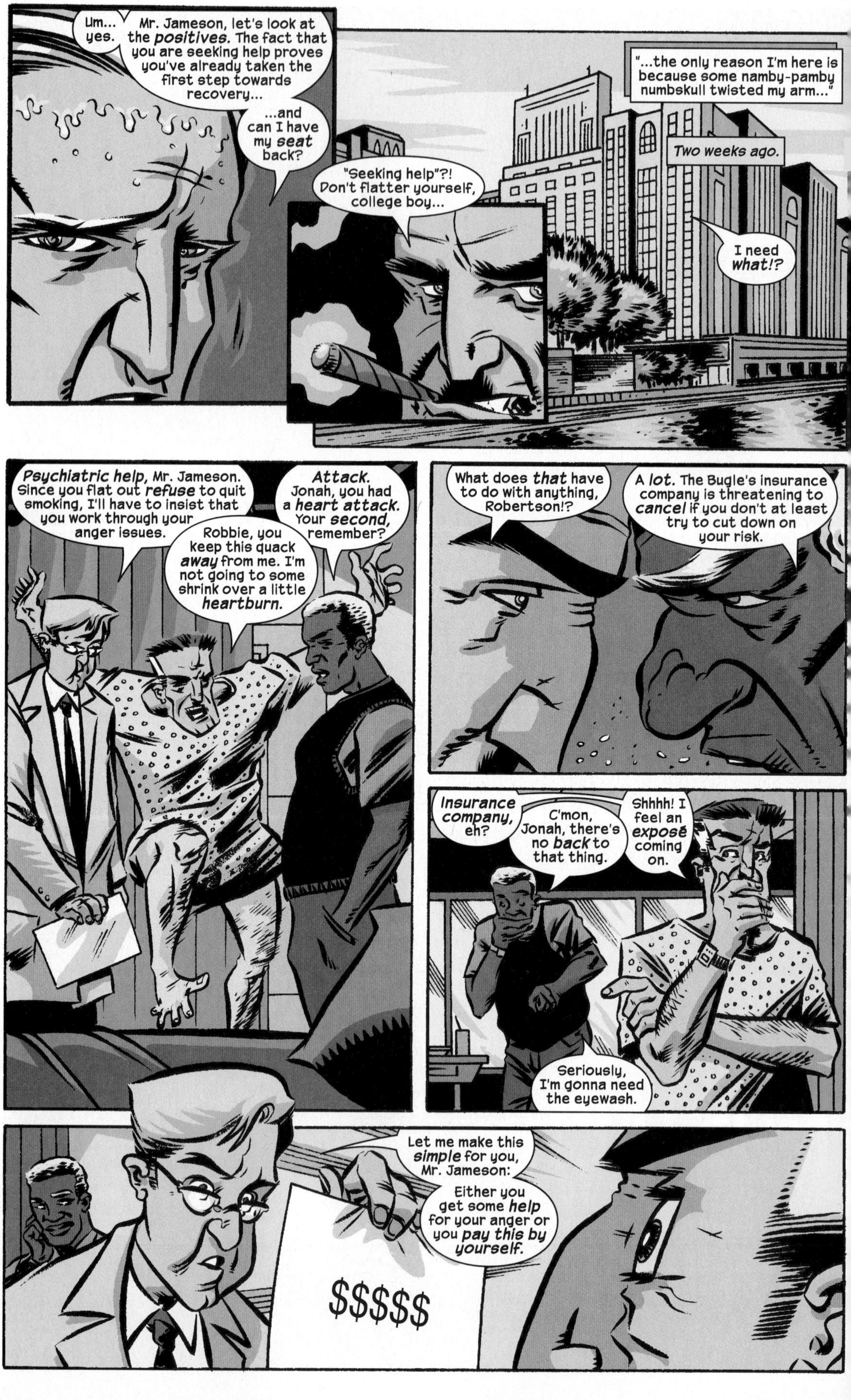
Um... yes.
Mr. Jameson, let's look at the positives. The fact that you are seeking help proves you've already taken the first step towards recovery...
...and can I have my seat back?
"Seeking help"?! Don't flatter yourself, college boy...
"...the only reason I'm here is because some namby-pamby numbskull twisted my arm..."
Two weeks ago.
I need what!?
Psychiatric help, Mr. Jameson. Since you flat out refuse to quit smoking, I'll have to insist that you work through your anger issues.
Robbie, you keep this quack away from me. I'm not going to some shrink over a little heartburn.
Attack. Jonah, you had a heart attack. Your second, remember?
What does that have to do with anything, Robertson!?
A lot. The Bugle's insurance company is threatening to cancel if you don't at least try to cut down on your risk.
Insurance company, eh?
C'mon, Jonah, there's no back to that thing.
Shhhh! I feel an exposé coming on.
Seriously, I'm gonna need the eyewash.
Let me make this simple for you, Mr. Jameson:
Either you get some help for your anger or you pay this by yourself.
$$$$$

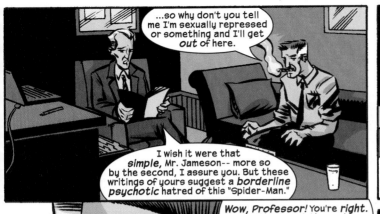

...so why don't you tell me I'm *sexually repressed* or something and I'll get *out* of here.

I wish it were that *simple*, Mr. Jameson-- more so by the second, I assure you. But these writings of yours suggest a *borderline psychotic* hatred of this "Spider-Man."

My *editorials!?!?*

Call them what you will, Mr. Jameson, if a high school student wrote these about a peer they'd call the S.W.A.T. team.

Wow, Professor! You're *right.* It's *me* that's got the problem. Why, I'm going to find the next egomaniac claiming to be a "hero" and give 'im a big hug!

Now let's not get--

No-- especially if he hides his face and goes around... *excreting...* "webbing" on people.

Mr. Jameson--

--the brighter the tights the better, doc, it's a whole new world for me!

Can I *go* now?

Interesting. Would you say you've *always* had a prejudice against this "Spider-Man" because of his *chosen* profession?

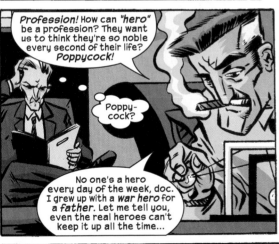

Profession! How can "hero" be a profession? They want us to think they're so noble every second of their life? *Poppycock!*

Poppy-cock?

No one's a hero every day of the week, doc. I grew up with a *war hero* for a *father.* Let me tell you, even the real heroes can't keep it up all the time...

Damn it-- what *are* these things anyway?! You think these are fun?

They relax most people.

Most people are idiots!

Should we pause and appreciate the irony of insulting people's intelligence while being outfoxed by five metal balls?

You misused "irony," college boy.

Mr. Jameson, why don't you turn around so I can be sure you're not making faces at me.

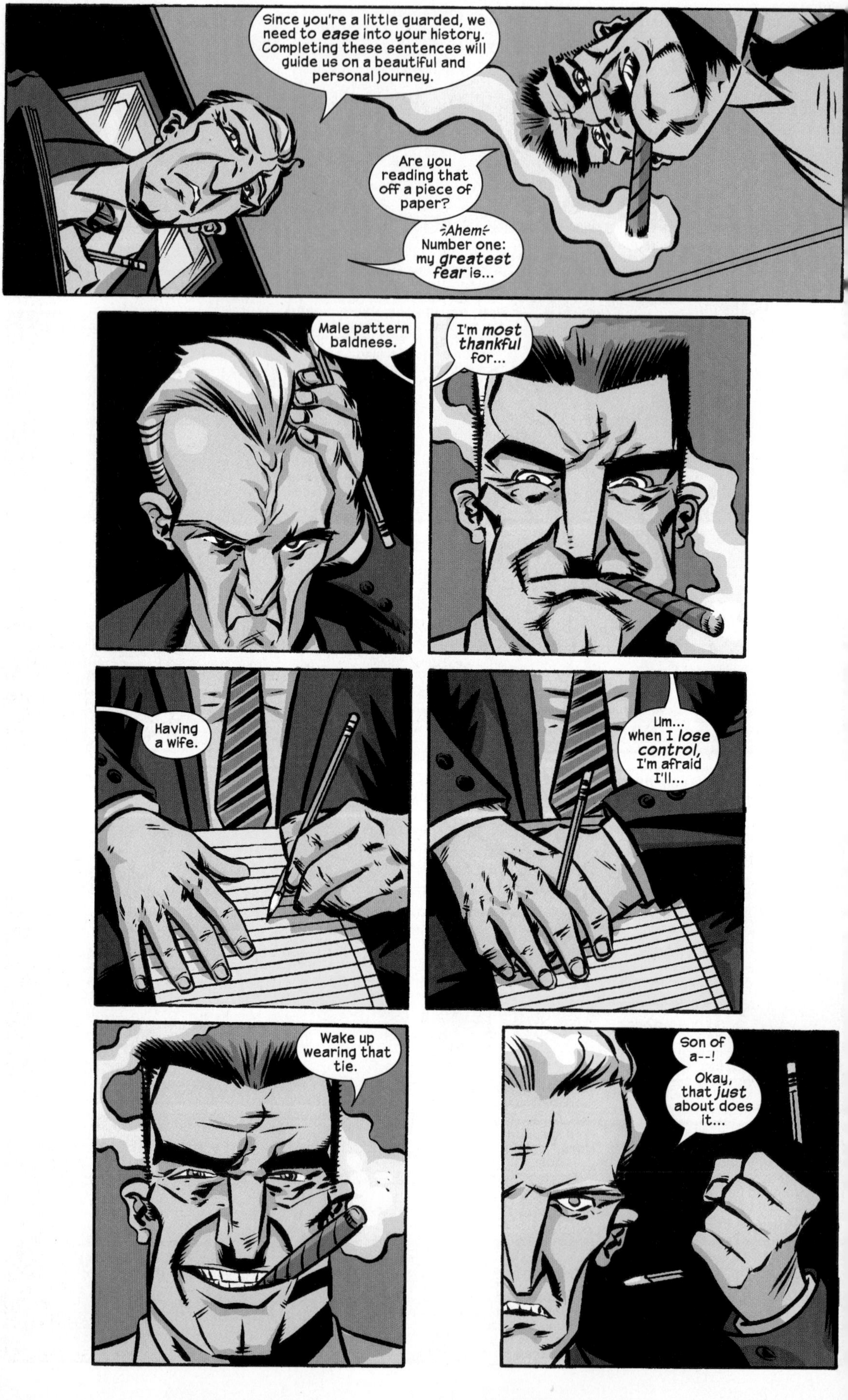
Since you're a little guarded, we need to *ease* into your history. Completing these sentences will guide us on a beautiful and personal journey.
Are you reading that off a piece of paper?
Ahem
Number one: my *greatest fear* is...
Male pattern baldness.
I'm *most thankful* for...
Having a wife.
Um... when I *lose control,* I'm afraid I'll...
Wake up wearing that tie.
Son of a--!
Okay, that *just* about does it...

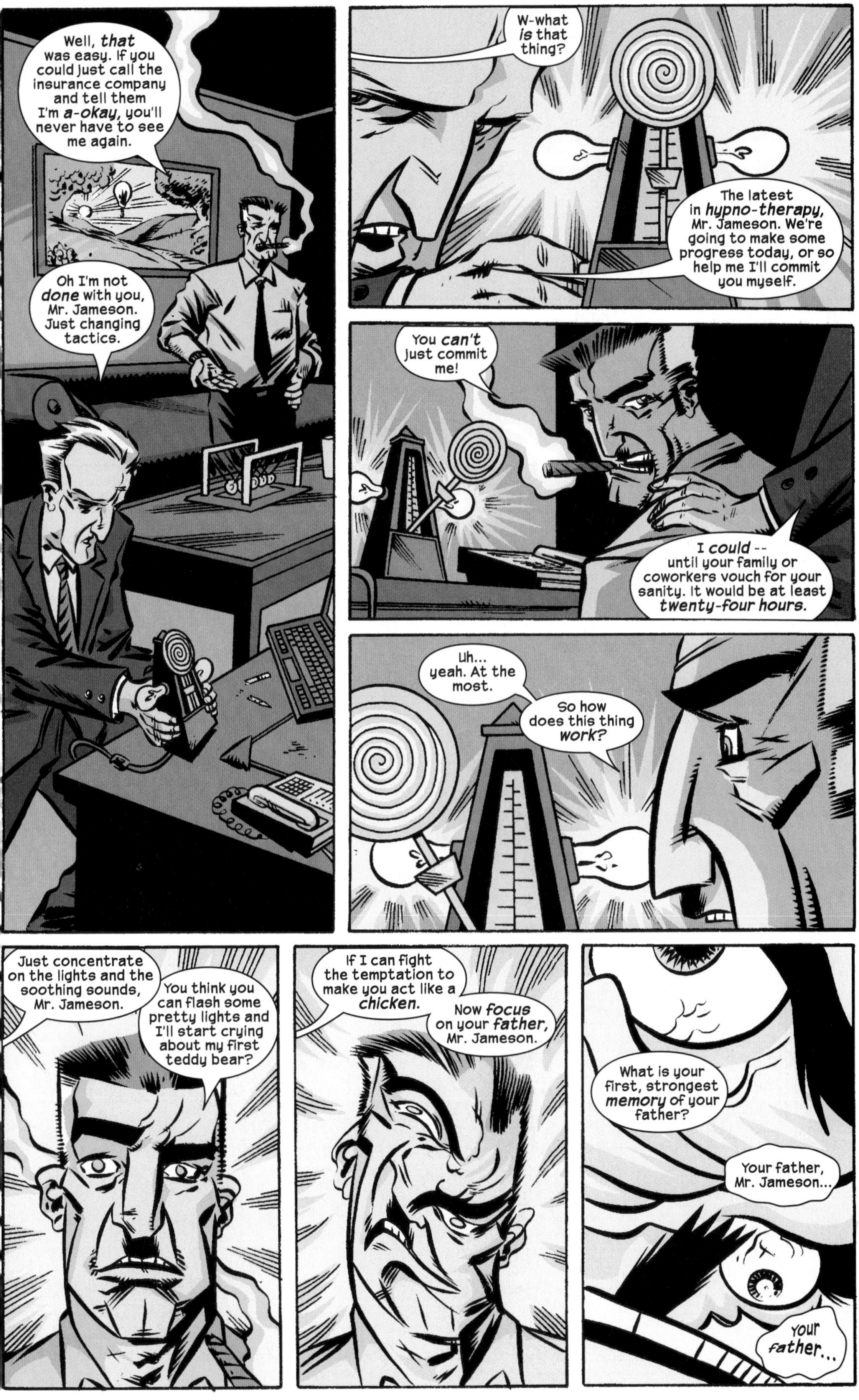
Well, that was easy. If you could just call the insurance company and tell them I'm a-okay, you'll never have to see me again.
Oh I'm not done with you, Mr. Jameson. Just changing tactics.
W-what is that thing?
The latest in hypno-therapy, Mr. Jameson. We're going to make some progress today, or so help me I'll commit you myself.
You can't just commit me!
I could -- until your family or coworkers vouch for your sanity. It would be at least twenty-four hours.
Uh... yeah. At the most.
So how does this thing work?
Just concentrate on the lights and the soothing sounds, Mr. Jameson.
You think you can flash some pretty lights and I'll start crying about my first teddy bear?
If I can fight the temptation to make you act like a chicken.
Now focus on your father, Mr. Jameson.
What is your first, strongest memory of your father?
Your father, Mr. Jameson...
Your father...

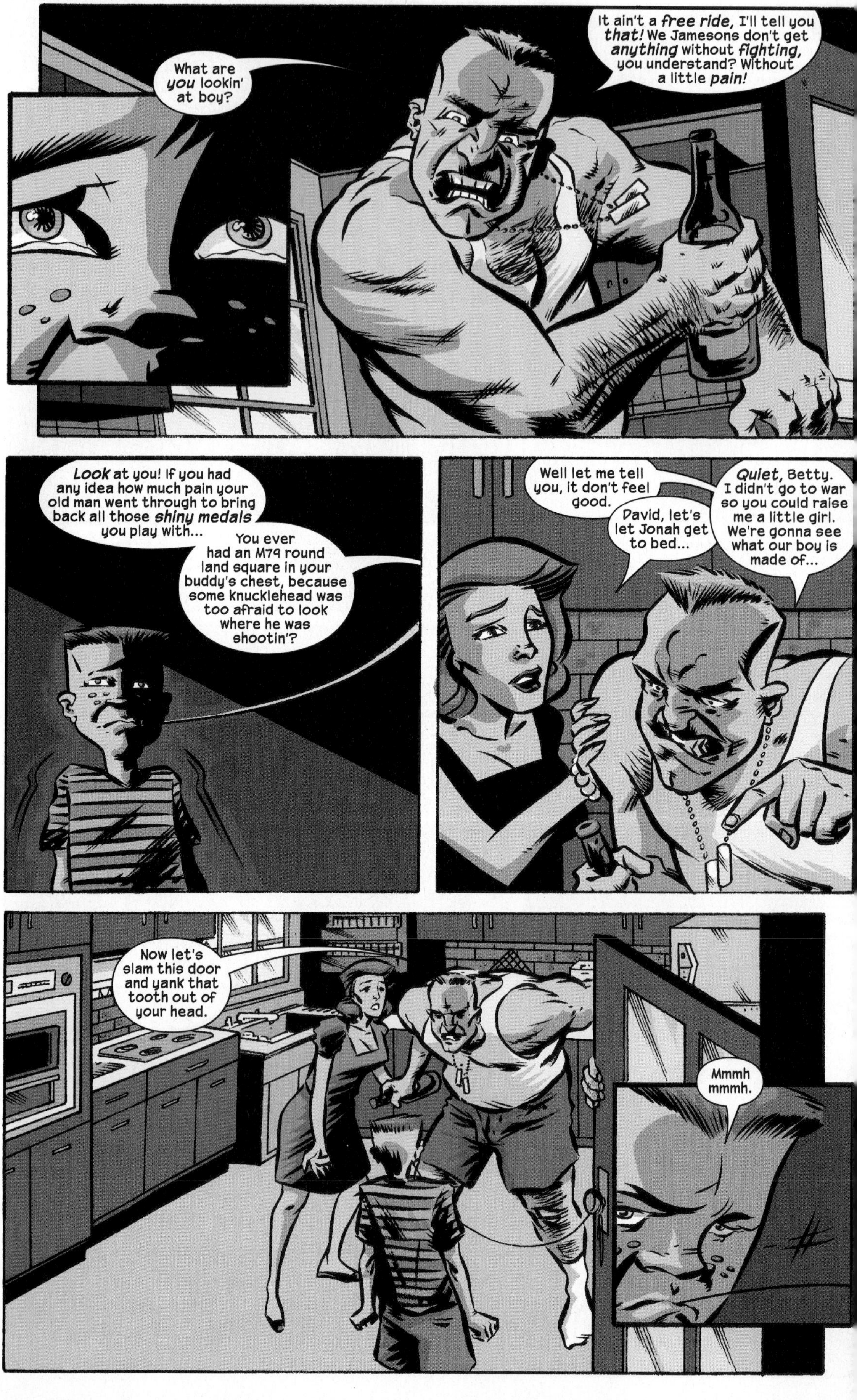
What are you lookin' at boy?
It ain't a free ride, I'll tell you that! We Jamesons don't get anything without fighting, you understand? Without a little pain!
Look at you! If you had any idea how much pain your old man went through to bring back all those shiny medals you play with...
You ever had an M79 round land square in your buddy's chest, because some knucklehead was too afraid to look where he was shootin'?
Well let me tell you, it don't feel good.
David, let's let Jonah get to bed...
Quiet, Betty. I didn't go to war so you could raise me a little girl. We're gonna see what our boy is made of...
Now let's slam this door and yank that tooth out of your head.
Mmmh mmmh.

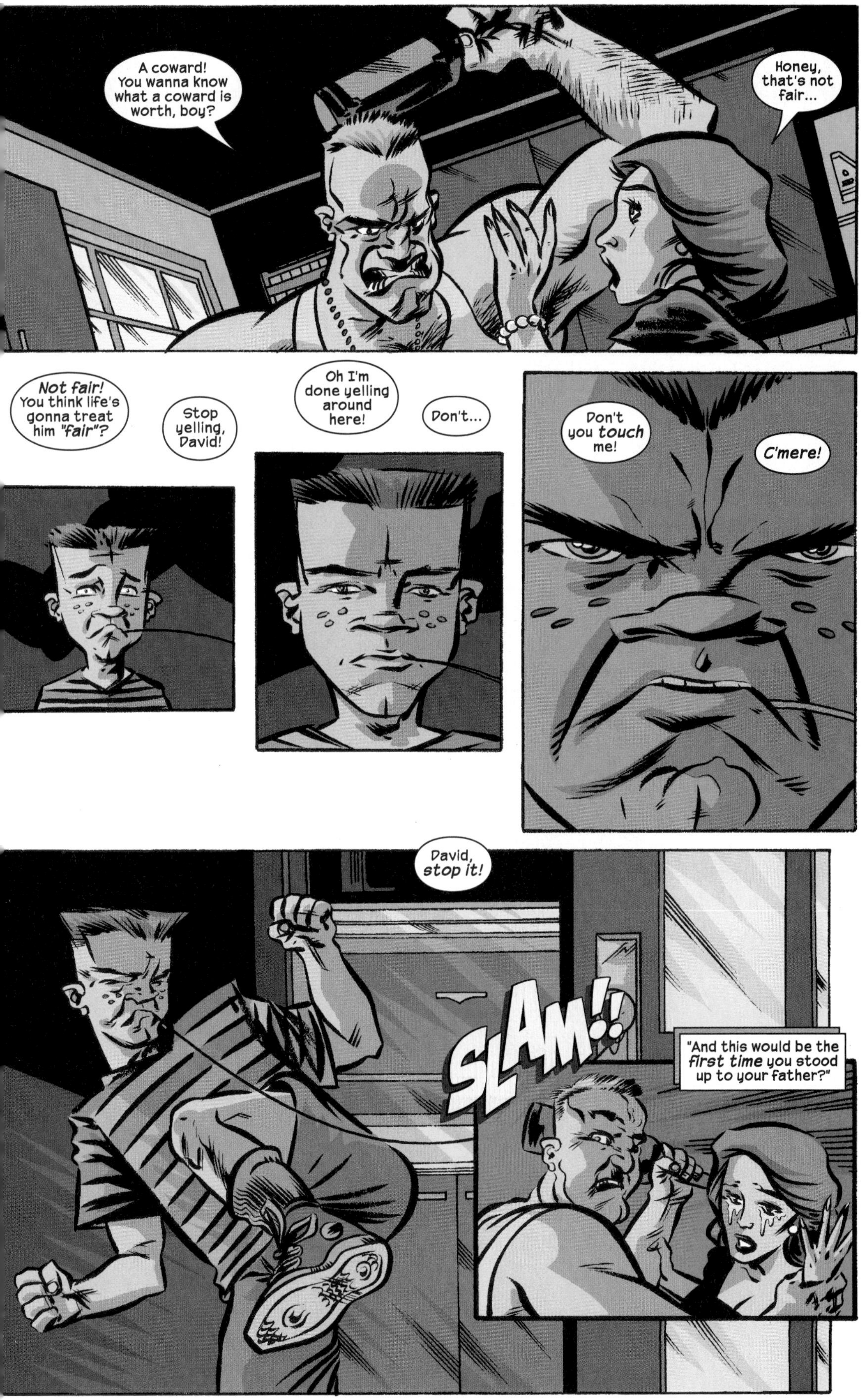
A coward! You wanna know what a coward is worth, boy?
Honey, that's not fair...
Not fair! You think life's gonna treat him "fair"?
Stop yelling, David!
Oh I'm done yelling around here!
Don't...
Don't you touch me!
C'mere!
David, stop it!
SLAM!!
"And this would be the first time you stood up to your father?"

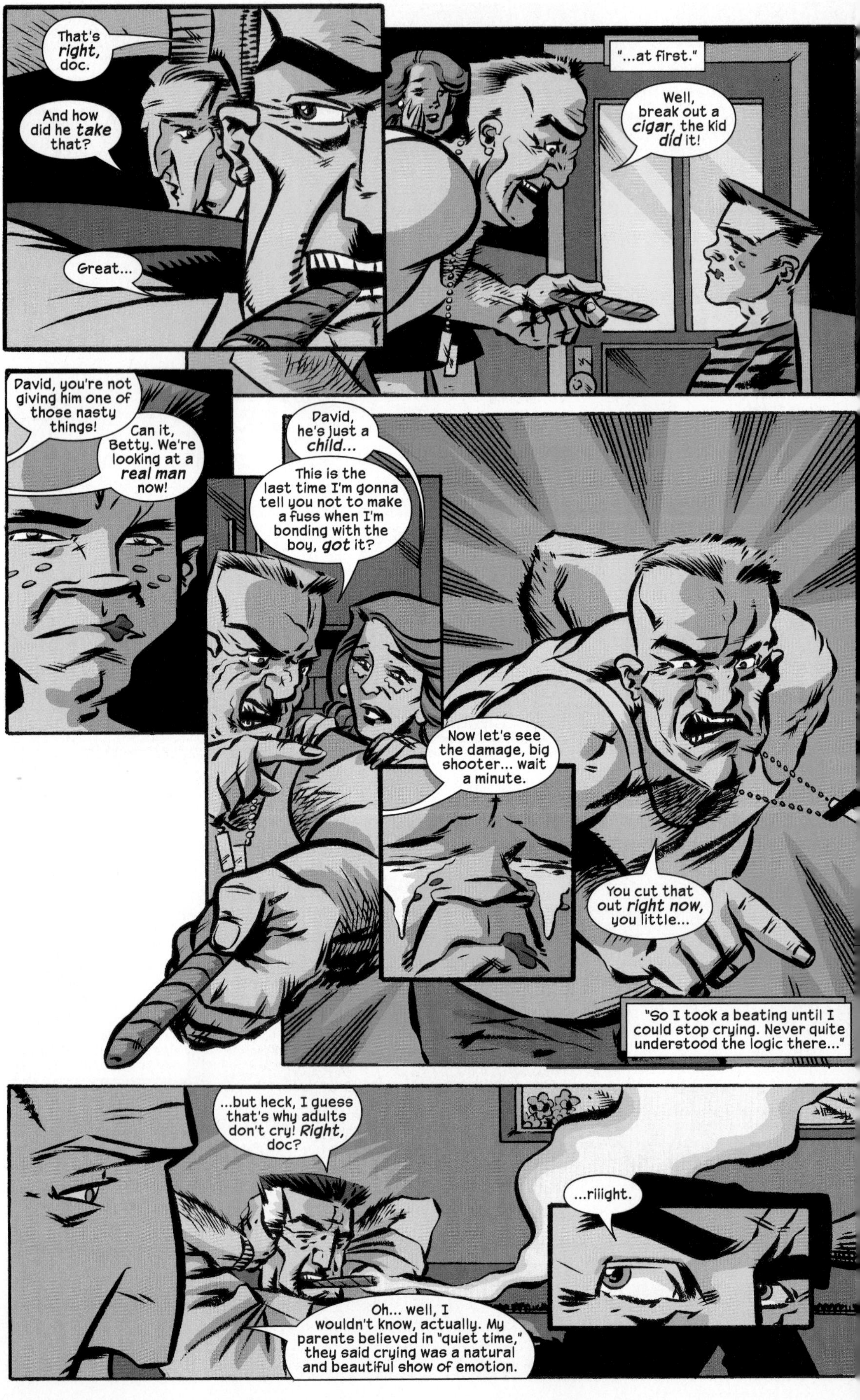
That's right, doc.
And how did he take that?
Great...
"...at first."
Well, break out a cigar, the kid did it!
David, you're not giving him one of those nasty things!
Can it, Betty. We're looking at a real man now!
David, he's just a child...
This is the last time I'm gonna tell you not to make a fuss when I'm bonding with the boy, got it?
Now let's see the damage, big shooter... wait a minute.
You cut that out right now, you little...
"So I took a beating until I could stop crying. Never quite understood the logic there..."
...but heck, I guess that's why adults don't cry! Right, doc?
...riiight.
Oh... well, I wouldn't know, actually. My parents believed in "quiet time," they said crying was a natural and beautiful show of emotion.

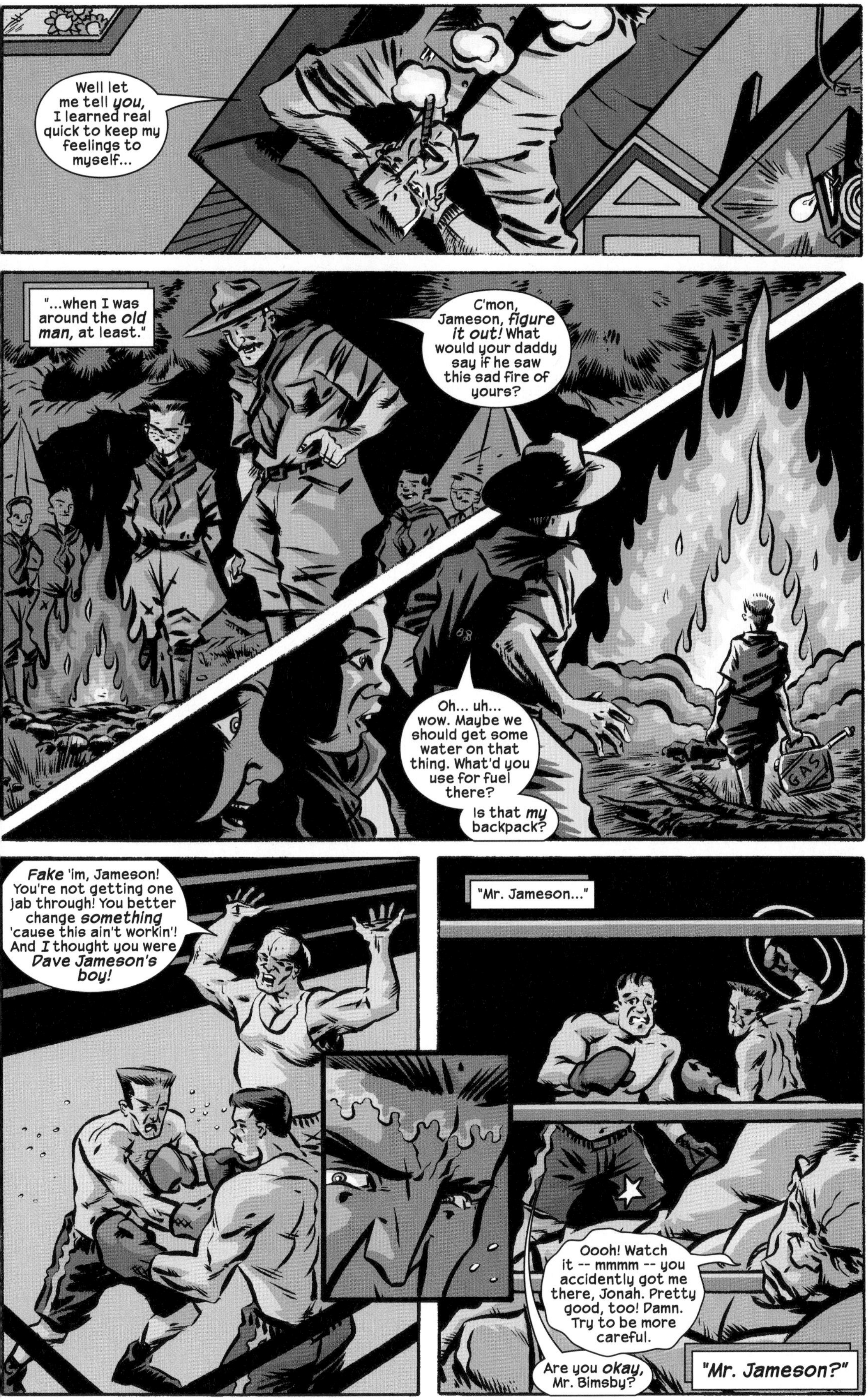
Well let me tell *you*, I learned real quick to keep my feelings to myself...
"...when I was around the *old man,* at least."
C'mon, Jameson, *figure it out!* What would your daddy say if he saw this sad fire of yours?
Oh... uh... wow. Maybe we should get some water on that thing. What'd you use for fuel there?
Is that *my* backpack?
GAS
Fake 'im, Jameson! You're not getting one jab through! You better change *something* 'cause this ain't workin'! And *I* thought you were *Dave Jameson's boy!*
"Mr. Jameson..."
Oooh! Watch it -- mmmm -- you accidently got me there, Jonah. Pretty good, too! Damn. Try to be more careful.
Are you *okay,* Mr. Bimsby?
"Mr. Jameson?"

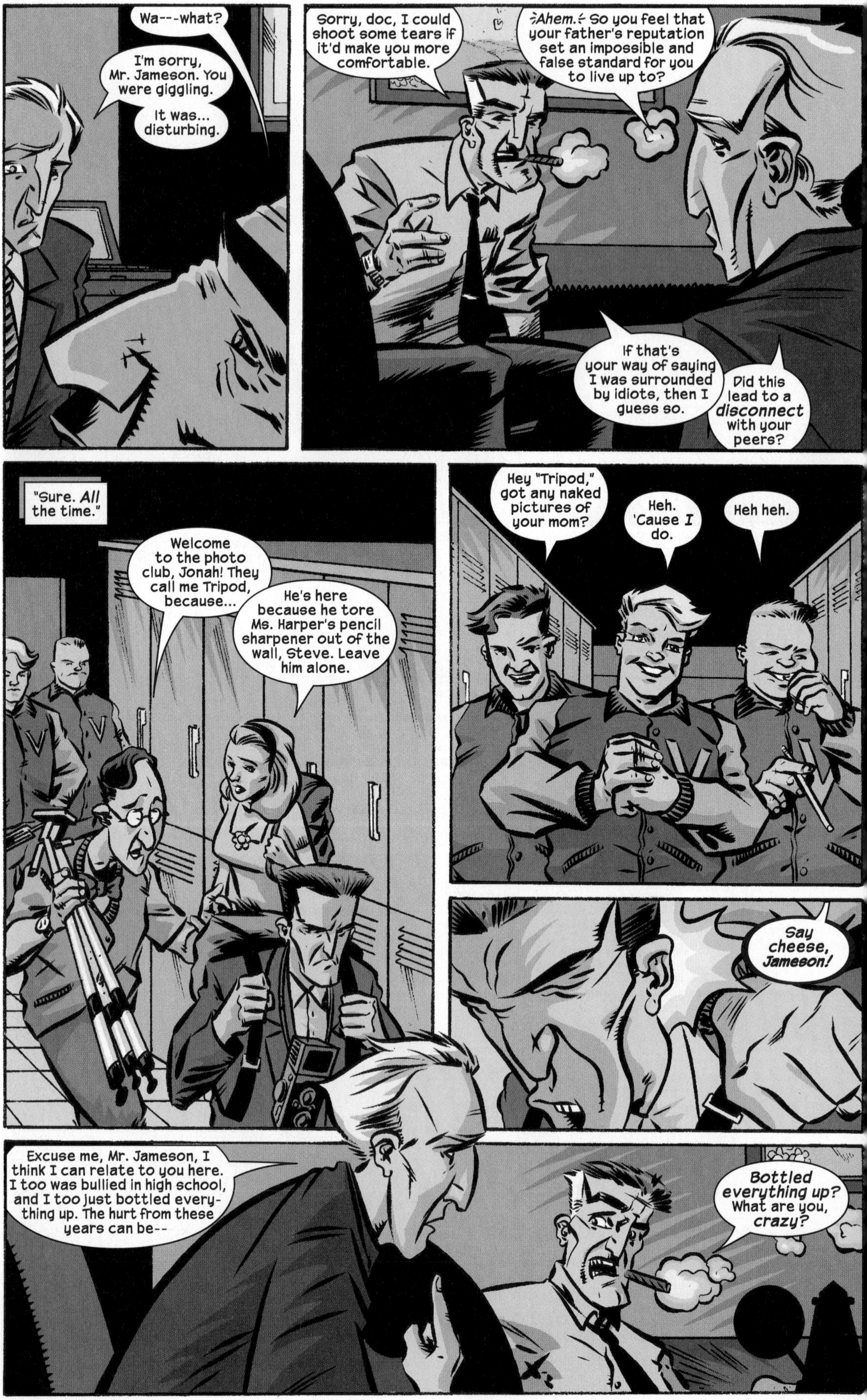
Wa---what?
I'm sorry, Mr. Jameson. You were giggling.
It was... disturbing.
Sorry, doc, I could shoot some tears if it'd make you more comfortable.
Ahem. So you feel that your father's reputation set an impossible and false standard for you to live up to?
If that's your way of saying I was surrounded by idiots, then I guess so.
Did this lead to a disconnect with your peers?
"Sure. All the time."
Welcome to the photo club, Jonah! They call me Tripod, because...
He's here because he tore Ms. Harper's pencil sharpener out of the wall, Steve. Leave him alone.
Hey "Tripod," got any naked pictures of your mom?
Heh. 'Cause I do.
Heh heh.
Say cheese, Jameson!
Excuse me, Mr. Jameson, I think I can relate to you here. I too was bullied in high school, and I too just bottled everything up. The hurt from these years can be--
Bottled everything up? What are you, crazy?

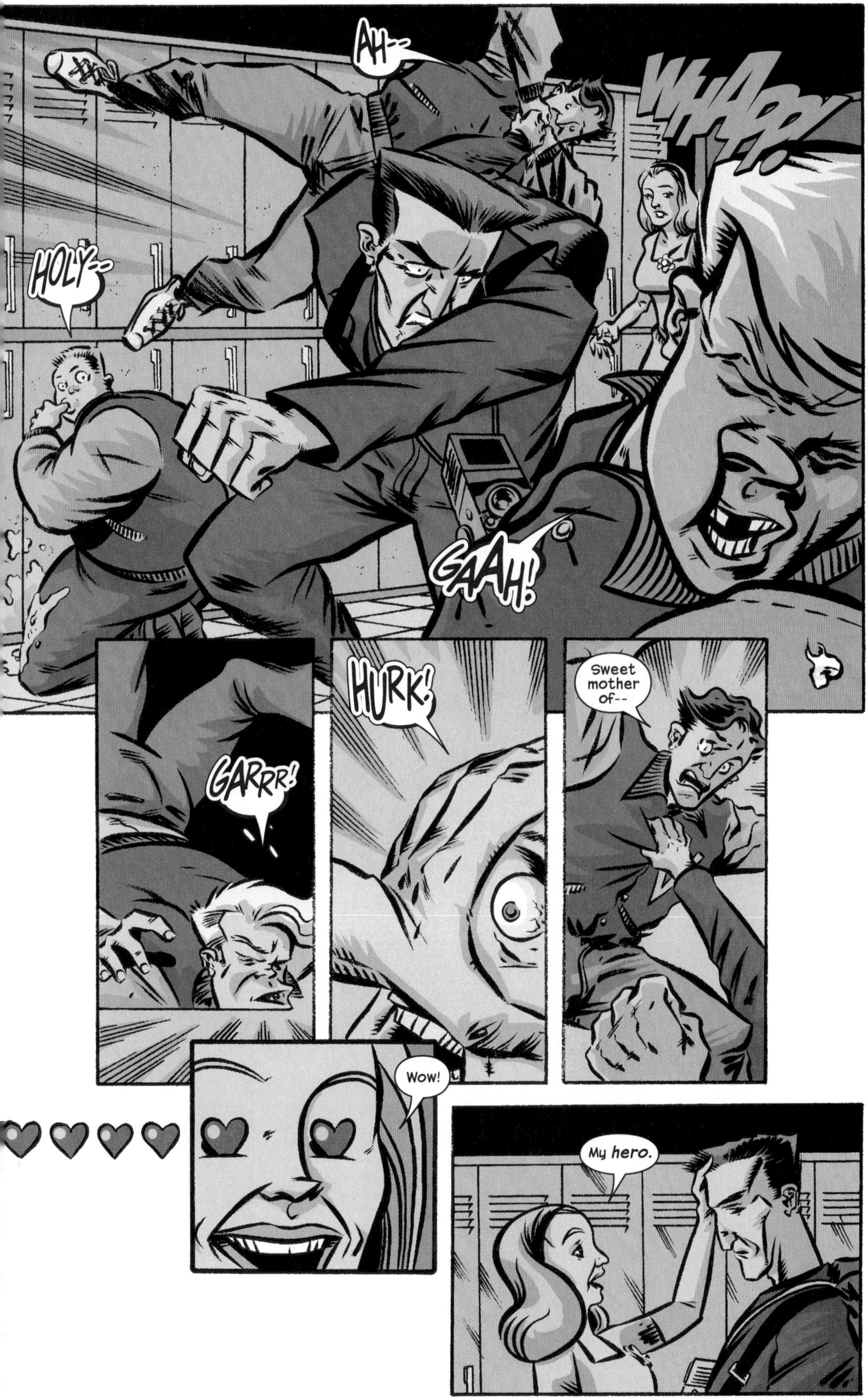
AH--
WHAPP!
HOLY--
GAAH!
GARRR!
HURK!
Sweet mother of--
Wow!
My hero.

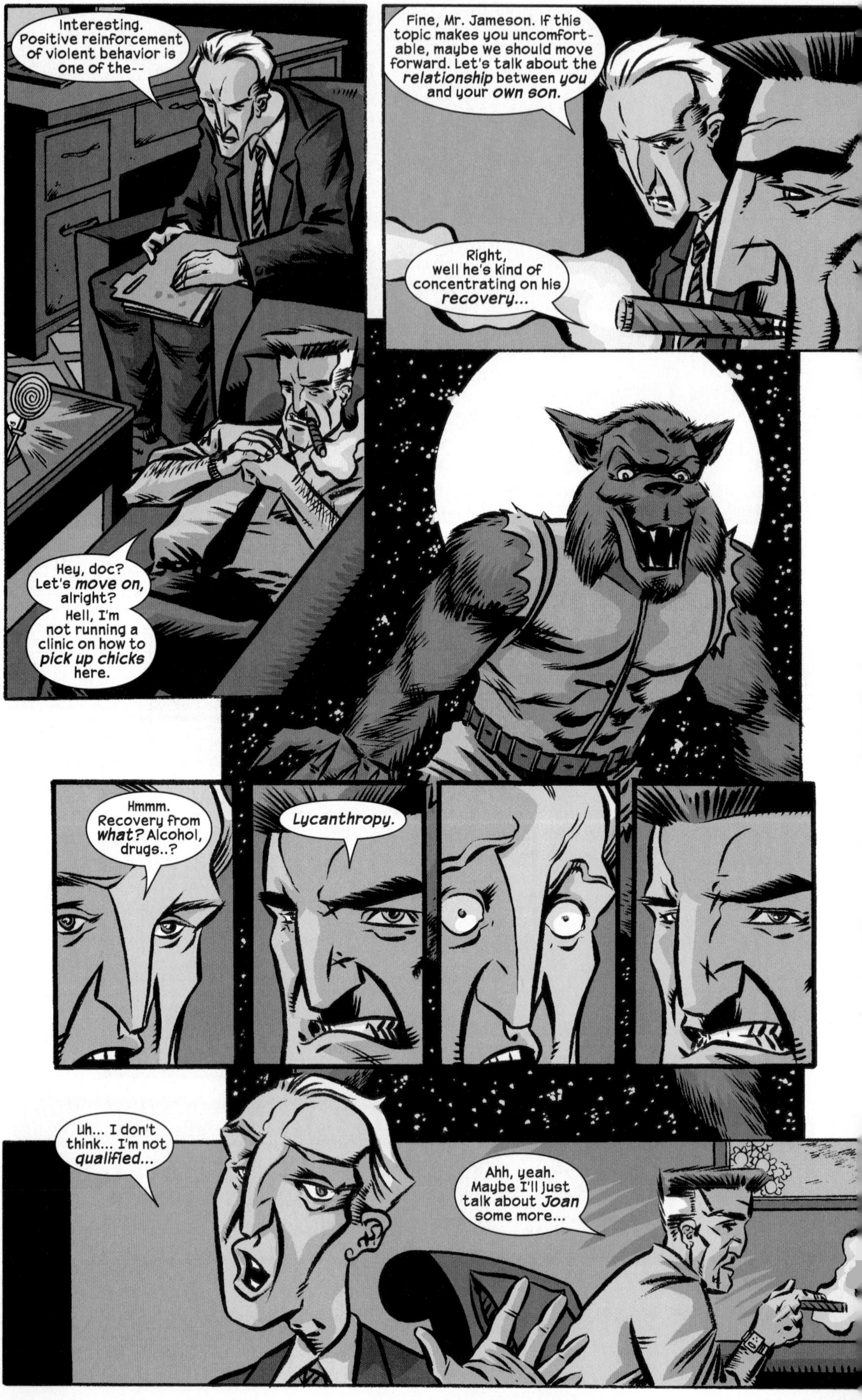
Interesting. Positive reinforcement of violent behavior is one of the--
Fine, Mr. Jameson. If this topic makes you uncomfortable, maybe we should move forward. Let's talk about the relationship between you and your own son.
Right, well he's kind of concentrating on his recovery...
Hey, doc? Let's move on, alright?
Hell, I'm not running a clinic on how to pick up chicks here.
Hmmm. Recovery from what? Alcohol, drugs..?
Lycanthropy.
Uh... I don't think... I'm not qualified...
Ahh, yeah. Maybe I'll just talk about Joan some more...

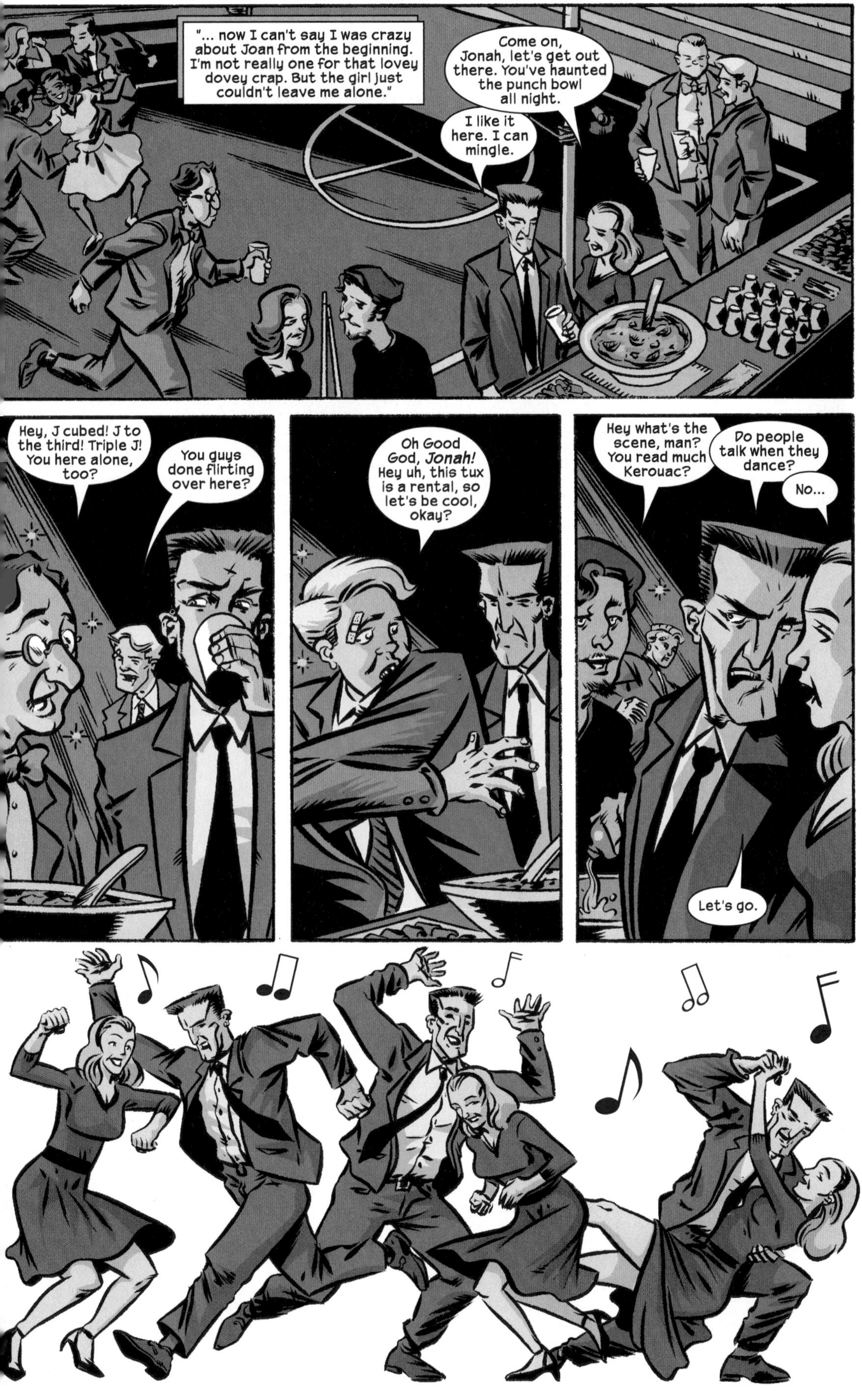
"... now I can't say I was crazy about Joan from the beginning. I'm not really one for that lovey dovey crap. But the girl just couldn't leave me alone."
Come on, Jonah, let's get out there. You've haunted the punch bowl all night.
I like it here. I can mingle.
Hey, J cubed! J to the third! Triple J! You here alone, too?
You guys done flirting over here?
Oh Good God, Jonah! Hey uh, this tux is a rental, so let's be cool, okay?
Hey what's the scene, man? You read much Kerouac?
Do people talk when they dance?
No...
Let's go.

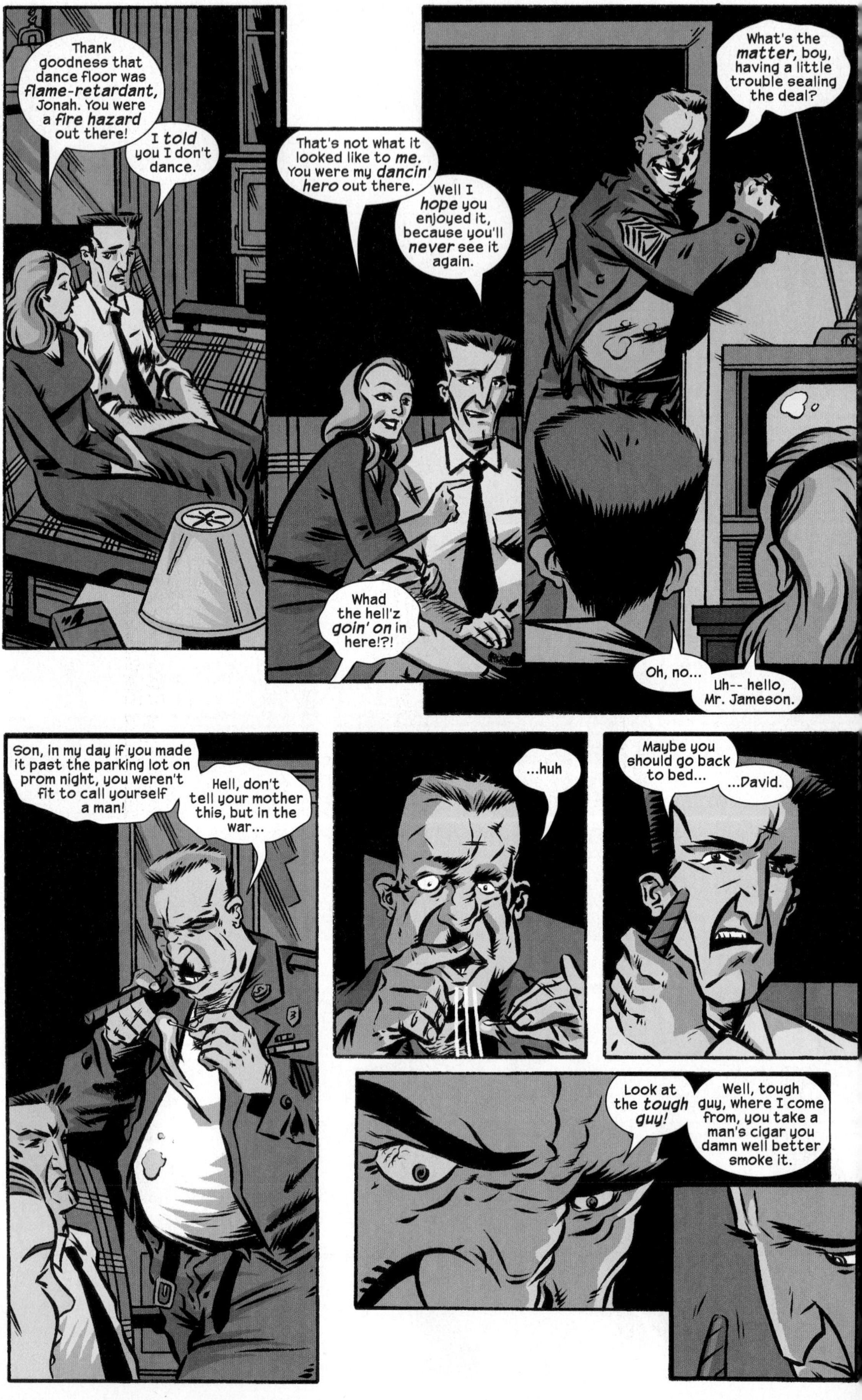

Thank goodness that dance floor was *flame-retardant*, Jonah. You were a *fire hazard* out there!
I *told* you I don't dance.
That's not what it looked like to *me.* You were my *dancin' hero* out there.
Well I *hope* you enjoyed it, because you'll *never* see it again.
Whad the hell'z *goin' on* in here!?!
What's the *matter*, boy, having a little trouble sealing the deal?
Oh, no...
Uh-- hello, Mr. Jameson.
Son, in my day if you made it past the parking lot on prom night, you weren't fit to call yourself a man!
Hell, don't tell your mother this, but in the war...
...huh
Maybe you should go back to bed...
...David.
Look at the *tough guy!*
Well, tough guy, where I come from, you take a man's cigar you damn well better smoke it.

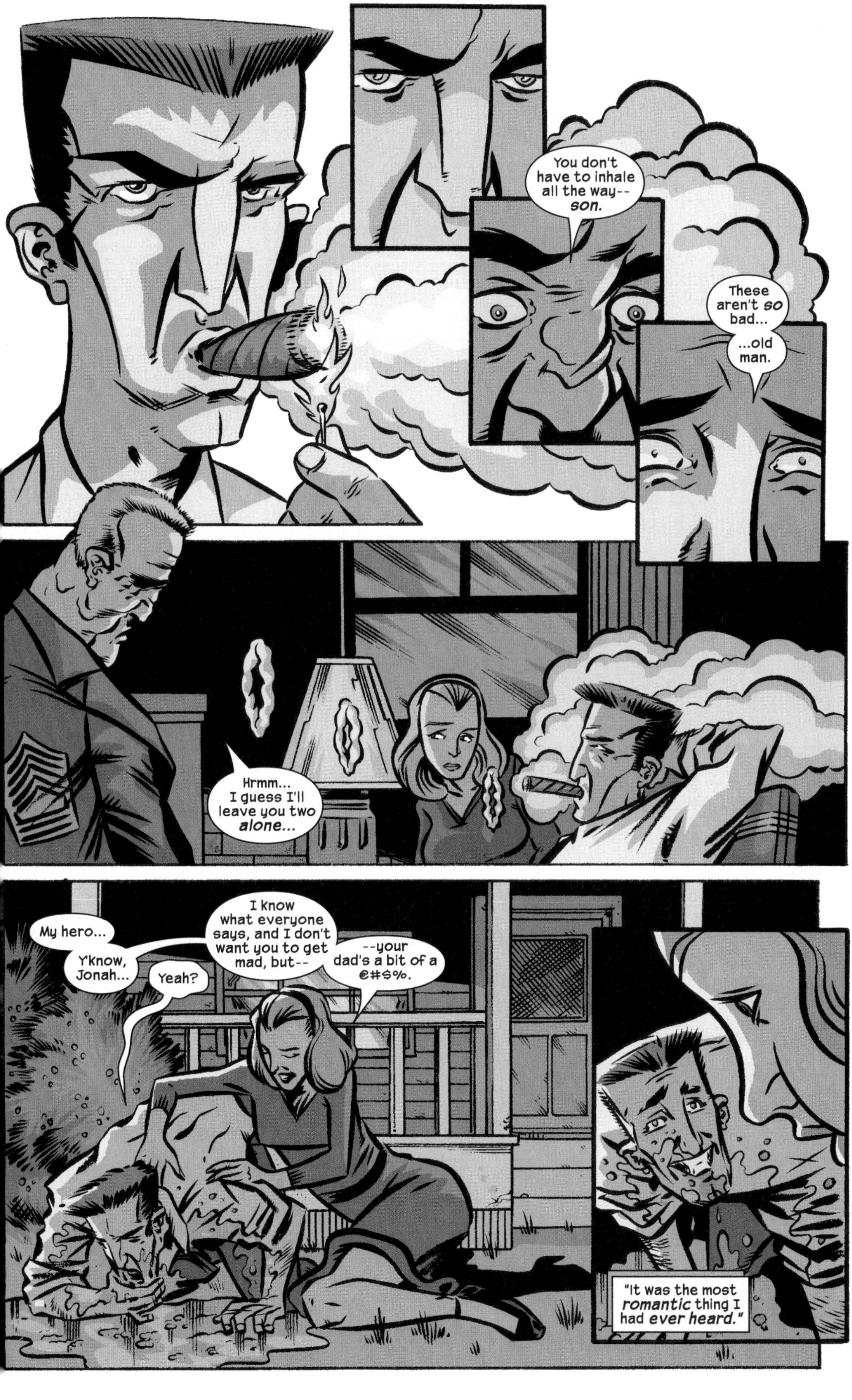

You don't have to inhale all the way-- son.
These aren't so bad...
...old man.
Hrmm... I guess I'll leave you two alone...
My hero...
Y'know, Jonah...
Yeah?
I know what everyone says, and I don't want you to get mad, but--
--your dad's a bit of a @#$%.
"It was the most romantic thing I had ever heard."

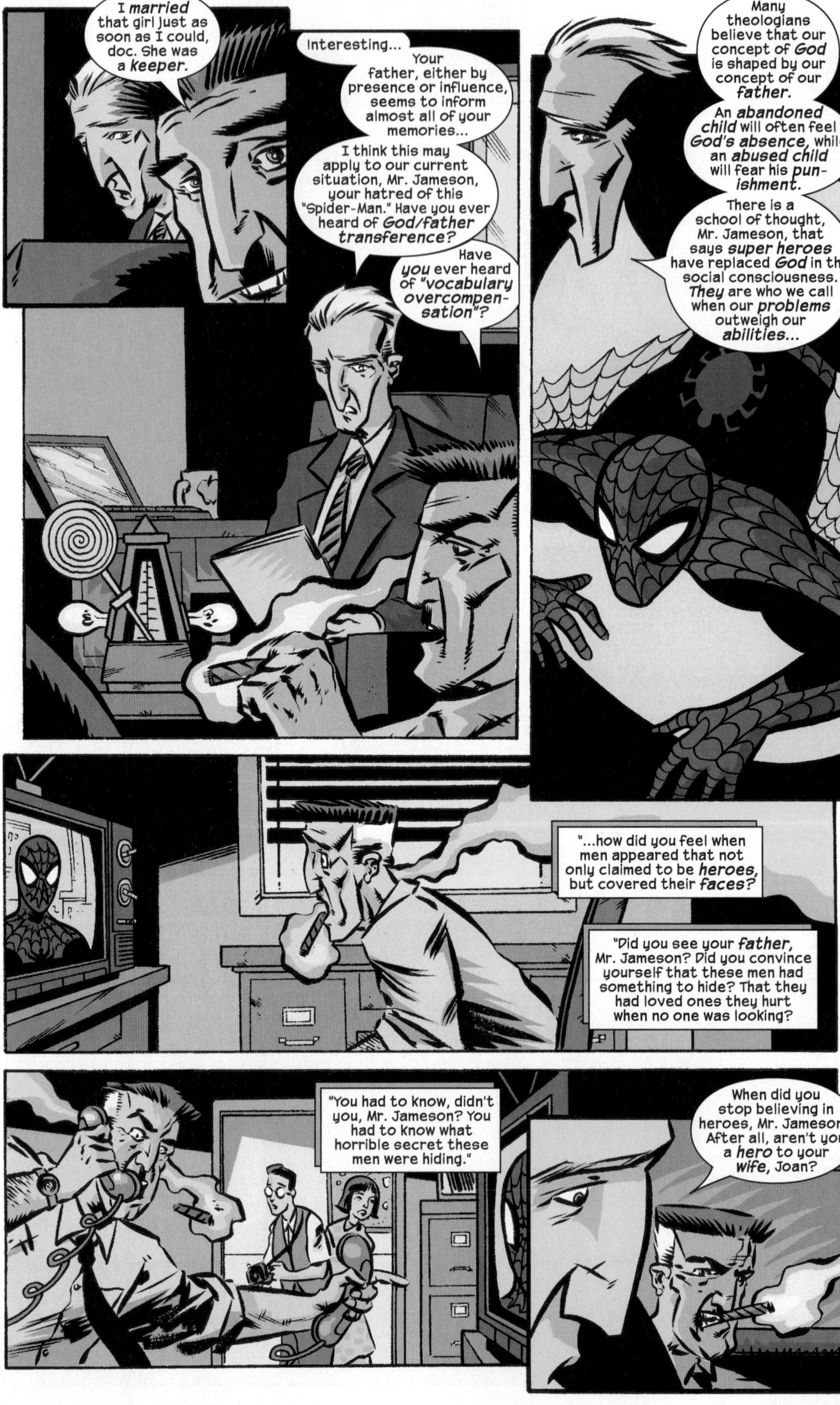

I married that girl just as soon as I could, doc. She was a keeper.
Interesting... Your father, either by presence or influence, seems to inform almost all of your memories...
I think this may apply to our current situation, Mr. Jameson, your hatred of this "Spider-Man." Have you ever heard of God/father transference?
Have you ever heard of "vocabulary overcompen-sation"?
Many theologians believe that our concept of God is shaped by our concept of our father.
An abandoned child will often feel God's absence, while an abused child will fear his pun-ishment.
There is a school of thought, Mr. Jameson, that says super heroes have replaced God in the social consciousness. They are who we call when our problems outweigh our abilities...
"...how did you feel when men appeared that not only claimed to be heroes, but covered their faces?
"Did you see your father, Mr. Jameson? Did you convince yourself that these men had something to hide? That they had loved ones they hurt when no one was looking?
"You had to know, didn't you, Mr. Jameson? You had to know what horrible secret these men were hiding."
When did you stop believing in heroes, Mr. Jameson? After all, aren't you a hero to your wife, Joan?

First wife.

Oh. Yes, I'm sorry. It says here that your first wife is deceased. How did she die, exactly?

... Mr. Jameson?

She *died alone.* I was in Korea, reporting for the Bugle...

...trying to impress the old man... prove to him that I wasn't scared--

Alone.

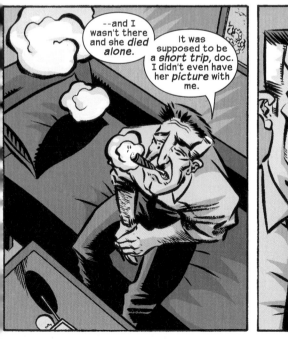

--and I wasn't there and she *died alone.*

It was supposed to be a *short trip*, doc. I didn't even have her *picture* with me.

All I could do was buy a *cigar*, like my dad used to smoke.

I smoked it and it reminded me of that night... of falling in love...

...with *her.*

They *still do...* sometimes.

No *one's* a hero, doc. *Especially* not me.

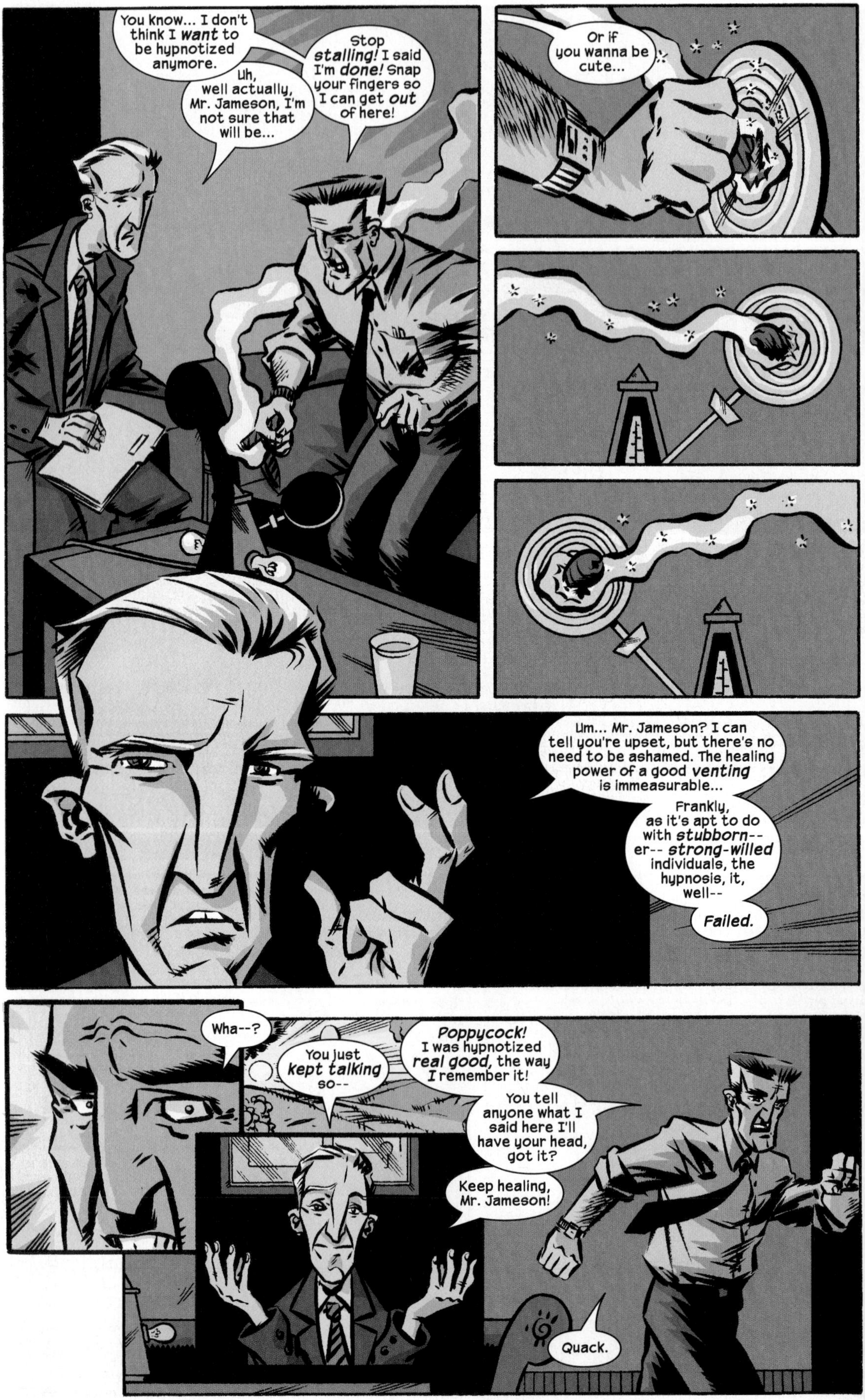
You know... I don't think I want to be hypnotized anymore.
Uh, well actually, Mr. Jameson, I'm not sure that will be...
Stop stalling! I said I'm done! Snap your fingers so I can get out of here!
Or if you wanna be cute...
Um... Mr. Jameson? I can tell you're upset, but there's no need to be ashamed. The healing power of a good venting is immeasurable...
Frankly, as it's apt to do with stubborn-- er-- strong-willed individuals, the hypnosis, it, well--
Failed.
Wha--?
You just kept talking so--
Poppycock! I was hypnotized real good, the way I remember it!
You tell anyone what I said here I'll have your head, got it?
Keep healing, Mr. Jameson!
Quack.

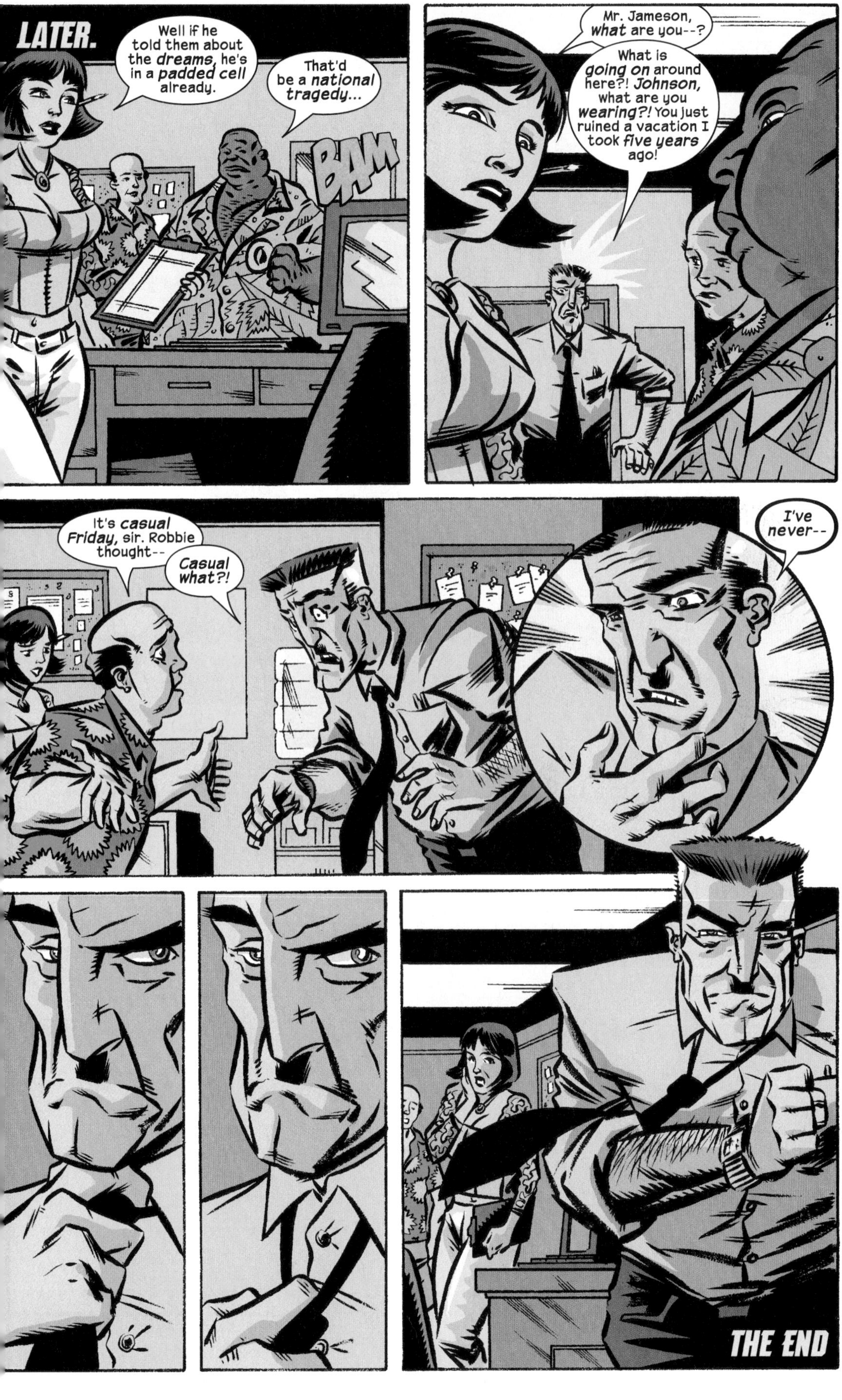
LATER.
Well if he told them about the dreams, he's in a padded cell already.
That'd be a national tragedy...
BAM
Mr. Jameson, what are you--?
What is going on around here?! Johnson, what are you wearing?! You just ruined a vacation I took five years ago!
It's casual Friday, sir. Robbie thought--
Casual what?!
I've never--
THE END

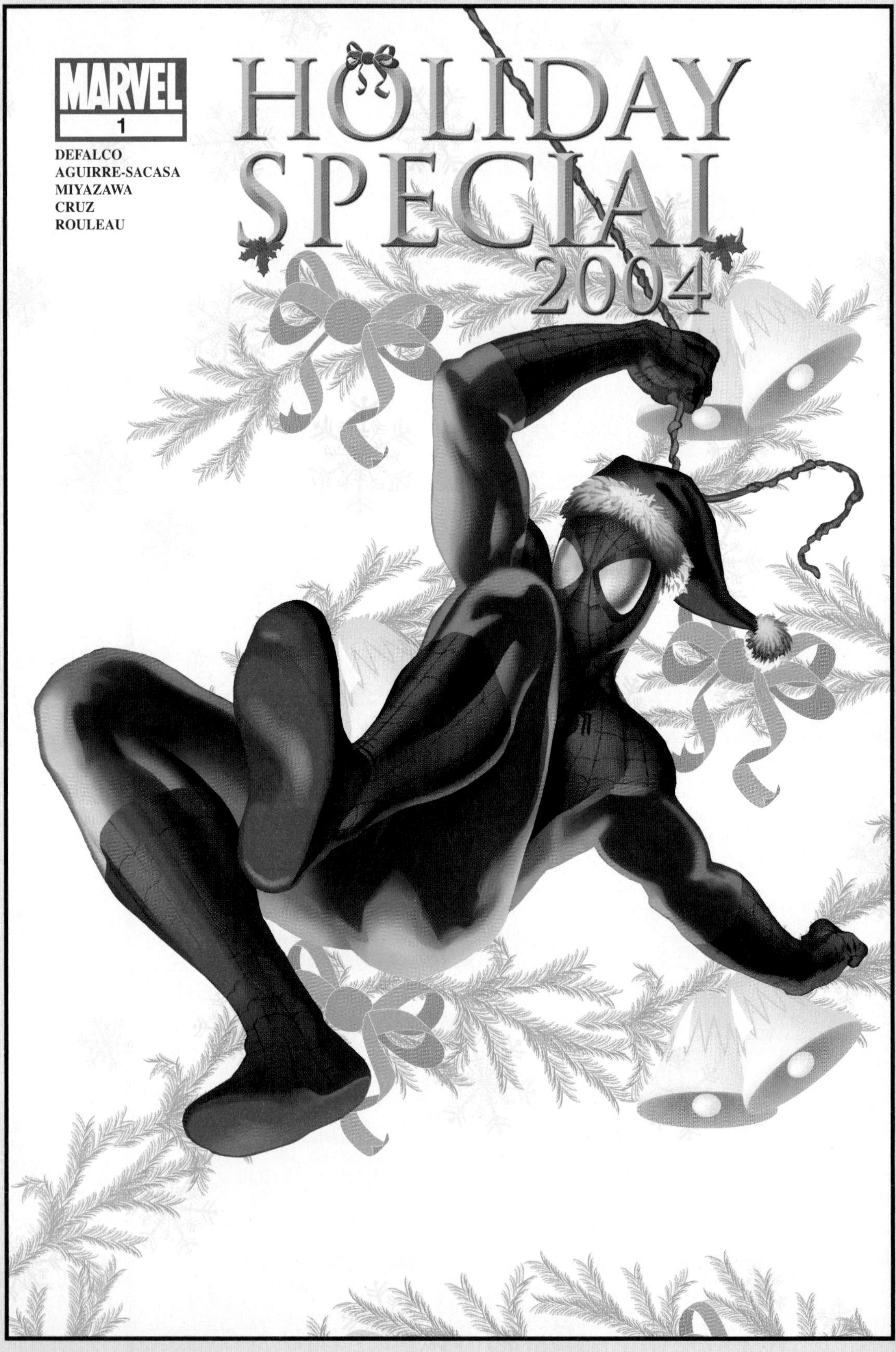
MARVEL
1
DEFALCO
AGUIRRE-SACASA
MIYAZAWA
CRUZ
ROULEAU
HOLIDAY SPECIAL 2004

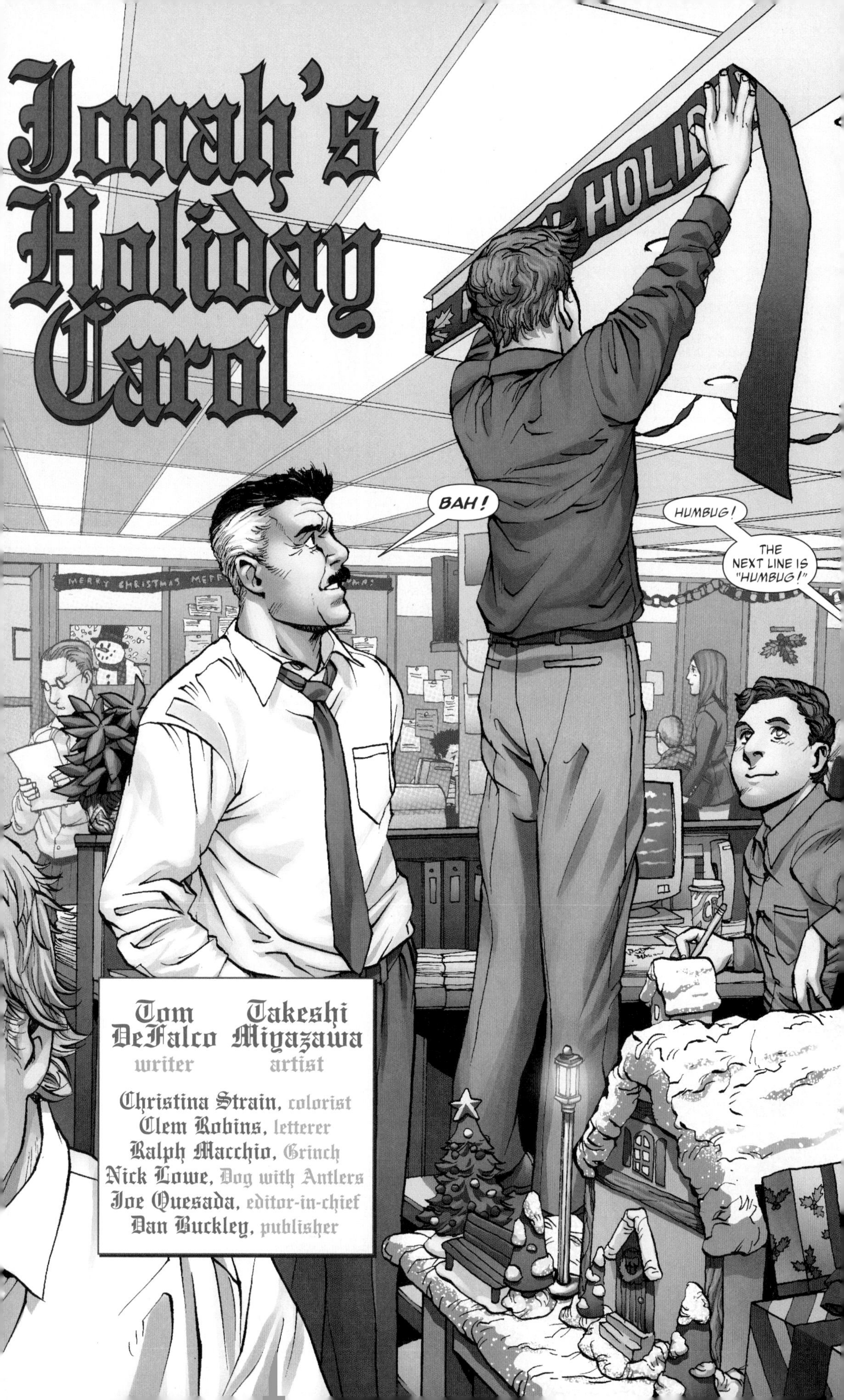
Jonah's Holiday Carol
BAH!
HUMBUG!
THE NEXT LINE IS "HUMBUG!"
Tom DeFalco writer
Takeshi Miyazawa artist
Christina Strain, colorist
Clem Robins, letterer
Ralph Macchio, Grinch
Nick Lowe, Dog with Antlers
Joe Quesada, editor-in-chief
Dan Buckley, publisher

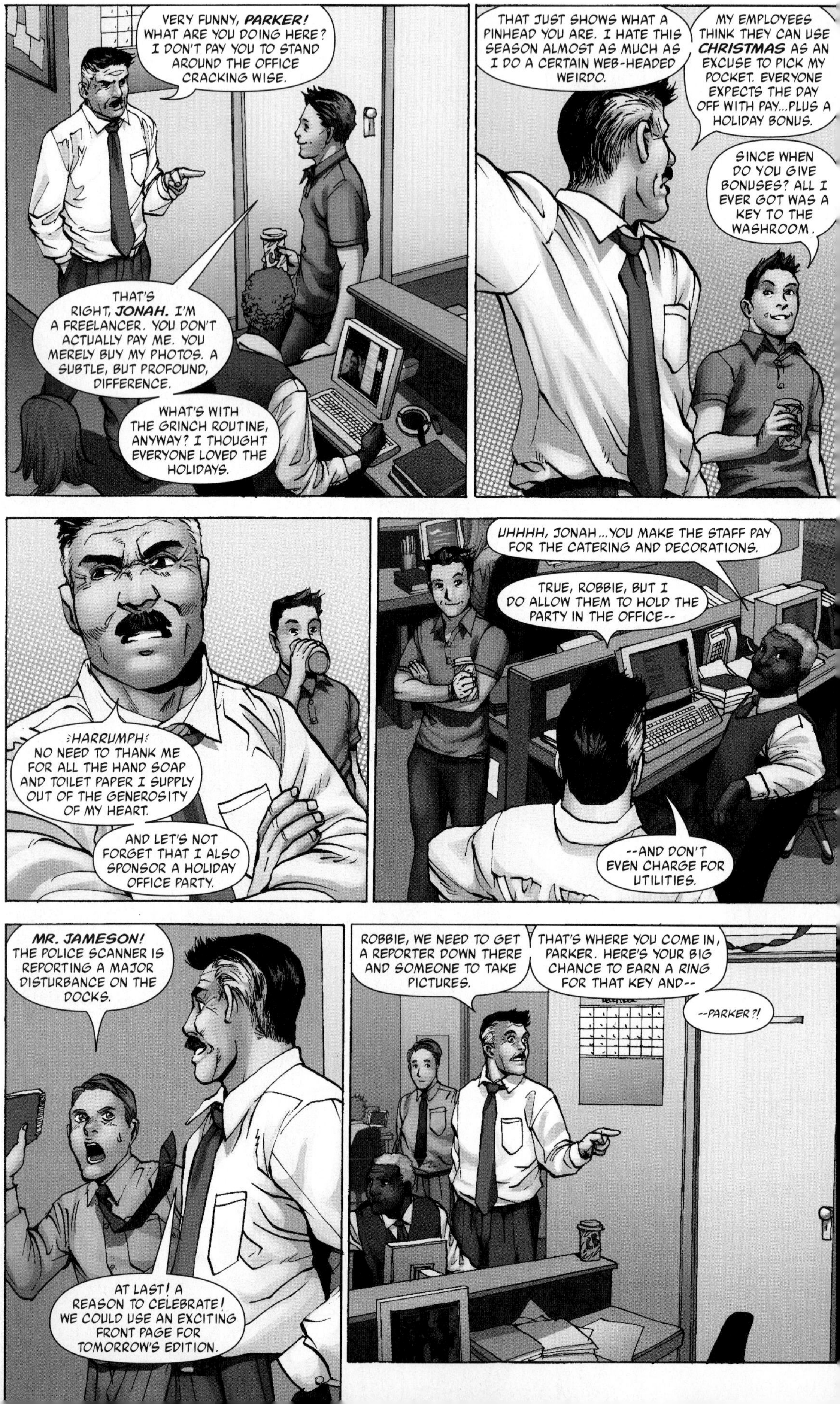
VERY FUNNY, PARKER! WHAT ARE YOU DOING HERE? I DON'T PAY YOU TO STAND AROUND THE OFFICE CRACKING WISE.
THAT'S RIGHT, JONAH. I'M A FREELANCER. YOU DON'T ACTUALLY PAY ME. YOU MERELY BUY MY PHOTOS. A SUBTLE, BUT PROFOUND, DIFFERENCE.
WHAT'S WITH THE GRINCH ROUTINE, ANYWAY? I THOUGHT EVERYONE LOVED THE HOLIDAYS.
THAT JUST SHOWS WHAT A PINHEAD YOU ARE. I HATE THIS SEASON ALMOST AS MUCH AS I DO A CERTAIN WEB-HEADED WEIRDO.
MY EMPLOYEES THINK THEY CAN USE CHRISTMAS AS AN EXCUSE TO PICK MY POCKET. EVERYONE EXPECTS THE DAY OFF WITH PAY...PLUS A HOLIDAY BONUS.
SINCE WHEN DO YOU GIVE BONUSES? ALL I EVER GOT WAS A KEY TO THE WASHROOM.
HARRUMPH NO NEED TO THANK ME FOR ALL THE HAND SOAP AND TOILET PAPER I SUPPLY OUT OF THE GENEROSITY OF MY HEART.
AND LET'S NOT FORGET THAT I ALSO SPONSOR A HOLIDAY OFFICE PARTY.
UHHHH, JONAH...YOU MAKE THE STAFF PAY FOR THE CATERING AND DECORATIONS.
TRUE, ROBBIE, BUT I DO ALLOW THEM TO HOLD THE PARTY IN THE OFFICE--
--AND DON'T EVEN CHARGE FOR UTILITIES.
MR. JAMESON! THE POLICE SCANNER IS REPORTING A MAJOR DISTURBANCE ON THE DOCKS.
AT LAST! A REASON TO CELEBRATE! WE COULD USE AN EXCITING FRONT PAGE FOR TOMORROW'S EDITION.
ROBBIE, WE NEED TO GET A REPORTER DOWN THERE AND SOMEONE TO TAKE PICTURES.
THAT'S WHERE YOU COME IN, PARKER. HERE'S YOUR BIG CHANCE TO EARN A RING FOR THAT KEY AND--
--PARKER?!

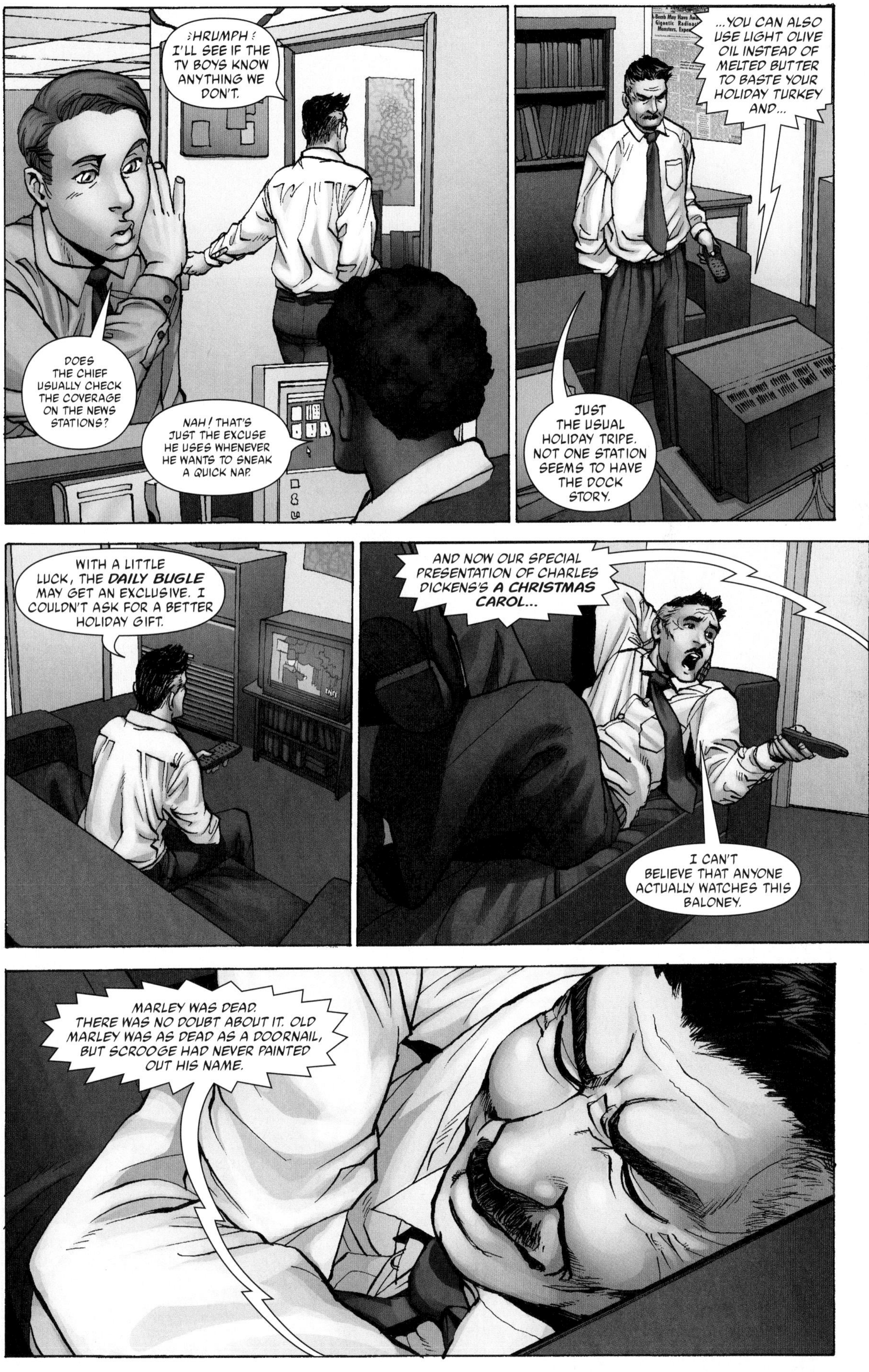
HRUMPH I'LL SEE IF THE TV BOYS KNOW ANYTHING WE DON'T.
DOES THE CHIEF USUALLY CHECK THE COVERAGE ON THE NEWS STATIONS?
NAH! THAT'S JUST THE EXCUSE HE USES WHENEVER HE WANTS TO SNEAK A QUICK NAP.
...YOU CAN ALSO USE LIGHT OLIVE OIL INSTEAD OF MELTED BUTTER TO BASTE YOUR HOLIDAY TURKEY AND...
JUST THE USUAL HOLIDAY TRIPE. NOT ONE STATION SEEMS TO HAVE THE DOCK STORY.
WITH A LITTLE LUCK, THE DAILY BUGLE MAY GET AN EXCLUSIVE. I COULDN'T ASK FOR A BETTER HOLIDAY GIFT.
AND NOW OUR SPECIAL PRESENTATION OF CHARLES DICKENS'S A CHRISTMAS CAROL...
I CAN'T BELIEVE THAT ANYONE ACTUALLY WATCHES THIS BALONEY.
MARLEY WAS DEAD. THERE WAS NO DOUBT ABOUT IT. OLD MARLEY WAS AS DEAD AS A DOORNAIL, BUT SCROOGE HAD NEVER PAINTED OUT HIS NAME.

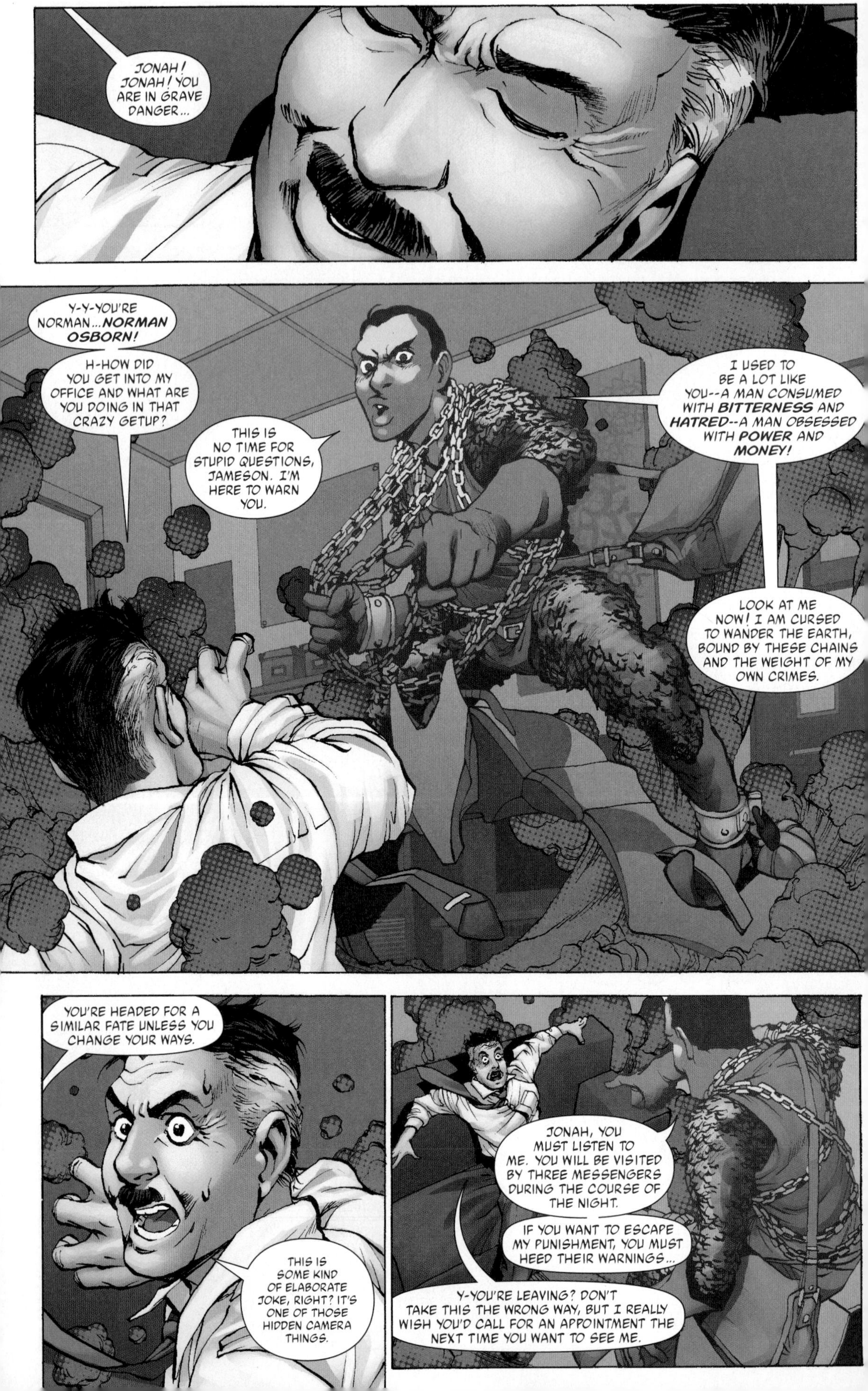
JONAH! JONAH! YOU ARE IN GRAVE DANGER...
Y-Y-YOU'RE NORMAN...**NORMAN OSBORN!**
H-HOW DID YOU GET INTO MY OFFICE AND WHAT ARE YOU DOING IN THAT CRAZY GETUP?
THIS IS NO TIME FOR STUPID QUESTIONS, JAMESON. I'M HERE TO WARN YOU.
I USED TO BE A LOT LIKE YOU--A MAN CONSUMED WITH **BITTERNESS** AND **HATRED**--A MAN OBSESSED WITH **POWER** AND **MONEY!**
LOOK AT ME NOW! I AM CURSED TO WANDER THE EARTH, BOUND BY THESE CHAINS AND THE WEIGHT OF MY OWN CRIMES.
YOU'RE HEADED FOR A SIMILAR FATE UNLESS YOU CHANGE YOUR WAYS.
THIS IS SOME KIND OF ELABORATE JOKE, RIGHT? IT'S ONE OF THOSE HIDDEN CAMERA THINGS.
JONAH, YOU MUST LISTEN TO ME. YOU WILL BE VISITED BY THREE MESSENGERS DURING THE COURSE OF THE NIGHT.
IF YOU WANT TO ESCAPE MY PUNISHMENT, YOU MUST HEED THEIR WARNINGS...
Y-YOU'RE LEAVING? DON'T TAKE THIS THE WRONG WAY, BUT I REALLY WISH YOU'D CALL FOR AN APPOINTMENT THE NEXT TIME YOU WANT TO SEE ME.

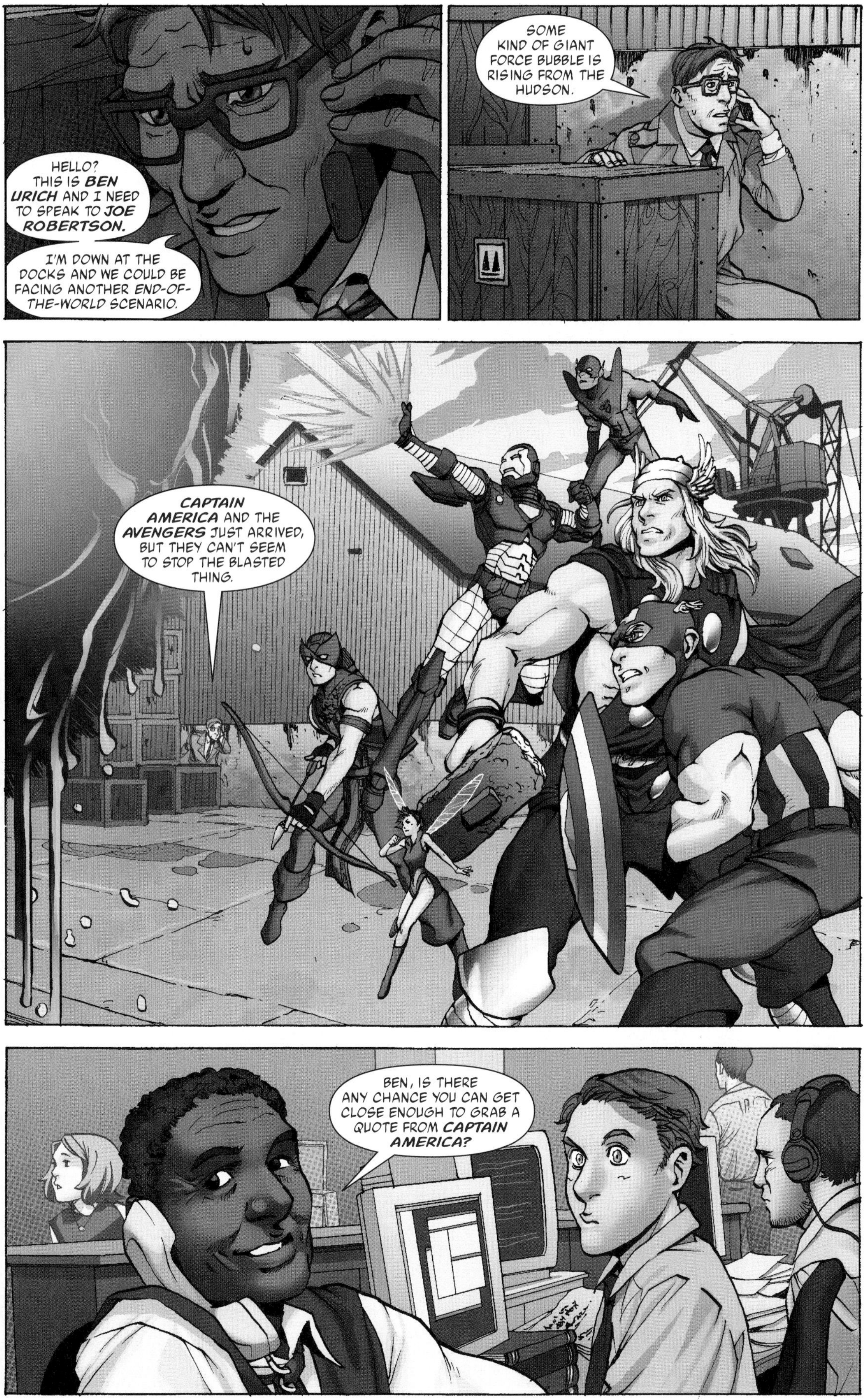
HELLO? THIS IS BEN URICH AND I NEED TO SPEAK TO JOE ROBERTSON.
I'M DOWN AT THE DOCKS AND WE COULD BE FACING ANOTHER END-OF-THE-WORLD SCENARIO.
SOME KIND OF GIANT FORCE BUBBLE IS RISING FROM THE HUDSON.
CAPTAIN AMERICA AND THE AVENGERS JUST ARRIVED, BUT THEY CAN'T SEEM TO STOP THE BLASTED THING.
BEN, IS THERE ANY CHANCE YOU CAN GET CLOSE ENOUGH TO GRAB A QUOTE FROM CAPTAIN AMERICA?

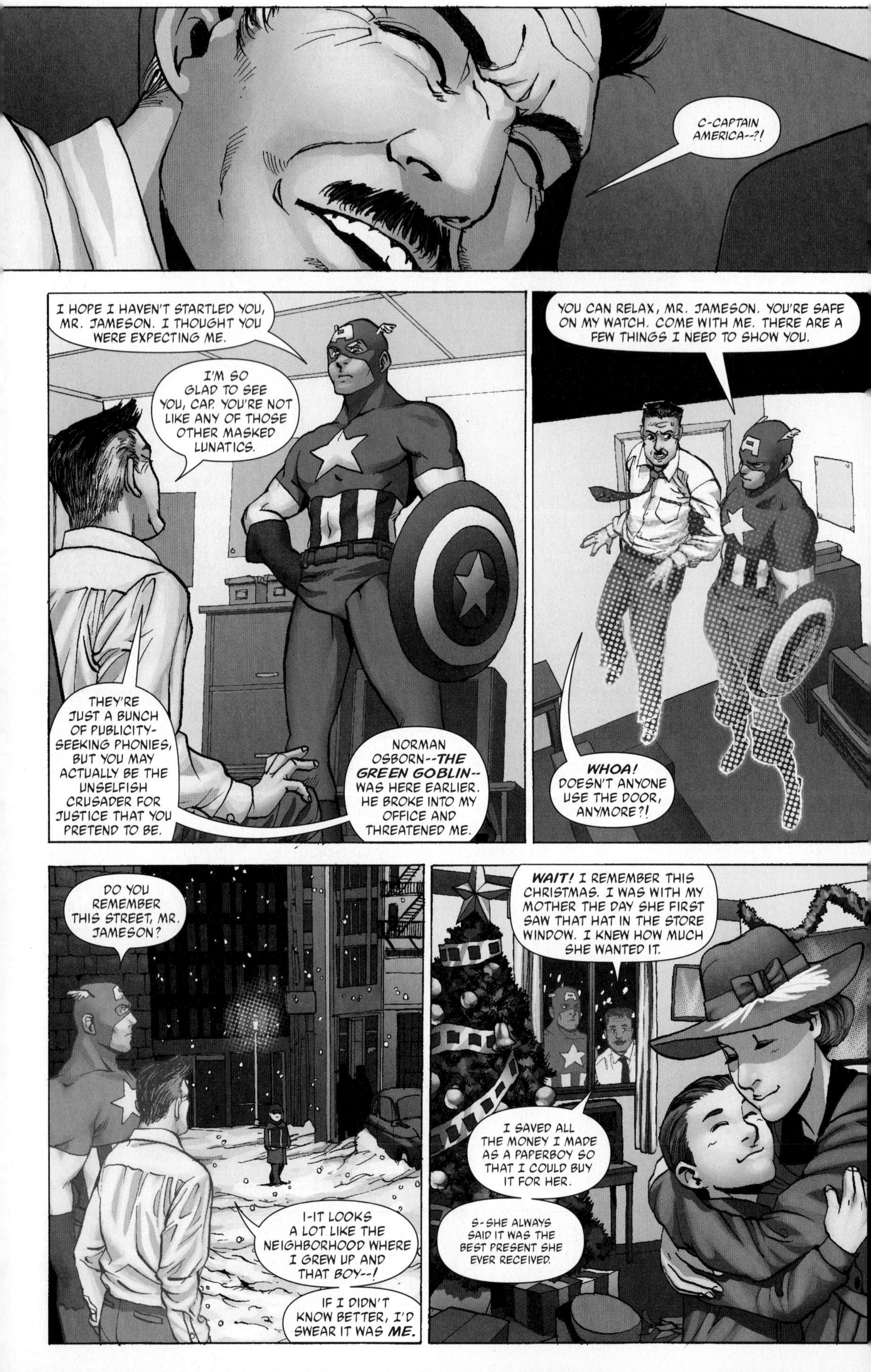
C-CAPTAIN AMERICA--?!
I HOPE I HAVEN'T STARTLED YOU, MR. JAMESON. I THOUGHT YOU WERE EXPECTING ME.
I'M SO GLAD TO SEE YOU, CAP. YOU'RE NOT LIKE ANY OF THOSE OTHER MASKED LUNATICS.
THEY'RE JUST A BUNCH OF PUBLICITY-SEEKING PHONIES, BUT YOU MAY ACTUALLY BE THE UNSELFISH CRUSADER FOR JUSTICE THAT YOU PRETEND TO BE.
NORMAN OSBORN--THE GREEN GOBLIN--WAS HERE EARLIER. HE BROKE INTO MY OFFICE AND THREATENED ME.
YOU CAN RELAX, MR. JAMESON. YOU'RE SAFE ON MY WATCH. COME WITH ME. THERE ARE A FEW THINGS I NEED TO SHOW YOU.
WHOA! DOESN'T ANYONE USE THE DOOR, ANYMORE?!
DO YOU REMEMBER THIS STREET, MR. JAMESON?
I-IT LOOKS A LOT LIKE THE NEIGHBORHOOD WHERE I GREW UP AND THAT BOY--!
IF I DIDN'T KNOW BETTER, I'D SWEAR IT WAS ME.
WAIT! I REMEMBER THIS CHRISTMAS. I WAS WITH MY MOTHER THE DAY SHE FIRST SAW THAT HAT IN THE STORE WINDOW. I KNEW HOW MUCH SHE WANTED IT.
I SAVED ALL THE MONEY I MADE AS A PAPERBOY SO THAT I COULD BUY IT FOR HER.
S-SHE ALWAYS SAID IT WAS THE BEST PRESENT SHE EVER RECEIVED.

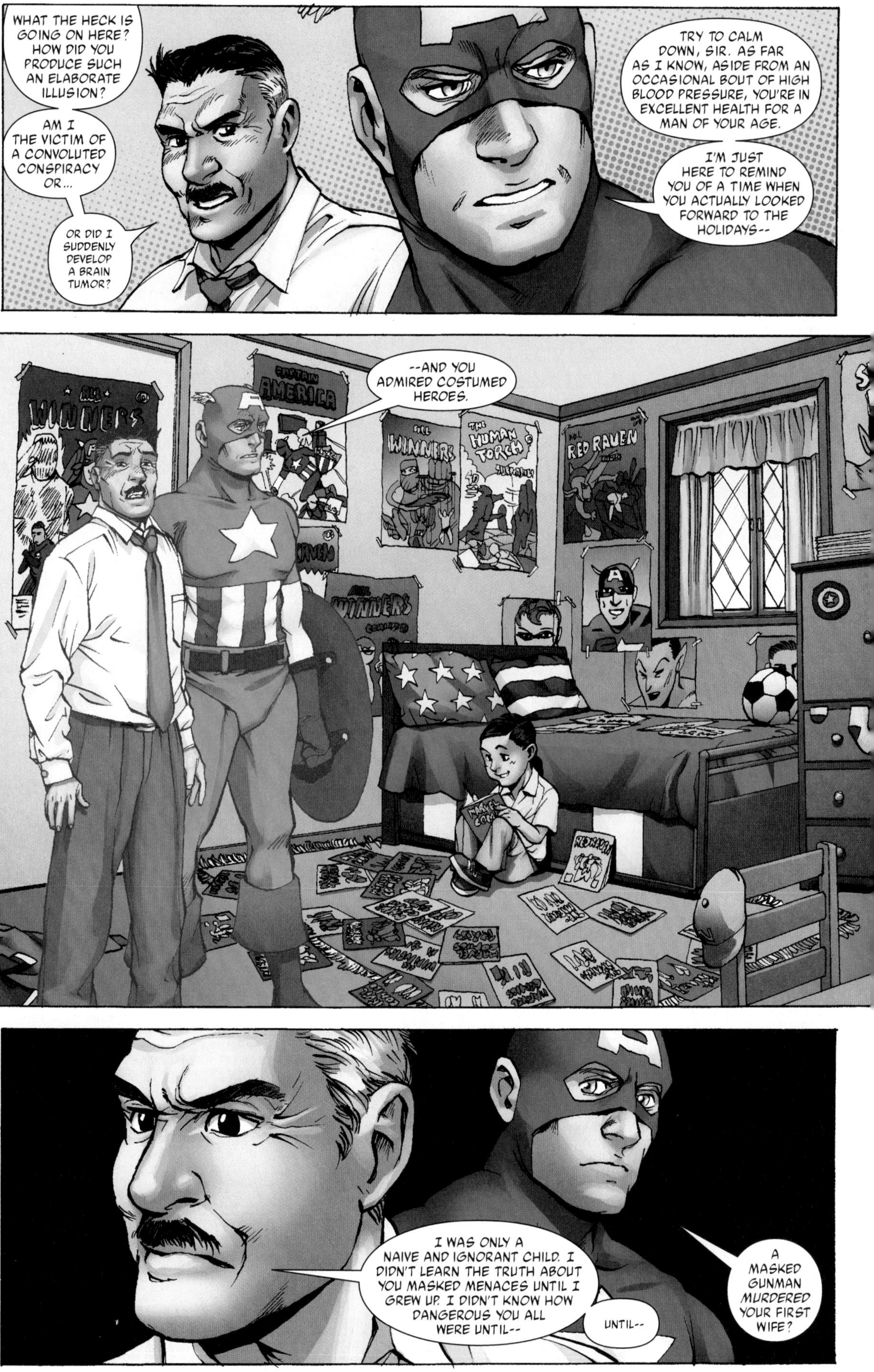
WHAT THE HECK IS GOING ON HERE? HOW DID YOU PRODUCE SUCH AN ELABORATE ILLUSION?
AM I THE VICTIM OF A CONVOLUTED CONSPIRACY OR...
OR DID I SUDDENLY DEVELOP A BRAIN TUMOR?
TRY TO CALM DOWN, SIR. AS FAR AS I KNOW, ASIDE FROM AN OCCASIONAL BOUT OF HIGH BLOOD PRESSURE, YOU'RE IN EXCELLENT HEALTH FOR A MAN OF YOUR AGE.
I'M JUST HERE TO REMIND YOU OF A TIME WHEN YOU ACTUALLY LOOKED FORWARD TO THE HOLIDAYS--
CAPTAIN AMERICA
--AND YOU ADMIRED COSTUMED HEROES.
THE HUMAN TORCH
RED RAVEN
I WAS ONLY A NAIVE AND IGNORANT CHILD. I DIDN'T LEARN THE TRUTH ABOUT YOU MASKED MENACES UNTIL I GREW UP. I DIDN'T KNOW HOW DANGEROUS YOU ALL WERE UNTIL--
UNTIL--
A MASKED GUNMAN MURDERED YOUR FIRST WIFE?

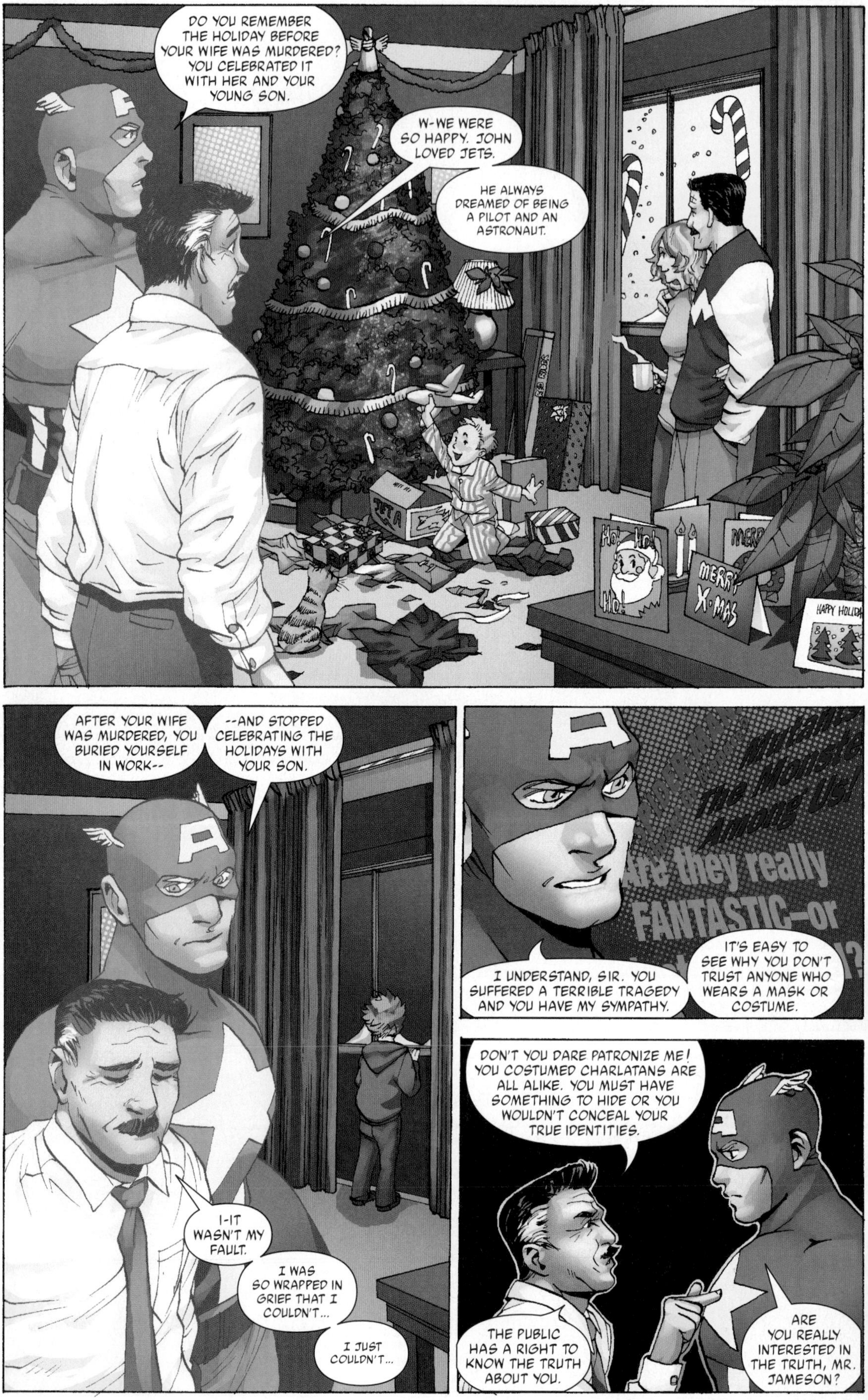
DO YOU REMEMBER THE HOLIDAY BEFORE YOUR WIFE WAS MURDERED? YOU CELEBRATED IT WITH HER AND YOUR YOUNG SON.
W-WE WERE SO HAPPY. JOHN LOVED JETS.
HE ALWAYS DREAMED OF BEING A PILOT AND AN ASTRONAUT.
HO! HO! HO!
MERRY X-MAS
AFTER YOUR WIFE WAS MURDERED, YOU BURIED YOURSELF IN WORK--
--AND STOPPED CELEBRATING THE HOLIDAYS WITH YOUR SON.
I-IT WASN'T MY FAULT.
I WAS SO WRAPPED IN GRIEF THAT I COULDN'T...
I JUST COULDN'T...
Are they really
FANTASTIC–or
I UNDERSTAND, SIR. YOU SUFFERED A TERRIBLE TRAGEDY AND YOU HAVE MY SYMPATHY.
IT'S EASY TO SEE WHY YOU DON'T TRUST ANYONE WHO WEARS A MASK OR COSTUME.
DON'T YOU DARE PATRONIZE ME! YOU COSTUMED CHARLATANS ARE ALL ALIKE. YOU MUST HAVE SOMETHING TO HIDE OR YOU WOULDN'T CONCEAL YOUR TRUE IDENTITIES.
THE PUBLIC HAS A RIGHT TO KNOW THE TRUTH ABOUT YOU.
ARE YOU REALLY INTERESTED IN THE TRUTH, MR. JAMESON?

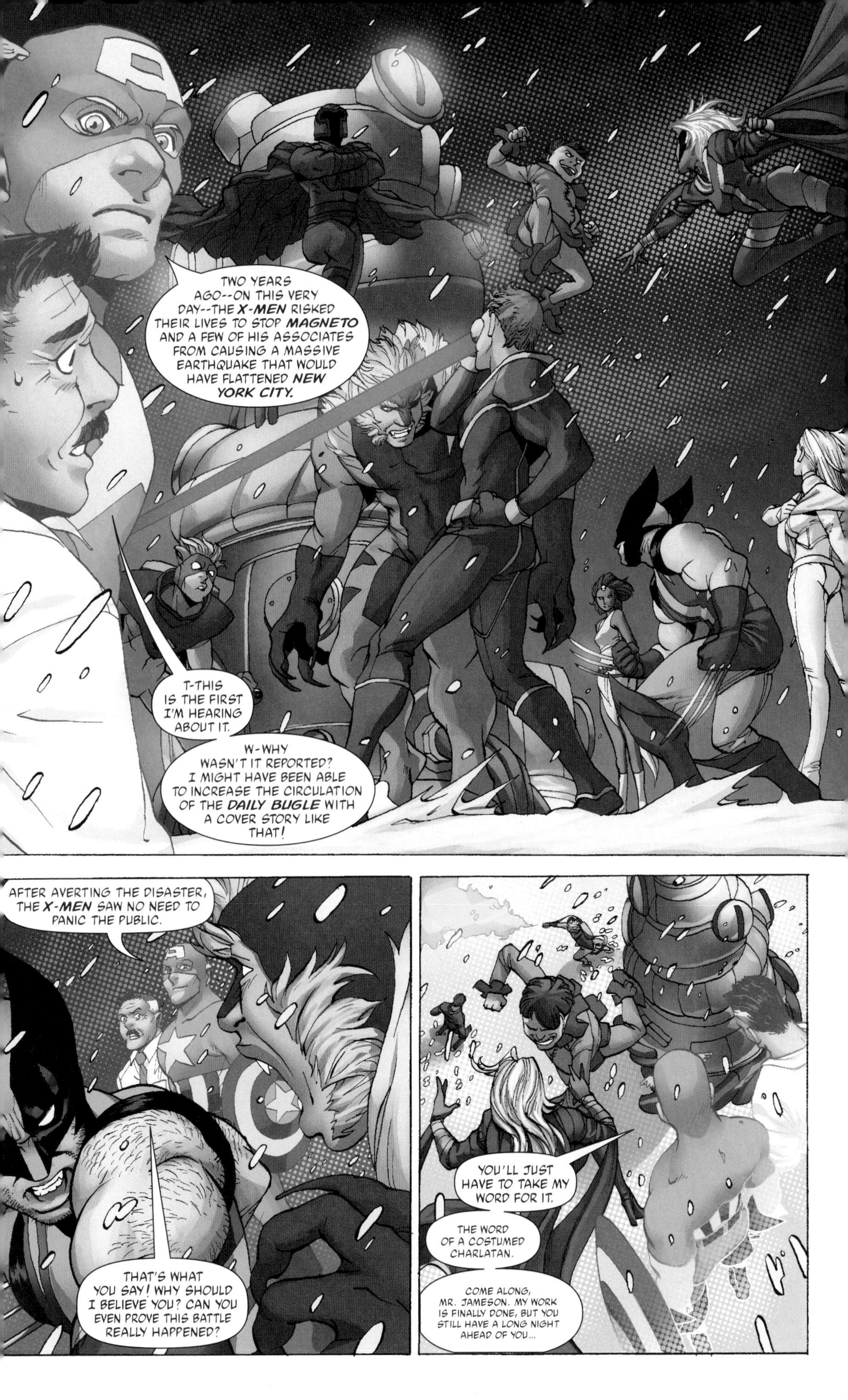

TWO YEARS AGO--ON THIS VERY DAY--THE X-MEN RISKED THEIR LIVES TO STOP MAGNETO AND A FEW OF HIS ASSOCIATES FROM CAUSING A MASSIVE EARTHQUAKE THAT WOULD HAVE FLATTENED NEW YORK CITY.
T-THIS IS THE FIRST I'M HEARING ABOUT IT.
W-WHY WASN'T IT REPORTED? I MIGHT HAVE BEEN ABLE TO INCREASE THE CIRCULATION OF THE DAILY BUGLE WITH A COVER STORY LIKE THAT!
AFTER AVERTING THE DISASTER, THE X-MEN SAW NO NEED TO PANIC THE PUBLIC.
THAT'S WHAT YOU SAY! WHY SHOULD I BELIEVE YOU? CAN YOU EVEN PROVE THIS BATTLE REALLY HAPPENED?
YOU'LL JUST HAVE TO TAKE MY WORD FOR IT.
THE WORD OF A COSTUMED CHARLATAN.
COME ALONG, MR. JAMESON. MY WORK IS FINALLY DONE, BUT YOU STILL HAVE A LONG NIGHT AHEAD OF YOU...

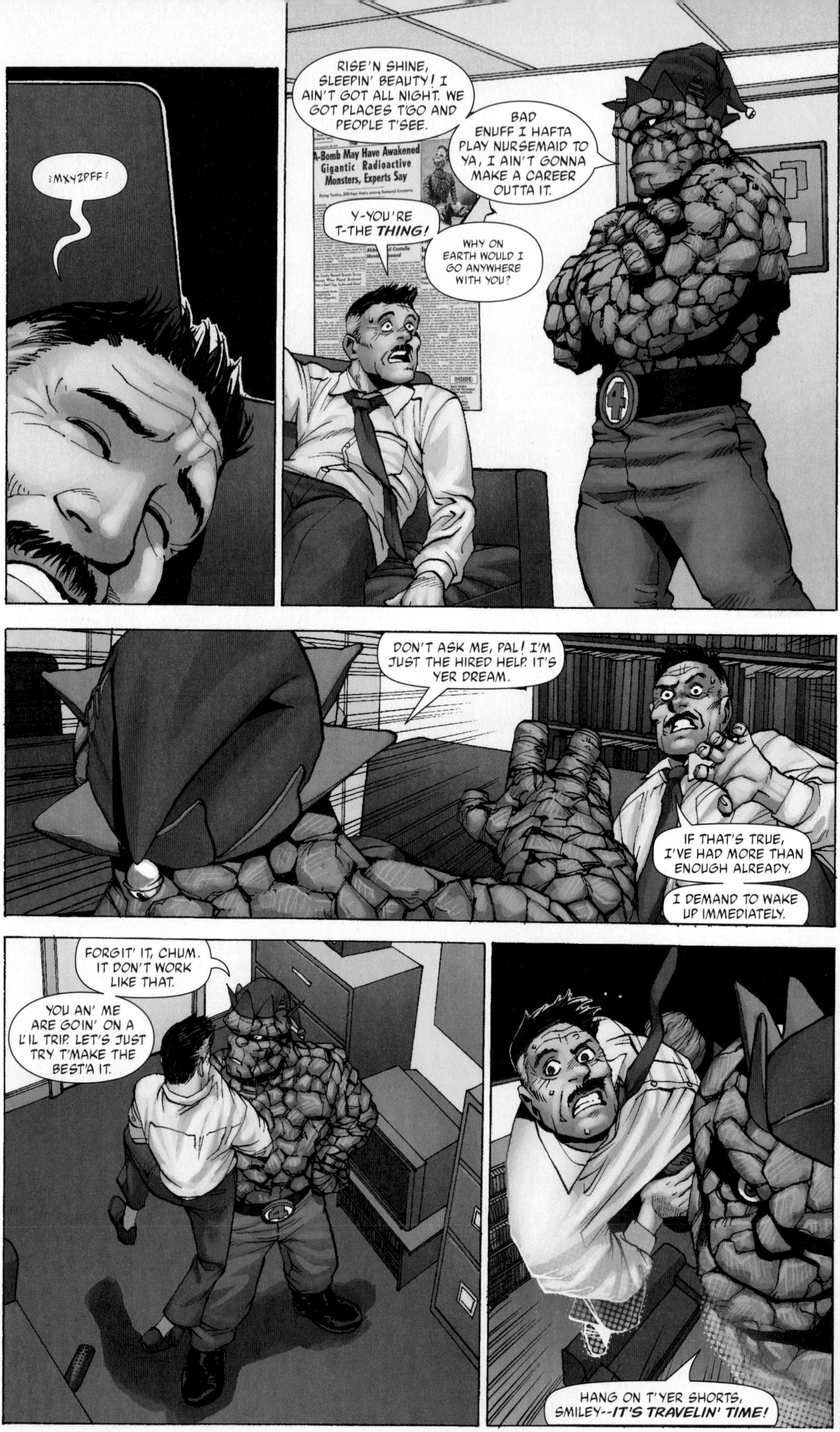

MXYZPFF
RISE'N SHINE, SLEEPIN' BEAUTY! I AIN'T GOT ALL NIGHT. WE GOT PLACES T'GO AND PEOPLE T'SEE.
BAD ENUFF I HAFTA PLAY NURSEMAID TO YA, I AIN'T GONNA MAKE A CAREER OUTTA IT.
A-Bomb May Have Awakened Gigantic Radioactive Monsters, Experts Say
Y-YOU'RE T-THE **THING!**
WHY ON EARTH WOULD I GO ANYWHERE WITH YOU?
DON'T ASK ME, PAL! I'M JUST THE HIRED HELP. IT'S YER DREAM.
IF THAT'S TRUE, I'VE HAD MORE THAN ENOUGH ALREADY.
I DEMAND TO WAKE UP IMMEDIATELY.
FORGIT' IT, CHUM. IT DON'T WORK LIKE THAT.
YOU AN' ME ARE GOIN' ON A L'IL TRIP. LET'S JUST TRY T'MAKE THE BEST'A IT.
HANG ON T'YER SHORTS, SMILEY--***IT'S TRAVELIN' TIME!***

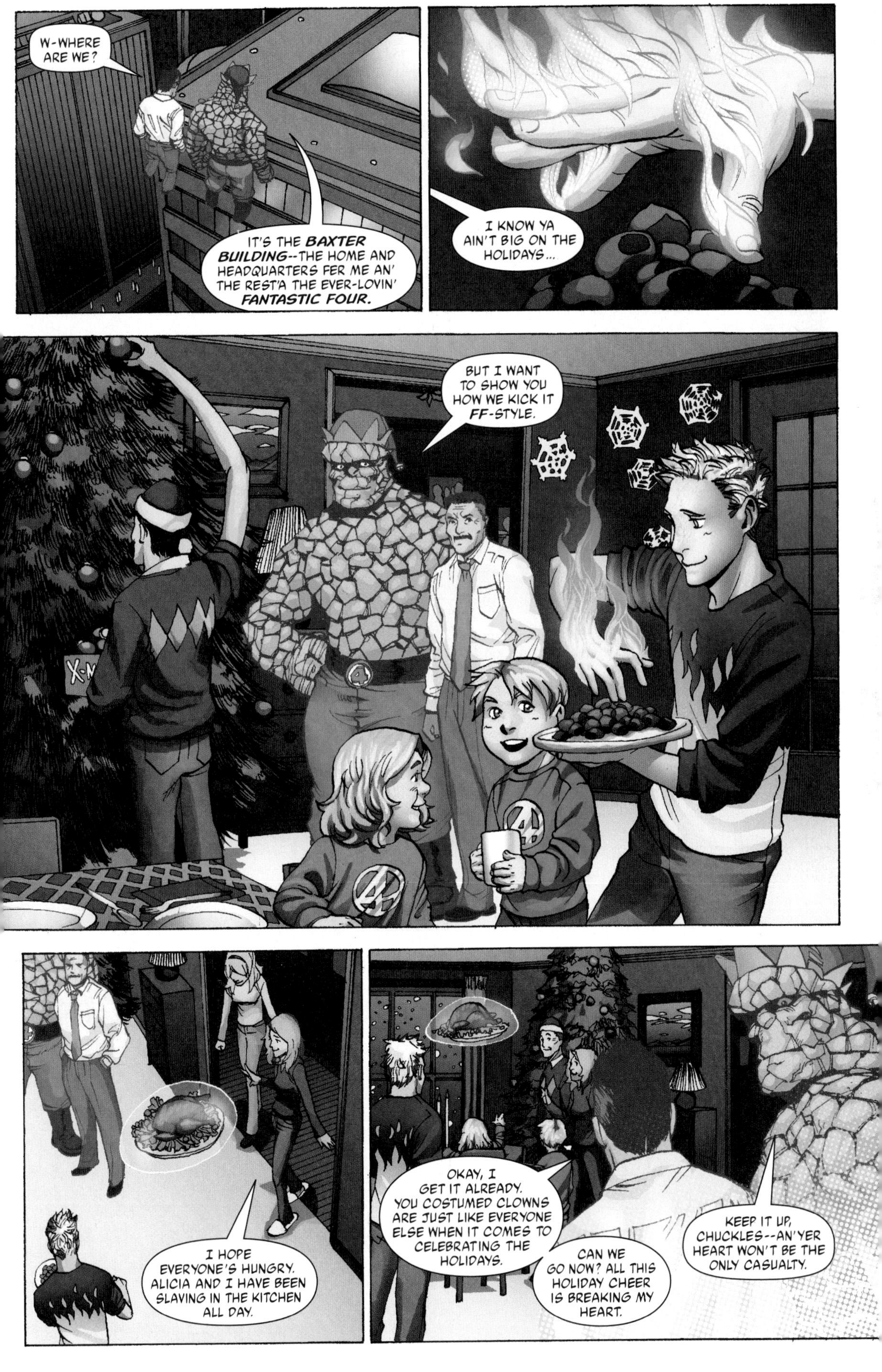
W-WHERE ARE WE?
IT'S THE **BAXTER BUILDING**--THE HOME AND HEADQUARTERS FER ME AN' THE REST'A THE EVER-LOVIN' **FANTASTIC FOUR.**
I KNOW YA AIN'T BIG ON THE HOLIDAYS...
BUT I WANT TO SHOW YOU HOW WE KICK IT **FF**-STYLE.
I HOPE EVERYONE'S HUNGRY. ALICIA AND I HAVE BEEN SLAVING IN THE KITCHEN ALL DAY.
OKAY, I GET IT ALREADY. YOU COSTUMED CLOWNS ARE JUST LIKE EVERYONE ELSE WHEN IT COMES TO CELEBRATING THE HOLIDAYS.
CAN WE GO NOW? ALL THIS HOLIDAY CHEER IS BREAKING MY HEART.
KEEP IT UP, CHUCKLES--AN'YER HEART WON'T BE THE ONLY CASUALTY.

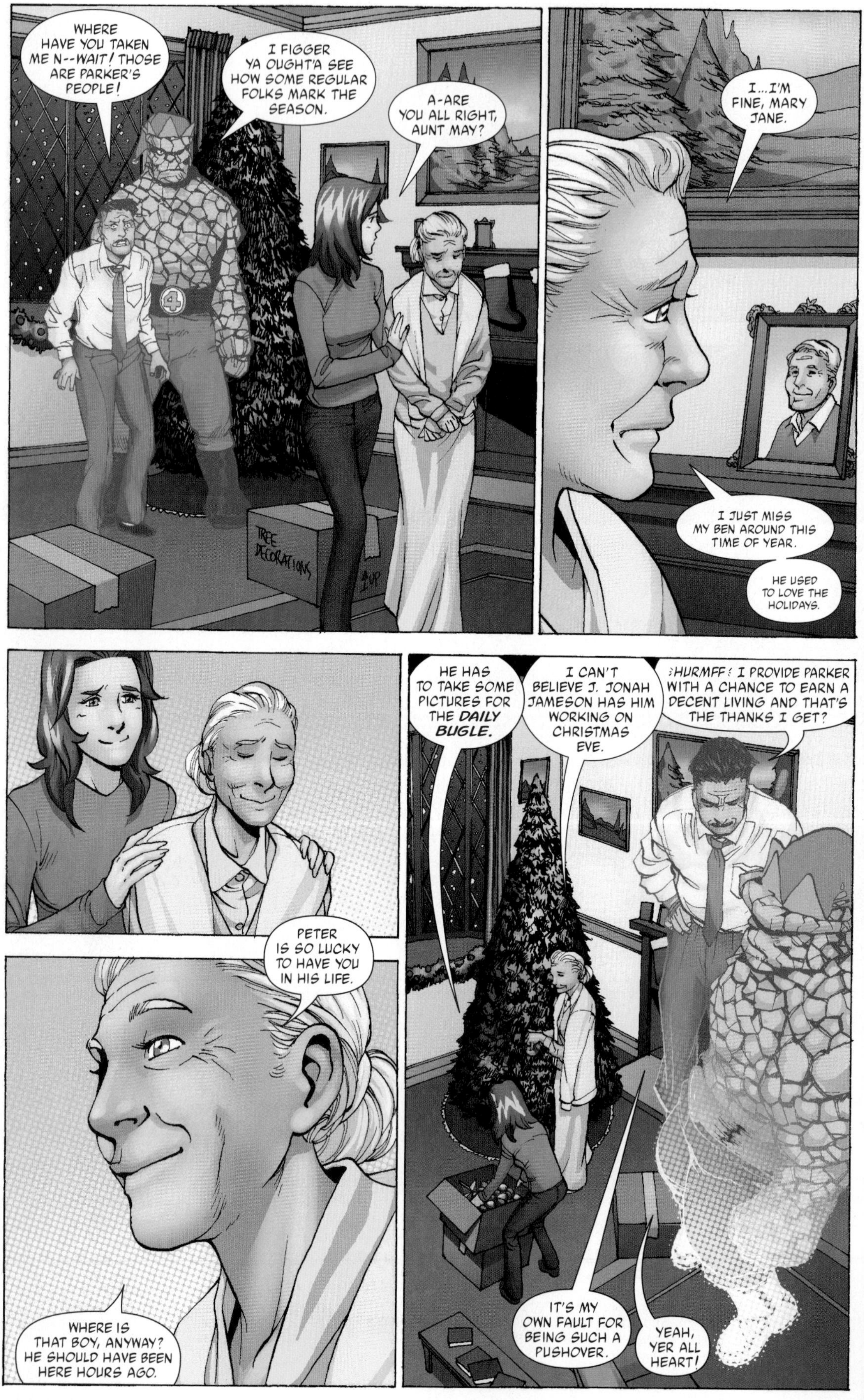
WHERE HAVE YOU TAKEN ME N--WAIT! THOSE ARE PARKER'S PEOPLE!
I FIGGER YA OUGHT'A SEE HOW SOME REGULAR FOLKS MARK THE SEASON.
A-ARE YOU ALL RIGHT, AUNT MAY?
TREE DECORATIONS
I...I'M FINE, MARY JANE.
I JUST MISS MY BEN AROUND THIS TIME OF YEAR.
HE USED TO LOVE THE HOLIDAYS.
PETER IS SO LUCKY TO HAVE YOU IN HIS LIFE.
WHERE IS THAT BOY, ANYWAY? HE SHOULD HAVE BEEN HERE HOURS AGO.
HE HAS TO TAKE SOME PICTURES FOR THE DAILY BUGLE.
I CAN'T BELIEVE J. JONAH JAMESON HAS HIM WORKING ON CHRISTMAS EVE.
HURMFF! I PROVIDE PARKER WITH A CHANCE TO EARN A DECENT LIVING AND THAT'S THE THANKS I GET?
IT'S MY OWN FAULT FOR BEING SUCH A PUSHOVER.
YEAH, YER ALL HEART!

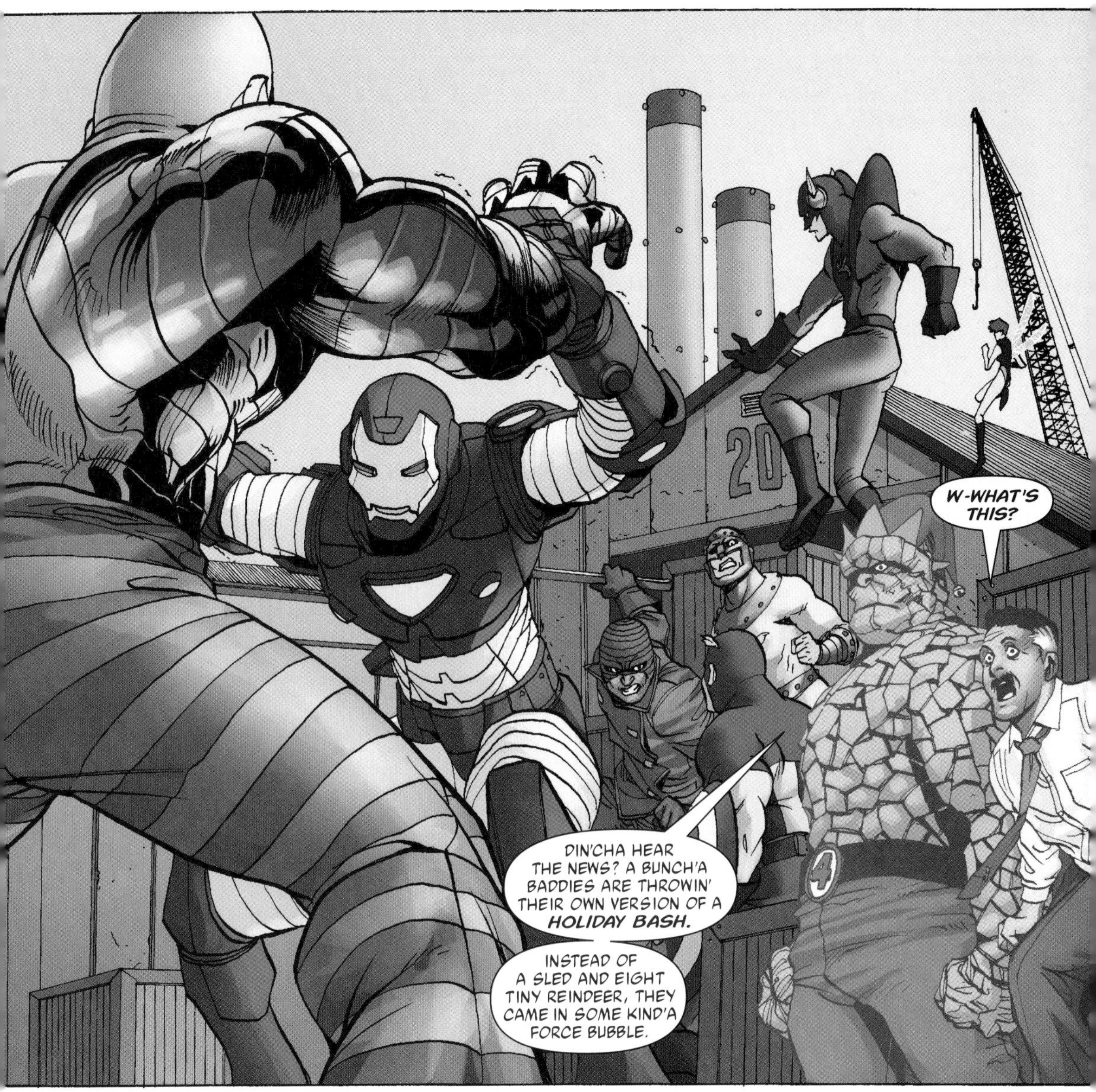
W-WHAT'S THIS?
DIN'CHA HEAR THE NEWS? A BUNCH'A BADDIES ARE THROWIN' THEIR OWN VERSION OF A **HOLIDAY BASH.**
INSTEAD OF A SLED AND EIGHT TINY REINDEER, THEY CAME IN SOME KIND'A FORCE BUBBLE.

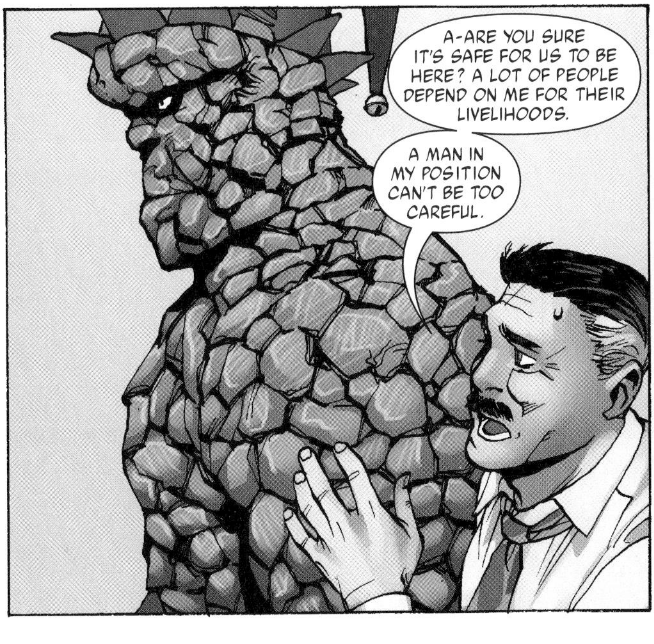
A-ARE YOU SURE IT'S SAFE FOR US TO BE HERE? A LOT OF PEOPLE DEPEND ON ME FOR THEIR LIVELIHOODS.
A MAN IN MY POSITION CAN'T BE TOO CAREFUL.

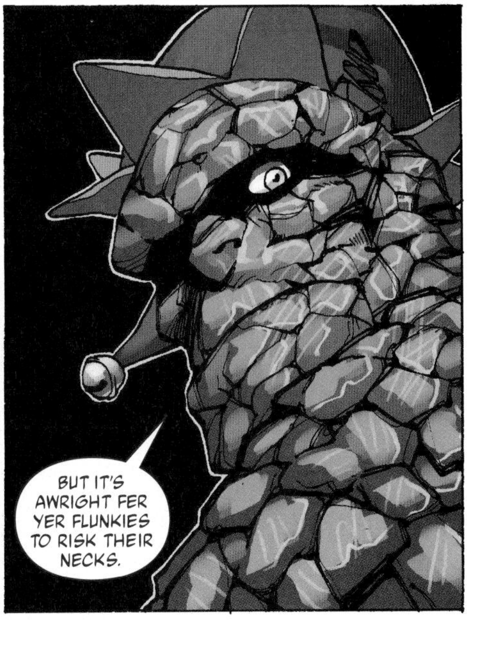
BUT IT'S AWRIGHT FER YER FLUNKIES TO RISK THEIR NECKS.

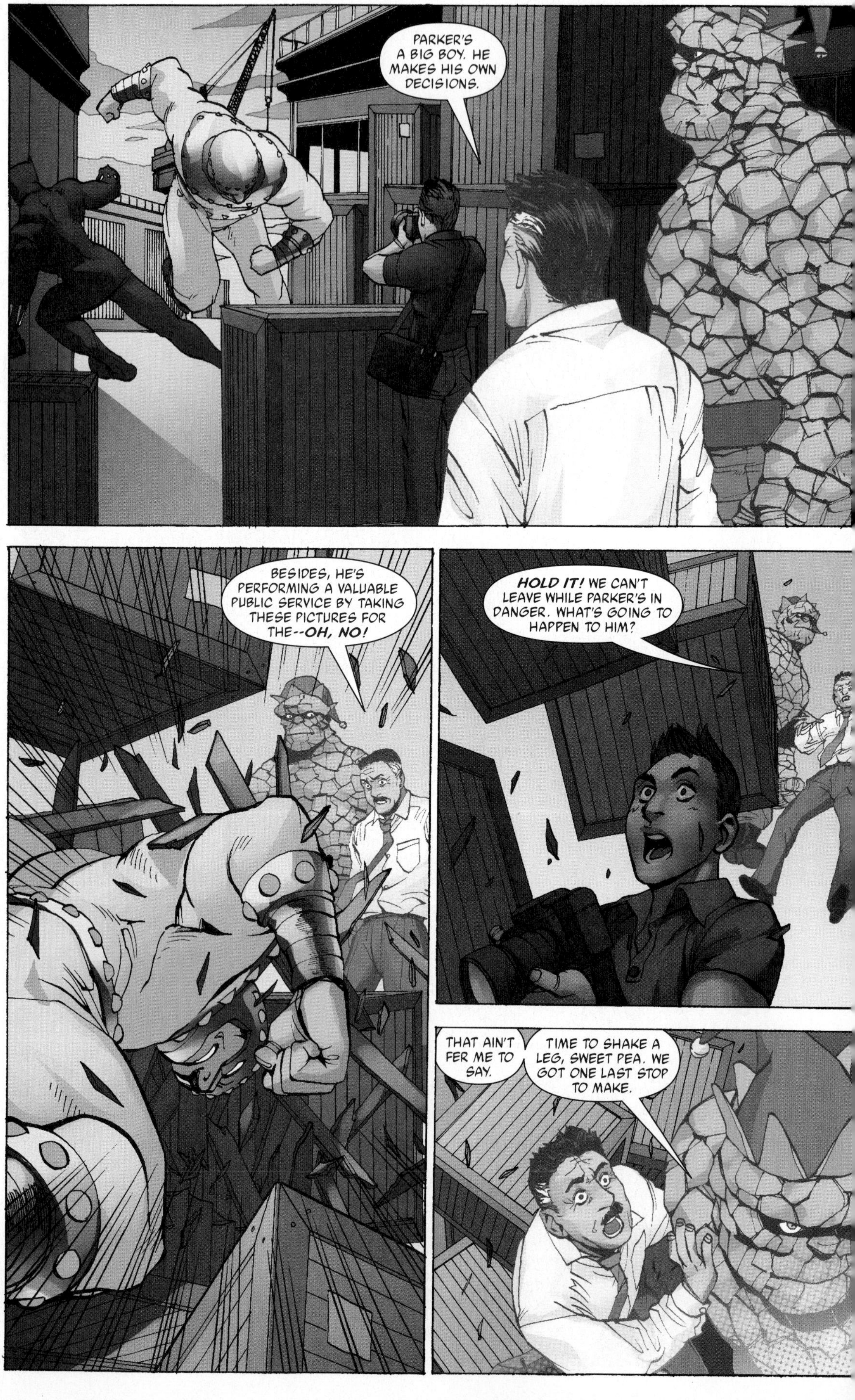
PARKER'S A BIG BOY. HE MAKES HIS OWN DECISIONS.
BESIDES, HE'S PERFORMING A VALUABLE PUBLIC SERVICE BY TAKING THESE PICTURES FOR THE--*OH, NO!*
HOLD IT! WE CAN'T LEAVE WHILE PARKER'S IN DANGER. WHAT'S GOING TO HAPPEN TO HIM?
THAT AIN'T FER ME TO SAY.
TIME TO SHAKE A LEG, SWEET PEA. WE GOT ONE LAST STOP TO MAKE.

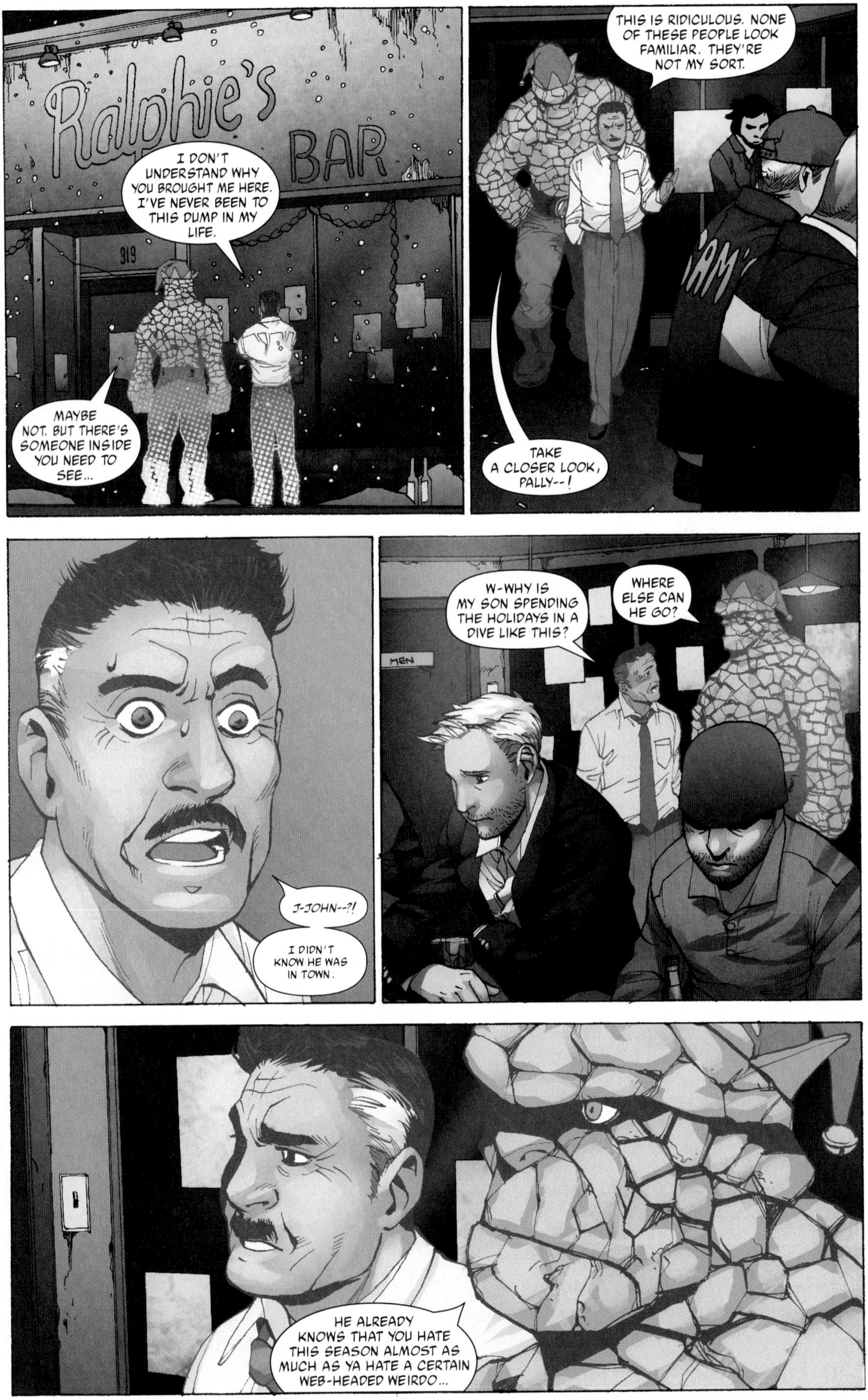
Ralphie's BAR
919
I DON'T UNDERSTAND WHY YOU BROUGHT ME HERE. I'VE NEVER BEEN TO THIS DUMP IN MY LIFE.
MAYBE NOT. BUT THERE'S SOMEONE INSIDE YOU NEED TO SEE...
THIS IS RIDICULOUS. NONE OF THESE PEOPLE LOOK FAMILIAR. THEY'RE NOT MY SORT.
TAKE A CLOSER LOOK, PALLY--!
J-JOHN--?!
I DIDN'T KNOW HE WAS IN TOWN.
MEN
W-WHY IS MY SON SPENDING THE HOLIDAYS IN A DIVE LIKE THIS?
WHERE ELSE CAN HE GO?
HE ALREADY KNOWS THAT YOU HATE THIS SEASON ALMOST AS MUCH AS YA HATE A CERTAIN WEB-HEADED WEIRDO...

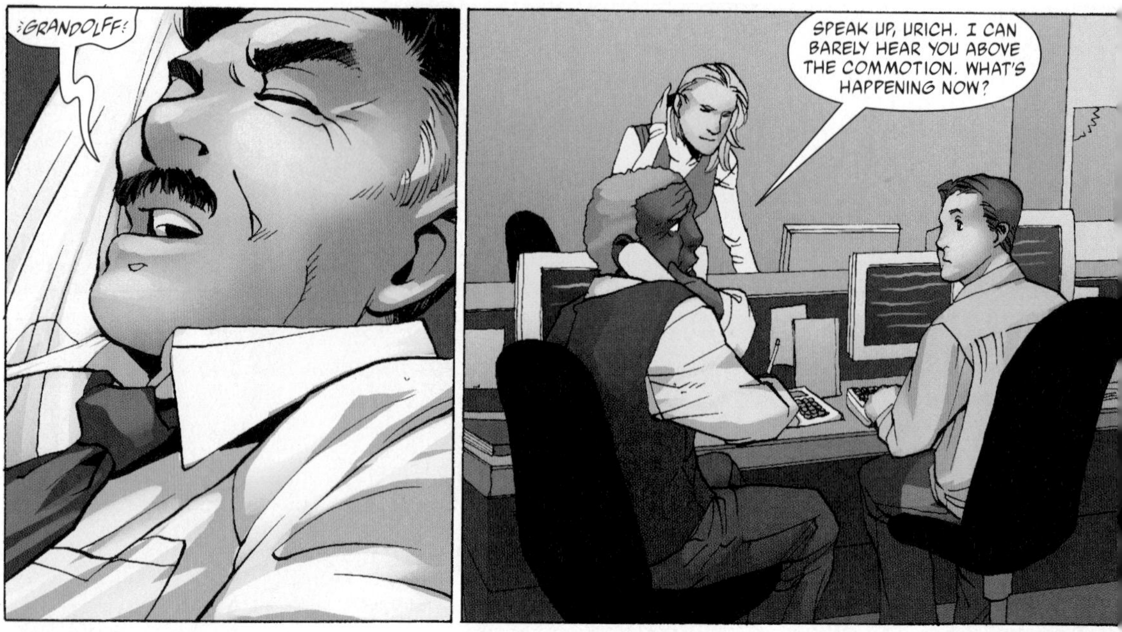
GRANDOLFF!
SPEAK UP, URICH. I CAN BARELY HEAR YOU ABOVE THE COMMOTION. WHAT'S HAPPENING NOW?

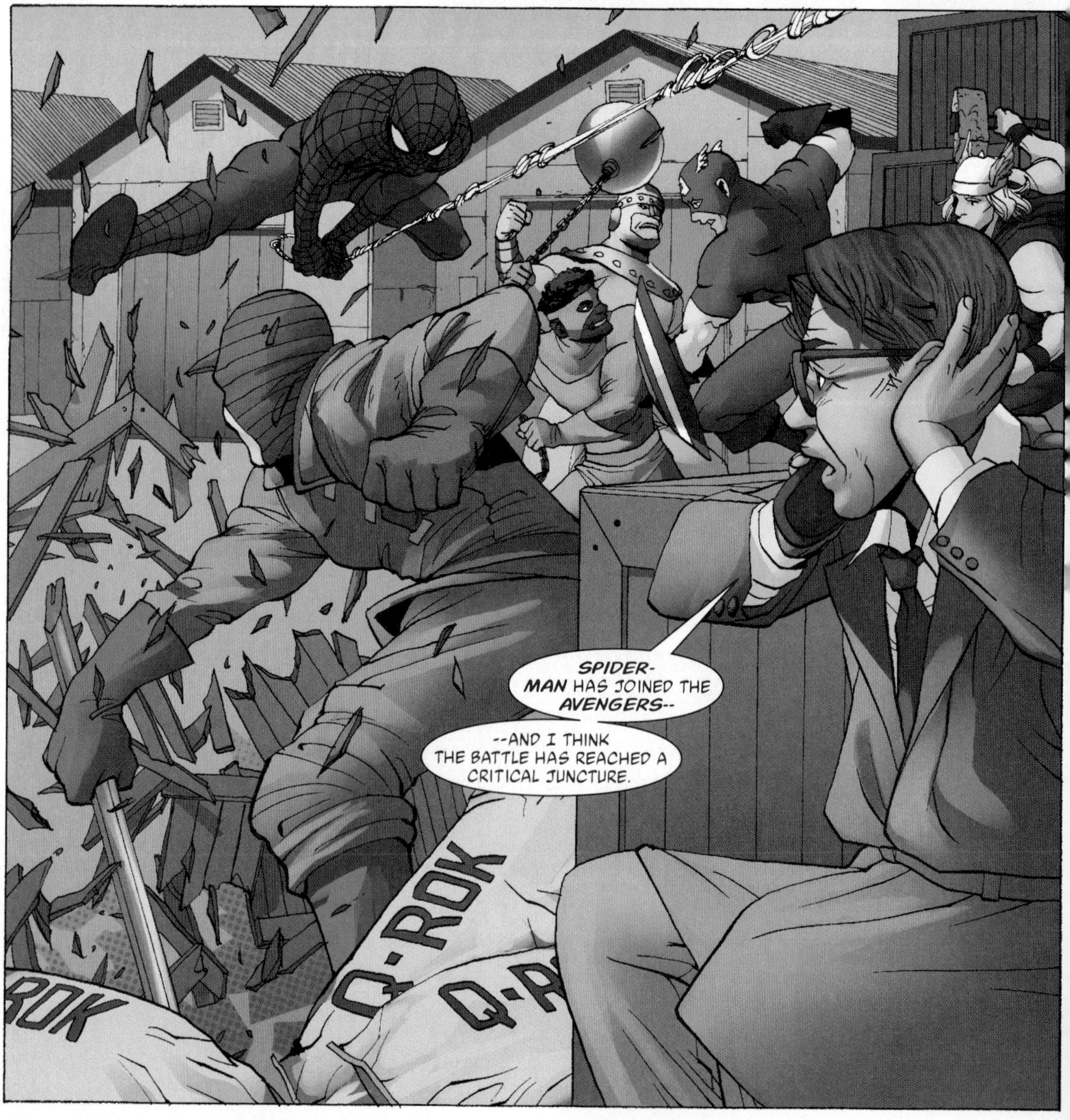
SPIDER-MAN HAS JOINED THE AVENGERS--
--AND I THINK THE BATTLE HAS REACHED A CRITICAL JUNCTURE.
Q-ROK
Q-R
ROK

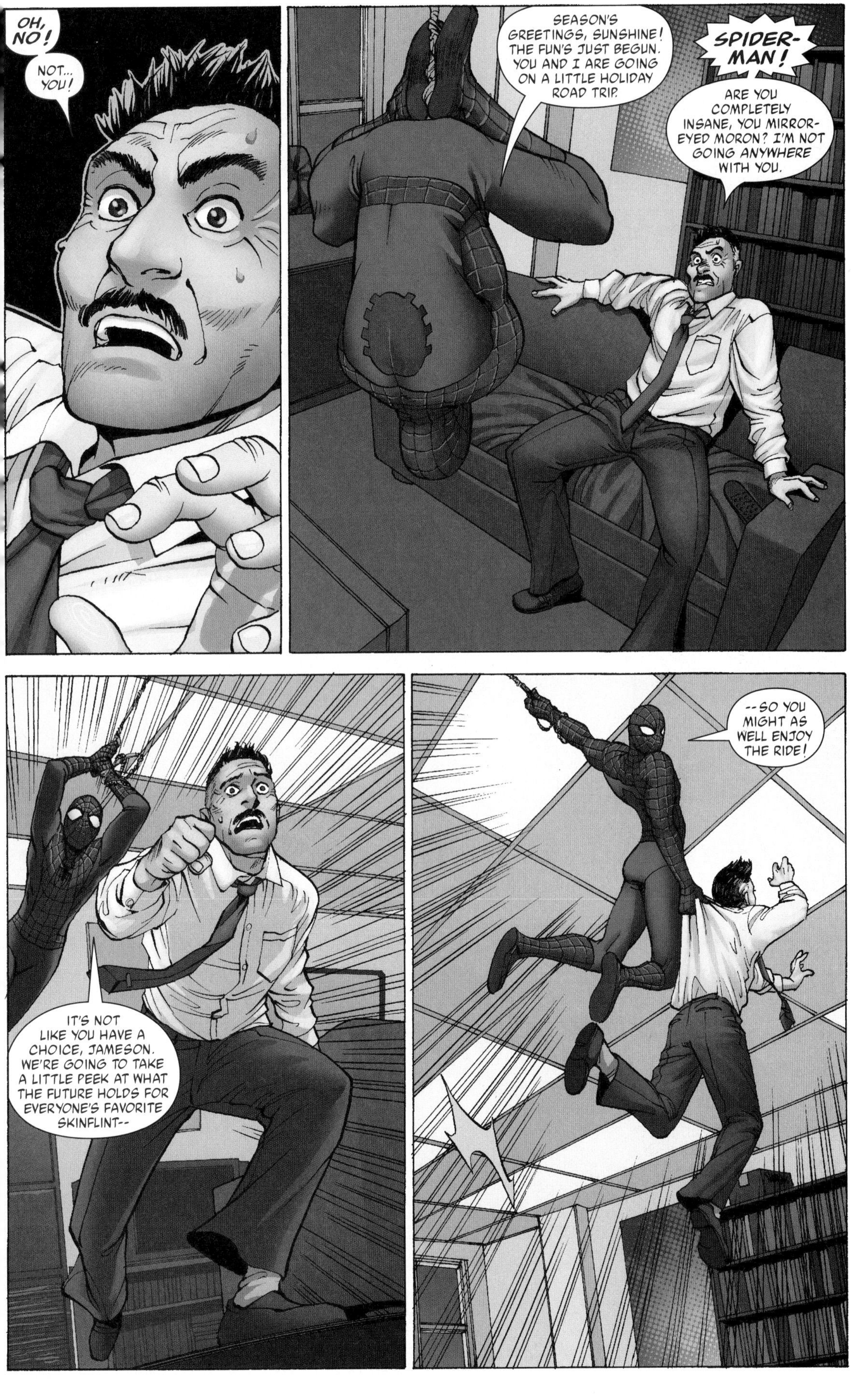
OH, NO!
NOT... YOU!
SEASON'S GREETINGS, SUNSHINE! THE FUN'S JUST BEGUN. YOU AND I ARE GOING ON A LITTLE HOLIDAY ROAD TRIP.
SPIDER-MAN!
ARE YOU COMPLETELY INSANE, YOU MIRROR-EYED MORON? I'M NOT GOING ANYWHERE WITH YOU.
IT'S NOT LIKE YOU HAVE A CHOICE, JAMESON. WE'RE GOING TO TAKE A LITTLE PEEK AT WHAT THE FUTURE HOLDS FOR EVERYONE'S FAVORITE SKINFLINT--
--SO YOU MIGHT AS WELL ENJOY THE RIDE!

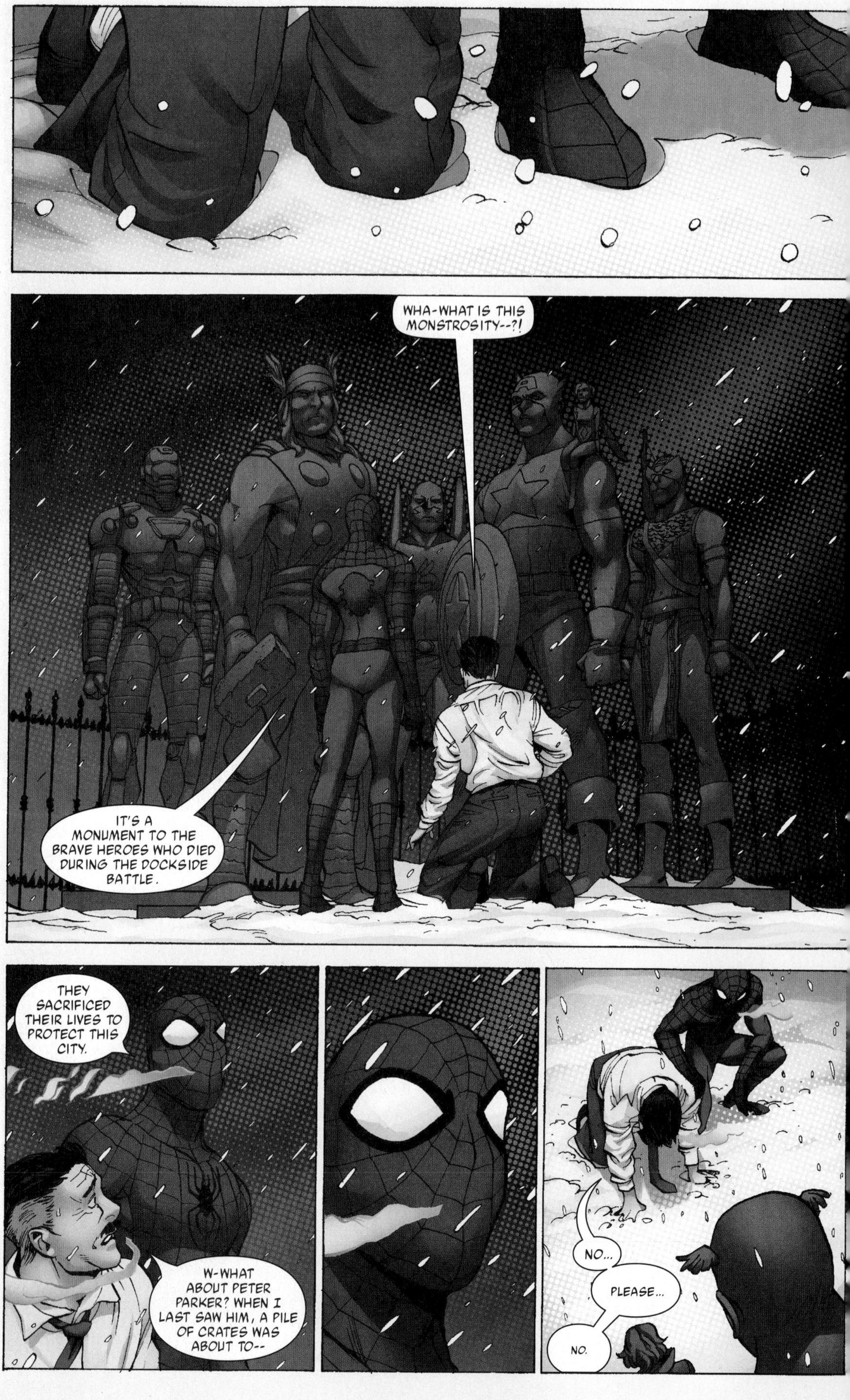
WHA-WHAT IS THIS MONSTROSITY--?!
IT'S A MONUMENT TO THE BRAVE HEROES WHO DIED DURING THE DOCKSIDE BATTLE.
THEY SACRIFICED THEIR LIVES TO PROTECT THIS CITY.
W-WHAT ABOUT PETER PARKER? WHEN I LAST SAW HIM, A PILE OF CRATES WAS ABOUT TO--
NO...
PLEASE...
NO.

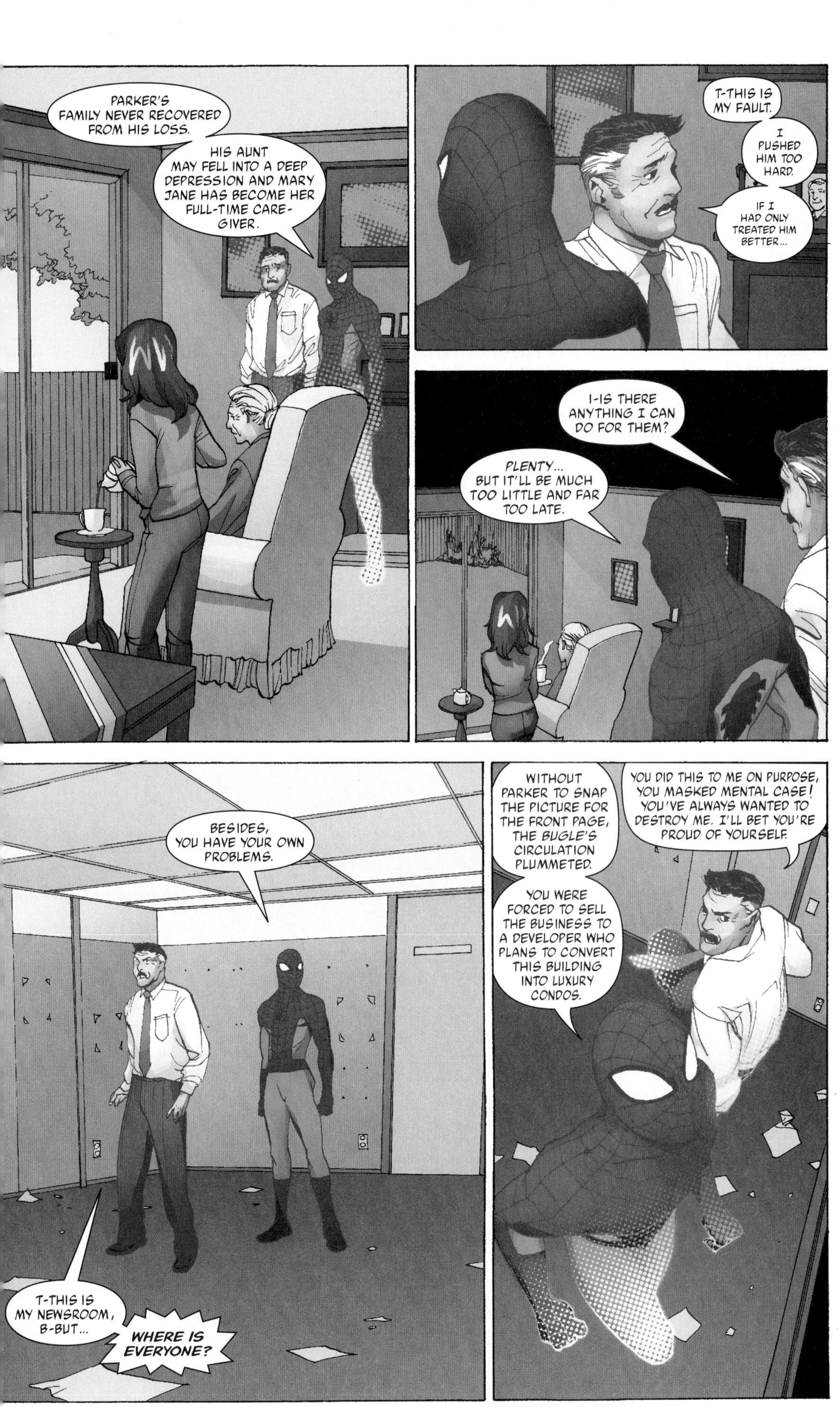
PARKER'S FAMILY NEVER RECOVERED FROM HIS LOSS.
HIS AUNT MAY FELL INTO A DEEP DEPRESSION AND MARY JANE HAS BECOME HER FULL-TIME CARE-GIVER.
T-THIS IS MY FAULT.
I PUSHED HIM TOO HARD.
IF I HAD ONLY TREATED HIM BETTER...
I-IS THERE ANYTHING I CAN DO FOR THEM?
PLENTY... BUT IT'LL BE MUCH TOO LITTLE AND FAR TOO LATE.
BESIDES, YOU HAVE YOUR OWN PROBLEMS.
T-THIS IS MY NEWSROOM, B-BUT...
WHERE IS EVERYONE?
WITHOUT PARKER TO SNAP THE PICTURE FOR THE FRONT PAGE, THE BUGLE'S CIRCULATION PLUMMETED.
YOU WERE FORCED TO SELL THE BUSINESS TO A DEVELOPER WHO PLANS TO CONVERT THIS BUILDING INTO LUXURY CONDOS.
YOU DID THIS TO ME ON PURPOSE, YOU MASKED MENTAL CASE! YOU'VE ALWAYS WANTED TO DESTROY ME. I'LL BET YOU'RE PROUD OF YOURSELF.

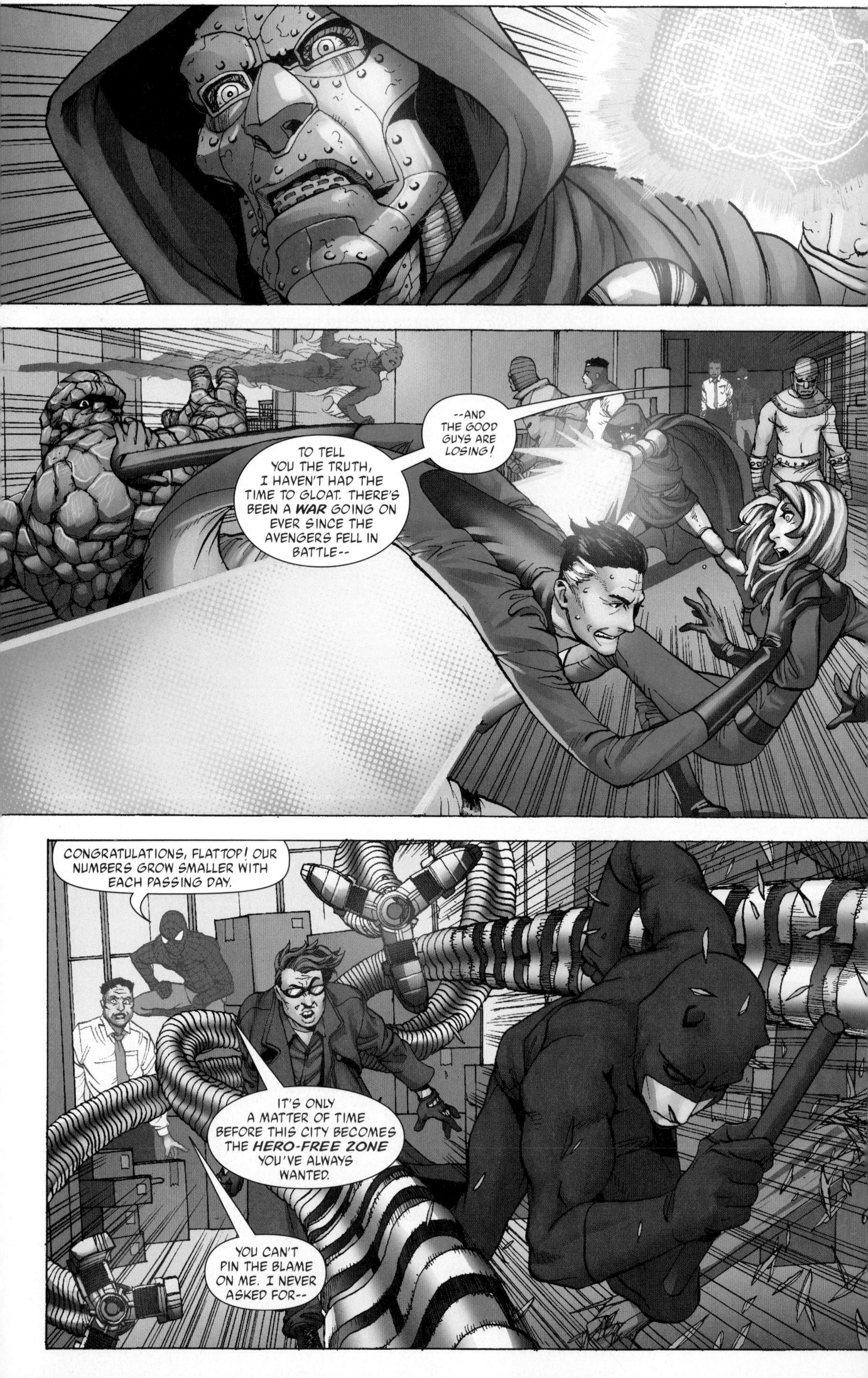
TO TELL YOU THE TRUTH, I HAVEN'T HAD THE TIME TO GLOAT. THERE'S BEEN A **WAR** GOING ON EVER SINCE THE AVENGERS FELL IN BATTLE--
--AND THE GOOD GUYS ARE LOSING!
CONGRATULATIONS, FLATTOP! OUR NUMBERS GROW SMALLER WITH EACH PASSING DAY.
IT'S ONLY A MATTER OF TIME BEFORE THIS CITY BECOMES THE **HERO-FREE ZONE** YOU'VE ALWAYS WANTED.
YOU CAN'T PIN THE BLAME ON ME. I NEVER ASKED FOR--

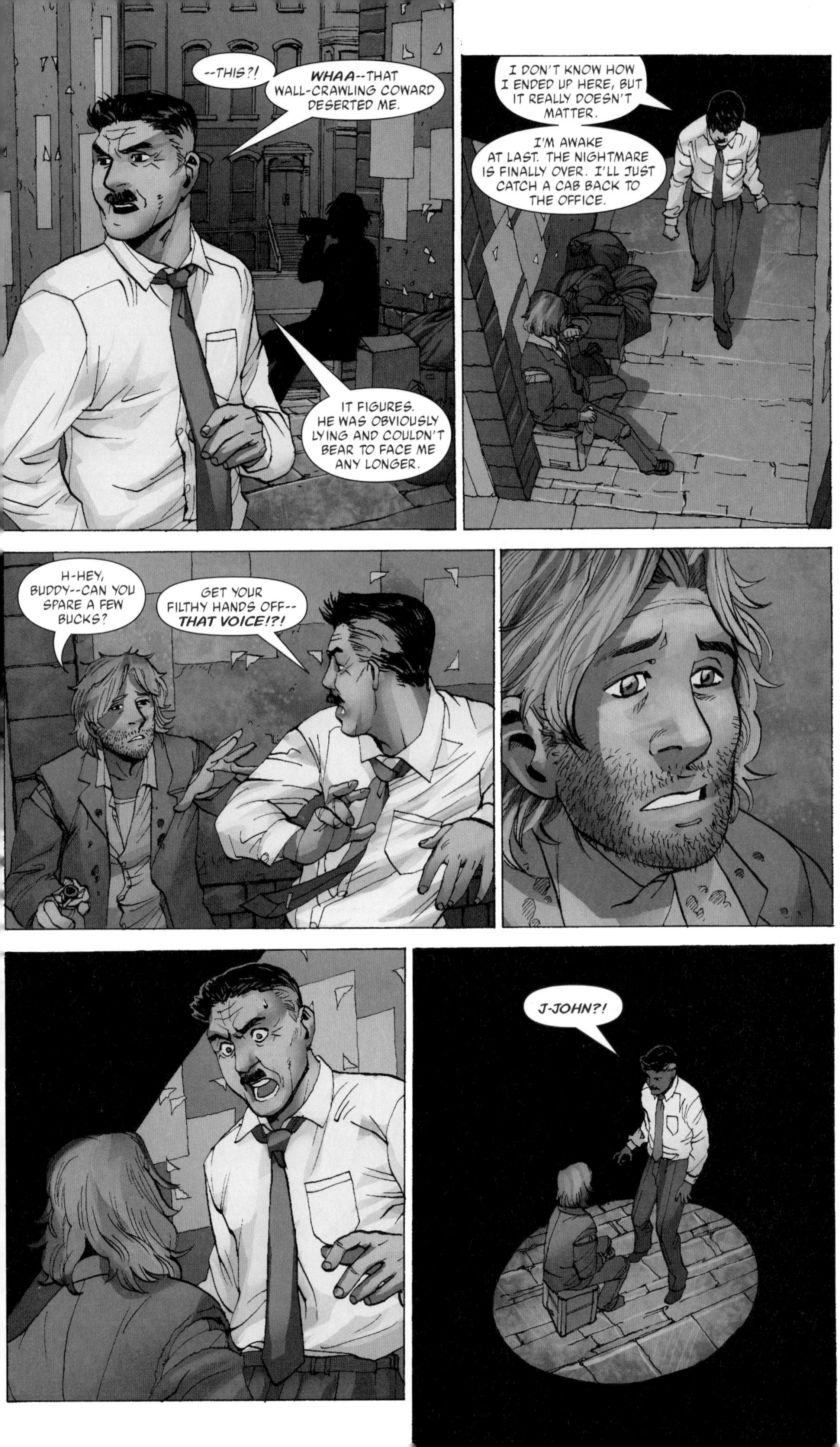
--THIS?!
WHAA--THAT WALL-CRAWLING COWARD DESERTED ME.
IT FIGURES. HE WAS OBVIOUSLY LYING AND COULDN'T BEAR TO FACE ME ANY LONGER.
I DON'T KNOW HOW I ENDED UP HERE, BUT IT REALLY DOESN'T MATTER.
I'M AWAKE AT LAST. THE NIGHTMARE IS FINALLY OVER. I'LL JUST CATCH A CAB BACK TO THE OFFICE.
H-HEY, BUDDY--CAN YOU SPARE A FEW BUCKS?
GET YOUR FILTHY HANDS OFF-- THAT VOICE!?!
J-JOHN?!

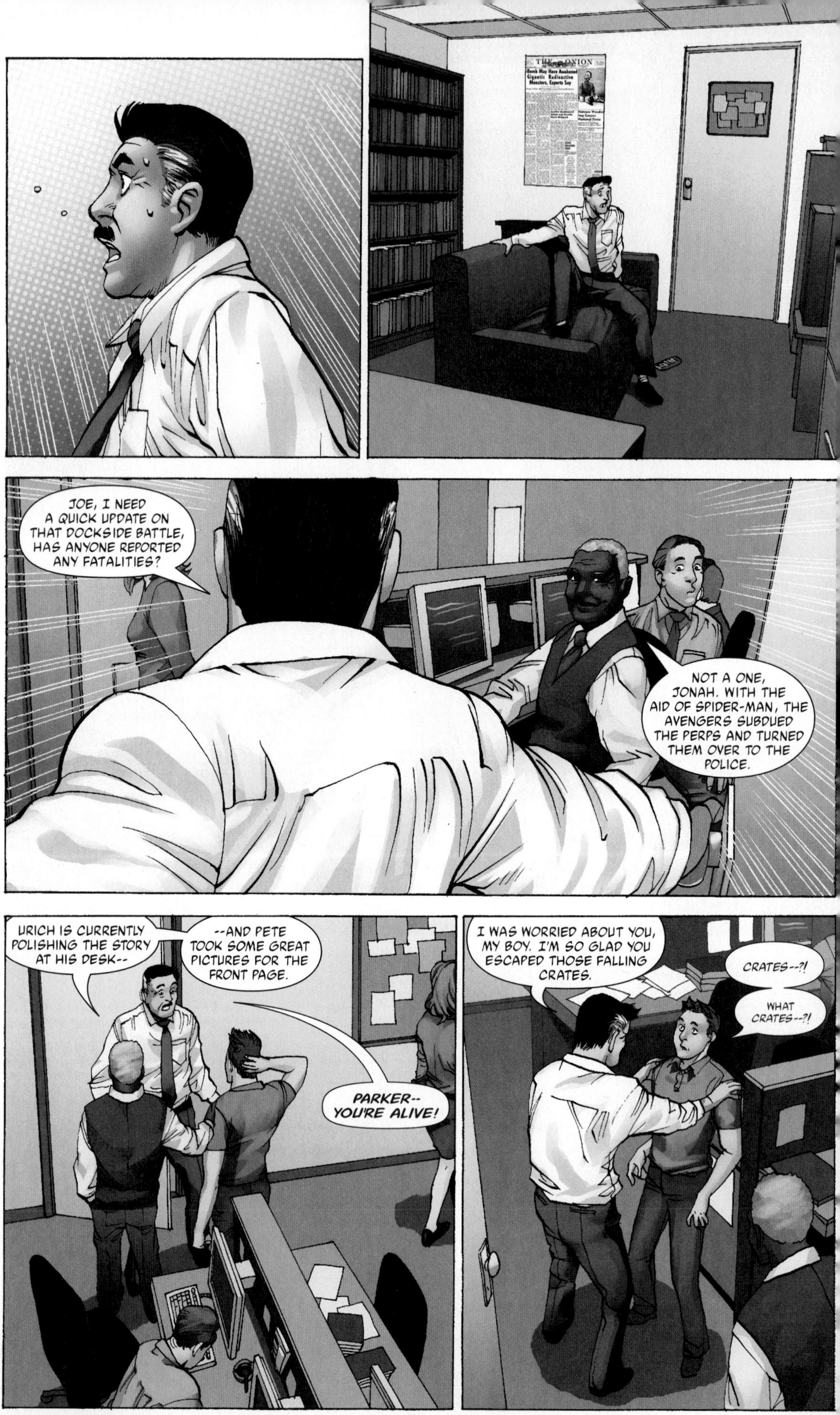
THE ONION
Bomb May Have Awakened Gigantic Radioactive Monsters, Experts Say
JOE, I NEED A QUICK UPDATE ON THAT DOCKSIDE BATTLE, HAS ANYONE REPORTED ANY FATALITIES?
NOT A ONE, JONAH. WITH THE AID OF SPIDER-MAN, THE AVENGERS SUBDUED THE PERPS AND TURNED THEM OVER TO THE POLICE.
URICH IS CURRENTLY POLISHING THE STORY AT HIS DESK--
--AND PETE TOOK SOME GREAT PICTURES FOR THE FRONT PAGE.
PARKER-- YOU'RE ALIVE!
I WAS WORRIED ABOUT YOU, MY BOY. I'M SO GLAD YOU ESCAPED THOSE FALLING CRATES.
CRATES--?!
WHAT CRATES--?!

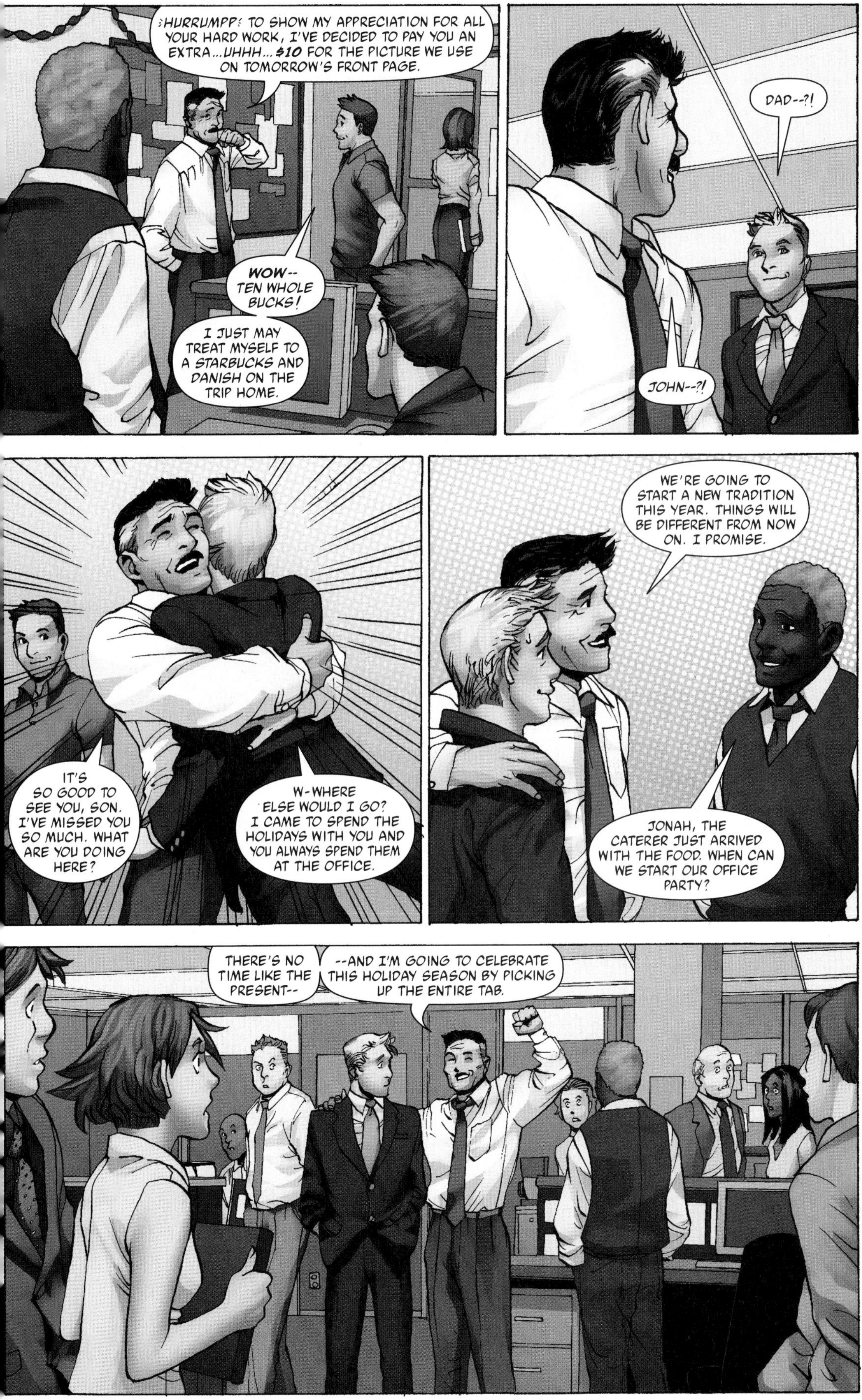

HURRUMPP! TO SHOW MY APPRECIATION FOR ALL YOUR HARD WORK, I'VE DECIDED TO PAY YOU AN EXTRA...UHHH...$10 FOR THE PICTURE WE USE ON TOMORROW'S FRONT PAGE.
WOW-- TEN WHOLE BUCKS!
I JUST MAY TREAT MYSELF TO A STARBUCKS AND DANISH ON THE TRIP HOME.
DAD--?!
JOHN--?!
IT'S SO GOOD TO SEE YOU, SON. I'VE MISSED YOU SO MUCH. WHAT ARE YOU DOING HERE?
W-WHERE ELSE WOULD I GO? I CAME TO SPEND THE HOLIDAYS WITH YOU AND YOU ALWAYS SPEND THEM AT THE OFFICE.
WE'RE GOING TO START A NEW TRADITION THIS YEAR. THINGS WILL BE DIFFERENT FROM NOW ON. I PROMISE.
JONAH, THE CATERER JUST ARRIVED WITH THE FOOD. WHEN CAN WE START OUR OFFICE PARTY?
THERE'S NO TIME LIKE THE PRESENT--
--AND I'M GOING TO CELEBRATE THIS HOLIDAY SEASON BY PICKING UP THE ENTIRE TAB.

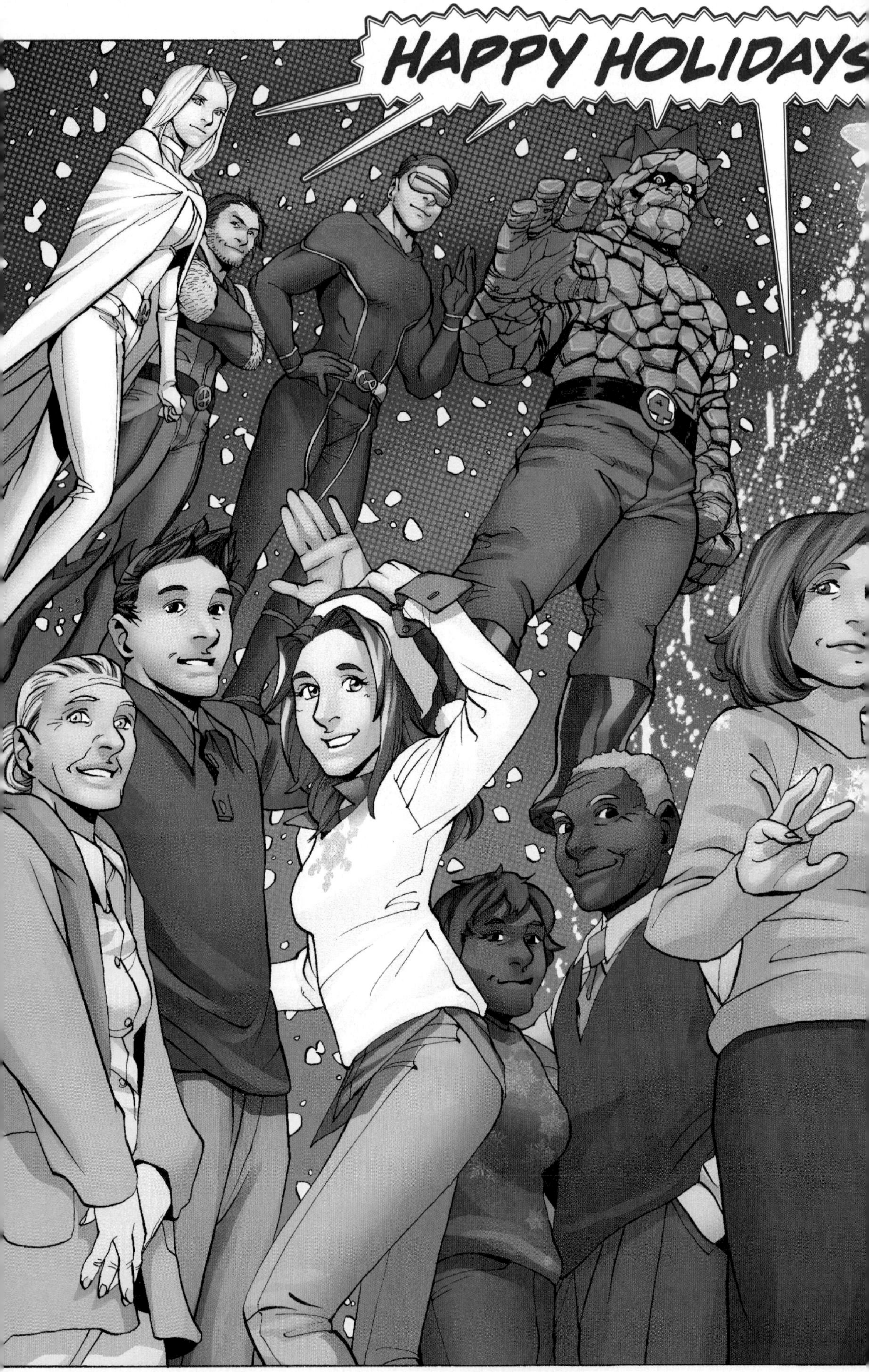
HAPPY HOLIDAYS

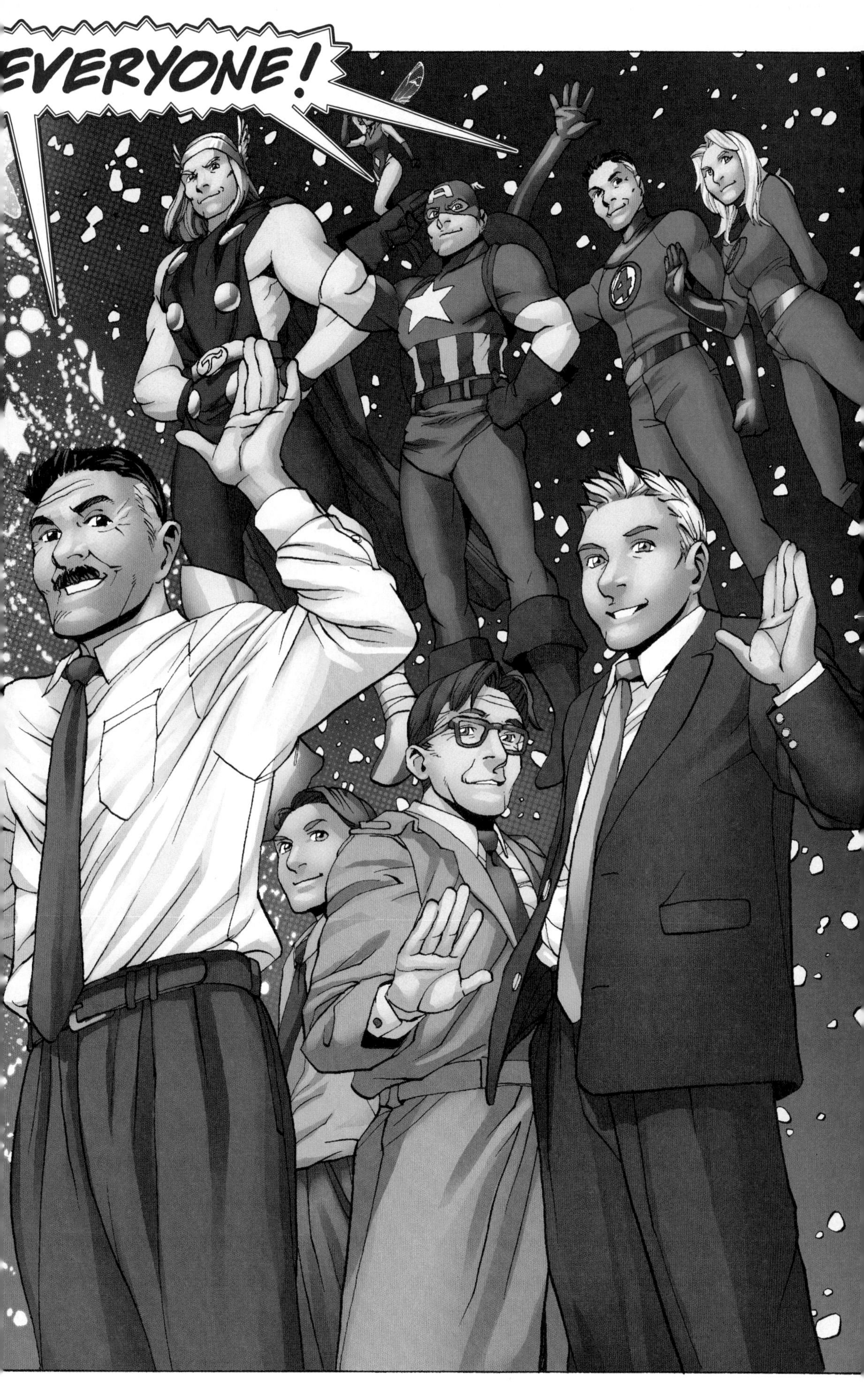
EVERYONE!

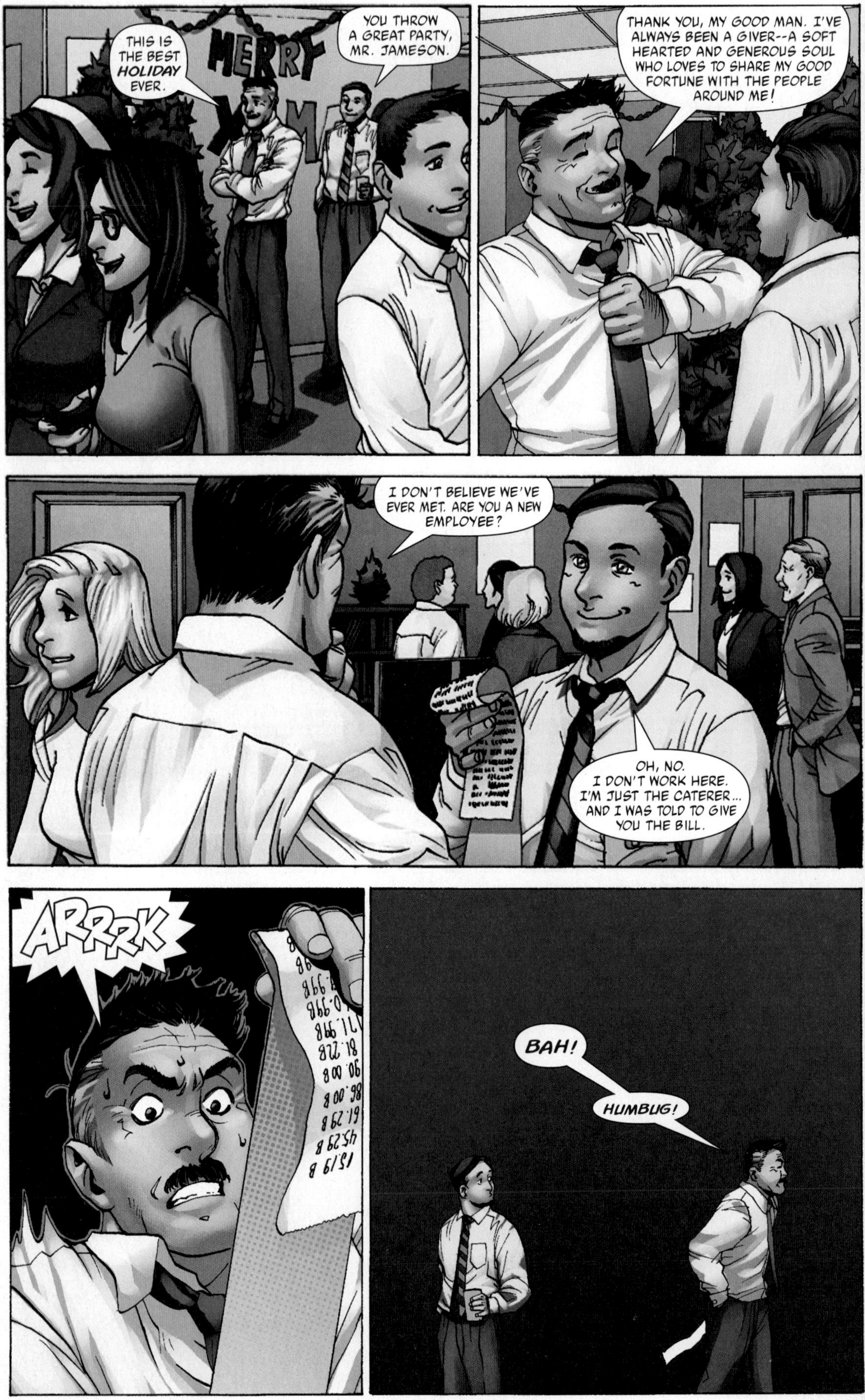
THIS IS THE BEST HOLIDAY EVER.
YOU THROW A GREAT PARTY, MR. JAMESON.
MERRY
THANK YOU, MY GOOD MAN. I'VE ALWAYS BEEN A GIVER--A SOFT HEARTED AND GENEROUS SOUL WHO LOVES TO SHARE MY GOOD FORTUNE WITH THE PEOPLE AROUND ME!
I DON'T BELIEVE WE'VE EVER MET. ARE YOU A NEW EMPLOYEE?
OH, NO. I DON'T WORK HERE. I'M JUST THE CATERER... AND I WAS TOLD TO GIVE YOU THE BILL.
ARRRK
BAH!
HUMBUG!